Quantitative Research Methods Course Slides

Seventh Edition

Dr. Johnathan Mun, Professor of Research
Quantitative Research Methods Course Slides
Seventh Edition, 2026, ROV Press

Course Professor

Dr. Johnathan Mun, *Ph.D., MBA, MS, BS, CRM, CQRM, CFC, FRM, MIFC*
Research Professor, Naval Postgraduate School
jcmun@nps.edu

❖ Professor and Chair, San Francisco Bay University; Research Professor, Naval Postgraduate School. Formerly Professor in Finance, Economics, and Statistics at the Swiss School of Management (Switzerland), University of Applied Sciences (Germany), and Adjunct Professor at Golden Gate University (California), St. Mary's College (California), San Francisco State University (California)

❖ Founder and CEO, Real Options Valuation, Inc. and Chair, IIPER (International Institute of Professional Education and Research)

❖ Author of 30+ books, including: Quantitative Research Methods, IIPER Press 2018; *Modeling Risk: Applying Monte Carlo Risk Simulation, Strategic Real Options, Stochastic Forecasting and Portfolio Optimization,* First and Second Edition, Wiley 2006, 2010; Third Edition, Thompson-Shore, 2015; *Real Options Analysis: Tools and Techniques,* First and Second Edition Wiley 2002 & 2005; *Credit Engineering,* Academic Press, 2010; *Advanced Analytical Models,* Wiley 2008; *Basel II Handbook on Credit Risk,* Elsevier Science, 2007-2008; *Real Options Analysis Course: Business Cases and Applications,* Wiley 2003; *Applied Risk Analysis: Moving Beyond Uncertainty,* Wiley 2003/2005; *Valuing Employee Stock Options 2004 FAS 123,* Wiley 2004.

❖ Holds 13 registered patents with another 10 patents pending

❖ Software Creator: *Risk Simulator, Real Options Super Lattice Solver, Project Economics Analysis Tool (PEAT), Employee Stock Options Toolkit (ESO), Modeling Toolkit, Health Economics Analysis Toolkit (HEAT), ROV Credit Market Operational Liquidity (CMOL), ROV BizStats, ROV Modeler, ROV Valuator, ROV Optimizer, ROV Visual Modeler, ROV Compiler, ROV Dashboard, Real Options Analysis Toolkit, etc.*

❖ Taught risk analytics, real options, simulation and optimization seminars worldwide (New York, San Francisco, Houston, Miami, Las Vegas, Tokyo, Singapore, Zurich, Ghana, London, Munich, Frankfurt, Paris, Colombia, Peru, Mexico, and many other places)

❖ Currently CEO of Real Options Valuation, Inc. Formerly Vice President of Analytics at Decisioneering Crystal Ball, Inc., and worked for KPMG Consulting in Global Financial Strategies performing strategic valuation and developing real options and simulation applications. Headed a group in Financial and Economic Forecasting for FDX (FedEx) group of companies.

❖ Certified in Financial Consulting, Certified in Financial Risk Management, Charter Member of the Institute of Financial Consultants, Certified Risk Analyst, Certified in Risk Management

❖ Published dozens of academic journal articles in the *Global Finance Journal; Journal of Acquisitions Research; Neural Network Journal; Reliability and Systems Engineering' Advances in Quantitative Finance and Accounting; Journal of Financial Economics; Journal of International Finance, Institutions, and Money; Journal of the Society of Petroleum Engineers; American Institute of Physics; Defense Acquisition University; Expert Systems; Financial Engineering; Applied Energy Journal; NPS Acquisitions Symposium,* and others

List of Topics

1. Research Basics
2. Overview of Applied Statistical and Quantitative Methods
3. Descriptive Statistics
4. Basic Probability
5. Discrete Probability Distributions
6. Continuous Probability Distributions
7. Hypothesis Testing Approaches
8. ROV BizStats
9. Statistical Methods for Two or More Variables
10. Quick Reference Guide: Analytics Summary
11. Forecasting and Predictive Modeling: Tomorrow's Forecast Today
12. Forecasting and Predictive Modeling: Using the Past to Predict the Future
13. Monte Carlo Simulation: On the Shores of Monaco
14. Test Driving Risk Simulator
15. Advanced Data Analytics: Pandora's Toolbox
16. Optimization: The Search for the Optimal Decision
17. Optimization Under Uncertainty
18. Analytics Exercises: Using R, Python, Minitab, SPSS, Excel, and EViews
19. Capital Budgeting and Portfolio Optimization
20. Artificial Intelligence, Machine Learning, and Data Science Methods
21. Appendix

DISTRIBUTIONAL MOMENTS

$$\bar{x} = \frac{\sum_{i=1}^{n} x_i}{n}$$

$$Median\ rank = \frac{n+1}{2}$$

$$Sturges'\ Rule:\ k = 1 + 3.3\log(n)$$

$$\sigma^2 = \sum_{i=1}^{N} \frac{(x_i - \mu)^2}{N}\ and\ s^2 = \sum_{i=1}^{n} \frac{(x_i - \bar{x})^2}{n-1}$$

$$\sigma = \sqrt{\sum_{i=1}^{N} \frac{(x_i - \mu)^2}{N}}\ and\ s = \sqrt{\sum_{i=1}^{n} \frac{(x_i - \bar{x})^2}{n-1}}$$

$$CV = \frac{s}{\bar{x}}\ or\ CV = \frac{\sigma}{\mu}$$

$$Skew\ g_1 = \frac{n}{(n-1)(n-2)} \sum_{i=1}^{n} \left(\frac{x_i - \bar{x}}{s}\right)^3$$

$$Excess\ Kurtosis\ g_2$$

$$= \frac{n(n+1)}{(n-1)(n-2)(n-3)} \sum_{i=1}^{n} \left(\frac{x_i - \bar{x}}{s}\right)^4 - \frac{3(n-1)^2}{(n-2)(n-3)}$$

BASIC PROBABILITY RULES

$$P(A|M) = \frac{P(A \cap M)}{P(M)} = \frac{P(A)P(M|A)}{P(M)}$$

$$= \frac{P(A)P(M|A)}{P(A \cap M) + P(B \cap M) + P(C \cap M)}$$

$$Bayes\ Theorem\ P(X_1|M)$$

$$= \frac{P(X_1)P(M|X_1)}{P(X_1)P(M|X_1) + P(X_2)P(M|X_2) + \cdots + P(X_n)P(M|X_n)}$$

$$Pairwise\ counts:\ m \times n$$

$$Permutations:\ P_x^n = \frac{n!}{(n-x)!}$$

$$Combinations:\ C_x^n = \frac{n!}{x!\,(n-x)!}$$

$$P(A \cup B) = P(A\ or\ B)$$
$$= P(A) + P(B) - P(A \cap B)\ not\ mutually\ exclusive$$

$$P(A \cup B) = P(A\ or\ B)$$
$$= P(A) + P(B)\ mutually\ exclusive$$

$$P(A \cap B) = P(A\ and\ B) = P(A) \cdot P(B|A)\ dependent$$

$$P(A \cap B) = P(A\ and\ B) = P(A) \cdot P(B)\ independent$$

DISCRETE PROBABILITY DISTRIBUTIONS

$$Binomial\ P(x) = \frac{n!}{x!\,(n-x)!} p^x (1-p)^{n-x};\ x_{int} \geq 0;$$

$$n_{int} \geq 0;\ and\ 0 < p < 1$$

$$\mu = np \qquad \sigma = \sqrt{np(1-p)}$$

$$skew\ g_1 = \frac{1-2p}{\sqrt{np(1-p)}}$$

$$kurt\ g_2 = \frac{6p^2 - 6p + 1}{np(1-p)}$$

$$Hypergeometric\ P(x)$$

$$= \frac{\frac{(N_x)!}{x!\,(N_x - x)!} \frac{(N - N_x)!}{(n-x)!\,(N - N_x - n + x)!}}{\frac{N!}{n!\,(N - n)!}}$$

$$for\ x = Max(n - (N - N_x), 0), \dots, Min(n, N_x)$$

$$\mu = \frac{N_x n}{N} \qquad \sigma = \sqrt{\frac{(N - N_x)N_x n(N - n)}{N^2(N-1)}}$$

$$skew\ g_1 = \frac{(N - 2N_x)(N - 2n)}{N-2} \sqrt{\frac{N-1}{(N - N_x)N_x n(N-n)}}$$

$$kurt\ g_2 = \frac{V(N, N_x, n)}{(N - N_x)N_x n(-3 + N)(-2 + N)(-N + n)}$$

$$where\ V(N, N_x, n)$$
$$= (N - N_x)^3 - (N - N_x)^5 + 3(N - N_x)^2 N_x - 6(N - N_x)^3 N_x$$
$$+(N - N_x)^4 N_x + 3(N - N_x) N_x^2 - 12(N - N_x)^2 N_x^2$$
$$+ 8(N - N_x)^3 N_x^2 + N_x^3$$
$$-6(N - N_x)N_x^3 + 8(N - N_x)^2 N_x^3 + (N - N_x)N_x^4 - N_x^5$$
$$- 6(N - N_x)^3 N_x$$
$$+6(N - N_x)^4 N_x + 18(N - N_x)^2 N_x n - 6(N - N_x)^3 N_x n$$
$$+ 18(N - N_x) N_x^2 n$$
$$-24(N - N_x)^2 N_x^2 n - 6(N - N_x)^3 n - 6(N - N_x) N_x^3 n$$
$$+ 6N_x^4 n + 6(N - N_x)^2 n^2$$
$$-6(N - N_x)^3 n^2 - 24(N - N_x) N_x n^2 + 12(N - N_x)^2 N_x n^2 + 6N_x^2 n^2 + 12(N - N_x) N_x^2 n^2 - 6N_x^3 n^2$$

$$Poisson\ P(x) = \frac{e^{-\lambda}\lambda^x}{x!}\ for\ x\ and\ \lambda > 0$$

$$\mu = \lambda \qquad \sigma = \sqrt{\lambda}$$

$$skew\ g_1 = \frac{1}{\sqrt{\lambda}} \qquad kurt\ g_2 = \frac{1}{\lambda}$$

$$Bernoulli\ P(x) = \begin{cases} 1-p & for\ x = 0 \\ p & for\ x = 1 \end{cases}$$
$$or$$
$$P(x) = p^x (1-p)^{1-x}$$

$$\mu = p \qquad \sigma = \sqrt{p(1-p)}$$

$$skew\ g_1 = \frac{1-2p}{\sqrt{p(1-p)}} \qquad kurt\ g_2 = \frac{6p^2 - 6p + 1}{p(1-p)}$$

$$Discrete\ Uniform\ P(x) = \frac{1}{N}$$

$$\mu = \frac{N+1}{2}\ rank \qquad \sigma = \sqrt{\frac{(N-1)(N+1)}{12}}\ rank$$

$$skew\ g_1 = 0 \qquad kurt = \frac{-6(N^2+1)}{5(N-1)(N+1)}\ rank$$

BASIC HYPOTHESIS TESTS

$$\mu \pm Z\left(\frac{\sigma}{\sqrt{n}}\right) \ or \ \mu \pm t\left(\frac{\sigma}{\sqrt{n}}\right)$$

$$FPC = \sigma_{\bar{x}} = \frac{\sigma}{\sqrt{n}}\sqrt{\frac{N-n}{N-1}} \ for \ \frac{n}{N} \geq 5\%$$

$$Z = \frac{\bar{x} - \mu_{\bar{x}}}{\sigma_{\bar{x}}} = \frac{\bar{x} - \mu_{\bar{x}}}{\frac{\sigma}{\sqrt{n}}} \ and \ Z = \frac{\bar{x}_1 - \bar{x}_2}{\sqrt{\frac{\sigma_1^2}{n_1} + \frac{\sigma_2^2}{n_2}}}$$

Null H_0	True	False
Accept	True Negative $(1-\alpha)$	Type II (β) False Negative
Reject	Type I (α) False Positive	Power $(1-\beta)$ True Positive

PARAMETRICS

$$Eq.Var.t = \frac{(\bar{x}_1 - \bar{x}_2) - (\mu_1 - \mu_2)}{\sqrt{s_p^2\left(\frac{1}{n_1} + \frac{1}{n_2}\right)}} \ with$$

$$s_p^2 = \frac{(n_1-1)s_1^2 + (n_2-1)s_2^2}{n_1 + n_1 - 2} \ and \ df = n_1 + n_2 - 2$$

$$Uneq.Var.t = \frac{(\bar{x}_1 - \bar{x}_2) - (\mu_1 - \mu_2)}{\sqrt{\left(\frac{s_1^2}{n_1} + \frac{s_2^2}{n_2}\right)}} \ with \ df = \frac{\left(\frac{s_1^2}{n_1} + \frac{s_2^2}{n_2}\right)^2}{\frac{\left(\frac{s_1^2}{n_1}\right)^2}{n_1 - 1} + \frac{\left(\frac{s_2^2}{n_2}\right)^2}{n_2 - 1}}$$

$$Dep.Var.t = \frac{\bar{d}}{\frac{s_d}{\sqrt{n}}} \ with \ df = n - 1 \ and \ d = (x_1 - x_2)$$

$$Ind.Var.F = max\left(\frac{s_1^2}{s_2^2}, \frac{s_2^2}{s_1^2}\right) with \ F\left(\frac{\alpha}{2}, n_L - 1, n_s - 1\right)$$

$$Proportions \ Z = \frac{p_1 - p_2}{\sqrt{\bar{p}(1-\bar{p})\left[\frac{1}{n_1} + \frac{1}{n_2}\right]}}$$

$$where \ \bar{p} = \frac{n_1 p_1 + n_2 p_2}{n_1 + n_2}$$

ANOVA Single Factor Multiple Treatments

$$x_{i,j} = \mu + \tau_j + \varepsilon_{ij}$$

$$\tilde{x} = \frac{\sum_{j=1}^{t}\sum_{i=1}^{t} x_{ij}}{n}$$

$$SS_{Treatment} = \sum_{j=1}^{t} n_j(\bar{x}_j - \tilde{x})^2$$

$$SS_{Error} = \sum_{j=1}^{t}\sum_{i=1}^{n_j}(x_{ij} - \bar{x}_j)^2$$

$$SS_{Total} = \sum_{j=1}^{t}\sum_{i=1}^{n_j}(x_{ij} - \tilde{x})^2$$

$$df_{Treatment} = t - 1$$

$$df_{Error} = n - t$$

$$F_{n-1,n-t} = \frac{MS_{Treatment}}{MS_{Error}}$$

ANOVA Randomized Block

$$x_{i,j} = \mu + \tau_j + \beta_j + \varepsilon_{ij}$$

$$\tilde{x} = \frac{\sum_{j=1}^{t}\sum_{i=1}^{t} x_{ij}}{n}$$

$$SS_{Treatment} = n\sum_{j=1}^{t}(\bar{x}_j - \tilde{x})^2$$

$$SS_{Block} = t\sum_{j=1}^{t}(\bar{x}_i - \tilde{x})^2$$

$$SS_{Total} = \sum_{j=1}^{t}\sum_{i=1}^{n_j}(x_{ij} - \tilde{x})^2$$

$$SS_{Error} = SS_{Total} - SS_{Treatment} - SS_{Block}$$

$$df_{Tr} = t - 1 \quad df_{Block} = n - 1 \quad df_{Err} = (n-1)(t-1)$$

$$F_{(t-1),(n-1)(t-1)} = \frac{MS_{Treatment}}{MS_{Error}} \ for \ n \ blocks$$

TWO WAY ANOVA $x_{i,j} = \mu + \alpha_i + \beta_j + (\alpha\beta)_{ij} + \varepsilon_{ijk}$

$$SS_A = rb\sum_{i=1}^{a}(\bar{x}_i - \tilde{x})^2 \quad SS_B = ra\sum_{j=1}^{b}(\bar{x}_j - \tilde{x})^2$$

$$SS_{Total} = \sum_{i=1}^{a}\sum_{j=1}^{b}\sum_{k=1}^{r}(x_{ijk} - \tilde{x})^2$$

$$SS_{Error} = \sum_{i=1}^{a}\sum_{j=1}^{b}\sum_{k=1}^{r}(x_{ijk} - \bar{x}_{ij})^2$$

$$SS_{AB} = SS_{Total} - SS_A - SS_B - SS_{Error}$$

$$df_A = a - 1 \quad df_B = b - 1 \quad df_{Error} = ab(r-1)$$

$$df_{Total} = abr - 1 \quad df_{AB} = (a-1)(b-1)$$

$$F_{(A,B,AB),ab(r-1)} = \frac{MS_{Factor(A,B,AB)}}{MS_{Error}}$$

ANOVA on Regression

$$SS_{Reg} = \sum_{i=1}^{n}(\hat{y}_i - \bar{y})^2$$

$$SS_{Error} = \sum_{i=1}^{n}(y_i - \hat{y}_i)^2$$

$$SS_{Total} = \sum_{i=1}^{n}(y_i - \bar{y})^2$$

$$df_{Reg} = k - 1 \quad df_{Error} = n - k - 1 \quad df_{Tot} = n - 1$$

$$F_{k-1,n-k-1} = \frac{MS_{Treatment}}{MS_{Error}}$$

The hypotheses tested are typically:

$H_0: \mu_1 = \mu_2$, or $\mu_1 - \mu_2 = 0$, that is, the two samples' means are statistically similar

$H_a: \mu_1 \neq \mu_2$, or $\mu_1 - \mu_2 \neq 0$, where the two samples' means are statistically significantly different

The null hypothesis (H_0) generally has the equivalence sign (i.e., =, ≥, ≤), whereas the alternate hypothesis (H_a) has its complement (i.e., ≠, <, >). The sign of the alternate hypothesis points to whether the test is a two-tailed test (≠) or a one-tailed test (right tail is denoted with >, whereas a left tail test uses <). In most situations, the p-values of this calculated t-statistic are calculated and compared against some predefined level of significance (i.e., the standard α significance levels of 0.10, 0.05, and 0.01 will be assumed throughout these examples) using the t-distribution with a certain degree of freedom (*df*). If the p-value is below these α significance levels, we reject the null hypothesis and accept the alternate hypothesis.

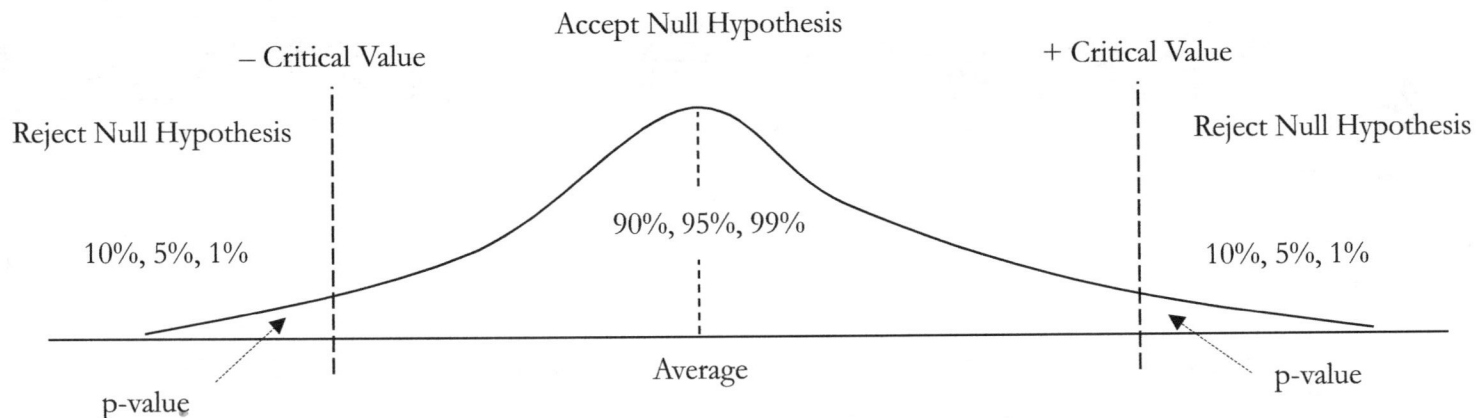

CORRELATION

$$r_{x,y} = \frac{cov_{x,y}}{s_x s_y} = \frac{n\sum x_i y_i - \sum x_i \sum y_i}{\sqrt{n\sum x_i^2 - (\sum x_i)^2}\sqrt{n\sum y_i^2 - (\sum y_i)^2}}$$

$$r_{x,y} = \frac{\sum_{i=1}^{n} x_i y_i - n\bar{x}\bar{y}}{(n-1)s_x s_y} = \frac{\sum_{i=1}^{n}(x_i - \bar{x})(y_i - \bar{y})}{(n-1)s_x s_y}$$

$$r_{x,y} = \frac{\sum_{i=1}^{n}(x_i - \bar{x})(y_i - \bar{y})}{\sqrt{\sum_{i=1}^{n}(x_i - \bar{x})^2 \sum_{i=1}^{n}(y_i - \bar{y})^2}}$$

$$r_{x,y} = \frac{n\sum_{i=1}^{n} x_i y_i - \sum_{i=1}^{n} x_i \sum_{i=1}^{n} y_i}{\sqrt{n\sum_{i=1}^{n} x_i^2 - (\sum_{i=1}^{n} x_i)^2}\sqrt{n\sum_{i=1}^{n} y_i^2 - (\sum_{i=1}^{n} y_i)^2}}$$

$$\sigma_p = \sqrt{\sum_{i=1}^{n}\omega_i^2\sigma_i^2 + \sum_{i=1}^{n}\sum_{j=1}^{m} 2\omega_i\omega_j\rho_{ij}\sigma_i\sigma_j} \;\; and \;\; t = \frac{r\sqrt{n-2}}{\sqrt{1-r^2}}$$

DISTRIBUTIONAL FITTING

$$Kolmogorov - Smirnov = \max_{1\le i\le N}\left|F(Y_i) - \frac{i}{N}\right|$$

$$\chi^2 = \sum_{i=1}^{k}(O_i - E_i)^2/E_i \quad E_i = N\big(F(Y_U) - F(Y_L)\big) \quad \chi^2(\alpha, k-c)$$

MULTIPLE REGRESSION

$$Y = \beta_0 + \beta_1 X_1 + \beta_2 X_2 + \beta_3 X_3 \ldots + \beta_k X_k + \varepsilon$$

$$\beta_1 = \frac{\sum_{i=1}^{n}(X_i - \bar{X})(Y_i - \bar{Y})}{\sum_{i=1}^{n}(X_i - \bar{X})^2} = \frac{\sum_{i=1}^{n} X_i Y_i - \frac{\sum_{i=1}^{n} X_i \sum_{i=1}^{n} Y_i}{n}}{\sum_{i=1}^{n} X_i^2 - \frac{(\sum_{i=1}^{n} X_i)^2}{n}}$$

$$\beta_0 = \bar{Y} - \beta_1\bar{X}$$

$$\hat{\beta}_2 = \frac{\sum Y_i X_{2,i} \sum X_{3,i}^2 - \sum Y_i X_{3,i} \sum X_{2,i} X_{3,i}}{\sum X_{2,i}^2 \sum X_{3,i}^2 - (\sum X_{2,i} X_{3,i})^2}$$

$$\hat{\beta}_3 = \frac{\sum Y_i X_{3,i} \sum X_{2,i}^2 - \sum Y_i X_{2,i} \sum X_{2,i} X_{3,i}}{\sum X_{2,i}^2 \sum X_{3,i}^2 - (\sum X_{2,i} X_{3,i})^2}$$

$Multicollinearity \; X_{3,i} = \lambda X_{2,i} \; for \; \lambda > 0:$

$$\hat{\beta}_2 = \frac{\sum Y_i X_{2,i} \sum \lambda^2 X_{2,i}^2 - \sum Y_i \lambda X_{2,i} \sum \lambda X_{2,i}^2}{\sum X_{2,i}^2 \sum \lambda^2 X_{2,i}^2 - (\sum \lambda^{\square} X_{2,i}^2)^2} = \frac{0}{0}$$

$$VIF_i = \frac{1}{(1 - R_i^2)}$$

$$SE_{y,x} = \sqrt{\frac{\sum(y_i - \hat{y})^2}{n-k}}$$

$$SE_{b1} = \frac{SE_{y,x}}{\sqrt{\sum x_i^2 - n(\bar{x})^2}} = \frac{SE_{y,x}}{\sqrt{\sum(x_i - \bar{x})^2}} = \sqrt{\frac{\frac{\sum error^2}{n-k}}{\sum(x_i - \bar{x})^2}}$$

$$SE_{b0} = SE_{y,x}\sqrt{\frac{1}{n} + \frac{\bar{x}^2}{SS_x}} \;\; and \;\; t = \frac{\hat{\beta}_i}{se_b}$$

$$R\;Squared = \frac{SS_{reg}}{SS_{total}} = 1 - \frac{SS_{error}}{SS_{total}} = 1 - \frac{\sum_{i=1}^{n}(y_i - \hat{y}_i)^2}{\sum_{i=1}^{n}(y_i - \bar{y})^2}$$

$$Adjusted\;R\;Squared = 1 - \left[\frac{(1-R^2)(n-1)}{n-k}\right]$$

$$Correlation\;R_{a,b} = \frac{n\sum a_i b_i - \sum a_i \sum b_i}{\sqrt{n\sum a_i^2 - (\sum a_i)^2}\sqrt{n\sum b_i^2 - (\sum b_i)^2}}$$

$$Partial\;R = -C^{-1}\left[\sqrt{D}C'^{-1}\right]^{-1} + 2I$$

$$\bar{R}^2 = 1 - \frac{\sum_{i=1}^{n}\frac{(Y_i - \hat{Y}_i)^2}{k-2}}{\sum_{i=1}^{n}\frac{(Y_i - \bar{Y})^2}{k-1}} = 1 - \frac{\frac{SSE}{k-2}}{\frac{TSS}{k-1}}$$

$$MLE = -\frac{1}{2}N ln(2\pi) - \left(\frac{N}{2}\right)ln\left(\frac{SE}{N}\right) - \frac{N}{2} = -\frac{1}{2}N\left(ln\left(\frac{2\pi SE}{N}\right) + 1\right)$$

$$AIC = \frac{-2MLE + 2K}{N} = ln\left(\frac{2\pi SE}{N}\right) + \left(\frac{2K+N}{N}\right)$$

$$BIC = \frac{-2MLE + Kln(N)}{N} = ln\left(\frac{2\pi SE}{N}\right) + \frac{Kln(N)+N}{N}$$

$$HQ = \frac{-2MLE + 2Kln[ln(N)]}{N} = ln\left(\frac{2\pi SE}{N}\right) + \frac{2Kln[ln(N)]+N}{N}$$

$$DW = \frac{\sum(\varepsilon_t - \varepsilon_{t-1})^2}{\sum \varepsilon_t^2} \;\; and \;\; DW_{Auto} = \frac{\sum \varepsilon_t \varepsilon_{t-1}}{\sum \varepsilon_t^2}$$

$Breusch-Godfrey \; Y = f(X_1, X_2, \ldots, X_k)$

$$Y = f(X_1, X_2, \ldots, X_k, \varepsilon_{t-1}, \varepsilon_{t-2}, \varepsilon_{t-p}) \quad with \; R^2(n-p) \sim \chi_{df=p}^2$$

NONPARAMETRICS

$$Runs = \frac{T - \left(\frac{2n_1 n_2}{n_1 + n_2} + 1\right)}{\sqrt{\frac{2n_1 n_2(2n_1 n_2 - n_1 - n_2)}{(n_1 + n_2)^2(n_1 + n_2 - 1)}}}$$

$$Lilliefors\;D = max|O_i - CDF_i|$$

$$Wilcoxon\;W = \Sigma\,(R+)$$

$$Kruskal\;Wallis\;H = \frac{12}{N(N+1)}\left[\frac{(\sum R_1)^2}{n_1} + \cdots + \frac{(\sum R_k)^2}{n_k}\right] - 3(N+1)$$

$$Friedman's\;F_r = \frac{12}{bt(t+1)}\sum_{j=1}^{t} R_j^2 - 3b(t+1)$$

TIME SERIES & STOCHASTIC PROCESSES

$$\frac{\delta S}{S} = \mu(\delta t) + \sigma\varepsilon\sqrt{\delta t}$$

$$\frac{\delta S}{S} = \left(\mu - \frac{\sigma^2}{2}\right)\delta t + \sigma\varepsilon\sqrt{\delta t}$$

$$\frac{\delta S}{S} = exp\left[\mu(\delta t) + \sigma\varepsilon\sqrt{\delta t}\right]$$

$$\frac{\delta S}{S} = \eta(\bar{S}e^{\mu(\delta t)} - S)\delta t + \mu(\delta t) + \sigma\varepsilon\sqrt{\delta t}$$

$$\frac{\delta S}{S} = \eta(\bar{S}e^{\mu(\delta t)} - S)\delta t + \mu(\delta t) + \sigma\varepsilon\sqrt{\delta t} + \theta F(\lambda)(\delta t)$$

$\theta = jump\;size\;of\;S, F(\lambda) = ICDF\;Poisson$

$\lambda = S\;jump\;rate + a_p y_{t-p} + \varepsilon_t$

$$Logit\;P(x) = \frac{EXP(\hat{Y})}{[1 + EXP(\hat{Y})]}$$

$Polynomial\;line\;y = a + b_1 x + b_2 x^2 + \cdots + + b_n x^n$

$$SMA_n = \frac{\sum_{i=1}^{n} Y_i}{n}$$

$$ESF_t = \alpha Y_{t-1} + (1 - \alpha)ESF_{t-1}$$

$$DMAt_{t+1} = 2MA_{1,t} - MA_{2,t} + \frac{2}{m-1}\left[MA_{1,t} - MA_{2,t}\right]$$

$$DES_t = \beta(SES_t - SES_{t-1}) + (1 - \beta)DES_{t-1}$$

$$SES_t = \alpha Y_t + (1 - \alpha)(SES_{t-1} + DES_{t-1})$$

$$F_t = SES_{t-1} + N \times DES_{t-1}$$

TIME SERIES MODELS

$$\hat{Y}_i \pm Z \left[\frac{RMSE}{N-T} \right] N$$

$$RMSE = \sqrt{\sum_{i=1}^{n} \frac{(y_i - \hat{y}_i)^2}{n}} \qquad MSE = \sum_{i=1}^{n} \frac{(y_i - \hat{y}_i)^2}{n}$$

$$MAD = \sum_{i=1}^{n} \frac{|y_i - \hat{y}_i|}{n} \qquad MAPE = \sum_{i=1}^{n} \frac{\left| \frac{y_i - \hat{y}_i}{y_i} \right|}{n}$$

$$U = \sqrt{\frac{\sum_{i=1}^{n} \left(\frac{\hat{y}_i - y_i}{y_{i-1}} \right)^2}{\sum_{i=1}^{n} \left(\frac{y_i - y_{i-1}}{y_{i-1}} \right)^2}} \qquad RMSLE = \sqrt{\frac{\sum_{i=1}^{n} \left[ln \left(\frac{1 + \hat{y}_i}{1 + y_i} \right) \right]^2}{n}}$$

$$RMSPE = \sqrt{\frac{\sum_{i=1}^{n} \left[\frac{y_i - \hat{y}_i}{y_i} \right]^2}{n}} \qquad sMAPE = \sum_{i=1}^{n} \frac{\left| \frac{y_i - \hat{y}_i}{\frac{y_i + \hat{y}_i}{2}} \right|}{n}$$

$$U1_{Acc} = \sqrt{\frac{\sum_{i=1}^{n} (\hat{y}_i - y_i)^2}{\sum_{i=1}^{n} y_i^2}} \qquad U2_{Qual} = \sqrt{\frac{\sum_{i=1}^{n} \frac{(\hat{y}_i - y_i)^2}{n}}{\frac{\sum_{i=1}^{n} y_i^2 \sum_{i=1}^{n} \hat{y}_i^2}{n^2}}}$$

$MA(q) \quad y_t = \varepsilon_t + b_1 \varepsilon_{t-1} + \cdots + b_q \varepsilon_{t-q}$

$ARMA(p,q) \quad y_t = a_1 y_{t-1} \ldots + a_p y_{t-p} + \varepsilon_t + b_1 \varepsilon_{t-1} \ldots + b_q \varepsilon_{t-q}$

$GARCH \quad y_t = x_t \gamma + \varepsilon_t \qquad$ where $\sigma_t^2 = \omega + \alpha \varepsilon_{t-1}^2 + \beta \sigma_{t-1}^2$

$SA: L_t = \alpha(Y_t - S_{t-s}) + (1 - \alpha)L_{t-1}$

$SA: S_t = \gamma(Y_t - L_t) + (1 - \gamma)S_{t-s}$

$SA: F_{t+m} = L_t + S_{t+m-s}$

$SM: L_t = \alpha \left(\frac{Y_t}{S_{t-s}} \right) + (1 - \alpha)L_{t-1}$

$SM: S_t = \gamma \left(\frac{Y_t}{L_t} \right) + (1 - \gamma)S_{t-s}$

$SM: F_{t+m} = L_t S_{t+m-s}$

$HWA: B_t = \beta(L_t - L_{t-1}) + (1 - \beta)B_{t-1}$

$HWA: S_t = \gamma(Y_t - L_t) + (1 - \gamma)S_{t-s}$

$HWA: F_{t+m} = L_t + mB_t + S_{t+m-s}$

$HWM: L_t = \alpha \left(\frac{Y_t}{S_{t-s}} \right) + (1 - \alpha)(L_{t-1} + B_{t-1})$

$HWM: B_t = \beta(L_t - L_{t-1}) + (1 - \beta)B_{t-1}$

$HWM: S_t = \gamma \left(\frac{Y_t}{L_t} \right) + (1 - \gamma)S_{t-s}$

$HWA: F_{t+m} = (L_t + mB_t)S_{t+m-s}$

	$Z_t \sim$ Normal Distribution	$Z_t \sim$ T-Distribution
GARCH-M Variance in Mean Equation	$y_t = c + \lambda \sigma_t^2 + \varepsilon_t$ $\varepsilon_t = \sigma_t z_t$ $\sigma_t^2 = \omega + \alpha \varepsilon_{t-1}^2 + \beta \sigma_{t-1}^2$	$y_t = c + \lambda \sigma_t^2 + \varepsilon_t$ $\varepsilon_t = \sigma_t z_t$ $\sigma_t^2 = \omega + \alpha \varepsilon_{t-1}^2 + \beta \sigma_{t-1}^2$
GARCH-M Standard Deviation in Mean Equation	$y_t = c + \lambda \sigma_t + \varepsilon_t$ $\varepsilon_t = \sigma_t z_t$ $\sigma_t^2 = \omega + \alpha \varepsilon_{t-1}^2 + \beta \sigma_{t-1}^2$	$y_t = c + \lambda \sigma_t + \varepsilon_t$ $\varepsilon_t = \sigma_t z_t$ $\sigma_t^2 = \omega + \alpha \varepsilon_{t-1}^2 + \beta \sigma_{t-1}^2$
GARCH-M Log Variance in Mean Equation	$y_t = c + \lambda \, ln(\sigma_t^2) + \varepsilon_t$ $\varepsilon_t = \sigma_t z_t$ $\sigma_t^2 = \omega + \alpha \varepsilon_{t-1}^2 + \beta \sigma_{t-1}^2$	$y_t = c + \lambda \, ln(\sigma_t^2) + \varepsilon_t$ $\varepsilon_t = \sigma_t z_t$ $\sigma_t^2 = \omega + \alpha \varepsilon_{t-1}^2 + \beta \sigma_{t-1}^2$
GARCH	$y_t = x_t \gamma + \varepsilon_t$ $\sigma_t^2 = \omega + \alpha \varepsilon_{t-1}^2 + \beta \sigma_{t-1}^2$	$y_t = \varepsilon_t$ $\varepsilon_t = \sigma_t z_t$ $\sigma_t^2 = \omega + \alpha \varepsilon_{t-1}^2 + \beta \sigma_{t-1}^2$
EGARCH	$y_t = \varepsilon_t$ $\varepsilon_t = \sigma_t z_t$ $ln(\sigma_t^2) = \omega + \beta \cdot ln(\sigma_{t-1}^2) +$ $\alpha \left[\left| \frac{\varepsilon_{t-1}}{\sigma_{t-1}} \right| - E(|\varepsilon_t|) \right] + r \frac{\varepsilon_{t-1}}{\sigma_{t-1}}$ $E(|\varepsilon_t|) = \sqrt{\frac{2}{\pi}}$	$y_t = \varepsilon_t$ $\varepsilon_t = \sigma_t z_t$ $ln(\sigma_t^2) = \omega + \beta \cdot ln(\sigma_{t-1}^2) +$ $\alpha \left[\left| \frac{\varepsilon_{t-1}}{\sigma_{t-1}} \right| - E(|\varepsilon_t|) \right] + r \frac{\varepsilon_{t-1}}{\sigma_{t-1}}$ $E(|\varepsilon_t|) = \frac{2\sqrt{\nu - 2} \, \Gamma \left(\frac{\nu + 1}{2} \right)}{(\nu - 1)\Gamma \left(\frac{\nu}{2} \right) \sqrt{\pi}}$
GJR-GARCH	$y_t = \varepsilon_t$ $\varepsilon_t = \sigma_t z_t$ $\sigma_t^2 = \omega + \alpha \varepsilon_{t-1}^2 +$ $r \varepsilon_{t-1}^2 d_{t-1} + \beta \sigma_{t-1}^2$ $d_{t-1} = \begin{cases} 1 & if \varepsilon_{t-1} < 0 \\ 0 & otherwise \end{cases}$	$y_t = \varepsilon_t$ $\varepsilon_t = \sigma_t z_t$ $\sigma_t^2 = \omega + \alpha \varepsilon_{t-1}^2 +$ $r \varepsilon_{t-1}^2 d_{t-1} + \beta \sigma_{t-1}^2$ $d_{t-1} = \begin{cases} 1 & if \varepsilon_{t-1} < 0 \\ 0 & otherwise \end{cases}$

Quantitative Research

1. Conceptual Framework
- Research Purpose
  - Purpose Statement
- Theory Development
  - Constructs, Propositions, Logic, Boundary Conditions
  - Research Structure, Data Source, Operationalize Variables
- Hypothesis Statements
  - Research Questions and Research Hypotheses
  - Statistical Test Hypotheses
- Identification of Dependent and Independent Variables
  - Endogenous, Exogenous, Interacting, Mediating
- Data Source
  - Experimentation, Field Work, Questionnaires, Secondary Data, Surveys
  - Sampling Issues (Probabilistic vs. Nonprobabilistic Sampling)
  - Biases (Attrition, Confirmation, Confounding, Cultural, Exclusion, Instrument, Maturation, Respondent, Self Selection, Survivorship, etc.)

2. Descriptive Statistics
- Histogram and Charts
  - PDF, CDF, ICDF
  - Control Charts (C, N, NP, R, U, X, XMR)
  - Contingency Tables (McNemar's), Cross Tabulation, Power Analysis
- Four Moments of Key Variables
  - Mean, Sigma, Skew, Kurtosis
  - Distributional and Curve Fitting
- Correlation of Key Variables
  - Dependent vs. Independent; Independent vs. Independent
  - Chi-Square Test for Independence

3. Data Reliability and Consistency
- Outliers
  - Grubbs' Test
  - Bartlett's Homogeneity of Variances
  - Volatility and Kurtosis (GARCH)
- Normality
  - Large Dataset (≥ 30)
    - Assume Central Limit Theorem
    - Parametric: Akaike Info Criterion, Anderson-Darling, Kolmogorov-Smirnov, Kuiper's, Schwarz Criterion
  - Small Dataset
    - Test for Normality
      - Chi-Square, D'Agostino-Pearson, Lilliefors, Shapiro-Wilk-Royston, Q-Q Test
      - Box-Cox Transformation
- Determination of Possible Tests
  - Parametric vs. Nonparametric
  - Nominal, Ordinal, Interval, Ratio (NOIR) Levels of Measurement
  - Alpha, Power, and Considerations of Type I to Type IV Errors
- Reliability and Consistency Tests
  - Binary Data: Cronback's Alpha
  - Pairwise Data: Cohen's Kappa
  - Categorical Data: Guttman's Lambda
  - Multivariate Data: Inter-Rater Reliability, ICC, Kendall's W, Kuder-Richardson
  - Homogeneity of Sample: Shannon-Brillouin-Simpson Diversity
- Data Structure
  - Accuracy and Past Performance (Akaike IC, Bayes IC, Diebold-Mariano, Hannan-Quinn, Pesaran-Timmerman)
  - Structural Breaks (Ramsey's RESET or Structural Break Chow's Test)
  - Euclidean Distance (Mahalanobis)
  - Randomness (Stochastic Fit and Runs Test)
- Data Diagnostics
  - Time-Series: Autocorrelation, Cyclicality, Endogeneity, Heteroskedasticity, Interactions, Leads and Lags, Multicollinearity, Nonlinearity, Nonstationarity, Out of Range, Outliers, Redundant and Omitted Variables, Seasonality, Specification Error, Sphericity of Errors, Stationarity, Stochastic Process, Structural Shift
    - Heteroskedasticity: Breusch-Pagan-Godfrey, Lagrange Multiplier, Wald-Glejser
  - Cross-Sectional: Endogeneity, Interactions, Multicollinearity, Nonlinearity, Out of Range, Outliers, Redundant and Omitted Variables, Specification Error, Sphericity of Errors, Structural Shift

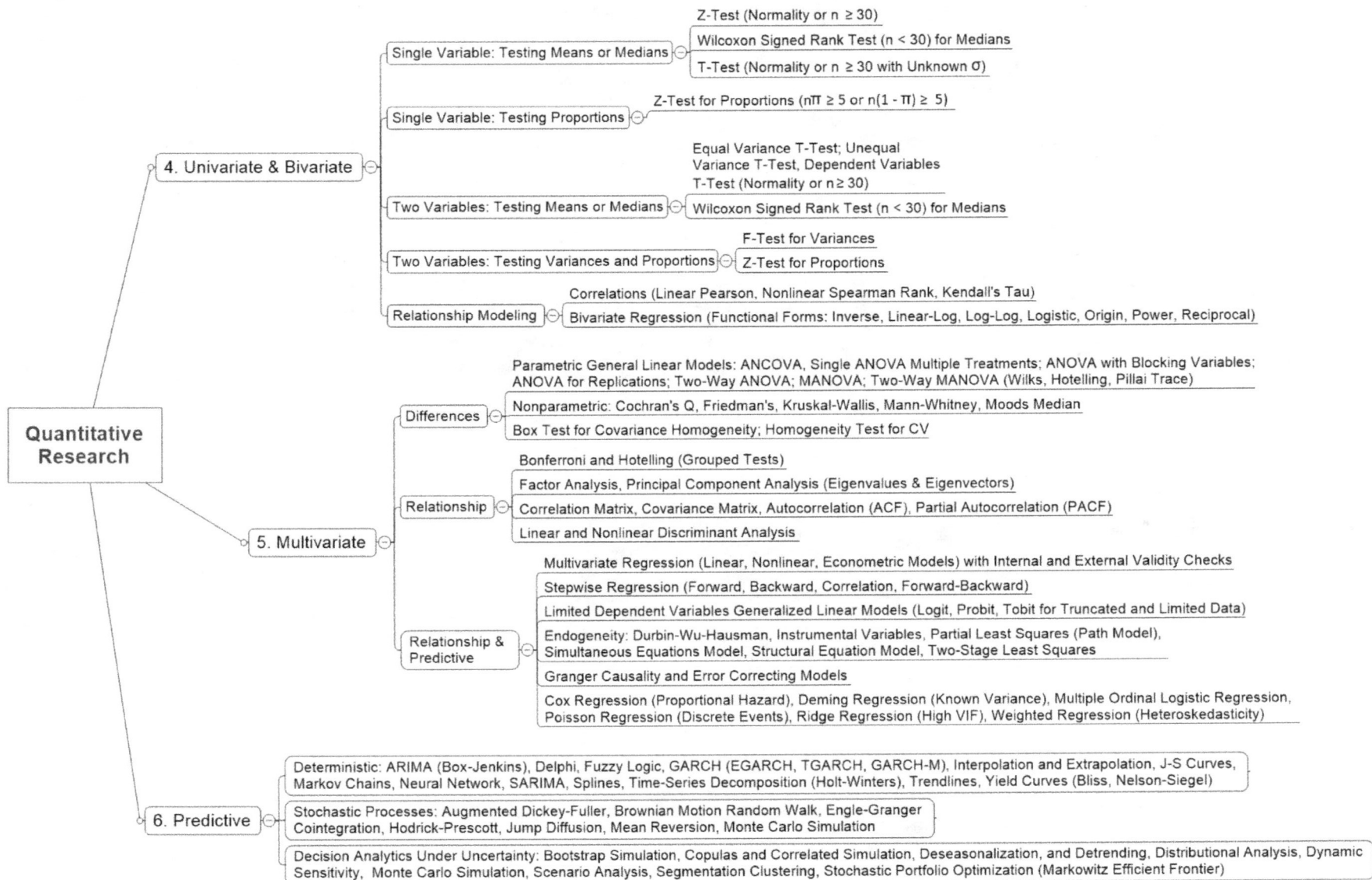

Quantitative Research

4. Univariate & Bivariate

- **Single Variable: Testing Means or Medians**
  - Z-Test (Normality or $n \geq 30$)
  - Wilcoxon Signed Rank Test ($n < 30$) for Medians
  - T-Test (Normality or $n \geq 30$ with Unknown σ)
- **Single Variable: Testing Proportions**
  - Z-Test for Proportions ($n\pi \geq 5$ or $n(1 - \pi) \geq 5$)
- **Two Variables: Testing Means or Medians**
  - Equal Variance T-Test; Unequal Variance T-Test, Dependent Variables T-Test (Normality or $n \geq 30$)
  - Wilcoxon Signed Rank Test ($n < 30$) for Medians
- **Two Variables: Testing Variances and Proportions**
  - F-Test for Variances
  - Z-Test for Proportions
- **Relationship Modeling**
  - Correlations (Linear Pearson, Nonlinear Spearman Rank, Kendall's Tau)
  - Bivariate Regression (Functional Forms: Inverse, Linear-Log, Log-Log, Logistic, Origin, Power, Reciprocal)

5. Multivariate

- **Differences**
  - Parametric General Linear Models: ANCOVA, Single ANOVA Multiple Treatments; ANOVA with Blocking Variables; ANOVA for Replications; Two-Way ANOVA; MANOVA; Two-Way MANOVA (Wilks, Hotelling, Pillai Trace)
  - Nonparametric: Cochran's Q, Friedman's, Kruskal-Wallis, Mann-Whitney, Moods Median
  - Box Test for Covariance Homogeneity; Homogeneity Test for CV
- **Relationship**
  - Bonferroni and Hotelling (Grouped Tests)
  - Factor Analysis, Principal Component Analysis (Eigenvalues & Eigenvectors)
  - Correlation Matrix, Covariance Matrix, Autocorrelation (ACF), Partial Autocorrelation (PACF)
  - Linear and Nonlinear Discriminant Analysis
- **Relationship & Predictive**
  - Multivariate Regression (Linear, Nonlinear, Econometric Models) with Internal and External Validity Checks
  - Stepwise Regression (Forward, Backward, Correlation, Forward-Backward)
  - Limited Dependent Variables Generalized Linear Models (Logit, Probit, Tobit for Truncated and Limited Data)
  - Endogeneity: Durbin-Wu-Hausman, Instrumental Variables, Partial Least Squares (Path Model), Simultaneous Equations Model, Structural Equation Model, Two-Stage Least Squares
  - Granger Causality and Error Correcting Models
  - Cox Regression (Proportional Hazard), Deming Regression (Known Variance), Multiple Ordinal Logistic Regression, Poisson Regression (Discrete Events), Ridge Regression (High VIF), Weighted Regression (Heteroskedasticity)

6. Predictive

- Deterministic: ARIMA (Box-Jenkins), Delphi, Fuzzy Logic, GARCH (EGARCH, TGARCH, GARCH-M), Interpolation and Extrapolation, J-S Curves, Markov Chains, Neural Network, SARIMA, Splines, Time-Series Decomposition (Holt-Winters), Trendlines, Yield Curves (Bliss, Nelson-Siegel)
- Stochastic Processes: Augmented Dickey-Fuller, Brownian Motion Random Walk, Engle-Granger Cointegration, Hodrick-Prescott, Jump Diffusion, Mean Reversion, Monte Carlo Simulation
- Decision Analytics Under Uncertainty: Bootstrap Simulation, Copulas and Correlated Simulation, Deseasonalization, and Detrending, Distributional Analysis, Dynamic Sensitivity, Monte Carlo Simulation, Scenario Analysis, Segmentation Clustering, Stochastic Portfolio Optimization (Markowitz Efficient Frontier)

SUMMARY OF KEY EQUATIONS & CONCEPTS IN STATISTICAL AND QUANTITATIVE ANALYTICAL METHODS

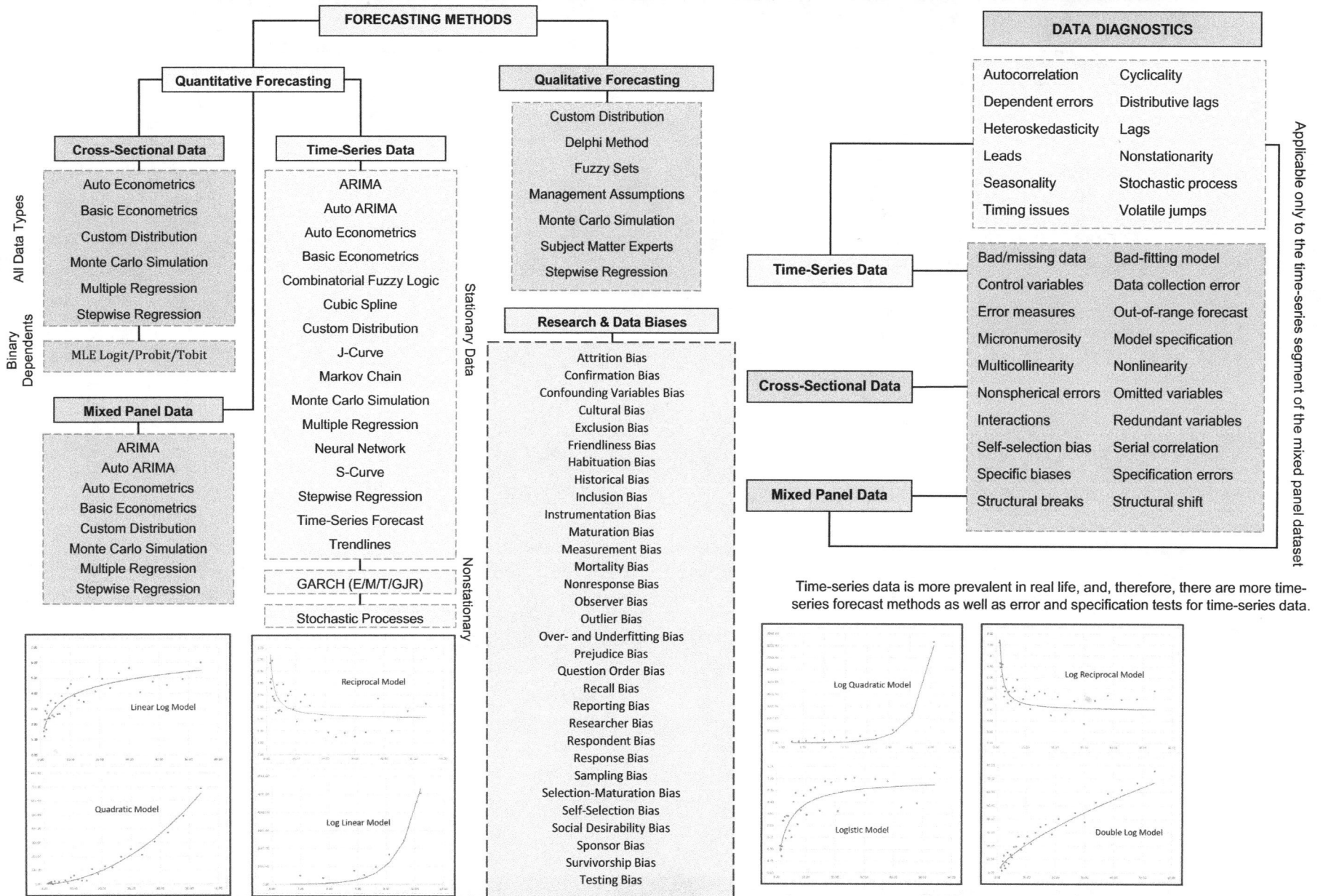

FORECASTING METHODS

Quantitative Forecasting

Cross-Sectional Data
(All Data Types)

Auto Econometrics
Basic Econometrics
Custom Distribution
Monte Carlo Simulation
Multiple Regression
Stepwise Regression

(Binary Dependents)

MLE Logit/Probit/Tobit

Mixed Panel Data

ARIMA
Auto ARIMA
Auto Econometrics
Basic Econometrics
Custom Distribution
Monte Carlo Simulation
Multiple Regression
Stepwise Regression

Time-Series Data

(Stationary Data)

ARIMA
Auto ARIMA
Auto Econometrics
Basic Econometrics
Combinatorial Fuzzy Logic
Cubic Spline
Custom Distribution
J-Curve
Markov Chain
Monte Carlo Simulation
Multiple Regression
Neural Network
S-Curve
Stepwise Regression
Time-Series Forecast
Trendlines

(Nonstationary)

GARCH (E/M/T/GJR)

Stochastic Processes

Qualitative Forecasting

Custom Distribution
Delphi Method
Fuzzy Sets
Management Assumptions
Monte Carlo Simulation
Subject Matter Experts
Stepwise Regression

Research & Data Biases

Attrition Bias
Confirmation Bias
Confounding Variables Bias
Cultural Bias
Exclusion Bias
Friendliness Bias
Habituation Bias
Historical Bias
Inclusion Bias
Instrumentation Bias
Maturation Bias
Measurement Bias
Mortality Bias
Nonresponse Bias
Observer Bias
Outlier Bias
Over- and Underfitting Bias
Prejudice Bias
Question Order Bias
Recall Bias
Reporting Bias
Researcher Bias
Respondent Bias
Response Bias
Sampling Bias
Selection-Maturation Bias
Self-Selection Bias
Social Desirability Bias
Sponsor Bias
Survivorship Bias
Testing Bias

DATA DIAGNOSTICS

Autocorrelation	Cyclicality
Dependent errors	Distributive lags
Heteroskedasticity	Lags
Leads	Nonstationarity
Seasonality	Stochastic process
Timing issues	Volatile jumps

Time-Series Data

Cross-Sectional Data

Mixed Panel Data

Bad/missing data	Bad-fitting model
Control variables	Data collection error
Error measures	Out-of-range forecast
Micronumerosity	Model specification
Multicollinearity	Nonlinearity
Nonspherical errors	Omitted variables
Interactions	Redundant variables
Self-selection bias	Serial correlation
Specific biases	Specification errors
Structural breaks	Structural shift

Applicable only to the time-series segment of the mixed panel dataset

Time-series data is more prevalent in real life, and, therefore, there are more time-series forecast methods as well as error and specification tests for time-series data.

Linear Log Model

Quadratic Model

Reciprocal Model

Log Linear Model

Log Quadratic Model

Logistic Model

Log Reciprocal Model

Double Log Model

PDF & CDF SHAPES OF MOMENTS

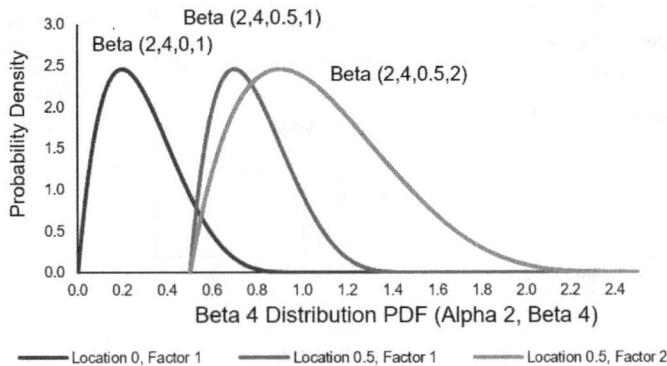

Beta 4 Distribution PDF (Location 10, Factor 2)

Beta 4 Distribution CDF (Location 10, Factor 2)

Beta 4 Distribution PDF (Location 10, Factor 2)

Beta 4 Distribution CDF (Location 10, Factor 2)

Beta 4 Distribution PDF (Alpha 2, Beta 4)

Beta 4 Distribution CDF (Alpha 2, Beta 4)

PROBABILITY DISTRIBUTIONS

$Geometric\ P(x) = p(1-p)^{x-1}\ for\ 0 < p < 1\ and\ x = 1, 2, \dots, n$

$\mu = \frac{1}{p} - 1 \qquad \sigma = \sqrt{\frac{1-p}{p^2}}$

$skew\ g_1 = \frac{2-p}{\sqrt{1-p}} \qquad kurt\ g_2 = \frac{p^2 - 6p + 6}{1-p}$

$Neg.\ Binomial\ P(x) = \frac{(x+r-1)!}{(r-1)!\,x!} p^r (1-p)^x$

$for\ x = r,\ r+1,\ \dots;\ and\ 0 < p < 1$

$\mu = \frac{r(1-p)}{p} \qquad \sigma = \sqrt{\frac{r(1-p)}{p^2}}$

$skew\ g_1 = \frac{2-p}{\sqrt{r(1-p)}} \qquad kurt\ g_2 = \frac{p^2 - 6p + 6}{r(1-p)}$

$Pascal\ F(x) = \begin{cases} \sum_{x=1}^{k} \frac{(x-1)!}{(x-s)!(s-1)!} p^s (1-p)^{x-s} & for\ all\ x \geq s \\ 0 & otherwise \end{cases}$

$\mu = \frac{s}{p} \qquad \sigma = \sqrt{s(1-p)p^2}$

$skew\ g_1 = \frac{2-p}{\sqrt{r(1-p)}} \qquad kurt\ g_2 = \frac{p^2 - 6p + 6}{r(1-p)}$

$Arcsine\ f(x) = \begin{cases} \frac{1}{\pi\sqrt{x(1-x)}} & for\ 0 \leq x \leq 1 \\ 0 & otherwise \end{cases}$

$F(x) = \begin{cases} 0 & x < 0 \\ \frac{2}{\pi} \sin^{-1}(\sqrt{x}) & for\ 0 \leq x \leq 1 \\ 1 & x > 1 \end{cases}$

$\mu = \frac{Min+Max}{2} \qquad \sigma = \sqrt{\frac{(Max-Min)^2}{8}}$

$skew\ g_1 = 0 \qquad kurt\ g_2 = 1.5$

$Beta\ f(x) = \frac{(x)^{(\alpha-1)}(1-x)^{(\beta-1)}}{\left[\frac{\Gamma(\alpha)\Gamma(\beta)}{\Gamma(\alpha+\beta)}\right]}\ for\ \alpha > 0;\ \beta > 0;\ x > 0$

$\mu = \frac{\alpha}{\alpha+\beta} \qquad \sigma = \sqrt{\frac{\alpha\beta}{(\alpha+\beta)^2(1+\alpha+\beta)}}$

$skew\ g_1 = \frac{2(\beta-\alpha)\sqrt{1+\alpha+\beta}}{(2+\alpha+\beta)\sqrt{\alpha\beta}} \quad kurt\ g_2 = \frac{3(\alpha+\beta+1)[\alpha\beta(\alpha+\beta-6)+2(\alpha+\beta)^2]}{\alpha\beta(\alpha+\beta+2)(\alpha+\beta+3)} - 3$

$Cauchy\ Lorentzian\ f(x) = \frac{1}{\pi} \frac{\frac{\gamma}{2}}{(x-m)^2 + \frac{\gamma^2}{4}}$

$Chi-Square\ f(x) = \frac{2^{-\frac{k}{2}}}{\Gamma(\frac{k}{2})} x^{\frac{k}{2}-1} e^{-\frac{x}{2}}\ for\ all\ x > 0$

$\mu = k \qquad \sigma = \sqrt{2k}$

$skew\ g_1 = 2\sqrt{\frac{2}{k}} \qquad kurt\ g_2 = \frac{12}{k}$

$Z_1^2 + Z_2^2 + \cdots + Z_k^2 \overset{d}{\sim} \chi_k^2$

$Cosine\ f(x) = \begin{cases} \frac{1}{2b} Cos\left[\frac{x-a}{b}\right] & for\ Min \leq x \leq Max \\ 0 & otherwise \end{cases}$

$where\ a = \frac{Min+Max}{2}\ and\ b = \frac{Max-Min}{\pi}$

$F(x) = \begin{cases} \frac{1}{2}\left[1 + Sin\left(\frac{x-a}{b}\right)\right] & for\ Min \leq x \leq Max \\ 1 & for\ x > Max \end{cases}$

$\mu = \frac{Min+Max}{2} \qquad \sigma = \sqrt{\frac{(Max-Min)^2(\pi^2-8)}{4\pi^2}}$

$skew\ g_1 = 0 \qquad kurt\ g_2 = \frac{6(90-\pi^4)}{5(\pi^2-6)^2}$

$Double\ Log\ f(x) = \begin{cases} \frac{-1}{2b} ln\left(\frac{|x-a|}{b}\right) & for\ Min \leq x \leq Max \\ 0 & otherwise \end{cases}$

$where\ a = \frac{Min+Max}{2}\ and\ b = \frac{Max-Min}{2}$

$F(x) = \begin{cases} \frac{1}{2} - \left(\frac{|x-a|}{2b}\right)\left[1 - ln\left(\frac{|x-a|}{b}\right)\right] & for\ Min \leq x \leq a \\ \frac{1}{2} + \left(\frac{|x-a|}{2b}\right)\left[1 - ln\left(\frac{|x-a|}{b}\right)\right] & for\ a \leq x \leq Max \end{cases}$

$\mu = \frac{Min+Max}{2} \qquad \sigma = \sqrt{\frac{(Max-Min)^2}{36}}$

$skew\ g_1 = 0 \qquad Kurtosis\ is\ a\ complex\ function$

$Gamma\ Erlang\ f(x) = \begin{cases} \frac{\left(\frac{x}{\beta}\right)^{\alpha-1} e^{-\frac{x}{\beta}}}{\beta(\alpha-1)} & for\ x \geq 0 \\ 0 & otherwise \end{cases}$

$F(x) = \begin{cases} 1 - e^{-\frac{x}{\beta}} \sum_{i=0}^{\alpha-1} \frac{(x/\beta)^i}{i!} & for\ x \geq 0 \\ 0 & otherwise \end{cases}$

$\mu = \alpha\beta \qquad \sigma = \sqrt{\alpha\beta^2}$

$skew\ g_1 = \frac{2}{\sqrt{\alpha}} \qquad kurt\ g_2 = \frac{6}{\alpha} - 3$

$Exponential\ f(x) = \lambda e^{-\lambda x}\ for\ x \geq 0;\ \lambda > 0$

$\mu = \frac{1}{\lambda} \qquad \sigma = \frac{1}{\lambda}$

$skew\ g_1 = 2 \qquad kurt\ g_2 = 6$

$EV\ Gumbel\ f(x) = \frac{1}{\beta} z e^{-z}\ where\ z = e^{\frac{x-m}{\beta}}\ for\ \beta > 0$

$\mu = m + 0.577215\beta \qquad \sigma = \sqrt{\frac{1}{6}\pi^2\beta^2}$

$skew\ g_1 = 1.13955 \qquad kurt\ g_2 = 5.4$

$Fisher-Snedecor\ \frac{\frac{\chi_n^2}{n}}{\frac{\chi_m^2}{m}} \overset{d}{\sim} F_{n,m}$

$f(x) = \frac{\Gamma\left(\frac{n+m}{2}\right)\left(\frac{n}{m}\right)^{\frac{n}{2}} x^{\frac{n}{2}-1}}{\Gamma\left(\frac{n}{2}\right)\Gamma\left(\frac{m}{2}\right)\left[x\left(\frac{n}{m}\right)+1\right]^{\frac{n+m}{2}}}$

$\mu = \frac{m}{m-2} \qquad \sigma = \frac{2m^2(m+n-2)}{n(m-2)^2(m-4)}\ for\ all\ m > 4$

$skew\ g_1 = \frac{2(m+2n-2)}{m-6}\sqrt{\frac{2(m-4)}{n(m+n-2)}}$

$kurt\ g_2 = 12(-16 + 20m - 8m^2 + m^3 + 44n - 32mn$
$+ 5m^2 n - 22n^2 + 5mn^2 n(m-6)(m-8)(n+m-2))$

Gamma $f(x) = \dfrac{\left(\frac{x}{\beta}\right)^{\alpha-1} e^{-\frac{x}{\beta}}}{\Gamma(\alpha)\beta}$ any value $\alpha > 0$ and $\beta > 0$

$\mu = \alpha\beta$ $\qquad \sigma = \sqrt{\alpha\beta^2}$

skew $g_1 = \frac{2}{\sqrt{\alpha}}$ kurt $g_2 = \frac{6}{\alpha}$

Laplace $f(x) = \dfrac{1}{2\beta} exp\left(-\dfrac{|x-\alpha|}{\beta}\right)$

$F(x) = \begin{cases} \dfrac{1}{2} exp\left[\dfrac{x-\alpha}{\beta}\right] & \text{when } x < \alpha \\ 1 - \dfrac{1}{2} exp\left[-\dfrac{x-\alpha}{\beta}\right] & \text{when } x \geq \alpha \end{cases}$

$\mu = \alpha$ $\qquad \sigma = 1.4142\beta$

skew $g_1 = 0$ kurt $g_2 = 3$

Logistic $f(x) = \dfrac{e^{\frac{\mu-x}{\alpha}}}{\alpha\left[1 + e^{\frac{\mu-x}{\alpha}}\right]^2}$ any value of α and μ

$\mu = \hat{\mu}$ $\qquad \sigma = \sqrt{\frac{1}{3}\pi^2\alpha^2}$

skew $g_1 = 0$ kurt $g_2 = 1.2$

Lognormal $f(x) = \dfrac{1}{x\sqrt{2\pi}\,ln(\sigma)} e^{\frac{-[ln(x)-ln(\mu)]^2}{2[ln(\sigma)]^2}}$; $x, \mu, \sigma > 0$

$\mu = exp\left(\mu + \frac{\sigma^2}{2}\right)$ $\sigma = \sqrt{exp(\sigma^2 + 2\mu)\,[exp(\sigma^2) - 1]}$

skew $g_1 = \left[\sqrt{exp(\sigma^2) - 1}\,\right](2 + exp(\sigma^2))$

kurt $g_2 = exp\,(4\sigma^2) + 2\,exp\,(3\sigma^2) + 3\,exp\,(2\sigma^2) - 6$

Normal $f(x) = \dfrac{1}{\sqrt{2\pi}\sigma} e^{\frac{-(x-\mu)^2}{2\sigma^2}}$ any value of x and μ; $\sigma > 0$

$\mu = \hat{\mu}$ $\qquad \sigma = \hat{\sigma}$ $\qquad$ skew $g_1 = 0$ $\qquad$ kurt 0

Parabolic $f(x) = \dfrac{(x)^{(\alpha-1)}(1-x)^{(\beta-1)}}{\left[\frac{\Gamma(\alpha)\Gamma(\beta)}{\Gamma(\alpha+\beta)}\right]}$ where $x > 0$; $\alpha = \beta = 2$

$\mu = \frac{Min+Max}{2}$ $\qquad \sigma = \sqrt{\frac{(Max-Min)^2}{20}}$

skew $g_1 = 0$ kurt $g_2 = -0.8571$

Pareto $f(x) = \dfrac{\beta L^\beta}{x^{(1+\beta)}}$ for $x > L$

$\mu = \frac{\beta L}{\beta-1}$ $\qquad \sigma = \sqrt{\frac{\beta L^2}{(\beta-1)^2(\beta-2)}}$

skew $g_1 = \sqrt{\frac{\beta-2}{\beta}}\left[\frac{2(\beta+1)}{\beta-3}\right]$

kurt $g_2 = \frac{6(\beta^3+\beta^2-6\beta-2)}{\beta(\beta-3)(\beta-4)}$

Pearson V $f(x) = \dfrac{x^{-(\alpha+1)}e^{-\frac{\beta}{x}}}{\beta^{-\alpha}\Gamma(\alpha)}$

$F(x) = \dfrac{\Gamma\left(\alpha, \frac{\beta}{x}\right)}{\Gamma(\alpha)}$

$\mu = \frac{\beta}{\alpha-1}$ $\qquad \sigma = \sqrt{\frac{\beta^2}{(\alpha-1)^2(\alpha-2)}}$

skew $g_1 = \frac{4\sqrt{\alpha-2}}{\alpha-3}$ kurt $g_2 = \frac{30\alpha-66}{(\alpha-3)(\alpha-4)} - 3$

Pearson VI $f(x) = \dfrac{(x/\beta)^{\alpha_1-1}}{\beta\,B(\alpha_1, \alpha_2)[1+(x/\beta)]^{\alpha_1+\alpha_2}}$

$F(x) = F_B\left(\dfrac{x}{x+\beta}\right)$

$\mu = \frac{\beta\alpha_1}{\alpha_2-1}$ $\qquad \sigma = \sqrt{\frac{\beta^2\alpha_1(\alpha_1+\alpha_2-1)}{(\alpha_2-1)^2(\alpha_2-2)}}$

skew $g_1 = 2\sqrt{\frac{\alpha_2-2}{\alpha_1(\alpha_1+\alpha_2-1)}}\left[\frac{2\alpha_1+\alpha_2-1}{\alpha_2-3}\right]$

kurt $g_2 = \frac{3(\alpha_2-2)}{(\alpha_2-3)(\alpha_2-4)}\left[\frac{2(\alpha_2-1)^2}{\alpha_1(\alpha_1+\alpha_2-1)} + (\alpha_2+5)\right] - 3$

PERT $f(x) = \dfrac{(x-M_1)^{A1-1}(M_3-x)^{A2-1}}{B(A1,A2)(M_3-M_1)^{A1+A2-1}}$

$A1 = 6\left[\dfrac{\frac{M_1+4M_2+M_3}{6}-M_1}{M_3-M_1}\right]$; $A2 = 6\left[\dfrac{M_3-\frac{M_1+4M_2+M_3}{6}}{M_3-M_1}\right]$

and B is the Beta function

$\mu = \frac{M_1+4M_2+M_3}{6}$ $\qquad \sigma = \sqrt{\frac{(\mu-M_1)(M_3-\mu)}{7}}$

skew $g_1 = \sqrt{\dfrac{7}{(\mu-M_1)(M_3-\mu)}}\left(\dfrac{M_1+M_3-2\mu}{4}\right)$

kurt g_2 is a complex function

Power $f(x) = \alpha x^{\alpha-1}$ and $F(x) = x^\alpha$

$\mu = \frac{\alpha}{1+\alpha}$ $\qquad \sigma = \sqrt{\frac{\alpha}{(1+\alpha)^2(2+\alpha)}}$

skew $g_1 = \sqrt{\frac{\alpha+2}{\alpha}}\left(\dfrac{2(\alpha-1)}{\alpha+3}\right)$ kurt $g_2 = complex\ function$

Student's T $f(t) = \dfrac{\Gamma\left[\frac{r+1}{2}\right]}{\sqrt{r\pi}\,\Gamma\left[\frac{r}{2}\right]}(1+t^2/r)^{-\frac{r+1}{2}}$

$\mu = 0$ $\qquad \sigma = \sqrt{\frac{r}{r-2}}$

skew $g_1 = 0$ $\qquad$ kurt $g_2 = \frac{6}{r-4}$ for all $r > 4$

Triangular $f(x) = \begin{cases} \dfrac{2(x-M_1)}{(M_3-M_1)(M_2-M_1)} & \text{for } M_1 < x < M_2 \\ \dfrac{2(M_3-x)}{(M_3-M_1)(Max-M_2)} & \text{for } M_2 < x < M_3 \end{cases}$

$\mu = \frac{1}{3}(M_1+M_2+M_3)$

$\sigma = \sqrt{\frac{1}{18}(M_1^2+M_2^2+M_3^2-M_1M_3-M_1M_2-M_2M_3)}$

skew $g_1 = \dfrac{\sqrt{2}(M_1+M_3-2M_2)(2M_1-M_3-M_2)(M_1-2M_3+M_2)}{5(M_1^2+M_2^2+M_3^2-M_1M_3-M_1M_2-M_2M_3)^{\frac{3}{2}}}$

kurt $g_2 = -0.6$

Uniform $f(x) = \dfrac{1}{Max-Min}$ all values of $Min < Max$

$\mu = \frac{Min+Max}{2}$ $\qquad \sigma = \sqrt{\frac{(Max-Min)^2}{12}}$

skew $g_1 = 0$ $\qquad$ kurt -1.2

Weibull $f(x) = \dfrac{\alpha}{\beta}\left[\dfrac{x}{\beta}\right]^{\alpha-1} e^{-\left(\frac{x}{\beta}\right)^\alpha}$ (Exponential when $\alpha = 1$)

$\mu = \beta\Gamma(1+\alpha^{-1})$ $\quad \sigma = \beta^2[\Gamma(1+2\alpha^{-1}) - \Gamma^2(1+\alpha^{-1})]$

skew $g_1 = \dfrac{2\Gamma^3(1+\beta^{-1})-3\Gamma(1+\beta^{-1})\Gamma(1+2\beta^{-1})+\Gamma(1+3\beta^{-1})}{[\Gamma(1+2\beta^{-1})-\Gamma^2(1+\beta^{-1})]^{\frac{3}{2}}}$

kurt $g_2 = complex\ function$

AI MACHINE LEARNING

```
                  ┌─────────────────────┐   ┌──────────────────┐   ┌──────────────────┐
                  │ Natural Language    │───│   ARTIFICIAL     │───│  Deep Learning   │
                  │ Processing          │   │   INTELLIGENCE   │   │                  │
                  └─────────────────────┘   └──────────────────┘   └──────────────────┘
                                                     │
                                            ┌──────────────────┐
                                            │ MACHINE LEARNING │
                                            └──────────────────┘
```

Known Groupings or Known Dependent Variables   Unknown Original Groupings

SUPERVISED   **UNSUPERVISED**

FORECASTING

CLASSIFICATION

| Linear multivariate regression | LINEAR FIT |
| Customized functional forms | NONLINEAR FIT |

BAGGING BOOTSTRAP AGGREGATION

One model re-run thousands of times with resampled original data with replacement

K-NEAREST NEIGHBOR (KNN)

CLASSIFICATION & FORECASTING

| Linear multivariate regression | LINEAR FIT |
| Customized functional forms | NONLINEAR FIT |

FITTING (TRAIN & TEST)

One model fitted using a training dataset for prediction using a testing dataset

CLASSIFICATION & REGRESSION TREES (CART)

Tree with binary splits

RANDOM FOREST

Bootstraps CART for prediction

Cross-sectional with interactions	COMMON FIT
Time-series with interactions	COMPLEX FIT
Compares different time-series methods	TIME-SERIES FIT

ENSEMBLE LEARNING

Tests thousands of model specifications to find the best fit using the same dataset

SUPPORT VECTOR MACHINES (SVM)

Learns and classifies data into linearly separable segments

- GAUSSIAN SVM
- LINEAR SVM
- POLYNOMIAL SVM

| COS HYPERBOLIC |
| HYPERBOLIC |
| LINEAR |
| LOGISTIC |

NEURAL NETWORK

Forecasting time-series data using multilayered perceptrons

CLASSIFICATION & PROBABILITIES

LOGISTIC (LOGIT)

NORMIT (PROBIT)

Binary dependent variable

DIMENSION REDUCTION

FACTOR ANALYSIS

Eigenvalues, eigenvectors, Varimax rotation, factor scores

PRINCIPAL COMPONENT ANALYSIS (PCA)

Eigenvalues, eigenvectors, reduced data matrix

CLASSIFICATION

GAUSSIAN MIX

Classification probabilities with multivariate normal

K-MEANS

Randomized iterations of classes and groups

PHYLOGENIC TREES

SEGMENTATION CLUSTERING

Clustering with centroids and Euclidean mean distances

CLASSIFICATION & FORECASTING

DISCRIMINANT ANALYSIS

- LINEAR LDA
- QUADRATIC QDA

1. Research Basics

Dr. Johnathan Mun, Professor of Research
Quantitative Research Methods Course Slides
Seventh Edition, 2026, ROV Press

Introduction to Research (I)

- The study of quantitative research methods typically revolves around the applications of statistics and statistical theory. Basic statistics can be divided into two categories: **descriptive** and **inferential**. Inferential statistics are the statistical methods used to arrive at conclusions about the associations and relationships among different variables through the testing of hypotheses, which are arrived at through the structured development of intelligent questions to be answered in the research. Descriptive statistics, in contrast, are explicitly designed to describe the fundamental characteristics of a dataset, such as its distributional moments.

- British philosopher Karl Popper once famously said that theories can never be proven, only disproven, apropos to inferential statistics and the applications of **hypothesis testing**. Therefore, the proper setup of any quantitative research method is to start with a testable theory from which hypotheses or research questions would emerge. Data would then be collected through probabilistic sampling methods, and quantitative methods can be applied to reject or "accept" said hypotheses.

Introduction to Research (II)

- Hypotheses cannot be truly accepted or proven to be true, we would never outrightly accept a hypothesis or accept a theory to be completely and perfectly true as specified. The problem with testing hypothesized relationships, especially in the areas of financial economics and social science research is that the dependent variable, the resulting variable that the researcher is interested in measuring and understanding, may be influenced by a large number of extraneous and exogenous variables, making it implausible to block, measure, control, or account for their effects. If variables are related in an observed sample dataset, they may not be truly related within the entire population. Hence, inferential statistics and the testing of hypotheses are never perfectly certain and deterministic. In fact, the testing of hypotheses will, at best, always be probabilistic in nature.

Why Learn Research Philosophy?

- How can understanding the basics of the underlying philosophy improve our research methodology and approach?
- Researchers' personal thoughts, feelings, backgrounds, biases, and beliefs shape the research design, outcomes, and results interpretation.
- The validity of the research will be dependent on the nature of the reality that is being studied.
- **Ontology** is defined as the reality that is being studied or researched. It helps researchers recognize how certain they can be about the nature and existence of the objects under study.
  - **Bounded Relativism.** All theoretical constructs are equally and relatively valuable within their boundaries.
  - **Naïve Realism.** Appropriate methods are required in order to study what "reality" means.
  - **Structural Realism.** The structure of reality can be described within theoretical constructs, but its true structure may remain unknown.
  - **Critical Realism.** Reality can be identified through a critical examination of patterns and facts.
  - **Relativism.** Realities can exist in different constructs and possibly even within different theoretical boundaries.

Epistemology (I)

- **Epistemology** is the knowledge of reality. It covers the aspects of validity, scope, and methodology of acquiring knowledge. What constitutes a knowledge claim; how knowledge is acquired or produced; and how transferability of knowledge can be assessed.

- **Objectivist** Epistemology: Assumes that reality exists outside, or independently, of the individual subject. Objectivist research focuses on providing reliability, consistency, external validity, generalizability, and applicability of the results to other contexts.

- **Constructionist** Epistemology: Rejects the idea that objective truth exists and is waiting to be discovered. The value of constructionist research is in generating contextual understandings of a specified topic or problem and relies on the subjective interpretations of the researcher when constructing realities of the object.

- **Subjectivist** Epistemology: Reality can be expressed in a range of subjective symbolic and linguistic systems. Individuals use such systems to impose understanding, interpretation, and meaning on an event in ways that makes sense to them.

Epistemology (II)

- **Positivism**: Assumes that there is independence between the researcher and the object under research. This implies an objective and evidence-based reality that can be empirically and mathematically interpreted. It further assumes that scientific inquiry should rely on observable and measurable facts rather than on subjective experiences. According to positivism, what counts as knowledge must be capturable via sensory information. If knowledge goes into subjective boundaries, such information does not qualify as knowledge. Positivists believed that science is the only medium where truth can be identified. This means that according to positivists, only the natural sciences such as physics, chemistry, and biology can be counted as science. Clearly, very few researchers ascribe to this stance.

- **Logical Positivism** or **Logical Empiricism**: Multiple methods are needed to identify a valid belief because all methods are considered to be imperfect when used to find the true meaning of reality. This view presupposes that scientific knowledge is the sole type of factual knowledge and all metaphysical doctrines are rejected as meaningless. Knowledge rests upon objective experimental verification or empirical confirmation and does not rely on personal subjective experience.

Epistemology (III)

- **Post-Positivism** or **Post-Empiricism**: This epistemological stance is not simply a revision of positivism, but a complete rejection of the core values of positivism. Post-positivism, which many quantitative researchers ascribe to, points out that scientific reasoning is like common-sense reasoning. Post-positivists reason that our observations cannot always be relied upon as they can also be subjected to error. Therefore, post-positivists are sometimes considered as critical realists, who are critical of the reality under study. Being critical of reality, post-positivists do not rely on a single methodology because each method can have errors or limitations. Therefore, a number of different methods are required to triangulate to an acceptable answer. Post-positivism assumes that scientists are never completely objective and are oftentimes culturally, experientially, or emotionally biased. Therefore, post-positivists assume that pure objectivity cannot be achieved.

The Concept of Theory: Constructs, Propositions, Logic, and Boundary Conditions (I)

- Knowledge that is obtained through a rigorous scientific method typically includes a collection of theories and laws. A theory is a system that incorporates a series of constructs or concepts as well as a series of propositions or the relationships between those constructs, where, collectively, these constructs and propositions present a logical, coherent, and systematic explanation of the researched phenomenon, within some assumptions, constraints, and boundary conditions.

- **Constructs** can be seen as the conceptual or theoretical level. They must be operationalized and measurable at the empirical and observational level in order to be tested. Operationalized constructs are known as variables. These operationalized variables are typically defined as independent (the input variable that may cause or impact a change in the dependent variable, which itself is not caused by any other variable, within the context of the research) or dependent (the output variable to be measured, whose output possibly depends on the independent variable). However, in most research problems, certain variables can also be considered as endogenous, mediating, interacting, or moderating. These variables will be modeled later in the book.

The Concept of Theory: Constructs, Propositions, Logic, and Boundary Conditions (II)

- **Propositions** are the relationships or associations hypothesized to exist among constructs, using deductive logic. Propositions within the concepts of a theory are typically declarative in nature and may indicate an association (e.g., a high level of A is associated with a high level of B) or even a direct cause and effect (e.g., A causes B). Propositions in a theory are usually conjectures but must be operationalizable and testable. Propositions can be rejected if not supported by empirical analysis. Constructs and propositions are stated at the theory level, and they can only be tested if operationalized as variables and measurable. Therefore, hypotheses are simply empirical formulations of constructs and propositions, stated as relationships between operationalized variables.

- **Logic** is the justification of the propositions of the constructs. It connects the theoretical constructs and provides an explanation of the relationships among these constructs. Without incorporating logic, constructs and propositions are simply be a collection of random thoughts devoid of meaning and would not constitute a required cohesive system that is required to form a theory.

- Theories are constrained and restricted by certain assumptions of space, time, and other **Boundary Conditions**. These constraints identify when and where the theory can or cannot be applied.

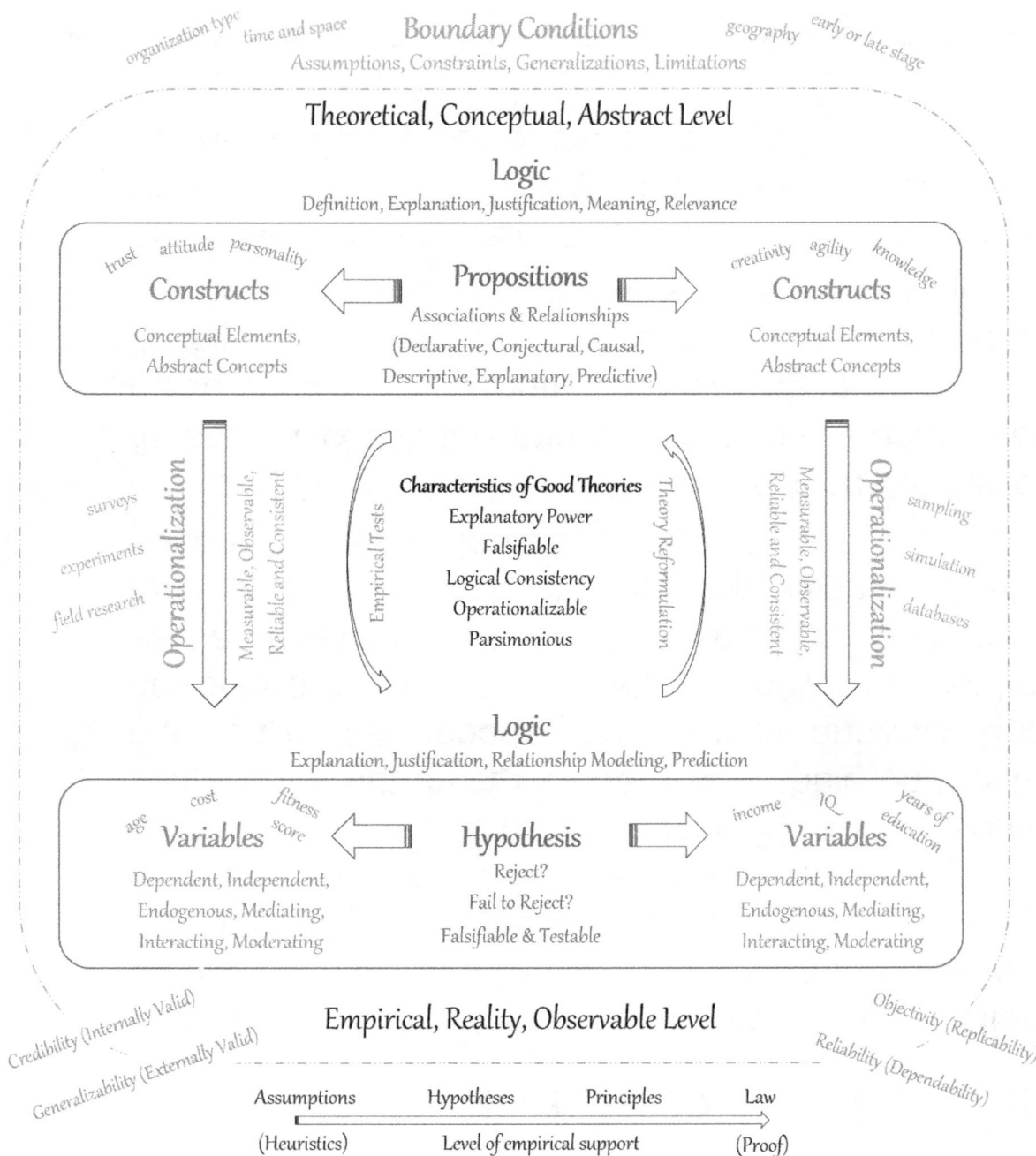

Boundary Conditions
organization type *time and space* *geography* *early or late stage*
Assumptions, Constraints, Generalizations, Limitations

Theoretical, Conceptual, Abstract Level

Logic
Definition, Explanation, Justification, Meaning, Relevance

trust *attitude* *personality*
Constructs
Conceptual Elements,
Abstract Concepts

Propositions
Associations & Relationships
(Declarative, Conjectural, Causal,
Descriptive, Explanatory, Predictive)

creativity *agility* *knowledge*
Constructs
Conceptual Elements,
Abstract Concepts

Operationalization
Measurable, Observable, Reliable and Consistent
surveys *experiments* *field research*

Empirical Tests

Characteristics of Good Theories
Explanatory Power
Falsifiable
Logical Consistency
Operationalizable
Parsimonious

Theory Reformulation

Operationalization
Measurable, Observable, Reliable and Consistent
sampling *simulation* *databases*

Logic
Explanation, Justification, Relationship Modeling, Prediction

age *cost* *fitness* *score*
Variables
Dependent, Independent,
Endogenous, Mediating,
Interacting, Moderating

Hypothesis
Reject?
Fail to Reject?
Falsifiable & Testable

income *IQ* *years of education*
Variables
Dependent, Independent,
Endogenous, Mediating,
Interacting, Moderating

Credibility (Internally Valid)
Generalizability (Externally Valid)

Empirical, Reality, Observable Level

Objectivity (Replicability)
Reliability (Dependability)

Assumptions — Hypotheses — Principles — Law
(Heuristics) — Level of empirical support — (Proof)

A theory can be heuristic and used to describe and explain a phenomenon.

Components of a Scientific Theory
- Constructs (What or Who)
- Propositions (How)
- Logic (Why)
- Boundary (When and Where)

Theory Building Approaches
- Inductive
  - Explanation of Observables
  - Grounded Theory
- Conceptual
  - Bottom Up
  - Cause-Effect
  - Input-Output
  - Interpretive
  - Process-Output
- Deductive
  - Extension to Existing Theory
  - Modify, Add, Fit to Context
- New Context
  - Deductive Approach to New Boundaries
  - Reasoning by Analogy

Attributes of a Good Theory

- **Explanatory Power:** Akaike Information Criterion or adjusted R-square can be used to measure a model's predictive and explanatory power, which in turn, allows the researcher to validate or invalidate the theory.

- **Principal of Parsimony:** Ockham's Razor states that among competing explanations that sufficiently explain the observed evidence, the simplest theory with the smallest number of independent variables having the least amount of assumptions and restrictions is typically the best.

- **Testability and Falsifiability:** For theories to be valid, they must be testable and falsifiable. Falsifiability means the theory can be potentially disprovable or rejected when empirical data is collected and modeled. A theory is not a valid theory unless it can be empirically tested.

- **Operationalizability:** In order to be tested, a theory needs its constructs and propositions to be operationalizable. That is, variables can be constructed from the constructs and propositions, data can be obtained on these variables, and the data can be empirically tested.

- **Logical Consistency:** The theoretical constructs, theoretical propositions, theoretical logic, and theoretical boundary conditions have to all be consistent with each other.

Approaches to Theory Building (I)

- **Grounded Theory (Inductive Reasoning)**. Theories can be built inductively using empirically observed events, behaviors, outcomes, and patterns. This approach is grounded on empirical observations and hence, aptly named grounded theory. It relies on the observations and interpretations of the researcher, and the theory may be subjective and difficult to test. The main difficulties involved in this approach include the need to go beyond a researcher's subjective interpretations and the large set of observations sufficient to generate consistent explanations for the observed patterns and events.

- **Conceptual Analysis (Bottom Up)**. A conceptual or bottom-up analysis identifies different sets of explanatory variables and predictors relevant to explain the event or pattern within certain predefined frameworks. Frameworks can take on various forms, such as interpretive, input-output, cause-effect, and process-output. This is similar to the grounded theory approach in that it relies heavily on the researcher's subjective interpretations.

Approaches to Theory Building (II)

- **Extension and Modification of Existing (Deductive Reasoning).** Another approach is to extend or modify existing theories to describe the phenomenon under a new context. Concepts, propositions, logic, and boundary conditions of the existing theory are retained, added, or modified to fit the new context. This approach is considered a deductive approach as it can appropriate and incorporate a large amount of existing theories and is the most efficient way of building new theories simply by taking advantage of existing ones. An example might be to create momentum investment theory by leveraging the inverse rationality of contrarian theory through empirically modeling the perceptions of economic agents during market downturns.

- **New Context.** The new context approach to theory building utilizes existing theories in entirely new contexts by applying their structural similarities. The difficulty with this approach is being able to use reasoning by analogy and creatively applying a deductive approach to a completely new set of boundaries. An example might be to apply quantum theory in physics to financial markets (new context and new boundaries) to create new theories on stochastic movements of equity prices.

Probabilistic Statistical Sampling

- Sampling theory, in its simplest form, states that if a sample is truly representative of the entire population, then the estimated sample statistics should be identical to corresponding theoretical population parameters. This rationale is based on the Central Limit Theorem and Sampling Distribution Theory.

- Top-Down Sampling Approach
  - **Target Population**
  - **Sampling Frame**
  - **Sampling Technique**

- Sampling Approaches
  - **Randomized Sampling Theory**
  - **Simple Random Sampling**
  - **Systematic Sampling**
  - **Stratified Sampling**
  - **Cluster Sampling**
  - **Matched Pairs Sampling**
  - **Multiple Stage Sampling**

Nonprobabilistic Statistical Sampling

- In nonprobabilistic statistical sampling, some units of the population have zero chance of selection or the probability of selection cannot be accurately determined. Typically, units are selected based on certain nonrandom criteria, such as quota or convenience. Because selection is nonrandom, nonprobability sampling does not allow the estimation of sampling errors and may be subjected to a sampling bias.

- Types of Nonprobabilistic Sampling
  - **Convenience Sampling**
  - **Quota Sampling**
  - **Subject Matter Expert Sampling (Delphi & Likert)**

Consistency, Reliability, Validity

- **Accuracy**. In Data: Accuracy refers to how close your measurements or predictions are to the true values. In Baking: Accuracy is like making sure you measure your ingredients exactly so your cake turns out as intended.

- **Bias**. In Data: Bias is a systematic error that skews your results in a particular direction. In Baking: Bias is like always using the same brand of flour that might be a bit heavier, so your cake always comes out denser.

- **Consistency**. In Data: Consistency means that results or data agree with each other over time, across sources, or across different parts of the dataset because the same rules and procedures are applied in the same way. In Baking: Consistency is like always following the same recipe and steps—same oven temperature, same mixing order, same baking time—so everything in the process is done the same way each time, helping your cakes turn out uniform from one batch to the next. Layers have the same level of softness and consistency.

- **Precision**. In Data: Precision refers to how consistent your measurements are when repeated under the same conditions. In Baking: Precision is like always measuring the exact same amount of sugar every time you bake, so your cake is consistently sweet.

- **Reliability**. In Data: Reliability means you get the same results consistently when you repeat the measurement. In Baking: It's like baking the same cake multiple times and having it turn out just as delicious each time.

- **Replicability**. In Data: Replicability is when other researchers can use your methods and data and get the same results. In Baking: It's like giving your recipe to a friend and having them bake the same cake successfully in their own kitchen.

- **Validity**. In Data: Validity is about how well your method measures what it's supposed to measure. In Baking: Validity is like making sure your recipe actually produces the type of cake you promised—like a fluffy sponge if that's what you claimed.

Threats to Validity

- **Internal Validity** asks if the treatments in an experiment make a difference in the specific boundary conditions of the research. For example, if a new teaching method helps improve students' test scores. **External Validity**, in contrast, looks to inductively identify how the results and conclusions can be generalized and under what boundary conditions, assumptions, settings, and treatments. Examples:

Attrition Bias	Confirmation Bias	Confounding Variables Bias
Cultural Bias	Exclusion Bias	Friendliness Bias
Habituation Bias	Historical Bias	Inclusion Bias
Instrumentation Bias	Maturation Bias	Measurement Bias
Mortality Bias	Nonresponse Bias	Observer Bias
Outlier Bias	Over- and Underfitting Bias	Question Order Bias
Prejudice Bias	Recall Bias	Reporting Bias
Researcher Bias	Respondent Bias	Response Bias
Sampling Bias	Selection-Maturation Bias	Self-Selection Bias
Social Desirability Bias	Sponsor Bias	Survivorship Bias
Testing Bias		

Qualitative Research Approaches (I)

- **Case Study**. Detailed analysis of a specific case, focusing on a specific facet, aspect, subject, process, or activity. The research instruments may include interviews, focus groups, questionnaires, project documentation, physical visits, observations, stories, and surveys.

- **Phenomenology**. Subjective interpretation of a problem from different points of view. In other words, how individuals feel or perceive a phenomenon. Typically, the researcher would find a specific phenomenon to study, then find exemplars of this phenomenon and identify subjects that might best fit having experienced the events. In-depth and detailed interviews and focus groups are usually held to understand the individual's and collective group's experiences. The typical characteristics of these interviews are that they tend to be detailed, lengthy, and might require subsequent follow-ups. The researchers are usually experienced in extracting open-ended responses and are highly trained in the phenomenon being researched.

- **Field Research**, **Field Studies**, or **Fieldwork**. Collection of data outside a laboratory or controlled setting, where subjects are observed in their natural state. Researchers typically take extensive notes of certain events, typically with modern videography and computer simulation models. Examples of field research may include observing animals in their original habitats, interacting with other animals, or social scientists observing people in their natural environment, observing, and learning their languages, political leanings, folklore, and social structures.

Qualitative Research Approaches (II)

- **Ethnographic Research**. Embeds the researcher into an organization or culture to study an entire culture, organization, or group and the interactions within entire groups. Extensive notes and recordings are usually made, and conclusions from the researchers typically include subjective observations and impressions of the interactions.

- **Grounded Theory (Inductive Reasoning)**. Development of theories about the phenomenon that is being researched grounded on empirical observation. Core theoretical concepts are identified simultaneously while the data are being gathered. Explanations, causalities, associations, or linkages between the theoretical concepts and the empirical data are created. Because each new observation can theoretically lead to a new linkage, the circular process never terminates. The research terminates only when the researcher decides to conclude the study. Grounded theory is an eccentric data analysis approach as it involves simultaneous data collection and data analysis. Researchers hope to reveal value-added insights as more data are gathered and their research direction changes. For this to happen, the data is analyzed from the moment data collection begins and continues until the research ends.

True Experimental Design

- The following slides are some sample classical experimental designs in the tradition of Campbell and Stanley as well as Isaac and Michael. To illustrate each of the design types below, let us assume that we wish to determine if a new math teaching method (e.g., Singapore Math) at a middle school is effective in increasing math aptitude, as measured through standardized test scores. Treatment X is the new math learning method that the students will be exposed to, for a specific amount of time. Tests (T) are administered at different times in the various designs. In some designs, there will be a pre-test, or first test (T1) applied to gauge the students' math abilities prior to the new teaching method, and, later, a post-test (T2) is employed to gauge the effects of the teaching method.

Design 0: Poor No-Control One-Shot Case Study

Treatment	Post Test
X	T2

Design 0 is a one-shot test, where no pre-tests were administered, only a post-test. This is considered a poor research design as there is no control and it provides no internal validity, making the results highly misleading because there is no basis for comparison. There might exist numerous exogenous effects that can impact T2 that are not considered or controlled for. This might be a good initial rough-cut design to quickly test if a problem is researchable, but no proper or valid conclusions can be drawn.

Design 1: Minimal Control One Group Pre- and Post-Test Design

Pre-Test	Treatment	Post-Test
T1	X	T2

Design 1 implements a pre-test as a control for the single group tested. In contrast to Design 0, this design provides a much-needed control or comparison. If the same subjects take T1 and T2, then we can eliminate any selection bias (different people taking the two tests) and mortality bias (possible loss of subjects over time) only if the experiment is performed in a time-constrained manner. The difference in scores (T2 − T1) is the test variable that is subjected to statistical hypothesis tests such as a parametric t-test for larger sample sizes with interval and ratio data, or nonparametric Wilcoxon signed-rank test and Mann–Whitney test, for smaller sample sizes or if the data is ordinal.

Potential issues with this design include history bias (some students might take external courses to help boost their scores between T1 and T2), maturation bias (students generally get better at a subject the more they practice and learn), testing bias (having a pre-test might increase a student's motivation to do well, or reduce morale and induce test anxiety), instrumentation bias (different pre- and post-test exam types), and outlier bias (there might be extreme cases with super achievers and low test scores in the class, biasing the regression line).

Design 2: Randomized Control Group Pre- and Post-Test Design

Group	Pre-Test	Treatment	Post-Test
Experimental Group	T1	X	T2
Control Group	T1	.	T2

Design 2 introduces a control group and randomization. All conditions are kept identical between the experimental and control groups except for the treatment, which the control group does not receive, and the students are randomly assigned to the two groups. The differences T2 – T1 for each group are computed. Compare the two difference variables to see if there is a statistical difference. A parametric pairwise t-test with independent variables and equal variance or a nonparametric two-variable Wilcoxon signed rank test and Mann–Whitney test can be applied.

Design 2: Randomized Control Group Pre- and Post-Test Design (EXTENSION)

Group	Pre-Test	Treatment	Post-Test
Experimental Group 1	T1	X (Method A)	T2
Experimental Group 2	T1	X (Method B)	T2
Control Group	T1	.	T2

Design 2 can be further extended to multiple experimental groups as shown next. A parametric ANOVA single factor multiple treatments test or nonparametric Kruskal–Wallis test can be employed to identify differences among all groups simultaneously. In addition, pairwise t-tests or the Wilcoxon and Mann–Whitney tests can be applied between pairs of experimental groups. The control group is not required in the model when comparing if there are differences between different groups. The different groups can also be subjected to different treatment types or treatment levels. Internal validity is strengthened in Design 2 but instrumentation bias (same tests need to be administered identically by the same teachers) and maturation bias (different teachers and teaching techniques in the different groups) may still exist.

Design 3: Randomized Solomon Four Group Design

Group	Pre-Test	Treatment	Post-Test
Pre-Tested	T1	X	T2
Pre-Tested	T1	.	T2
No Pre-Test		X	T2
No Pre-Test		.	T2

Design 3 has four groups where two of these groups were not subjected to any pre-test, thereby eliminating any potential external validity issues (e.g., students not subjected to pre-tests may not feel the extra pressure to perform or be unmotivated and end up under-performing due to the added stress of testing). The reduction of a pre-test (T1) takes away any additional anxiety, which may create an interacting effect on the students' learning experience and eventual test scores (T2), which may or may not impact the experimental results.

Design 4: Randomized Control Group Post-Test Only Design

Group	Pre-Test	Treatment	Post-Test
Experimental Group		X	T2
Control Group		.	T2

Design 4 consists of the last two groups of Design 3, where the possible interacting effects of a pre-test are removed. Although this looks similar to Design 0 with a control group, the students are randomly selected. The randomization, when performed correctly, can be used to assume that both groups have an equal distribution of abilities. Interestingly, in some respects, Design 4 is superior to Design 2 in that the confounding and interacting effects have been removed, and it also reduces the cost and time required by not having to perform a pre-test.

Design 5: Non-Randomized Control Group Pre- and Post-Test Design

Group	Pre-Test	Treatment	Post-Test
Experimental Group	T1	X	T2
Control Group	T1	.	T2

Design 5 is similar to Design 2 except that the students are not randomized but pre-assigned and pre-assembled into the various groups. The same validity threats exist in this design as in Design 2, but the benefits are that these pre-assembled groups are convenient and we further reduce any added anxiety or stress in the subjects as their classes are kept intact, without any further random redistribution into new cohorts and groups.

Design 6: Counterbalanced Design

Replication	Treatment X(a)	Treatment X(b)	Treatment X(c)	Treatment X(d)
1	A	B	C	D
2	B	D	A	C
3	C	A	D	B
4	D	C	B	A

Design 6 is an enhancement to Design 5 in that if intact and pre-assembled groups are required and random assignments are not possible, then a counterbalanced design might be appropriate. When multiple treatments are tested (a, b, c, d), where one of these treatments can be a control (no treatment is applied), then groups of student cohorts (A, B, C, D) can be exposed to each treatment in a rotational fashion. A post-test is administered after each treatment. This design reduces the weakness of nonrandomization in Design 5 but adds additional biases in terms of maturation (student fatigue in so many experiments and tests) and interaction or confounding variables bias (learning materials from one treatment type versus another might create confusion for the students).

Design 7: One Group Time-Series Design

Pre-Test	Treatment	Post-Test
T1, T2, T3, T4	X	T5, T6, T7, T8

Design 7 is similar to Design 1 except that multiple pre- and post-tests are administered over time. This helps control for internal validity issues that exist in Design 1. If the scores T1 to T4 are comparable, and T5 to T8 are comparable, we can state that the internal validity issues of maturation bias and instrumentation bias are reduced. However, the external validity threats of interaction between the pre- and post-tests remain.

Design 8: Control Group Time-Series Design

Group	Pre-Test	Treatment	Post-Test
Experimental Group	T1, T2, T3, T4	X	T5, T6, T7, T8
Control Group	T1, T2, T3, T4	.	T5, T6, T7, T8

Design 8 is like Design 7 except for a new control group. This eliminates any contemporaneous history bias especially if there is little difference between T5 and T4 in the control group, but the experimental group shows statistically significant gains. Contemporaneous history bias implies that there might be some event (e.g., Math Olympiad or math week on television) that might confound the results in the post-test.

Factorial Design

2 × 2 Factorial Design	Factor A1	Factor A2
Factor B1	…	…
Factor B2	…	…

The classical research designs shown previously apply to single-factor treatments. These designs can be further improved with a factorial design structure, when more than one factor is tested. The design shown next is a 2 × 2 factorial design where we test two factors, A and B, and their interactions. Factor A can be the two different math courses; whereas B can be the length of time the courses are taught (one semester versus one academic year); and we can also model the potential interactions among A and B. The Parametric Two Factor ANOVA model or regression model can be used to test this factorial experimental design. Extensions of this Factorial Design might be done with replication. A Two Factor ANOVA model with Replication can be applied in such instances. If the second factor needs to be controlled, we can apply the ANOVA with Blocking Variables method. Additional factors beyond this 2 × 2 factorial design can be created, such as an M × N design or even a P × Q × R design, where MANOVA models and multiple regression (all factors and all possible combinations of interacting factors are set as independent variables) methods can be employed.

Quasi-Experimental Design

Unlike a true experiment, a quasi-experiment does not rely on random assignment. Instead, subjects are assigned to groups based on nonrandom criteria. In fact, Design 6 can be classified as a quasi-experimental design in that subjects were not randomized, and counterbalancing is used to reduce maturation and confounding variables biases. A Latin Cube and Latin Hypercube approach can be used when randomization is impractical and when the sample size is small. A true experimental design requires a larger sample size, proper randomization, and proper designing of the experimental process.

Doctoral Dissertation Chapters and Sections

- ## Title of Research
  - Succinct but also descriptive
  - Highlights the main idea and purpose of your research topic
  - Contains relevant keywords for easier archiving and searching

- ## Abstract
  - The most important paragraph in the doctoral dissertation
  - Brief single-paragraph summary (100–300 words)
  - Identify the problem or research issue, purpose of the study, summary of the data collected, the main statistical results, and practical applications, as well as why this research is important
  - Concise, precise, readable, and simple
  - One of the first items to be written, the single paragraph that is edited the most, and one of the last things that you rewrite

Doctoral Dissertation Chapters and Sections

A. INTRODUCTION CHAPTER

- ## Purpose Statement
    - Clear, concise, informative, and specific
    - Written in one or several sentences and encapsulates the intent of the entire study, making it probably the most important singular statement in the entire article or dissertation
    - Don't include the research problem or hypothesis, or the circumstances that led you to perform the research as those appear elsewhere
    - Use words such as *purpose, goal, objective,* or *intent*
    - Examples: "The purpose of this study is to explore/investigate the effects of…" or "This research seeks to explain why…" or "This research describes a quantitative study of…" or "This study attempts to link [some variable] to the effects of [some variable] …" or "The purpose of the current research is to examine and find the statistical relationship between…"

Doctoral Dissertation Chapters and Sections

A. INTRODUCTION CHAPTER

- ## Research Question and Hypotheses

    – Narrow down the purpose statement to a more defined and quantifiable set of criteria. Therefore, use specific variables whenever possible.

    – Present either the research questions or a set of hypotheses to test.

    – Hypotheses tend to be simpler to write in that they tend to follow a more formulaic sentence structure.

    – There are usually multiple hypotheses to test. It is good practice to always include both a null and an alternate hypothesis for each item tested. The alternate hypotheses can be nondirectional or unidirectional.

    – The null hypothesis means that there are no statistically significant effects of one or more independent variables on a dependent variable.

    – The alternate hypothesis states that either there is some effect (nondirectional) or that the value of the dependent variable increases or decreases (unidirectional) based on the effects applied in the independent variables.

    – Example of unidirectional null and alternate hypotheses: "There is no relationship between parents' wealth and their children's educational achievement" and "Children of wealthier parents' tend to do better academically."

Doctoral Dissertation Chapters and Sections

A. INTRODUCTION CHAPTER

- ## Contribution to Knowledge
  - This section can either be simple to write or incredibly difficult.
  - To write this section, you usually must first speculate as to what your theoretical contributions may be, continue with the research, and then come back and properly complete the section.

- ## Report Layout
  - The last section of the introduction should state the layout of the rest of the report and explain what to expect in the second and subsequent chapters, providing only cursory highlights and an outline of the content.

Doctoral Dissertation Chapters and Sections

B. LITERATURE REVIEW CHAPTER

- ## Review of Literature
  - A search of the literature or a literature review is the next section.
  - A detailed search of the studies on the main topic related to your research as well as reviewing and summarizing them.
  - Sources could come from academic journals, books, periodicals, articles, web blogs, and other research studies.
  - The focus should be on legitimate academically-based sources such as books and published academic articles, preferably from peer-reviewed and notable journals.

- ## Review of Relevant Theory and Deficiencies
  - You should also review existing theories that pertain both directly and indirectly to your current study. A literature review is not a book report, simply regurgitating all the information ingested. Rather, it requires the distilling, culling, combining, and integrating of various studies into a coherent story, setting the stage and supporting the need for your current research work.

Doctoral Dissertation Chapters and Sections

C. RESEARCH METHODOLOGY CHAPTER

- Details of the survey, experiment, and data collection mechanisms.
- Before deciding on the research instrument to collect your data and what type of data to collect, you need to first understand the types of data that exist and what you can do with said data. Then, you explain how your experiment works.
- How do you propose to obtain the data? A survey, a live audience experiment, a computer simulation, secondary data resources, and databases, etc.? What data would you require to model the hypotheses you have laid out? If you are performing an experiment, how are participants selected, that is, according to any specific criteria or background? How are these participants stratified or grouped? How would the data be collected?
- This section essentially tells the story of your approach such that any knowledgeable person would be able to follow along with the story and instructions provided and, in theory, be able to replicate the study.
- Detailed descriptions of surveys, questionnaires, and interview questions should all be collated and integrated into an appendix.
- Caution is required if there are ethical considerations or privacy laws and restrictions involved in your research. For example, HIPPA rules forbid releasing personal health records and information, information pertaining to the identity of individuals should not be released, programs that are classified by the government or military organizations need to be held in confidence, and so forth.

Doctoral Dissertation Chapters and Sections

D. ANALYSIS CHAPTER

- # Data Overview and Biases

  - Are there any data collection issues such as survivorship bias, self-selection bias, and other types of sampling biases?

- # Descriptive Statistics

  - Data collected should be subjected to some basic descriptive statistics and visualization.

  - Histograms or bar and line charts would go a long way in explaining the layout of the data and provide a high-level overview of the data structure.

  - Basic descriptive statistics such as mean, median, standard deviation, coefficient of variation, and cross-correlations should be done to help the researcher get a better sense and grasp of the data. Are there any outliers in the data? Are there significantly high or low correlations between certain variables, and why or why not? Are any variables wildly fluctuating about their means and why? Descriptive statistics help validate the data quality as well as lay the foundations for additional tests.

Doctoral Dissertation Chapters and Sections

D. ANALYSIS CHAPTER

- ## Statistical Inferences and Hypothesis Tests
  - Lay out the hypotheses and show the tests used and the results obtained from these tests.

- ## Results and Interpretation
  - The results of the hypotheses tests are collated and grouped into tables. Hypotheses are rejected or accepted based upon the researcher's predefined thresholds.
  - Interpret the results, look for interconnectivity and links.

Doctoral Dissertation Chapters and Sections

E. CONCLUSION CHAPTER

- ## Conclusion and Recommendations
  - Draw additional conclusions and showcase how the work will benefit society or how the work can be made practical.
  - State your recommendations as a researcher.

- ## Research Limitations and Next Steps
  - Any research worth its weight should have a specific and narrow focus. Trying to take on the entire topic in a single research would be both foolish and intractable. Therefore, there will always be missing pieces in the research you performed.
  - List all deficiencies in this section. Note the limitations you faced in the current research, such as insufficient data, low response rate, too narrow a sample, limited resources, and so forth.
  - Expand upon how the research can be continued, or the next steps to be taken, should a fellow researcher who comes after you wish to take over the mantle and continue to pursue the research.

Doctoral Dissertation Chapters and Sections

- ## Appendices
  - Appendices can include all the miscellaneous details that a reader would find too cumbersome to read in the main text of your research. For a doctoral dissertation or graduate thesis, they are where any details of the survey design, survey questions, experimental procedures and steps, raw data, analysis settings, method calculations, screenshots of software applications, and other items are provided. Appendices should be separated into different sections either based on the order in which they are referred to in the main body of the research or by relevant topics.

- ## References
  - Follow your academic institution's or journal's requirements when it comes to the style to use for references. The standard approach is to apply the APA (American Psychological Association) style and format. The rule of thumb is to have at least 30 references for any master's level thesis and at least 50 references for any doctoral dissertations. References should be listed alphabetically.

Doctoral Dissertation Chapters and Sections

- ## Miscellaneous Items

  Front Matter
  - Cover Page
  - Signature Page (advisors' approval)
  - Declaration Page (declaring the work is original)
  - Acknowledgments and Tribute
  - Table of Contents
  - List of Figures
  - List of Tables
  - List of Acronyms Used

  End Material
  - Additional Appendices
  - Endnotes
  - Glossary of Terms
  - Index
  - Biography or Curriculum Vitae

2. Overview of Applied Statistical and Quantitative Methods

Dr. Johnathan Mun, Professor of Research
Quantitative Research Methods Course Slides
Seventh Edition, 2026, ROV Press

Probability Theory and Probability Distributions

Bayes' Theorem

$$P(A|M) = \frac{P(A \cap M)}{P(M)} = \frac{P(A)P(M|A)}{P(M)} = \frac{P(A)P(M|A)}{P(A \cap M) + P(B \cap M) + P(C \cap M)} = \frac{P(A)P(M|A)}{P(A)P(M|A) + P(B)P(M|B) + P(C)P(M|C)}$$

$$P(X_1|M) = \frac{P(X_1)P(M|X_1)}{P(X_1)P(M|X_1) + P(X_2)P(M|X_2) + P(X_3)P(M|X_3) + \dots + P(X_n)P(M|X_n)}$$

Combinations and Permutations

$$C_x^n = \frac{n!}{x!(n-x)!} \qquad P_x^n = \frac{n!}{(n-x)!}$$

Binomial Distribution

$$P(x) = \frac{n!}{x!(n-x)!}p^x(1-p)^{(n-x)} \quad \text{for } n > 0; \ x = 0, 1, 2, \dots n; \text{ and } 0 < p < 1$$

For each trial, only two outcomes are possible that are mutually exclusive. The trials are independent—what happens in the first trial does not affect the next trial. The probability of an event occurring remains the same from trial to trial.

Poisson Distribution

$$P(x) = \frac{e^{-\lambda}\lambda^x}{x!}$$

The number of possible occurrences in any interval is unlimited. The occurrences are independent. The number of occurrences in one interval does not affect the number of occurrences in other intervals. The average number of occurrences must remain the same from interval to interval. The values x and $\lambda > 0$.

Hypergeometric Distribution

$$P(x) = \frac{\dfrac{(N_x)!}{x!(N_x-x)!}\dfrac{(N-N_x)!}{(n-x)!(N-N_x-n+x)!}}{\dfrac{N!}{n!(N-n)!}} \quad \text{for } x = Max(n-(N-N_x),0), \ \dots, \ Min(n,N_x)$$

The total number of items or elements (the population size) is a fixed number, a finite population. The population size must be less than or equal to 1,750. The sample size (the number of trials) represents a portion of the population. The known initial probability of success in the population changes after each trial.

Normal Distribution

$$f(x) = \frac{1}{\sqrt{2\pi}\sigma}e^{\frac{-(x-\mu)^2}{2\sigma^2}} \quad \text{for all values of } x$$

Some value of the uncertain variable is the most likely (the mean of the distribution). The uncertain variable could as likely be above the mean as it could be below the mean (symmetrical about the mean). The uncertain variable is more likely in the vicinity of the mean than further away.

Hypothesis Testing

The hypotheses tested are typically:

H_0: $\mu_1 = \mu_2$, or $\mu_1 - \mu_2 = 0$, that is, the two samples' means are statistically similar

H_a: $\mu_1 \neq \mu_2$, or $\mu_1 - \mu_2 \neq 0$, where the two samples' means are statistically significantly different

The null hypothesis (H_0) generally has the equivalence sign (i.e., =, ≥, ≤), whereas the alternate hypothesis (H_a) has its complement (i.e., ≠, <, >). The sign of the alternate hypothesis points to whether the test is a two-tailed test (≠) or a one-tailed test (right tail is denoted with >, whereas a left tail test uses <). As an example, to get started in a two-sample hypothesis test, a dataset with some number of data points for two variables (with n_1 and n_2 sample sizes) are put side by side. Then, their respective sample averages ($\bar{x}_1$ and $\bar{x}_2$) and sample standard deviations (s_1 and s_2) are computed. The t-statistic is then calculated using the relevant formula (depending on the specific test) and compared against the critical t-values. In most situations, the p-values of this calculated t-statistic are calculated and compared against some predefined level of significance (i.e., the standard α significance levels of 0.10, 0.05, and 0.01 will be assumed throughout these examples) using the t-distribution with a certain degree of freedom (df). If the p-value is below these α significance levels, we reject the null hypothesis and accept the alternate hypothesis.

Statistical Methods for One Variable

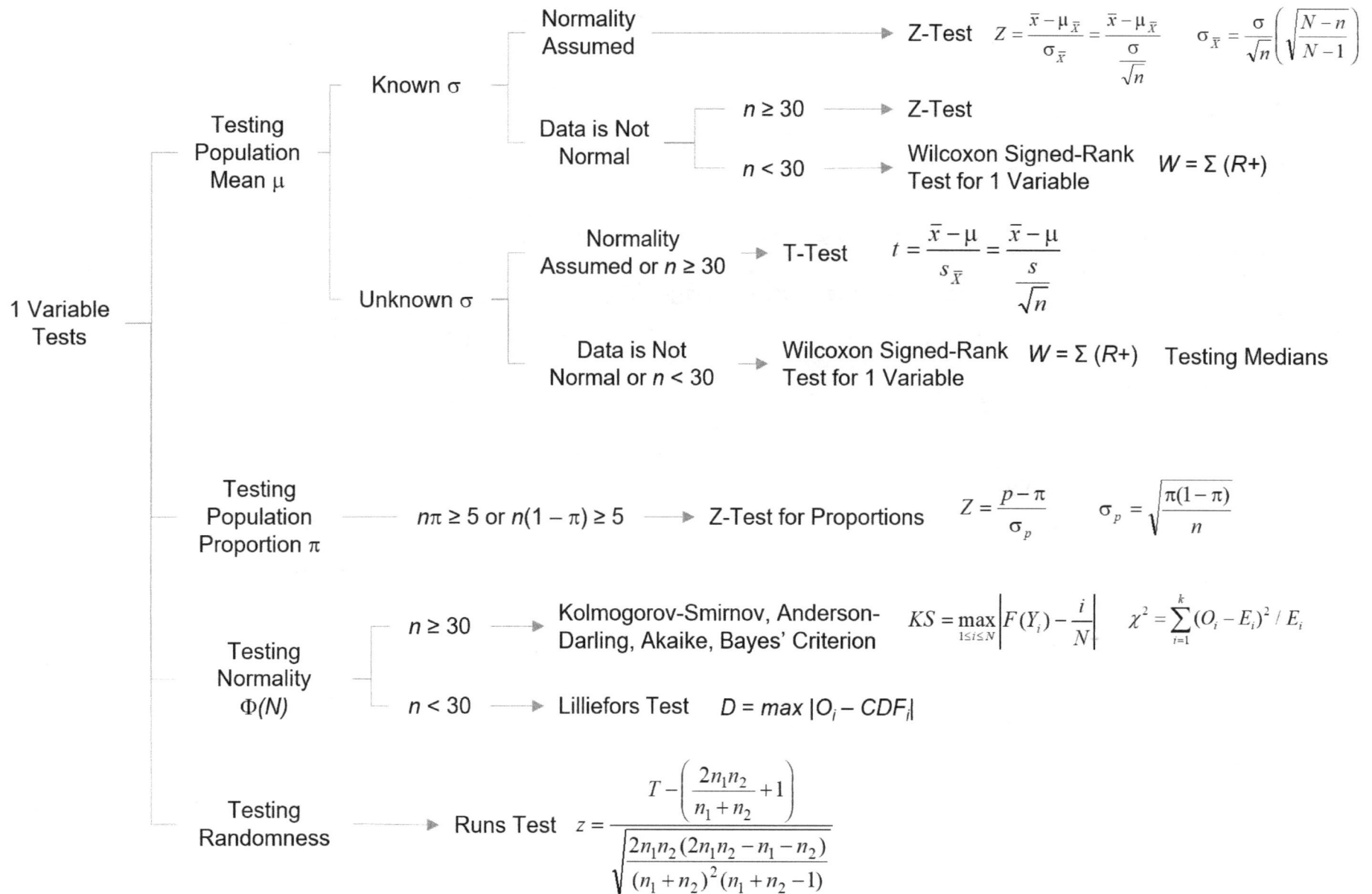

Testing Population Mean μ

Known σ

Normality Assumed → Z-Test
$$Z = \frac{\bar{x} - \mu_{\bar{x}}}{\sigma_{\bar{x}}} = \frac{\bar{x} - \mu_{\bar{x}}}{\frac{\sigma}{\sqrt{n}}} \qquad \sigma_{\bar{x}} = \frac{\sigma}{\sqrt{n}}\left(\sqrt{\frac{N-n}{N-1}}\right)$$

Data is Not Normal
- $n \geq 30$ → Z-Test
- $n < 30$ → Wilcoxon Signed-Rank Test for 1 Variable $\quad W = \Sigma\,(R+)$

Unknown σ

Normality Assumed or $n \geq 30$ → T-Test
$$t = \frac{\bar{x} - \mu}{s_{\bar{X}}} = \frac{\bar{x} - \mu}{\frac{s}{\sqrt{n}}}$$

Data is Not Normal or $n < 30$ → Wilcoxon Signed-Rank Test for 1 Variable $\quad W = \Sigma\,(R+) \quad$ Testing Medians

Testing Population Proportion π

$n\pi \geq 5$ or $n(1 - \pi) \geq 5$ → Z-Test for Proportions
$$Z = \frac{p - \pi}{\sigma_p} \qquad \sigma_p = \sqrt{\frac{\pi(1-\pi)}{n}}$$

Testing Normality $\Phi(N)$

- $n \geq 30$ → Kolmogorov-Smirnov, Anderson-Darling, Akaike, Bayes' Criterion
$$KS = \max_{1 \leq i \leq N}\left|F(Y_i) - \frac{i}{N}\right| \qquad \chi^2 = \sum_{t=1}^{k}(O_i - E_i)^2 / E_i$$
- $n < 30$ → Lilliefors Test $\quad D = max\,|O_i - CDF_i|$

Testing Randomness

Runs Test
$$z = \frac{T - \left(\frac{2n_1 n_2}{n_1 + n_2} + 1\right)}{\sqrt{\frac{2n_1 n_2 (2n_1 n_2 - n_1 - n_2)}{(n_1 + n_2)^2 (n_1 + n_2 - 1)}}}$$

1 Variable Tests

Statistical Methods for Two Variables

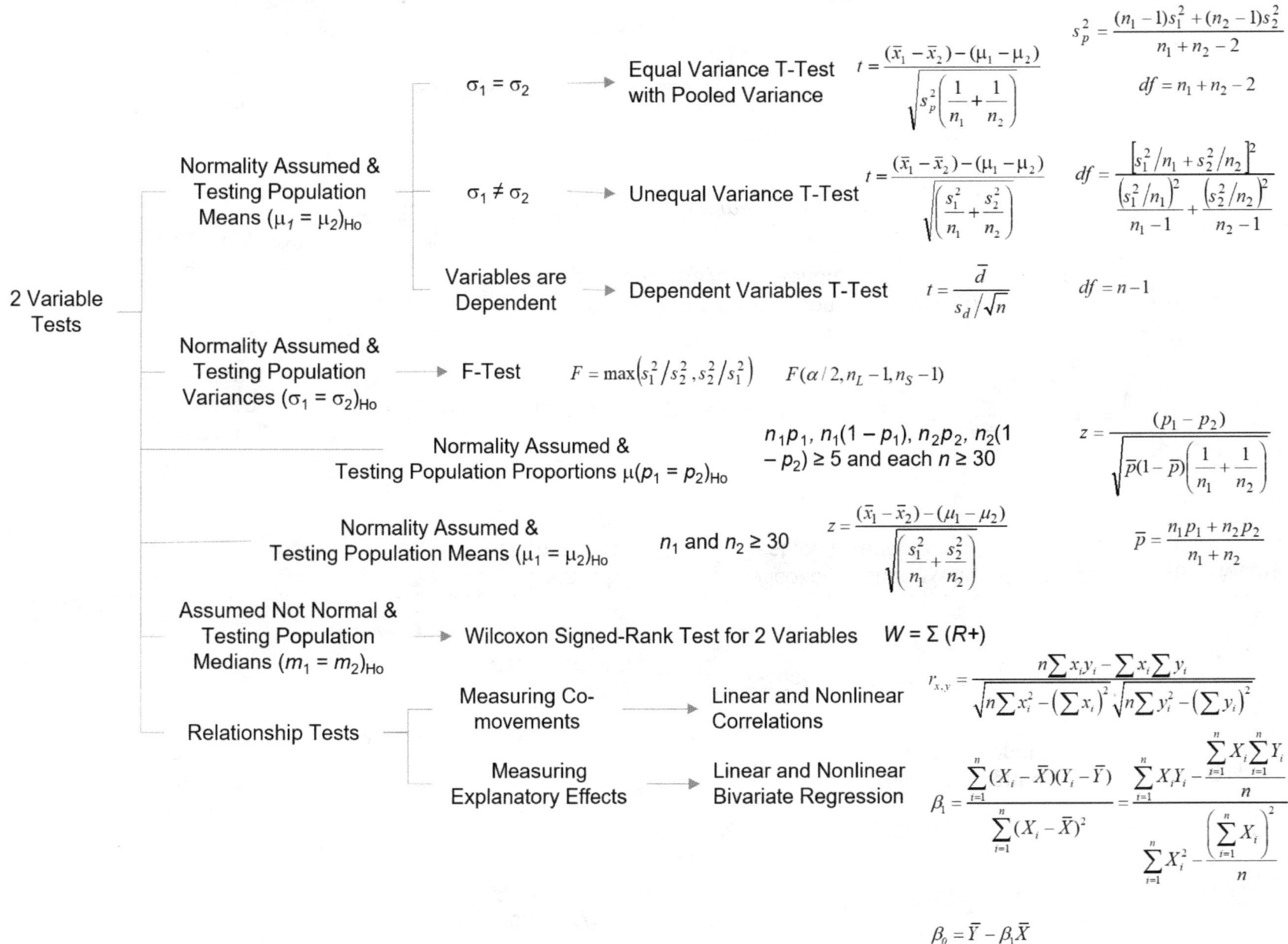

2 Variable Tests

Normality Assumed & Testing Population Means $(\mu_1 = \mu_2)_{Ho}$

$\sigma_1 = \sigma_2$ → **Equal Variance T-Test with Pooled Variance**

$$t = \frac{(\bar{x}_1 - \bar{x}_2) - (\mu_1 - \mu_2)}{\sqrt{s_p^2 \left(\frac{1}{n_1} + \frac{1}{n_2} \right)}}$$

$$s_p^2 = \frac{(n_1 - 1)s_1^2 + (n_2 - 1)s_2^2}{n_1 + n_2 - 2}$$

$$df = n_1 + n_2 - 2$$

$\sigma_1 \neq \sigma_2$ → **Unequal Variance T-Test**

$$t = \frac{(\bar{x}_1 - \bar{x}_2) - (\mu_1 - \mu_2)}{\sqrt{\left(\frac{s_1^2}{n_1} + \frac{s_2^2}{n_2} \right)}}$$

$$df = \frac{\left[s_1^2/n_1 + s_2^2/n_2 \right]^2}{\frac{\left(s_1^2/n_1 \right)^2}{n_1 - 1} + \frac{\left(s_2^2/n_2 \right)^2}{n_2 - 1}}$$

Variables are Dependent → **Dependent Variables T-Test**

$$t = \frac{\bar{d}}{s_d/\sqrt{n}}$$

$$df = n - 1$$

Normality Assumed & Testing Population Variances $(\sigma_1 = \sigma_2)_{Ho}$ → **F-Test**

$$F = \max\left(s_1^2/s_2^2, s_2^2/s_1^2 \right) \qquad F(\alpha/2, n_L - 1, n_S - 1)$$

Normality Assumed & Testing Population Proportions $\mu(p_1 = p_2)_{Ho}$

$n_1 p_1, n_1(1 - p_1), n_2 p_2, n_2(1 - p_2) \geq 5$ and each $n \geq 30$

$$z = \frac{(p_1 - p_2)}{\sqrt{\bar{p}(1 - \bar{p})\left(\frac{1}{n_1} + \frac{1}{n_2} \right)}}$$

Normality Assumed & Testing Population Means $(\mu_1 = \mu_2)_{Ho}$

n_1 and $n_2 \geq 30$

$$z = \frac{(\bar{x}_1 - \bar{x}_2) - (\mu_1 - \mu_2)}{\sqrt{\left(\frac{s_1^2}{n_1} + \frac{s_2^2}{n_2} \right)}}$$

$$\bar{p} = \frac{n_1 p_1 + n_2 p_2}{n_1 + n_2}$$

Assumed Not Normal & Testing Population Medians $(m_1 = m_2)_{Ho}$ → **Wilcoxon Signed-Rank Test for 2 Variables**

$$W = \Sigma (R+)$$

Relationship Tests

Measuring Co-movements → **Linear and Nonlinear Correlations**

$$r_{x,y} = \frac{n\sum x_i y_i - \sum x_i \sum y_i}{\sqrt{n\sum x_i^2 - \left(\sum x_i\right)^2} \sqrt{n\sum y_i^2 - \left(\sum y_i\right)^2}}$$

Measuring Explanatory Effects → **Linear and Nonlinear Bivariate Regression**

$$\beta_1 = \frac{\sum_{i=1}^{n}(X_i - \bar{X})(Y_i - \bar{Y})}{\sum_{i=1}^{n}(X_i - \bar{X})^2} = \frac{\sum_{i=1}^{n} X_i Y_i - \frac{\sum_{i=1}^{n} X_i \sum_{i=1}^{n} Y_i}{n}}{\sum_{i=1}^{n} X_i^2 - \frac{\left(\sum_{i=1}^{n} X_i\right)^2}{n}}$$

$$\beta_0 = \bar{Y} - \beta_1 \bar{X}$$

Statistical Methods for Two or More Variables

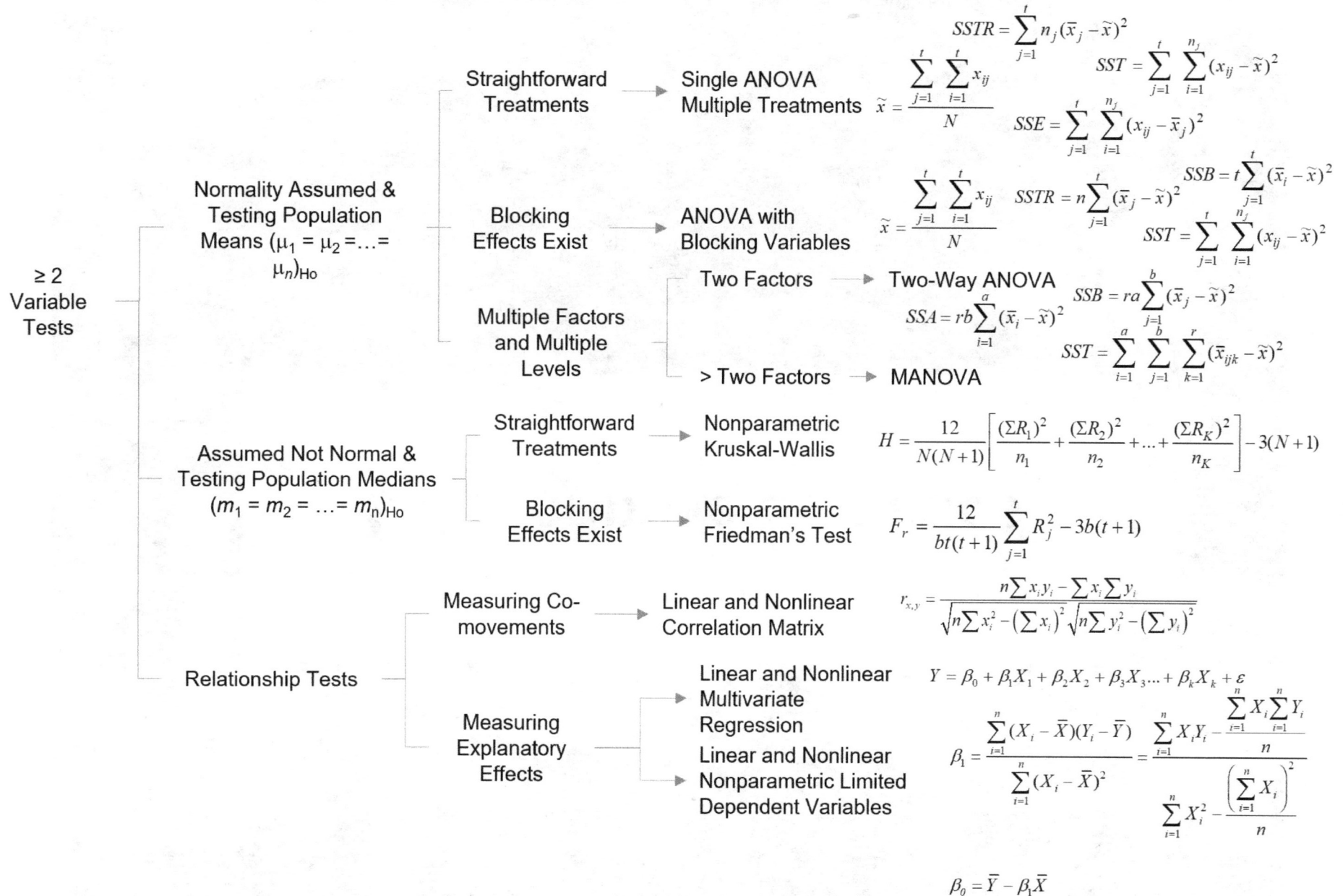

≥ 2 Variable Tests

Normality Assumed & Testing Population Means $(\mu_1 = \mu_2 = \ldots = \mu_n)_{Ho}$

Straightforward Treatments → **Single ANOVA Multiple Treatments**

$$SSTR = \sum_{j=1}^{t} n_j (\overline{x}_j - \widetilde{x})^2$$

$$\widetilde{x} = \frac{\sum_{j=1}^{t} \sum_{i=1}^{t} x_{ij}}{N}$$

$$SST = \sum_{j=1}^{t} \sum_{i=1}^{n_j} (x_{ij} - \widetilde{x})^2$$

$$SSE = \sum_{j=1}^{t} \sum_{i=1}^{n_j} (x_{ij} - \overline{x}_j)^2$$

Blocking Effects Exist → **ANOVA with Blocking Variables**

$$\widetilde{x} = \frac{\sum_{j=1}^{t} \sum_{i=1}^{t} x_{ij}}{N}$$

$$SSTR = n \sum_{j=1}^{t} (\overline{x}_j - \widetilde{x})^2$$

$$SSB = t \sum_{j=1}^{t} (\overline{x}_i - \widetilde{x})^2$$

$$SST = \sum_{j=1}^{t} \sum_{i=1}^{n_j} (x_{ij} - \widetilde{x})^2$$

Multiple Factors and Multiple Levels

- **Two Factors** → **Two-Way ANOVA**

$$SSA = rb \sum_{i=1}^{a} (\overline{x}_i - \widetilde{x})^2$$

$$SSB = ra \sum_{j=1}^{b} (\overline{x}_j - \widetilde{x})^2$$

$$SST = \sum_{i=1}^{a} \sum_{j=1}^{b} \sum_{k=1}^{r} (\overline{x}_{ijk} - \widetilde{x})^2$$

- **> Two Factors** → **MANOVA**

Assumed Not Normal & Testing Population Medians $(m_1 = m_2 = \ldots = m_n)_{Ho}$

Straightforward Treatments → **Nonparametric Kruskal-Wallis**

$$H = \frac{12}{N(N+1)} \left[\frac{(\Sigma R_1)^2}{n_1} + \frac{(\Sigma R_2)^2}{n_2} + \ldots + \frac{(\Sigma R_K)^2}{n_K} \right] - 3(N+1)$$

Blocking Effects Exist → **Nonparametric Friedman's Test**

$$F_r = \frac{12}{bt(t+1)} \sum_{j=1}^{t} R_j^2 - 3b(t+1)$$

Relationship Tests

Measuring Co-movements → **Linear and Nonlinear Correlation Matrix**

$$r_{x,y} = \frac{n \sum x_i y_i - \sum x_i \sum y_i}{\sqrt{n \sum x_i^2 - \left(\sum x_i \right)^2} \sqrt{n \sum y_i^2 - \left(\sum y_i \right)^2}}$$

Measuring Explanatory Effects

- → **Linear and Nonlinear Multivariate Regression**

$$Y = \beta_0 + \beta_1 X_1 + \beta_2 X_2 + \beta_3 X_3 \ldots + \beta_k X_k + \varepsilon$$

- → **Linear and Nonlinear Nonparametric Limited Dependent Variables**

$$\beta_1 = \frac{\sum_{i=1}^{n} (X_i - \overline{X})(Y_i - \overline{Y})}{\sum_{i=1}^{n} (X_i - \overline{X})^2} = \frac{\sum_{i=1}^{n} X_i Y_i - \frac{\sum_{i=1}^{n} X_i \sum_{i=1}^{n} Y_i}{n}}{\sum_{i=1}^{n} X_i^2 - \frac{\left(\sum_{i=1}^{n} X_i \right)^2}{n}}$$

$$\beta_0 = \overline{Y} - \beta_1 \overline{X}$$

3. Descriptive Statistics

Dr. Johnathan Mun, Professor of Research
Quantitative Research Methods Course Slides
Seventh Edition, 2026, ROV Press

Descriptive Statistics and Distributional Moments

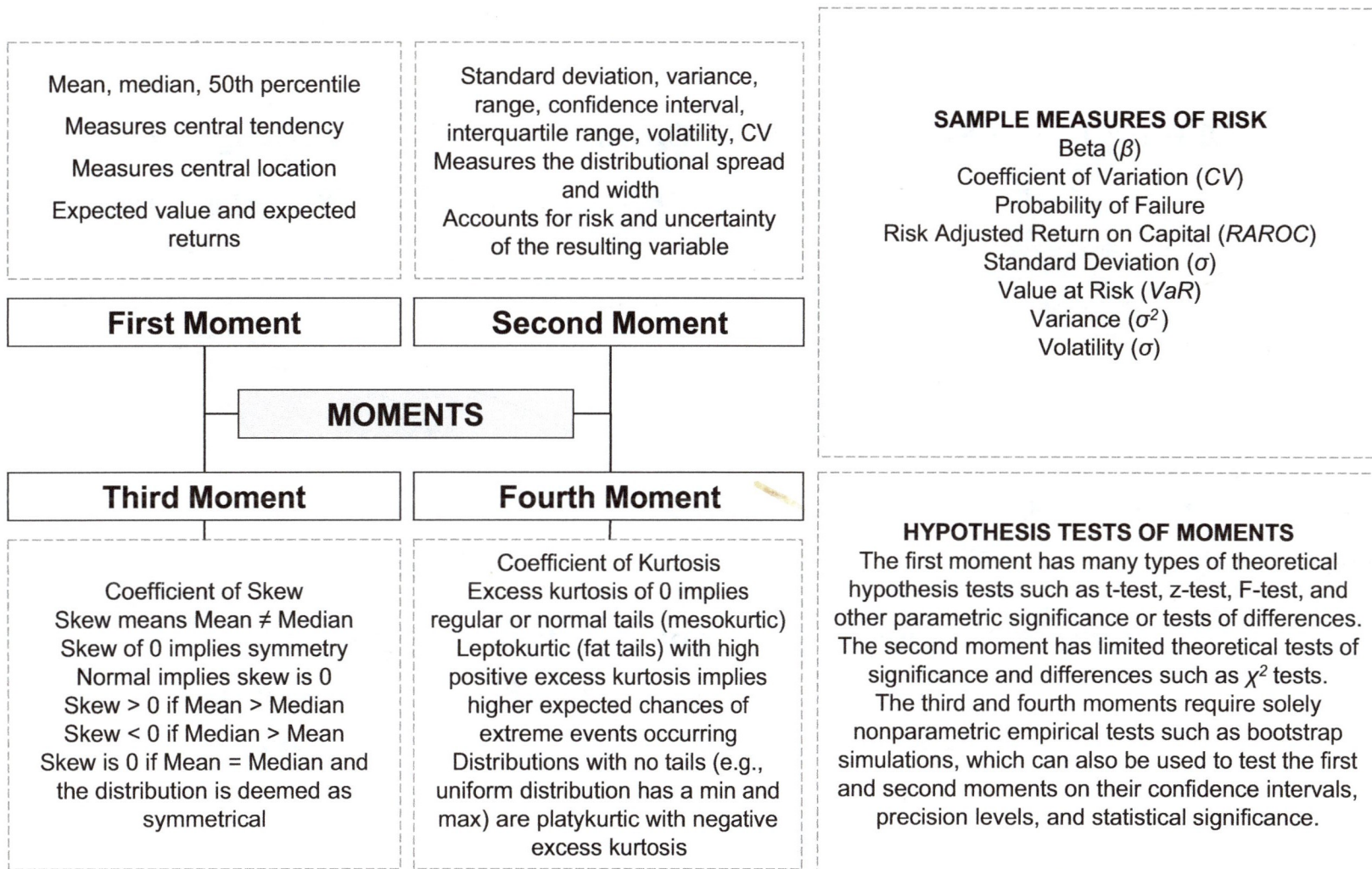

Mean, median, 50th percentile

Measures central tendency

Measures central location

Expected value and expected returns

Standard deviation, variance, range, confidence interval, interquartile range, volatility, CV
Measures the distributional spread and width
Accounts for risk and uncertainty of the resulting variable

SAMPLE MEASURES OF RISK
Beta (β)
Coefficient of Variation (CV)
Probability of Failure
Risk Adjusted Return on Capital ($RAROC$)
Standard Deviation (σ)
Value at Risk (VaR)
Variance (σ^2)
Volatility (σ)

First Moment	**Second Moment**

MOMENTS

Third Moment	**Fourth Moment**

Coefficient of Skew
Skew means Mean ≠ Median
Skew of 0 implies symmetry
Normal implies skew is 0
Skew > 0 if Mean > Median
Skew < 0 if Median > Mean
Skew is 0 if Mean = Median and the distribution is deemed as symmetrical

---

Coefficient of Kurtosis
Excess kurtosis of 0 implies regular or normal tails (mesokurtic)
Leptokurtic (fat tails) with high positive excess kurtosis implies higher expected chances of extreme events occurring
Distributions with no tails (e.g., uniform distribution has a min and max) are platykurtic with negative excess kurtosis

---

HYPOTHESIS TESTS OF MOMENTS
The first moment has many types of theoretical hypothesis tests such as t-test, z-test, F-test, and other parametric significance or tests of differences. The second moment has limited theoretical tests of significance and differences such as χ^2 tests. The third and fourth moments require solely nonparametric empirical tests such as bootstrap simulations, which can also be used to test the first and second moments on their confidence intervals, precision levels, and statistical significance.

Interpreting the Forecast Statistics

First Moment – A Measure of Returns

- Central Tendency – Mean, Median, and Mode
- A measure of location or shift
- Conveys the *Expected Value* of an uncertain variable

Sample Statistic for Mean: $\bar{x} = \dfrac{\sum x_i}{n}$

Population Parameter for Mean: $\mu = \dfrac{\sum x_i}{N}$

Mean 1   Mean 2

- May be deceiving… *Flaw of Averages* example
- Probability that the average will occur is very close to 0%

Interpreting the Forecast Statistics

Second Moment – A Measure of Risk

- A measure of width, range, risk, and uncertainty
- Standard deviation, volatility, uncertainty, variance, width, percentiles, inter-quartile ranges, coefficient of variation…

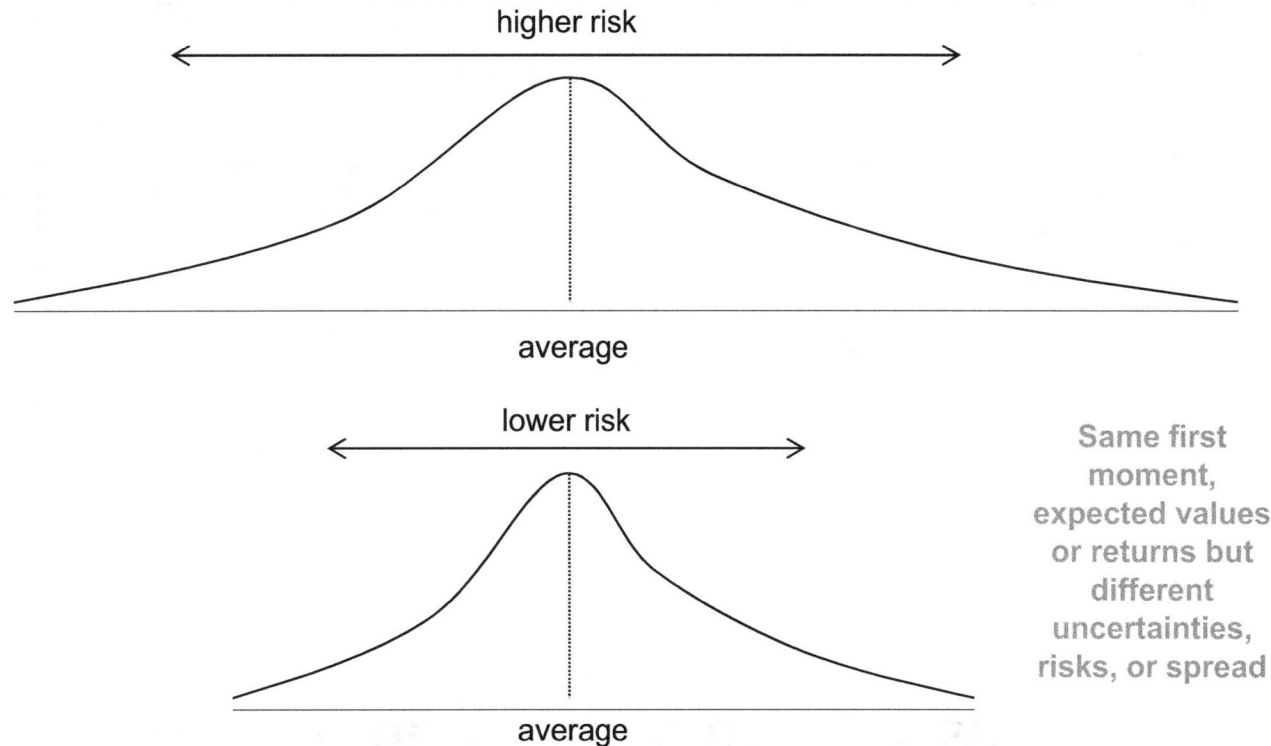

higher risk

average

lower risk

average

Same first moment, expected values or returns but different uncertainties, risks, or spread

The Intuition – Measuring Risk

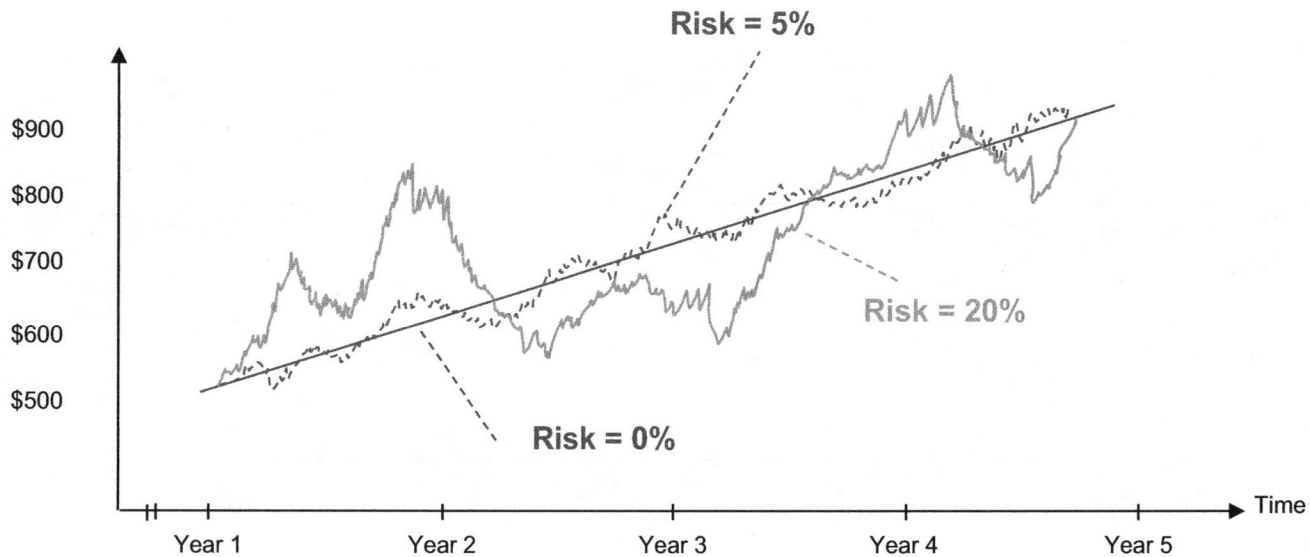

So, What Is This Standard Deviation?

Simply defined as the average deviation
of each point around the mean!

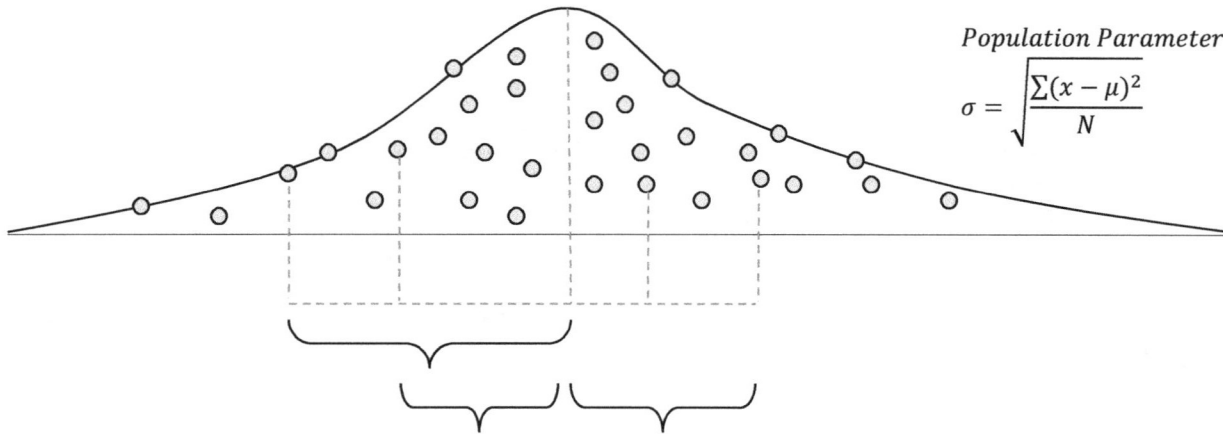

Sample Statistic for Standard Deviation:

$$s = \sqrt{\frac{\Sigma(x - \bar{x})^2}{n - 1}}$$ **STDEV in Excel**

Population Parameter for Standard Deviation:

$$\sigma = \sqrt{\frac{\Sigma(x - \mu)^2}{N}}$$ **STDEVP in Excel**

Take all the deviations or distances between the mean and average them!

Note that standard deviation (and by extension, variance) is an *absolute* measure of variability whereas CV is a *relative* measure of variability. Suppose we have three stocks:

Stock A: $1.25, $1.45, $1.55, $1.75, $2.05 $\bar{x}$ = $1.61, s = $0.304, CV = 18.94%

Stock B: $12.5, $14.5, $15.5, $17.5, $20.5 $\bar{x}$ = $16.1, s = $3.049, CV = 18.94%

Stock C: $1250, $1450, $1550, $1750, $2050 $\bar{x}$ = $1610, s = $304.9, CV = 18.94%

Value at Risk (VaR)

Same returns but
different VaR

average

-$50M	-$10M	$0M	+$10M	LOSSES/GAINS
$1M	$10M	$50M	$90M	PROFITS

Which project has a higher risk and which project is more desirable?

Skew: Mean vs. Median

Skew < 0
Left Skew

A   B   C

Skew > 0
Right Skew

D   E   F

Where are the Mean, Median, and Mode of the two distributions?

Interpreting the Forecast Statistics

Third Moment – A Measure of Skewness

Simply taking into account the first and second moments could be dangerous…

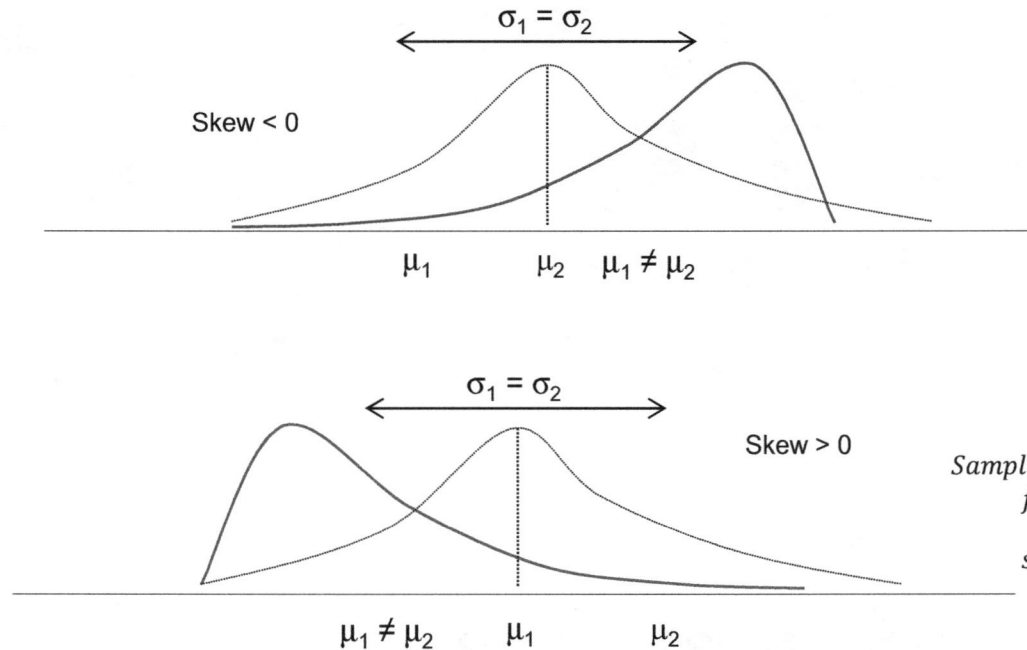

These two distributions of outcomes may have identical means and standard deviations, but they are very different!

Sample Statistic and Population Paremeter for Skew Coefficient:

$$skew = \frac{n}{(n-1)(n-2)} \sum \left(\frac{x_i - \bar{x}}{s}\right)^3$$

Interpreting the Forecast Statistics

Fourth Moment – A Measure of Kurtosis

Kurtosis measures the probabilities of extreme events… catastrophic losses (e.g., Sept. 11, stock market crashes)

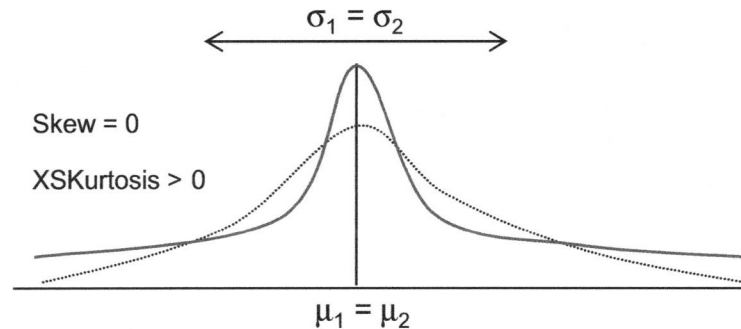

$$\sigma_1 = \sigma_2$$

Skew = 0

XSKurtosis > 0

$$\mu_1 = \mu_2$$

A higher kurtosis means a higher chance of extreme events occurring… the essence of risk management!

Notes:

Risk Simulator reports the Excess Kurtosis, which means we set 0 as the baseline.

Sample Statistic and Population Paremeter for Excess Kurtosis Coefficient:

$$excess\ kurtosis = \frac{n(n+1)}{(n-1)(n-2)(n-3)}\sum\left(\frac{x_i - \bar{x}}{s}\right)^4 - \frac{3(n-1)^2}{(n-2)(n-3)}$$

Pearson's linear product moment correlation coefficient

Correlation

$$r_{x,y} = \frac{n\sum x_i y_i - \sum x_i \sum y_i}{\sqrt{n\sum x_i^2 - \left(\sum x_i\right)^2}\sqrt{n\sum y_i^2 - \left(\sum y_i\right)^2}}$$

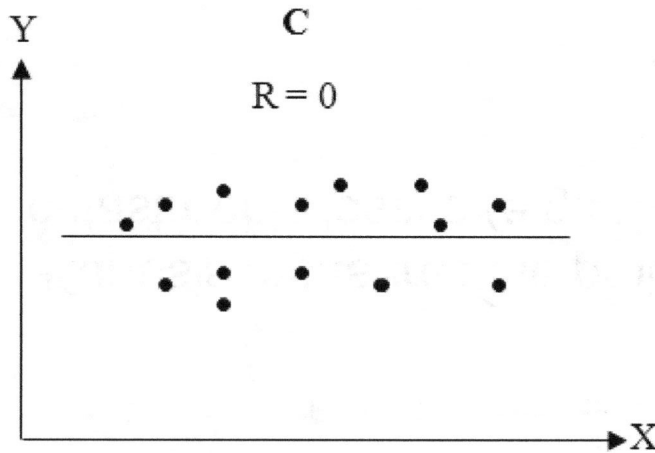

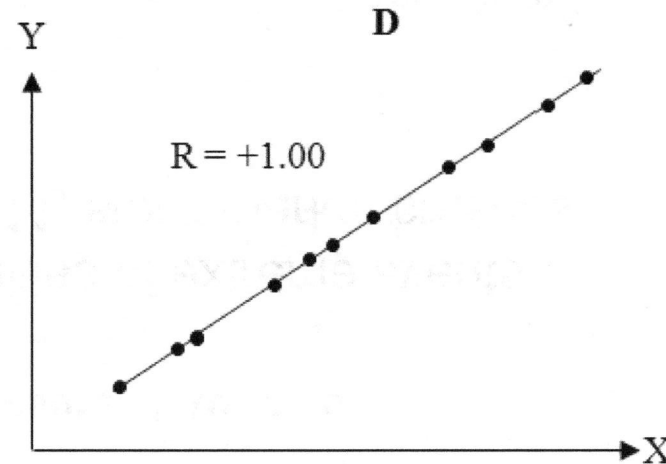

A R = + 0.70

B R = − 0.85

C R = 0

D R = +1.00

Correlation

Spearman's nonlinear nonparametric rank correlation coefficient

Don't forget:

Kendall's Tau

E

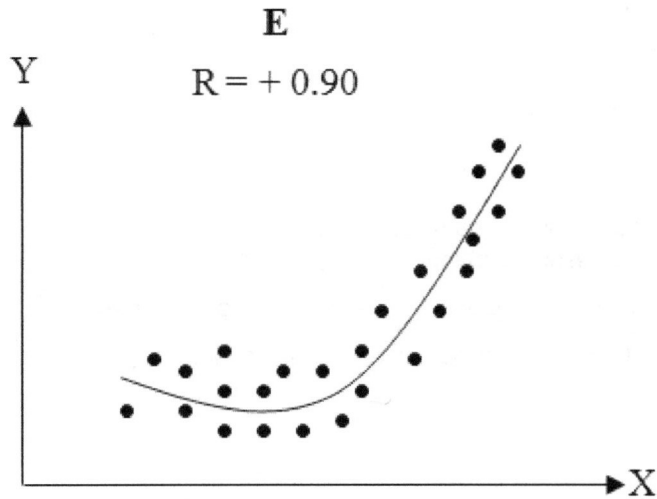

R = + 0.90

F

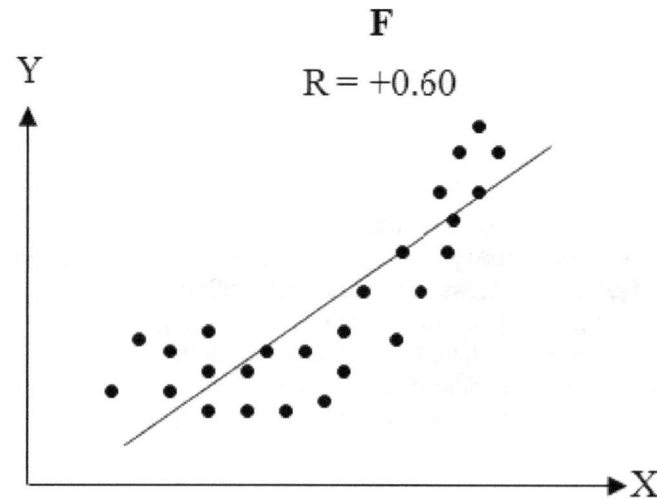

R = +0.60

G

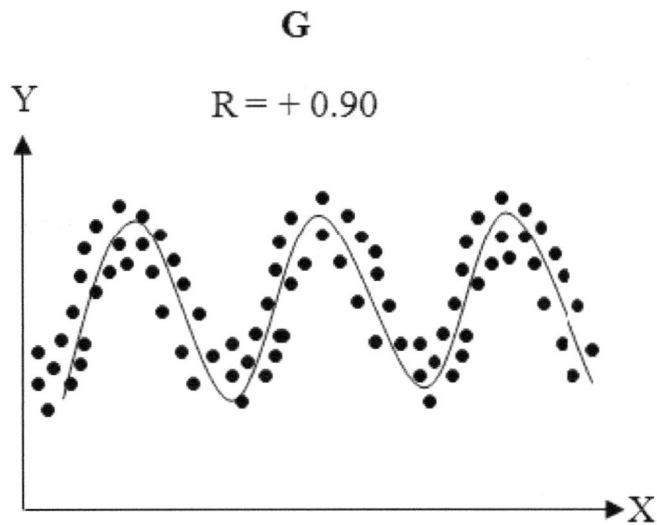

R = + 0.90

H

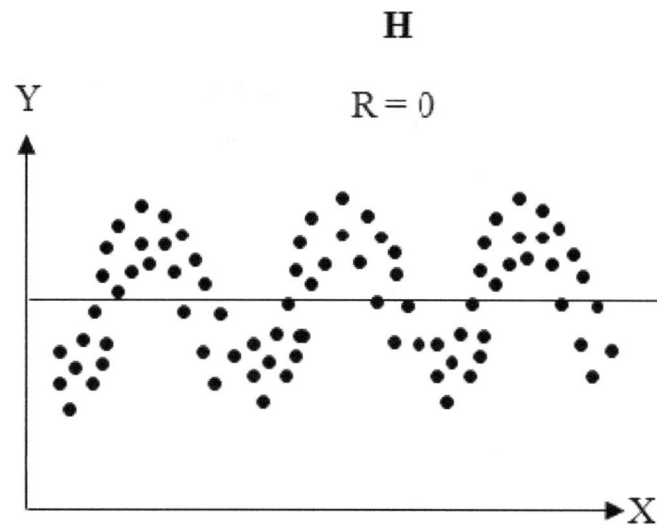

R = 0

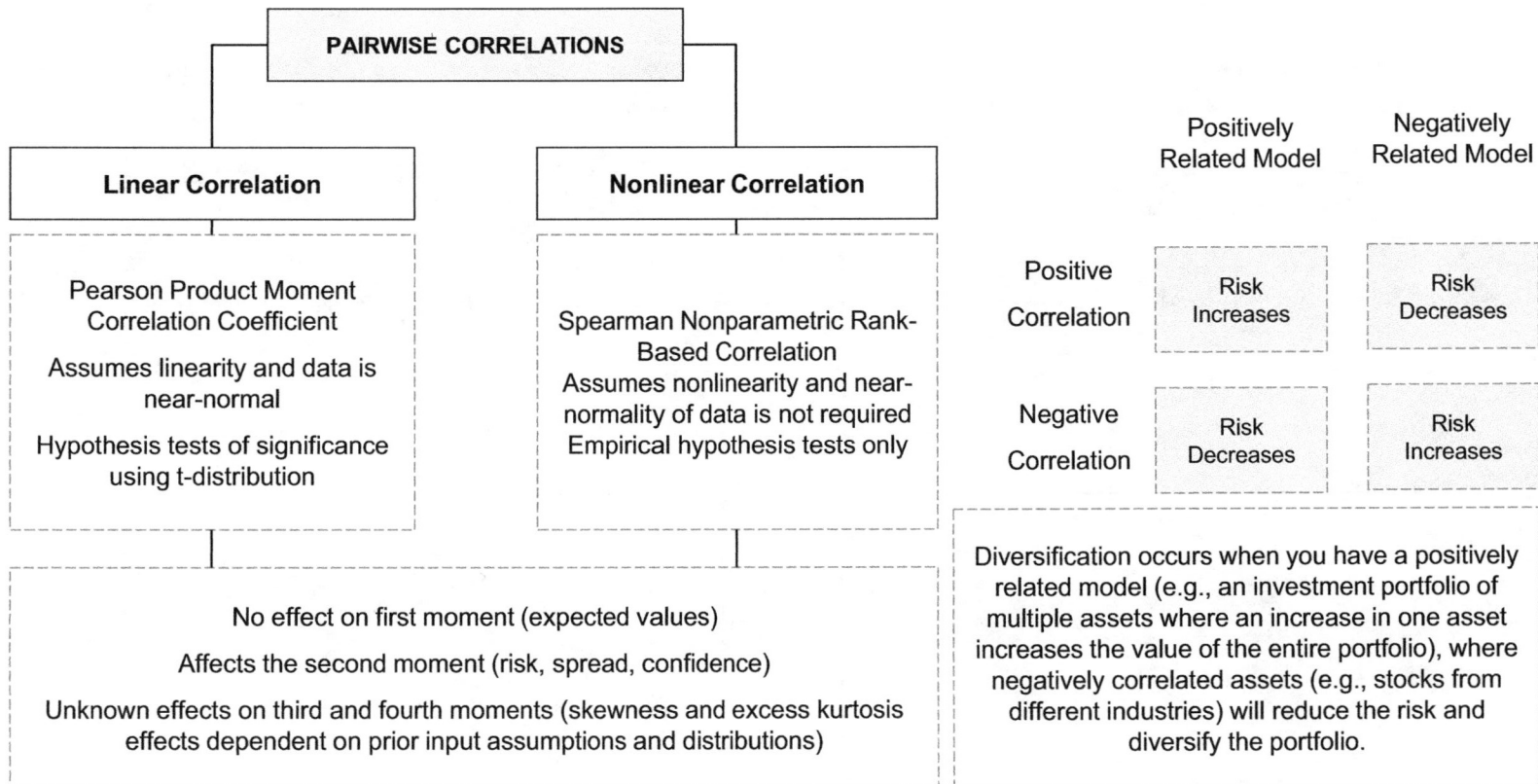

PAIRWISE CORRELATIONS

Linear Correlation

Pearson Product Moment Correlation Coefficient

Assumes linearity and data is near-normal

Hypothesis tests of significance using t-distribution

Nonlinear Correlation

Spearman Nonparametric Rank-Based Correlation
Assumes nonlinearity and near-normality of data is not required
Empirical hypothesis tests only

No effect on first moment (expected values)

Affects the second moment (risk, spread, confidence)

Unknown effects on third and fourth moments (skewness and excess kurtosis effects dependent on prior input assumptions and distributions)

	Positively Related Model	Negatively Related Model
Positive Correlation	Risk Increases	Risk Decreases
Negative Correlation	Risk Decreases	Risk Increases

Diversification occurs when you have a positively related model (e.g., an investment portfolio of multiple assets where an increase in one asset increases the value of the entire portfolio), where negatively correlated assets (e.g., stocks from different industries) will reduce the risk and diversify the portfolio.

Example: Descriptive Statistics I

Example 1: (i) What is the mode of 2   3   5   6   7?   No mode

(ii) What is the mode of 3   3   5   6   7?   3 Unimodal

(iii) What is the mode of 2   3   5   6   7   99?   No mode

(iv) Does the existence of an outlier affect the results?   No

Example 2: (i) What is the mean of 2   3   5   6   7?   4.6

(ii) What is the mean of 1   3   5   6   8?   4.6

(iii) What is the mean of 2   3   5   6   7   99?   20.3

(iv) Does the existence of an outlier affect the results?   Yes

Example 3: (i) What is the median of 2   3   5   6   7?   5

(ii) What is the median of 1   3   5   6   8?   5

(iii) What is the median of 2   3   5   6   7   99?   5.5

(iv) Does the existence of an outlier affect the results?   Not much

What can you conclude from these three examples?
That is, which measure is most sensitive to outliers
and which is least sensitive to outliers?

**Most sensitive is Mean, and less sensitive are
Mode and Median**

Example 4: An extension of the median is the quartile, one of the three points that divide a range of data or population into four equal parts. Thus, Q_1 denotes the first quartile; Q_2, the median; and Q_3, the third quartile. Note that quartiles can be a little tricky to work with.

(i) Get the Range, Median, Q_1, Q_3, and IQR for

9   7   15   2   5   17   12

First, rank them! 2   5   7   9   12   15   17

Max = 17 and Min = 2

Range = Max – Min = 17 – 2 = 15

Median = $(7 + 1)/2$ = 4th term, or 9

Since odd, bring the median to both sides, we have $n = 4$, hence, $Q_1 = (4+1)/2 = 2.5$th term, or $(5+7)/2 = 6$

$Q_3 = 2.5$th term from the right, or $(12+15)/2 = 13.5$

IQR = $Q_3 - Q_1 = 13.5 - 6 = 7.5$

(ii) Get the Range, Median, Q_1, Q_3, and IQR for

9   7   15   2   5   17   12   19

First, rank them! 2   5   7   9   12   15   17   19

Max = 19 and Min = 2

Range = Max – Min = 19 – 2 = 17

Median = $(8 + 1)/2$ = 4.5th term, or $(9+12)/2 = 10.5$

Since even, we have $n = 4$

$Q_1 = (4+1)/2 = 2.5$th term = $(5+7)/2 = 6$

$Q_3 = 2.5$th term from the right, or $(15+17)/2 = 16$

IQR = $Q_3 - Q_1 = 16 - 6 = 10$

Example: Descriptive Statistics II

Sturges' Rule: $k = 1 + 3.3\log(n)$ $\bar{x} = \dfrac{\sum\limits_{i=1}^{n} x_i}{n}$ $(n + 1)/2^{\text{th}}$ value after it is ranked

frequency

Example 5:   Draw a histogram to represent the following data:

20.5	15.4	16.9	13.4	8.8	19.5	12.7	7.8
14.3	22.1	15.6	5.4	23.3	19.2	20.8	24.1
17.0	11.8	9.2	12.6	9.9	28.6	18.4	16.8
15.9							

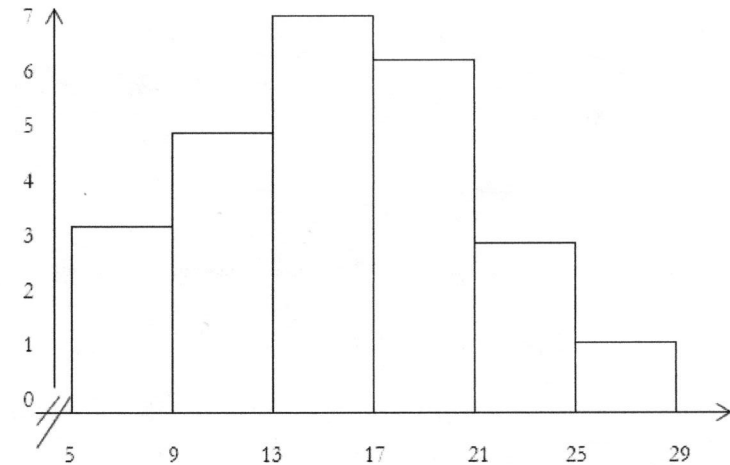

STEP 1: $n = 25$, so, using Sturges' Rule, $k = 1 + 3.3\log(25) = 5.61$, or 6 classes

STEP 2: MAX – MIN = 28.6 – 5.4 = 23.2, the RANGE

STEP 3: Class Width = $23.3/6 \approx 4$

STEP 4: Class Intervals: starting from 5.0, we have:

Class Boundaries	Frequency	Relative Frequency
5.0 – 8.99	3	3/25
9.0 – 12.99	5	5/25
13.0 – 16.99	7	7/25
17.0 – 20.99	6	6/25
21.0 – 24.99	3	3/25
25.0 – 28.99	1	1/25
	$\Sigma = 25$	$\Sigma = 1.0$

Example 6: Taken randomly from an enrollment of 120, the following is the number of cans of beer consumed by 5 college sophomores right after taking a statistics class at a local university: 2, 9, 11, 5, 6.

(i)   What is the average consumption of beer? $(2 + 9 + 11 + 5 + 6)/5$ = 6.6

(ii)   Is this the sample or population mean? **Sample**

(iii) Is this an arithmetic mean, geometric mean, harmonic mean or weighted mean? Why? **Arithmetic mean, since $\Sigma x/n$**

Example: Descriptive Statistics III

Example 7: Calculate the sample mean, median, mode, range, first and third quartile, inter-quartile range, standard deviation, variance, and coefficient of variation for the following data: 2 3 5 6 7

Sample mean: $\bar{x} = \dfrac{\sum_{i=1}^{n} x_i}{n} = 4.6$

Sample median: $\dfrac{n+1}{2}$ rank = 5

Sample mode: most frequently recurring = none

Range: max − min = 7 − 2 = 5

Q_1: first quartile = 3

Q_3: third quartile = 6

IQR: $Q_3 − Q_1 = 6 − 3 = 3$

Sample standard deviation: $s = \sqrt{\dfrac{\sum_{i=1}^{n}(x_i - \bar{x})^2}{n-1}} = 2.073$

$$\sqrt{\dfrac{(2-4.6)^2 + (3-4.6)^2 + (5-4.6)^2 + (6-4.6)^2 + (7-4.6)^2}{5-1}} = \sqrt{\dfrac{6.76 + 2.56 + 0.16 + 1.96 + 5.76}{4}}$$

Sample variance: $s^2 = \dfrac{\sum_{i=1}^{n}(x_i - \bar{x})^2}{n-1} = 2.073^2 = 4.3$

Sample coefficient of variation: $CV = \dfrac{s}{\bar{x}} = 2.073/4.6 = 0.45$

What are parameters and what are statistics?

Which of these statistics can take on negative inputs?

Which of these statistics always yields only positive results?

Example 8: Now multiply the numbers in the preceding example by 10, giving you 20 30 50 60 70. Recalculate the sample mean, median, mode, range, first and third quartile, inter-quartile range, standard deviation, variance, and coefficient of variation. What do you observe?

Sample mean: $\bar{x} = \dfrac{\sum_{i=1}^{n} x_i}{n} = 46$

Sample median: $\dfrac{n+1}{2}$ rank = 50

Sample mode: most frequently recurring = none

Range: max − min = 70 − 20 = 50

Q_1: first quartile = 30

Q_3: third quartile = 60

IQR: inter-quartile range = 60 − 30 = 30

Sample standard deviation: $s = \sqrt{\dfrac{\sum_{i=1}^{n}(x_i - \bar{x})^2}{n-1}} = 20.73$

$$\sqrt{\dfrac{(20-46)^2 + (30-46)^2 + (50-46)^2 + (60-46)^2 + (70-46)^2}{5-1}} = \sqrt{\dfrac{676 + 256 + 16 + 196 + 576}{4}}$$

Sample variance: $s^2 = \dfrac{\sum_{i=1}^{n}(x_i - \bar{x})^2}{n-1} = 20.73^2 = 430$

Sample coefficient of variation: $CV = \dfrac{s}{\bar{x}} = 20.73/46 = 0.45$

OBSERVATIONS? Mean, median, range, Q_1, Q_3, IQR, and s up 10×. CV is constant, while s^2 goes up 10 × 10, or 100×.

Example: Descriptive Statistics III

Example 9: Calculate the sample mean, median, mode, range, first and third quartile, inter-quartile range, standard deviation, variance, and coefficient of variation for the following data: 2 3 5 6 7 99. What happens here? Compare to the calculations to the previous examples.

mean = 20.33, median = 5.5, mode = none, range = 97, Q_1 = 3, Q_3 = 7, IQR = 4, S = 38.58, s^2 = 1488 and CV = 1.897

Example 10: If you multiply the numbers in Example 1 by 3, that is, using the following numbers, 6 9 15 18 21, what do you expect the mean, mode, median, range, Q_1, Q_3, IQR, s, s^2, and CV to be? You do not have to show the work; just take an educated guess.

mean median, Q_1, Q_3, IQR, range, and s are up 3×, while s^2 is up 9× and CV stays the same

Example 11: Now, increase by 5 the numbers in the previous example and calculate the sample mean, median, mode, range, first and third quartile, inter-quartile range, standard deviation, variance, and coefficient of variation for the following data: 7 8 10 11 12. What happens here? Compare with previous examples.

mean, median, Q_1, and Q_3 go up by +5, while s, s^2, IQR, and range remain the same and CV changes a little

Example 12: Let's now be a little creative … Suppose we take the numbers from the previous examples and transform them according to the following formula: $^2/_3 X + 6$, resulting in 7.33 8 9.33 10 10.67. What happens to the mean, standard deviation, variance, and coefficient of variation?

$^2/_3 (2) + 6 = 7.33$

$^2/_3 (3) + 6 = 8.00$ mean = 9.06, or $^2/_3$ (4.6 old mean) + 6

$^2/_3 (5) + 6 = 9.33$ $s = ^2/_3 (X) = 1.3825$, and $s^2 = (^2/_3)^2 (X) = 1.9112$

$^2/_3 (6) + 6 = 10.00$

$^2/_3 (7) + 6 = 10.67$

4. Basic Probability

Dr. Johnathan Mun, Professor of Research
Quantitative Research Methods Course Slides
Seventh Edition, 2026, ROV Press

83

Basic Probability Rules

$P(A \cup B) = P(A \text{ or } B) = P(A) + P(B) - P(A \cap B)$ when not mutually exclusive

$P(A \cup B) = P(A \text{ or } B) = P(A) + P(B)$ when mutually exclusive as $P(A \cap B) = 0$

$P(A \cap B) = P(A \text{ and } B) = P(A) \cdot P(B|A)$ when dependent

$P(A \cap B) = P(A \text{ and } B) = P(A) \cdot P(B)$ when independent as $P(B|A) = P(B)$

Pairwise counts: $m \times n$

Permutations: $P_x^n = \dfrac{n!}{(n-x)!}$

Combinations: $C_x^n = \dfrac{n!}{x!(n-x)!}$

Mutually Exclusive

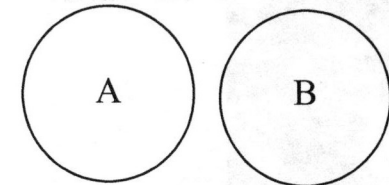

Not Mutually Exclusive

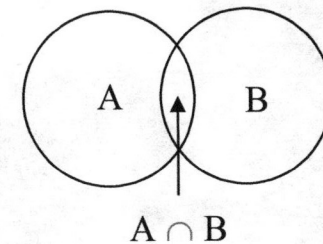

$A \cap B$

Probability Solution Methods

o Probability Tables or Contingency Tables

o Bayes' Theorem

o Probability Trees

o Combinations, Permutations, and Counting Rules

Basic Probability Examples

$P(A \cup B) = P(A \text{ or } B) = P(A) + P(B) - P(A \cap B)$ when not mutually exclusive

$P(A \cup B) = P(A \text{ or } B) = P(A) + P(B)$ when mutually exclusive since $P(A \cap B) = 0$

$P(A \cap B) = P(A \text{ and } B) = P(A).P(B \mid A)$ when dependent

$P(A \cap B) = P(A \text{ and } B) = P(A).P(B)$ when independent as $P(B \mid A) = P(B)$

Example 1: $P(6 \text{ or } 5 \text{ on a die}) = P(6) + P(5)$ as mutually exclusive $= 1/6 + 1/6 = 1/3$

Example 2: Given 20% of BMWs are manufactured in Canada, 10% in Mexico, and 70% in the U.S., find the P(car manufactured not in US) = P(Canada or Mexico) = P(Canada) + P(Mexico) = 0.2 + 0.1 = 0.3 or 30%.

Example 3: $P(\text{Ace} \cup \text{Spades}) = P(\text{Ace}) + P(\text{Spades}) - P(\text{Ace} \cap \text{Spades})$ since not mutually exclusive, we double count, hence, take out the intersection $= 4/52 + 13/52 - 1/52 = 16/52 = 31\%$.

Example 4: When flipping 2 coins, what is the P(HH)? $P(HH) = P(H_1 \text{ and } H_2) = P(H_1) \times P(H_2)$ as independent events, $P(H_1)$ and $P(H_2) = 1/2 \times 1/2 = 1/4$.

Example 5: If selecting from a deck of cards *with replacement*, what is the probability of obtaining two aces?

$P(A_1 \cap A_2) = P(A_1)P(A_2) = 4/52 \times 4/52$.

Example 6: If selecting from a deck of cards *without replacement*, what is the probability of obtaining two aces?

$P(A_1 \cap A_2) = P(A_1)P(A_2 \mid A_1)$ since dependent, $4/52 \times 3/51$.

Example 7: Given a bag filled with 20 marbles, of which there 10 red (R), 4 green (G), and 6 blue (B), we randomly select 2. Find the following probabilities:

  If the selection was *without replacement*:

    P(Green on the first and Blue on the second) $= P(G_1)P(B_2 \mid G_1) = (4/20)(6/19) = 0.063$

    P(Green on both times) $= P(G_1)P(G_2 \mid G_1) = (4/20)(3/19) = 0.032$

  If the selection was *with replacement*:

    P(Green on the first and Blue on the second) $= P(G_1)P(B_2) = (4/20)(6/20) = 0.06$

    P(Green on both times) $= P(G_1)P(G_2) = (4/20)(4/20) = 0.04$

Basic Probability Examples II

Example 8: Suppose that a telemarketer gets a sale once every 10 customers, and that on a given day, she calls 2 customers. Find the following probabilities:

i. P(sale on both calls) = $P(S_1)P(S_2)$ = (1/10)(1/10) = 0.01

ii. P(sale on either call) = $P(S_1)+P(S_2) - P(S_1 \cap S_2)$

$$= (1/10) + (1/10) - 0.01 = 0.19$$

iii. P(only 1 sale) = $P(S_1 \cap NS_2)$ or $P(NS_1 \cap S_2)$ compound event

$$= P(S_1)P(NS_2)+P(NS_1)P(S_2) = (1/10)(9/10)+(9/10)(1/10)=0.18$$

iv. P(no sales) = $P(NS_1 \cap NS_2)$ = (9/10)(9/10) = 0.81

v. P(at least 1 sale) can be solved several ways:

    (A)   P(2 sales) + P(1 sale) = $\{P(S_1 \cap S_2)\}$ + $\{P(S_1 \cap NS_2) + P(NS_1 \cap S_2)\}$ = {.01] + {.09 + .09} = 0.19 = 19%.

    (B)   P(at least 1 sale) = 1 – P(no sale) = $1 - P(NS_1 \cap NS_2)$ = 1 – 0.81 = 0.19 = 19%.

    (C) $P(S_1 \cup S_2) = P(S_1) + P(S_2) - P(S_1 \cap S_2)$ = 0.1 + 0.1 – 0.01 = 0.19 = 19%.

Bayes' Theorem: The Basics

For example, suppose you find yourself standing outside of three darkened rooms labeled A, B, and C, and you know that in each room there are two people, either male (MM), female (FF), or one of each (MF). Therefore, $P(M|A) = 1.0$; $P(M|B) = 0.5$ and $P(M|C) = 0$. See the following diagram:

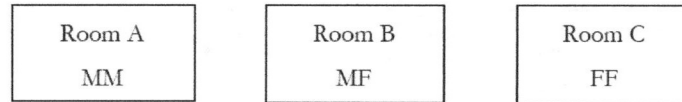

Room A	Room B	Room C
MM	MF	FF

You take a flashlight and enter a room at random where you first shine the light on a male. What is the probability that you have entered room A? In other words, find $P(A|M)$.

Seeing that we know the probably rule where $P(M\ and\ A) = P(M \cap A) = P(M)P(A|M)$

Solving for $P(A|M)$, we get

$$P(A|M) = \frac{P(M \cap A)}{P(M)}$$

$$P(A|M) = \frac{P(M \cap A)}{P(M)} = \frac{P(M)P(A|M)}{P(M)} = P(A|M)$$

but here, we are stuck in a circular loop! We need to use Bayes' Theorem to solve the problem:

$$P(A|M) = \frac{P(M \cap A)}{P(M)} = \frac{P(A \cap M)}{P(M)}$$

since commutability holds where $P(M \cap A) = P(A \cap M)$. Hence, from here,

$$P(A|M) = \frac{P(A \cap M)}{P(M)} = \frac{P(A)P(M|A)}{P(M)} = \frac{P(A)P(M|A)}{P(A \cap M) + P(B \cap M) + P(C \cap M)}$$

$$P(A|M) = \frac{P(A)P(M|A)}{P(A)P(M|A) + P(B)P(M|B) + P(C)P(M|C)}$$

represents the Bayes' Theorem. So,

$$P(A|M) = \frac{(1/3)(1)}{(1/3)(1)\ +\ (1/3)(1/2)\ +\ (1/3)(0)} = 2/3$$

Bayes' Theorem can be generalized to:

$$P(X_1|M) = \frac{P(X_1)P(M|X_1)}{P(X_1)P(M|X_1) + P(X_2)P(M|X_2) + P(X_3)P(M|X_3) + \ldots + P(X_n)P(M|X_n)}$$

Bayes' Theorem: Card Game

In the bar trick, suppose you hang out at a local bar to test your analytical skills. You take out three blank cards and write something down on each of the six sides. On the first card, you have Red and Red, the second card has Black and Black, and the third card has Red and Black. You then cover the cards with a napkin, and shuffle them, and proceed to ask the hostess to take one card out, showing only the top. Neither of you sees the bottom of the card. Now, suppose the top of the card says Red. You then insist that being the gentleman you are, you will also select Red on the bottom. If the bottom is indeed Red, you win, but if it is Black, the hostess wins. You then proceed to tell a fake statistical tale. You say that since the top card is Red, there is no way it is the Black-Black card. Therefore, it must be either the Red-Red or Red-Black card, thereby having a 50:50 chance of being either Red or Black. And the payoff is that if you win, she brings you a free drink, but if she wins, you will double her tip (by the way, you have not yet told her what her tip was going to be, so, the double of nothing is still nothing, or the double of something fairly little is still little). The question is, what is the probability that you win or that she wins? In this situation, a Bayes-update calculation is needed, and we can boldly say that the chances of being Red or Black are not 50%.

The calculations are shown next, however, before we jump into the math, it would be nice to understand the concept a little better and see if we can answer the question as to who wins (i.e., is the bottom of the card Red or Black) using basic logic. As mentioned, it can never be the Black-Black card. Hence, we are left with only the Red-Black or Red-Red card. Now, if you had selected the Red-Black card with the Red showing, then the other side must be Black. Score one for the Black team. Next, if she had selected the Red-Red card, you both could have been looking at the first side of the Red-Red card, or the second side of the Red-Red card. And in either scenario, the other side is Red, meaning there are two possible Red outcomes. Hence, the probability of Red at the bottom is 2/3 and the probability of Black at the bottom is 1/3.

Card 1 (C1) Red & Red	Card 2 (C2) Black & Black	Card 3 (C3) Red & Black

$$P(A|M) = \frac{P(A)P(M|A)}{P(A)P(M|A) + P(B)P(M|B) + P(C)P(M|C)}$$

$$P(C1|Red) = \frac{P(C1)P(Red|C1)}{P(C1)P(Red|C1) + P(C2)P(Red|C2) + P(C3)P(Red|C3)}$$

$$P(C1|Red) = \frac{(1/3)(1)}{(1/3)(1) + (1/3)(1/2) + (1/3)(0)} = 2/3$$

Bayes' Theorem: Monty Hall

In the final segment of the old Monty Hall television game show, the host, Monty, would show the contestant three closed doors. Behind these doors were three rooms, where one room had a brand new car and the other two a Billy goat each. Clearly, to win the grand prize, the contestant must select the room with the shiny new car. Now, suppose the contestant selects Room 1. Monty then proceeds to the back and sees where the car is actually located. And he then opens a room door that was not previously chosen by the contestant, and which has a goat. Monty then gives the contestant a choice: stay with your current selection or switch to the last remaining room. The question is, should the contestant stay or switch? Which option provides a higher probability of winning?

Let's use some basic logic on this one. In the figure below, the car can be in any of the rooms and the other two rooms will be the goats. Now, suppose Room 1 was selected, and if the car is in Room 1, then staying will win and switching will lose the car. Score one for staying. In this case, Monty will open either Room 2 or Room 3 as both have Billy goats. However, if the car is in Room 2, Monte has no choice but to open Room 3 because Room 2 has the car and the contestant has already selected Room 1. Hence, switching will guarantee a win as the only room the contestant can switch to is Room 2. The same happens when the car is in Room 3, where Monty has no choice but to open Room 2, and, hence, if the switch is made, only Room 3 can be selected and it is a win. Therefore, there is a 2/3 probability of winning if the contestant switches and 1/3 if the contestant stays put.

Room 1	Room 2	Room 3	Selects Room 1	Stays with Room 1	Monty Opens Room(s)	If Switch…
Car	Goat	Goat	1	win	2 or 3	lose
Goat	Car	Goat	1	lose	3	win
Goat	Goat	Car	1	lose	2	win

Bayes' Theorem: COVID-19

COVID-19 is highly contagious and at one point, 25% of the population has been infected. Suppose there is a low-priced rapid test kit that claims to have 99% accuracy in detecting the COVID-19 virus without PCR. Accuracy in this case means that if a person is truly sick, the test returns a positive result. However, the kit also has a possibility of false positives, creating mistakes in diagnosing healthy persons and identifying them as sick (i.e., the test shows a positive result even if the person is really not sick or infected). In the case of a person being tested with this kit showing a positive result, what is the probability that the person is really sick or infected, or shows negative when the person is, in fact, not sick or infected (correct diagnosis)? What is the probability of false positives and false negatives (incorrect diagnosis)? Is Type I Error or Type II Error a bigger problem in this case? An interesting phenomenon occurs in this case. Rare diseases (low population with the sickness) even with higher levels of test accuracy tend to create a higher probability of false positives, but the false negatives are still relatively low. This is why it is so hard to diagnose exotic and uncommon illnesses. With a regular percentage of the population infected and sick (e.g., 25%), a lower accuracy test will yield significantly high false positives and false negatives. However, false positives usually outweigh false negatives in this situation.

$P(positive|sick) = 0.99$ which means $P(negative|sick) = 0.01$

$P(positive|{\sim}sick) = 0.01$ which means $P(negative|{\sim}sick) = 0.99$

$P(sick) = 0.25$ which means $P({\sim}sick) = 0.75$

$$Bayes\ Theorem = P(A|M) = \frac{P(A).P(M|A)}{P(A).P(M|A) + P(B).P(M|B)}$$

$$P(sick|positive) = \frac{P(sick).P(positive|sick)}{P(sick).P(positive|sick) + P({\sim}sick).P(positive|{\sim}sick)}$$

$$\boldsymbol{P(sick|positive)} = \frac{0.25 \times 0.99}{0.25 \times 0.99 + 0.75 \times 0.01} = \frac{0.2475}{0.2550} = 97.06\%\ correct\ diagnosis$$

$$P({\sim}sick|positive) = \frac{P({\sim}sick).P(positive|{\sim}sick)}{P({\sim}sick).P(positive|{\sim}sick) + P(sick).P(positive|sick)}$$

$$\boldsymbol{P({\sim}sick|positive)} = \frac{0.75 \times 0.01}{0.75 \times 0.01 + 0.25 \times 0.99} = \frac{0.0075}{0.2550} = 2.94\%\ false\ positive$$

$Check\ for\ Complement: P(sick|positive) + P({\sim}sick|positive) = 97.06\% + 2.94\% = 100\%$

$$P(sick|negative) = \frac{P(sick).P(negative|sick)}{P(sick).P(negative|sick) + P({\sim}sick).P(negative|{\sim}sick)}$$

$$\boldsymbol{P(sick|negative)} = \frac{0.25 \times 0.01}{0.25 \times 0.01 + 0.75 \times 0.99} = \frac{0.0025}{0.7450} = 0.34\%\ false\ negative$$

$$P({\sim}sick|negative) = \frac{P({\sim}sick).P(negative|{\sim}sick)}{P({\sim}sick).P(negative|{\sim}sick) + P(sick).P(negative|sick)}$$

$$\boldsymbol{P({\sim}sick|negative)} = \frac{0.75 \times 0.99}{0.75 \times 0.99 + 0.25 \times 0.01} = \frac{0.7425}{0.7450} = 99.66\%\ correct\ diagnosis$$

$Check\ for\ Complement: P(sick|negative) + P({\sim}sick|negative) = 0.34\% + 99.66\% = 100\%$

Bayes' Theorem: COVID-19

P(X|Y)	Sick	Not Sick	Expected
	25.0% (c)	75.0% (c)	Value
Positive	99.0% (a)	1.0% (b)	25.50% (d)
Negative	1.0% (b)	99.0% (a)	74.50% (d)
Sum Check	100.00%	100.00%	100.00%

P(X|Y)		Positive	Negative	
Sick	25.0% (c)	97.06% (e)	0.34% (e)	
Not Sick	75.0% (c)	2.94% (e)	99.66% (e)	
Expected Value		25.50% (d)	74.50% (d)	100.00%
Sum Check		100.00%	100.00%	

Correct Diagnostic:	Prob (sick | positive)	97.06%		
False Positive:	Prob (not sick | positive)	2.94%	Type I Error	
Correct Diagnostic:	Prob (not sick | negative)	99.66%		
False Negative:	Prob (sick | negative)	0.34%	Type II Error	

a: The assumed accuracy of 99%, with positive results if the person is truly sick or returns negative if the person is not truly sick.

b: The error rate and is simply the complement probability to the accuracy rate or 100%–99%.

That is, the test shows a positive result when the person is not sick, or negative when the person is sick.

c: The percentage of sick population vs. not sick population.

d: 25% × 99% + 75% × 1% = 25.50% and 25% × 1% + 75% × 99% = 74.50%

e: 25% × 99%/25.50% = 97.06%

25% × 1%/74.50% = 0.34%

75% × 1%/25.50% = 2.94%

75% × 99%/74.50% = 99.66%

Finally, the following slide shows that when different Sick % and Accuracy % are run through the computations, we see that rare diseases are very difficult to diagnose correctly and lead to higher levels of false positives (1% sick with 99% accuracy has a 50% false positive) whereas more prevalent diseases are more easily diagnosed correctly (80% sick with 99% accuracy) has a 0.25% false positive. In addition, with moderate diseases (25% sick), low levels of test accuracy can lead to very misleading results. For instance, a test with 30% accuracy has 87.50% false positives and 43.75% false negatives. Even a 90% test accuracy can lead to 25% false positives.

Bayes' Theorem: COVID-19

Rare diseases are very difficult to diagnose correctly and lead to more false positives

Scenario 1

Sick	1.0%
Accuracy	99.0%

P(X|Y) Table	Sick 1.0%	Not Sick 99.0%	Expected Value
Positive	99.0%	1.0%	1.98%
Negative	1.0%	99.0%	98.02%
Check	100.00%	100.00%	100.00%

P(X|Y) Table		Positive	Negative	
Sick	1.0%	50.00%	0.01%	
Not Sick	99.0%	50.00%	99.99%	
Expected Value		1.98%	98.02%	100.00%
		100.00%	100.00%	

Correct Diagnostic	Prob (sick|positive)	50.00%
False Positive (Type I Error)	Prob (~sick|positive)	**50.00%**
Correct Diagnostic	Prob (~sick|negative)	99.99%
False Negative (Type II Error)	Prob (sick|negative)	**0.01%**

Scenario 2

Sick	25.0%
Accuracy	99.0%

P(X|Y) Table	Sick 25.0%	Not Sick 75.0%	Expected Value
Positive	99.0%	1.0%	25.50%
Negative	1.0%	99.0%	74.50%
Check	100.00%	100.00%	100.00%

P(X|Y) Table		Positive	Negative	
Sick	25.0%	97.06%	0.34%	
Not Sick	75.0%	2.94%	99.66%	
Expected Value		25.50%	74.50%	100.00%
		100.00%	100.00%	

Correct Diagnostic	Prob (sick|positive)	97.06%
False Positive (Type I Error)	Prob (~sick|positive)	**2.94%**
Correct Diagnostic	Prob (~sick|negative)	99.66%
False Negative (Type II Error)	Prob (sick|negative)	**0.34%**

Scenario 3

Sick	80.0%
Accuracy	99.0%

P(X|Y) Table	Sick 80.0%	Not Sick 20.0%	Expected Value
Positive	99.0%	1.0%	79.40%
Negative	1.0%	99.0%	20.60%
Check	100.00%	100.00%	100.00%

P(X|Y) Table		Positive	Negative	
Sick	80.0%	99.75%	3.88%	
Not Sick	20.0%	0.25%	96.12%	
Expected Value		79.40%	20.60%	100.00%
		100.00%	100.00%	

Correct Diagnostic	Prob (sick|positive)	99.75%
False Positive (Type I Error)	Prob (~sick|positive)	**0.25%**
Correct Diagnostic	Prob (~sick|negative)	96.12%
False Negative (Type II Error)	Prob (sick|negative)	**3.88%**

Accuracy and efficacy levels can be very misleading as low test accuracy leads to high Type I and Type II Errors

Scenario 4

Sick	25.0%
Accuracy	30.0%

P(X|Y) Table	Sick 25.0%	Not Sick 75.0%	Expected Value
Positive	30.0%	70.0%	60.00%
Negative	70.0%	30.0%	40.00%
Check	100.00%	100.00%	100.00%

P(X|Y) Table		Positive	Negative	
Sick	25.0%	12.50%	43.75%	
Not Sick	75.0%	87.50%	56.25%	
Expected Value		60.00%	40.00%	100.00%
		100.00%	100.00%	

Correct Diagnostic	Prob (sick|positive)	12.50%
False Positive (Type I Error)	Prob (~sick|positive)	**87.50%**
Correct Diagnostic	Prob (~sick|negative)	56.25%
False Negative (Type II Error)	Prob (sick|negative)	**43.75%**

Scenario 5

Sick	25.0%
Accuracy	60.0%

P(X|Y) Table	Sick 25.0%	Not Sick 75.0%	Expected Value
Positive	60.0%	40.0%	45.00%
Negative	40.0%	60.0%	55.00%
Check	100.00%	100.00%	100.00%

P(X|Y) Table		Positive	Negative	
Sick	25.0%	33.33%	18.18%	
Not Sick	75.0%	66.67%	81.82%	
Expected Value		45.00%	55.00%	100.00%
		100.00%	100.00%	

Correct Diagnostic	Prob (sick|positive)	33.33%
False Positive (Type I Error)	Prob (~sick|positive)	**66.67%**
Correct Diagnostic	Prob (~sick|negative)	81.82%
False Negative (Type II Error)	Prob (sick|negative)	**18.18%**

Scenario 6

Sick	25.0%
Accuracy	90.0%

P(X|Y) Table	Sick 25.0%	Not Sick 75.0%	Expected Value
Positive	90.0%	10.0%	30.00%
Negative	10.0%	90.0%	70.00%
Check	100.00%	100.00%	100.00%

P(X|Y) Table		Positive	Negative	
Sick	25.0%	75.00%	3.57%	
Not Sick	75.0%	25.00%	96.43%	
Expected Value		30.00%	70.00%	100.00%
		100.00%	100.00%	

Correct Diagnostic	Prob (sick|positive)	75.00%
False Positive (Type I Error)	Prob (~sick|positive)	**25.00%**
Correct Diagnostic	Prob (~sick|negative)	96.43%
False Negative (Type II Error)	Prob (sick|negative)	**3.57%**

5. Discrete Probability Distributions

Dr. Johnathan Mun, Professor of Research
Quantitative Research Methods Course Slides
Seventh Edition, 2026, ROV Press

Discrete Distribution: Binomial

The three conditions underlying the binomial distribution are:

- For each trial, only two outcomes are possible that are mutually exclusive.

- The trials are independent—what happens in the first trial does not affect the next trial.

- The probability of an event occurring remains the same from trial to trial.

$$P(x) = \frac{n!}{x!\,(n-x)!}p^x(1-p)^{(n-x)} \quad \text{for } n > 0;\ x = 0, 1, 2, \ldots n;\ \text{and } 0 < p < 1$$

The probability P of x events is a function of the combinatorial outcomes and the probabilities of occurrence. Here, n is the total number of trials, small p is the probability of success, and x is the number of successful events.

Discrete Distribution: Hypergeometric

The three conditions underlying the hypergeometric distribution are:

- The total number of items or elements (the population size) is a fixed number, a finite population. The population size must be less than or equal to 1,750.

- The sample size (the number of trials) represents a portion of the population.

- The known initial probability of success in the population changes after each trial.

$$P(x) = \frac{\dfrac{(N_x)!}{x!\,(N_x - x)!}\dfrac{(N - N_x)!}{(n - x)!\,(N - N_x - n + x)!}}{\dfrac{N!}{n!\,(N - n)!}} \quad \text{for } x$$

$$= Max(n - (N - N_x), 0), \;...,\; Min(n, N_x)$$

N is the population, *Nx* is the number of successes in the population, *n* is the number of trials, and *x* is the exact number of successes for which we wish to find the exact probability.

Discrete Distribution: Poisson

The three conditions underlying the Poisson distribution are:

- The number of possible occurrences in any interval is unlimited.

- The occurrences are independent. The number of occurrences in one interval does not affect the number of occurrences in other intervals.

- The average number of occurrences must remain the same from interval to interval.

$$P(x) = \frac{e^{-\lambda}\lambda^x}{x!}$$

λ is the average per period and x is the exact number of successes for which we wish to find the exact probability.

Example: Binomial PMF

A new office complex consists of 16 office suites, each of which is rented on a lease. There is a 20% chance that any one-office suite will be vacated before the lease is up.

a. What discrete probability distribution should you be using and why?

> Binomial, as there are 2 outcomes, finite trials, fixed probabilities, discrete events, and independence.

b. What is the probability that at least one suite will be vacated before the lease expires?

> We require $P(\text{At least one vacated}) = P(x = 1) + P(x = 2) + \ldots + P(x = 16)$, which is the same as getting $P(\text{At least one vacated}) = 1 - P(x = 0)$ since they are complementary:

$$1 - P(x=0) = 1 - C_x^n p^x (1-p)^{n-x} = 1 - C_0^{16}(0.2)^0(1-0.2)^{16-0}$$

$$1 - \frac{16!}{0!(16-0)!}(0.2)^0(0.8)^{16} = 1 - 0.0281 = 0.9719$$

c. What is the probability that no more than one suite will be vacated?

> $P(\text{No more than one}) = P(x = 0) + P(x = 1)$ and using the binomial, we have

$$P(x=0) + P(x=1) = C_0^{16}(0.2)^0(1-0.2)^{16-0} + C_1^{16}(0.2)^1(1-0.2)^{16-1}$$

$$\frac{16!}{0!(16-0)!}(0.2)^0(0.8)^{16} + \frac{16!}{1!(16-1)!}(0.2)^1(0.8)^{15} = 0.0281 + 0.1126 = 0.1407$$

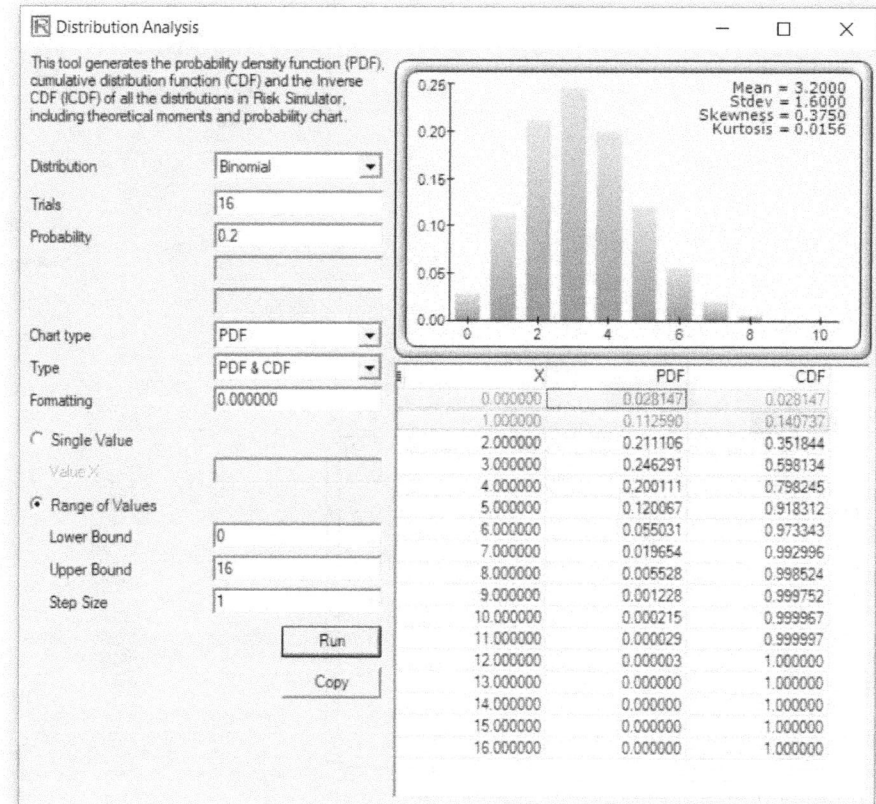

Distribution Analysis

This tool generates the probability density function (PDF), cumulative distribution function (CDF) and the Inverse CDF (ICDF) of all the distributions in Risk Simulator, including theoretical moments and probability chart.

Distribution	Binomial
Trials	16
Probability	0.2
Chart type	PDF
Type	PDF & CDF
Formatting	0.000000

○ Single Value
  Value X
● Range of Values
  Lower Bound: 0
  Upper Bound: 16
  Step Size: 1

Run
Copy

Mean = 3.2000
Stdev = 1.6000
Skewness = 0.3750
Kurtosis = 0.0156

X	PDF	CDF
0.000000	0.028147	0.028147
1.000000	0.112590	0.140737
2.000000	0.211106	0.351844
3.000000	0.246291	0.598134
4.000000	0.200111	0.798245
5.000000	0.120067	0.918312
6.000000	0.055031	0.973343
7.000000	0.019654	0.992996
8.000000	0.005528	0.998524
9.000000	0.001228	0.999752
10.000000	0.000215	0.999967
11.000000	0.000029	0.999997
12.000000	0.000003	1.000000
13.000000	0.000000	1.000000
14.000000	0.000000	1.000000
15.000000	0.000000	1.000000
16.000000	0.000000	1.000000

Example: Binomial PMF

In a 2016 article *Consumer Reports* found widespread contamination and mislabeling of seafood in New York supermarkets. The study revealed that 40% of the swordfish pieces available for sale had levels of mercury above the Food and Drug Administration maximum amounts. In a random sample of 5 swordfish pieces, find the following probabilities:

    a. Four have mercury levels above the maximum levels

$$P(x=4) = C_x^n p^x (1-p)^{n-x} = C_4^5 (0.4)^4 (1-0.4)^{5-4}$$

$$\frac{5!}{4!(5-4)!}(0.4)^4(0.6)^1 = 0.0768$$

    b. Two have mercury levels above the maximum levels

$$P(x=2) = C_x^n p^x (1-p)^{n-x} = C_2^5 (0.4)^2 (1-0.4)^{5-2}$$

$$\frac{5!}{2!(5-2)!}(0.4)^2(0.6)^3 = 0.3456$$

    c. Which discrete probability distribution should you be using and why?

Binomial, since there are two outcomes, finite trials, discrete, fixed probabilities, and independence between trials.

Distribution Analysis

This tool generates the probability density function (PDF), cumulative distribution function (CDF) and the Inverse CDF (ICDF) of all the distributions in Risk Simulator, including theoretical moments and probability chart.

Distribution	Binomial
Trials	5
Probability	0.4

Chart type: PDF
Type: PDF & CDF
Formatting: 0.000000

○ Single Value
  Value X

◉ Range of Values
  Lower Bound: 0
  Upper Bound: 5
  Step Size: 1

Run
Copy

Mean = 2.0000
Stdev = 1.0954
Skewness = 0.1826
Kurtosis = -0.3667

X	PDF	CDF
0.000000	0.077760	0.077760
1.000000	0.259200	0.336960
2.000000	0.345600	0.682560
3.000000	0.230400	0.912960
4.000000	0.076800	0.989760
5.000000	0.010240	1.000000

Example: Hypergeometric PMF (I)

A commercial for Tasteless sugarless chewing gum claims that 3 out of 4 dentists who recommend sugarless gum to their patients recommend Tasteless. Suppose this claim was established following a survey of 4 dentists randomly selected from a group of 20 dentists. What is the probability that at least 3 of the 4 dentists would recommend Tasteless if, in fact, only 50% of the original group of 20 dentists favor that brand? What discrete distribution should you use?

P(At least 3) $= P(3) + P(4)$, using the hypergeometric distribution since sampling without replacement, which creates dependence. We thus have:

$$P(3) + P(4) = \frac{C_3^{10} C_1^{10}}{C_4^{20}} + \frac{C_4^{10} C_0^{10}}{C_4^{20}}$$

$$= \frac{\dfrac{10!}{3!\,7!} \cdot \dfrac{10!}{1!\,9!}}{\dfrac{20!}{4!\,16!}} + \frac{\dfrac{10!}{4!\,6!} \cdot \dfrac{10!}{0!\,10!}}{\dfrac{20!}{4!\,16!}}$$

$$= 0.2477 + 0.0433 = 0.2910$$

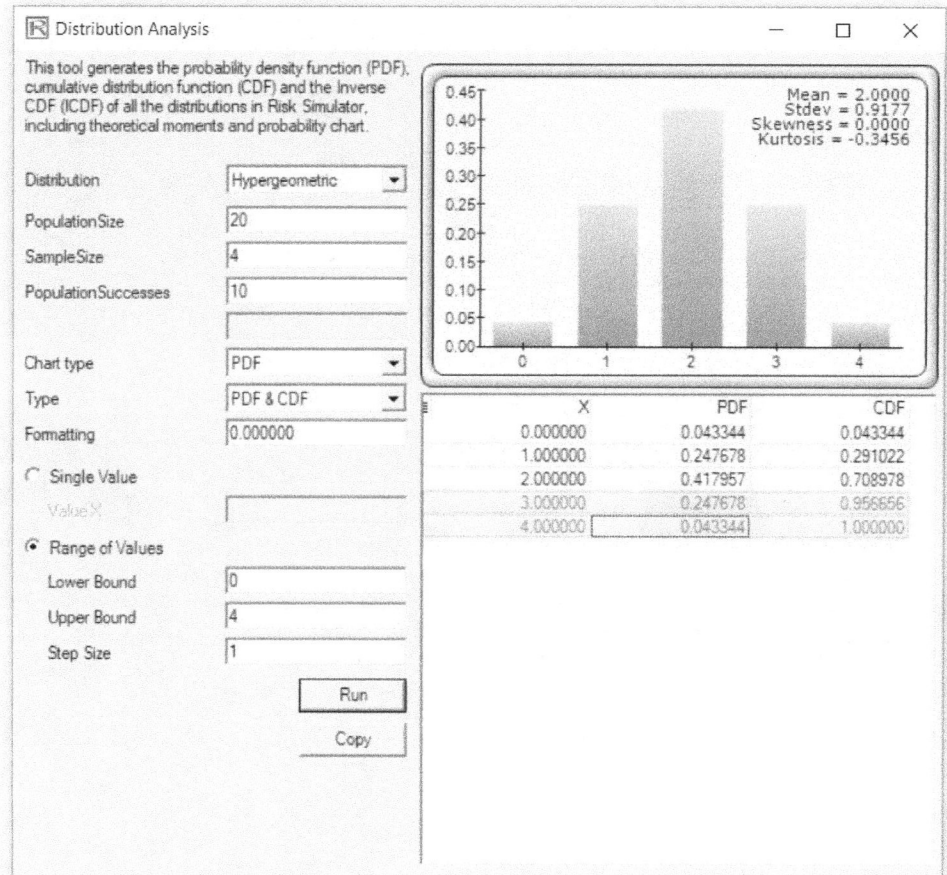

Example: Hypergeometric PMF (II)

Suppose there are 420 applicants for 7 positions at a certain company, and the company is able to narrow the field to 22 equally qualified applicant finalists. Of the finalists, 9 are minority candidates. Assume that the 7 who are chosen are selected at random from this final group of 22. Calculate the probability that:

a. 4 of the 7 hired are minority candidates

$$P(x=4) = \frac{C_4^9 C_3^{13}}{C_7^{22}} = \frac{\dfrac{9!}{4!\,5!}\dfrac{13!}{3!\,10!}}{\dfrac{22!}{7!\,15!}} = 0.2113$$

b. None of the minority candidates is hired

$$P(x=0) = \frac{C_0^9 C_7^{13}}{C_7^{22}} = \frac{\dfrac{9!}{0!\,9!}\dfrac{13!}{7!\,6!}}{\dfrac{22!}{7!\,15!}} = 0.0101$$

c. Only 1 of those hired is a minority candidate

$$P(x=1) = \frac{C_1^9 C_6^{13}}{C_7^{22}} = \frac{\dfrac{9!}{1!\,8!}\dfrac{13!}{6!\,7!}}{\dfrac{22!}{7!\,15!}} = 0.0906$$

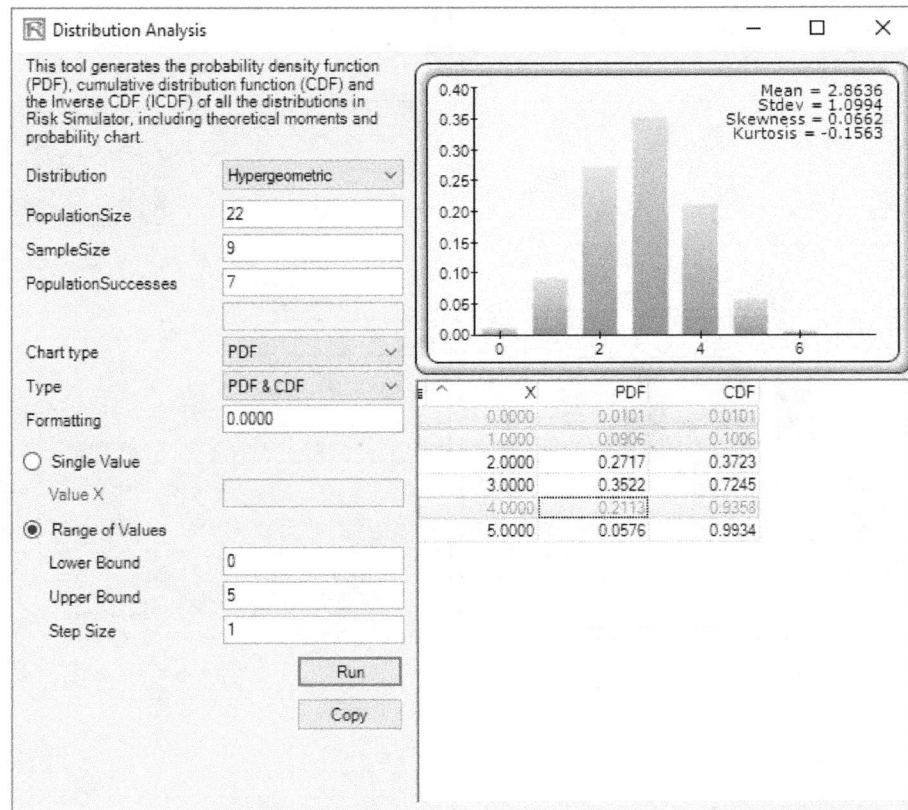

Distribution Analysis

This tool generates the probability density function (PDF), cumulative distribution function (CDF) and the Inverse CDF (ICDF) of all the distributions in Risk Simulator, including theoretical moments and probability chart.

Distribution	Hypergeometric
PopulationSize	22
SampleSize	9
PopulationSuccesses	7
Chart type	PDF
Type	PDF & CDF
Formatting	0.0000

○ Single Value
　Value X

● Range of Values
　Lower Bound　0
　Upper Bound　5
　Step Size　1

Run

Copy

Mean = 2.8636
Stdev = 1.0994
Skewness = 0.0662
Kurtosis = -0.1563

X	PDF	CDF
0.0000	0.0101	0.0101
1.0000	0.0906	0.1006
2.0000	0.2717	0.3723
3.0000	0.3522	0.7245
4.0000	0.2113	0.9358
5.0000	0.0576	0.9934

Example: Poisson PMF

The Labor Management Reporting and Disclosure Act of 1959 prescribes fiduciary responsibilities for union officials and makes embezzlement of union funds a crime. In the 38 years since the act was passed, civil suits have been filed under the law randomly and independently of one another at an average rate of 2.7 suits per month.

a. What is the probability that NO suits are filed in given month? This follows a Poisson distribution where

$$P(0) = \frac{\mu^x e^{-\mu}}{x!} = \frac{2.7^0 e^{-2.7}}{0!} = e^{-2.7} = 0.0672$$

b. What is the probability of no more than 2 suits being filed?

$$P(0) + P(1) + P(2) = \frac{2.7^0 e^{-2.7}}{0!} + \frac{2.7^1 e^{-2.7}}{1!} + \frac{2.7^2 e^{-2.7}}{2!}$$
$$= 0.0672 + 0.1814 + 0.2449 = 0.4935$$

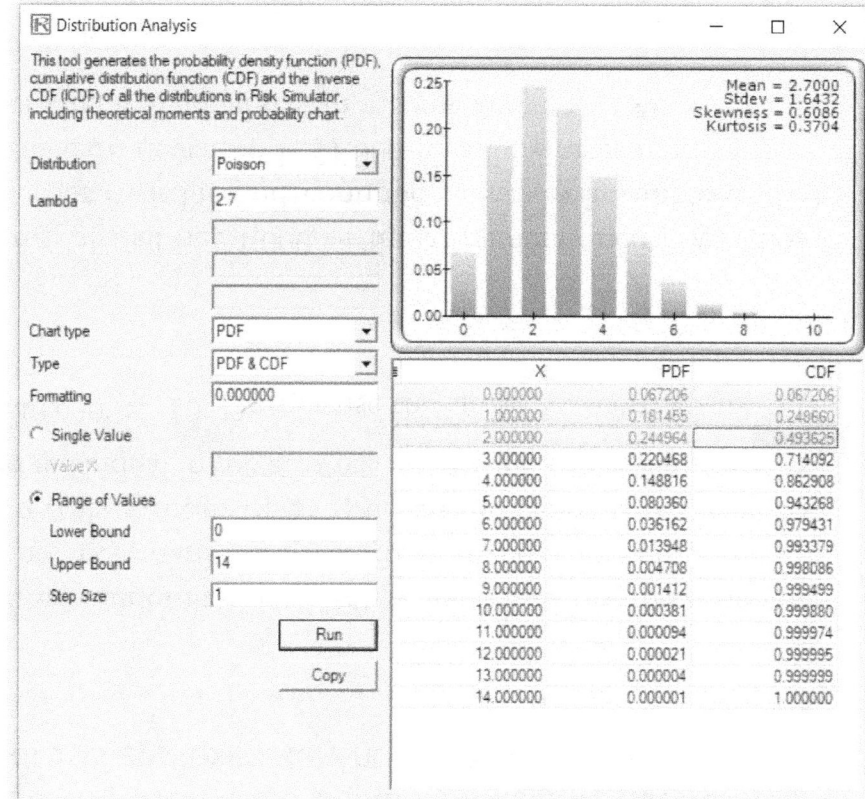

Distribution Analysis

This tool generates the probability density function (PDF), cumulative distribution function (CDF) and the Inverse CDF (ICDF) of all the distributions in Risk Simulator, including theoretical moments and probability chart.

Mean = 2.7000
Stdev = 1.6432
Skewness = 0.6086
Kurtosis = 0.3704

Distribution: Poisson
Lambda: 2.7

Chart type: PDF
Type: PDF & CDF
Formatting: 0.000000

○ Single Value
  Value X
● Range of Values
  Lower Bound: 0
  Upper Bound: 14
  Step Size: 1

Run
Copy

X	PDF	CDF
0.000000	0.067206	0.067206
1.000000	0.181455	0.248660
2.000000	0.244964	0.493625
3.000000	0.220468	0.714092
4.000000	0.148816	0.862908
5.000000	0.080360	0.943268
6.000000	0.036162	0.979431
7.000000	0.013948	0.993379
8.000000	0.004708	0.998086
9.000000	0.001412	0.999499
10.000000	0.000381	0.999880
11.000000	0.000094	0.999974
12.000000	0.000021	0.999995
13.000000	0.000004	0.999999
14.000000	0.000001	1.000000

Sampling Distribution and Central Limit Theorem

The sampling distribution looks nothing like the original uniform distribution. In fact, according to the Central Limit Theorem, all sampling distributions given will tend toward a normal distribution, thereby justifying the times we assume normality if our sample size is large enough, typically when $n > 30$. According to the Central Limit Theorem, even if the population itself is not normal, for large enough n, the random variable's mean or $\bar{x}$ is approximately normal with mean μ and:

$$\sigma_{\bar{x}} = \frac{\sigma}{\sqrt{n}}$$

Example 1: From a population of 550,000 in the area, we randomly select 100 people to survey their income. From economic theory, we know that incomes are not necessarily normally distributed, depending on the income stratification of the population. The sample reveals a mean of $35,000 and a standard deviation of $5,000. What is the probability that a randomly selected individual in the area has an income above $40,000?

> $Z = (40 - 35)/(5/\text{root}100) = 10$, so, the $P(x \geq 40,000) = 0.0$. Do not use the simple Z score where $Z = (40 - 35)/5 = 1.0$ with $P(x) = .5 - .3413 = 0.1587$.

Example 2: Suppose a virulent strain of the Ebola virus kills all but 1,000 of the aforementioned population. Being such staunch statisticians, ignore the threats to your own life and continue to survey a sample of 100 people. The new sample income mean is $5,000 and standard deviation is $1,000 (deadly viruses tend to mess up business). What is the probability that a randomly selected individual has an income above $5,500?

> We must use the finite population correction factor:

> FPC corrected $\sigma_{\bar{x}} = (1000/\text{root}100)\text{root}([1000 - 100]/[1000 - 1]) = 94.915$ and,
> hence, $Z = (5500 - 5000)/94.915 = 5.26$ and we have $P(x \geq 5500) = 0\%$.

Note: We should *not* be calculating regular $Z = (5500 - 5000)/(1000) = 0.5$ with a corresponding $P(x \geq 5500) = 0.5 - 0.1915 = 0.3085$, which is incorrect.

Sampling Distribution and Central Limit Theorem

Example 3: Suppose we take a single die with 6 sides and throw it 100,000 times. We see that the resulting mean and standard deviation are theoretically 3.50 and 1.71. We know that the theoretical mean for a discrete uniform distribution is $rank\left[\frac{n+1}{2}\right] = 3.5th\, rank = 3.5$ and the standard deviation is $rank\sqrt{\frac{(n-1)(n+1)}{12}} = rank\sqrt{\frac{(6-1)(6+1)}{12}} = rank(1.71) = 1.71$. In fact, a computational Monte Carlo simulation was run, and we see the simulated empirical results (3.50 and 1.71, rounded) match our theoretical results (see Figure 7.1).

Now, suppose instead of tossing a single die 100,000 times, we now toss 4 dice at once, for 25,000 times. This is similar to throwing the single die 100,000 times because we would record a total of 100,000 outcomes. The results are shown in Figure 7.2. We see the same 3.50 mean, but the standard deviation is now 0.85. This case is a sampling distribution problem, where the sample size each time is 4. We just empirically proved that $\frac{1.71}{\sqrt{4}} = 0.85$ (rounded).

Similarly, if we tossed 10 dice simultaneously for 10,000 times, we obtain the results shown in Figure 7.3, where the mean is still 3.50 and the standard deviation is 0.54 (rounded). We can empirically prove that $\frac{1.71}{\sqrt{10}} = 0.54$ (rounded).

These three examples show the power of Central Limit Theorem and statistical sampling. The mean of the sample approaches the population mean, and the sampling standard deviation approaches the population standard deviation divided by the square root of the sample size.

Sampling Distribution and Central Limit Theorem

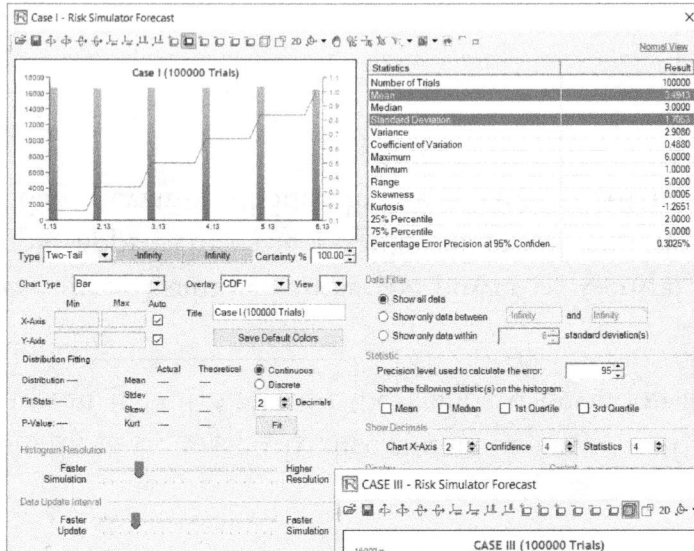

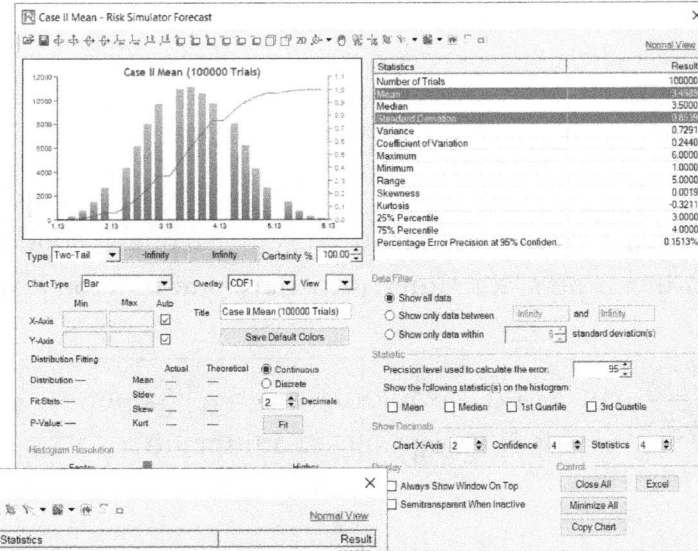

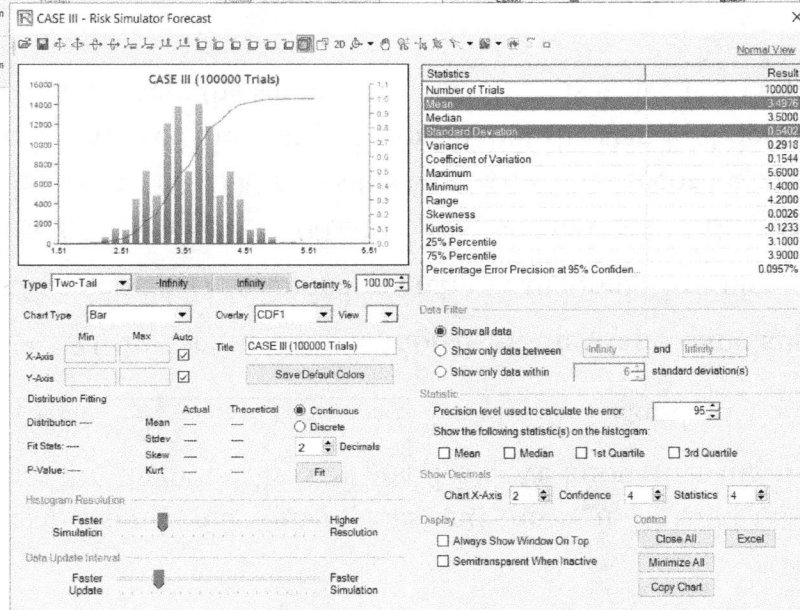

6. Continuous Probability Distributions

Dr. Johnathan Mun, Professor of Research
Quantitative Research Methods Course Slides
Seventh Edition, 2026, ROV Press

Continuous Distribution: Normal

The normal distribution is the most important distribution in probability theory because it describes many natural phenomena, such as people's IQs or heights. Decision makers can use the normal distribution to describe uncertain variables such as the inflation rate or the future price of gasoline. Input requirements: Standard deviation > 0 and can be any positive value whereas mean can be any value.

The three conditions underlying the normal distribution are:

- Some value of the uncertain variable is the most likely (the mean of the distribution).

- The uncertain variable could as likely be above the mean as it could be below the mean (symmetrical about the mean).

- The uncertain variable is more likely in the vicinity of the mean than further away.

$$f(x) = \frac{1}{\sqrt{2\pi}\sigma} e^{\frac{-(x-\mu)^2}{2\sigma^2}} \quad \textit{for all values of } x$$

Continuous Distribution: Student's T

The Student's t-distribution is the most widely used distribution in hypothesis testing. This distribution is used to estimate the mean of a normally distributed population when the sample size is small, and is used to test the statistical significance of the difference between two sample means or confidence intervals for small sample sizes.

The t-distribution is related to the F-distribution as follows: the square of a value of t with r degrees of freedom is distributed as F with 1 and r degrees of freedom. The overall shape of the probability density function of the t-distribution also resembles the bell shape of a normally distributed variable with mean 0 and variance 1, except that it is a bit lower and wider or is leptokurtic (fat tails at the ends and peaked center). As the number of degrees of freedom grows (say, above 30), the t-distribution approaches the normal distribution with mean 0 and variance 1. Input requirements: Degrees of freedom ≥ 1 and must be an integer.

$$f(t) = \frac{\Gamma[(r+1)/2]}{\sqrt{r\pi}\,\Gamma[r/2]}(1+t^2/r)^{-(r+1)/2}$$

Continuous Distribution: F

The F-distribution, also known as the Fisher–Snedecor distribution, is another continuous distribution used most frequently for hypothesis testing. Specifically, it is used to test the statistical difference between two variances in analysis of variance tests and likelihood ratio tests. The F-distribution with the numerator degree of freedom n and denominator degree of freedom m is related to the chi-square distribution in that:

$$\frac{\chi_n^2 / n}{\chi_m^2 / m} \overset{d}{\sim} F_{n,m}$$

The numerator degree of freedom n and denominator degree of freedom m are the only distributional parameters. Input requirements: Degrees of freedom numerator and denominator are both > 0 integers.

$$f(x) = \frac{\Gamma\left(\dfrac{n+m}{2}\right)\left(\dfrac{n}{m}\right)^{n/2} x^{n/2-1}}{\Gamma\left(\dfrac{n}{2}\right)\Gamma\left(\dfrac{m}{2}\right)\left[x\left(\dfrac{n}{m}\right)+1\right]^{(n+m)/2}}$$

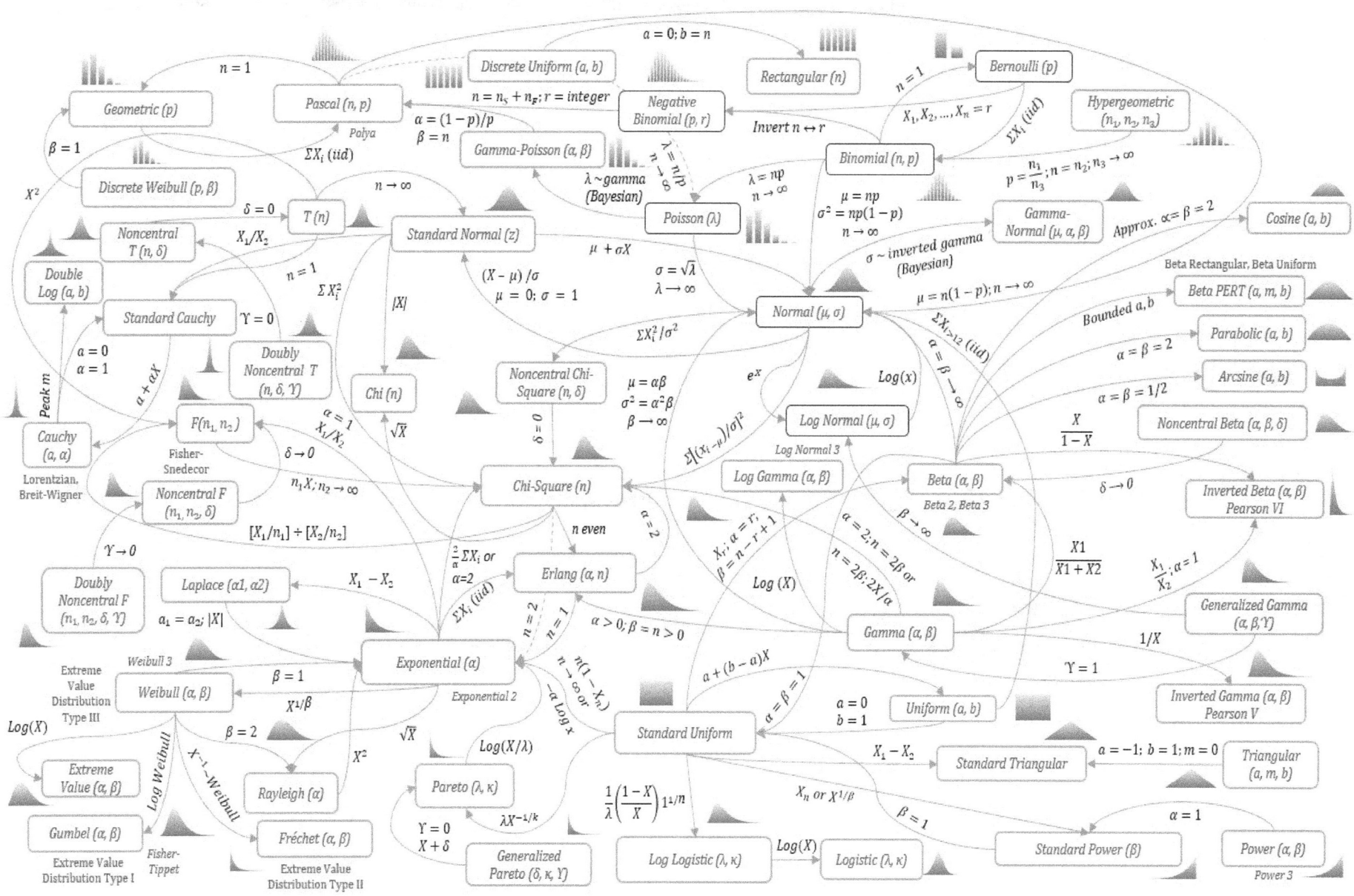

Discrete Uniform (a, b) — $a = 0; b = n$ — Rectangular (n)

Bernoulli (p) — Hypergeometric (n_1, n_2, n_3)

Geometric (p) — $n = 1$ — Pascal (n, p) — $n = n_s + n_F; r = integer$ — Negative Binomial (p, r) — Invert $n \leftrightarrow r$ — $X_1, X_2, \ldots, X_n = r$ — ΣX_i (iid)

Polya — $\alpha = (1-p)/p$; $\beta = n$

Gamma-Poisson (α, β) — $\lambda \sim gamma$ (Bayesian)

Discrete Weibull (p, β) — ΣX_i (iid) — $n \to \infty$ — Binomial (n, p) — $p = \frac{n_1}{n_3}; n = n_2; n_3 \to \infty$

X^2 — $\beta = 1$ — $\lambda = np$; $n \to \infty$ — Poisson (λ) — $\mu = np$; $\sigma^2 = np(1-p)$; $n \to \infty$

$\delta = 0$ — T (n) — Standard Normal (z) — $\mu + \sigma X$ — $\sigma = \sqrt{\lambda}$; $\lambda \to \infty$

Noncentral T (n, δ) — X_1/X_2 — $(X - \mu)/\sigma$; $\mu = 0; \sigma = 1$

Gamma-Normal (μ, α, β) — $\sigma \sim$ inverted gamma (Bayesian) — Approx. $\alpha = \beta = 2$ — Cosine (a, b)

$n = 1$ — ΣX_i^2

Double Log (a, b) — Standard Cauchy — $\Upsilon = 0$ — $|X|$ — $\Sigma X_i^2/\sigma^2$ — Normal (μ, σ) — $\mu = n(1-p); n \to \infty$ — Beta Rectangular, Beta Uniform

Beta PERT (a, m, b)

$\alpha = 0$; $\alpha = 1$ — Doubly Noncentral T (n, δ, Υ) — Chi (n) — Noncentral Chi-Square (n, δ) — $\mu = \alpha\beta$; $\sigma^2 = \alpha^2\beta$; $\beta \to \infty$ — e^x — Log(x) — Bounded a, b — Parabolic (a, b)

$a + \alpha X$ — $\sqrt{X}$ — $\delta = 0$ — $\Sigma[(x_i - \mu)/\sigma]^2$ — Log Normal (μ, σ) — $\frac{X}{1-X}$ — $\alpha = \beta = 2$ — Arcsine (a, b)

Peak m — Cauchy (a, α) — $\alpha = 1$; X_1/X_2 — $F(n_1, n_2)$ — Log Normal 3 — Noncentral Beta (α, β, δ)

Lorentzian, Breit-Wigner — Fisher-Snedecor — $\delta \to 0$ — $n_1 X; n_2 \to \infty$ — Chi-Square (n) — Log Gamma (α, β) — Beta (α, β) — $\beta \to \infty$ — Inverted Beta (α, β) Pearson VI

Noncentral F (n_1, n_2, δ) — $[X_1/n_1] \div [X_2/n_2]$ — n even — $\alpha = 2$ — $X_i, \alpha = r; \beta = n - r + 1$ — Beta 2, Beta 3 — $\frac{X1}{X1+X2}$ — $\frac{X_1}{X_2}; \alpha = 1$

$\Upsilon \to 0$ — Doubly Noncentral F $(n_1, n_2, \delta, \Upsilon)$ — Laplace (α1, α2) — $X_1 - X_2$ — $\frac{2}{\pi}\Sigma X_i$ or $\alpha = 2$ — Erlang (α, n) — $\alpha = 2; n = 2\beta$ or $n = 2\beta; 2X/\alpha$ — Log (X) — Generalized Gamma (α, β, Υ)

$a_1 = a_2; |X|$ — ΣX_i (iid) — $n = 2$ — $\alpha > 0; \beta = n > 0$ — Gamma (α, β) — $1/X$

$n = 1$ — $a + (b-a)X$ — $\alpha = \beta = 1$ — $a = 0$; $b = 1$ — Uniform (a, b) — $\Upsilon = 1$ — Inverted Gamma (α, β) Pearson V

Extreme Value Distribution Type III — Weibull 3 — Weibull (α, β) — $\beta = 1$ — Exponential (α) — $n \to \infty$ or $-\alpha \log x$ — Standard Uniform — $X_1 - X_2$ — Standard Triangular — $a = -1; b = 1; m = 0$ — Triangular (a, m, b)

$X^{1/\beta}$ — Exponential 2 — $n(1 - X_n)$

Log(X) — $\beta = 2$ — X^2 — $\sqrt{X}$ — $Log(X/\lambda)$ — $\frac{1}{\lambda}\left(\frac{1-X}{X}\right)^{1/n}$ — X_n or $X^{1/\beta}$ — $\beta = 1$ — $\alpha = 1$

Extreme Value (α, β) — Log Weibull — X^{-1}—Weibull — Rayleigh (α) — Pareto (λ, κ) — Log Logistic (λ, κ) — $Log(X)$ — Logistic (λ, κ) — Standard Power (β) — Power (α, β)

Gumbel (α, β) — Fréchet (α, β) — $\Upsilon = 0$; $X + \delta$ — $\lambda X^{-1/k}$ — Generalized Pareto (δ, κ, Υ)

Extreme Value Distribution Type I — Fisher-Tippet — Extreme Value Distribution Type II — Power 3

Continuous PDF (Area Chart)

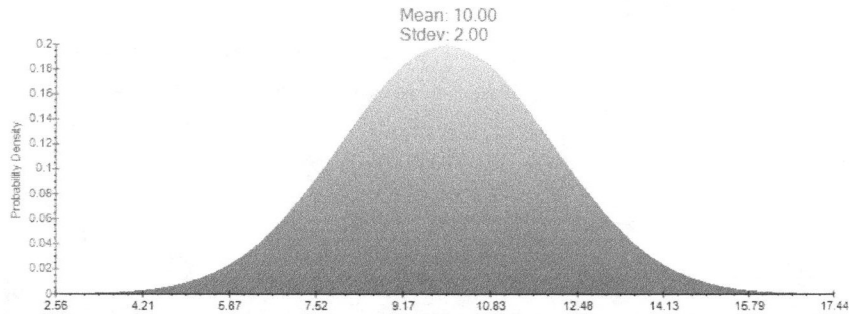

Discrete PMF (Bar Chart)

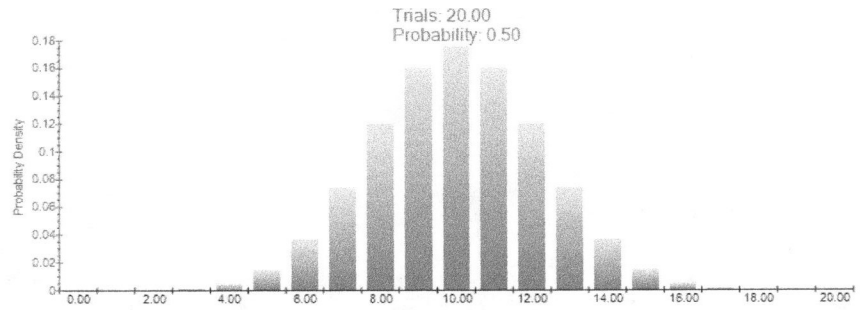

Multiple Continuous PDF Overlay Charts

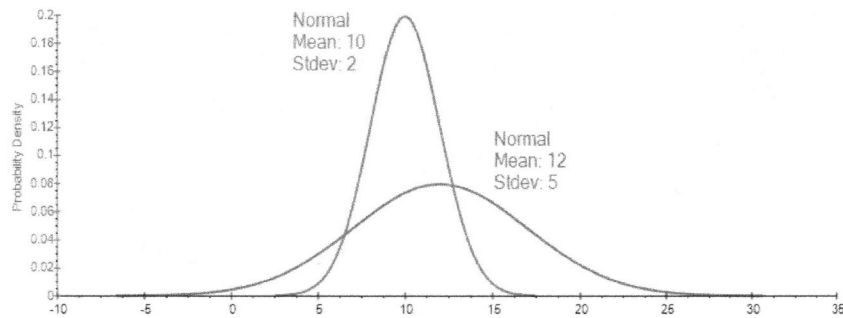

CDF Overlay Charts

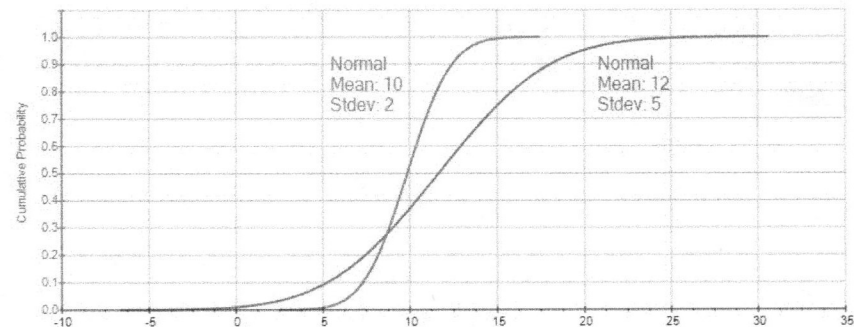

Interpreting PDF and CDF

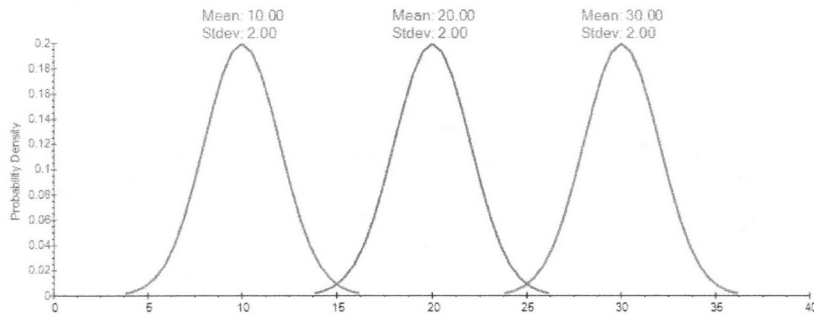

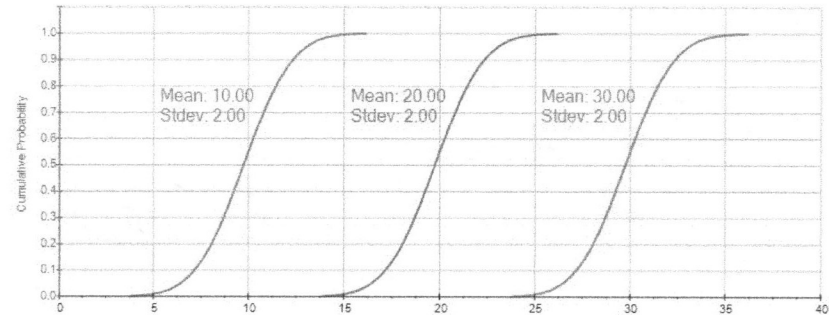

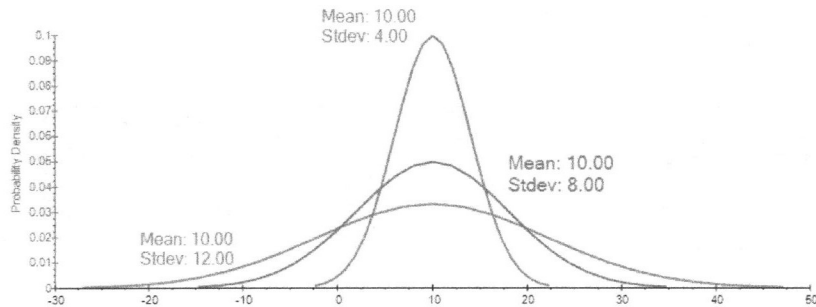

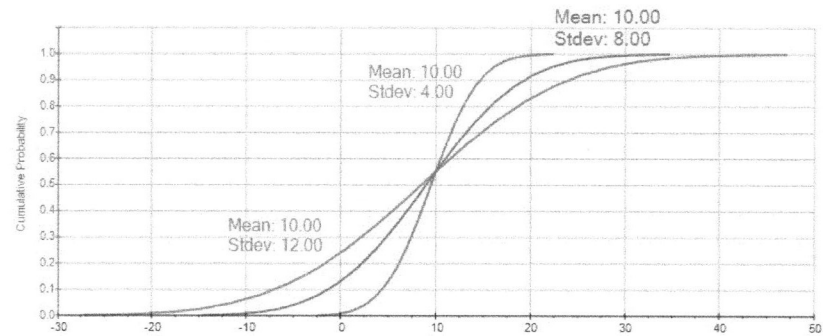

PDF Characteristics of the Beta Distribution

PDF of a Negatively Skewed Beta Distribution

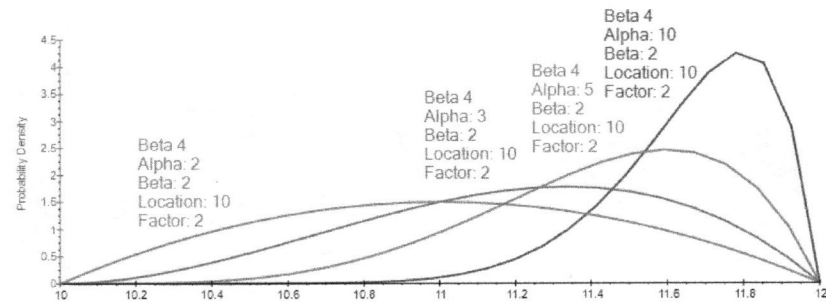

CDF of a Positively Skewed Distribution

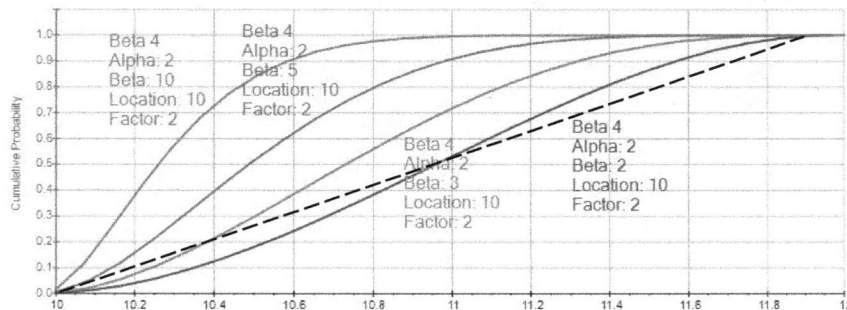

CDF of a Negatively Skewed Distribution

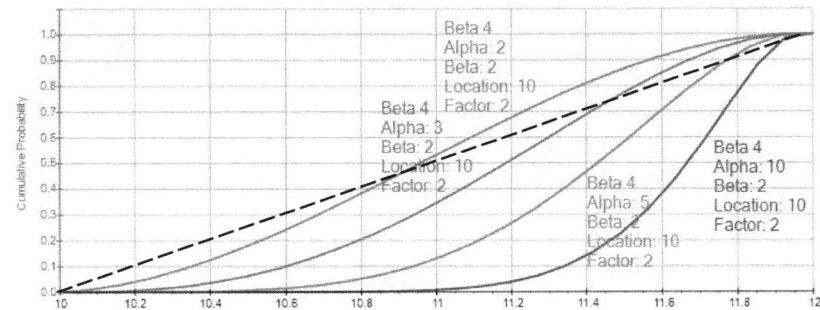

PDF Characteristics of a Shift

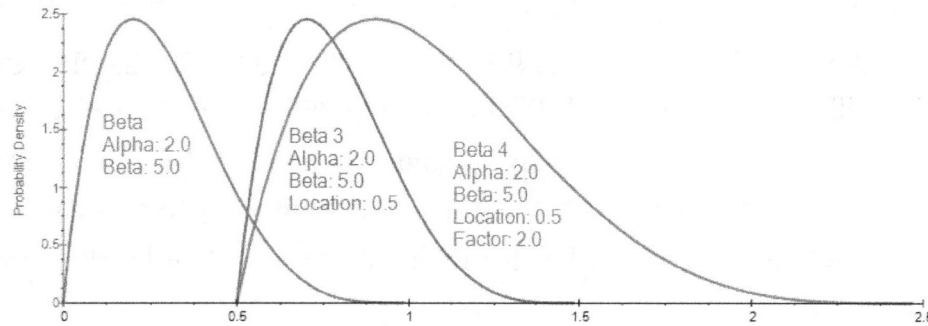

CDF Characteristics of a Shift

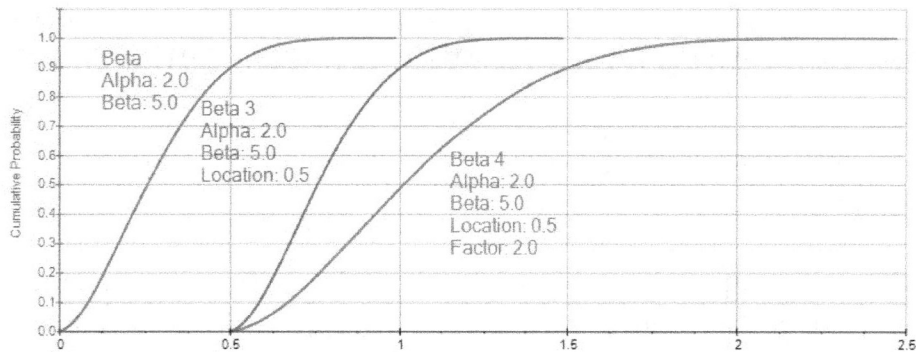

Examples: Standard Normal Distribution $Z = \dfrac{x - \mu}{\sigma}$

Example 1: The batteries from a particular watch battery manufacturer last, on average, for 15 months with a standard deviation of 1.5 months. Assume that the battery life is normally distributed. If a battery is randomly selected from the manufacturer's production line, find the probability that it has a life of:

(i) $P(x = 15 \text{ months}) = 0$ since for a point, the probability is 0.

(ii) $P(x \geq 15 \text{ months}) = 0.50$ as half of the curve or $Z = (15 - 15)/1.5$ yields the value $Z = 0$ or an area of 0.0, hence, $0.5 - 0.0 = 0.5$.

(iii) $P(x \geq 16.5 \text{ months}) \Rightarrow Z = (16.5 - 15)/1.5 = 1$ or $A = 0.3413$. Hence, we have $0.5 - 0.3413 = 0.1587 = 15.87\%$. See the chart below.

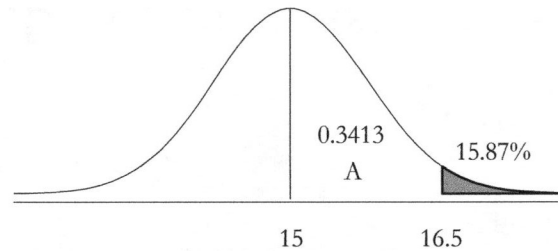

A Z-value of 1 on a Normal (0,1) can be obtained using Risk Simulator's Distributional Analysis Tool as shown on the left in the accompanying figure. The CDF is the left tail and the 1 – CDF value is the right tail. For the problem above, the right tail is required, which yields 15.87%.

Alternatively, use Excel and enter the function "=NORMSDIST(1)" which will return the CDF of 84.13% for the left tail, or "=1-NORMSDIST(1)" which will return 15.87% for the right tail.

An even simpler approach may be to use Risk Simulator's Distributional Analysis Tool to enter the mean of 15 and standard deviation of 1.5 into a normal distribution and compute the CDF of 16.5 months (see on the right in the figure). The tool returns the 1 – CDF or right tail of 15.87%. The tool makes the computations directly without the need to obtain the Z-scores and convert them into probabilities.

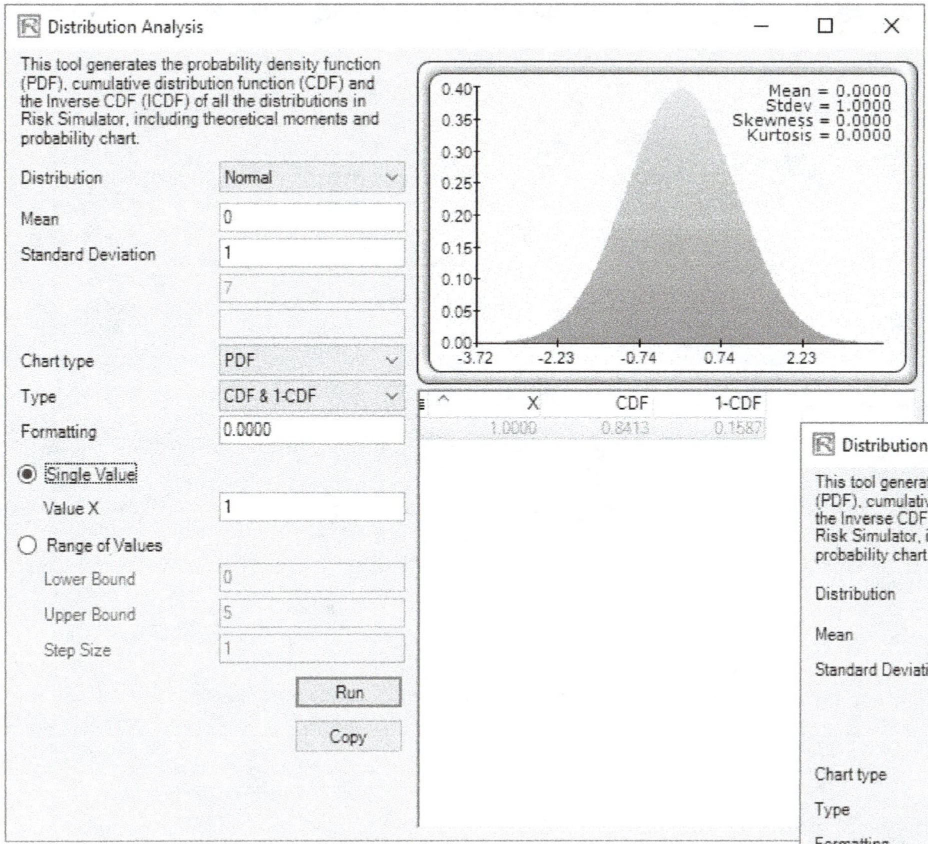

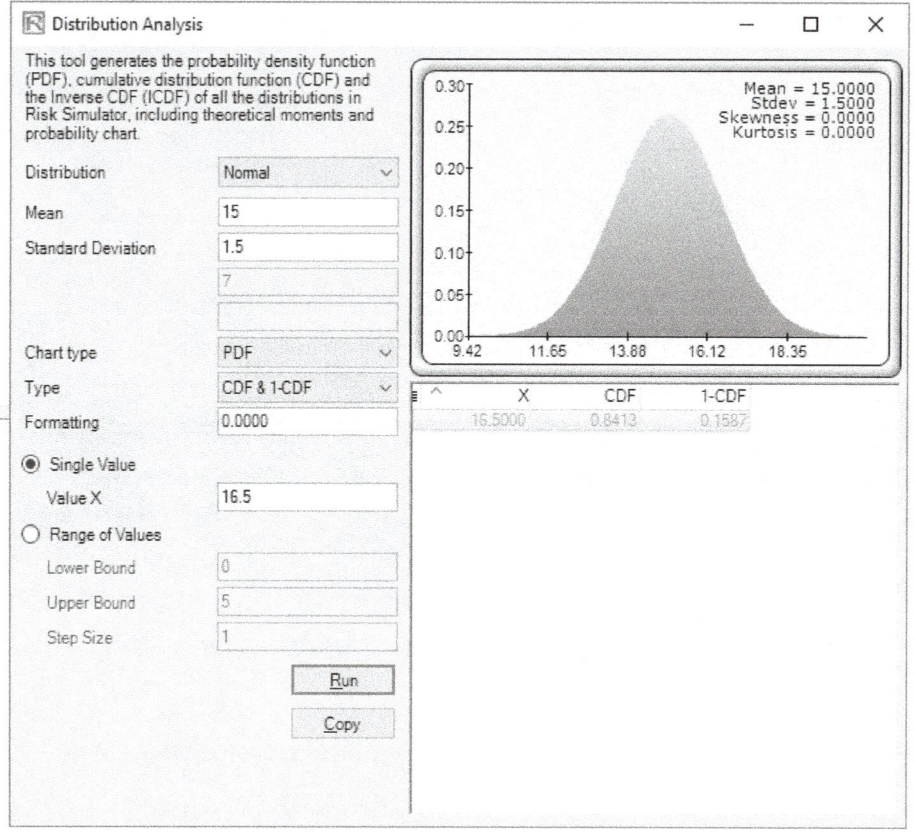

Example 2: The battery manufacturer from example 1 wants to offer a 12-month warranty on her batteries: a full refund if the battery dies before 12 months. What are the chances that this refund will have to be provided?

So, we get $P(x \leq 12) \Rightarrow Z = (12 - 15)/1.5 = -2.0$ or $A = 0.4772$ to the left since a negative Z. Hence, $0.5 - 0.4772 = 0.0228$ or 2.28% probability.

Using a Z score of -2.0, we get 2.28% using Risk Simulator (below, left) and in Excel, "=NORMSDIST(-2)" yields 2.28%. Alternatively, direct calculations using a normal distribution's CDF also yields 2.28% (below, right).

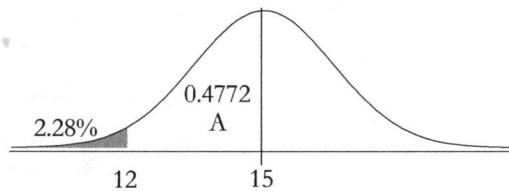

Example 3: Suppose the probability calculated in example 2 is too high and, hence, too costly for the manufacturer. To minimize the cost and lower the probability of having to make a refund to a 1% probability, what would be a suitable warranty date (in months)?

Working backwards, to obtain a $P(x \leq X) = 0.01$, first look at the graph and then find the Z value for A = 0.49, which yields Z = 2.33 Hence, Z = $-2.33 = (x - 15)/1.5$. Solving, x = $(-2.33 \times 1.5) + 15 = 11.5$ months. Watch out! If you use 2.33 without the negative sign, you get 18 months, which does not make any sense! Similarly, you can easily solve the problem by using Risk Simulator to compute the Inverse CDF (ICDF) on a 1% CDF left-tail probability, which yields 11.5 months (see the figure below).

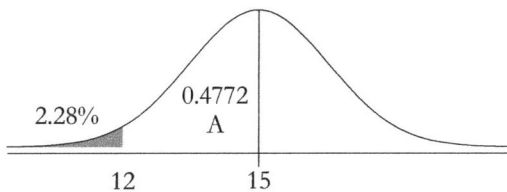

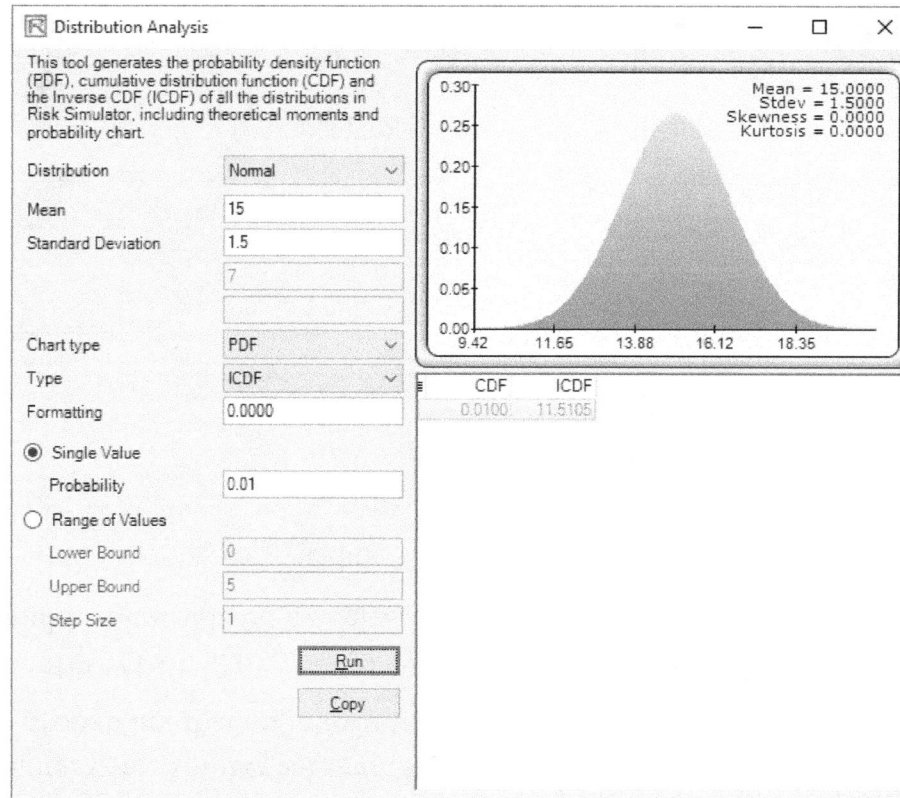

Example 4: The population mean of an IQ test based on the Cattel scale is 100, and its standard deviation is 15; the *genius threshold* is 140 points, while the *not-so-genius threshold* is 50. What is the probability that an individual is a genius? What is the probability that an individual is an idiot?

(i) For $P(x \geq 140) \Rightarrow Z = (140 - 100)/15 = 2.67$, $A = 0.4962$. Hence, $0.5 - 0.4962 = 0.0038$ or 0.38% or about 4 people in 1,000 would be considered a genius.

(ii) For $P(x \leq 50) \Rightarrow Z = (50 - 100)/15 = -3.33$ yielding $A = 0.4996$, the probability of being not so smart is $0.5 - 0.4996 = 0.0004$ or 0.04%

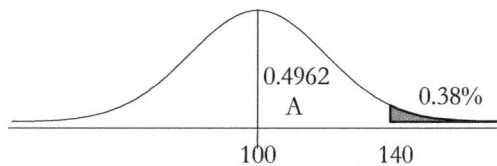

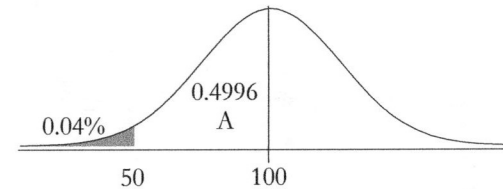

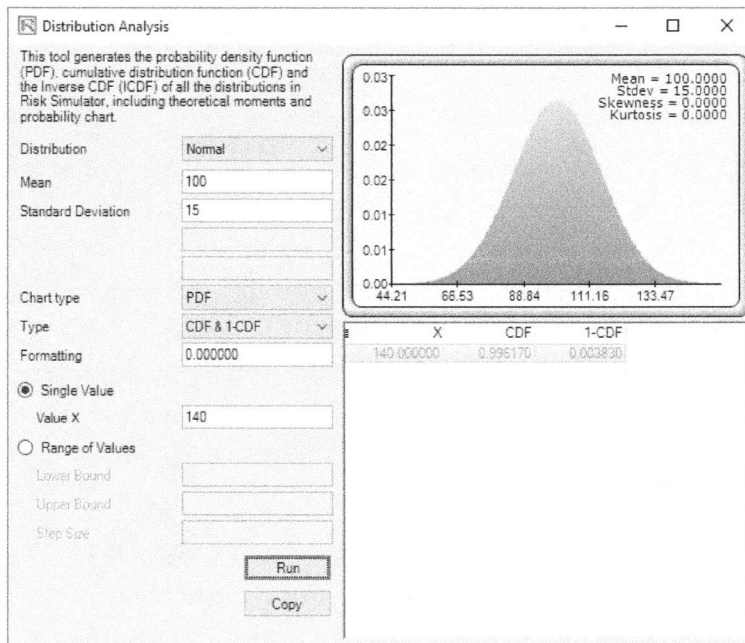

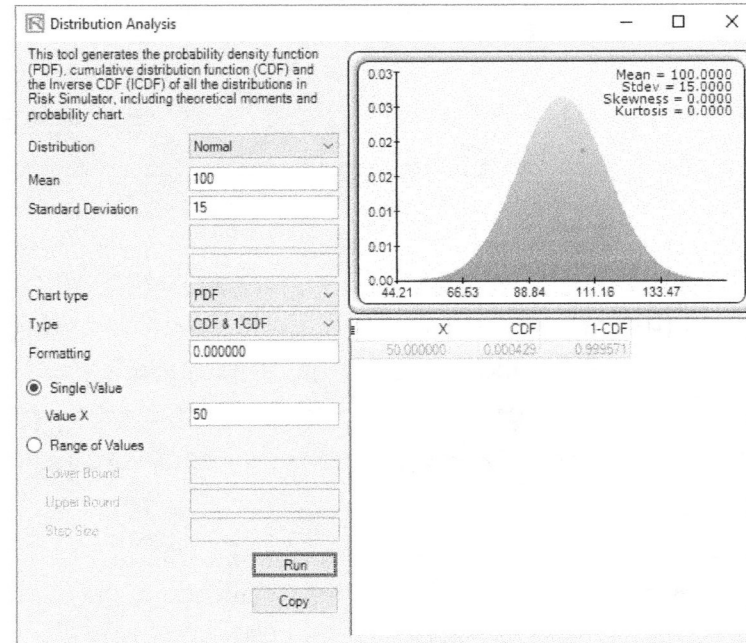

Example 5: Use the table of standard normal probability distribution at the end of the book or ROV BizStats to determine the following. To facilitate answering the question, draw a standard normal curve and shade in the area you are attempting to calculate.

a. $P(0.00 < z < 1.96) = 47.5\%$

    $A = 0.4750$

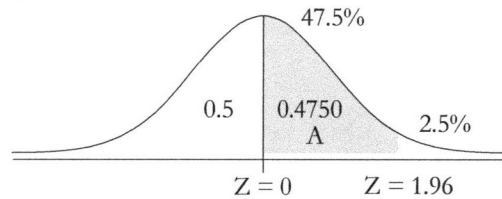

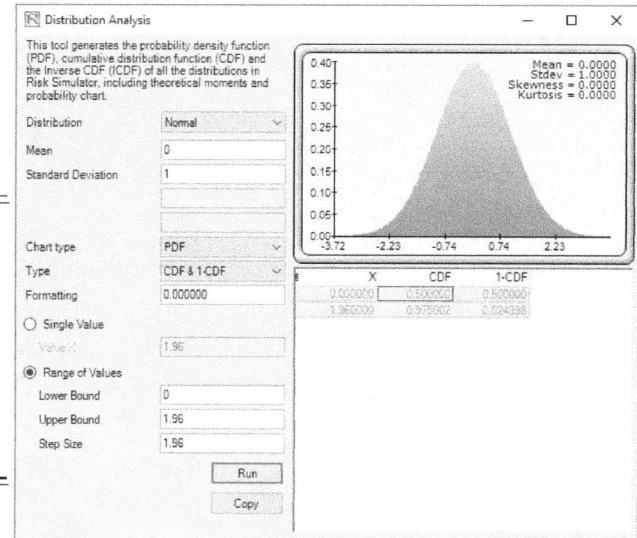

b. $P(z > 1.64) = 1 - (0.5 + 0.4495) = 5\%$

    $A = 0.4495$

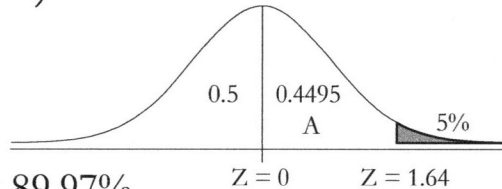

c. $P(z < 1.28) = 0.5 + 0.3997 = 89.97\%$

    $A = 0.3997$

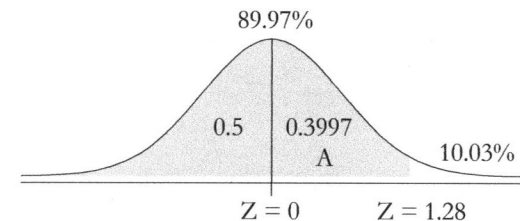

d. $P(-2.00 < z < 2.00) = 0.4772 + 0.4772 = 95.44\%$

    $A1 = A2 = 0.4772$

e. $P(z < 1.50) = 0.4332 + 0.5 = 93.32\%$

    $A = 0.4332$

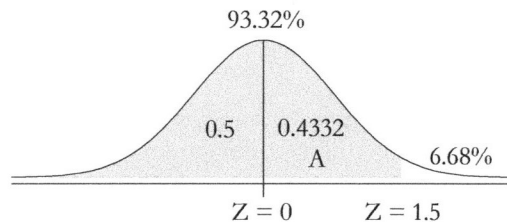

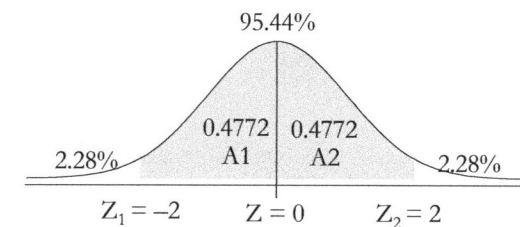

Example 6: The operating life of 50-gallon hot water heaters is known to be normally distributed with a mean of 12 years and a standard deviation of 3 years. The heaters are all sold with an 8-year guarantee. Sketch a normal distribution and shade the appropriate areas.

a.   What proportion of customers will get double the guaranteed life, that is, an operating life of 16 years?

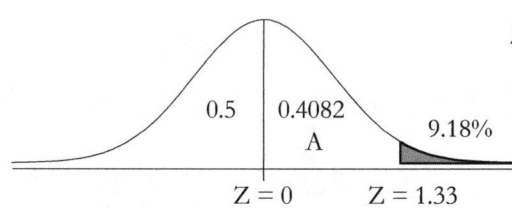

$$Z_{16} = \frac{16-12}{3} = 1.33 \; which \; yields \; an \; A = 0.4082 \; while \; P(x \geq 16) = 1 - (0.5 + 0.4082) = 9.18\%$$

0.5   0.4082
       A   9.18%

Z = 0   Z = 1.33

b.   What proportion of heaters will be eligible to be returned for failing to satisfy the guarantee?

9.18%   0.4082   0.5
          A

Z = −1.33   Z = 0
x = 8   μ = 12

$$Z_8 = \frac{8-12}{3} = -1.33 \; which \; yields \; an \; A = 0.4082 \; while \; P(x \leq 8) = 0.5 - 0.4082 = 9.18\%$$

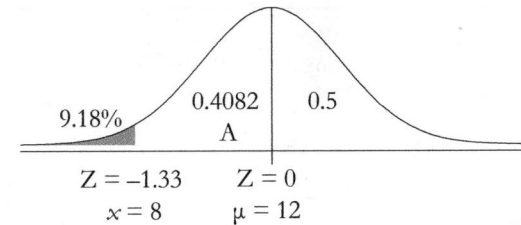

Example 7: Calculate the 95% confidence interval for a population mean for each condition:

a. $\bar{x} = 680 \;\; \sigma = 20 \;\; n = 70$

$680 \pm 1.96 \dfrac{20}{\sqrt{70}}$ means a confidence range of 675.315 to 684.685

b. $\bar{x} = 31 \;\; \sigma = 9 \;\; n = 50$

$31 \pm 1.96 \dfrac{9}{\sqrt{50}}$ means a confidence range of 28.505 to 33.495

c. $\bar{x} = 26{,}000 \;\; \sigma = 48{,}000 \;\; n = 500$

$26000 \pm 1.96 \dfrac{48000}{\sqrt{500}}$ means a confidence range of 21792 to 30207

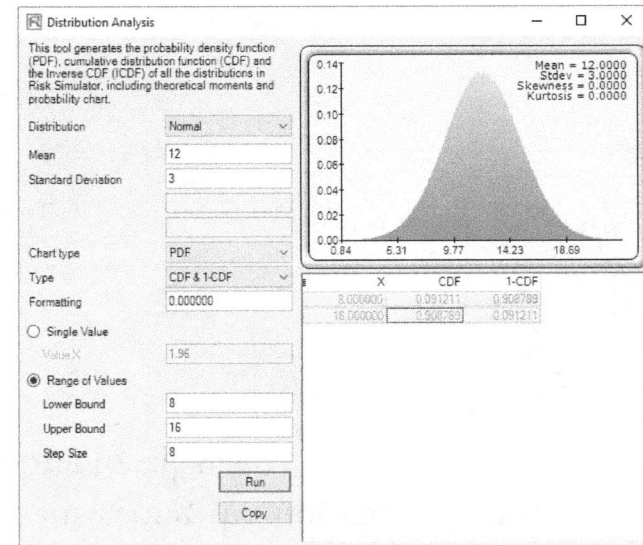

Example 8: The following amounts from telephone bills for 10 residential homes in a particular town have historically been found to follow a normal distribution: $20.95, $123.50, $55.00, $38.95, $75.00, $155.00, $23.50, $79.90, $50.50, $100.50

a. Estimate the monthly telephone bill for the town using a point estimate and calculate the 95% confidence interval.

Calculated $\bar{x} = 72.28$ and $s = 43.7493$

b. How large a sample of telephone bills would have to be taken to make the error of estimate no more than $5.00?

$$72.28 \pm 1.96 \frac{43.7493}{\sqrt{10}} \ implies \ a \ range \ of \ 45.1639 \ to \ 99.3961$$

$$5 = 1.96 \frac{43.7493}{\sqrt{n}} \quad means \quad n = \frac{1.96^2 (43.7493)^2}{5^2} = 294$$

Although we have not yet started using the BizStats software, there is a function called "Parametric: Percentiles and Confidence Intervals (Z & T)" where after entering the data above, the following table is generated in BizStats and we can read the confidence interval directly from the table (see results table on the right).

The 95% confidence interval (95% in the center of the distribution's body, with 2.5% on the left and 2.5% on the right) means a CDF of 2.50% and 97.50% or a confidence interval between 45.164 and 99.396. Similarly, a 90% confidence interval is between 49.524 and 95.036 (CDF of 5.00% and 95.00%, with a body of 90% and 5% in each of the two tails).

Another approach is to use Excel's function for the 95% confidence
=72.28-CONFIDENCE.NORM(0.05,43.7493,10) which yields 45.164 and
=72.28+CONFIDENCE.NORM(0.05,43.7493,10) which yields 99.396

And the following for the 90% confidence interval:
=72.28-CONFIDENCE.NORM(0.10,43.7493,10) for 49.524 and
=72.28+CONFIDENCE.NORM(0.10,43.7493,10) for 95.036

CDF(Z)	ICDF(Z)	CDF(Z)	ICDF(Z)
0.50%	36.644	95.00%	95.036
1.00%	40.095	95.50%	95.735
1.50%	42.257	96.00%	96.500
2.00%	43.866	97.00%	98.300
2.50%	45.164	97.50%	99.396
3.00%	46.259	98.00%	100.693
3.50%	47.212	98.50%	102.302
4.00%	48.059	99.00%	104.464
4.50%	48.824	99.50%	107.915
5.00%	49.524	99.90%	115.032

Note that the Confidence.Norm(alpha, stdev, size) function in Excel computes $1.96 \frac{43.7493}{\sqrt{10}}$ and assumes a two-tailed distribution and alpha is simply 1 – Confidence Interval. For a one-tailed distribution, simply double the value of alpha. Any slight discrepancies from the manual computations and Excel or BizStats is due to rounding.

7. Hypothesis Testing Approaches

Dr. Johnathan Mun, Professor of Research
Quantitative Research Methods Course Slides
Seventh Edition, 2026, ROV Press

Hypothesis Testing

- A hypothesis test is performed when testing the means and variances of two distributions to determine if they are statistically identical or statistically different from one another. That is, to see if the differences between the means and variances of two different forecasts that occur are based on random chance or they are in fact statistically significantly different from one another.

- This analysis is related to bootstrap simulation with several differences. Classical hypothesis testing uses mathematical models and is based on theoretical distributions. This means that the precision and power of the test are higher than bootstrap simulation's empirically based method of simulating a simulation and letting the data tell the story. However, a classical hypothesis test is only applicable for testing two distributions' means and variances (and by extension, standard deviations) to see if they are statistically identical or different. In contrast, nonparametric bootstrap simulation can be used to test for any distributional statistics, making it more useful, but the drawback is its lower testing power. Risk Simulator provides both techniques to choose from.

Hypothesis Testing Fundamentals

An example two-tailed hypothesis test is shown below. The null hypothesis is that the values x, y, or z are each identical to the mean. If the computed p-value is less than the specified value (typically 0.10, 0.05, and 0.01), we then reject the null hypothesis and state that the value is statistically significantly different from the mean value. If it is greater than the specified critical value, we then cannot reject the null hypothesis or accept the null hypothesis, and state that the value is statistically similar to the mean value.

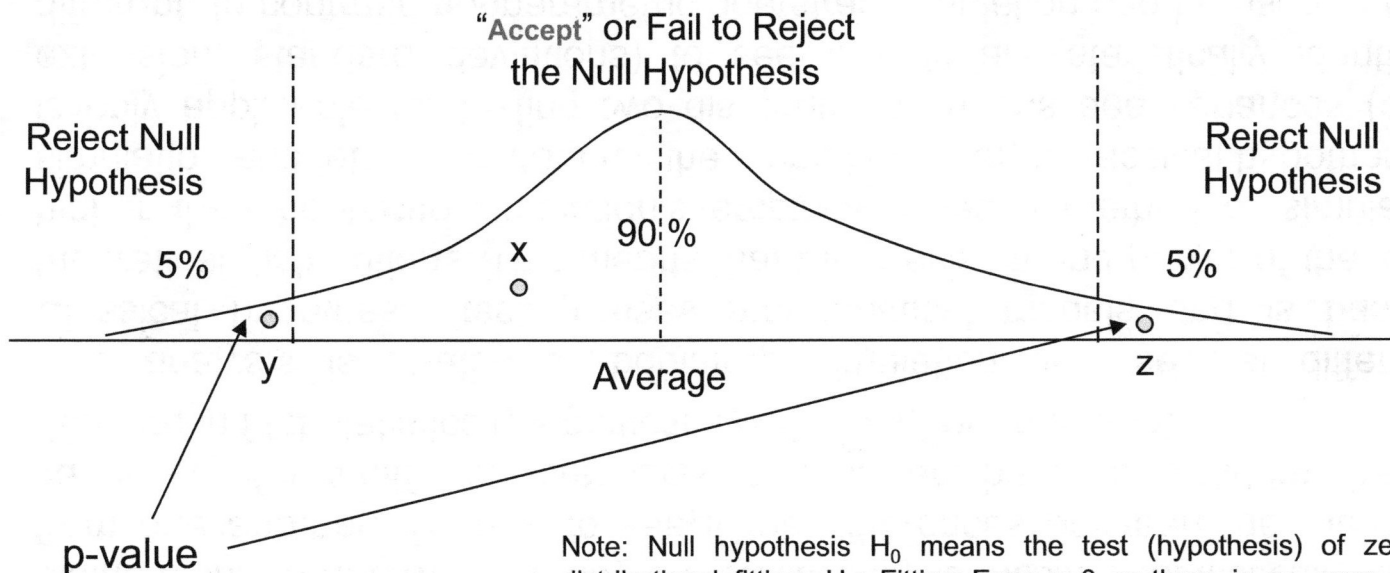

"Accept" or Fail to Reject
the Null Hypothesis

Reject Null
Hypothesis

5%

Reject Null
Hypothesis

5%

90 %

x

y

Average

z

p-value

Note: Null hypothesis H_0 means the test (hypothesis) of zero (null); e.g., in distributional fitting, H_0: Fitting Error = 0 or there is no error, which means the distribution is correct, therefore we do not want to reject H_0, where a high p-value indicates a good distributional fit. In contrast, in hypothesis tests of differences, correlation coefficients, or in multiple regression where H_0: Mean = 0, Difference = 0, or Effect = 0, we want to reject the H_0, meaning we want a low p-value to prove that there is a statistically significant effect or that there is a difference.

Central Limit Theorem (I)

Since attempting to measure a whole population is oftentimes very costly, time consuming, and difficult, we usually take a sample and use it to infer about the population. For example, trying to figure out the percentage of voters who like a certain politician would consist of polling every voter (N), up to several million of them; hence, we use a small sample (n) of, say, a thousand instead. Then we need a way to quantify these samples, and this is where sampling theory comes in. Example: Assume there exists a population with a uniform distribution, we then sample $n = 2$ on $N = 4$.

X	$1	2	3	4
P(x)	0.25	0.25	0.25	0.25

Here, the population $\mu = \Sigma x P(x) = 1(.25) + 2(.25) + 3(.25) + 4(.25) = \$2.50$.

Also, the population $\sigma^2 = \Sigma(x - \mu)^2 P(x) = \$1.25$.

If we take samples of $n = 2$, the following shows all the possible sets of samples we can take:

1,1	1,2	1,3	1,4
2,1	2,2	2,3	2,4
3,1	3,2	3,3	3,4
4,1	4,2	4,3	4,4

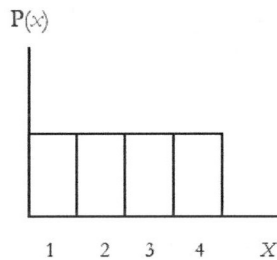

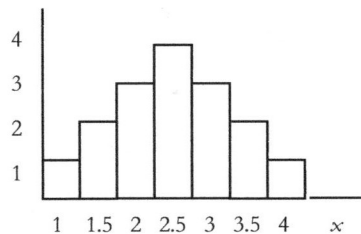

Hence, all the $\bar{x}$ average sample values possible in a probability distribution:

X	$1	1.5	2	2.5	3	3.5	4
P(x)	1/16	2/16	3/16	4/16	3/16	2/16	1/16

The sampling distribution looks nothing like the original uniform distribution! In fact, according to the Central Limit Theorem, all sampling distributions given will tend toward a normal distribution, thereby justifying the times we assume normality if our sample size is large enough, typically when $n > 30$.

Central Limit Theorem (II)

In fact, here, the sampling distribution's mean is:

$$\mu_{\bar{x}} = \sum \bar{x} P(\bar{x}) = 1(1/16) + 1.5(2/16) + \ldots = \$2.50$$

which is the same as the population mean of $\mu = \$2.50$. So, the sample mean is an unbiased estimator of the population mean.

Next, the sampling distribution's variance is:

$$\sigma_{\bar{x}}^2 = \sum (\bar{x} - \mu_{\bar{x}}) P(\bar{x}) = (1 - 0.25)^2 (1/16) + (1.5 - 0.25)^2 (2/16) + \ldots = 0.625$$

compared to $\sigma^2 = 1.25$, which is twice that. In general, for sampling distributions,

$$\sigma_{\bar{x}}^2 = \frac{\sigma^2}{n}$$ or similarly, $\sigma_{\bar{x}} = \frac{\sigma}{\sqrt{n}}$ which always holds. Here, $n = 2$ and $1.25/2 = 0.625$.

According to the Central Limit Theorem, even if the population itself is not normal, for large enough n, the random variable's mean or $\bar{x}$ is approximately normal with mean μ and $\sigma_{\bar{x}} = \frac{\sigma}{\sqrt{n}}$.

So, from now, if we use a sample and not the population itself, the standard deviation will have to reflect that of the sampling distribution's standard deviation, $\sigma_{\bar{x}} = \frac{\sigma}{\sqrt{n}}$.

In other words, we have $$Z = \frac{\bar{x} - \mu_{\bar{x}}}{\sigma_{\bar{x}}} = \frac{\bar{x} - \mu_{\bar{x}}}{\frac{\sigma}{\sqrt{n}}}.$$

In addition, according to the Finite Population Correction Factor (FPC), , when the population is too small, and the sample is too large, or $n/N \geq 5\%$, then when n is small, the FPC approaches unity. This FPC factor increases the accuracy of the estimates.

$$FPC = \sigma_{\bar{x}} = \frac{\sigma}{\sqrt{n}} \sqrt{\frac{N-n}{N-1}} \text{ for } \frac{n}{N} \geq 5\%$$

Basic Hypothesis Testing Example

Example 1: A light bulb manufacturing company wants to test the hypothesis that its bulbs can last, on average, 1,000 burning hours. It employs a student who is currently taking statistics and bribed the instructor to allow this student to perform this project for them in lieu of a final exam. So, for an A– in the class (since it's an easy problem): If the manager randomly selects 100 sample bulbs, and finds that the sample's mean is 980 hours and standard deviation is 80 hours, at a 5% significance level, what is the conclusion?

H_0: $\mu = 1000$ and H_a: $\mu \neq 1000$

Since $n > 30$, we can assume normality and we can estimate σ

For $\alpha = 0.05$ level, the $Z = \pm 1.96$ for a two-tail test or $\alpha/2 = 0.025$

If the calculated values lie in the tails beyond the critical, reject H_0

Classical—Critical limits:

$$X_{critical} = \mu \pm Z\left(\frac{s}{\sqrt{n}}\right) = 1{,}000 \pm 1.96\left(\frac{80}{\sqrt{100}}\right)$$

$X_{upper} = 1015.68$ and $X_{lower} = 984.32$;

$980 < X_{lower}$ and we reject H_0

Standardized—Z-scores:

$$Z = \frac{\bar{x} - \mu}{\sigma_{\bar{x}}} = \frac{\bar{x} - \mu}{\frac{\sigma}{\sqrt{n}}} = \frac{\bar{x} - \mu}{\frac{s}{\sqrt{n}}} = \frac{980 - 1{,}000}{\frac{80}{\sqrt{100}}} = -2.5$$

$-2.5 < -1.96$ means it lies in the tail and we reject H_0

P-Value: For the calculated Z value of –2.5, we have p-value $= 0.5 - 0.4938$ yielding p-value 0.0062, which is less than α of 0.05, and so we reject H_0.

Confidence Interval: The confidence interval has already been calculated above using the classical method. Hence, C.I. ranges from 984.32 to 1015.68, and since the measured sample $\bar{x} = 980$ does not fall within this region, we reject H_0. In all cases, the approaches might be slightly different but yield similar conclusions, that is, reject H_0. Hence, we accept H_a stating that the population mean is significantly different from 1000.

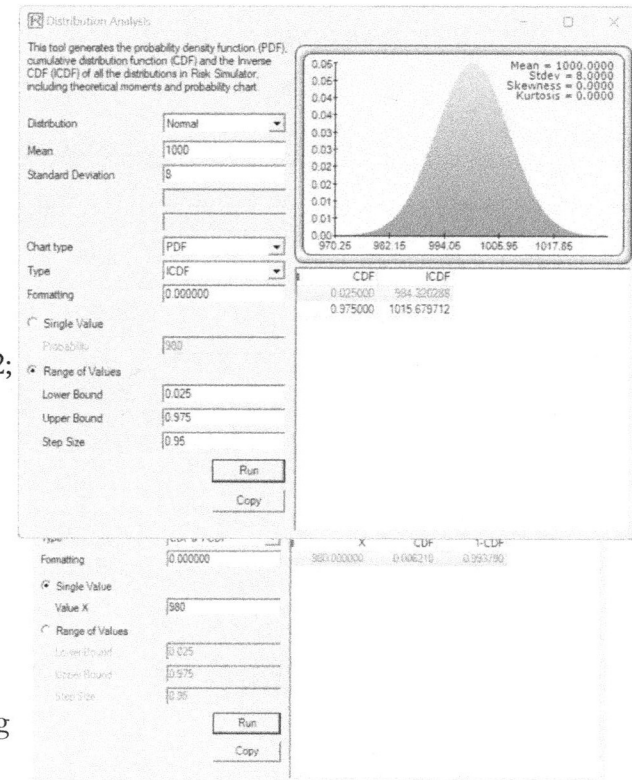

Basic Hypothesis Testing Example

Example 2: A firm wants to know with a 95% level of confidence if it can claim that the boxes of detergent it sells contain more than 500 g of detergent. From past experience, the firm knows that the amount of detergent in the boxes is normally distributed. Taking a random sample of $n = 25$, the average was found to be 520 g

and the standard deviation, 75 g. Perform a hypothesis test.

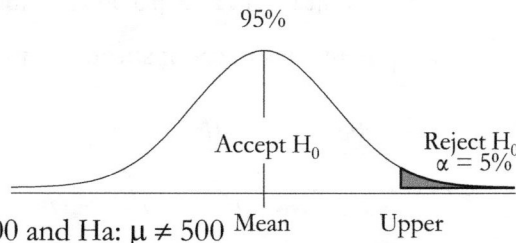

H_0: $\mu = 500$ and Ha: $\mu \neq 500$

Since $n = 25$, we use a t-distribution

Critical t for $df = n - 1 = 25 - 1 = 24$ is 1.711 at $\alpha = 0.05$ for a one-tail test

Classical Approach: $X_{critical}^{upper} = \mu \pm t\left(\frac{s}{\sqrt{n}}\right) = 500 + 1.711\left(\frac{75}{\sqrt{25}}\right) = 525.66$

Since $520 <$ critical level 525.66, we accept H_0

Standardized Approach: $t = \dfrac{\bar{x} - \mu}{\sigma_{\bar{x}}} = \dfrac{\bar{x} - \mu}{\dfrac{\sigma}{\sqrt{n}}} = \dfrac{\bar{x} - \mu}{\dfrac{s}{\sqrt{n}}} = \dfrac{520 - 500}{\dfrac{75}{\sqrt{25}}} = 1.33$ which falls within the acceptance region; so, accept H_0

P-value Approach: With the calculated t-value as 1.33, for df = 24, the p-value is between 0.05 and 0.10, which means we will accept the H_0 since it is above α of 0.05.

Confidence Interval: Using the results from the classical method, C.I. ranges from 0.00 to 525.66, and since 520 falls within this C.I. region, we accept H_0.

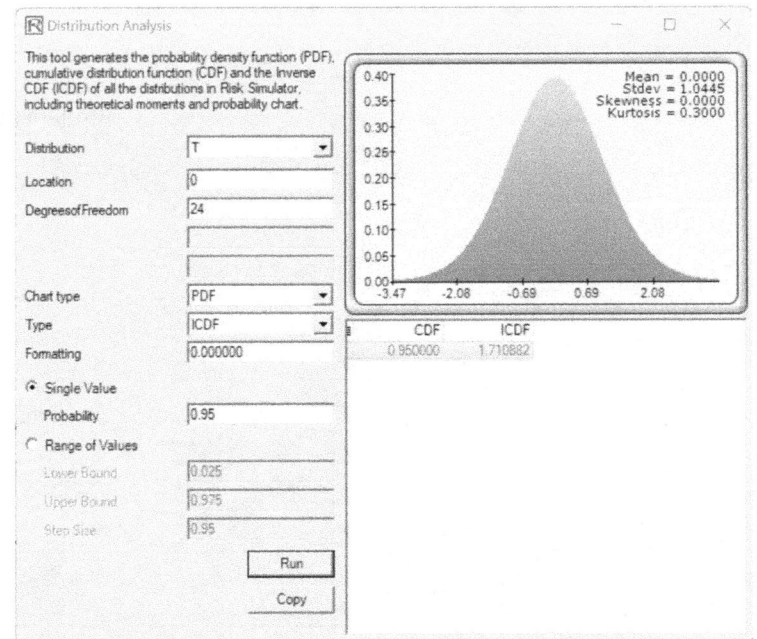

Type I – Type IV Errors

A related issue to consider is that of Types I–IV errors. The significance level α is actually a control for the Type I error. Type I error is the probability that you will *reject the null hypothesis when it is true*. Another name for Type I error is *alpha error* or *false positives*. We want this to be set low, of course. This error is committed when we reject the null when it is actually true and should not be rejected. Stated another way, we say that there is an effect when in fact no effect exists at all. A simple analogy might better explain this concept. We can all agree that for a civilized society, it is better to let a guilty man go free rather than incarcerate an innocent man. Hence, if we assume that innocence is true, the null hypothesis is innocence or that there is zero guilt. So, if we reject this null hypothesis, we reject innocence and zero guilt, which means you throw an innocent person in jail. This creates a false positive (*false* because he is innocent, but we say he is guilty; and *positive* because we found him guilty). Therefore, in this situation, you would want that false positive error to be small, i.e., a low alpha, which traditionally is set at 1%, 5%, or 10%.

Type II errors occur when we *accept a null hypothesis that is false*. We use the term "accept" here interchangeably with "failure to reject," as discussed above. This error is also known as a *beta error* or *false negative*. Accepting or failing to reject the null hypothesis when it is false means that we miss or ignore an effect when that effect actually exists. A simple analogy would be that of a fire alarm in your home. Let us assume a binary condition where the alarm could either go off or not go off. Further, this binary state also includes whether there is a house fire or there is no fire. The null hypothesis is that there is zero instances of a fire. In this case, a Type I error means that you reject when the null hypothesis is true (i.e., alarm goes off when there is no fire, no big deal, it just wakes you up and you get annoyed). However, a Type II error is a much bigger deal because it means that you accept the null hypothesis when it is false (i.e., the alarm does not go off when there really is a fire). In this example, we would want to minimize beta error, or maximize $1 - \beta$, its complement. Another name for this complement is the *power of the test* (Power = $1 - \beta$). The following matrix summarizes the first two types of errors.

Type I – Type IV Errors

There are also less commonly known Type III and Type IV errors. A Type III error occurs when the correct conclusion is made but for the wrong reason. For instance, you incorrectly used a one-tailed hypothesis instead of a two-tailed hypothesis, or vice versa, a wrong question was posed, if the hypothesis is incorrectly formulated. A Type IV error occurs when there is data aggregation bias, mistakes interpreting the results, or you correctly reject the null hypothesis, but the dataset has multicollinearity issues or data collection biases.

Type IV errors are more difficult to quantitatively measure. The chapter on regression modeling and data diagnostics covers how to test for some of these biases, whereas the chapter on hypothesis testing covers some examples of using the Shannon Diversity Index model, Grubbs Outliers test, Runs model for randomness, and others.

Null Hypothesis	True	False
Accept	True Negative $(1-\alpha)$	TYPE II (β) False Negative
Reject	Type I (α) False Positive	Power $(1-\beta)$ True Positive

One-Tailed Power Analysis: Sample Calculations
(Without Non-centrality Corrections)

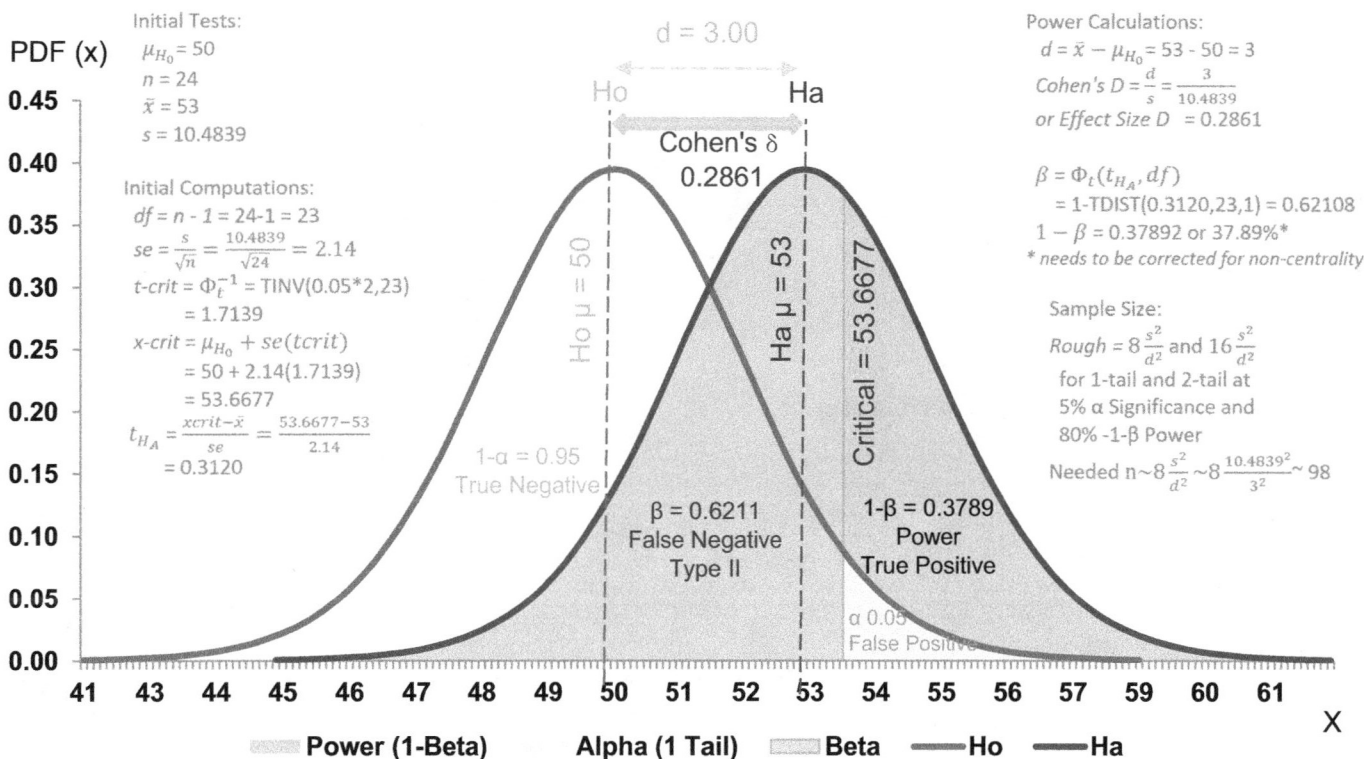

PDF (x)

Initial Tests:
$\mu_{H_0} = 50$
$n = 24$
$\bar{x} = 53$
$s = 10.4839$

Initial Computations:
$df = n - 1 = 24-1 = 23$
$se = \frac{s}{\sqrt{n}} = \frac{10.4839}{\sqrt{24}} = 2.14$
$t\text{-crit} = \Phi_t^{-1} = \text{TINV}(0.05*2,23)$
$= 1.7139$
$x\text{-crit} = \mu_{H_0} + se(tcrit)$
$= 50 + 2.14(1.7139)$
$= 53.6677$
$t_{H_A} = \frac{xcrit-\bar{x}}{se} = \frac{53.6677-53}{2.14}$
$= 0.3120$

$d = 3.00$

Ho   Ha

Cohen's δ
0.2861

Ho $\mu = 50$

Ha $\mu = 53$

Critical = 53.6677

$1-\alpha = 0.95$
True Negative

$\beta = 0.6211$
False Negative
Type II

$1-\beta = 0.3789$
Power
True Positive

$\alpha\ 0.05$
False Positive

Power Calculations:
$d = \bar{x} - \mu_{H_0} = 53 - 50 = 3$
$Cohen's\ D = \frac{d}{s} = \frac{3}{10.4839}$
$or\ Effect\ Size\ D = 0.2861$

$\beta = \Phi_t(t_{H_A}, df)$
$= 1\text{-TDIST}(0.3120,23,1) = 0.62108$
$1 - \beta = 0.37892\ or\ 37.89\%*$
* needs to be corrected for non-centrality

Sample Size:
$Rough = 8\frac{s^2}{d^2}\ and\ 16\frac{s^2}{d^2}$
for 1-tail and 2-tail at
5% α Significance and
80% -1-β Power

$Needed\ n \sim 8\frac{s^2}{d^2} \sim 8\frac{10.4839^2}{3^2} \sim 98$

X axis: 41 43 44 45 46 47 48 49 50 51 52 53 54 55 56 57 58 59 60 61   X

Legend: Power (1-Beta) Alpha (1 Tail) Beta Ho Ha

Test Dataset ($n = 24$):
41, 56, 71, 38, 61, 51
58, 49, 52, 39, 42, 34
72, 48, 62, 54, 45, 58
52, 67, 56, 52, 46, 68

Notes:
- You can replicate using the typical Z, T, F, χ^2 distributions
- Apply $\alpha/2$ on both tails for a two-tailed hypothesis, or leave as α for one tail
- You can replicate this for a left-tail test of a two-tailed test
- The analysis requires a Non-Central T-Distribution, but seeing that Excel only has a central T-Distribution (TINV, TDIST functions), the results above are for illustration and used as approximations only (albeit pretty decent ones)... we need to use BizStats, G-Power (hard to use and untested), SPSS, Minitab, R (need to know how to code), to obtain the exact results

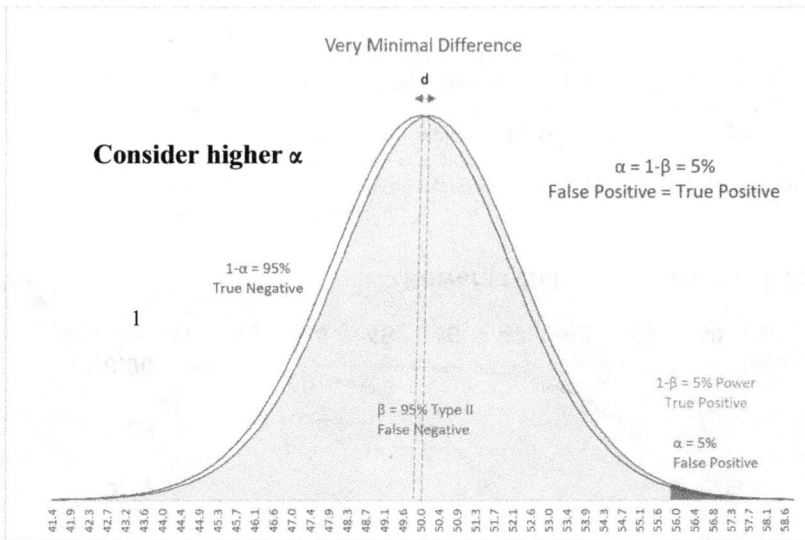

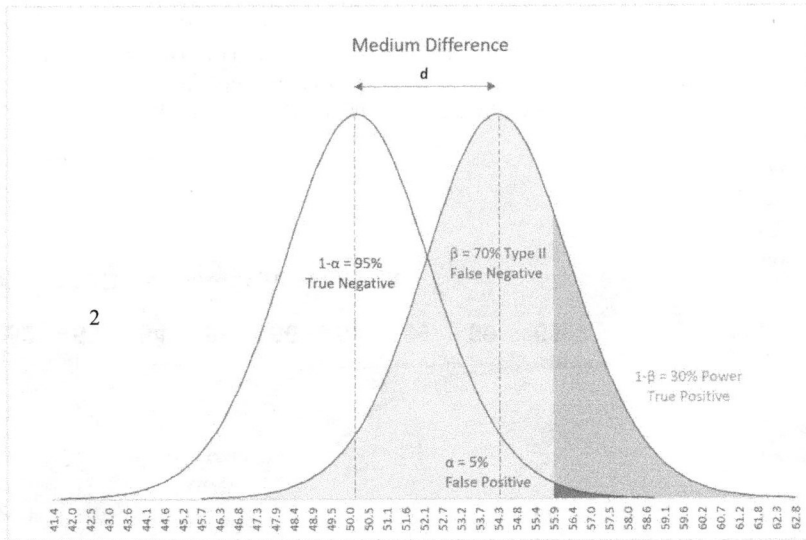

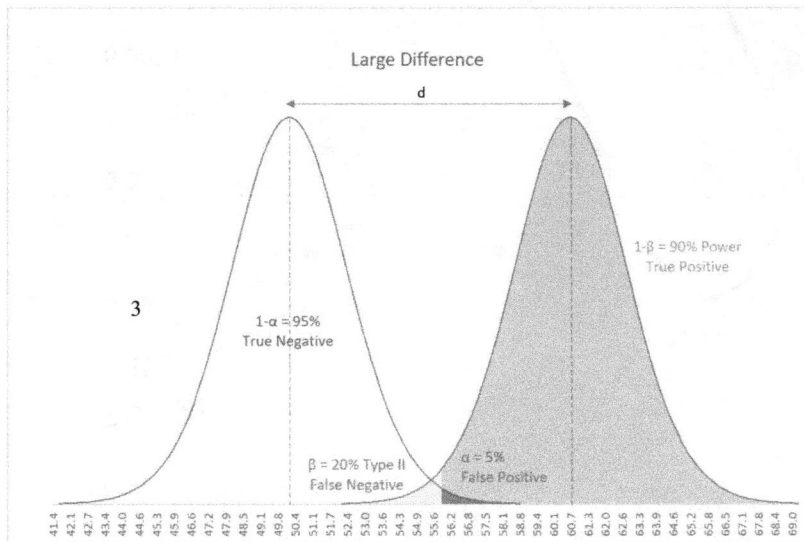

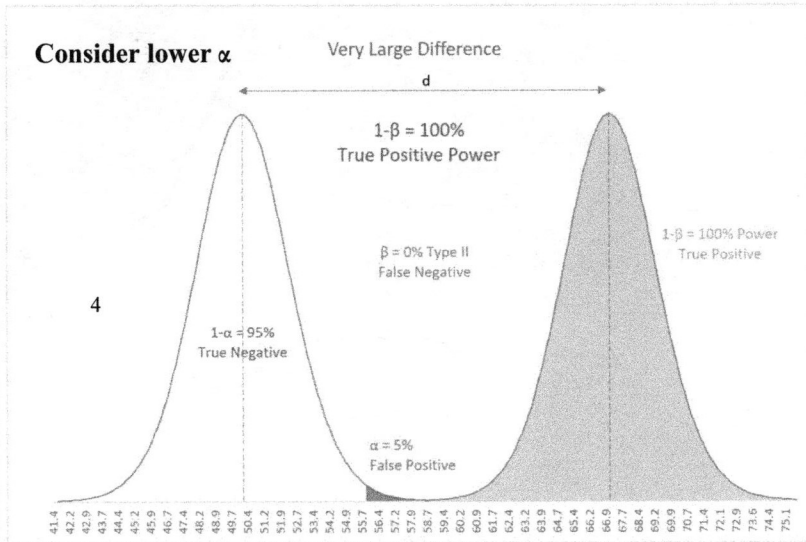

Symmetrical Two-Tailed Power Curve (Non-centrality Corrected, n = 24, $\alpha = 0.05$)

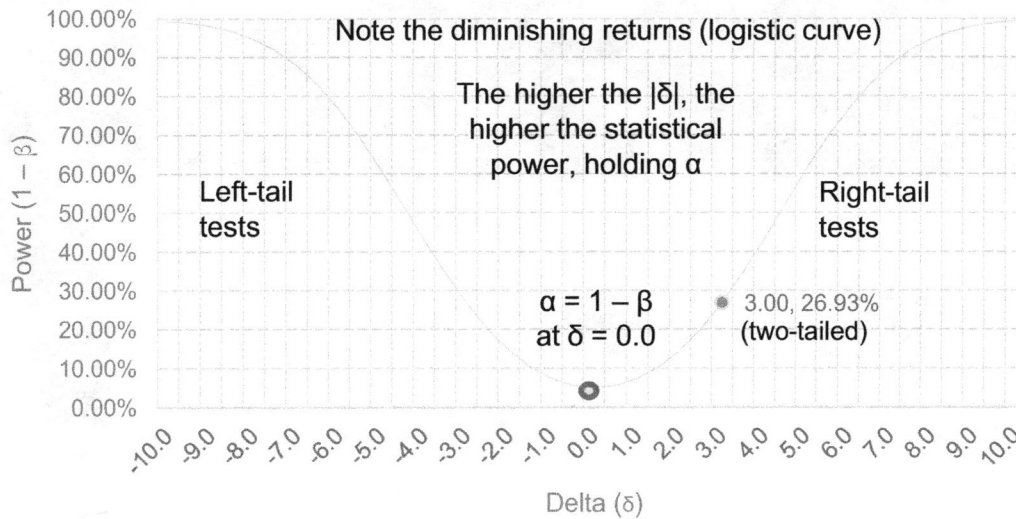

Note the diminishing returns (logistic curve)

The higher the $|\delta|$, the higher the statistical power, holding α

Left-tail tests

Right-tail tests

$\alpha = 1 - \beta$ at $\delta = 0.0$

3.00, 26.93% (two-tailed)

Power (1 − β): 100.00%, 90.00%, 80.00%, 70.00%, 60.00%, 50.00%, 40.00%, 30.00%, 20.00%, 10.00%, 0.00%

Delta (δ): -10.0, -9.0, -8.0, -7.0, -6.0, -5.0, -4.0, -3.0, -2.0, -1.0, 0.0, 1.0, 2.0, 3.0, 4.0, 5.0, 6.0, 7.0, 8.0, 9.0, 10.0

BZSTATS: Power for a Single Variable Test (corrected for noncentral t-distribution)

Delta	Hypothesis	Effect δ	Beta	Power (=)	Power (>)	Power (<)
-10.00	43.00	-0.9538	0.0060	99.40%	0.00%	99.80%
-9.50	43.50	-0.9061	0.0111	98.89%	0.00%	99.61%
-9.00	44.00	-0.8585	0.0195	98.05%	0.00%	99.25%
-8.50	44.50	-0.8108	0.0328	96.72%	0.00%	98.63%
-8.00	45.00	-0.7631	0.0528	94.72%	0.00%	97.62%
-7.50	45.50	-0.7154	0.0815	91.85%	0.00%	96.03%
-7.00	46.00	-0.6677	0.1207	87.93%	0.00%	93.67%
-6.50	46.50	-0.6200	0.1715	82.85%	0.00%	90.34%
-6.00	47.00	-0.5723	0.2342	76.58%	0.00%	85.88%
-5.50	47.50	-0.5246	0.3079	69.21%	0.00%	80.19%
-5.00	48.00	-0.4769	0.3904	60.96%	0.00%	73.30%
-4.50	48.50	-0.4292	0.4782	52.18%	0.01%	65.37%
-4.00	49.00	-0.3815	0.5670	43.30%	0.03%	56.71%
-3.50	49.50	-0.3338	0.6525	34.75%	0.06%	47.70%
-3.00	50.00	-0.2862	0.7307	26.93%	0.13%	38.81%
-2.50	50.50	-0.2385	0.7985	20.15%	0.27%	30.47%
-2.00	51.00	-0.1908	0.8542	14.58%	0.53%	23.04%
-1.50	51.50	-0.1431	0.8969	10.31%	1.00%	16.74%
-1.00	52.00	-0.0954	0.9267	7.33%	1.79%	11.68%
-0.50	52.50	-0.0477	0.9442	5.58%	3.06%	7.81%
0.00	53.00	0.0000	0.9500	5.00%	5.00%	5.00%
0.50	53.50	0.0477	0.9442	5.58%	7.81%	3.06%
1.00	54.00	0.0954	0.9267	7.33%	11.68%	1.79%
1.50	54.50	0.1431	0.8969	10.31%	16.74%	1.00%
2.00	55.00	0.1908	0.8542	14.58%	23.04%	0.53%
2.50	55.50	0.2385	0.7985	20.15%	30.47%	0.27%
3.00	56.00	0.2862	0.7307	26.93%	38.81%	0.13%
3.50	56.50	0.3338	0.6525	34.75%	47.70%	0.06%
4.00	57.00	0.3815	0.5670	43.30%	56.71%	0.03%
4.50	57.50	0.4292	0.4782	52.18%	65.37%	0.01%
5.00	58.00	0.4769	0.3904	60.96%	73.30%	0.00%
5.50	58.50	0.5246	0.3079	69.21%	80.19%	0.00%
6.00	59.00	0.5723	0.2342	76.58%	85.88%	0.00%
6.50	59.50	0.6200	0.1715	82.85%	90.34%	0.00%
7.00	60.00	0.6677	0.1207	87.93%	93.67%	0.00%

The higher the $|\delta|$, the higher the statistical power, holding α constant

8. Statistical Methods for Two or More Variables

Dr. Johnathan Mun, Professor of Research
Quantitative Research Methods Course Slides
Seventh Edition, 2026, ROV Press

Two Variable Equal Variance T-Test

As a reminder, the null hypothesis (H_0) generally has the equivalence sign (i.e., =, ≥, ≤), whereas the alternate hypothesis (H_a) has its complement (i.e., ≠, <, >). The sign of the alternate hypothesis points to whether the test is a two-tailed test (≠) or a one-tailed test (right tail is denoted with >, whereas a left tail test uses <).

To get started, two datasets with some number of data points (with n_1 and n_2 sample sizes) are put side by side (see Figure 9.2). Then, their respective sample averages ($\overline{x_1}$ and $\overline{x_2}$) and sample standard deviations (s_1 and s_2) are computed. The t-statistic is then calculated using the formula below and compared against the critical t-values. In most situations, the p-values of this calculated t-statistic are calculated and compared against some predefined level of significance (i.e., the standard α significance levels of 0.10, 0.05, and 0.01 will be assumed throughout these examples) using the t-distribution with a certain degree of freedom (df). If the p-value is below these α significance levels, we reject the null hypothesis and accept the alternate hypothesis.

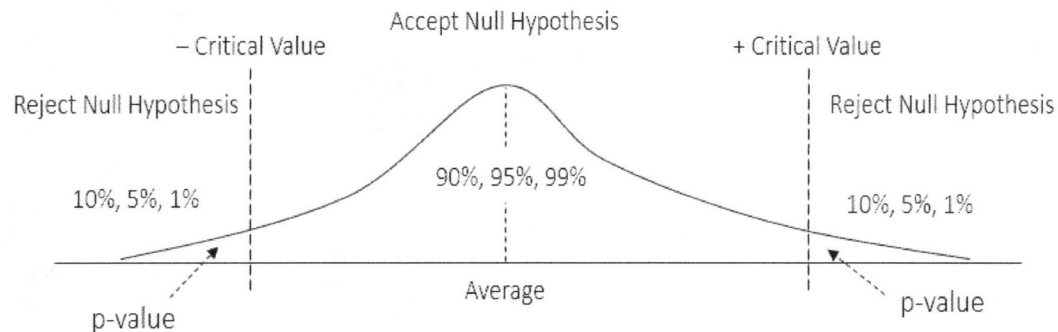

Two Variable Equal Variance T-Test

The two-sample equal variance t-test, as its name suggests, compares two sample datasets against each other to determine if there is a statistically significant difference between their population means (μ). In other words, the test can identify if a certain event or experiment has an effect. This t-test assumes that the unknown population standard deviations (σ) of both samples are roughly equal, and the populations are roughly normal. The t-distribution is appropriate here as the true standard deviations of the populations are unknown, and when smaller sample sizes are available (typically < 30). This test is also known as the pooled-variances t-test because it takes the standard deviations of both samples and pools them into a single parameter in the model.

The hypotheses tested are typically:

H_0: $\mu_1 = \mu_2$, that is, the two samples' means are statistically similar

H_a: $\mu_1 \neq \mu_2$, that is, the two samples' means are statistically significantly different

$$t = \frac{(\bar{x}_1 - \bar{x}_2) - (\mu_1 - \mu_2)}{\sqrt{s_p^2\left(\frac{1}{n_1} + \frac{1}{n_2}\right)}} \qquad s_p^2 = \frac{(n_1-1)s_1^2 + (n_2-1)s_2^2}{n_1 + n_2 - 2}$$

$$df = n_1 + n_2 - 2$$

Note: When we test $H_0: \mu_1 = \mu_2$, this means we set $\mu_1 - \mu_2 = 0$ in the equation above and we set 0 as the hypothesized mean in BizStats.

	VAR 1	VAR 2				
	11	10	Average 1	6.0000	=AVERAGE(B3:B12)
	8	11	Average 2	7.8000	=AVERAGE(C3:C12)
	8	9	Sample Variance 1	9.7778	=VAR(B3:B12)
	3	7	Sample Variance 2	11.7333	=VAR(C3:C12)
	7	2	Pooled Variance	10.7556	=((COUNT(B3:B12)-1)*G5+(COUNT(C3:C12)-1)*G6)/(COUNT(B3:B12)+COUNT(C3:C12)-2)
	5	11	Paired T Statistic	-1.2273	=(G3-G4)/SQRT(G7*(1/COUNT(B3:B12)+1/(COUNT(C3:C12))))
	9	12	P-value One Tail	0.1178	=TDIST(-G8,COUNT(B3:B12)+COUNT(C3:C12)-2,1)
	5	3	P-value Two Tail	0.2355	=TDIST(-G8,COUNT(B3:B12)+COUNT(C3:C12)-2,2)
	1	6			
	3	7			

ROV Biz Stats

File Data Language

STEP 1: Data — Manually enter your data, paste from another application, or load an example dataset with analysis

Example

Visualize

Dataset | Visualize | Command

N	VAR1	VAR2	VAR3	VAR4	VAR5	VAR6	VAR7	VAR8	VAR9	VAR10
NOTES										
1	11	10								
2	8	11								
3	8	9								
4	3	7								
5	7	2								
6	5	11								
7	9	12								

STEP 2: Analysis — Choose analysis and enter parameters required (see example inputs below)

View: Alphabetical

VAR1; VAR2
0

Nonparametric: Chi-Square Independence
Nonparametric: Chi-Square Population Variance
Nonparametric: Friedman's Test
Nonparametric: Kruskal-Wallis Test
Nonparametric: Lilliefors Test
Nonparametric: Runs Test
Nonparametric: Wilcoxon Signed-Rank (One Var)
Nonparametric: Wilcoxon Signed-Rank (Two Var)
Parametric: One Variable (T) Mean
Parametric: One Variable (Z) Mean
Parametric: One Variable (Z) Proportion
Parametric: Two Variable (F) Variances
Parametric: Two Variable (T) Dependent Means
Parametric: Two Variable (T) Independent Equal Variance
Parametric: Two Variable (T) Independent Unequal Variance
Parametric: Two Variable (Z) Independent Means
Parametric: Two Variable (Z) Independent Proportions
Power

Data (=2), Hypothesized Mean:
> Var1; Var2
> 5

STEP 3: Run

Run — Run the current analysis in Step 2 or the selected saved analysis in Step 4, view the results, charts and statistics, copy the results and charts to clipboard, or generate reports

○ Use All Data
○ Use Rows 1 ~ 20

Copy
Report

Results | Charts

```
Column 2 Observations : 10
Column 2 Sample Mean : 7.800000
Column 2 Sample Standard Deviation : 3.425395
Sample Mean Difference : -1.800000
t-Statistic : -1.227273
Hypothesized Mean : 0.000000

p-Value Left Tailed : 0.117765
not significant at any of the following significance levels: 1%, 5%, and 10%
not rejected
not significantly less than the hypothesized mean difference.

p-Value Right Tailed : 0.882235
not significant at any of the following significance levels: 1%, 5%, and 10%
not rejected
not significantly greater than the hypothesized mean difference.

p-Value Two Tailed : 0.235530
not significant at any of the following significance levels: 1%, 5%, and 10%
not rejected
not significantly different than the hypothesized mean difference.
```

STEP 4: Save (Optional) — You can save multiple analyses and notes in the profile for future retrieval

Name:
Notes:

ADD
EDIT
DEL
Save
Exit

Two Variable Unequal Variance T-Test

If the standard deviations of the two sample datasets are still unknown but assumed to be different, combining them into a single pooled estimate as done previously would be inappropriate. Therefore, the sample standard deviations (s) will be used independently to estimate the population standard deviations (σ).

Nonetheless, normality of the underlying dataset is assumed, although this assumption becomes less important with larger datasets. The two-sample unequal variance t-test would be needed. The hypotheses tested are typically:

H_0: $\mu_1 = \mu_2$, that is, the two samples' means are statistically similar

H_a: $\mu_1 \neq \mu_2$, that is, the two samples' means are statistically significantly different

As a reminder, the null hypothesis (H_0) generally has the equivalence sign (i.e., =, $\geq$, $\leq$), whereas the alternate hypothesis (H_a) has its complement (i.e., $\neq$, <, >). The sign of the alternate hypothesis points to whether the test is a two-tailed test ($\neq$) or a one-tailed test (right tail is denoted with >, whereas a left tail test uses <).

$$t = \frac{(\bar{x}_1 - \bar{x}_2) - (\mu_1 - \mu_2)}{\sqrt{\left(\frac{s_1^2}{n_1} + \frac{s_2^2}{n_2}\right)}} \qquad df = \frac{\left[s_1^2/n_1 + s_2^2/n_2\right]^2}{\frac{\left(s_1^2/n_1\right)^2}{n_1 - 1} + \frac{\left(s_2^2/n_2\right)^2}{n_2 - 1}}$$

Note: When we test H_0: $\mu_1 = \mu_2$, this means we set $\mu_1 - \mu_2 = 0$ in the equation above and we set 0 as the hypothesized mean in BizStats.

Mean 1	18.2229		
Stdev 1	2.6319		
Count 1	35		
Mean 2	20.1000		
Stdev 2	3.8865		
Count 2	35		
Calculated T	-2.3659	=((C3-C6)-0)/SQRT((C4^2/C5)+(C7^2/C8))	
Calculated DF	60	=ROUND((((C4^2/C5)+(C7^2/C8))^2/(((C4^2/C5)^2/(C5-1))+((C7^2/C8)^2/(C8-1)))),0)	
P-Value	0.0212	2 Tails	=TDIST(C10,C11,2)
Critical T @ 0.10	1.6706	2 Tails	=TINV(0.1,C11)
Critical T @ 0.05	2.0003	2 Tails	=TINV(0.05,C11)
Critical T @ 0.01	2.6603	2 Tails	=TINV(0.01,C11)
P-Value	0.0106	1 Tail	=TDIST(C10,C11,1)
Critical T @ 0.10	1.2958	1 Tail	=TINV(0.1*2,C11)
Critical T @ 0.05	1.6706	1 Tail	=TINV(0.05*2,C11)
Critical T @ 0.01	2.3901	1 Tail	=TINV(0.01*2,C11)

Two Variable Dependent Means T-Test

In situations when the two datasets are dependent on each other, the two-sample t-test with dependent means is used. This test is also known as the paired observations test, which means that the number of observations in each of the two datasets has to be the same ($n = n_1 = n_2$). For example, if the researcher is interested in testing the before and after effects on productivity of the same sample of employees after a change in work hours, the data is obtained from the same dataset (i.e., the same employees are tested).

The hypotheses tested are the typical two-tailed or one-tailed test. Example of a one-tail left-tail test:

H_0: $\mu_1 \geq \mu_2$, that is, the two samples' means are statistically similar

H_a: $\mu_1 < \mu_2$, that is, the two samples' means are statistically significantly different

In the book, Figure 9.7 provides an example of the productivity study where X_1 measured after the change in work hours, compared to the before-change measured in X_2. The numbers indicate the total hours it takes to complete a certain activity, and each row of the dataset represents an individual.

$$t = \frac{\bar{d}}{s_d / \sqrt{n}} \qquad d = x_1 - x_2 \qquad df = n - 1$$

	B	C	D
	X1	X2	Difference (d)
3	25.5	43.6	-18.10
4	59.2	69.9	-10.70
5	38.4	39.8	-1.40
6	66.8	73.4	-6.60
7	44.9	50.2	-5.30
8	47.4	53.9	-6.50
9	41.6	40.3	1.30
10	48.9	58.0	-9.10
11	60.7	66.9	-6.20
12	41.0	66.5	-25.50
13	36.1	27.4	8.70
14	34.4	33.7	0.70
16	Average	-6.5583	=AVERAGE(D3:D14)
17	Stdev	9.0010	=STDEV(D3:D14)
18	Calculated T	-2.5240	=D16/(D17/SQRT(COUNT(D3:D14)))
19	DF	11	=COUNT(D3:D14)-1
20	P-value (2 Tail)	0.0283	=TDIST(ABS(D18),COUNT(D3:D14)-1,2)
21	P-value (1 Tail)	0.0141	=TDIST(ABS(D18),COUNT(D3:D14)-1,1)

Two Variable F-Test of Variances from Independent Variables

On occasion, we may need to compare the variances of two independent sample sets. For instance, when comparing the mean time between failure (MTBF) of two different equipment setups and measuring the amount of variation that exists, we can determine if the variation of MTBF of the old or new equipment is greater. The F-test is used in this instance, where we test the following hypotheses:

H_0: $\sigma_1^2 = \sigma_2^2$ there is no difference in variation between the two samples

H_a: $\sigma_1^2 \neq \sigma_2^2$ there is a difference in variation between the two samples

In the book, see the example provided in Figure 9.9. Suppose two equipment sets were each implemented in seven different locations and their respective MTBF in months were collected. The sample standard deviations were calculated as 0.7091 and 0.5350 for these two equipment sets. The F statistic is computed as 1.7571 with a corresponding one-tail p-value of 0.2552, which means we do not reject the null hypothesis and conclude that there is no statistically significant difference in variation of the MTBF.

$$F = \max\left(s_1^2 / s_2^2 , s_2^2 / s_1^2\right)$$

$$F(\alpha / 2, n_L - 1, n_S - 1)$$

	A	B	C	D	E	F	G
1							
2		X1	X2				
3		2.5	5.2				
4		2.6	5.6				
5		3.4	5.4				
6		2.9	5.9				
7		4.3	5.9				
8		4.1	6.2				
9		3.6	6.8				
10							
11	Mean	3.3429	5.8571	=AVERAGE(B3:B9) and =AVERAGE(C3:C9)			
12	Stdev	0.7091	0.5350	=STDEV(B3:B9) and =STDEV(C3:C9)			
13	Count	7	7	=COUNT(B3:B9) and =COUNT(C3:C9)			
14	F Statistic	1.7571	One Tail	=MAX(B12^2/C12^2,C12^2/B12^2)			
15	P-value	0.2552	One Tail	=FDIST(B14,B13-1,C13-1)			

ROV Biz Stats

File   Data   Language

STEP 1: Data   Manually enter your data, paste from another application, or load an example dataset with analysis   Example   STEP 2: Analysis   Choose analysis and enter parameters required (see example inputs below)

Dataset Visualize Command   Visualize   View: Alphabetical   VAR1; VAR2

N	VAR1	VAR2	VAR3	VAR4	VAR5	VAR6	VAR7	VAR8	VAR9	VAR10
NOTES										
1	2.5	5.2								
2	2.6	5.6								
3	3.4	5.4								
4	2.9	5.9								
5	4.3	5.9								
6	4.1	6.2								
7	3.6	6.8								

Parametric: One Variable (T) Mean
Parametric: One Variable (Z) Mean
Parametric: One Variable (Z) Proportion
Parametric: Two Variable (F) Variances
Parametric: Two Variable (T) Dependent Means
Parametric: Two Variable (T) Independent Equal Variance
Parametric: Two Variable (T) Independent Unequal Variance
Parametric: Two Variable (Z) Independent Means
Parametric: Two Variable (Z) Independent Proportions
Power
Principal Component Analysis
Rank Ascending
Rank Descending
Regression Through Origin
Relative LN Returns
Relative Returns
Seasonality
Segmentation Clustering

Data (=2):
> Var1; Var2

STEP 3: Run   Run   Run the current analysis in Step 2 or the selected saved analysis in Step 4, view the results, charts and statistics, copy the results and charts to clipboard, or generate reports
◉ Use All Data   Copy
○ Use Rows   1 ~ 20   Report

Results Charts

Two Variable (F) Variances
Column 1 Observations : 7
Column 1 Sample Mean : 3.342857
Column 1 Sample Standard Deviation : 0.709124
Column 2 Observations : 7
Column 2 Sample Mean : 5.867143
Column 2 Sample Standard Deviation : 0.534968
F-Statistic : 1.757072
Hypothesized Mean : 0.000000

p-Value Left Tailed : 0.762714
not significant at any of the following significance levels: 1%, 5%, and 10%
not rejected
not significantly less than the hypothesized mean difference.

p-Value Right Tailed : 0.237286
not significant at any of the following significance levels: 1%, 5%, and 10%
not rejected
not significantly greater than the hypothesized mean difference.

STEP 4: Save (Optional)   You can save multiple analyses and notes in the profile for future retrieval

Name:
Notes:
ADD
EDIT
DEL
Save
Exit

Box Test of Covariance & CV Test for Homogeneity

A related test is the Box Test of Covariance Homogeneity, which extends the F-test for variances. The latter tests two variables at once for similarities between their variances, whereas the former looks at multiple variables in two distinct groups. The null hypothesis is such that the covariance matrix of the first group is the same as the second group. For example, the results below are based on running the Box test where the first group has three variables and the second group also has three variables. The Chi-Square test and F-test can be applied in this example. Both p-values for these tests indicate we cannot reject the null hypothesis, indicating that the covariances are similar between the two groups of variables. This test is also useful when looking at consistency of data variations between two groups.

Another related test is the Coefficient of Variation Homogeneity (CV Homogeneity) test, where instead of looking at variances (F-test) or covariance matrices (Box Test), we can test the similarities among coefficients of variation. Recall that CV is a relative measure of risk, spread, and uncertainty of a distribution. It is unitless and can be used to compare the dispersion among distributions with differing units (e.g., we can compare kilograms with meters, millions of dollars against multibillion dollar investment risks). Hence, testing the homogeneity of CV is sometimes important. The following is an example set of results from BizStats, where the CV Homogeneity tests the null hypothesis that the CVs are equal across multiple variables. A low p-value indicates we can reject the null hypothesis and conclude that the CVs are not similar among the test variables.

```
Box Test of Covariance Homogeneity

Group 1 Covariance
        1.25674       -9.94263        3.26632
       -9.94263      169.31316      -38.30000
        3.26632      -38.30000       31.80000

Group 2 Covariance
        1.49673      -10.43072        0.64771
      -10.43072      175.15359      -28.56209
        0.64771      -28.56209       24.45752

Pooled Covariance
        1.37007      -10.17312        2.02975
      -10.17312      172.07114      -33.70154
        2.02975      -33.70154       28.33272
```

```
Box's Test with Chi-Square
Chi-Square    2.85467
P-Value       0.82685


Box's Test with F-Test
F-Stat        0.47543
P-Value       0.82709


Homogeneity of Coefficients of Variation

    Average CV: 0.128503
    Pooled CV: 0.129837
    Chi-Square: 7.324772
    P-Value: 0.025671
Null hypothesis tested is that all CVs are equal or homogeneous
```

Two Variable Z-Test for Proportions and Means

In certain situations, proportions (p) are used instead of raw values. In such situations, when there are two sets of data, the two proportions can be tested using the following hypotheses:

H_0: $\mu(p_1 - p_2) = 0$, there is no difference between the two datasets
H_a: $\mu(p_1 - p_2) \neq 0$, there is a difference between the two datasets

This approach assumes that $n_1 p_1$, $n_1(1 - p_1)$, $n_2 p_2$, and $n_2(1 - p_2) \geq 5$ and each $n \geq 30$ so that the underlying binomial distribution (a proportion is equivalent to a binomial probability distribution with two outcomes) approaches the normal distribution, hence the ability to use the z-test.

For the independent means test, the two samples' means are tested using:

H_0: $\mu(\bar{x}_1 - \bar{x}_2) = 0$, there is no difference between the two datasets
H_a: $\mu(\bar{x}_1 - \bar{x}_2) \neq 0$, there is a difference between the two datasets

$$z = \frac{(p_1 - p_2)}{\sqrt{\bar{p}(1 - \bar{p})\left(\dfrac{1}{n_1} + \dfrac{1}{n_2}\right)}}$$

$$z = \frac{(\bar{x}_1 - \bar{x}_2) - (\mu_1 - \mu_2)}{\sqrt{\dfrac{s_1^2}{n_1} + \dfrac{s_2^2}{n_2}}}$$

$$\bar{p} = \frac{n_1 p_1 + n_2 p_2}{n_1 + n_2}$$

	A	B	C	D	E	F	G	H
1								
2		Proportion 1	0.0815					
3		Proportion 2	0.0983					
4		Count 1	1903					
5		Count 2	1903					
6								
7		Pooled P	0.0899		=(C4*C2+C5*C3)/(C4+C5)			
8		Z-Score	-1.8117		=(C2-C3)/SQRT(C7*(1-C7)*(1/C4+1/C5))			
9		P-Value	0.0350	1 Tail	=NORMSDIST(C8)			
10		P-Value	0.0700	2 Tail	=NORMSDIST(C8)*2			
11		Z Critical @ 0.10	-1.2816	Left 1 Tail	=NORMSINV(0.1)			
12		Z Critical @ 0.05	-1.6449	Left 1 Tail	=NORMSINV(0.05)			
13		Z Critical @ 0.01	-2.3263	Left 1 Tail	=NORMSINV(0.01)			

ROV Biz Stats

File   Data   Language

STEP 1: Data — Manually enter your data, paste from another application, or load an example dataset with analysis   [Example]

[Visualize]

STEP 2: Analysis — Choose analysis and enter parameters required (see example inputs below)

View: Alphabetical

Dataset | Visualize | Command

N	VAR1	VAR2	VAR3	VAR4	VAR5	VAR6	VAR7	VAR8	VAR9	VAR10
NOTES										
1	1	1								
2	1	1								
3	1	1								
4	1	1								
5	1	1								
6	1	1								
7	1	1								

Parametric: One Variable (T) Mean
Parametric: One Variable (Z) Mean
Parametric: One Variable (Z) Proportion
Parametric: Two Variable (F) Variances
Parametric: Two Variable (T) Dependent Means
Parametric: Two Variable (T) Independent Equal Variance
Parametric: Two Variable (T) Independent Unequal Variance
Parametric: Two Variable (Z) Independent Means
Parametric: Two Variable (Z) Independent Proportions
Power
Principal Component Analysis
Rank Ascending
Rank Descending
Regression Through Origin
Relative LN Returns
Relative Returns
Seasonality
Segmentation Clustering

VAR1; VAR2
0

Data (=2), Hypothesized Mean:
> Var1; Var2
> 5

STEP 3: Run   [Run]   Run the current analysis in Step 2 or the selected saved analysis in Step 4, view the results, charts and statistics, copy the results and charts to clipboard, or generate reports   [Copy]   [Report]

● Use All Data
○ Use Rows   1 ~ 20

Results | Charts

```
Column 1 Observations : 1903
Column 1 Sample Mean : 0.081450
Column 1 Sample Standard Deviation : 0.273697
Column 2 Observations : 1903
Column 2 Sample Mean : 0.098266
Column 2 Sample Standard Deviation : 0.297752
Z-Statistic : -1.813771
Hypothesized Mean : 0.000000

p-Value Left Tailed : 0.034857
significant at 10% and 5%
rejected
significantly less than the hypothesized mean.

p-Value Right Tailed : 0.965143
not significant at any of the following significance levels: 1%, 5%, and 10%
not rejected
not significantly greater than the hypothesized mean.

p-Value Two Tailed : 0.069713
```

STEP 4: Save (Optional)   You can save multiple analyses and notes in the profile for future retrieval

Name:
Notes:
[ADD]
[EDIT]
[DEL]
[Save]
[Exit]

Single ANOVA with Multiple Treatment Variables

The previously described t-tests, z-tests, and F-tests are applied to two variables at a time to determine if their means, proportions, or variances are statistically significantly different or if the small differences are attributable to random chance. When two or more sample means need to be tested at the same time, we resort to Analysis of Variance (ANOVA) tests.

The single ANOVA with multiple treatments tests *one* categorical independent variable (with multiple treatment levels, types, or categories) and *one* numerical dependent variable (randomly allocated into the multiple treatment categories) to determine if their population means are equal. Each data column will have a different treatment (e.g., a new method of manufacturing, a new training regimen, a new technology employed). This test assumes that the treatments are completely and randomly assigned to all the persons in the experiment and the underlying data is normally distributed with equal variance. Note that the nonparametric equivalent is the Kruskal–Wallis test, which is presented later in the chapter.

Example: Nine staff members in an organization were randomly divided into three teams each consisting of three individuals, and each team was provided a different type of training. There are three distinct training courses or treatments in this case. Upon completing the training course, each individual was assigned a task to complete and the time it took to complete the task was recorded and shown in the data grid. Because the selection is random, we use the randomized single ANOVA with multiple treatments the test the following hypotheses:

H_0: $\mu_1 = \mu_2 = \ldots = \mu_t$ for treatments 1 to t (there is no effect in the treatments)
H_a: Population means are not equal (there is an effect in at least one of the treatments)

$$Global\ Average\ \tilde{x} = \frac{\displaystyle\sum_{j=1}^{t}\sum_{i=1}^{t} x_{ij}}{N} \qquad SS\ Treatment = \sum_{j=1}^{t} n_j(\bar{x}_j - \tilde{x})^2 \qquad SS\ Error = \sum_{j=1}^{t}\sum_{i=1}^{n_j}(x_{ij} - \bar{x}_j)^2 \qquad SS\ Total = \sum_{j=1}^{t}\sum_{i=1}^{n_j}(x_{ij} - \tilde{x})^2$$

Mean Squares of Between Treatment (MS Treatment) = (SS Treatment)/(Number of Treatments – 1)

Mean Squares of Errors or Mean Squares Within Treatments (MS Error) = (SS Error)/(Total Observations – Number of Treatments)

F Statistic is computed as MS Treatment / MS Error

	Method 1	Method 2	Method 3
Person 1	15	10	18
Person 2	20	15	19
Person 3	19	11	23

EXCEL ANALYSIS TOOL PAK

Anova: Single Factor

SUMMARY

Groups	Count	Sum	Average	Variance
Column 1	3	54	18	7
Column 2	3	36	12	7
Column 3	3	60	20	7

ANOVA

Source of Variation	SS	df	MS	F	P-value	F crit
Between Groups	104	2	52	7.4286	0.0238	5.1433
Within Groups	42	6	7			
Total	146	8				

Results of Single ANOVA with Multiple Treatment Variables

ANOVA with Randomized Block Test

In the previous single ANOVA test, the assumption was that the treatments were completely and randomly assigned to all the persons in the experiment. This approach may result in overrepresentation and underrepresentation in some treatment groups simply by chance. If the properties or characteristics of the individuals participating in the experiment have a strong influence on the measurements and data obtained, the single ANOVA may end up measuring the differentials inside this experimental group instead of the effects of the treatments. To resolve this issue, ANOVA with Randomized Block can be used. Note that the nonparametric equivalent is the Friedman's test.

The specification tested in this ANOVA is $x_{i,j} = \mu + \tau_j + \beta_i + \varepsilon_{ij}$

H_0: $\tau_j = 0$ for treatments j = 1 to t (there is no effect in the treatments)
H_a: $\tau_j \neq 0$ for at least one treatment j = 1 to t (one or more treatments has an effect)
where τ is the treatments and β is the blocking variable.

Example: Suppose that there are four auto headlamps under development. The manufacturer wishes to test the visibility of each lamp design by measuring how far someone can see using each of these headlamps. Now suppose 12 individuals were randomly selected to participate in this experiment, and suppose we categorize these participants as young (Y), middle aged (M), and old (O). If we completely randomize the selection of these individuals, each of the method may be over- or underrepresented in terms of age groups, as seen in the first data grid below on the left. Now, further suppose that the participants' properties (e.g., age) has an influence on their vision (e.g., older participants cannot see as far as someone much younger). Consequently, completely randomizing the participants into these groups will yield biased results. The better approach is to "block" this intervening age variable. The second data grid below on the right shows how to set up an ANOVA dataset with blocks. In this example, there are three blocks, and they are stratified into rows.

ANOVA One-Way Randomized Design

	Method 1	Method 2	Method 3	Method 4
Person 1	Y	M	O	Y
Person 2	Y	O	Y	M
Person 3	O	O	M	Y

ANOVA with Blocking Variable

	Method 1	Method 2	Method 3	Method 4
Block 1	Y	Y	Y	Y
Block 2	M	M	M	M
Block 3	O	O	O	O

ANOVA with Randomized Block Test

$$Global\ Average = \tilde{x} = \frac{\sum_{j=1}^{t}\sum_{i=1}^{t} x_{ij}}{N}$$

$$SS\ Treatment = n\sum_{j=1}^{t}(\bar{x}_j - \tilde{x})^2$$

$$SS\ Block = t\sum_{j=1}^{t}(\bar{x}_i - \tilde{x})^2$$

$$SS\ Total = \sum_{j=1}^{t}\sum_{i=1}^{n_j}(x_{ij} - \tilde{x})^2$$

$$SS\ Error = SS\ Total - SS\ Treatment - SS\ Block$$

	Method 1	Method 2	Method 3	Method 4	Average
Block 1	90	87	93	85	88.7500
Block 2	86	79	87	83	83.7500
Block 3	76	74	77	73	75.0000
Average	84.0000	80.0000	85.6667	80.3333	

		A	B	C
7	Global Average	82.5000	=AVERAGE(B2:E4)
8	Number of Rows (Blocks)	3	=COUNT(B2:B4)
9	Number of Columns (Treatments)	4	=COUNT(B2:E2)
10	SS Total	473.0000	=(B2-B7)^2+(B3-B7)^2+(B4-B7)^2+(C2-B7)^2+(C3-B7)^2+(C4-B7)^2+(D2-B7)^2+(D3-B7)^2+(D4-B7)^2+(E2-B7)^2+(E3-B7)^2+(E4-B7)^2
11	SS Blocking (Rows)	387.5000	=B9*((F2-B7)^2+(F3-B7)^2+(F4-B7)^2)
12	SS Treatment (Columns)	69.6667	=B8*((B5-B7)^2+(C5-B7)^2+(D5-B7)^2+(E5-B7)^2)
13	SS Errors	15.8333	=B10-B12-B11
14	MS Block	193.7500	=B11/B17
15	MS Treatment	23.2222	=B12/B18
16	MS Error	2.6389	=B13/B19
17	DF Block	2	=B8-1
18	DF Treatment	3	=B9-1
19	DF Error	6	=B17*B18
20	F Statistic (Treatment)	8.8000	=B15/B16
21	P-Value (Treatment)	0.0129	=FDIST(B20,B18,B19)
22	F Statistic (Blocking)	73.4211	=B14/B16
23	P-Value (Blocking)	0.0001	=FDIST(B22,B17,B19)
24	F Critical (Treatment) @ 0.10	3.2888	=FINV(0.1,B18,B19)
25	F Critical (Treatment) @ 0.05	4.7571	=FINV(0.05,B18,B19)
26	F Critical (Treatment) @ 0.01	9.7795	=FINV(0.01,B18,B19)
27	F Critical (Blocking) @ 0.10	3.4633	=FINV(0.1,B17,B19)
28	F Critical (Blocking) @ 0.05	5.1433	=FINV(0.05,B17,B19)
29	F Critical (Blocking) @ 0.01	10.9248	=FINV(0.01,B17,B19)
30	The blocking variable has statistically significant effect at Alpha 5% on at least one of the levels		
31	The treatment variable has statistically significant effect at Alpha 1% on at least one of the levels		

ANOVA Randomized Blocks Multiple Treatments

	DF	Sums of Squares	Mean Square	F Stat	p-Value
Block Factor (Row)	2	387.50	193.75	73.4211	0.0001
Treatment Factor (Column)	3	69.67	23.22	8.8000	0.0129
Error	6	15.83	2.64		
Total	11	473.00			

F Critical (Treatment) @ 0.10: 3.288761
F Critical (Treatment) @ 0.05: 4.757062
F Critical (Treatment) @ 0.01: 9.779639
F Critical (Blocking) @ 0.10: 3.463304
F Critical (Blocking) @ 0.05: 5.143253
F Critical (Blocking) @ 0.01: 10.924768
The blocking variable has statistically significant effect at Alpha 5% on at least one of the levels
The treatment variable has statistically significant effect at Alpha 1% on at least one of the levels

Mean Squares of Between Treatment (MS Treatment) = (SS Treatment)/(Number of Treatments – 1)

Mean Squares of Blocks (MS Block) = (SS Block)/(Total Observations – 1)

Mean Squares of Errors or Mean Squares Within Treatments (MS Error) = (SS Error)/((Total Observations – 1)(Number of Treatments – 1)

F Statistic is computed as MS Treatment / MS Error

F statistic df = (Number of Treatments – 1) in the numerator and (Total Observations – 1)(Number of Treatments – 1) in the denominator

Two-Way ANOVA

The one-way ANOVA models presented above look at a single factor on the dependent variable. In this section, we introduce the two-way ANOVA, a method that simultaneously examines the effects of two factors (*two* categorical independent variables) on the *one* numerical dependent variable, as well the interactions of different levels of the two factors. That is, random assignments are made such that two or more participants are subjected to each possible combination of the factor levels. The number of persons or participants within each of these combinations is termed the *number of replications* (r) and r has to be ≥ 2.

The specification tested in this ANOVA is $x_{i,j} = \mu + \alpha_i + \beta_j + (\alpha\beta)_{ij} + \varepsilon_{ijk}$

Testing the main effect, factor A:
H_0: $\alpha_i = 0$ for each level of factor A, for $i = 1$ to a (no level of factor A has an effect)
H_a: $\alpha_i \neq 0$ for at least one value of i, where $i = 1$ to a (at least one level has an effect)

Testing the main effect, factor B:
H_0: $\beta_j = 0$ for each level of factor B, for $j = 1$ to b (no level of factor B has an effect)
H_a: $\beta_j \neq 0$ for at least one value of j, where $j = 1$ to b (at least one level has an effect)

Testing the interaction effects, between levels of factors A and B:
H_0: $\alpha\beta_{ij} = 0$ for each combination of i and j (there are no interaction effects)
H_a: $\alpha\beta_{ij} \neq 0$ for at least one combination of i and j (at least one combination has effect)

Example: Suppose an aircraft manufacturer is testing three different alloys (B1, B2, and B3) for its wing construction of a new plane, and each alloy type can be produced in four different thickness (A1 to A4). The number of twists and flexes are recorded until stress failure is detected.

	Factor B1	Factor B2	Factor B3
Factor A1	804	836	804
Factor A1	816	828	808
Factor A2	819	844	807
Factor A2	813	836	819
Factor A3	820	814	819
Factor A3	821	811	829
Factor A4	806	811	827
Factor A4	805	806	835

$$SSA = rb \sum_{i=1}^{a} (\bar{x}_i - \tilde{x})^2 \qquad SSB = ra \sum_{j=1}^{b} (\bar{x}_j - \tilde{x})^2$$

$$SSE = \sum_{i=1}^{a} \sum_{j=1}^{b} \sum_{k=1}^{r} (x_{ijk} - \bar{x}_{ij})^2 \qquad SST = \sum_{i=1}^{a} \sum_{j=1}^{b} \sum_{k=1}^{r} (x_{ijk} - \tilde{x})^2$$

Degrees of freedom (*df*) for factor A is *(a − 1)*, factor B is *(b − 1)*, Interaction AB is *(a − 1)(b − 1)*, Error is *ab(r − 1)*, and Total is *(abr − 1)*.

Mean Squares (MS) for factor A is *SSA/df(A)*, factor B is *SSB/df(B)*, factor AB is *SSAB/df(AB)*, Error is *SSE/df(E)*.

The calculated F Statistic for factor A is MS(A)/MS(E), factor B is MS(B)/MS(E), and AB interaction is MS(AB)/MS(E).

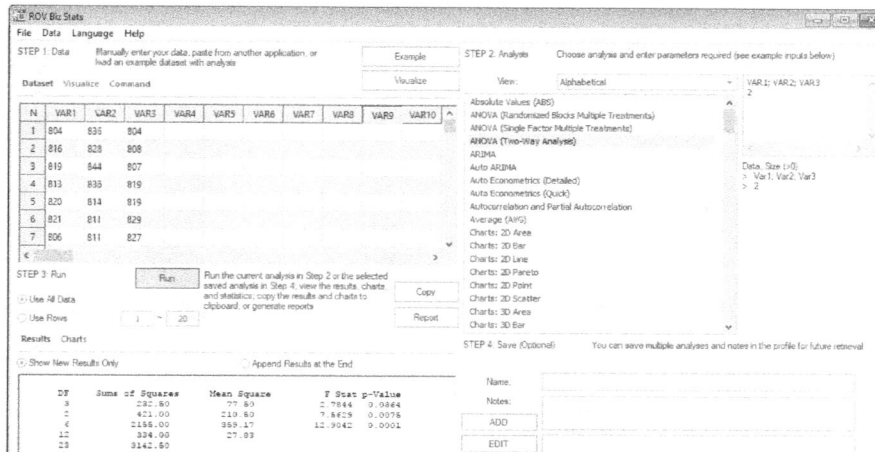

ROV Biz Stats — File Data Language Help

STEP 1: Data — Manually enter your data, paste from another application, or load an example dataset with analysis

Dataset | Visualize | Command

N	VAR1	VAR2	VAR3	VAR4	VAR5	VAR6	VAR7	VAR8	VAR9	VAR10
1	804	836	804							
2	816	828	808							
3	819	844	807							
4	813	835	819							
5	820	814	819							
6	821	811	829							
7	806	811	827							

STEP 2: Analyze — Choose analysis and enter parameters required (see example inputs below)

View: Alphabetical — VAR1; VAR2; VAR3

Absolute Values (ABS)
ANOVA (Randomized Blocks Multiple Treatments)
ANOVA (Single Factor Multiple Treatments)
ANOVA (Two-Way Analysis)
ARIMA
Auto ARIMA
Auto Econometrics (Detailed)
Auto Econometrics (Quick)
Autocorrelation and Partial Autocorrelation
Average (AVG)
Charts: 2D Area
Charts: 2D Bar
Charts: 2D Line
Charts: 2D Pareto
Charts: 2D Point
Charts: 3D Scatter
Charts: 3D Area
Charts: 3D Bar

Data, Size i>0;
> Var1, Var2, Var3
> 2

STEP 3: Run — Run the current analysis in Step 2 or the selected saved analysis in Step 4, view the results, charts and statistics; copy the results and charts to clipboard, or generate reports
Use All Data
Use Rows 1 - 20

Results Charts
Show New Results Only   Append Results at the End

DF	Sums of Squares	Mean Square	F Stat	p-Value
3	232.50	77.50	2.7844	0.0864
2	421.00	210.50	7.5629	0.0075
6	2155.00	359.17	12.9042	0.0001
12	334.00	27.83		
23	3142.50			

STEP 4: Save (Optional) — You can save multiple analyses and notes in the profile for future retrieval
Name:
Notes:
ADD
EDIT

	Factor B1	Factor B2	Factor B3	Average
Factor A1	804	836	804	
Factor A1	816	828	808	816.0000
Factor A2	819	844	807	
Factor A2	813	836	819	823.0000
Factor A3	820	814	819	
Factor A3	821	811	829	819.0000
Factor A4	806	811	827	
Factor A4	805	806	835	815.0000
Average	813.0000	823.2500	818.5000	

Two Way ANOVA

Careful with column E. We average the number
of rows based on user input of number of
Replication/Rows there are

Replication/Rows (User Input)	2	This is a user input
Number of Rows	8	=COUNT(B2:B9)
Factors/Rows	4	=B14/B13
Factors/Columns	3	=COUNT(B2:D2)
Global Average	818.2500	=AVERAGE(B2:D9)
SS Total	3142.5000	see equation on the right
SS Factors Rows	232.5000	=B13*B16*((E3-B17)^2+(E5-B17)^2+(E7-B17)^2+(E9-B17)^2)
SS Factors Columns	421.0000	=B13*B15*((B11-B17)^2+(C11-B17)^2+(D11-B17)^2)
SS Interaction	2155.0000	=B18-B19-B20 watch out on this one… example has 2 Replication so we average two rows only, if replication 5 then average of all 5 rows and do the difference and square for all five items…
SS Errors	334.0000	see equation on the right
MS Factor Rows	77.5000	=B19/(B15-1)
MS Factor Columns	210.5000	=B20/(B16-1)
MS Interaction	359.1667	=B21/((B15-1)*(B16-1))
MS Errors	27.8333	=B22/(B15*B16*(B13-1))
F Statistic for Row Factors	2.7844	=B23/B26
F Statistic for Column Factors	7.5629	=B24/B26
F Statistic for Interaction	12.9042	=B25/B26
DF Row Factors	3	=B15-1
DF Column Factors	2	=B16-1
DF Interaction	6	=(B15-1)*(B16-1)
DF Both Factors	12	=B15*B16*(B13-1)
P-Value for Row Factors	0.0864	=FDIST(B27,B30,B33)
P-Value for Column Factors	0.0075	=FDIST(B28,B31,B33)
P-Value for Interaction	0.0001	=FDIST(B29,B32,B33)

$B18=(B2-\$B\$17)^2+(B3-\$B\$17)^2+(B4-\$B\$17)^2+(B5-\$B\$17)^2+(B6-\$B\$17)^2+(B7-\$B\$17)^2+(B8-\$B\$17)^2+(B9-\$B\$17)^2+(C2-\$B\$17)^2+(C3-\$B\$17)^2+(C4-\$B\$17)^2+(C5-\$B\$17)^2+(C6-\$B\$17)^2+(C7-\$B\$17)^2+(C8-\$B\$17)^2+(C9-\$B\$17)^2+(D2-\$B\$17)^2+(D3-\$B\$17)^2+(D4-\$B\$17)^2+(D5-\$B\$17)^2+(D6-\$B\$17)^2+(D7-\$B\$17)^2+(D8-\$B\$17)^2+(D9-\$B\$17)^2$

'B22=(B2-AVERAGE(B2:B3))^2+(B3-AVERAGE(B2:B3))^2 + (B4-AVERAGE(B4:B5))^2+(B5-AVERAGE(B4:B5))^2 + (B6-AVERAGE(B6:B7))^2+(B7-AVERAGE(B6:B7))^2 + (B8-AVERAGE(B8:B9))^2+(B9-AVERAGE(B8:B9))^2 + (C2-AVERAGE(C2:C3))^2+(C3-AVERAGE(C2:C3))^2 + (C4-AVERAGE(C4:C5))^2+(C5-AVERAGE(C4:C5))^2 + (C6-AVERAGE(C6:C7))^2+(C7-AVERAGE(C6:C7))^2 + (C8-AVERAGE(C8:C9))^2+(C9-AVERAGE(C8:C9))^2 + (D2-AVERAGE(D2:D3))^2+(D3-AVERAGE(D2:D3))^2 + (D4-AVERAGE(D4:D5))^2+(D5-AVERAGE(D4:D5))^2 + (D6-AVERAGE(D6:D7))^2+(D7-AVERAGE(D6:D7))^2 + (D8-AVERAGE(D8:D9))^2+(D9-AVERAGE(D8:D9))^2

Two Way ANOVA Results

	DF	SS	MS	F	P
Row Factor	3	232.5000	77.5000	2.7844	0.0864
Column Factor	2	421.0000	210.5000	7.5629	0.0075
Interaction	6	2155.0000	359.1667	12.9042	0.0001
Error	12	334.0000	27.8333		

General Linear Models

GENERAL LINEAR MODEL	Dependent Variable(s)	Independent Variable(s)	Notes
ANOVA Single Factor Multiple Treatments	One	One	One factor with multiple treatment types.
ANOVA Single Factor with Repeated Measures	One	One	Repeating similar tests for reliability.
ANOVA with Blocking Variables	One	One	Controls and tests for exogenous impacts.
Two-Way ANOVA	One	Two	Two factors with multiple treatment types each and testing for their interactions. M x N factorial design.
Three-Way ANOVA	One	Three	Three factors with multiple treatment types each and testing for their interactions. P x Q x R factorial design.
ANCOVA	One	One	Controls for baselines using covariates.
MANOVA	Multiple	One	Simultaneous ANOVA by testing multiple dependent variables at once.
Two-Way MANOVA	Multiple	Two	Two factors with multiple treatment types each and testing for their interactions on multiple dependent variables at once. M x N factorial design.

Factorial Design (DOE) Combinatorics

2×2 or 2^2
2 IV with 2 levels on IV(1) and 2 levels on IV(2)
2 Main Effects + 1 Interaction Effect +
4 Experimental Conditions

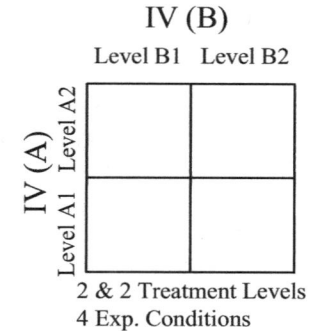

IV (B)

Level B1   Level B2

IV (A)   Level A2   Level A1

2 & 2 Treatment Levels
4 Exp. Conditions

Two IV
/ \

3×3 or 3^2

2 IV with 3 levels on IV(1) and 3 levels on IV(2)
2 Main + 1 Interaction + 9 Conditions

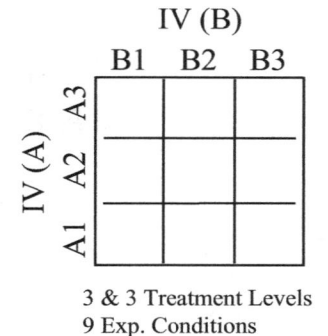

IV (B)

B1   B2   B3

IV (A)   A3   A2   A1

3 & 3 Treatment Levels
9 Exp. Conditions

Three IV
/ | \

$2 \times 2 \times 4$ or $2^2 4$

3 IV with 2 levels on IV(1), 2 levels on IV(2), and
4 levels on IV(3)
3 Main + 4 Interaction + 16 Conditions
Hint: AB, AC, BC, ABC

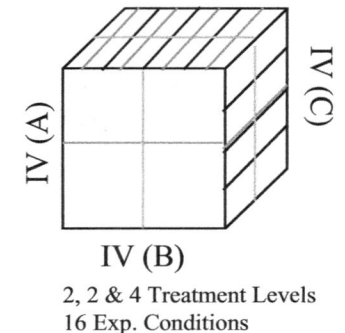

IV (A)   IV (C)

IV (B)

2, 2 & 4 Treatment Levels
16 Exp. Conditions

Design of Experiment DOE

N	Block	A	B	C
1	1	A1	B1	C1
2	1	A1	B1	C2
3	1	A1	B1	C3
4	1	A1	B1	C4
5	1	A1	B2	C1
6	1	A1	B2	C2
7	1	A1	B2	C3
8	1	A1	B2	C4
9	1	A2	B1	C1
10	1	A2	B1	C2
11	1	A2	B1	C3
12	1	A2	B1	C4
13	1	A2	B2	C1
14	1	A2	B2	C2
15	1	A2	B2	C3
16	1	A2	B2	C4

ANOVA vs. Regression

ANOVA

Dep. Var.	Continuous
Indep. Var.	Categorical [1]
Requirements	Normality of data [2]

[1] If dependent variable is categorical, use Discriminant Analysis, clustering, segmentation, and other AI/ML grouping methods; if dependent variable is binary, bivariate, or truncated, use GLM methods
[2] Use nonparametric equivalence if nonlinear (Kruskal-Wallis, Freidman, Mood's Median)

REGRESSION

Dep. Var.	Continuous [3]
Indep. Var.	Continuous [4]
Requirements	Multivariate normality and sphericity of errors, homoskedasticity, expected error is zero, no autocorrelation, no micronumerosity (k > n), non-stochastic, no multicollinearity, and so forth…

[3] Use Generalized Linear Models (Logit, Probit, Tobit) for Binary, Bivariate, and Truncated Data
[4] Dummy Variables (binary), Index Variables (1, 2, 3) can be used in multiple regression

SIMPLE RULES

Do not exceed ANOVA Three-Way or MANOVA Two-Way. Use regression instead.

Only differences is needed: ANOVA. Marginal impacts and predictions: regression.

MANOVA has difficulty in identifying the source of the difference, only that there is one.

Regression provides additional validity indicators: R-Sq, Akaike, Hannan-Quinn, Bayes…

Careful as categorical and dummy variables can sometimes cause multicollinearity issues. Select the right regression (Autoeconometrics, Correlated, Cox, Deming, Functional Forms, Instrumental Variables, Origin, Stepwise, Weighted, etc.).

Conclusion: Collect interval data if possible and run both! Each provides a different set of insights…

ANOVA for Single Factor Multiple Treatments
1 Dependent Variable vs. 1 Independent Variable (One Factor Multiple Treatments)

Participants	Method 1 Treatment	Method 2 Treatment	Method 3 Treatment
Person 1	58	80	96
Person 2	68	82	92
Person 3	70	88	90
...	...	...	...
...	...	...	...
Person 30	72	86	88

* Method 1: Russian Math; Method 2: Singapore Math; Method 3: U.S. Math
* The Single Factor Tested: Different Teaching Techniques
* Dependent Variable = Math Scores (continuous numerical values in the table)
* Independent Variable = Teaching Techniques (column groups)

ANOVA for Single Factor Repeated Measures
1 Dependent Variable vs. 1 Independent Variable (Repeated Tests)

Participants	Test 1	Test 2	Test 3
Person 1	50	52	50
Person 2	88	90	92
Person 3	60	62	58
...	...	...	...
...	...	...	...
Person 30	78	80	80

* The same treatment is used but the participants are tested multiple times
* Dependent Variable = Math Scores (continuous numerical values in the table)
* The same students are subjected to multiple tests

ANOVA with Blocking Variable
1 Dependent Variable vs. 1 Independent Variable with Blocking Variable

Blocks	Method 1 Treatment	Method 2 Treatment	Method 3 Treatment
Private School	66	82	94
Public School	68	84	90
Home School	70	88	90

* Method 1: Russian Math; Method 2: Singapore Math; Method 3: U.S. Math
* The Single Factor Tested: Different Teaching Techniques
* Dependent Variable = Math Scores (continuous numerical values in the table)
* Independent Variable = Teaching Techniques (column groups)
* Blocking Variable = Type of school (variable to control)

TWO-WAY ANOVA
1 Dependent Variable vs. 2 Independent Variable (One Factor Multiple Treatments)

Factor B	Method 1 Factor A1	Method 2 Factor A2	Method 3 Factor A3
Factor B1: 1 Month	68	82	96
Factor B2: 3 Months	72	84	86
Factor B3: 6 Months	66	90	92

* The Two Factors Tested: Different Teaching Techniques vs. Length of Time Taught
* Factor A:: Method 1: Russian Math; Method 2: Singapore Math; Method 3: U.S. Math
* Factor B:: 1 Month, 3 Month, 6 Months
* Dependent Variable = Math Scores (continuous numerical values in the table)
* This example is a 3 x 3 Factorial Model

MANOVA
Multiple Dependent Variables vs. 1 Independent Variable

Independent Var Schools	Dependent Var 1 Math Scores	Dependent Var 2 Satisfaction	Dependent Var 3 Teacher Ratings
Public	76.7	29.5	7.5
Public	60.5	32.1	6.3
Public	96.1	40.7	4.2
Private	76.9	20.4	3.0
Private	66.9	23.9	1.1
Private	55.4	29.1	5.0
Charter	62.8	25.9	2.9
Charter	45.0	15.9	1.2
Charter	47.8	36.1	4.1
Home School	52.5	39.0	3.1
Home School	80.0	54.2	4.0
Home School	54.7	32.1	5.7

* Multiple Dependent Variables = The numerical values in the table include test scores, student satisfaction survey scores, and teacher ratings
* One Independent Variable = Type of school

TWO WAY MANOVA
Multiple Dependent Variables vs. 2 Independent Variables

Independent Var 1 Schools	Independent Var 2 Economic	Dependent Var 1 Math Scores	Dependent Var 2 Satisfaction	Dependent Var 3 Teacher Ratings
Public	Wealthy	29.50	29.50	7.50
Public	Wealthy	32.10	32.10	6.30
Public	Middle	40.70	40.70	4.20
Public	Middle	29.50	29.50	7.50
Public	Poor	32.10	32.10	6.30
Public	Poor	40.70	40.70	4.20
Private	Wealthy	20.40	20.40	3.00
Private	Wealthy	23.90	23.90	1.10
Private	Middle	29.10	29.10	5.00
Private	Middle	25.90	25.90	2.90
Private	Poor	15.90	15.90	1.20
Private	Poor	36.10	36.10	4.10
Home School	Wealthy	39.00	39.00	3.10
Home School	Wealthy	54.20	54.20	4.00
Home School	Middle	32.10	32.10	5.70
Home School	Middle	39.00	39.00	3.10
Home School	Poor	54.20	54.20	4.00
Home School	Poor	32.10	32.10	5.70

* Multiple Dependent Variables = The numerical values in the table include test scores, student satisfaction survey scores, and teacher ratings
* Two Independent Variable = Type of school vs. Economic status of the school district

MANOVA

Screenshot: [EXAMPLE] - ROV Biz Stats

File Data Language Help

STEP 1: Data — Manually enter your data, paste from another application, or load an example dataset with analysis

STEP 2: Analysis — Choose analysis and enter parameters required (see example inputs below)

View: All Methods

Analysis list:
- ANCOVA (Single Factor Multiple Treatments)
- ANOVA (MANOVA 2 Factor Replication)
- ANOVA (MANOVA General Linear Model)
- ANOVA (Randomized Blocks Multiple Treatm...
- ANOVA (Single Factor Multiple Treatments)
- ANOVA (Single Factor Repeated Measures)
- ANOVA (Two-Way Analysis)
- ARIMA
- ARIMA Seasonal (SARIMA)
- Auto ARIMA
- Auto Econometrics (Detailed)
- Auto Econometrics (Quick)
- Autocorrelation and Partial Autocorrelation
- Autocorrelation Durbin-Watson AR(1) Test
- Bonferroni Test (Single Variable with Repetiti...
- Bonferroni Test (Tw...
- Box's Test for Homo...
- Box-Cox Normal Tra
- Charts: 2D Area
- Charts: 2D Bar
- Charts: 2D Column

General Linear Model: MANOVA

	Stat	F	DF1	DF2	P-value
Pillai Trace	0.53450	2.02340	9.00	84.00	0.04641
Wilk's Lambda	0.48941	2.40496	9.00	63.43	0.02047
Hotelling Trace	0.99464	2.72605	9.00	74.00	0.00840
Roy's Root	0.94364				

Null hypothesis: There is zero mean difference among all the variables.

SSCP Matrix Adjusted for Type (H)
911.41594	62.97406	162.45969
62.97406	121.90594	23.64531
162.45969	23.64531	32.34844

Between Subjects Effects Test

	Sum of Squares	DF	Mean Square	F Stat	P-Value
Variable A on Treatment 1	0.8313	2	0.4157	8.0235	0.0032
Variable A on Treatment 2	1.6406	2	0.8203	7.6865	0.0039
Variable A on Treatment 3	0.6323	2	0.3162	0.2977	0.7461
Variable B on Treatment 1	1.4715	2	0.7357	14.2013	0.0002
Variable B on Treatment 2	0.0287	2	0.0144	0.1346	0.8749
Variable B on Treatment 3	0.6737	2	0.3368	0.3172	0.7322
Interactions AB on Treatment 1	2.6117	4	0.6529	12.6030	0.0000
Interactions AB on Treatment 2	0.6232	4	0.1558	1.4599	0.2556
Interactions AB on Treatment 3	1.8303	4	0.4576	0.4308	0.7845
Errors on Treatment 1	0.9325	18	0.0518		
Errors on Treatment 2	1.9209	18	0.1067		
Errors on Treatment 3	19.1167	18	1.0620		

Multivariate Tests

VAR A	Stat	DF1	DF2	F Stat	P-Value
Pillai's Trace	0.6935	6.0000	34.0000	3.0082	0.0182
Wilk's Lambda	0.3302	6.0000	32.0000	3.9486	0.0046
Hotelling's Trace	1.9571	6.0000	30.0000	4.8926	0.0014
Roy's Largest Root	1.9197				

VAR B	Stat	DF1	DF2	F Stat	P-Value
Pillai's Trace	0.6541	6.0000	34.0000	2.7542	0.0273
Wilk's Lambda	0.3594	6.0000	32.0000	3.5631	0.0081
Hotelling's Trace	1.7448	6.0000	30.0000	4.3621	0.0028
Roy's Largest Root	1.7230				

VAR AB	Stat	DF1	DF2	F Stat	P-Value
Pillai's Trace	0.7855	12.0000	54.0000	1.5962	0.1205
Wilk's Lambda	0.2233	12.0000	42.6235	2.7076	0.0083
Hotelling's Trace	3.4382	12.0000	44.0000	4.2022	0.0002
Roy's Largest Root	3.4266				

Normality and Probability Distribution Fitting of Data

Akaike Information Criterion, Anderson–Darling, Kuiper's Statistic, and Schwarz/Bayes Criterion

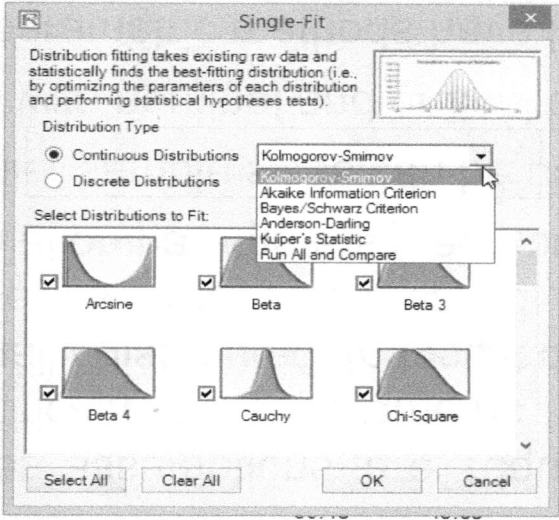

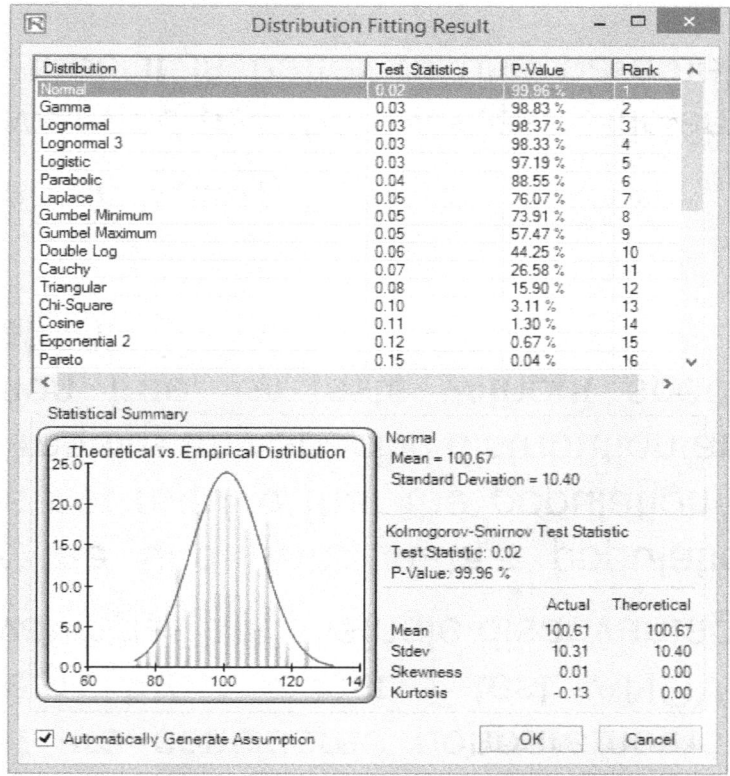

Nonparametric Tests

There are some methods and tests that are considered nonparametric in nature. Compared to parametric tests (e.g., t-test, z-test, F-test, ANOVA), nonparametric tests have the following advantages and a single disadvantage:

- Fewer assumptions are required for the underlying data's population. Specifically, a nonparametric test does not require that the population be normally distributed. In fact, it does not require any specific distribution and, hence, is sometimes called distribution free, or tests without specific population parameters (i.e., nonparametric).

- Smaller sample sizes can be used.

- Data with nominal and ordinal scales can be tested.

- Nonparametric methods have lower power and use the data less efficiently. Therefore, if assumptions have been met, it is better to use parametric tests whenever possible.

Some of most common nonparametric tests are the Runs test for randomness, Wilcoxon test, Lilliefors test, Kruskal–Wallis test, and Friedman's test.

Nonparametric Chi-Square Test

The chi-square distribution is used to model three different types of tests:

1. Goodness-of-Fit Test

  H_0: The sample is from the specified distribution.

  H_a: The sample is not from the specified distribution.

2. Test of Independence

  H_0: The variables are independent of each other.

  H_a: The variables are not independent of each other.

3. Comparing Proportions of Multiple Independent Samples

  H_0: $\pi_1 = \pi_2 = \ldots = \pi_k$ for the $j = 1$ to k populations.

  H_a: At least one of the π_j values differs from the others.

Nonparametric Runs Test for Data Randomness

The Runs test evaluates the randomness of a series of observations by analyzing the number of runs it contains. A run is a consecutive appearance of one or more observations that are similar. The null hypothesis tested is whether the data sequence is random, versus the alternate hypothesis that the data sequence is not random.

H_0: The sequence is random
H_a: The sequence is not random

For nominal data with two outcomes (e.g., heads and tails in a coin toss, arrival of male and female customers in a bank), the series of events are captured, and the number of runs are computed. For instance, in the series F M M M F F M, there would be a total of 4 runs, or in the series H H T T T T H H, there would be 3 runs. For ordinal, interval, and ratio data, the median is first calculated, and the runs are converted into + and − signs for above and below the median. Then, a z-statistic is computed based on the number of runs (T) observed, and the total number of observations in each of the types (n_1 and n_2):

$$z = \frac{T - \left(\dfrac{2n_1 n_2}{n_1 + n_2} + 1 \right)}{\sqrt{\dfrac{2n_1 n_2 (2n_1 n_2 - n_1 - n_2)}{(n_1 + n_2)^2 (n_1 + n_2 - 1)}}}$$

The standard normal p-value is then calculated, if sample sizes $n_1 \geq 10$ and $n_2 \geq 10$.

Nonparametric Runs Test for Data Randomness

Nonparametric Wilcoxon Signed-Rank Test (One Variable)

Nonparametric techniques make no assumptions about the specific shape or distribution from which the sample is drawn. This lack of assumptions is different from the other hypothesis tests such as ANOVA or t-tests (parametric tests) where the sample is assumed to be drawn from a population that is normally or approximately normally distributed. If normality is assumed, the power of the test is higher due this normality restriction. However, if flexibility on distributional requirements is needed, then nonparametric techniques are superior.

The nonparametric Wilcoxon Signed-Rank Test (WSRT) for Single Variable looks at whether a sample dataset could have been randomly drawn from a particular population whose *median* is being hypothesized. The corresponding parametric test is the one-sample t-test, which should be used if the underlying population is assumed to be normal, providing a higher power on the test. In this single variable test, the following hypotheses are tested:

H_0: Population Median = m

H_a: Population Median ≠ m

Of course, the null hypothesis can take the standard equality signs of =, ≥, or ≤, and m can be any hypothesized value to test. The alternate hypothesis will have the appropriate complementary sign of ≠, <, or >.

The WSRT uses a W-statistic, and its corresponding critical values are usually provided in a statistics table (these will be automatically calculated in a statistics software package such as ROV BizStats). The first step in calculating W is to take the difference $d_i = x_i - m$. All $d = 0$ values are ignored. Then, these $|d_i|$ values are ranked from smallest (rank of 1) to largest. All tied ranks are assigned their average values. For all ranks that have a positive value or where $x_i > m$, we sum all these positive ranks to obtain the W, that is, $W = \Sigma (R+)$.

The next slide shows an example of the WSRT for a single variable. The calculated W statistic is 13, and the two-tailed critical limits at a 0.05 significance are 9 and 46. The W falls within these critical limits, which means we fail to reject the null hypothesis and conclude that the population median is statistically not different than the hypothesized median (in this example it is set as 40 in ROV BizStats, as seen in the next slide).

Nonparametric Wilcoxon Signed-Rank Test (One Variable)

Nonparametric Wilcoxon Signed-Rank Test (Two Variables)

In contrast, the Nonparametric WSRT for Paired Variables looks at whether the *medians* of the differences between the two paired variables are equal. This test is specifically formulated for testing the same or similar samples before and after an event (e.g., measurements that are taken before a medical treatment are compared against those measurements taken after the treatment to see if there is a difference). The corresponding parametric test is the two-sample t-test with dependent means, which should be used if the underlying population is assumed to be normal, providing a higher power on the test. In this paired variable test, the following hypotheses are tested:

H_0: Population Median of Differences $m_d = 0$

H_a: Population Median of Differences $m_d \neq 0$

The approach is similar to the single variable WSRT with the exception that the difference d is computed as $d_i = x_i - y_i$ where x and y are the two variables being tested. The next slide shows the WSRT for two variables. The calculated W is 44.5 with a hypothesized difference of 0, and the 0.05 significance. The conclusion is we cannot reject the two-tailed null hypothesis and state that the differences are statistically close enough to 0.

Nonparametric Wilcoxon Signed-Rank Test (Two Variables)

Parametric and Nonparametric Normality Tests

- **Distributional Fitting.** Which distribution does an analyst or engineer use for an input variable in a model? What are the relevant distributional parameters? The null hypothesis tested is that the fitted distribution is the same distribution as the population from which the sample data to be fitted comes.
    - **Akaike Information Criterion (AIC).** Rewards goodness-of-fit but also includes a penalty that is an increasing function of the number of estimated parameters (although AIC penalizes the number of parameters less strongly than other methods).
    - **Anderson–Darling (AD).** When applied to testing if a normal distribution adequately describes a set of data, it is one of the most powerful statistical tools for detecting departures from normality and is powerful for testing normal tails. However, in non-normal distributions, this test lacks power compared to others.
    - **Kolmogorov–Smirnov (KS).** A nonparametric test for the equality of continuous probability distributions that can be used to compare a sample with a reference probability distribution, making it useful for testing abnormally shaped distributions and non-normal distributions.
    - **Kuiper's Statistic (K).** Related to the KS test, Kuiper's Statistic is as sensitive in the tails as at the median and is invariant under cyclic transformations of the independent variable. This test is invaluable when testing for cyclic variations over time. In comparison, the AD provides equal sensitivity at the tails as the median, but it does not provide the cyclic invariance.
    - **Schwarz/Bayes Information Criterion (SC/BIC).** The SC/BIC introduces a penalty term for the number of parameters in the model, with a larger penalty than AIC.
    - **Discrete (Chi-Square).** The Chi-Square test is used to perform distributional fitting on discrete data.

- **Box–Cox Normal Transformation.** Although this is not strictly a test for normality, it takes your existing dataset and transforms it into normally distributed data. The original dataset is tested using the Shapiro–Wilk test for normality (H_0: data is assumed to be normal), then transformed using the Box–Cox method either using your custom Lambda parameter or internally optimized Lambda. The transformed data is tested again for normality using Shapiro–Wilk.

- **Grubbs Test for Outliers.** The Grubbs test is used to identify potential outliers and to test the null hypothesis that all the values are from the same normal population with no outliers.

Parametric and Nonparametric Normality Tests

- **Nonparametric Chi-Square Goodness-of-Fit for Normality (Grouped Data).** The chi-square test for goodness-of-fit is used to examine if a sample dataset could have been drawn from a population having a specified probability distribution. The probability distribution tested here is the normal distribution. The null hypothesis tested is such that the sample is randomly drawn from the normal distribution.

- **Nonparametric Lilliefors Test for Normality.** The Lilliefors test evaluates the null hypothesis of whether the data sample was drawn from a normally distributed population, versus an alternate hypothesis that the data sample is not normally distributed. If the calculated p-value is less than or equal to the alpha significance value, then reject the null hypothesis and accept the alternate hypothesis. Otherwise, if the p-value is higher than the alpha significance value, do not reject the null hypothesis. This test relies on two cumulative frequencies: one derived from the sample dataset and one from a theoretical distribution based on the mean and standard deviation of the sample data. An alternative to this test is the chi-square test for normality. The chi-square test requires more data points to run compared to the Lilliefors test.

- **Nonparametric: D'Agostino–Pearson Normality Test.** The D'Agostino–Pearson test it used to nonparametrically determine if there is near-normality in the dataset. This tests the null hypothesis that the data is normally distributed.

- **Nonparametric: Shapiro–Wilk–Royston Normality Test.** The Shapiro–Wilk test for normality uses the Royston algorithm to test the null hypothesis that the data is normally distributed.

- **Q-Q Normal Chart.** The Quantile-Quantile chart is a normal probability plot, which is a graphical method for comparing a probability distribution with the normal distribution by plotting their quantiles against each other. It only provides a visual inspection of the near normality of your dataset.

- **Skew and Kurtosis: Shapiro–Wilk and D'Agostino–Pearson.** You can run the Skew and Kurtosis tests to see if the data has both statistics equal to zero. A normal distribution has skew and kurtosis equal to zero. The D'Agostino–Pearson tests if both skew and kurtosis of the data are simultaneously statistically equal zero. The null hypothesis is the data has zero skew and zero kurtosis, approximating normality.

Nonparametric Lilliefors, Q-Q Chart, D'Agostino–Pearson, and Shapiro–Wilk–Royston Tests

The Lilliefors test evaluates the null hypothesis of whether the data sample was drawn from a normally distributed population, versus an alternate hypothesis that the data sample is not normally distributed. This test relies on two cumulative frequencies: one derived from the sample dataset and one from a theoretical distribution based on the mean and standard deviation of the sample data. An alternative to this test is the chi-square test for normality. The chi-square test requires more data points to run compared to the Lilliefors test.

H_0: The sample is from a Normal Distribution

H_a: The sample is not from a Normal Distribution

In this test, the sample dataset is first arranged in order, from the smallest value to the largest value. Its observed (O) cumulative frequency is calculated and a corresponding cumulative distribution function (CDF) of the normal distribution is computed based on the observed dataset's mean and standard deviation. The differences D between O and CDF are calculated, and the D statistic is computed as $D = max\ |O_i - CDF_i|$. Figure 9.30 illustrates a small sample set of five observations with the Lilliefors test administered. The computed D is 0.2782, which is less than the α = 5% significance level threshold of 0.3370, which means we are unable to reject the null hypothesis and conclude that the small sample size is normally distributed. Note that nonparametric methods have less power but are applicable in smaller sample sizes as illustrated in this example. However, if a larger dataset is available, it is always better to perform parametric distributional fitting such as those described previously (Kolmogorov–Smirnov, Akaike, Bayes Criterion, Kuiper, and so forth). There are other nonparametric approaches in BizStats used for normality tests, which are slightly more powerful than the Lilliefors test:

- **Nonparametric D'Agostino–Pearson Normality Test**. The D'Agostino–Pearson test it used to nonparametrically determine if there is near-normality in the dataset. This tests the null hypothesis that the data is normally distributed.
- **Nonparametric Shapiro–Wilk–Royston Normality Test**. The Shapiro–Wilk test for normality uses the Royston algorithm to test the null hypothesis that the data is normally distributed. This test does require more data points to compute than the Lilliefors and D'Agostino–Pearson tests. For example, the small dataset in Figure 9.35 will be insufficient to run this test.
- **Q-Q Normal Chart**. This Quantile-Quantile chart is a normal probability plot, which is a graphical method for comparing a probability distribution with the normal distribution by plotting their quantiles against each other. It only pro-vides a visual inspection of the near normality of your dataset. However, if a larger dataset is available, it is always better to perform parametric distributional fitting such as those described previously (Kolmogorov–Smirnov, Akaike, Bayes Criterion, Kuiper, and so forth).

Nonparametric Lilliefors, Q-Q Chart, D'Agostino–Pearson, and Shapiro–Wilk–Royston Tests

Model Inputs:
VAR1

Nonparametric d'Agostino-Pearson Test for Normality

DAP Stat: 2.554537
DAP P-Value: 0.278798

Null hypothesis: The data is normally distributed

Model Inputs:
VAR1

Lilliefors Test

Average: 278.600000
Stdev: 141.800212
D Statistic: 0.278183
D Critical at 1%: 0.315000
D Critical at 5%: 0.337000
D Critical at 10%: 0.405000

The data is statistically normal at the 1%, 5% and 10% significance level
  (null hypothesis tested is that the data is normally distributed).

Data	Relative Frequency	Observed	Expected
137.000000	0.200000	0.200000	0.158997
181.000000	0.200000	0.400000	0.245634
213.000000	0.200000	0.600000	0.321817
424.000000	0.200000	0.800000	0.847410
438.000000	0.200000	1.000000	0.869518

Box–Cox Transformation

In our focus to test for data normality so that most parametric tests can be run, we sometimes get ahead of ourselves and perform modifications to existing data in order to normalize said data. For instance, the dataset 4.5, 1.8, 9.3, 6.1, 8.2, 13.9, 23.5, 3.2, 56.8, 80.7 is subjected to BizStats' Box–Cox Transformation and the resulting data becomes 0.55492, 1.03910, 1.30106, 1.52037, 1.72135, 1.80337, 2.05196, 2.34839, 2.78224, 2.93490. In fact, the before- and after-transformation results look rather astounding. The original data rejects normality with a p-value of 0.0017 versus the post-transformation p-value of 0.9691, with a very high normality fit. However, the data completely loses its efficacy and meaning with such a drastic change. Nonetheless, there are applications in Six Sigma, such as computing the process capability, that require such a transformation in order to obtain valid estimates.

```
Original Data
Shapiro-Wilk: 0.723918
P-value: 0.001719
Null Hypothesis: Normality
R-Squared to Normal Fit: 0.613784

Box-Cox Transformed Data
Shapiro-Wilk: 0.980764
P-value: 0.969126
Null Hypothesis: Normality
R-Squared to Normal Fit: 0.987518
```

Nonparametric Kruskal–Wallis Test

The Kruskal–Wallis test is the extension of the Wilcoxon Signed-Rank test by comparing more than two independent samples. The corresponding parametric test is the One-Way ANOVA, but unlike the ANOVA, the Kruskal–Wallis does not require that the dataset be randomly sampled from normally distributed populations with equal variances. The Kruskal–Wallis test is a two-tailed hypothesis test where the null hypothesis is such that the population medians of each treatment are statistically identical to the rest of the group; that is, there is no effect among the different treatment groups. Similar to the ANOVA method, the Kruskal–Wallis tests the following hypotheses:

H_0: $m_1 = m_2 = \ldots = m_K$ for $i = 1$ to k (population medians are identical)

H_a: At least one of the medians m differs from the others

The method starts off with k variables to be tested. For each variable, the data is ranked from smallest to largest, with the smallest value receiving the rank of 1, and all tied ranks are assigned their average values. Then, sum all the ranks for each variable, yielding a list of summed ranks $\Sigma(R_1)$, $\Sigma(R_2)$, ..., $\Sigma(R_K)$.

$$H = \frac{12}{N(N+1)}\left[\frac{(\Sigma R_1)^2}{n_1} + \frac{(\Sigma R_2)^2}{n_2} + \ldots + \frac{(\Sigma R_K)^2}{n_K}\right] - 3(N+1)$$

Nonparametric Kruskal–Wallis Test

Nonparametric Friedman's Test

The Friedman test is the extension of the Wilcoxon Signed-Rank test for paired samples. The corresponding parametric test is the Randomized Block Multiple Treatment ANOVA, but unlike the ANOVA, the Friedman test does not require that the dataset be randomly sampled from normally distributed populations with equal variances. The Friedman test uses a two-tailed hypothesis test where the null hypothesis is such that the population medians of each treatment are statistically identical to the rest of the group; that is, there is no effect among the different treatment groups. Similar to the ANOVA method, the Friedman tests the following hypotheses:

H_0: $m_1 = m_2 = \ldots = m_K$ for $i = 1$ to k (population medians are identical)

H_a: At least one of the medians m differs from the others

Similar to the ANOVA with Blocking Variable, the data needs to be set up in a $B \times T$ fashion, where the blocking variables (B) are listed in rows and the treatments (T) are in columns as different variables. The next slide illustrates an example with the correct data setup. As an example, assume that a company is testing a new stain remover liquid, and the company has come up with four distinct formulations. These formulations are listed as the treatments, T, as different variables (columns). For each formulation or treatment, the stain remover was applied to various stain types (the blocking variable, B). In the example, there were six types of stains tested (e.g., chocolate, red wine, coffee, ink, paint, crayon) and these are listed in the rows. Each row represents one specific type of stain (e.g., row 1 may represent red wine). The numerical data in the grid is a value between 1 and 10, with a high number indicating that the stain was completely removed. The computed F_r statistic is 8.45, which is statistically significant at the 5% alpha level, so we can reject the null hypothesis and conclude that at least one of the formulations is different than the rest.

Nonparametric Friedman's Test

Inter-rater Reliability, Intra-rater Reliability, Consistency, Credibility, Diversity, Internal Validity, External Validity, and Predictability

The concept of data reliability can be complicated and can take many forms. In general, reliability can be defined as how accurate the data is and the level of consistency of the collected data. In other words, the extent to which an experiment, test, or measuring procedure yields the same results on repeated trials is the measure of its reliability. For example, if one were to take a tape measure and find the length of a specific table, measuring the table repeatedly should yield the same result. If this is the case, then the data obtained are reliable.

Reliability can also be characterized as inter-rater (different people using the same measuring tape and measuring the same table multiple times) vs. intra-rater (the same person measuring the same table several times, using the same measuring tape). There are statistical tests that can be run to identify the data's reliability and consistency.

Inter-Rater Reliability with Pairwise Cohen's Kappa

In Case A, there are 50 patients, and the first rater (physician or healthcare worker) judges 15 of them as being psychotic, 24 borderline, and 11 neither. In comparison, the second rater or judge finds 16, 23, and 11 patients within these respective categories. The patients that fall within the same judgment categories are shown in the grid. Both judges agree that 10 are psychotic, 16 are borderline, and 8 are neither, with a total of 34 findings in agreement out of 50 cases (this can be read off the diagonal in the data grid). The results from BizStats indicate that Cohen's Kappa = 0.4959 or 49% agreement. In Case B, we see that the data grid is equally distributed with 200 patients in each block, and the computed Cohen's Kappa = 0.0000, indicating absolutely no consistency and reliability between these two raters spread evenly. Case C, as you would imagine, returns Cohen's Kappa = 1.0000. Finally, Case D, where reliability is actually not just zero, but there is no value between the corresponding pairs, we obtain a Cohen's Kappa = –0.50902. Clearly, a high positive Cohen's Kappa measure is desirable for inter-rater reliability.

Cohen's Kappa test can be applied to test for the reliability of two raters. The null hypothesis tested is that both sets of judgments agree and are consistent. In the following table, we see 4 example cases. In each situation, there are two judges or raters.

CASE A	Judge 2 Psychotic (16)	Judge 2 Borderline (23)	Judge 2 Neither (11)
Judge 1 Psychotic (15)	10	4	1
Judge 1 Borderline (24)	6	16	2
Judge 1 Neither (11)	0	3	8

CASE B	Judge 2 Psychotic (600)	Judge 2 Borderline (600)	Judge 2 Neither (600)
Judge 1 Psychotic (600)	200	200	200
Judge 1 Borderline (600)	200	200	200
Judge 1 Neither (600)	200	200	200

CASE C	Judge 2 Psychotic (100)	Judge 2 Borderline (100)	Judge 2 Neither (100)
Judge 1 Psychotic (100)	100	0	0
Judge 1 Borderline (100)	0	100	0
Judge 1 Neither (100)	0	0	100

CASE D	Judge 2 Psychotic (135)	Judge 2 Borderline (99)	Judge 2 Neither (114)
Judge 1 Psychotic (124)	0	55	69
Judge 1 Borderline (95)	50	0	45
Judge 1 Neither (129)	85	44	0

Internal Consistency and Reliability with Cronback's Alpha for Binary Data

When there exist more than two raters or judges, we can use the Cronback's Alpha Analysis of Internal Consistency and Reliability. The null hypothesis for the Cronback's Alpha is that there is zero alpha reliability, and, therefore, there is no internal consistency among the different raters. We see in Case E, there are 12 respondents to a survey comprising 11 different questions. Note that to run the Cronback's Alpha test, the data obtained must be binary. If you look at the data carefully by *row*, we see that there are respondents such as Albert and Bob who tend to respond with the value 1 regardless of the question, whereas Kim and Larry might do the opposite, with a 0 response. One might even think that some respondents are too lazy to actually answer the questions and will simply fill in the blanks with similar responses throughout. In fact, the calculated Cronback's Alpha p-value = 0.6659 in BizStats, which means we cannot reject the null hypothesis and conclude that in Case E, there is no internal consistency among the different respondents. The survey data is, therefore, not consistent and not reliable.

Conversely, in Case F, we see that if you look down each *column*, there seems to be consistency among all the respondents. For instance, in Questions 6 and 7 (Q6 and Q7), almost all respondents agreed it would be a 0, as opposed to Q5, with all 1s in the column. Q2 and Q3 show that the respondents are equally spread between 0s and 1s. In this Case F, the computed Cronback's Alpha p-value = 0.002723 in BizStats, indicating that the null can be rejected, and we conclude that there is, indeed, statistically significant alpha-level reliability among the respondents.

CASE E	Q1	Q2	Q3	Q4	Q5	Q6	Q7	Q8	Q9	Q10	Q11
Albert	1	1	1	1	1	1	1	1	1	1	1
Bob	1	1	1	1	1	1	1	1	0	1	0
Cathy	1	0	1	1	1	1	1	1	1	0	0
Derek	1	1	1	0	1	1	0	1	1	0	0
Eric	1	1	1	1	1	0	0	0	1	0	0
Flo	0	1	1	0	1	1	1	1	0	0	0
Gale	1	1	1	1	0	0	1	0	0	0	0
Henry	1	1	1	1	1	0	0	0	0	0	0
Indi	0	1	0	1	1	0	0	0	0	1	0
Jack	1	0	0	1	0	1	0	0	0	0	0
Kim	1	1	1	0	0	0	0	0	0	0	0
Larry	1	0	0	1	0	0	0	0	0	0	0

CASE F	Q1	Q2	Q3	Q4	Q5	Q6	Q7
Andy	1	1	0	1	1	0	1
Becky	0	1	0	1	1	0	0
Colin	1	1	0	0	1	0	0
Dave	0	1	0	0	1	0	0
Even	1	1	0	1	1	0	0
Flynn	0	1	0	1	1	0	0
George	1	0	1	0	1	0	0
Hope	0	0	1	0	1	0	0
Isaac	1	0	1	1	1	0	0
John	0	0	1	1	1	0	0
Kern	1	0	1	0	1	0	0
Lisa	0	0	1	0	1	0	0

Internal Consistency and Reliability with Guttman's Lambda

When the responses are not binary but categorical, we can use the Guttman's Lambda test for inter-rater consistency and reliability. A quick scan of Case G indicates a familiar problem, where the vertical entries are almost identical in each column, but the columns themselves are not consistent across the different raters. For instance, Alex might always select a low score regardless of the question or issue posed, whereas Cory is an optimist and consistently provides a high score. The raters themselves might be consistent with themselves, but they are certainly not consistent with other raters. The computed Guttman's Lambda = 0.07563, with a corresponding Spearman–Brown Correlation Correction Factor = 0.07782 using BizStats (note that if multiple correlation correction factors are presented, we usually look at the more conservative measure). Low correlation corrections and low lambda scores mean there is low reliability and low consistency among the raters. Note that the data matrix is inverted in this test, as opposed to the Cronback's test, where we show the questions as rows and respondents or judges/raters as columns. In comparison, for Case H, Guttman's Lambda = 0.99004 and the conservative Spearman-Brown Correlation Correction Factor = 0.9909. This indicates a very high consistency and reliability of the responses. For instance, Question A received a very low score regardless of the rater, whereas Question C scores high consistently. Looking across the rows shows consistency and reliability in the data.

Case G	Alex	Ben	Cory	Dick	Emma	Flo	Ginny	Hale	Izzy	John
Question A	1	4	8	2	7	5	6	2	5	3
Question B	1	4	8	2	7	1	6	3	5	3
Question C	1	4	8	2	7	2	6	2	5	3
Question D	1	5	8	2	7	2	6	3	5	3
Question E	1	4	8	3	7	2	5	2	5	3
Question F	1	4	9	2	8	2	6	3	6	3
Question G	1	4	8	2	8	2	6	2	5	3
Question H	1	5	8	2	7	2	6	3	5	3
Question I	2	4	8	2	7	2	5	2	5	3
Question J	1	4	9	3	7	2	6	3	5	3
Question K	1	4	8	2	7	2	6	2	6	3
Question L	1	4	8	2	7	1	6	3	5	4
Question M	1	4	8	2	7	1	6	2	5	3
Question N	2	4	8	2	7	2	6	3	5	3
Question O	1	4	8	2	7	1	6	2	5	3

Case H	Arlo	Bex	Cal	Dale	Elsa	Fox	Guy	Ham	Illy	Jay
Question A	1	1	1	1	1	1	1	1	2	1
Question B	4	4	4	5	4	4	4	5	4	4
Question C	8	8	8	8	8	9	8	8	8	9
Question D	2	2	2	2	3	2	2	2	2	3
Question E	7	7	7	7	7	8	8	7	7	7
Question F	5	1	2	2	2	2	2	2	2	2
Question G	6	6	6	6	5	6	6	6	5	6
Question H	2	3	2	3	2	3	2	3	2	3
Question I	5	5	5	5	5	6	5	5	5	5
Question J	3	3	3	3	3	3	3	3	3	3

Inter-Rater Reliability using Inter-Class Correlation (ICC)

If we wish to test for both inter-rater and intra-rater reliability, we can use the Inter-Class Correlation (ICC) test. Cases I and J show some example data where we perform a double-blind test on 8 wines (the wine bottles look identical, labels removed, and replaced with a generic label such as Wine 1, Wine 2, and so forth). And suppose 4 sommeliers or expert wine judges were asked to grade the wines, from a value of 1 (low quality) to 10 (high quality).

In Case I, we see that for each of the different wines, all four judges scored the wines consistently. For example, Wine 1 is by far the worst, whereas wines 7 and 8 are highly rated by all judges. This would indicate a high level of consistency and reliability in each row. The ICC test returns an Interclass Correlation = 0.9841, the row's p-value = 0.0000, and the column's p-value = 0.8538. This means there is a high level of consistency, as measured by the ICC, and we can reject the null hypothesis of having the same values in the rows and fail to reject regarding the columns. In other words, all the judges tend to be fairly consistent in their tastes (high ICC), possibly because they all have a similar judging or sommelier training. In addition, the wines are different as compared to one another (p-value of 0.0000 for the rows), where we can say based on the scores, which we have now concluded are consistent and reliable, that the wines are certainly of varying quality. In contrast, when comparing the columns (i.e., comparing among the judges), we have a consistency and statistically no difference in their ratings (high p-value of the columns at 0.8538), or in other words, the judges have similar judgments.

Case J shows a very different situation. We see that Judge 1 is probably a snob, whereby no wine is considered good. Hence, Judge 1 is internally consistent with himself, or has high intra-rater reliability. In contrast, Judge 4 simply loves wine and scores any and all wines highly. Judge 4 is also internally reliable to himself, but not to the other judges. The computed Interclass Correlation = 0.00149 (low inter-rater consistency and low reliability among the judges) with a row p-value of 0.3958 (we cannot reject the null hypothesis and state that the rows, when taken together, are statistically similar to each other, indicating, in this case, that there is high intra-rater reliability) and a column p-value of 0.0000 (we reject the null hypothesis and state that there is a statistically significant difference among the columns or judges, which means that there is no inter-rater consistency and no reliability in the wine scores).

Case I	Judge 1	Judge 2	Judge 3	Judge 4
Wine 1	1	1	1	1
Wine 2	2	3	3	2
Wine 3	3	3	3	3
Wine 4	6	6	6	6
Wine 5	6	5	5	6
Wine 6	2	2	2	2
Wine 7	8	9	9	9
Wine 8	9	9	9	8

Case J	Judge 1	Judge 2	Judge 3	Judge 4
Wine 1	1	3	5	8
Wine 2	2	3	5	9
Wine 3	3	3	6	9
Wine 4	1	2	6	7
Wine 5	1	2	5	9
Wine 6	1	2	5	9
Wine 7	2	3	4	9
Wine 8	3	1	5	8

Kendall's W Measure of Concordance Inter-rater Reliability Test (With or Without Ties)

Another test for the inter-rater reliability is the Kendall's W measure, which can be run with ties or without ties. A tie means there are multiple data points with the same value, and hence, we must split the difference between these ties. Regardless, the null hypothesis for these tests is that there is zero agreement (W = 0) among all the judges.

Case K returns a calculated Kendall's W = 1.1068, Kendall's R = 1.124646, and p-value = 0.0000. We reject the null hypothesis and conclude that there is agreement among the judges. For instance, we see that Issue 1 is critical for all judges, whereas Issues 3, 7, and 8 are rated lower. All ratings are consistent among all the judges.

In Case L, Kendall's W = 0.2261, Kendall's R = 0.0971, and p-value = 0.1352. This indicates that we cannot reject the null hypothesis and conclude that there is no statistical concordance among the different respondents answering the survey questions.

Finally, in Case M, Kendall's W = 0.0028, Kendall's R = -0.1633, and p-value = 0.9999. This certainly indicates extremely low consistency and reliability among the respondents.

Case K	Issue 1	Issue 2	Issue 3	Issue 4	Issue 5	Issue 6	Issue 7	Issue 8
Judge 1	8	8	2	5	3	5	2	1
Judge 2	8	7	2	6	3	5	1	1
Judge 3	8	7	2	5	3	6	2	1
Judge 4	8	7	3	5	2	5	1	2
Judge 5	8	7	2	6	3	5	1	2
Judge 6	8	8	2	5	3	6	1	2
Judge 7	7	7	3	5	2	5	2	1

Case L	Q1	Q2	Q3	Q4	Q1	Q2	Q3	Q4
Person 1	7	8	5	4	1	7	2	1
Person 2	1	7	10	6	2	6	3	1
Person 3	3	1	7	10	3	5	10	1
Person 4	10	3	1	5	4	4	10	2
Person 5	3	2	1	1	5	3	1	4.5
Person 6	2	6	7.5	2.5	6	2	5	2.5
Person 7	6	10	4	8	7	1	6	1

Case M	Issue 1	Issue 2	Issue 3	Issue 4	Issue 5	Issue 6	Issue 7	Issue 8
Judge 1	5	5	5	5	5	5	5	5
Judge 2	8	8	8	8	7	8	7	8
Judge 3	1	1	1	2	2	1	1	1
Judge 4	5	5	5	5	5	5	5	5
Judge 5	6	7	6	7	6	7	6	7
Judge 6	9	9	9	9	9	9	9	9
Judge 7	2	1	2	2	3	2	2	1

Data Diversity with Shannon, Brillouin, and Simpson Diversity and Homogeneity Test

Another issue with regards to data reliability and consistency pertains to the randomized and stratified sampling that is performed. For instance, we may get a high level of data consistency and reliability but if the people sampled are from the same group or category, then the data may not be entirely reliable. As an example, suppose we wish to survey voter sentiment on a particular issue in a state. If all the voters selected were Democrats or predominantly Republicans, then the data might be skewed one way. Hence, to test for the diversity of a randomized and stratified sampling group, we can apply the Shannon, Brillouin, and Simpson model. In Case N, suppose we have five categories of self-described voters (highly conservative, conservative, moderate, liberal, and highly liberal) and the data grid shows the number of people sampled within each category. The following shows the results of the four samples. The higher the diversity index is to the maximum index, the higher the level of diversity. Clearly, we see that Scenario 1 has the highest homogeneity score and the diversity index is closest to the maximum index value. Scenario 2 has a 94.71% homogeneity score, while Scenarios 3 and 4 have the lowest diversity index relative to the maximum value.

Case N	Scenario 1	Scenario 2	Scenario 3	Scenario 4
Category A	5	5	1	11
Category B	5	8	1	11
Category C	5	6	21	1
Category D	5	2	1	1
Category E	5	4	1	1

Sample 1 Results	Shannon	Brillouin	Simpson
Diversity Index	1.6094	0.5918	0.2000
Max Index	1.6094	0.5918	
Homogeneity	1.0000	1.0000	

Sample 2 Results	Shannon	Brillouin	Simpson
Diversity Index	1.5243	0.5587	0.2320
Max Index	1.6094	0.5918	
Homogeneity	0.9471	0.9441	

Sample 3 Results	Shannon	Brillouin	Simpson
Diversity Index	0.6615	0.2193	0.7120
Max Index	1.6094	0.5918	
Homogeneity	0.4110	0.3706	

Sample 4 Results	Shannon	Brillouin	Simpson
Diversity Index	1.1087	0.3995	0.3920
Max Index	1.6094	0.5918	
Homogeneity	0.6889	0.6751	

Internal Validity

A related issue is that of model validity. When we discuss the validity of a model, we typically mean if the specified model does what it is intended to do. In other words, does the model actually model what we are looking to model? To answer the question, we look at the internal validity of a model and its external validity.

The internal validity of a model, such as a multivariate regression, looks at whether the independent variables used are statistically significant; that is, are the internal constructs of the model valid? We typically use the p-value of a regression to measure this internal validity. The null hypothesis tested is that each of the independent variables has zero effect on the dependent variable. Hence, low p-values, at or below the alpha significance level, imply that it is statistically significant and impacts the dependent variable. Hence, a model with only significant independent variables is deemed internally valid.

	Coeff	Std. Error	T-stat	**P-value**	Lower 5%	Upper 95%
Intercept	57.95550	108.79014	0.53273	0.59690	-161.29661	277.20762
VAR X1	-0.00354	0.00352	-1.00656	0.31965	-0.01064	0.00355
VAR X2	0.46437	0.25353	1.83159	**0.01379**	-0.04659	0.97533
VAR X3	25.23770	14.11723	1.78772	**0.02071**	-3.21371	53.68911
VAR X4	-0.00856	0.10156	-0.08433	0.93317	-0.21325	0.19612
VAR X5	16.55792	14.79957	1.11881	**0.03929**	-13.26866	46.38449

External Validity

A statistically significant and internally valid model may or may not have practical significance. This is where external validity comes in. While internal validity looks at the individual constructs of the model, external validity looks at the entire model and measures how much that model may explain the predicted variable. Typically, external validity is measured using a variety of error formulae. The typical measure is the R-square and adjusted R-square (the coefficient of determination and adjusted coefficient of determination). The R-square is simply the linear correlation (R) between the actual and predicted values, squared. While R has a domain between −1.00 and +1.00, its squared value will always lie between 0.00 and 1.00. Hence, the R-square is a percentage measure, which shows how much of the variation of the dependent variable can be explained simultaneously by all of the independent variables in the model. The higher the R-square, the higher the external validity of the model. However, in multivariate models, adding additional exogenous variables that may or may not be internally valid will usually increase the R-square value. This is where the adjusted R-square comes in. The adjusted R-square will adjust for the added independent variables and penalizes the R-square for having too many independent variables that do not statistically significantly increase the R-square sufficiently. This means that with added extraneous variables, the adjusted R-square may actually decline, making it a more conservative and better estimate of a model's external validity.

In addition, along the lines of penalizing added variables, where holding everything else constant, if the predictive powers of two models are identical but one uses fewer predictor variables, then the more parsimonious model wins out. Based on the theory of parsimony and penalization of too many extraneous variables, other measures of external validity were created, such as the Akaike Information Criterion or the Bayes–Schwarz Criterion. These are relative measures of external model errors and are typically used to compare different model specifications to identify the lower error scores. The following are additional external validity error measures. Those denoted with an asterisk * are values that we would rather see increase, versus the remaining error measures where the lower the error, the higher the external validity of the model.

*R-Squared
*Adjusted R-Squared
*Maximum Likelihood

Akaike Information Criterion (AIC)
Bayes and Schwarz Criterion (BSC)
Hannan–Quinn Criterion (HQC)
Mean Absolute Deviation (MAD)
Mean Absolute Percentage Error (MAPE)
Mean Squared Error (MSE)

Median Absolute Error (MdAE)
Median Absolute Percentage Error (MdAPE)
Root Mean Square Log Error (RMSLE)
Root Mean Square Percentage Error Loss (RMSPE)
Root Mean Squared Error (RMSE)
Root Median Square Percentage Error Loss (RMdSPE)
Sum of Squared Errors (SSE)
Symmetrical Mean Absolute Percentage Error (sMAPE)
Theil's U1 Accuracy (U1)
Theil's U2 Quality (U2)

Predictability and Accuracy: Akaike, Bayes, Hannan–Quinn, Diebold–Mariano, Pesaran–Timmermann

Another concept in data and modeling is that of predictability and accuracy. Multiple methods can be used to measure the accuracy of a predictive model. As previously mentioned, in a multivariate regression setting, we can use the R-square, Akaike Information Criterion, Bayes–Schwarz Criterion and others. As an example, suppose we are comparing between two models' accuracy. One simple way is to look at the model predicted values and compare them against the historical actuals. The difference would constitute the model's prediction errors. The following shows two example sets of errors. We can see that model 2's errors are a lot smaller than model 1's errors. The computed results using BizStats' Forecast Accuracy model shows that the second model has a lot lower errors and is, therefore, the preferred model with a higher level of accuracy.

Even if the two models show a different level of forecast accuracy, the next question is whether the two forecasts are statistically significantly different from one another. The Diebold–Mariano Test of Forecast Differences and the Harvey, Leybourne, and Newbold Test allow us to determine if the errors are statistically significant. The null hypothesis tested is that there is no significant difference between the two forecasts. Finally, sometimes the exact forecast accuracy is not in question. Rather, it is the ability to predict directional change that is critical. The Pesaran–Timmerman tests for whether a model can adequately predict and track the directional changes over time. The null hypothesis tested is that the forecast does not track directional changes in the data.

Errors 1	Errors 2
221.4876	0.112161248
-120.1243	0.535868655
88.6704	0.635762518
...	...
...	...
-174.1671	0.234313273
-36.3149	0.530179776

```
Error Measures for Model 1
Maximum Log-Likelihood: -318.173405
Akaike Info Criterion (AIC): 12.926936
AIC Correction (AICC): 15.593603
Bayes and Schwarz Criterion (BSC): 13.118139
Hannan-Quinn Criterion (HQC): 12.999747
Mean Absolute Deviation (MAD): 114.467810
Mean Squared Errors (MSE): 19713.503554
Root Mean Squared Error (RMSE): 140.404785

Error Measures for Model 2
Maximum Log-Likelihood: -41.017947
Akaike Info Criterion (AIC): 1.840718
AIC Correction (AICC): 4.507385
Bayes and Schwarz Criterion (BSC): 2.031920
Hannan-Quinn Criterion (HQC): 1.913529
Mean Absolute Deviation (MAD): 0.475521
Mean Squared Errors (MSE): 0.302051
Root Mean Squared Error (RMSE): 0.549592
```

$$\text{Normal } N(\mu, \sigma): f(x|\mu, \sigma) = \frac{1}{\sqrt{2\pi\sigma^2}} exp\left[-\frac{(x-\mu)^2}{2\sigma^2}\right]$$

$$f[N_{iid} \text{ of } N(\mu, \sigma)] = \prod_{i=1}^{n} f(x_i|\mu_i, \sigma_i) = \left[\frac{1}{\sqrt{2\pi\sigma^2}}\right]^{n/2} exp\left[-\frac{\sum_{i=1}^{n}(x-\mu)^2}{2\sigma^2}\right]$$

$$\text{General Log-Likelihood: } \ln[L(\mu, \sigma)] = -\frac{n}{2}\ln(2\pi\sigma^2) - \frac{1}{2\sigma^2}\sum_{i=1}^{n}(x_i - \mu)^2$$

$$\text{OLS Log-Likelihood: } \ln[L(\mu=0, \sigma=1)] = -\frac{n}{2}\ln(2\pi) - \frac{n}{2}ln\left[\frac{SE}{n}\right] - \frac{n}{2}$$

$$MLE = -\frac{1}{2}N\ln(2\pi) - \left(\frac{N}{2}\right)ln\left(\frac{SE}{N}\right) - \frac{N}{2} = -\frac{1}{2}N\left(ln\left(\frac{2\pi SE}{N}\right) + 1\right)$$

$$AIC = \frac{-2MLE + 2K}{N} = ln\left(\frac{2\pi SE}{N}\right) + \left(\frac{2K + N}{N}\right)$$

$$BIC = \frac{-2MLE + Kln(N)}{N} = ln\left(\frac{2\pi SE}{N}\right) + \frac{Kln(N) + N}{N}$$

$$HQ = \frac{-2MLE + 2Kln[ln(N)]}{N} = ln\left(\frac{2\pi SE}{N}\right) + \frac{2Kln[ln(N)] + N}{N}$$

Grubbs Test for Outliers & Mahalanobis Distance

Outliers, as discussed, will impact the validity and consistency of your data. The Grubbs test for outliers is used to test the null hypothesis that all the values are from the same normal population without any outliers. In other words, if we fail to reject the null hypothesis, we can safely state that there are no outliers. To illustrate, suppose we have the two variables below, each with 11 data points. Notice that VAR1 has a clear outlier (bold value, 3).

> VAR1: 145, 125, 190, 135, 220, 130, 210, **3**, 165, 165, 150

> VAR2: 145, 125, 190, 135, 220, 130, 210, **203**, 165, 165, 150

When we run Grubb's test in BizStats, the results are shown below. We see that for VAR1, the Grubbs statistic for the smallest data point (i.e., 3) exceeds the critical values of all three alpha significance values, indicating that we can reject the null hypothesis and conclude that the value 3 is, indeed, a statistical outlier. In contrast, VAR2's results indicate a Grubbs statistic under the critical limits, which means we cannot reject the null hypothesis and we have to conclude that the data does not have any statistical outliers.

A related test is the Mahalanobis Distance, that measures the distance between point X and a distribution Y, based on multidimensional generalizations of the number of standard deviations X is away from the average of Y. This multidimensional Mahalanobis distance is equivalent to standard Euclidean distance. The null hypothesis tested is that there are no outliers in each of the data rows.

Grubbs Test for Outliers:	VAR1	VAR2
Grubbs Stat (Smallest Data):	**2.523906**	1.245483
Grubbs Stat (Largest Data):	1.229716	1.565597
G Critical @ 0.01:	2.484279	2.484279
G Critical @ 0.05:	2.233908	2.233908
G Critical @ 0.10:	2.088014	2.088014
Minimum:	3.000000	125.0000
Average:	148.9090	167.0909
Maximum:	220.0000	220.0000
Outlier Tested:	3.000000	220.0000

Null: All data values are from the same normal population (no outliers)

Linear & Quadratic Discriminant Analysis

Linear Discriminant Analysis is related to ANOVA and multivariate regression analysis, which attempt to model one dependent variable as a linear combination of other independent variables. Discriminant analysis typically has multiple continuous independent variables and a single categorical dependent variable. The Quadratic Discriminant Analysis is the nonlinear counterpart, where we assume there are nonlinear combinations of the independent variables that best explain the dependent variable.

As an illustration, the following shows part of a dataset used in BizStats, where the dependent variable is the categorical variable. For example, each row may constitute an individual, where the Category may be something like Agree, Neutral, and Agree, while the independent predictor variables X1 to X3 may be years of education, knowledge of the product, experience using the product, and so forth.

In the results, the "True Group" versus "Put into Group" matrix illustrates that, statistically, 68 individuals who should be categorized as Group 1 are indeed put into this group in the raw data, with 13 and 4 others incorrectly put into groups 2 and 3, respectively. This indicates an 80% accuracy. For groups 2 and 3, the grouping accuracy is 72% and 76%, respectively. The linear discriminant function shows that variable X2 (1.2406 and 1.0380 are the highest factors) has the highest impact on whether an individual is in Group 1 and 2, while variable X3 (1.1057 is the highest factor) has the highest impact on whether individuals should be in Group 3. Using this method, certain types of data can be tested to see how the statistically predicted groupings match up against the actual group membership, as an additional layer of data validity checking.

Linear & Quadratic Discriminant Analysis

Category	X1	X2	X3
VAR1	VAR2	VAR3	VAR4
1	10	22	25
1	14	17	66
1	19	33	77
...	...	...	...
...	...	...	...
2	14	29	12
2	14	25	37
...	...	...	...
...	...	...	...
3	20	25	12
3	16	18	48

Model Inputs:
VAR1
VAR2; VAR3; VAR4

Linear Discriminant Analysis (LDA)

Group	1	2	3
Count	85	93	66
Prior	0.3484	0.3811	0.2705

Classification Results

		True Group	
Put into Group	1	2	3
1	**68**	16	3
2	**13**	67	13
3	**4**	10	50
Total N	85	93	66
N Correct	68	67	50
Proportion	**0.8000**	**0.7204**	**0.7576**

N: 244
N Correct: 185
Proportion Correct: 0.758197

VAR	1	2	3
Global Mean Vector	15.6393	20.6762	10.5902

	Linear Discriminant Function for Groups		
Betas Group 1	0.6263	**1.2406**	0.6865
Intercept1	-23.0975		
Betas Group 2	0.9966	**1.0380**	0.7956
Intercept2	-25.2063		
Betas Group 3	0.8427	0.7221	**1.1057**
Intercept3	-20.7715		

Principal Component Analysis

Principal Component Analysis is related to another method called Factor Analysis. Principal component analysis makes multivariate data easier to model and summarize. Figure 15.27 illustrates an example where we start with 9 independent variables that are unlikely to be independent of one another, such that changing the value of one variable will change another variable. Recall that this multicollinearity effect can cause biases in a multiple regression model. Both principal component and factor analysis can help identity and eventually replace the original independent variables with a new set of smaller variables that are less than the original but are uncorrelated to one another, while, at the same time, each of these new variables is a linear combination of the original variables. This means most of the variation can be accounted for by using fewer explanatory variables. Similarly, factor analysis is used to analyze interrelationships within large numbers of variables and simplifying said factors into a smaller number of common factors. The method condenses information contained in the original set of variables into a smaller set of implicit factor variables with minimal loss of information. The analysis is related to the principal component analysis by using the correlation matrix and applying principal component analysis coupled with a varimax matrix rotation to simplify the factors.

In the next slide, we start with an example of 9 independent variables, which means the factor analysis or principal component analysis results will return a 9×9 matrix of eigenvectors, and 9 eigenvalues. Typically, we are only interested in components with eigenvalues > 1. Hence, in the results, we are only interested in the first three or four factors or components (some researchers would plot these eigenvalues and call it a scree plot, which can be useful for identifying where the kinks are in the eigenvalues). Notice that the fourth factor (the fourth column in the figure) returns a cumulative proportion of 72.31%. This means that using these four factors will explain approximately three-quarters of the variation in all the independent factors themselves. Next, we look at the absolute values of the eigenvalue matrix. It seems that variables 2, 3, 7, and 8 can be combined into a new variable in factor 1, variables 1 and 9 as the second factor, variable 6 by itself as the third factor, and variable 4 by itself as a new variable. This can be done separately and outside of principal component analysis.

Principal Component Analysis

Model Inputs:
VAR105; VAR106; VAR107; VAR108; VAR109; VAR110; VAR111; VAR112; VAR113
Factor Analysis: Eigenvalues and Eigenvectors

Eigenvalue	2.8804	1.4387	1.1639	1.0245	0.7052	0.6476	0.5624	0.3452	0.2321
Proportion	0.3200	0.1599	0.1293	0.1138	0.0258	0.0384	0.0784	0.0720	0.0625
Cum Proportion	0.3200	0.4799	0.6092	0.7231	0.7488	0.7872	0.8656	0.9375	1.0000

Eigenvectors	Factor 1	Factor 2	Factor 3	Factor 4	Factor 5	Factor 6	Factor 7	Factor 8	Factor 9
VAR1	0.1087	-0.6392	0.2573	0.1138	-0.4171	0.0959	0.4808	0.2842	0.0724
VAR2	-0.4116	0.2531	0.1811	-0.2616	-0.3396	-0.0000	0.4365	-0.5925	0.0914
VAR3	-0.4443	-0.2907	0.1873	-0.3022	-0.0301	0.1325	-0.3009	0.0640	-0.6918
VAR4	-0.2156	-0.1355	0.1829	0.8396	-0.0282	0.0082	-0.2214	-0.3788	-0.0578
VAR5	-0.3407	-0.0368	-0.4196	0.1560	0.4236	0.5599	0.4245	0.0882	-0.0352
VAR6	-0.1766	-0.0253	-0.7145	0.0630	-0.6325	-0.0296	-0.2161	0.0730	0.0257
VAR7	-0.4815	-0.1996	0.1803	-0.1644	0.0891	0.0992	-0.3614	0.1678	0.7016
VAR8	-0.4053	-0.0294	-0.1076	0.1162	0.2150	-0.7828	0.2818	0.2591	-0.0651
VAR9	-0.1776	0.6179	0.3190	0.2312	-0.2744	0.1903	0.0417	0.5587	-0.0782

Dr. Johnathan Mun, Professor of Research
Quantitative Research Methods Course Slides
Seventh Edition, 2026, ROV Press

MULTIVARIATE ANALYTICS

OPTIMIZATION PROFILE

18:45 PM

AI Machine Learning

9. Multiple Regression and Multivariate Methods

ECONOMETRIC MODELING

FORECASTING

01.12.2022   05.12.2022

Linear, Nonlinear, Bivariate, and Multivariate Regression

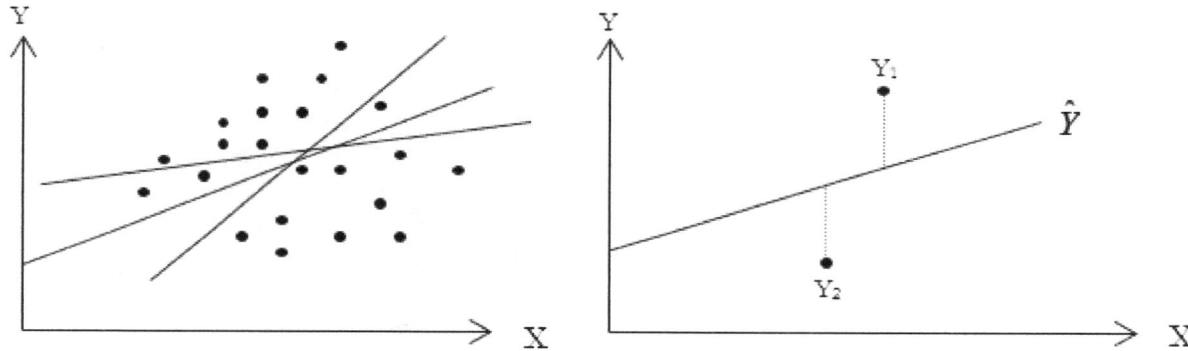

$$Y_i = \beta_1 + \beta_2 X_{2,i} + \beta_3 X_{3,i} + \varepsilon_i$$

$$Min \sum_{i=1}^{n} (Y_i - \hat{Y}_i)^2$$

$$\frac{d}{d\beta_0} \sum_{i=1}^{n} (Y_i - \hat{Y}_i)^2 = 0 \ \ and \ \ \frac{d}{d\beta_1} \sum_{i=1}^{n} (Y_i - \hat{Y}_i)^2 = 0$$

$$\beta_1 = \frac{\sum_{i=1}^{n}(X_i - \bar{X})(Y_i - \bar{Y})}{\sum_{i=1}^{n}(X_i - \bar{X})^2} = \frac{\sum_{i=1}^{n} X_i Y_i - \frac{\sum_{i=1}^{n} X_i \sum_{i=1}^{n} Y_i}{n}}{\sum_{i=1}^{n} X_i^2 - \frac{\left(\sum_{i=1}^{n} X_i\right)^2}{n}}$$

$$\hat{\beta}_2 = \frac{\sum Y_i X_{2,i} \sum X_{3,i}^2 - \sum Y_i X_{3,i} \sum X_{2,i} X_{3,i}}{\sum X_{2,i}^2 \sum X_{3,i}^2 - \left(\sum X_{2,i} X_{3,i}\right)^2}$$

$$\hat{\beta}_3 = \frac{\sum Y_i X_{3,i} \sum X_{2,i}^2 - \sum Y_i X_{2,i} \sum X_{2,i} X_{3,i}}{\sum X_{2,i}^2 \sum X_{3,i}^2 - \left(\sum X_{2,i} X_{3,i}\right)^2}$$

$$\beta_0 = \bar{Y} - \beta_1 \bar{X}$$

Linear, Nonlinear, Bivariate, and Multivariate Regression

Multiple Regression Analysis Data Set

Aggravated Assault	Bachelor's Degree	Police Expenditure Per Capita	Population in Millions	Population Density (Persons/Sq Mile)	Unemployment Rate
521	18308	185	4.041	79.6	7.2
367	1148	600	0.55	1	8.5
443	18068	372	3.665	32.3	5.7
365	7729	142	2.351	45.1	7.3
614	100484				
385	16728				
286	14630				
397	4008				
764	38927				
427	22322				
153	3711				
231	3136				
524	50508				
328	28886				
240	16996				
286	13035				
285	12973				
569	16309				
96	5227				
498	19235				
481	44487				
468	44213				
177	23619				
198	9106				
458	24917				
108	3872				
246	8945				
291	2373				
68	7128				
311	23624	349	7.73	1042	6.6

Multiple Regression Analysis

Multiple Regression Analysis can be used to run linear regressions with multiple independent variables. These variables can be applied through a series of lags or nonlinear transformations, or regressed in a stepwise fashion starting with the most correlated variable.

Multivariate Regression Y = F(X)

Dependent Variable: Aggravated Assault

☑ Aggravated Assault	☑ Bachelor's Degree	☑ Police Expenditure Per Capita	☑ Popu
521	18308	185	4.041
367	1148	600	0.55
443	18068	372	3.665
365	7729	142	2.351
614	100484	432	29.76
385	16728	290	3.294
286	14630	346	3.287
397	4008	328	0.666

Options

☐ Lag Regressors [1] Period(s)   ☐ Nonlinear Regression

☐ Stepwise Correlation Method   ☐ Show All Steps   OK

p-Value: 0.1   Cancel

Bootstrap Simulation

Linear, Nonlinear, Bivariate, and Multivariate Regression

Regression Analysis Report

Regression Statistics

R-Squared (Coefficient of Determination)	0.3272
Adjusted R-Squared	0.2508
Multiple R (Multiple Correlation Coefficient)	0.5720
Standard Error of the Estimates (SEy)	149.6720
Number of Observations	50

The R-Squared or Coefficient of Determination indicates that 0.33 of the variation in the dependent variable can be explained and accounted for by the independent variables in this regression analysis. However, in a multiple regression, the Adjusted R-Squared takes into account the existence of additional independent variables or regressors and adjusts this R-Squared value to a more accurate view of the regression's explanatory power. Hence, only 0.25 of the variation in the dependent variable can be explained by the regressors.

The Multiple Correlation Coefficient (Multiple R) measures the correlation between the actual dependent variable (Y) and the estimated or fitted (Y) based on the regression equation. This is also the square root of the Coefficient of Determination (R-Squared).

The Standard Error of the Estimates (SEy) describes the dispersion of data points above and below the regression line or plane. This value is used as part of the calculation to obtain the confidence interval of the estimates later.

Regression Results

	Intercept	Bachelor's Degree	Police Expenditure Per Capita	Population in Millions	Population Density (Persons/Sq Mile)	Unemployment Rate
Coefficients	57.9555	-0.0035	0.4644	25.2377	-0.0086	16.5579
Standard Error	108.7901	0.0035	0.2535	14.1172	0.1016	14.7996
t-Statistic	0.5327	-1.0066	1.8316	1.7877	-0.0843	1.1188
p-Value	0.5969	0.3197	0.0738	0.0807	0.9332	0.2693
Lower 5%	-161.2966	-0.0106	-0.0466	-3.2137	-0.2132	-13.2687
Upper 95%	277.2076	0.0036	0.9753	53.6891	0.1961	46.3845

Degrees of Freedom

		Hypothesis Test	
Degrees of Freedom for Regression	5	Critical t-Statistic (99% confidence with df of 44)	2.6923
Degrees of Freedom for Residual	44	Critical t-Statistic (95% confidence with df of 44)	2.0154
Total Degrees of Freedom	49	Critical t-Statistic (90% confidence with df of 44)	1.6802

The Coefficients provide the estimated regression intercept and slopes. For instance, the coefficients are estimates of the true; population b values in the following regression equation Y = b0 + b1X1 + b2X2 + ... + bnXn. The Standard Error measures how accurate the predicted Coefficients are, and the t-Statistics are the ratios of each predicted Coefficient to its Standard Error.

The t-Statistic is used in hypothesis testing, where we set the null hypothesis (Ho) such that the real mean of the Coefficient = 0, and the alternate hypothesis (Ha) such that the real mean of the Coefficient is not equal to 0. A t-test is is performed and the calculated t-Statistic is compared to the critical values at the relevant Degrees of Freedom for Residual. The t-test is very important as it calculates if each of the coefficients is statistically significant in the presence of the other regressors. This means that the t-test statistically verifies whether a regressor or independent variable should remain in the regression or it should be dropped.

The Coefficient is statistically significant if its calculated t-Statistic exceeds the Critical t-Statistic at the relevant degrees of freedom (df). The three main confidence levels used to test for significance are 90%, 95% and 99%. If a Coefficient's t-Statistic exceeds the Critical level, it is considered statistically significant. Alternatively, the p-Value calculates each t-Statistic's probability of occurrence, which means that the smaller the p-Value, the more significant the Coefficient. The usual significant levels for the p-Value are 0.01, 0.05, and 0.10, corresponding to the 99%, 95%, and 90% confidence levels.

The Coefficients with their p-Values highlighted in blue indicate that they are statistically significant at the 90% confidence or 0.10 alpha level, while those highlighted in red indicate that they are not statistically significant at any other alpha levels.

Analysis of Variance

	Sums of Squares	Mean of Squares	F-Statistic	p-Value	Hypothesis Test	
Regression	479388.49	95877.70	4.28	0.0029	Critical F-statistic (99% confidence with df of 5 and 44)	3.4651
Residual	985675.19	22401.71			Critical F-statistic (95% confidence with df of 5 and 44)	2.4270
Total	1465063.68				Critical F-statistic (90% confidence with df of 5 and 44)	1.9828

The Analysis of Variance (ANOVA) table provides an F-test of the regression model's overall statistical significance. Instead of looking at individual regressors as in the t-test, the F-test looks at all the estimated Coefficients' statistical properties. The F-Statistic is calculated as the ratio of the Regression's Mean of Squares to the Residual's Mean of Squares. The numerator measures how much of the regression is explained, while the denominator measures how much is unexplained. Hence, the larger the F-Statistic, the more significant the model. The corresponding p-Value is calculated to test the null hypothesis (Ho) where all the Coefficients are simultaneously equal to zero, versus the alternate hypothesis (Ha) that they are all simultaneously different from zero, indicating a significant overall regression model. If the p-Value is smaller than the 0.01, 0.05, or 0.10 alpha significance, then the regression is significant. The same approach can be applied to the F-Statistic by comparing the calculated F-Statistic with the critical F values at various significance levels.

Forecasting

Period	Actual (Y)	Forecast (F)	Error (E)
1	521.0000	299.5124	221.4876
2	367.0000	487.1243	(120.1243)
3	443.0000	353.2789	89.7211
4	365.0000	276.3296	88.6704
5	614.0000	776.1336	(162.1336)
6	385.0000	298.9993	86.0007
7	286.0000	354.8718	(68.8718)
8	397.0000	312.6155	84.3845
9	764.0000	529.7550	234.2450
10	427.0000	347.7034	79.2966
11	153.0000	266.2526	(113.2526)
12	231.0000	264.6375	(33.6375)
13	524.0000	406.8009	117.1991
14	328.0000	272.2226	55.7774
15	240.0000	231.7882	8.2118
16	286.0000	257.8862	28.1138
17	285.0000	314.9521	(29.9521)
18	569.0000	335.3140	233.6860
19	96.0000	282.0356	(186.0356)
20	498.0000	370.2062	127.7938
21	481.0000	340.8742	140.1258
22	468.0000	427.5118	40.4882
23	177.0000	274.5298	(97.5298)
24	198.0000	294.7795	(96.7795)
25	458.0000	295.2180	162.7820

RMSE: 140.4048

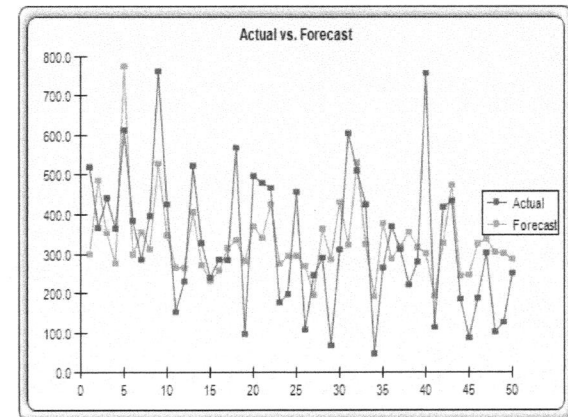
Actual vs. Forecast

Example: Given the following sales amounts ($ millions) and advertising sizes (measured as linear inches by summing up all the sides of an ad) for a local newspaper, answer the following questions.

Advertising size (inch)	12	18	24	30	36	42	48
Sales ($ millions)	5.9	5.6	5.5	7.2	8.0	7.7	8.4

(a) Which is the dependent variable and which is the independent variable?
   The independent variable is advertising size, whereas the dependent variable is sales.

(b) Manually calculate the slope (β_1) and the intercept (β_0) terms.

X	Y	XY	X^2	Y^2
12	5.9	70.8	144	34.81
18	5.6	100.8	324	31.36
24	5.5	132.0	576	30.25
30	7.2	216.0	900	51.84
36	8.0	288.0	1296	64.00
42	7.7	323.4	1764	59.29
48	8.4	403.2	2304	70.56
$\Sigma(X)=210$	$\Sigma(Y)=48.3$	$\Sigma(XY)=1534.2$	$\Sigma(X^2)=7308$	$\Sigma(Y^2)=342.11$

$$\beta_1 = \frac{1534.2 - \dfrac{210(48.3)}{7}}{7308 - \dfrac{210^2}{7}} = 0.0845 \quad and \quad \beta_0 = \frac{48.3}{7} - 0.0845\left[\frac{210}{7}\right] = 4.3643$$

(c) What is the estimated regression equation?
   $Y = 4.3643 + 0.0845X$ or Sales $= 4.3643 + 0.0845$(Size)

(d) What would the level of sales be if we purchase a 28-inch ad?
   $Y = 4.3643 + 0.0845 (28) = \$6.73$ million dollars in sales

Note that we only predict or forecast and cannot say for certain. This is only an expected value or on average.

The R-squared (R^2), or coefficient of determination, is an error measurement that looks at the percent variation of the dependent variable that can be explained by the variation in the independent variable for a regression analysis. The coefficient of determination can be calculated by:

$$R^2 = 1 - \frac{\sum_{i=1}^{n}(Y_i - \hat{Y}_i)^2}{\sum_{i=1}^{n}(Y_i - \bar{Y})^2} = 1 - \frac{SSE}{TSS}$$

where the coefficient of determination is one less the ratio of the sums of squares of the errors (SSE) to the total sums of squares (TSS). In other words, the ratio of SSE to TSS is the unexplained portion of the analysis, thus, one less the ratio of SSE to TSS is the explained portion of the regression analysis.

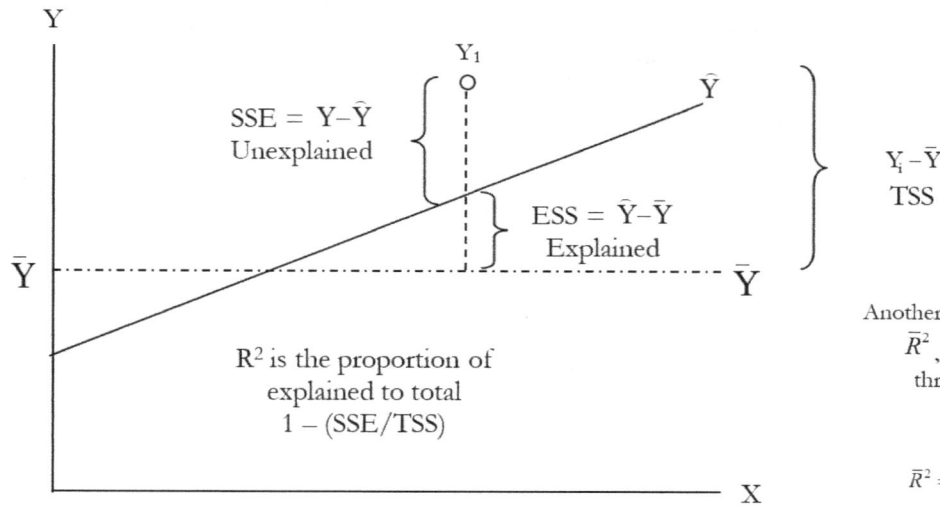

SSE = Y−$\hat{Y}$ Unexplained

ESS = $\hat{Y}$−$\bar{Y}$ Explained

$Y_i - \bar{Y}$ TSS

R^2 is the proportion of explained to total
1 − (SSE/TSS)

Another related statistic, the adjusted coefficient of determination, or the adjusted R-squared $\bar{R}^2$, corrects for the number of independent variables (k) in a multivariate regression through a degrees of freedom correction to provide a more conservative estimate:

$$\bar{R}^2 = 1 - \frac{\sum_{i=1}^{n}(Y_i - \hat{Y}_i)^2 / (k-2)}{\sum_{i=1}^{n}(Y_i - \bar{Y})^2 / (k-1)} = 1 - \frac{SSE / (k-2)}{TSS / (k-1)}$$

The adjusted R-squared should be used instead of the regular R-squared in multivariate regressions because every time an independent variable is added into the regression analysis, the R-squared will increase; indicating that the percent variation explained has increased. This increase occurs even when nonsensical regressors are added. The adjusted R-squared takes the added regressors into account and penalizes the regression accordingly, providing a much better estimate of a regression model's goodness-of-fit.

Regression Statistics

R-Squared (Coefficient of Determination)	0.8146
Adjusted R-Squared	0.7776
Multiple R (Multiple Correlation Coefficient)	0.9026
Standard Error of the Estimates (SEy)	0.5725
Number of Observations	7

Regression Results

	Intercept	Ad Size
Coefficients	4.3643	0.0845
Standard Error	0.5826	0.0180
t-Statistic	7.4911	4.6877
p-Value	0.0007	0.0054
Lower 5%	2.8667	0.0382
Upper 95%	5.8619	0.1309

ANOVA

	df	SS	MS	F	Significance F
Regression	1	7.2014	7.2014	21.9747	0.0054
Residual	5	1.6386	0.3277		
Total	6	8.8400			

	Coefficients	Standard Error	t Stat	P-value	Lower 95%	Upper 95%
Intercept	4.3643	0.5826	7.4911	0.0007	2.8667	5.8619
X Variable 1	0.0845	0.0180	4.6877	0.0054	0.0382	0.1309

Example: Given the information from the regression analysis output, interpret the following:

(a) Perform a hypothesis test on the slope and intercept to see if they are *each* significant at a two-tailed alpha (α) of 0.05. The null hypothesis H_0 is such that the slope $\beta_1 = 0$ and the alternate hypothesis H_a is such that $\beta_1 \neq 0$. The t-statistic calculated is 4.6877, which exceeds the t-critical (2.9687 obtained from the t-statistic table at the end of this book) for a two-tailed alpha of 0.05 and degrees of freedom $n - k = 7 - 1 = 6$.[36] Therefore, the null hypothesis is rejected, and one can state that the slope is statistically significantly different from 0, indicating that the regression's estimate of the slope is statistically significant. This hypothesis test can also be performed by looking at the t-statistic's corresponding p-value (0.0054), which is less than the alpha of 0.05, which means the null hypothesis is rejected. The hypothesis test is then applied to the intercept, where the null hypothesis H_0 is such that the intercept $\beta_0 = 0$ and the alternate hypothesis H_a is such that $\beta_0 \neq 0$. The t-statistic calculated is 7.4911, which exceeds the critical t value of 2.9687 for $n - k$ ($7 - 1 = 6$) degrees of freedom, so, the null hypothesis is rejected indicating that the intercept is statistically significantly different from 0, meaning that the regression's estimate of the intercept if statistically significant. The calculated p-value (0.0007) is also less than the alpha level, which means the null hypothesis is also rejected.

(b) Perform a hypothesis test to see if both the slope and intercept are significant as a whole. In other words, if the estimated model is statistically significant at an alpha (α) of 0.05. The simultaneous null hypothesis H_0 is such that $\beta_0 = \beta_1 = 0$ and the alternate hypothesis H_a is $\beta_0 \neq \beta_1 \neq 0$. The calculated F-value is 21.9747, which exceeds the critical F-value (5.99 obtained from the table at the end of this book) for k (1) degrees of freedom in the numerator and $n - k$ ($7 - 1 = 6$) degrees of freedom for the denominator, so the null hypothesis is rejected indicating that both the slope and intercept are simultaneously significantly different from 0 and that the model as a whole is statistically significant. This result is confirmed by the p-value of 0.0054 (significance of F), which is less than the alpha value, thereby rejecting the null hypothesis and confirming that the regression as a whole is statistically significant.

(c) Using Risk Simulator's regression output, interpret the R^2 value. How is it related to the correlation coefficient? The calculated R^2 is 0.8146, meaning that 81.46% of the variation in the dependent variable can be explained by the variation in the independent variable. The R^2 is simply the square of the correlation coefficient, that is, the correlation coefficient between the independent and dependent variable is 0.9026.

Manual Regression Calculations

Manual Computations of Simple Regression, Coefficients, Standard Errors, Akaike, Bayes, Schwarz, Hannan Quinn, R-Squared, Adjusted R-Squared, ANOVA for Regression, T-Stat, etc.

		SS Error:			SS Total:	SS Regression:
SUM	1192442.249	23513989216.42	80065082.16		1465063.68	272621.43
	SUM(O6:O55)	SUM(P6:P55)	SUM(Q6:Q55)		SUM(R6:R55)	SUM(S6:S55)

Left data / calculations

Y	X1	Label	Value	Formula
521	18308	N (Rows)	50	<< COUNTA(F6:F55)
367	1148	K (Variables)	2	<< COUNTA(F5:G5)
443	18068	Multiple R	0.43137	<< CORREL(F6:F55,N6:N55)
365	7729	R-Squared	0.18608	<< J8*J8
614	100484	Adj R-Squared	0.16912	<< 1-(((1-J9)*(J5-1))/(J5-J6))
385	16728	S.E. Estimates	157.61519	<< SQRT(P3/(J5-J6))
286	14630			
397	4008	Max Likelihood	-322.93420	<< -J5/2*LN(2*PI())-J5/2*LN(P3/J5)-J5/2
764	38927	Akaike Criterion	12.99737	<< -2*J13/J5+2*J6/J5
427	22322	Bayes and Schwarz	13.07385	<< -2*J13/J5+J6*LN(J5)/J5
153	3711	Hannan-Quinn	13.02649	<< -2*J13/J5+2*J6*LN(LN(J5))/J5
231	3136			
524	50508	Slope B1	0.00340	<< R3/Q3
328	28886	SE Slope	0.00103	<< J11/SQRT(Q3)
240	16996	T-Stat B1	3.31270	<< J18/J19
286	13035	P-value	0.00176	<< TDIST(J20,$I$5-$I$6,2)
285	12973	CI Lower B1	0.00134	<< J18-TINV(0.05,$I$5-$I$6)*J19
569	16309	CI Upper B1	0.00547	<< J18+TINV(0.05,$I$5-$I$6)*J19
96	5227			
498	19235	Intercept	258.14207	<< AVERAGE($E$6:$E$55)-J18*AVERAGE(G6:G55)
481	44487	SE Intercept Bo	31.50967	<< J11*(SQRT(1/J5+(AVERAGE(G6:G55)*AVERAGE(G6:G55)/Q3)
468	44213	T-Stat Bo	8.19247	<< J25/J26
177	23619	P-value	0.00000	<< TDIST(J27,$I$5-$I$6,2)
198	9106	CI Upper Bo	194.78764	<< J25-TINV(0.05,$I$5-$I$6)*J26
458	24917	CI Upper Bo	321.49651	<< J25+TINV(0.05,$I$5-$I$6)*J26
108	3872			
246	8945	DF Regression	1	<< J6-1
291	2373	DF Residual	48	<< J5-J6
68	7128	DF Total	49	<< J5-1
311	23624	SS Regression	272621.43	<< T3
606	5242	SS Residual	1192442.25	<< P3
512	92629	SS Total	1465063.68	<< S3
426	28795	MS Regression	272621.43	<< J35/J32
47	4487	MS Residual	24842.55	<< J36/J33
265	48799	F Statistic	10.97397	<< J38/J39
370	14067	P-value	0.00176	<< FDIST(J40,J32,J33)
312	12693	Eta-Square	0.18608	<< J35/J37
222	62184			
280	9153	MATRIX:		
759	14250		258.14207	<< =MMULT(MINVERSE(MMULT(TRANSPOSE(AD94:AE143),
114	3680		0.00340	AD94:AE143)),MMULT(TRANSPOSE(AD94:AE143),W94:W143))
419	18063			

Right computation table

Y Pred	Error	Error^2	(X - X Avg)^2	(X - X Avg)(Y - Y Avg)	(Y - Y Avg)^2	(Y Pred - Y Avg)^2
320.48	200.52	40207.96	11286509.01	-635221.82	35751.25	130.86
262.05	104.95	11014.29	421051521.81	-719825.46	1230.61	4881.68
319.66	123.34	15211.87	12956688.21	-399836.90	12338.77	150.22
284.46	80.54	6486.80	194282897.33	-461086.90	1094.29	2252.52
600.29	13.71	187.97	6212034366.93	22232547.04	79569.13	72022.39
315.10	69.90	4885.89	24399055.41	-262190.78	2817.49	282.88
307.96	-21.96	482.12	49526969.25	323163.84	2108.65	574.22
271.79	125.21	15677.72	311859353.01	-1149282.86	4235.41	3615.70
390.69	373.31	139361.53	297888959.49	7457467.48	186693.13	3453.73
334.15	92.85	8621.41	428317.89	62226.06	9040.21	4.97
270.78	-117.78	13871.66	322437328.77	3212784.14	32012.37	3738.34
268.82	-37.82	1430.36	343417974.77	1870203.02	10184.85	3981.59
430.12	93.88	8813.13	831772133.01	5539675.56	36894.73	9643.57
356.50	-28.50	812.18	52106164.77	-28296.36	15.37	604.12
316.01	-76.01	5778.04	21823285.97	429407.96	8449.29	253.02
302.53	-16.53	273.12	74520746.85	396406.24	2108.65	863.99
302.32	-17.32	299.81	75595025.81	407947.82	2201.49	876.45
313.67	255.33	65191.27	28713950.93	-1270402.66	56206.93	332.91
275.94	-179.94	32378.40	270291355.49	3878652.20	55658.25	3133.76
323.64	174.36	30402.38	5917250.85	-403996.24	27582.57	68.60
409.62	71.38	5095.07	520727754.69	3401925.10	22224.85	6037.32
408.69	59.31	3518.00	508297766.61	3067986.20	18517.77	5893.21
338.56	-161.56	26103.16	3808196.13	-302309.19	24000.21	44.15
289.15	-91.15	8307.91	157792287.17	1682241.44	17934.57	1829.45
342.98	115.02	13228.59	10558990.29	409691.92	15896.17	122.42
271.33	-163.33	26675.46	316681243.89	3984777.32	50140.17	3671.61
288.60	-42.60	1814.74	161863024.05	1093120.64	7382.25	1876.64
266.22	24.78	613.94	372279273.81	789532.58	1674.45	4316.21
282.41	-214.41	45972.89	211398223.41	3837275.40	69653.77	2450.95
338.58	-27.58	760.75	3827735.73	-40929.14	437.65	44.38
275.99	330.01	108905.89	269798364.29	-4501912.00	75119.85	3128.04
573.54	-61.54	3787.62	5035528805.33	12778739.72	32428.81	58381.97
356.19	69.81	4873.58	50800686.05	670551.44	8851.05	588.98
273.42	-226.42	51266.15	295170954.69	4895079.46	81179.41	3422.22
424.30	-159.30	25377.31	736116121.73	-1815637.30	4478.29	8534.54
306.04	63.96	4090.86	57768208.29	-289428.56	1450.09	669.77
301.36	10.64	113.17	80542368.21	178772.84	396.81	933.81
469.88	-247.88	61443.73	1641583530.93	-4453569.28	12082.41	19032.54
289.31	-9.31	86.64	156613711.41	649754.92	2695.69	1815.78
306.66	452.34	204608.50	55019899.65	-3167882.98	182397.33	637.90
270.67	-156.67	24546.26	323551595.25	3919844.72	47489.13	3751.26
319.65	99.35	9871.11	12992708.61	-313883.34	7582.93	150.64

Manual Regression Calculations with Matrices

OLS Residuals $\varepsilon_i = y_i - f(x_i, \beta)$ where $f(x_i, \beta) = \beta_0 + \beta_1 x$

Sums of Squares of Errors (Residuals) $SSE = \sum_{i=1}^{n} \varepsilon_i^2$

For multiple regressions, $f(x_i, \beta) = \sum_{j=1}^{m} \beta_j \phi_j(x)$

We set $X_{i,j} = \phi_j(x_i)$ for a dataset D, and Y, X dependent and independent variables

OLS Likelihood Function: $L(D, \beta) = \|X\beta - Y\|^2$

$\|X\beta - Y\|^2 = [X\beta - Y]'[X\beta - Y]$

$\|X\beta - Y\|^2 = Y'Y + \beta'X'X\beta - Y'X\beta - \beta'X'Y$

Minimizing Error $\dfrac{\delta L(D, \beta)}{\delta \beta} = \dfrac{\delta(Y'Y + \beta'X'X\beta - Y'X\beta - \beta'X'Y)}{\delta \beta} = 0$

$\dfrac{\delta L(D, \beta)}{\delta \beta} = -2X'Y + 2X'X\beta = 0$

Solving, we have $2X'Y = 2X'X\beta$ which means that $\beta = [X'X]^{-1}X'Y$

MMULT(MINVERSE(MMULT(TRANSPOSE(xmatrix), xmatrix)),
MMULT(TRANSPOSE(xmatrix), ymatrix))

	W	X	Y	Z	AA	AB	AC	AD	AE
84	MATRIX APPROACH:								
85	258.14207	<< =MMULT(MINVERSE(MMULT(TRANSPOSE(AD94:AE143),							
86	0.00340	AD94:AE143)),MMULT(TRANSPOSE(AD94:AE143),W94:W143))							
87									
88									
89	Using Excel:	0.43137	<< =CORREL(W94:W143,X94:X143)						
90	Correlation R	0.43137	<< =SUM(AA94:AA143)/SQRT(SUM(AB94:AB143)*SUM(AC94:AC143))						
91	R-Squared	0.18608	<< =Y90*Y90						
92									

	Y	Y Pred	Y-Mu	Y Pred - Mu	Product	Sq Y-Mu	Sq Y Pred - Mu	UNIT	X
93									
94	521	320.481	189.0800	-11.4392	-2162.93	35751.2	130.8559005	1	18308
95	367	262.051	35.0800	-69.8690	-2451	1230.61	4881.675636	1	1148
96	443	319.664	111.0800	-12.2564	-1361.44	12338.8	150.2199752	1	18068
97	365	284.459	33.0800	-47.4607	-1570	1094.29	2252.517892	1	7729
98	614	600.290	282.0800	268.3699	75701.8	79569.1	72022.38978	1	100484
99	385	315.101	53.0800	-16.8191	-892.759	2817.49	282.8828972	1	16728
100	286	307.957	-45.9200	-23.9628	1100.37	2108.65	574.2161864	1	14630
101	397	271.789	65.0800	-60.1307	-3913.31	4235.41	3615.700518	1	4008
102	764	390.688	432.0800	58.7684	25392.7	186693	3453.727633	1	38927
103	427	334.148	95.0800	2.2284	211.88	9040.21	4.965922002	1	22322
104	153	270.778	-178.9200	-61.1420	10939.5	32012.4	3738.341677	1	3711
105	231	268.820	-100.9200	-63.0999	6368.04	10184.8	3981.5915	1	3136
106	524	430.122	192.0800	98.2017	18862.6	36894.7	9643.57459	1	50508
107	328	356.499	-3.9200	24.5788	-96.3491	15.3664	604.1194055	1	28886
108	240	316.013	-91.9200	-15.9066	1462.13	8449.29	253.0194	1	16996
109	286	302.526	-45.9200	-29.3938	1349.76	2108.65	863.9942987	1	13035
110	285	302.315	-46.9200	-29.6049	1389.06	2201.49	876.4494999	1	12973
111	569	313.674	237.0800	-18.2458	-4325.72	56206.9	332.9098398	1	16309
112	96	275.940	-235.9200	-55.9800	13206.8	55658.2	3133.760731	1	5227
113	498	323.637	166.0800	-8.2828	-1375.61	27582.6	68.6046667	1	19235
114	481	409.620	149.0800	77.7002	11583.5	22224.8	6037.322896	1	44487
115	468	408.687	136.0800	76.7672	10446.5	18517.8	5893.209488	1	44213
116	177	338.565	-154.9200	6.6447	-1029.4	24000.2	44.15226477	1	23619
117	198	289.148	-133.9200	-42.7720	5728.03	17934.6	1829.445386	1	9106
118	458	342.984	126.0800	11.0644	1395	15896.2	122.4210411	1	24917
119	108	271.326	-223.9200	-60.5938	13568.2	50140.2	3671.60557	1	3872
120	246	288.600	-85.9200	-43.3202	3722.07	7382.25	1876.641551	1	8945
121	291	266.222	-40.9200	-65.6979	2688.36	1674.45	4316.209696	1	2373
122	68	282.413	-263.9200	-49.5071	13065.9	69653.8	2450.953157	1	7128
123	311	338.582	-20.9200	6.6617	-139.364	437.646	44.37880709	1	23624
124	606	275.991	274.0800	-55.9289	-15329	75119.8	3128.044986	1	5242
125	512	573.544	180.0800	241.6236	43511.6	32428.8	58381.9723	1	92629
126	426	356.189	94.0800	24.2690	2283.23	8851.05	588.983672	1	28795
127	47	273.420	-284.9200	-58.4997	16667.7	81179.4	3422.215058	1	4487
128	265	424.303	-66.9200	92.3826	-6182.24	4478.29	8534.53782	1	48799
129	370	306.040	38.0800	-25.8798	-985.504	1450.09	669.7651958	1	14067
130	312	301.362	-19.9200	-30.5583	608.721	396.806	933.8090381	1	12693
131	222	469.878	-109.9200	137.9585	-15164.4	12082.4	19032.53619	1	62184
132	280	289.308	-51.9200	-42.6120	2212.41	2695.69	1815.780967	1	9153
133	759	306.663	427.0800	-25.2567	-10786.6	182397	637.9012775	1	14250
134	114	270.672	-217.9200	-61.2475	13347.1	47489.1	3751.260494	1	3680
135	419	319.647	87.0800	-12.2735	-1068.77	7582.93	150.6375961	1	18063
136	435	479.848	103.0800	147.9283	15248.4	10625.5	21882.77953	1	65112
137	186	296.755	-145.9200	-35.1653	5131.31	21292.6	1236.594895	1	11340
138	87	273.645	-244.9200	-58.2750	14272.7	59985.8	3395.972302	1	4553
139	188	356.751	-143.9200	24.8308	-3573.65	20713	616.5691474	1	28960
140	303	323.521	-28.9200	-8.3986	242.886	836.366	70.53586613	1	19201
141	102	283.792	-229.9200	-48.1281	11065.6	52863.2	2316.311889	1	7533
142	127	347.840	-204.9200	15.9199	-3262.31	41992.2	253.4442073	1	26343
143	251	263.730	-80.9200	-68.1903	5517.96	6548.05	4649.920445	1	1641

Bivariate Functional Forms Specification

Regression models can also take many functional forms or specifications. For instance, a linear regression will take the form of $Y = \beta_0 + \beta_1 X_1 + \beta_2 X_2 \ldots + \beta_n X_n + \varepsilon$ whereas a nonlinear regression can take the standard form of $Y = \beta_0 + \beta_1 ln(X_1) + \beta_2 ln(X_2) \ldots + \beta_n ln(X_n) + \varepsilon$. However, there are other functional forms depending on the relationship of the variables. Typically, to test for functional form specifications, we revert to using a single independent variable at a time. The following are the most commonly used bivariate functional forms:

Linear	$Y = \beta_0 + \beta_1 X_1 + \varepsilon$
Linear Log	$Y = \beta_0 + \beta_1 ln(X_1) + \varepsilon$
Reciprocal	$Y = \beta_0 + \beta_1 (1/X_1) + \varepsilon$
Quadratic	$Y = \beta_0 + \beta_1 X_1 + \beta_2 X_1^2 + \varepsilon$
Log Linear	$ln(Y) = \beta_0 + \beta_1 X_1 + \varepsilon$
Log Reciprocal	$ln(Y) = \beta_0 + \beta_1 (1/X_1) + \varepsilon$
Log Quadratic	$ln(Y) = \beta_0 + \beta_1 X_1 + \beta_2 X_1^2 + \varepsilon$
Double Log	$ln(Y) = \beta_0 + \beta_1 ln(X_1) + \varepsilon$
Logistic	$Y/(1 - Y) = \beta_0 + \beta_1 X_1 + \varepsilon$

These functional forms are tested with one dependent variable with one independent variable. In the case of multivariate regressions, simply run the pairwise models and take the resulting functional forms and combine them into a more complex multivariate structure, with the understanding that when combining different functional forms, some previously statistically significant functions may drop out of the comprehensive model and integrate with other functions in the larger model.

Bivariate Functional Forms Specification

Additional Regression Methods

- **Cointegration Test or Engle–Granger Cointegration Test.** The Engle–Granger test is used to identify if there exists any cointegration of two nonstationary time-series variables. First of all, the two variables need to be nonstationary, otherwise a simple linear and nonlinear correlation would typically suffice in identifying if there is a co-movement relationship between them. If two time-series variables are nonstationary to order one, I(1), and if a linear combination of these two series is stationary at I(0), then these two variables are, by definition, cointegrated. Many macroeconomic data are I(1), and conventional forecasting and modeling methods do not apply due to the nonstandard properties of unit root I(1) processes. This cointegration test can be applied to identify the presence of cointegration, and if confirmed to exist, a subsequent Error Correction Model can then be used to forecast the time-series variables.

- **Cox Regression.** The Cox's proportional hazards model for survival time is used to test the effect of several variables at the time a specified event takes to happen. For example, in medical research, we can use the Cox model to investigate the association between the survival time of patients using one or more predictor variables.

- **Discriminate Analysis (Linear and Nonlinear).** A discriminant analysis is related to ANOVA and multivariate regression analysis, where it attempts to model one dependent variable as a linear or nonlinear combination of other independent variables. A Discriminant Analysis has continuous independent variables and a categorical dependent variable. Think of the discriminant analysis as a statistical analysis using a linear or nonlinear discriminant function to assign data to one of two or more categories or groups.

- **Endogeneity Test with Two Stage Least Squares (Durbin–Wu–Hausman).** This tests if a regressor is endogenous using the two-stage least squares (2SLS) method and applying the Durbin–Wu–Hausman test. A Structural Model and a (2SLS) Reduced Model are both computed in a 2SLS paradigm, and a Hausman test is administered to test if one of the variables is endogenous.

- **Endogenous Model (Instrumental Variables with Two-Stage Least Squares).** If the regressor is endogenous, we can apply a two-stage least squares (2SLS) with instrumental variables (IV) on a bivariate model to estimate the model.

- **Error Correction Model (Engle–Granger).** This is also known as an Error Correction Model where we assume that the variables exhibit cointegration. That is, if two time-series variables are nonstationary in the first order, I(1), and when both variables are found to be cointegrated (the I(0) relationship is stationary), we can run an error correction model for estimating short-term and long-term effects of one time series on another. The error correction comes from previous periods' deviation from a long-run equilibrium, where the error influences its short-run dynamics.

- **Granger Causality.** This test is applied to see if one variable Granger causes another variable and vice versa, using restricted autoregressive lags and unrestricted distributive lag models. Predictive causality in finance and economics is tested by measuring the ability to predict the future values of a time series using prior values of another time series. A simpler definition might be that a time-series variable X Granger causes another time-series variable Y if predictions of the value of Y are based solely on its own prior values and on the prior values of X, and these are comparatively better than predictions of Y based solely on its own past values. The causality loop is modeled using these data leads and lags.

Regression-Related Methods

- **Multiple Poisson Regression (Population and Frequency).** The Poisson Regression is like the Logit Regression in that the dependent variables can only take on non-negative values, but also that the underlying distribution of the data is a Poisson distribution, drawn from a known population size.

- **Multiple Regression (Deming Regression with Known Variance).** In regular multivariate regressions, the dependent variable Y is modeled and predicted by independent variables X_i with some error ε. However, in a Deming regression, we further assume that the data collected for Y and X have additional uncertainties and errors, or variances, that are used to provide a more relaxed fit in a Deming model.

- **Multiple Regression (Ordinal Logistic Regression).** This model runs a multivariate ordinal logistic regression with two dependent variables and multiple independent variables. Ordinal logistic regression models the relationship between one or more predictors and an ordinal response variable. The ordinal or categorical variable needs to have three or more levels with a natural ordering, such as those in a survey, with coded responses for strongly disagree, disagree, neutral, agree, and strongly agree.

- **Multiple Regression (Through Origin).** This model runs a multiple linear regression but without an intercept. This method is used when an intercept may not conceptually or theoretically apply to the data being modeled. As examples, a factory cannot produce outputs if the equipment is not running or the gravitational force of a large object does not exist when there is zero mass.

- **Multiple Ridge Regression (Low Variance, High Bias, High VIF).** A Ridge Regression model's results come with a higher bias than an Ordinary Least Squares standard multiple regression but has less variance. It is more suitable in situations with high Variance Inflation Factors and multicollinearity or when there is a high number of variables compared to data points. Clearly, in the case of high VIF with multicollinearity, some of the highly colinear variables will need to be dropped, but for whatever reason these colinear variables need to be included, a ridge-based regression is a better alternative.

- **Multiple Weighted Regression for Heteroskedasticity.** The Multivariate Regression on Weighted Variables is used to correct for heteroskedasticity in all the variables. The weights used to adjust these variables are the user input standard deviations. Clearly, this method is only applicable for time-series variables, due to the heteroskedastic assumption.

- **Stepwise Regression.** When there are multiple independent variables vying to be in a multivariate regression model, it can be cumbersome to identify and specify the correct combinations of variables in the model. A stepwise regression can be run to systematically identify which variables are statistically significant and should be inserted into the final model. Several simple algorithms exist for running stepwise regressions:

    - **Stepwise Regression (Backward)**

    - **Stepwise Regression (Correlation)**

    - **Stepwise Regression (Forward)**

    - **Stepwise Regression (Forward and Backward)**

Multicollinearity, Heteroskedasticity, Autocorrelation...

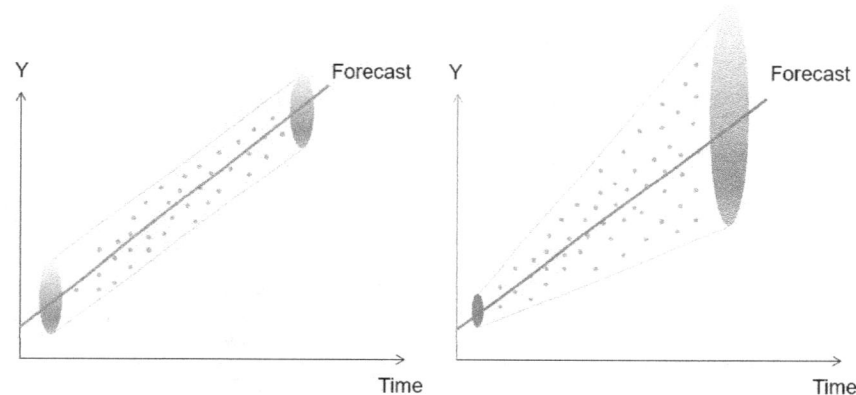

$$Y_i = \beta_1 + \beta_2 X_{2,i} + \beta_3 X_{3,i} + \varepsilon_i$$

$$\hat{\beta}_2 = \frac{\sum Y_i X_{2,i} \sum X_{3,i}^2 - \sum Y_i X_{3,i} \sum X_{2,i} X_{3,i}}{\sum X_{2,i}^2 \sum X_{3,i}^2 - \left(\sum X_{2,i} X_{3,i}\right)^2}$$

$$\hat{\beta}_3 = \frac{\sum Y_i X_{3,i} \sum X_{2,i}^2 - \sum Y_i X_{2,i} \sum X_{2,i} X_{3,i}}{\sum X_{2,i}^2 \sum X_{3,i}^2 - \left(\sum X_{2,i} X_{3,i}\right)^2}$$

$$\hat{\beta}_2 = \frac{\sum Y_i X_{2,i} \sum \lambda^2 X_{2,i}^2 - \sum Y_i \lambda X_{2,i} \sum \lambda X_{2,i}^2}{\sum X_{2,i}^2 \sum \lambda^2 X_{2,i}^2 - \left(\sum \lambda\, X_{2,i}^2\right)^2} = \frac{0}{0}$$

$$VIF_i = \frac{1}{(1 - R_i^2)}$$

Understand the concepts of heteroskedasticity versus homoskedasticity, autocorrelation versus serial correlation, lags versus leads, correlation versus causation, micronumerosity.

Understand where they apply and to what types of data.

Understand the tests that can be performed to identify and correct for these issues in your models.

Multicollinearity, Heteroskedasticity, Autocorrelation…

Heteroskedasticity, Micronumerosity, Outliers and Nonlinearity

Diagnostic Results

Variable	Heteroskedasticity W-Test p-value	Heteroskedasticity Hypothesis Test result	Micronumerosity Approximation result	Outliers Natural Lower Bound	Outliers Natural Upper Bound	Number of Potential Outliers	Nonlinearity Nonlinear Test p-value	Nonlinearity Hypothesis Test result
Y			no problems	-7.86	671.70	2		
X1	0.2543	Homoskedastic	no problems	-21377.95	64713.03	3	0.2458	linear
X2	0.3371	Homoskedastic	no problems	77.47	445.93	2	0.0335	nonlinear
X3	0.3649	Homoskedastic	no problems	-5.77	15.69	3	0.0305	nonlinear
X4	0.3066	Homoskedastic	no problems	-295.96	628.21	4	0.9298	linear
X5	0.2495	Homoskedastic	no problems	3.35	9.38	3	0.2727	linear

Autocorrelation

Time Lag	AC	PAC	Lower Bound	Upper Bound	Q-Stat	Prob
1	0.0580	0.0580	-0.2828	0.2828	0.1786	0.6726
2	-0.1213	-0.1251	-0.2828	0.2828	0.9754	0.6140
3	0.0590	0.0756	-0.2828	0.2828	1.1679	0.7607
4	0.2423	0.2232	-0.2828	0.2828	4.4865	0.3442
5	0.0067	-0.0078	-0.2828	0.2828	4.4890	0.4814
6	-0.2654	-0.2345	-0.2828	0.2828	8.6516	0.1941
7	0.0814	0.0939	-0.2828	0.2828	9.0524	0.2489
8	0.0634	-0.0442	-0.2828	0.2828	9.3012	0.3175
9	0.0204	0.0673	-0.2828	0.2828	9.3276	0.4076
10	-0.0190	0.0865	-0.2828	0.2828	9.3512	0.4991
11	0.1035	0.0790	-0.2828	0.2828	10.0648	0.5246
12	0.1658	0.0978	-0.2828	0.2828	11.9466	0.4500
13	-0.0524	-0.0430	-0.2828	0.2828	12.1394	0.5162
14	-0.2050	-0.2523	-0.2828	0.2828	15.1738	0.3664
15	0.1782	0.2089	-0.2828	0.2828	17.5315	0.2881
16	-0.1022	-0.2591	-0.2828	0.2828	18.3296	0.3050
17	-0.0861	0.0808	-0.2828	0.2828	18.9141	0.3335
18	0.0418	0.1987	-0.2828	0.2828	19.0559	0.3884
19	0.0869	-0.0821	-0.2828	0.2828	19.6894	0.4135
20	-0.0091	-0.0269	-0.2828	0.2828	19.6966	0.4770

Multicollinearity and Stationarity Tests

Nonstationarity Analysis of Dependent Variable

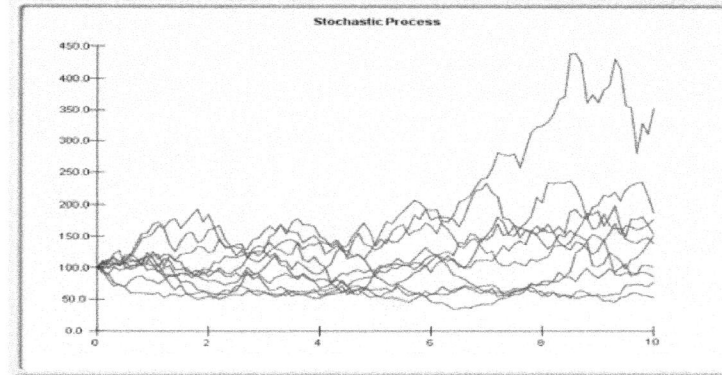

Multicollinearity Analysis of Independent Variables

Correlation Matrix

CORRELATION	X2	X3	X4	X5
X1	0.333	0.959	0.242	0.237
X2	1.000	0.349	0.319	0.120
X3		1.000	0.196	0.227
X4			1.000	0.290
				1.000

Variance Inflation Factor

VIF	X2	X3	X4	X5
X1	1.12	12.46	1.06	1.06
X2	N/A	1.14	1.11	1.01
X3		N/A	1.04	1.05
X4			N/A	1.09
				N/A

Statistical Summary

Periodic					
Drift Rate	-1.48%	Reversion Rate	283.89%	Jump Rate	20.41%
Volatility	88.84%	Long-Term Value	327.72	Jump Size	237.89

Probability of stochastic model fit: 46.48%

A high fit means a stochastic model is better than conventional models.

Runs	22	Standard Normal	-1.1432
Positive	26	P-Value (1-tail)	0.1265
Negative	24	P-Value (2-tail)	0.2530
Expected Run	26		

A low p-value (below 0.10, 0.05, 0.01) means that the sequence is not random and hence suffers from stationarity problems, and an ARIMA model might be more appropriate. Conversely, higher p-values indicate randomness and stochastic process models might be appropriate.

Testing for Heteroskedasticity

The **Breusch–Pagan–Godfrey test** for heteroskedasticity uses the main model to obtain error estimates and, using squared estimates, a restricted model is run and the Breusch–Pagan–Godfrey test is computed. The **Lagrange Multiplier test** for heteroskedasticity also uses the main model to obtain error estimates and, using squared estimates, a restricted model is run, and the Lagrange Multiplier test is computed. The Wald–Glejser test for heteroskedasticity again uses the main model to obtain error estimates and, using squared estimates, a restricted model is run and the **Wald–Glejser test** is computed. The Wald's Individual Variables test for heteroskedasticity runs multiple tests to see if the volatilities or uncertainties (standard deviation or variance of a variable) are nonconstant over time. Regardless of the test used, the results typically agree as to whether the null hypothesis can be rejected. If there is disagreement among any of these tests, we typically use the smallest p-value to determine if there is heteroskedasticity.

```
Model Inputs:
VAR141
VAR142; VAR143; VAR144

Breusch-Pagan-Godfrey Test for
Heteroskedasticity
Observations: 88
Restricted R-Square: 0.160141
Breusch-Pagan Stat: 14.092386
P-Value: 0.002782

Null hypothesis: homoskedasticity
```

Beyond Regression: Stepwise Regression

One powerful automated approach to regression analysis is *stepwise regression* and, based on its namesake, the regression process proceeds in multiple steps. There are several ways to set up these stepwise algorithms including the correlation approach, forward method, backward method, and the forward and backward method (these methods are all available in Risk Simulator).

In the correlation method, the dependent variable (Y) is correlated to all the independent variables (X), and starting with the X variable with the highest absolute correlation value, a regression is run, then subsequent X variables are added until the p-values indicate that the new X variable is no longer statistically significant. This approach is quick and simple but does not account for interactions among variables, and an X variable, when added, will statistically overshadow other variables.

In the forward method, we first correlate Y with all X variables, run a regression for Y on the highest absolute value correlation of X, and obtain the fitting errors. Then, correlate these errors with the remaining X variables and choose the highest absolute value correlation among this remaining set and run another regression. Repeat the process until the p-value for the latest X variable coefficient is no longer statistically significant then stop the process.

In the backward method, run a regression with Y on all X variables and reviewing each variable's p-value, systematically eliminate the variable with the largest p-value, then run a regression again, repeating each time until all p-values are statistically significant.

In the forward and backward method, apply the forward method to obtain three X variables then apply the backward approach to see if one of them needs to be eliminated because it is statistically insignificant. Then repeat the forward method, and then the backward method until all remaining X variables are considered.

The table on the next slide illustrates the sample results using the same dataset as in the multiple regression model run previously. Using the Stepwise Regression: Backward method, we see that the model starts by using all independent variables (Arrangement 1: Y to X1; X2; X3; X4; X5), identifies the least significant variable as X4, and re-runs the second regression model (Arrangement 2: Y to X1; X2; X3; X5). The algorithm then drops variables X1 and X5 in the subsequent two runs. The final result indicates the best-fitting model of Y to X2; X3. This result confirms the previous multiple regression, where we see that "Bachelor's Degree" (VAR1), "Population Density" (VAR4), and "Unemployment Rate" (VAR5) are not significant and should be removed and that the multiple regression should be re-run with only significant variables.

Beyond Regression: Stepwise Regression

```
Model Inputs:
VAR28
VAR29; VAR30; VAR31; VAR32; VAR33
Y against X1, X2, X3, X4, X5
```

Stepwise Regression (Backward)

ARRANGEMENT 1
Y<->X1;X2;X3;X4;X5

OVERALL FIT

Multiple R	0.57203	Maximum Log Likelihood	-318.17341
R-Square	0.32721	Akaike Info Criterion (AIC)	12.96694
Adjusted R-Square	0.25076	Bayes Schwarz Criterion (BSC)	13.19638
Standard Error	149.67200	Hannan-Quinn Criterion (HQC)	13.05431
Observations	50	Cohen's F-Squared	0.48636

	Coeff	Std. Error	T-stat	P-value	Lower 5%	Upper 95%
Intercept	57.95550	108.79014	0.53273	0.59690	-161.29661	277.20762
X1	-0.00354	0.00352	-1.00656	0.31965	-0.01064	0.00355
X2	0.46437	0.25353	1.83159	0.07379	-0.04659	0.97533
X3	25.23770	14.11723	1.78772	0.08071	-3.21371	53.68911
X4	-0.00856	0.10156	-0.08433	0.93317	-0.21325	0.19612
X5	16.55792	14.79957	1.11881	0.26929	-13.26866	46.38449

ARRANGEMENT 2
Y<->X1;X2;X3;X5

Multiple R	0.57193	Maximum Log Likelihood	-318.17745
R-Square	0.32710	Akaike Info Criterion (AIC)	12.92710
Adjusted R-Square	0.26729	Bayes Schwarz Criterion (BSC)	13.11830
Standard Error	148.01160	Hannan-Quinn Criterion (HQC)	12.99991
Observations	50	Cohen's F-Squared	0.48612

	Coeff	Std. Error	T-stat	P-value	Lower 5%	Upper 95%
Intercept	60.27060	104.10171	0.57896	0.56550	-149.40100	269.94220
X1	-0.00360	0.00342	-1.05382	0.29759	-0.01048	0.00328
X2	0.45846	0.24094	1.90276	0.06348	-0.02683	0.94374
X3	25.43968	13.75824	1.84905	0.07103	-2.27084	53.15020
X5	16.25036	14.18406	1.14568	0.25799	-12.31781	44.81853

ARRANGEMENT 3
Y<->X2;X3;X5

Multiple R	0.55722	Maximum Log Likelihood	-318.78692
R-Square	0.31050	Akaike Info Criterion (AIC)	12.91148
Adjusted R-Square	0.26553	Bayes Schwarz Criterion (BSC)	13.06444
Standard Error	148.18933	Hannan-Quinn Criterion (HQC)	12.96973
Observations	50	Cohen's F-Squared	0.45032

	Coeff	Std. Error	T-stat	P-value	Lower 5%	Upper 95%
Intercept	56.90111	104.17754	0.54619	0.58757	-152.79740	266.59962
X2	0.46096	0.24122	1.91093	0.06226	-0.02460	0.94651
X3	11.63902	4.22268	2.75631	0.00835	3.13920	20.13884
X5	15.17953	14.16461	1.07165	0.28947	-13.33234	43.69140

ARRANGEMENT 4
Y<->X2;X3

Multiple R	0.54156	Maximum Log Likelihood	-319.40341
R-Square	0.29328	Akaike Info Criterion (AIC)	12.89614
Adjusted R-Square	0.26321	Bayes Schwarz Criterion (BSC)	13.01086
Standard Error	148.42315	Hannan-Quinn Criterion (HQC)	12.93982
Observations	50	Cohen's F-Squared	0.41500

	Coeff	Std. Error	T-stat	P-value	Lower 5%	Upper 95%
Intercept	146.04706	62.81359	2.32509	0.02444	19.68243	272.41170
X2	0.47249	0.24136	1.95761	0.05623	-0.01306	0.95805
X3	12.53958	4.14475	3.02541	0.00402	4.20143	20.87774

Beyond Regression: Logit, Probit, Tobit

Limited Dependent Variables describe the situation where the dependent variable contains data that are limited in scope and range, such as binary responses (*0* or *1*), truncated, ordered, or censored data. For instance, given a set of independent variables (e.g., age, income, education level of credit card or mortgage loan holders), we can model the probability of defaulting on mortgage payments, using maximum likelihood estimation (MLE). The response or dependent variable *Y* is binary, that is, it can have only two possible outcomes that we denote as *1* and *0* (e.g., *Y* may represent presence/absence of a certain condition, defaulted/not defaulted on previous loans, success/failure of some device, answer yes/no on a survey, etc.) and we also have a vector of independent variable regressors *X*, which are assumed to influence the outcome *Y*. A typical ordinary least squares regression approach is invalid because the regression errors are heteroskedastic and non-normal, and the resulting estimated probability estimates will return nonsensical values of above *1* or below *0*. MLE analysis handles these problems using an iterative optimization routine to maximize a log likelihood function when the dependent variables are limited.

A Logit or Logistic regression is used for predicting the probability of occurrence of an event by fitting data to a logistic curve. It is a generalized linear model used for binomial regression, and like many forms of regression analysis, it makes use of several predictor variables that may be either numerical or categorical. MLE applied in a binary multivariate logistic analysis is used to model dependent variables to determine the expected probability of success of belonging to a certain group. The estimated coefficients for the Logit model are the logarithmic odds ratios and they cannot be interpreted directly as probabilities. A quick computation is first required, and the approach is simple.

Specifically, the Logit model is specified as $Estimated\ Y = LN[P_i/(1-P_i)]$ or, conversely, $P_i = EXP(Estimated\ Y)/(1 + EXP(Estimated\ Y))$, and the coefficients β_i are the log odds ratios. So, taking the antilog or $EXP(\beta_i)$ we obtain the odds ratio of $P_i/(1-P_i)$. This means that with an increase in a unit of β_i the log odds ratio increases by this amount. Finally, the rate of change in the probability $dP/dX = \beta_i P_i(1-P_i)$. The Standard Error measures how accurate the predicted Coefficients are, and the t-statistics are the ratios of each predicted Coefficient to its Standard Error and are used in the typical regression hypothesis test of the significance of each estimated parameter. To estimate the probability of success of belonging to a certain group (e.g., predicting if a smoker will develop respiratory complications given the amount smoked per year), simply compute the $Estimated\ Y$ value using the MLE coefficients. For example, if the model is $Y = 1.1 + 0.005\ (Cigarettes)$ then someone smoking 100 packs per year has an $Estimated\ Y = 1.1 + 0.005(100) = 1.6$. Next, compute the inverse antilog of the odds ratio by doing: $EXP(Estimated\ Y)/[1 + EXP(Estimated\ Y)] = EXP(1.6)/(1 + EXP(1.6)) = 0.8320$. So, such a person has an 83.20% chance of developing some respiratory complications in his lifetime.

Beyond Regression: Logit, Probit, Tobit

A Probit model (sometimes also known as a Normit model) is a popular alternative specification for a binary response model, which employs a Probit function estimated using maximum likelihood estimation, and the approach is called Probit regression. The Probit and Logistic regression models tend to produce very similar predictions where the parameter estimates in a logistic regression tend to be 1.6 to 1.8 times higher than they are in a corresponding Probit model. The choice of using a Probit or Logit is entirely up to convenience, and the main distinction is that the logistic distribution has a higher kurtosis (fatter tails) to account for extreme values. For example, suppose that house ownership is the decision to be modeled, and this response variable is binary (home purchase or no home purchase) and depends on a series of independent variables X_i such as income, age, and so forth, such that $I_i = \beta_0 + \beta_1 X_1 + \cdots + \beta_n X_n$, where the larger the value of I_i, the higher the probability of home ownership. For each family, a critical I^*threshold exists, where if exceeded, the house is purchased, otherwise, no home is purchased, and the outcome probability (P) is assumed to be normally distributed, such that $P_i = CDF(I)$ using a standard-normal cumulative distribution function (CDF). Therefore, use the estimated coefficients exactly like those of a regression model and using the $Estimated\,Y$ value, apply a standard-normal distribution (you can use Excel's *NORMSDIST* function or Risk Simulator's *Distributional Analysis* tool by selecting Normal distribution and setting the mean to be *0* and standard deviation to be *1*). Finally, to obtain a Probit or probability unit measure, set $I_i + 5$ (this is because whenever the probability $P_i < 0.5$, the estimated I_i is negative, due to the fact that the normal distribution is symmetrical around a mean of zero).

The Tobit model (Censored Tobit) is an econometric and biometric modeling method used to describe the relationship between a non-negative dependent variable Y_i and one or more independent variables X_i. A Tobit model is an econometric model in which the dependent variable is censored; that is, the dependent variable is censored because values below zero are not observed. The Tobit model assumes that there is a latent unobservable variable Y^*. This variable is linearly dependent on the X_i variables via a vector of β_i coefficients that determine their inter-relationships. In addition, there is a normally distributed error term U_i to capture random influences on this relationship. The observable variable Y_i is defined to be equal to the latent variables whenever the latent variables are above zero and Y_i is assumed to be zero otherwise. That is, $Y_i = Y^*\ if\ Y^* > 0;\ Y_i = 0\ if\ Y^* = 0$. If the relationship parameter β_i is estimated by using ordinary least squares regression of the observed Y_i on X_i, the resulting regression estimators are inconsistent and yield downward-biased slope coefficients and an upward-biased intercept. Only MLE would be consistent for a Tobit model. In the Tobit model, there is an ancillary statistic called sigma, which is equivalent to the standard error of estimate in a standard Ordinary Least Squares (OLS) regression, and the estimated coefficients are used the same way as in a regression analysis.

Beyond Regression: Logit, Probit, Tobit

Default	Age	Education	Work	Address	Income	Debt to Income	Credit	Other
1	41	3	17	12	176	9.3	11.36	5.01
0	27	1	10	6	31	17.3	1.36	4
.	..	.	..	..	..	...	...	...
.	..	.	..	..	..	...	...	...
1	24	2	2	0	28	17.3	1.79	3.06
0	41	2	5	5	25	10.2	0.39	2.16
0	39	1	20	9	67	30.6	3.83	16.67

Model Inputs:
VAR120
VAR121; VAR122; VAR123; VAR124; VAR125; VAR126; VAR127; VAR128

Generalized Linear Model (Logit with Binary Outcomes)

	Coefficient	Std. Error	Wald Test	P-value	Exp(B)	Lower	Upper
Intercept	-1.782757	0.751968	5.620634	0.017750	0.168174	0.000000	0.000000
VAR1	0.029975	0.020489	2.140280	0.143476	1.030428	0.989869	1.072650
VAR2	0.076260	0.144824	0.277272	0.598495	1.079243	0.812539	1.433487
VAR3	-0.253392	0.039145	41.9014	0.000000	0.776163	0.718841	0.838057
VAR4	-0.096522	0.027163	12.6271	0.000380	0.907989	0.860914	0.957639
VAR5	0.001268	0.012560	0.010193	0.919583	1.001269	0.976921	1.026223
VAR6	0.076775	0.039667	3.746016	0.052934	1.079799	0.999029	1.167099
VAR7	0.549211	0.132125	17.2787	0.000032	1.731886	1.336764	2.243799
VAR8	0.042293	0.100545	0.176940	0.674017	1.043201	0.856611	1.270433

Log Likelihood	-200.5005
Restricted Log Likelihood	-285.4773
McFadden R-Squared	0.297666
Cox and Snell R-Squared	0.288164
Nagelkerke R-Squared	0.423278
Raw Akaike Info. Criterion	419.0009
Raw Bayes Criterion	456.9324

Log Likelihood	-200.5005
Restricted Log Likelihood	-285.4773
Chi-Square	169.9536
Degrees of Freedom	8
P-value	0.000000

Beyond Regression: Structural Equation Modeling (SEM) with Partial Least Squares (PLS)

Another extension to multiple regression analysis is the Structural Equation Model (SEM), which uses the Partial Least Squares (PLS) method. SEM is typically used to solve path-dependent structures such as the one illustrated in the next slide. Suppose that there are five variables in your research, where the final dependent variable is technology acceptance (VAR5). We are trying to determine what drives and predicts the level of technology acceptance in different organizations. If we collected data on the corporate culture of the various organizations (VAR1) using a Likert scale in terms of openness to new technology, we can run a simple bivariate regression. However, we also understand from organizational behavior theory and decision theory that other intervening variables can also contribute to an organization's acceptance of new technology, such as what types of decisions are relegated to technology, that is, the decision criticality (VAR2) and whether new artificial intelligence (AI) technology is used or more traditional technology is used (VAR3). For example, letting a smart AI computer system make frequent orders of paperclips is a lot less critical than allowing AI complete access to the nation's nuclear arsenal. Mistakes made on the former have little consequence compared to the latter. However, we also know from technology acceptance theory that there are other latent and hidden effects that drive technology trust (VAR4). If a technology is not trusted, then the technology is probably not going to be accepted for use in the organization. Technology trust might include whether the AI technology has transparent algorithms or comes as a black box.

In such a research paradigm, one might be inclined to simply run the first four independent variables on the fifth dependent variable. That would be a major mistake and the results will be erroneous at best, because VAR2, VAR3, and VAR4 are endogenous. That is, based on various theories, we know that the type of organization drives the types of decision criticality (a local office-supplies store versus the U.S. Department of Defense, VAR1 drives VAR2), the type of advanced AI technology employed (paperclip reordering system has rudimentary code versus national cybersecurity defense against state-sponsored actors that requires much more sophisticated AI technology, VAR1 drives VAR3), and so forth. In addition, the level of decision criticality drives whether AI is needed (VAR2 drives VAR3). Whether AI is applied will drive trust in the new technology (VAR3 drives VAR4) and then acceptance. The next slide shows the tangled web known as a path model. A simple multiple regression analysis cannot be used. Instead, partial least squares or sequential regression models will need to be applied. The SEM approach is used to handle such complex path models.

Beyond Regression: Structural Equation Modeling (SEM) with Partial Least Squares (PLS)

In typical path models, the pathways move in a single direction, where one or multiple paths can originate from a box and one or many paths can recombine into a box, and the pathways all end at the main dependent model (in this example, that would be VAR5). The direct effects on VAR5 are pathways C, F, I, and J, from the four independent variables. However, these variables also have indirect effects (e.g., VAR3 has indirect impacts on VAR5 through path HJ; VAR2 has indirect effects on VAR5 through paths EJ, GI, and GHJ; and VAR1 has indirect impacts on VAR5 through paths AEJ, AF, AGI, AGHJ, BJ, DHJ, and DI). Notice that VAR4 does not have any indirect effects on VAR5, only a single direct impact path. The summation of the direct and indirect effects equals the total effects.

The indirect effects are:

VAR1 on VAR5: $0.94828 = (0.48406 \times -0.56521 \times 0.43355) + (0.48406 \times 0.2447) + (0.48406 \times 0.00253 \times 0.45264) + (0.48406 \times 0.00253 \times 0.98713 \times 0.43355) + (0.15673 \times 0.43355) + (0.99864 \times 0.98713 \times 0.43355) + (0.99864 \times 0.45264)$

VAR2 on VAR5: $-0.24282 = (-0.56521 \times 0.43355) + (0.00253 \times 0.45264) + (0.00253 \times 0.98713 \times 0.43355)$

VAR3 on VAR5: $0.42798 = (0.98713 \times 0.43355)$

VAR4 on VAR5: no indirect effects; only direct effects exist

Beyond Regression: Structural Equation Modeling (SEM) with Partial Least Squares (PLS)

Model Inputs:
VAR1;VAR2; VAR3; VAR4; VAR5
VAR1;VAR2; VAR3; VAR4
VAR1;VAR2; VAR3
VAR1;VAR2

Direct Effects Path

	Dep. Var:	VAR5	Tech Acceptance
	R-Square	0.99990	
	Disturbance	0.01000	

Var Name	Coeff	P-Value	Std. Beta	
Intercept	0.34030	0.34366		
Culture Org.VAR1	0.51562	0.21713	0.05159	C
Criticality VAR2	7.74992	0.00000	0.24470	F
New AI Tech VAR3	1.68941	0.00000	0.45264	I
Tech Trust VAR4	15.49786	0.00000	0.43355	J

Partial Direct Effects Path

	Dep. Var:	VAR4	Tech Trust
	R-Square	0.99980	
	Disturbance	0.01414	

Var Name	Coeff	P-Value	Std. Beta	
Intercept	0.11916	0.00000		
Culture Org.VAR1	0.04382	0.17074	0.15673	B
Criticality VAR2	-0.5007	0.00000	-0.5652	E
New AI Tech VAR3	0.10307	0.00000	0.98713	H

Partial Direct Effects Path

	Dep. Var:	VAR3	New AI Tech
	R-Square	0.99974	
	Disturbance	0.01612	

Var Name	Coeff	P-Value	Std. Beta	
Intercept	0.89306	0.00036		
Culture Org. VAR1	2.67416	0.00000	0.99864	D
Criticality VAR2	0.02146	0.35062	0.00253	G

Partial Direct Effects Path

	Dep. Var:	VAR2	Criticality
	R-Square	0.23432	
	Disturbance	0.87503	

Var Name	Coeff	P-Value	Std. Beta	
Intercept	-0.0335	0.98190		
Culture Org. VAR1	0.15276	0.00037	0.48406	A

Total Effects

	Dep. Var	VAR5	Tech Acceptance

Var Name	Coeff	P-Value	Std. Beta
Culture Org. VAR1	9.99326	0.00000	0.99987
Criticality VAR2	0.05966	0.47689	0.00188
New AI Tech VAR3	3.28678	0.00000	0.88061
Tech Trust VAR4	15.49786	0.00000	0.43355

Summary Standardized Path Effects

	Dep. Var	VAR5	Tech Acceptance

Var Name	Direct		Indirect	Total
Culture Org. VAR1	0.05159	C	**0.94828**	0.99987
Criticality VAR2	0.24470	F	**-0.2428**	0.00188
New AI Tech VAR3	0.45264	I	**0.42798**	0.88061
Tech Trust VAR4	0.43355	J	**0.00000**	0.43355

Beyond Regression: Endogeneity and Simultaneous Equations Methods with Two-stage Least Squares

Endogeneity occurs when a dependent variable in a model is also the independent variable in another model. The simplest example would be the structural equation model with partial least squares as shown previously. The SEM model is best used when there are complex combinations of pathways. Sometimes there are only two equations in the system, and, hence, these can be solved using a simultaneous equations model approach. Recall from basic algebra when you have two equations and two unknowns, you can solve them using simultaneous equations. The same applies here when we have a system of two equations.

Suppose we have two equations:

$$M_t = a_0 + a_1 Y_t + u_{1t}$$

$$Y_t = b_0 + b_1 M_t + b_2 I_t + u_{2t}$$

M_t is money supply at time t, Y_t is income at time t, and I_t is investment at time t. We see that M depends on Y in the first equation, but Y depends on M and I in the second equation. In this example, M and Y are endogenous or jointly determined, meaning that they cannot be modeled by themselves, and must be modeled together or simultaneously. However, I is an exogenous variable, which can be determined outside of this system of equations. In this example, the number of endogenous variables (k) is 2 and the number of exogenous variables (r) is 1. If $r = k - 1$, then it is considered to be exactly identified. The system of equations is overidentified or underidentified if r exceeds or is smaller than $k - 1$. The system can only be modeled when the system is exactly identified or overidentified.

As another example, when we have an overidentification system, where the second equation above has an additional exogenous variable G, such that:

$$Y_t = b_0 + b_1 M_t + b_2 I_t + b_3 G_t + u_{2t}$$

Beyond Regression: Endogeneity and Simultaneous Equations Methods with Two-stage Least Squares

Model Inputs:
VAR1
VAR2
VAR3

$$M_t = 85.853 + 0.132Y_t$$

Endogeneity Model Results with Instrumental Variables
and Two Stage Least Squares
 Intercept Coefficient: 85.853014
 Slope Coefficient: 0.132062
 Std. Error of Slope: 0.043941
 T-Stat of Slope: 3.005471
 P-Value of Slope: 0.007961

Model Inputs:
VAR1
VAR2
VAR3; VAR4

$$M_t = 84.398 + 0.133Y_t$$

Endogeneity Model Results with Instrumental Variables
and Two Stage Least Squares
 Intercept Coefficient: 84.398855
 Slope Coefficient: 0.133285
 Std. Error of Slope: 0.074370
 T-Stat of Slope: 1.792196
 P-Value of Slope: 0.090917

Beyond Regression: Durbin–Wu–Hausman Endogeneity Test

Sometimes, with random data, it is hard to determine if a certain variable is endogenous. The Durbin–Wu–Hausman test can be used to determine endogeneity. The null hypothesis is that there is no endogeneity. With a low p-value of 0.003, we reject this null hypothesis and conclude that there is, indeed, endogeneity among the variables.

Model Inputs:
VAR1
VAR2
VAR3
VAR4

Durbin-Wu-Hausman Test for Endogeneity
Correlation (Structural Error
   and Test Variable): -0.000000
P-Value for Error Coefficient: 0.010720
Hausman Test for Endogeneity: 8.653626
Hausman P-Value for Endogeneity: 0.003264

Error Coefficient Null: No endogeneity exists
   in the test variable
Hausman Null: No endogeneity exists in
   the test variable

Beyond Regression: Granger Causality and Engle–Granger Methods

The Granger causality tests if one variable "Granger causes" another variable and vice versa, using restricted autoregressive lags and unrestricted distributive lag models. Typically, predictive causality in finance and economics is tested by measuring the ability to predict the future values of a time series using prior values of another time series. A simpler definition might be that a time-series variable A can Granger cause another time-series variable B if predictions of the value of B based solely on its own prior values and on the prior values of A are comparatively better than predictions of B based solely on its own past values. For example, Figure 9.49 illustrates two time-series variables, A and B. The two null hypotheses tested are that there is no Granger causality of A on B and also between B and A. We see that the p-values for both directions are greater than an alpha of 0.05, so we cannot reject the null hypothesis and conclude that neither A Granger causes B nor B Granger causes A, when both are lagged for 3 periods (this is the value 3 in the input box). The Granger causality model can only be run pairwise and assumes that the time-series variable is stationary or not stochastic.

```
Model Inputs:

  VAR138
  VAR139
  3


Granger Causality
Effect              VAR2 on VAR1:     VAR1 on VAR2:
Wald Test             1.37224           0.76841
P-Value               0.26511           0.51852


Null hypothesis: VAR(i) does not Granger cause VAR(j)
```

Beyond Regression: Nonstationarity (Augmented Dickey–Fuller)

If a time-series is suspected to have nonstationary effects, we can run the Augmented Dickey–Fuller test, where the null hypothesis is that the series is nonstationary, has a unit root, or I(1) process, and is potentially stochastic. The example BizStats results indicate that the variable is stationary (the null hypothesis is rejected with a p-value of 0.0442).

```
Model Inputs:
VAR280

Augmented Dickey-Fuller Stationarity Test for AR(p)

With Constant and With Trend
Tau Statistic: -3.745611
Tau Critical: -3.659125
Stationary? Yes
Akaike Information Criterion: 1.752735
Bayes Info Criterion: 2.042456
Optimal Lags: 3
Coefficient: -2.772352
P-value: 0.044286

Null Hypothesis: Time Series is Unit Root and Not Stationary
```

Beyond Regression: Nonstationarity

If a time series variable is nonstationary and stochastic, you can still attempt to forecast this series several ways:

• Compute the difference to potentially make the series stationary. For example, stock prices are nonstationary and stochastic, whereas its difference, i.e., the calculated stock returns, tend to be stationary and more predictable than the raw stock prices.

• Run a stochastic process model, for example, a **geometric Brownian motion random walk process**, mean-reversion process, jump-diffusion process, or other mixed processes. These are typically used to forecast stock prices for the purposes of modeling and valuing stock options, real options, and employee stock options.

• If there is another nonstationary variable, you can test if these two series are cointegrated. For example, you can use the **Engle–Granger Error Correction Model** assuming the variables exhibit cointegration. If two time-series variables are nonstationary in the first order, I(1), as tested using the Augmented Dickey–Fuller test, and when both variables are cointegrated, the error correction model can be used for estimating short-term and long-term effects of one time series on the another. The error correction comes from previous periods' deviation from a long-run equilibrium, where the error influences its short-run dynamics.

• Apply a data filter to smooth out the disturbances such as the **Hodrick–Prescott filter**. This filter allows you to remove cyclicality effects of raw time-series data. The filter helps generate a smoothed-curve of a time-series variable that is sensitive to longer-term fluctuations rather than short-term impacts. The key is to choose the correct smoothing parameter, which can sometimes require trial and error.

Beyond Regression: Error-Correction Model

Model Inputs:

VAR103

VAR104

Error Correction Model

Multiple R	0.16264
R-Square	0.02645
Adjusted R-Square	0.02060
Standard Error	0.23979
Observations	503
Cohen's F-Squared	0.02717

	Coeff	Std. Error	T-stat	P-value	Lower	Upper
Intercept	-0.18466	0.06789	-2.71989	0.00676	-0.31805	-0.05127
Delta X	0.06146	0.02453	2.50556	0.01254	0.01327	0.10965
Lagged Error	-0.03542	0.01549	-2.28612	0.02267	-0.06587	-0.00498
Original Y	0.01479	0.00557	2.65783	0.00812	0.00386	0.02573

Beyond Regression: Poisson Regression

The Poisson regression is like the Logit regression in that the dependent variable can only take on non-negative values, but also that the underlying distribution of the data is a Poisson distribution, drawn from a known population size. Recall that the Poisson distribution is a discrete distribution used to model the probability that an event occurs within the context of time and area. Typically, this generalized linear model approach runs a loglinear regression model, where the dependent variable is the event count (see VAR1 in the sample dataset below), and an additional variable for the population size (VAR2) and categorical independent variables (VAR3 to VAR5) are needed.

Poisson Regression Example Dataset

VAR1 Cancer (Y)	VAR2 Population	VAR3 X1	VAR4 X2	VAR5 X3
45	24786	1	0	0
77	32125	1	0	0.5
95	34706	1	0	1
...	...	...	...	...
...	...	...	...	...
62	41707	0	0	1
57	26319	0	0	1.5
71	22978	0	0	2

```
Model Inputs:
VAR1
VAR2
VAR3; VAR4; VAR5
Multiple Poisson Regression
R-Square              0.96413
AIC                  19.62304
Pearson Phi           1.07152
Sqrt Phi              1.03514
Cohen's F-Squared    26.87470
```

	Coeff	Std. Error	Wald Test	P-value	Lower	Upper
Intercept	-7.30714	0.08931	6693.69972	0.00000	-7.48219	-7.13209
X1	**0.76457**	0.07958	92.29805	0.00000	0.60859	0.92055
X2	**0.38873**	0.09882	15.47465	0.16178	0.19505	0.58241
X3	0.76612	0.05376	203.06012	0.00000	0.66075	0.87149

With Phi Correction   1.035141

	Coeff	Std. Error	Wald Test	P-value	Lower	Upper
Intercept	-7.30714	0.09245	6693.69972	0.00000	-7.48834	-7.12593
X1	0.76457	0.08238	92.29805	0.00000	0.60311	0.92603
X2	0.38873	0.10229	15.47465	0.16178	0.18824	0.58921
X3	0.76612	0.05565	203.06012	0.00000	0.65704	0.87520

Beyond Regression: Poisson Regression

In a Poisson regression, the logarithm of the expected value is a linear combination of the independent variables, that is, $\log[E(Y \mid \mathbf{x})] = \alpha + \beta'\mathbf{x}$. In the sample results below, we can say that the coefficient for X_1 is 0.76457, which is the expected log count of each unit increase in X_1. Alternatively, $\exp(0.76457) = 2.148$, which means that there is a 114.8% (a 2.148-fold) increase in Y for every unit increase in X_1. Similarly, X_2 has an expected log count of 0.38873, or $\exp(0.38873) = 1.475$, which means that there is a 47.5% (a 1.475-fold) increase in Y for every unit increase in X_2. In addition, the interpretation of the p-values, R-square, and Akaike Information Criterion (AIC) are the same as a regular multiple regression. The new goodness-of-fit and error measures, such as Pearson's Phi and Cohen's F-Squared, test the null hypothesis that the current model is a good fit (null hypothesis states that the error is zero), which means we want these error measures to be small. These measures are typically used to compare against running other Poisson regression models, where a model with lower Pearson's Phi, F-squared, and AIC indicates a better fit. R-square is an *absolute* measure in the sense that it has a fixed domain between 0 and 1 and can be readily interpreted (the percent variation in the dependent variable that can be explained by the variation in the independent variable). However, these other goodness-of-fit error measures like Phi, F-squared, and AIC are *relative* measures, where there is little interpretation by themselves, and are only used when comparing across multiple models.

Beyond Regression: Deming Regression
(Known Variance)

In regular multivariate regressions, the dependent variable Y is modeled and predicted by independent variables X_i with some error ε. However, in a Deming regression, we further assume that the data collected for the X variables have additional uncertainties and errors, or variances, that are used to provide a more relaxed fit in a Deming model. This implies that the predicted Y values will have a higher level of variance and uncertainty. The estimated variances are used to determine the lambda, where $\lambda = s_x^2/s_y^2$, and this parameter is minimized to determine the value of the slope and intercept coefficients. The optimized coefficients will be unbiased estimators of the true population parameters, and the error residuals are assumed to be normally distributed. The following illustrates a sample dataset needed when using BizStats to compute a Deming regression, as well as the required input parameters. This bivariate model requires the dependent and independent variables, followed by the known variance for both variables.

Deming Regression
Example Dataset

VAR1	VAR2
Dep	Indep
5.4	5.1
5.6	5.6
6.3	6.8
...	...
...	...
6.8	6.7
4.6	5.2
4.1	4.5

Model Inputs:
VAR1
VAR2
0.02
0.09

Deming Regression

	Coefficient	S.E.	DF	T-Stat	P-value
Intercept	-0.30704	1.29693	9	-0.23674	0.81816
Slope	1.04233	0.21194	9	4.91812	0.00083
Lambda	4.500000				

Beyond Regression: Multinomial Ordinal Logistic Regression

An Ordinal Logistic regression runs a multivariate ordinal logistic regression with two predictor variables and multiple frequencies of ordered variables, for instance, the two categorical variables of Gender (0/1) and Age (1–5), with five variables filled with the numbers or frequencies of people who responded Strongly Agree, Agree, Neutral, Disagree, or Strongly Disagree, which are presumably ordered. Note that this is an ordinal dataset where the Age variables are ordered, and it is multinomial because we are forecasting the four variables VAR3–VAR6 values.

Note that this is an extension of the binary logistic model, but in this example, there are multiple probability or frequency forecasts (VAR3–VAR6). Alternatively, you can collapse these four variables into a single variable and run the Logit regression multiple times. For instance, combine these four variables into a single variable that is binary (e.g., Strongly Agree = 1 and All Others = 0) to run a Logit model. Then, repeat the process with Agree = 1 and All Others = 0, and repeat the process. Remember to run only $k - 1$ models, where k is the number of frequency or count variables, and the last variable's predicted probability should be the complement of the remaining variables such that the total probability equals 100%. Hence, in the results below, although there are four variables VAR3–VAR6, the results only return VAR4–VAR6.

The next slide illustrates some sample datasets used in BizStats, the required input parameter format, and the results. Typically, the computed coefficients are interpreted in a log logistic function and can seem complicated at times. Nonetheless, it is much simpler to look at the predicted probabilities (relative frequencies) and forecasted values (frequencies) given all the possible combinations of the two predictor variables of gender and age. Unfortunately, this approach can only accommodate two predictor variables. If more predictors are needed, use the Logit model as described above.

Beyond Regression: Multinomial Ordinal Logistic Regression

Ordinal Logistic Regression Example Dataset

VAR1 Gender	VAR2 Age	VAR3 Strongly Agree	VAR4 Agree	VAR5 Disagree	VAR6 Strongly Disagree
0	0	3	9	18	24
0	1	6	13	16	28
0	5	9	13	17	20
. .	. .	. .	. .	. .	. .
. .	. .	. .	. .	. .	. .
1	2	10	15	16	12
1	3	5	14	12	8

Model Inputs:
VAR1; VAR2
VAR3; VAR4; VAR5; VAR6

Multiple Ordinal Logistic Regression

	VAR4	VAR5	VAR6
Intercept	0.70462	1.30649	1.91678
VAR1	0.03091	-0.29433	-0.51153
VAR2	-0.06285	-0.15006	-0.39874

Maximum Log Likelihood	-88.16470
Initial Log Likelihood	-58.71436
Chi-Square Statistic	-58.90066
Degrees of Freedom	6
P-value	N/A

Predicted Probabilities

VAR1	VAR2	VAR3	VAR4	VAR5	VAR6	Total
0.00	0.00	7.40%	14.97%	27.33%	50.31%	100.00%
0.00	1.00	9.40%	17.85%	29.87%	42.88%	100.00%
0.00	2.00	11.65%	20.79%	31.87%	35.69%	100.00%
0.00	3.00	14.11%	23.65%	33.23%	29.01%	100.00%
1.00	0.00	10.09%	21.05%	27.75%	41.12%	100.00%
1.00	1.00	12.40%	24.30%	29.37%	33.93%	100.00%
1.00	2.00	14.89%	27.41%	30.35%	27.35%	100.00%
1.00	3.00	17.50%	30.24%	30.70%	21.57%	100.00%

Forecasted Values

VAR1	VAR2	VAR3	VAR4	VAR5	VAR6	Total
0.00	0.00	4.00	8.08	14.76	27.17	54.00
0.00	1.00	5.92	11.25	18.82	27.02	63.00
0.00	2.00	6.87	12.27	18.81	21.05	59.00
0.00	3.00	6.21	10.40	14.62	12.76	44.00
1.00	0.00	4.84	10.10	13.32	19.74	48.00
1.00	1.00	7.44	14.58	17.62	20.36	60.00
1.00	2.00	7.89	14.52	16.09	14.49	53.00
1.00	3.00	6.82	11.79	11.97	8.41	39.00

Beyond Regression: Ridge Regression
(Low Variance, High Bias, High VIF, Multicollinearity)

A Ridge regression comes with higher bias than an Ordinary Least Squares (OLS) multiple regression but has less variance. It is more suitable in situations with high Variance Inflation Factors (VIF) and multicollinearity or when there is a high number of variables compared to data points. In a standard multiple regression model, we minimize the fitted sum of squared errors where $SSE = \sum_{i=1}^{n}(y_i - \hat{y}_i)^2$, but in a high VIF dataset with near perfect collinearity, the matrix is not invertible and cannot be solved. In this situation, the sum of squares is penalized with an added term where $SSE = \sum_{i=1}^{n}(y_i - \hat{y}_i)^2 + \lambda \sum_{j=0}^{k} b_i^{2}$ and λ is considered the adjustment parameter. When $\lambda = 0$, the results revert to an OLS approach. A small λ generates estimates with less bias but with a higher variance, versus a large λ that generates higher bias with less variance. The idea is to select a value that balances bias and variance, which might require trial and error. Finally, ridge-based regressions are suitable only when there are high VIF or significant multicollinearity. As discussed, multicollinearity can be solved by simply removing the offending independent variable(s) and running a standard regression. A sample dataset and results from BizStats are shown below.

Ridge Regression Example Dataset

VAR1	VAR2	VAR3	VAR4	VAR5
Y	X1	X2	X3	X4
3	3	6	2	8
15	7	7	11	14
19	11	11	23	33
...	...	...	...	...
...	...	...	...	...
23	23	17	16	10
31	28	22	22	15
39	31	16	28	24

Beyond Regression: Ridge Regression
(Low Variance, High Bias, High VIF, Multicollinearity)

```
Model Inputs:
VAR1
VAR2; VAR3; VAR4; VAR5
```

Multiple Ridge Regression

OVERALL FIT

Multiple R	0.96818	Maximum Log Likelihood	-0.09243
R-Square	0.93737	Akaike Info Criterion (AIC)	0.56583
Adjusted R-Square	0.91947	Bayes Schwarz Criterion (BSC)	0.81315
Standard Error	0.27578	Hannan-Quinn Criterion (HQC)	0.59993
Observations	18	Cohen's F-Squared	14.96580

ANOVA

	DF	SS	MS	F	p-Value
Regression	4	15.93522	3.98381	52.38029	0.00000
Residual	14	1.06478	0.07606		
Total	18	17.00000			

	Coeff	Std. Error	T-stat	P-value	Lower 5%	Upper 95%
VAR X1	0.42021	0.26106	1.60965	0.12978	-0.13970	0.98012
VAR X2	-0.12370	0.25386	-0.48727	0.63361	-0.66817	0.42077
VAR X3	0.79884	0.26794	2.98141	0.00991	0.22416	1.37351
VAR X4	-0.26279	0.11732	-2.23987	0.04184	-0.51443	-0.01116

*Ridge Regression has higher bias than OLS regression but with less variance.
It is more suitable in situations with high VIF and multicollinearity or a high
number of variables compared to data points.

Lambda	0.00000	0.00170	0.01700	0.17000	1.70000	17.00000	170.00000
VAR X1	0.41543	0.41602	0.42020	0.42021	0.36398	0.25379	0.07428
VAR X2	-0.37140	-0.36783	-0.33685	-0.12370	0.23040	0.23845	0.07251
VAR X3	1.11241	1.10725	1.06388	0.79884	0.39040	0.22834	0.07024
VAR X4	-0.38094	-0.37902	-0.36284	-0.26279	-0.09478	0.01508	0.02177

Beyond Regression: Weighted Regression (Heteroskedastic Model)

A Multiple Weighted regression runs a Multivariate Regression on Weighted Variables (also known as weighted least squares, or WLS) to correct for heteroskedasticity in all the variables. The weights used to adjust these variables are the user input standard deviations. As mentioned, the standard OLS approach minimizes the sum of squares of the errors $SSE = \sum_{i=1}^{n}(y_i - \hat{y}_i)^2$, but in a weighted least squares approach, we add an additional weight variable w_i such that we have $SSE = \sum_{i=1}^{n} w_i(y_i - \hat{y}_i)^2$. Similarly, in matrix notation, the standard regression's $B = (X'X)^{-1}(X'Y)$ becomes $B = (X'WX)^{-1}(X'WY)$. These weights are used as an additional input variable to the model in situations where the errors are heteroskedastic.

The following provides an example dataset and results from BizStats using a weighted regression model. Notice that a new input variable called standard deviation is required.

Finally, the regression results will show $1/Stdev$ as a representation of the weighted intercept and $X/Stdev$ as a representation of the weighted X variable. These variables can be used exactly as in a standard regression model to determine the predicted dependent variable's values. In fact, the results from a WLS should be relatively close to those in an OLS model.

Beyond Regression: Weighted Regression
(Heteroskedastic Model)

```
           Weighted Regression
             Example Dataset
         VAR1      VAR2        VAR3
          Y         X          Stdev
         266.7    2.60269      60.5
         342.5    3.62434      68.3
         418.1    4.31749      81.4
         ...       ...         98.8
         608.3    5.92693      110.6
         798.3    6.62007      145.6
         950.6    8.00637      173.1
        1216.5    8.92266      238.3
```

Model Inputs:
VAR221
VAR222
VAR223

Multiple Weighted Regression

OVERALL FIT

Multiple R	0.99552	Maximum Log Likelihood	-5.59816
R-Square	0.99107	Akaike Info Criterion (AIC)	2.14954
Adjusted R-Square	0.98809	Bayes Schwarz Criterion (BSC)	2.17933
Standard Error	0.56252	Hannan-Quinn Criterion (HQC)	1.94861
Observations	8	Cohen's F-Squared	110.93199

ANOVA

	DF	SS	MS	F	p-Value
Regression	2	210.61	105.31	332.79596	0.00000
Residual	6	1.90	0.32		
Total	8	212.51			

	Coeff	Std. Error	T-stat	P-value	Lower 5%	Upper 95%
X1/Stdev	126.84523	11.82915	10.72311	0.00004	97.90035	155.79012
1/Stdev	-100.84543	53.29659	-1.89216	0.10733	-231.25749	29.56662

Beyond Regression: Bootstrap Regression

Bootstrap regression is the process of re-running hundreds to thousands of the same regression model via resampled data to generate the best consensus forecasts. The idea is that in a random selection of data, taking the average forecast of an ensemble of models provides a more accurate prediction than a single sample. This is the same concept as the wisdom of the crowd. Risk Simulator provides variations of this bootstrap regression by resampling the residual errors as well as generating probabilistic Monte Carlo simulation assumptions as a result.

Bootstrapping works well in situations where the dataset consists of independent and identically distributed (*i.i.d.*) data points. This means that the sequential order of the data points is not important in fitting the underlying process. For example, if we sufficiently resample rows of data (one row may consist of multiple columns of independent variables) with replacement, the fitted parameters will be distributed around the true population parameters. Because we assume that order is not important, bootstrap regression is typically used in cross-sectional data only. In addition, there might be situations where bootstrap regression is problematic, especially when the data points are not *i.i.d.* such as when the data points are clumpy or sensitive to extreme values.

In a traditional Empirical Bootstrap, given the original data of i rows of observations of k independent variables, $(Y_i, X_{ij}, \ldots X_{ik})$, we resample and generate a new set of *i.i.d.* observations $(Y_i^*, X_{ij}^*, \ldots X_{ij}^*)$ with replacement, such that for each l, $P(Y_l^* = Y_i, X_l^* = X_i) = \frac{1}{n} \forall i = 1, \ldots, n$. Each time, we generate n new observations (typically less than the original total number of observations) from the original dataset and the regression is run to obtain the coefficients. The process is then repeated B times in the bootstrap. The fitted coefficients $\hat{\beta}_i$ will be approximately normally distributed around the true values of β_i. This method is fast and effective but can run afoul if the original sample size is small and certain data elements are highly susceptible to extreme values. For example, if certain influential and outlier data points are not resampled, the estimated regression equation may increase the spread or the skew of the final coefficients' distributions. This methodology is available in *Risk Simulator | Forecasting | Multiple Regression | Bootstrap Regression | Random X Case Resampling*.

An alternative approach is Parametric Residual Bootstrap (sometimes also known as the wild residual bootstrap), which helps reduce the impact of influential outlier data points. Using the residuals from the regression $e_i = Y_i - \hat{\beta}_0 - \hat{\beta}_i X_i$, we generate *i.i.d.* $\hat{e}_i^*, \ldots, \hat{e}_n^*$. Then, we fix the covariates $X_i^* = X_i$ for each i and resample only the value of Y_i using the residual e_i. The bootstrap sampling is then obtained by $Y_i^* = \hat{\beta}_0 + \hat{\beta}_i X_i + \Phi_i e_i$, where $\Phi \sim N(0,1)$. The *i.i.d.* normal random variable is applied to reduce any heteroskedasticity issues in the event the variance of the error is unstable over time. This approach is preferred when there are influential outliers or heteroskedasticity issues in the data, whereas the empirical bootstrap approach is preferred in almost all other cases. This is available in *Risk Simulator | Forecasting | Multiple Regression | Bootstrap Regression | Fixed X Parametric Residual Resampling*.

Summary of Exotic Regression Methods

Bayesian Regression

Used when you want to incorporate prior beliefs about parameters and update them with data, producing a full probability distribution for coefficients (not just point estimates). You specify a prior $p(\beta)$ and a likelihood $p(y \mid X, \beta)$, and compute the posterior $p(\beta \mid y, X)$ using Bayes' rule. It's especially useful with small samples, hierarchical structure, or when uncertainty quantification matters. Computation is often done via MCMC or variational inference.

Bootstrap Regression

Used to assess the stability and uncertainty of regression estimates by repeatedly resampling the data and refitting the model. You draw many bootstrap samples, compute $\hat{\beta}^{(b)}$ for each sample b, and use the empirical distribution of $\hat{\beta}^{(b)}$ to estimate standard errors, confidence intervals, and bias. It is helpful when analytic standard errors are unreliable or assumptions are questionable. It can be applied to OLS, logistic regression, and many other models.

Cointegration Test (Engle–Granger)

Used to test whether two (or more) nonstationary time series share a stable long-run relationship, even though each series individually has a unit root. In the Engle–Granger approach, you first estimate the long-run regression $y_t = \alpha + \beta x_t + u_t$, then test whether residuals u_t are stationary using an ADF-type test. If $u_t \sim I(0)$ while $x_t, y_t \sim I(1)$, the series are cointegrated. If cointegration exists, an Error Correction Model is typically used next.

Cox Regression (Survival Regression)

Used for time-to-event outcomes (e.g., time until failure, death, churn) when some observations are censored. The Cox proportional hazards model specifies $h(t \mid X) = h_0(t)\exp(X\beta)$, separating the baseline hazard from covariate effects. It estimates how predictors multiplicatively change the hazard rate without requiring you to fully specify $h_0(t)$. It's widely used in medical, reliability, and customer analytics.

Deming Regression

Used when both the predictor X and response Y are measured with error, which violates ordinary least squares assumptions. Unlike OLS, it fits a line by minimizing squared *orthogonal* distances from data points to the line. The fit is weighted by the ratio of measurement error variances in X and Y. This is common in lab calibration and method-comparison studies.

Difference-in-Differences Regression (DiD)

A quasi-experimental method used to estimate a treatment's causal effect by comparing outcome changes over time between treated and control groups. The key assumption is parallel trends: in the absence of treatment, treated and control would have evolved similarly. A standard model is
$Y_{it} = \beta_0 + \beta_1 Post_t + \beta_2 Treat_i + \beta_3 (Treat_i \times Post_t) + \varepsilon_{it}$ where β_3 is the estimated treatment effect. It's common in policy evaluation, program impact, and business interventions.

Summary of Exotic Regression Methods

Discriminant Analysis (LDA / QDA)

Used to classify observations into two or more groups using continuous predictors and a categorical outcome. LDA assumes each class is normally distributed with a shared covariance matrix Σ, leading to a linear decision boundary; QDA allows class-specific covariance matrices Σ_k, producing nonlinear boundaries. Classification is based on a discriminant score, e.g.

$\delta_k(x) = x^{\mathsf{T}} \Sigma^{-1} \mu_k - \frac{1}{2} \mu_k^{\mathsf{T}} \Sigma^{-1} \mu_k + \ln \pi_k$. It is related to regression/ANOVA in that it models group separation using linear combinations of predictors.

Elastic Net Regression

Used when you have many predictors, especially correlated ones, and want both shrinkage and variable selection. It combines Lasso and Ridge penalties:

$\min_{\beta} \sum (y_i - x_i^{\mathsf{T}} \beta)^2 + \lambda(\alpha \parallel \beta \parallel_1 + (1 - \alpha) \parallel \beta \parallel_2^2)$. The Ridge component helps keep groups of correlated variables together, while the Lasso component can set some coefficients exactly to zero. It's widely used in high-dimensional prediction problems.

Endogeneity Test (Durbin–Wu–Hausman using 2SLS)

Used to test whether a regressor is endogenous (correlated with the error term), which would bias OLS estimates. A common approach is to run a first-stage regression using instruments, obtain residuals, and include them in the structural equation; significance implies endogeneity. Conceptually, it compares OLS vs IV/2SLS estimates and checks whether the difference is systematic. This is a core diagnostic step before committing to IV methods.

Endogenous Model (Instrumental Variables with 2SLS)

Used when a regressor is endogenous and you have valid instruments that affect the regressor but not the outcome error term. In 2SLS, you first predict the endogenous regressor from instruments (and exogenous controls), then regress the outcome on that predicted regressor:

Stage 1: $X_{end} = Z\pi + X_{exo}\gamma + u$,
Stage 2: $y = \hat{X}_{end}\beta + X_{exo}\theta + \varepsilon$.

This isolates the variation in X_{end} that is plausibly exogenous. Validity depends heavily on instrument relevance and exclusion.

Error Correction Model (ECM, Engle–Granger)

Used after cointegration is established, to model short-run dynamics while enforcing long-run equilibrium. The model includes an "error correction term" (ECT) that measures last period's deviation from equilibrium, e.g.

$$\Delta y_t = \alpha + \lambda(y_{t-1} - \beta x_{t-1}) + \sum \phi_i \Delta y_{t-i} + \sum \psi_i \Delta x_{t-i} + \varepsilon_t.$$

The coefficient λ captures the speed of adjustment back toward the long-run relationship. ECMs are common in macro/finance where levels are nonstationary but tied together long-run.

Summary of Exotic Regression Methods

Generalized Additive Models (GAMs)

Used to model nonlinear relationships flexibly while preserving additivity across predictors. A GAM typically has the form

$$g(E[Y \mid X]) = \beta_0 + f_1(X_1) + \cdots + f_p(X_p),$$

where $f_j(\cdot)$ are smooth functions (often splines) learned from data. This gives more flexibility than linear regression without going fully "black box." GAMs are popular when interpretability of each predictor's shape matters.

Granger Causality

Used to test whether lagged values of one time series improve prediction of another time series beyond its own lags. A common setup is

$$y_t = c + \sum_{i=1}^{p} a_i\, y_{t-i} + \sum_{i=1}^{p} b_i\, x_{t-i} + \varepsilon_t,$$

and you test $H_0: b_1 = \cdots = b_p = 0$. Rejection suggests "Granger causality," meaning predictive (not necessarily structural) causality. It's widely used in econometrics and finance for lead–lag relationships.

Lasso Regression

Used when you want automatic variable selection and coefficient shrinkage in one step. It minimizes squared error plus an L_1 penalty $\lambda \parallel \beta \parallel_1$, which can drive some coefficients exactly to zero. This makes it useful in sparse, high-dimensional settings. It can be sensitive when predictors are highly correlated (often motivating Elastic Net).

Linear Regression (OLS)

Used to model a linear relationship between a continuous outcome and one or more predictors. It assumes $y = X\beta + \varepsilon$ and estimates $\hat{\beta}$ by minimizing $\sum(y_i - x_i^\mathsf{T}\beta)^2$. OLS is simple, interpretable, and often a baseline model. Its reliability depends on assumptions like linearity, exogeneity, and error behavior.

Logistic Regression

Used to model the probability of a binary outcome (0/1) as a function of predictors. It models the log-odds as linear: $\log\frac{p}{1-p} = X\beta$, with $p = P(Y = 1 \mid X)$. Coefficients interpret as changes in log-odds (or odds ratios after exponentiation). It is a workhorse for classification with strong interpretability.

Multinomial Logistic Regression

Used when the outcome has more than two unordered categories (e.g., choose A/B/C). It models each non-reference category via

$$\log\frac{P(Y = k \mid X)}{P(Y = K \mid X)} = X\beta_k, k = 1, \ldots, K - 1.$$

Predicted probabilities across categories sum to 1, enabling multi-class classification. Common in choice modeling and segmentation.

Summary of Exotic Regression Methods

Nonparametric Regression (Kernel & Local)

Used when you don't want to assume a fixed parametric relationship between X and Y. Instead, it estimates $m(x) = E[Y \mid X = x]$ directly from local neighborhoods, e.g. kernel smoothing:

$$\hat{m}(x) = \frac{\sum K_h(x - X_i)Y_i}{\sum K_h(x - X_i)}.$$

This allows the data to shape the curve but can require more data and careful bandwidth selection. It's great for exploratory modeling and flexible fits.

Ordinal Regression (Proportional Odds)

Used when the outcome is ordered categories (e.g., low/medium/high) and you want the model to respect ordering. A common specification is the proportional odds model:

$$\log\frac{P(Y \leq j \mid X)}{P(Y > j \mid X)} = \theta_j - X\beta.$$

It assumes the effect of predictors is consistent across thresholds ("parallel lines"). It's common in survey and rating-scale modeling.

Partial Least Squares (PLS) Regression

Used when predictors are many and collinear, and you want dimension reduction targeted toward predicting Y. PLS constructs latent components as linear combinations of X that maximize covariance with Y. Then Y is regressed on these components rather than the raw predictors. It's often used in chemometrics, marketing analytics, and high-dimensional settings.

Poisson Regression

Used for modeling count outcomes $(0,1,2,\ldots)$ as a function of predictors. It assumes $Y \sim$ Poisson (μ) with $\log(\mu) = X\beta$, making effects multiplicative on the expected count. It is the standard GLM for counts but can struggle with overdispersion. In practice it's often paired with checks or alternatives (negative binomial).

Poisson Regression (Exposure & Population Offset)

Used when counts depend on an underlying exposure such as time at risk, population size, or number of trials. You include an offset term so the model predicts rates:

$$\log(\mu_i) = X_i\beta + \log(\text{exposure}_i).$$

This makes interpretation about incidence rates rather than raw counts. Common in epidemiology, insurance frequency, event modeling.

Quantile Regression

Used to model conditional quantiles of Y (median, 90th percentile, etc.) instead of the conditional mean. It estimates β_τ by minimizing the check-loss $\sum \rho_\tau(y_i - x_i^{\top}\beta)$, where $\rho_\tau(u) = u(\tau - 1[u < 0])$. This is useful when effects differ in the tails or when you care about risk/inequality. It is robust to certain outlier patterns compared to OLS.

Summary of Exotic Regression Methods

Regression Discontinuity Design (RDD)

A quasi-experimental method that identifies causal effects by exploiting a cutoff in a running variable. The key idea is that units just above and below the cutoff are comparable, so a jump at the threshold is attributed to treatment. A common local linear specification is

$$Y_i = \alpha + \tau D_i + \beta_1(R_i - c) + \beta_2(R_i - c)D_i + \varepsilon_i,$$

$D_i = 1[R_i \geq c]$. Validity depends on no manipulation around the cutoff and smooth potential outcomes.

Ridge Regression

Used when predictors are highly correlated or when p is large, to stabilize estimates and reduce variance. It adds an L_2 penalty $\lambda \parallel \beta \parallel_2^2$, shrinking coefficients toward zero but typically not to exactly zero. Ridge often improves prediction when multicollinearity inflates OLS variance. It is a common baseline regularization method.

Robust Regression (Huber)

Used when outliers or heavy-tailed errors would overly influence OLS. It replaces squared loss with a robust loss $\rho(\cdot)$ that grows more slowly for large residuals (e.g., Huber). This down-weights extreme observations rather than letting them dominate the fit. It's useful for messy real-world data or when you suspect contamination.

Spatial Regression

Used when observations are spatially located and neighboring units are correlated, violating independence assumptions. Common forms include a spatial lag model $y = \rho W y + X\beta + \varepsilon$ or a spatial error model $\varepsilon = \lambda W \varepsilon + u$, where W encodes neighborhood weights. These models separate covariate effects from spatial spillovers/dependence. They are common in real estate, epidemiology, and regional economics.

Spline Regression

Used to model nonlinear relationships by stitching together low-degree polynomials while enforcing smoothness at knots. It represents the relationship using spline-basis functions (e.g., B-splines) so the curve can bend where needed without becoming overly wiggly. This is a structured alternative to fully nonparametric methods. Splines are building blocks of GAMs.

Stepwise Regression

Used to select a subset of predictors in a multiple regression when many candidates exist. Variants include forward selection, backward elimination, and combined forward/backward, often using p-values or information criteria (AIC/BIC) to decide adds/drops. It can be quick and practical, but it may overfit or yield unstable variable choices. It's best treated as a heuristic rather than definitive inference.

Stepwise Regression (Backward)

Starts with all predictors, then iteratively removes the least significant variable (largest p-value) and refits. The process continues until all remaining predictors meet a significance criterion (or improve an information criterion). This can be effective when you believe most variables matter but want to simplify. Results can still be sensitive to collinearity and sampling noise.

Summary of Exotic Regression Methods

Stepwise Regression (Correlation)

Begins by correlating Y with each candidate X, selecting the strongest correlation first and building the model incrementally. It adds variables until newly added variables become insignificant. This is fast and intuitive but can be misleading because correlations ignore joint effects and interactions. Strong predictors added early may "mask" others.

Three-Stage Least Squares (3SLS)

Used for simultaneous equation systems where regressors are endogenous and error terms are correlated across equations. It combines 2SLS to address endogeneity with a GLS step to exploit cross-equation correlation for efficiency. This can improve estimates when the system structure is correct. It's common in structural econometric modeling.

Through-Origin Regression (No Intercept)

Used when theory or measurement implies the regression line should pass through zero. The model is $y = X\beta + \varepsilon$ with no constant term, so predictions are forced to be 0 when all predictors are 0. This is appropriate in some physical or production settings but can be dangerous if the true intercept isn't actually zero. Fit statistics can also behave differently, so interpretation needs care.

Tobit Regression

Used when the dependent variable is censored (e.g., values pile up at a lower bound like 0). It assumes an underlying latent variable $y_i^* = x_i^\mathsf{T}\beta + \varepsilon_i$, but observed y_i is censored, such as $y_i = \max(c, y_i^*)$. Estimation uses the censored normal likelihood rather than OLS. It's common for expenditures, demand, and limited outcomes.

Two-Stage Least Squares (2SLS)

Used to handle endogeneity using instrumental variables that shift regressors without directly affecting the outcome error term. In stage 1, endogenous regressors are predicted using instruments; in stage 2, the outcome is regressed on those fitted values. This produces consistent estimates under valid instruments, though standard errors must account for the two-stage procedure. It's foundational in causal econometrics.

Vector Autoregression (VAR)

Used for multivariate time series where each variable depends on its own lags and the lags of other variables. A VAR(p) is $y_t = A_1 y_{t-1} + \cdots + A_p y_{t-p} + \varepsilon_t$, with y_t a vector and A_j coefficient matrices. VARs are used for forecasting and impulse response analysis (shock propagation). They require stationarity or differencing/cointegration when nonstationary.

Weighted Least Squares (WLS)

Used when observations have different error variances (heteroskedasticity), so OLS is inefficient and standard errors can be misleading. WLS gives higher weight to more precise observations by minimizing $\sum w_i(y_i - x_i^\mathsf{T}\beta)^2$, often with $w_i \propto 1/\sigma_i^2$. It can improve both estimation and inference when weights are correctly specified. It is common in meta-analysis and models with known measurement variance.

10. Quick Reference Guide: Analytics Summary (see textbook for details)

Dr. Johnathan Mun, Professor of Research
Quantitative Research Methods Course Slides
Seventh Edition, 2026, ROV Press

11. Forecasting and Predictive Modeling: Tomorrow's Forecast Today

Dr. Johnathan Mun, Professor of Research
Quantitative Research Methods Course Slides
Seventh Edition, 2026, ROV Press

23

What Is Forecasting?

Forecasting is a means of predicting the future where the
- Data can be time-series
- Data can be cross-sectional
- Data can be mixed

The main techniques of forecasting that are required in the CQRM exam

- Monte Carlo Simulation
  - Using the Delphi Method, expert opinion, and custom distribution
  - Applicable for time-series, cross-sectional, and mixed panel data
- Time-Series Analysis
  - Examines historical data to predict future trends and for time-series data only
  - Method selection based on statistical goodness-of-fit and error minimization
- Nonlinear Extrapolation
  - Applicable only to time-series data and uses historical cycles and trends to predict the future outcomes
- Multivariate Regression Analysis
  - Uses past relationships between variables and is applicable for time-series data, cross-sectional data, and mixed panel data
- Stochastic Processes
  - Applicable only on time-series data and uses only minimal assumptions to forecast the future; adapts Monte Carlo simulation and stochastic mathematics to predict the future
- Box–Jenkins ARIMA
  - Applicable only on time-series data and is an advanced econometric modeling technique

The Forecasting Methodologies

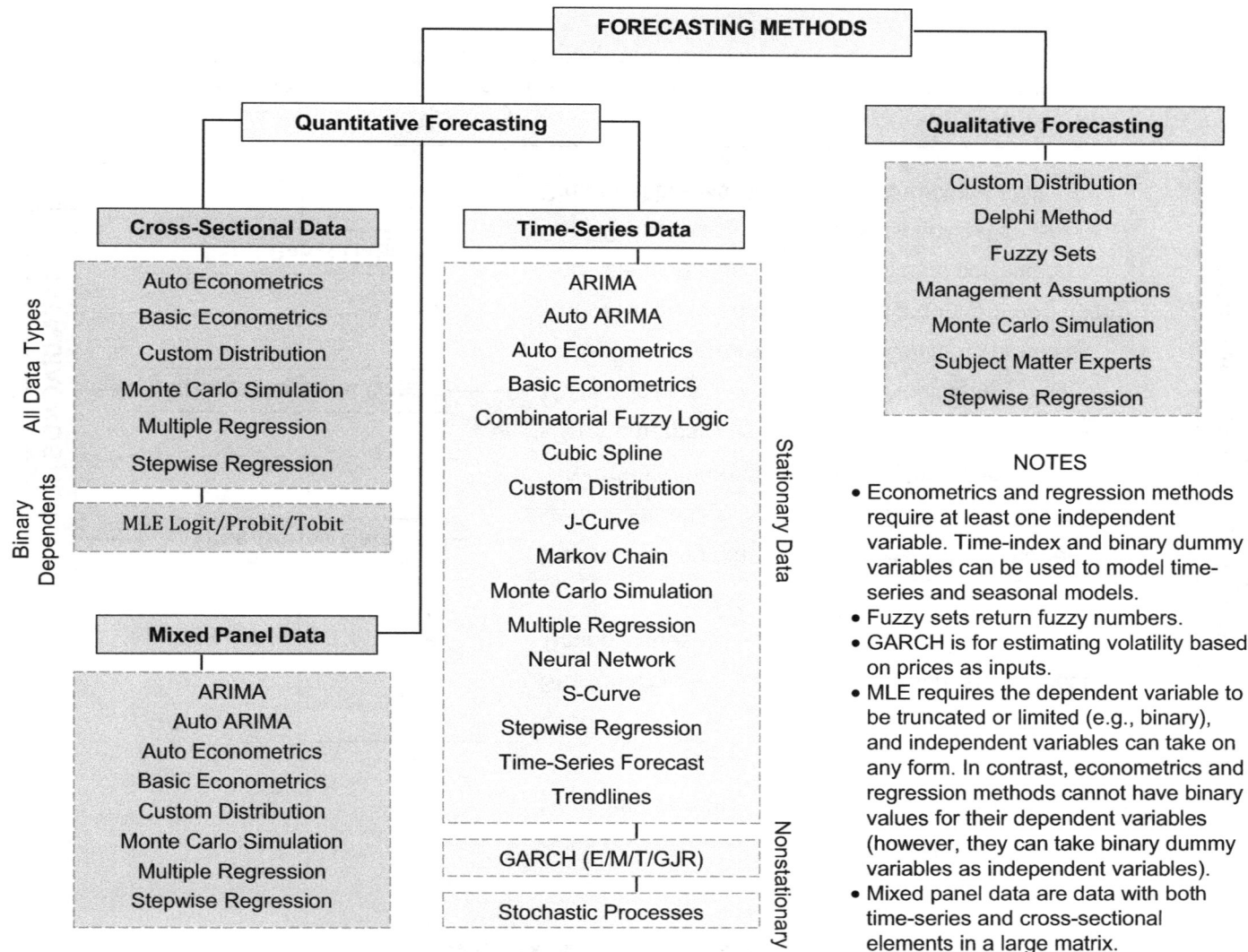

FORECASTING METHODS

Quantitative Forecasting

Cross-Sectional Data

All Data Types

Auto Econometrics
Basic Econometrics
Custom Distribution
Monte Carlo Simulation
Multiple Regression
Stepwise Regression

Binary Dependents

MLE Logit/Probit/Tobit

Mixed Panel Data

ARIMA
Auto ARIMA
Auto Econometrics
Basic Econometrics
Custom Distribution
Monte Carlo Simulation
Multiple Regression
Stepwise Regression

Time-Series Data

Stationary Data

ARIMA
Auto ARIMA
Auto Econometrics
Basic Econometrics
Combinatorial Fuzzy Logic
Cubic Spline
Custom Distribution
J-Curve
Markov Chain
Monte Carlo Simulation
Multiple Regression
Neural Network
S-Curve
Stepwise Regression
Time-Series Forecast
Trendlines

Nonstationary

GARCH (E/M/T/GJR)

Stochastic Processes

Qualitative Forecasting

Custom Distribution
Delphi Method
Fuzzy Sets
Management Assumptions
Monte Carlo Simulation
Subject Matter Experts
Stepwise Regression

NOTES

- Econometrics and regression methods require at least one independent variable. Time-index and binary dummy variables can be used to model time-series and seasonal models.
- Fuzzy sets return fuzzy numbers.
- GARCH is for estimating volatility based on prices as inputs.
- MLE requires the dependent variable to be truncated or limited (e.g., binary), and independent variables can take on any form. In contrast, econometrics and regression methods cannot have binary values for their dependent variables (however, they can take binary dummy variables as independent variables).
- Mixed panel data are data with both time-series and cross-sectional elements in a large matrix.

Data Diagnostics

Autocorrelation   Cyclicality

Dependent errors   Distributive lags

Heteroskedasticity   Lags

Leads   Nonstationarity

Seasonality   Stochastic process

Timing issues   Volatile jumps

DATA DIAGNOSTICS

Time-Series Data

Cross-Sectional Data

Mixed Panel Data

Bad or missing data	Bad-fitting model
Control variables	Data collection error
Error measurements	Interactions
Micronumerosity	Model specification
Multicollinearity	Nonlinearity
Nonspherical errors	Omitted variables
Out-of-range forecast	Redundant variables
Self-selection bias	Serial correlation
Specific biases	Specification errors
Structural breaks	Structural shift

Applicable only to the time-series segment of the mixed panel dataset

Time-series data is more prevalent in real life, and, therefore, there are more time-series forecast methods as well as error and specification tests for time-series data.

Time-Series Forecasting

The eight most common time-series models, segregated by seasonality and trend, are listed below. For instance, if the data variable has no trend or seasonality, then a single moving-average model or a single exponential-smoothing model would suffice. However, if seasonality exists but no discernable trend is present, either a seasonal additive or seasonal multiplicative model would be better, and so forth.

	NO SEASONALITY	WITH SEASONALITY
WITHOUT TREND	Single Moving Average	Seasonal Additive
WITHOUT TREND	Single Exponential Smoothing	Seasonal Multiplicative
WITH TREND	Double Moving Average	Holt–Winters Additive
WITH TREND	Double Exponential Smoothing	Holt–Winters Multiplicative

Year	Quarter	Period	Sales
2010	1	1	$684.20
2010	2	2	$584.10
2010	3	3	$765.40
2010	4	4	$892.30
2011	1	5	$885.40
2011	2	6	$677.00
2011	3	7	$1,006.60
2011	4	8	$1,122.10
2012	1	9	$1,163.40
2012	2	10	$993.20
2012	3	11	$1,312.50
2012	4	12	$1,545.30
2013	1	13	$1,596.20
2013	2	14	$1,260.40
2013	3	15	$1,735.20
2013	4	16	$2,029.70
2014	1	17	$2,107.80
2014	2	18	$1,650.30
2014	3	19	$2,304.40
2014	4	20	$2,639.40

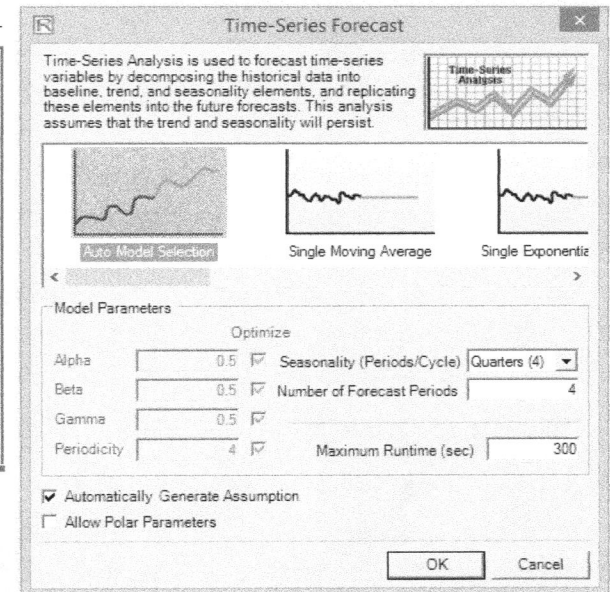

Time-Series Forecast

Time-Series Analysis is used to forecast time-series variables by decomposing the historical data into baseline, trend, and seasonality elements, and replicating these elements into the future forecasts. This analysis assumes that the trend and seasonality will persist.

Auto Model Selection | Single Moving Average | Single Exponentia

Model Parameters

Optimize

Alpha	0.5	☑ Seasonality (Periods/Cycle)	Quarters (4) ▼
Beta	0.5	☑ Number of Forecast Periods	4
Gamma	0.5	☑	
Periodicity	4	☑ Maximum Runtime (sec)	300

☑ Automatically Generate Assumption
☐ Allow Polar Parameters

OK   Cancel

Due Diligence on Forecasting: Beware of the Black Box

- Out of Range Forecasts
- Model Errors (Granger Causality and Causality Loops)
- Nonlinearities and Interactions
- Bad-fitting Model (Bad Goodness-of-Fit)
- Structural Breaks and Shifts
- Specification Errors and Incorrect Econometric Methods
- Omitted Variables
- Multicollinearity
- Redundant Variables
- Micronumerosity and Nonstationary Data
- Heteroskedasticity and Homoskedasticity
- Autocorrelation and Serial Correlation
- Seasonality and Cyclicality
- Non-spherical and Dependent Errors
- Random Walks, Non-Predictability, and Stochastic Processes:
  - Brownian Motion
  - Mean-Reversion
  - Jump-Process
  - Mixed Process
- And many, many, many other technical issues…

Homoskedasticity vs. Heteroskedasticity

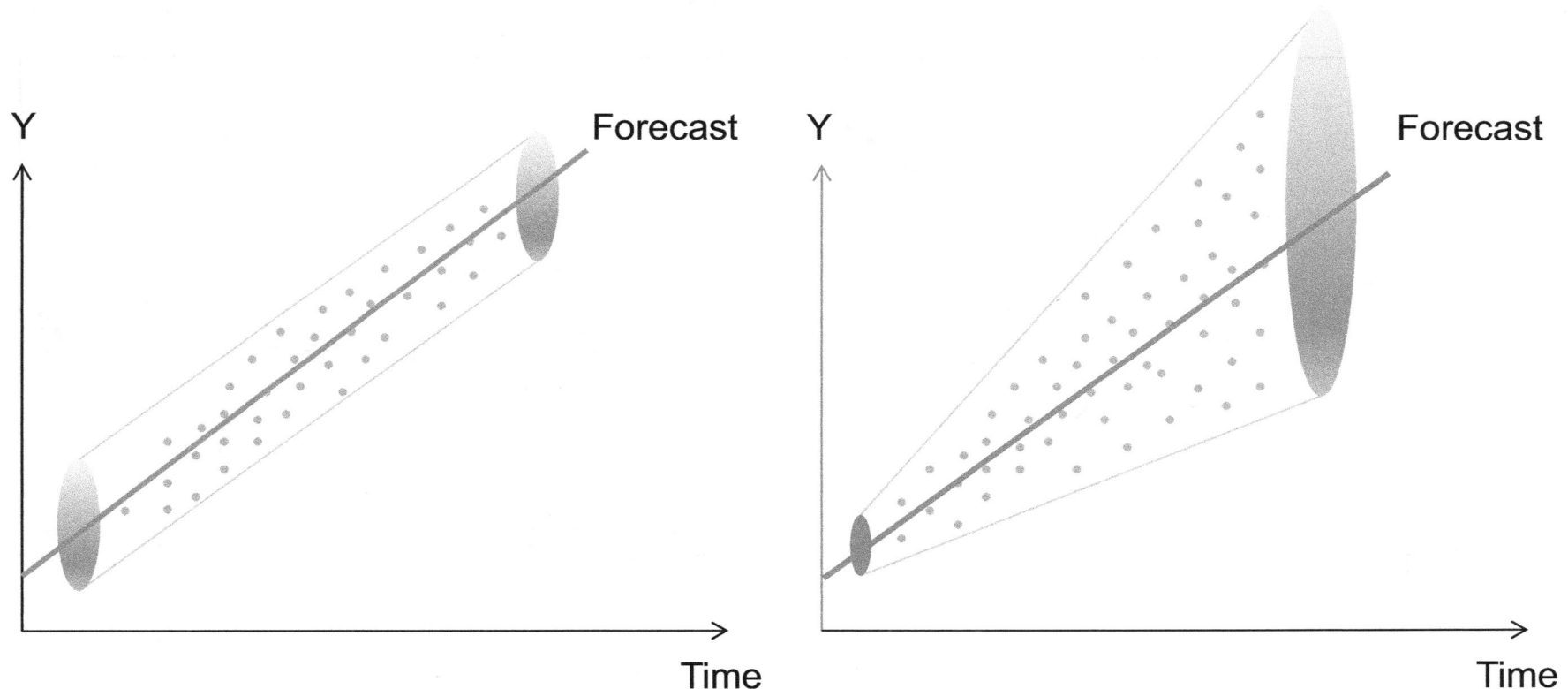

The best-fitting line that minimizes the vertical errors (fitted line versus actual data) is the forecast line (e.g., regression analysis). The errors can be visualized as either constant over time (homoskedastic) like a tube (the forecast error is the wiggle room of the forecast line inside this tube) or it can fan out over time (heteroskedastic) where the further out you go, the higher the level of forecast uncertainty…

Homoskedasticity vs. Heteroskedasticity

Forecast error is constant over time on homoskedastic data, whereas forecast errors increase over time (uncertainty increases the further out in time) for heteroskedastic data. If heteroskedasticity is not accounted for or modeled, forecast accuracy in the short term is high (low uncertainty) but this condition is misleading as the uncertainty increases the further out in time you go.

Qualitative versus Quantitative Forecasts

- Generally, forecasting can be divided into quantitative and qualitative approaches. Qualitative forecasting is used when little to no reliable historical, contemporaneous, or comparable data exists. Several qualitative methods exist such as the Delphi or expert opinion approach (a consensus-building forecast by field experts, marketing experts, or internal staff members), management assumptions (target growth rates set by senior management), as well as market research or external data or polling and surveys (data obtained through third-party sources, industry and sector indexes, or from active market research). These estimates can be either single-point estimates (an average consensus) or a set of prediction values (a distribution of predictions). The latter can be entered into Risk Simulator as a custom distribution and the resulting predictions can be simulated, that is, to run a nonparametric simulation using the prediction data points as the distribution.

- On the quantitative side of forecasting, the available data or data that need to be forecasted can be divided into time-series (values that have a time element to them, such as revenues at different years, inflation rates, interest rates, market share, failure rates, and so forth), cross-sectional (values that are time-independent, such as the grade point average of sophomore students across the nation in a particular year, given each student's levels of SAT scores, IQ, and the number of alcoholic beverages consumed per week), or mixed panel (a mixture between time-series and panel data, e.g., predicting sales over the next 10 years given budgeted marketing expenses and market share projections, this means that the sales data is time-series but exogenous variables such as marketing expenses and market share exist to help to model the forecast predictions).

Using Custom Distribution for Qualitative Forecasting

- Great for the DELPHI METHOD
- Obtain the general set of expert values and tabulate them, i.e., count the frequencies of occurrence of each value and put these values into the Custom Distribution:
  - Define an assumption as usual and choose Custom Distribution.
  - Click on Create a Distribution.
  - Start entering the X values (the set of expert values) and the Weights (Frequency of Occurrence).
  - Click on Update Chart to view the chart to make sure the custom distribution looks as expected.
  - Click on Apply to insert the distribution into the Assumption Gallery and close this form.
  - Back in the Assumption Gallery, click OK to confirm the creation of this custom assumption.

Close this distribution maker to go back to the main Assumption Gallery

1. Enter the relevant X and Weight or Frequency values and hit TAB

2. Click on Update Chart to see the graphical view of the data entered

3. Click on Apply to set the assumption into the Distributional Gallery

3. Hit File, Save to save the newly created distribution, then close this designer and set an assumption (use Custom and choose the created distribution)

EXERCISES

ARIMA

Autoregressive Integrated Moving Average (ARIMA) forecasts apply advanced econometric modeling techniques to forecast time-series data by first *back-fitting* to historical data and then *forecasting* the future. Advanced knowledge of econometrics is required to properly model ARIMA. Please see the ARIMA example Excel model for more details. However, to get started quickly, follow the instructions below:

1. Start Excel and open the example model *Risk Simulator | Example Models | 01 Advanced Forecast Models*.
2. Go to the *ARIMA and AUTO ARIMA* worksheet.
3. Select the data area *B5:B440* and click on *Risk Simulator | Forecasting | ARIMA* and click *OK* (you can keep the default settings for now). Spend some time reviewing the generated ARIMA report.
4. Next, go back to the worksheet and rerun ARIMA. This time you can try different P, D, Q values and enter a different Forecast Period of choice (e.g., *1,0,0* for P, D, Q, and *5* for Forecast… remember that these inputs have to be 0 or positive integers).
5. Run ARIMA again, but this time, click on the link icon to select the dataset *B5:B440* on the worksheet for the time-series variable and *C5:D445* for the exogenous variables.
   - Exercise Question: What does exogenous variable mean?
   - Exercise Question: What types of variables might be well-suited for ARIMA forecasting?
   - Exercise Question: What types of data are appropriate for ARIMA? Time-series, cross-sectional, or mixed-panel data?
   - Exercise Question: What are the P, D, Q values used for?
   - Exercise Question: How does ARIMA compare with multiple regression analysis?

Note: For ARIMA and AUTO ARIMA, you can run as many forecast periods as you wish if you only use the time-series variable (*Y*). If you add exogenous variables (*X*), note that your forecast period is limited to the number of exogenous variables' data periods minus the time-series variable's data periods. For example, you can only forecast up to 5 periods if you have time-series historical data of 100 periods and only if you have exogenous variables of 105 periods (100 historical periods to match the time-series variable and 5 additional future periods of independent exogenous variables to forecast the time-series dependent variable).

EXERCISES

BASIC ECONOMETRICS & AUTO ECONOMETRICS

To run an econometric model, follow the instructions below:

1. Start Excel and open the example model Risk Simulator | Example Models | 01 Advanced Forecast Models.
2. Go to the Basic Econometrics worksheet.
3. Select the data area B5:G55 and click on Risk Simulator | Forecasting | Basic Econometrics and then type in the variables and their modifications for the dependent and independent variables.
   - Dependent Variable: VAR1
   - Independent Variables: VAR2; VAR3; VAR4; VAR5; VAR6
4. Click on Show Results to preview the computed model and click OK to generate the econometric model report.
5. Go back to the data and rerun Basic Econometrics. This time, set up the model:
   - Dependent Variable: LN(VAR1)
   - Independent Variable: LN(VAR2); VAR3*VAR4; LAG(VAR5,1); DIFF(VAR6); TIME
6. Go back to the data one more time and rerun Basic Econometrics. This time, select the Multiple Models option. Run the initial model with VAR1 as the dependent variable and LAG(VAR5,INTEGER1); VAR3*VAR4 as the independent variable, set INTEGER1 to be between 1 and 3, Sort by Adjusted R-Square, and Shift Data 1 Row Down 5 Times and click OK.
   - Exercise Question: What happens when you perform a shift to multiple econometric models?
   - Exercise Question: How do you model linear, nonlinear, interacting, lag, lead, log, natural log, time-series, difference, and ratios?
7. Go back to the data, select Risk Simulator | Forecasting | Auto Econometrics and this time select Linear and Nonlinear Interacting, and then click OK. Review the generated report.

Note: Only one variable is allowed as the Dependent Variable (Y), whereas multiple variables are allowed in the Independent Variables (X) section, separated by a semicolon (;) and basic mathematical functions can be used (e.g., LN, LOG, LAG, +, -, /, *, TIME, RESIDUAL, DIFF). You can also automatically generate Multiple Models by entering a sample model and using the predefined 'INTEGER(N)' variable as well as Shifting Data up or down specific rows repeatedly. For instance, if you use the variable LAG(VAR1, INTEGER1) and you set INTEGER1 to be between MIN = 1 and MAX = 3, then the following three models will be run: LAG(VAR1,1), then LAG(VAR1,2), and, finally, LAG(VAR1,3). Using this Multiple Models section in Basic Econometrics, you can run hundreds of models by simply entering a single model equation if you use these predefined integer variables and shifting methods.

EXERCISES

MULTIPLE REGRESSION

To run the multiple regression analysis, follow these steps:
1. Start Excel and open the example model Risk Simulator | Example Models | 01 Advanced Forecast Models.
2. Go to the Regression worksheet.
3. Select the data area including the headers or cells B5:G55 and click on Risk Simulator | Forecasting | Regression Analysis. Select the Dependent Variable as the variable Y, leave everything else alone, and click OK. Review the generated report.
    *   Exercise Question: Which of the independent variables are statistically insignificant and how can you tell? That is, which statistic did you use?
    *   Exercise Question: How good is the initial model's fit?
    *   Exercise Question: Delete the entire variable columns of data that are insignificant and rerun the regression (i.e., select the column headers in Excel's grid, right-click and delete). Compare the R-Square and Adjusted R-Square values for both regressions. What can you determine?
    *   Exercise Question: Will R-Square always increase when you have more independent variables, regardless of their being statistically significant? How about Adjusted R-Square? Which is a more conservative and appropriate goodness-of-fit measure?
    *   Exercise Question: What can you do to increase the Adjusted R-Square of this model? Hint: Consider nonlinearity and some other econometric modeling techniques.
    *   Exercise Question: Run an Auto Econometric model on this dataset and select the nonlinear and interacting option and see what happens. Does the generated model better fit the data?

EXERCISES

TIME-SERIES DECOMPOSITION

Time-series forecasting decomposes the historical data into the baseline, trend, and seasonality, if any. The models then apply an optimization procedure to find the alpha, beta, and gamma parameters for the baseline, trend, and seasonality coefficients and then recompose them into a forecast. In other words, this methodology first applies a backcast to find the best-fitting model and best-fitting parameters of the model that minimizes forecast errors, and then proceeds to forecast the future based on the historical data that exist. This process, of course, assumes that the same baseline growth, trend, and seasonality hold going forward. Even if they do not, say, when there exists a structural shift (e.g., company goes global, has a merger, spin-off, and so forth), the baseline forecasts can be computed and then the required adjustments can be made to the forecasts.

To run these forecast models, follow the steps below:

1. Start Excel and open the example model Risk Simulator | Example Models | 01 Advanced Forecast Models.
2. Go to the Time Series Decomposition worksheet.
3. Create a new profile at Risk Simulator | New Simulation Profile if you wish the software to automatically generate assumptions for the forecast. Otherwise, if you do not need the assumption, a new profile is not required.
4. Select the data excluding the headers or cells E25:E44.
5. Click on Risk Simulator | Forecasting | Time Series Analysis and choose Auto Model Selection, set Forecast = 4, Periods and Seasonality = 4. Note that you can only select Create Simulation Assumptions if an existing Simulation Profile exists. Click OK to run the analysis. Review the generated report and chart.
    *   Exercise Question: What do the alpha, beta, and gamma mean or represent?
    *   Exercise Question: What are the three elements that a time-series analysis decomposes into?
    *   Exercise Question: Can time series analysis be used to forecast cross-sectional data? How about for panel data?
    *   Exercise Question: How accurate are the forecast results? How can you tell? What does each of the error measures represent in the report?
    *   Exercise Question: How is heteroskedasticity modeled in this forecast method? Hint: Look at each of the input assumptions automatically set up in the report.

Interpreting Time-Series Analysis Report

The figure here illustrates the sample results generated by using the *Forecasting* tool. The model selected by the software as the best-fitting model was a Holt-Winters' Multiplicative model. Notice that in the report, the model-fitting and forecast chart indicate that the trend and seasonality are picked up nicely by the Holt-Winters' Multiplicative model. The time-series analysis report provides the relevant optimized alpha, beta, and gamma parameters; the error measurements; fitted data; forecast values; and fitted-forecast graph. The parameters are simply for reference. Alpha captures the memory effect of the base level changes over time, beta is the trend parameter that measures the strength of the trend, while gamma measures the seasonality strength of the historical data. The analysis decomposes the historical data into these three elements and then recomposes them to forecast the future. The fitted data illustrates the historical data as well as the fitted data using the recomposed model and shows how close the forecasts are in the past (a technique called *backcasting*). The forecast values are either single-point estimates or assumptions (if the Automatically Generate Assumptions option is chosen and if a simulation profile exists). The graph illustrates these historical, fitted, and forecast values. The chart is a powerful communication and visual tool to see how good the forecast model is.

This time-series analysis module contains the eight time-series models. You can choose the specific model to run based on the trend and seasonality criteria or choose the Auto Model Selection, which will automatically iterate through all eight methods, optimize the parameters, and find the best-fitting model for your data. Alternatively, if you choose one of the eight models, you can also deselect the *optimize* checkboxes and enter your own alpha, beta, and gamma parameters. In addition, you would need to enter the relevant seasonality periods if you choose the automatic model selection or any of the seasonal models.

Holt-Winter's Multiplicative

Summary Statistics

Alpha, Beta, Gamma	RMSE	Alpha, Beta, Gamma	RMSE
0.00, 0.00, 0.00	914.824	0.00, 0.00, 0.00	914.824
0.10, 0.10, 0.10	415.322	0.10, 0.10, 0.10	415.322
0.20, 0.20, 0.20	187.202	0.20, 0.20, 0.20	187.202
0.30, 0.30, 0.30	118.795	0.30, 0.30, 0.30	118.795
0.40, 0.40, 0.40	101.794	0.40, 0.40, 0.40	101.794
0.50, 0.50, 0.50	102.143		

The analysis was run with alpha = 0.2429, beta = 1.0000, gamma = 0.7797, and seasonality = 4

Time-Series Analysis Summary

When both seasonality and trend exist, more advanced models are required to decompose the data into their base elements: a base-case level (L) weighted by the alpha parameter; a trend component (b) weighted by the beta parameter; and a seasonality component (S) weighted by the gamma parameter. Several methods exist but the two most common are the Holt-Winters' additive seasonality and Holt-Winters' multiplicative seasonality methods. In the Holt-Winter's additive model, the base case level, seasonality, and trend are added together to obtain the forecast fit.

The best-fitting test for the moving average forecast uses the root mean squared errors (RMSE). The RMSE calculates the square root of the average squared deviations of the fitted values versus the actual data points.

Mean Squared Error (MSE) is an absolute error measure that squares the errors (the difference between the actual historical data and the forecast-fitted data predicted by the model) to keep the positive and negative errors from canceling each other out. This measure also tends to exaggerate large errors by weighting the large errors more heavily than smaller errors by squaring them, which can help when comparing different time-series models. Root Mean Square Error (RMSE) is the square root of MSE and is the most popular error measure, also known as the quadratic loss function. RMSE can be defined as the average of the absolute values of the forecast errors and is highly appropriate when the cost of the forecast errors is proportional to the absolute size of the forecast error. The RMSE is used as the selection criteria for the best-fitting time-series model.

Mean Absolute Percentage Error (MAPE) is a relative error statistic measured as an average percent error of the historical data points and is most appropriate when the cost of the forecast error is more closely related to the percentage error than the numerical size of the error. Finally, an associated measure is the Theil's U statistic, which measures the naivety of the model's forecast. That is, if the Theil's U statistic is less than 1.0, then the forecast method used provides an estimate that is statistically better than guessing.

Period	Actual	Forecast Fit
1	684.20	
2	584.10	
3	765.40	
4	892.30	
5	885.40	684.20
6	677.00	667.55
7	1006.60	935.45
8	1122.10	1198.09
9	1163.40	1112.48
10	993.20	887.95
11	1312.50	1348.38
12	1545.30	1546.53
13	1596.20	1572.44
14	1260.40	1299.20
15	1735.20	1704.77
16	2029.70	1976.23
17	2107.80	2026.01
18	1650.30	1637.28
19	2304.40	2245.93
20	2639.40	2643.09
Forecast21		2713.69
Forecast22		2114.79
Forecast23		2900.42
Forecast24		3293.81
Forecast25		3346.55
Forecast26		2580.81
Forecast27		3506.19
Forecast28		3947.61
Forecast29		3979.41
Forecast30		3046.83

Error Measurements	
RMSE	71.8132
MSE	5157.1348
MAD	53.4071
MAPE	4.50%
Theil's U	0.3054

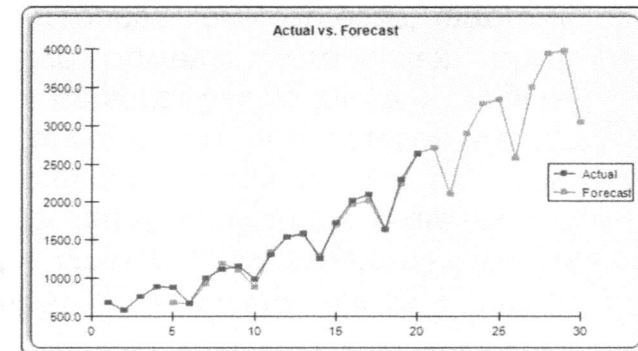

Actual vs. Forecast

Nonlinear Extrapolation Forecasts

- Extrapolation involves making statistical projections by using historical trends that are projected for a specified period of time into the future. It is only used for time-series forecasts. For cross-sectional or mixed panel data (time-series with cross-sectional data), multivariate regression is more appropriate. This methodology is useful when major changes are not expected, that is, causal factors are expected to remain constant or when the causal factors of a situation are not clearly understood. It also helps discourage the introduction of personal biases into the process. Extrapolation is fairly reliable, relatively simple, and inexpensive. However, extrapolation, which assumes that recent and historical trends will continue, produces large forecast errors if discontinuities occur within the projected time period. That is, pure extrapolation of time-series data assumes that all we need to know is contained in the historical values of the series that is being forecasted. If we assume that past behavior is a good predictor of future behavior, extrapolation is appealing. This makes it a useful approach when all that is needed are many short-term forecasts.

- This methodology estimates the $f(x)$ function for any arbitrary x value, by interpolating a smooth nonlinear curve through all the x values, and using this smooth curve, extrapolates future x values beyond the historical dataset. The methodology employs either the polynomial functional form or the rational functional form (a ratio of two polynomials). Typically, a polynomial functional form is sufficient for well-behaved data, however, rational functional forms are sometimes more accurate (especially with polar functions, i.e., functions with denominators approaching zero).

- When the historical data is smooth and follows some nonlinear patterns and curves, extrapolation is better than time-series analysis. However, when the data patterns follow seasonal cycles and a trend, time-series analysis will provide better results. It is always advisable to run both time-series analysis and extrapolation and compare the results to see which has a lower error measure and a better fit.

- To run a nonlinear extrapolation, type in or open an existing set of historical data as a basis to forecast from. The data needs to be arranged in a single column. Select the entire data series (excluding the title) and click on *Risk Simulator | Forecasting | Nonlinear Extrapolation*.

ℝ 🅧 Running and Interpreting Nonlinear Extrapolation

The generated report shows the historical data, the fitted forecasts, errors in fit, and forecast values, as well as the relevant error parameters and forecast chart. You can now compare the chart and forecast statistics with those generated from Time-Series Analysis.

To run a nonlinear extrapolation forecast:

- Type in or open existing time-series data.

- Select the entire column of data and start *Risk Simulator | Forecasting | Nonlinear Extrapolation.*

- Choose Automatic Selection and enter the number of periods to forecast and run the analysis.

Nonlinear Extrapolation

Statistical Summary

Extrapolation involves making statistical projections by using historical trends that are projected for a specified period of time into the future. It is only used for time-series forecasts. For cross-sectional or mixed panel data (time-series with cross-sectional data), multivariate regression is more appropriate. This methodology is useful when major changes are not expected, that is, causal factors are expected to remain constant or when the causal factors of a situation are not clearly understood. It also helps discourage the introduction of personal biases into the process. Extrapolation is fairly reliable, relatively simple, and inexpensive. However, extrapolation, which assumes that recent and historical trends will continue, produces large forecast errors if discontinuities occur within the projected time period. That is, pure extrapolation of time series assumes that all we need to know is contained in the historical values of the series that is being forecasted. If we assume that past behavior is a good predictor of future behavior, extrapolation is appealing. This makes it a useful approach when all that is needed are many short-term forecasts.

This methodology estimates the f(x) function for any arbitrary x value, by interpolating a smooth nonlinear curve through all the x values, and using this smooth curve, extrapolates future x values beyond the historical data set. The methodology employs either the polynomial functional form or the rational functional form (a ratio of two polynomials). Typically, a polynomial functional form is sufficient for well-behaved data, however, rational functional forms are sometimes more accurate (especially with polar functions, i.e., functions with denominators approaching zero).

Error Measurements
RMSE   19.6799
MSE   387.2974
MAD   10.2095
MAPE   31.56%
Theil's U   1.1210

Function Type: Rational

Historical Sales Revenues
Polynomial Growth Rates

Year	Month	Period	Sales
2014	1	1	$1.00
2014	2	2	$6.73
2014	3	3	$20.52
2014	4	4	$45.25
2014	5	5	$83.59
2014	6	6	$138.01
2014	7	7	$210.87
2014	8	8	$304.44
2014	9	9	$420.89
2014	10	10	$562.34
2014	11	11	$730.85
2014	12	12	$928.43

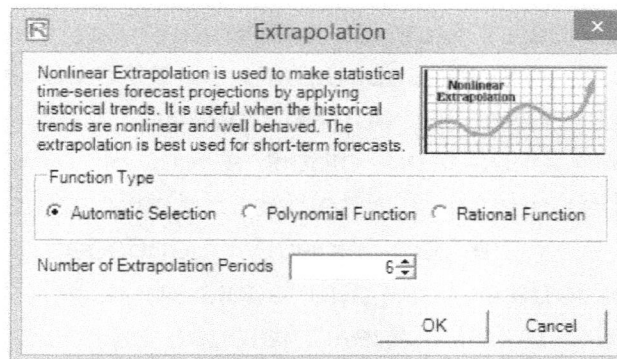

Extrapolation dialog: Nonlinear Extrapolation is used to make statistical time-series forecast projections by applying historical trends. It is useful when the historical trends are nonlinear and well behaved. The extrapolation is best used for short-term forecasts.

Function Type: ● Automatic Selection ○ Polynomial Function ○ Rational Function

Number of Extrapolation Periods: 6

OK   Cancel

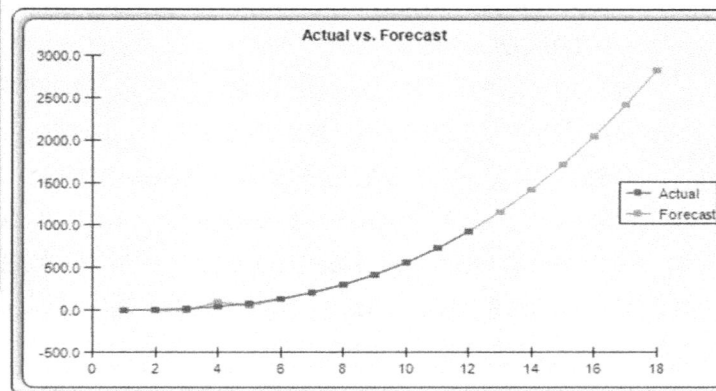

Actual vs. Forecast

Multivariate Regression Analysis

- It is assumed that the user is sufficiently knowledgeable about the fundamentals of regression analysis. The general bivariate linear regression equation takes the form where β_0 is the intercept, β_1 is the slope, and ε is the error term. It is bivariate as there are only two variables, a Y or dependent variable, and an X or independent variable, where X is also known as the regressor (sometimes a bivariate regression is also known as a univariate regression as there is only a single independent variable X). The dependent variable is named as such as it *depends* on the independent variable, for example, sales revenue depends on the amount of marketing costs expended on a product's advertising and promotion, making the dependent variable sales and the independent variable marketing costs. An example of a bivariate regression is seen as simply inserting the best-fitting line through a set of data points in a two-dimensional plane. In other cases, a multivariate regression can be performed, where there are multiple or k number of independent X variables or regressors, where the general regression equation will now take the functional form of $Y = \beta_0 + \beta_1 X_1 + \beta_2 X_2 + \ldots + \beta_k X_k + \varepsilon$. In this case, the best-fitting line will be within a $k + 1$ dimensional plane.

- To run a multivariate regression, type in or open an existing set of historical data as a basis to forecast from. The data variables need to be arranged in multiple columns. Select the entire data series (you can include the title) and click *Risk Simulator | Forecasting | Multiple Regression Analysis*.

Running a Multivariate Regression Analysis

Multivariate Regression

Y	X1	X2	X3	X4	X5
521	18308	185	4.041	79.6	7.2
367	1148	600	0.55	1	8.5
443	18068	372	3.665	32.3	5.7
365	7729	142	2.351	45.1	7.3
614	100484	432	29.76	190.8	7.5
385	16728	290	3.294	31.8	5
286	14630	346	3.287	678.4	6.7
397	4008				
764	38927				
427	22322				
153	3711				
231	3136				
524	50508				
328	28886				
240	16996				
286	13035				
285	12973				
569	16309				
96	5227				
498	19235				
481	44487				
468	44213				
177	23619				
198	9106				
458	24917				
108	3872				
246	8945				
291	2373				
68	7128				
311	23624				
606	5242				
512	92629				
426	28795				
47	4487				
265	48799				

To run a multiple regression analysis:

- Type in or open existing time-series or cross-sectional data and select the entire columns of data and click on
Risk Simulator | Forecasting | Multiple Regression Analysis.

- Review that the data are entered correctly or make any required changes and edits here, including changes to the variable names.

- Select any of the options required and click OK to run the multiple regression analysis.

Multiple Regression Analysis

Multiple Regression Analysis can be used to run linear regressions with multiple independent variables. These variables can be applied through a series of lags or nonlinear transformations, or regressed in a stepwise fashion starting with the most correlated variable.

Multivariate Regression
Y = F(X)

Dependent Variable [Y ▾]

☑ Y	☑ X1	☑ X2	☑ X3	☑ X4	☑ X5
521	18308	185	4.041	79.6	7.2
367	1148	600	0.55	1	8.5
443	18068	372	3.665	32.3	5.7
365	7729	142	2.351	45.1	7.3
614	100484	432	29.76	190.8	7.5
385	16728	290	3.294	31.8	5
286	14630	346	3.287	678.4	6.7
397	4008	328	0.666	340.8	6.2

Options

☐ Lag Regressors [1 ▲▼] Period(s)   ☐ Nonlinear Regression

☐ Stepwise Correlation Method [▾]   ☐ Show All Steps

p-Value: [0.1]

[OK] [Cancel]

[Bootstrap Simulation]

Regression Report I

Regression Statistics

R-Squared (Coefficient of Determination)	0.3272
Adjusted R-Squared	0.2508
Multiple R (Multiple Correlation Coefficient)	0.5720
Standard Error of the Estimates (SEy)	149.6720
Number of Observations	50

The R-Squared or Coefficient of Determination indicates that 0.33 of the variation in the dependent variable can be explained and accounted for by the independent variables in this regression analysis. However, in a multiple regression, the Adjusted R-Squared takes into account the existence of additional independent variables or regressors and adjusts this R-Squared value to a more accurate view of the regression's explanatory power. Hence, only 0.25 of the variation in the dependent variable can be explained by the regressors.

The Multiple Correlation Coefficient (Multiple R) measures the correlation between the actual dependent variable (Y) and the estimated or fitted (Y) based on the regression equation. This is also the square root of the Coefficient of Determination (R-Squared).

The Standard Error of the Estimates (SEy) describes the dispersion of data points above and below the regression line or plane. This value is used as part of the calculation to obtain the confidence interval of the estimates later.

Regression Results

	Intercept	X1	X2	X3	X4	X5
Coefficients	57.9555	-0.0035	0.4644	25.2377	-0.0086	16.5579
Standard Error	108.7901	0.0035	0.2535	14.1172	0.1016	14.7996
t-Statistic	0.5327	-1.0066	1.8316	1.7877	-0.0843	1.1188
p-Value	0.5969	0.3197	0.0738	0.0807	0.9332	0.2693
Lower 5%	-161.2966	-0.0106	-0.0466	-3.2137	-0.2132	-13.2687
Upper 95%	277.2076	0.0036	0.9753	53.6891	0.1961	46.3845

Degrees of Freedom		Hypothesis Test	
Degrees of Freedom for Regression	5	Critical t-Statistic (99% confidence with df of 44)	2.6923
Degrees of Freedom for Residual	44	Critical t-Statistic (95% confidence with df of 44)	2.0154
Total Degrees of Freedom	49	Critical t-Statistic (90% confidence with df of 44)	1.6802

The Coefficients provide the estimated regression intercept and slopes. For instance, the coefficients are estimates of the true; population b values in the following regression equation $Y = b0 + b1X1 + b2X2 + ... + bnXn$. The Standard Error measures how accurate the predicted Coefficients are, and the t-Statistics are the ratios of each predicted Coefficient to its Standard Error.

The t-Statistic is used in hypothesis testing, where we set the null hypothesis (Ho) such that the real mean of the Coefficient = 0, and the alternate hypothesis (Ha) such that the real mean of the Coefficient is not equal to 0. A t-test is performed and the calculated t-Statistic is compared to the critical values at the relevant Degrees of Freedom for Residual. The t-test is very important as it calculates if each of the coefficients is statistically significant in the presence of the other regressors. This means that the t-test statistically verifies whether a regressor or independent variable should remain in the regression or it should be dropped.

The Coefficient is statistically significant if its calculated t-Statistic exceeds the Critical t-Statistic at the relevant degrees of freedom (df). The three main confidence levels used to test for significance are 90%, 95% and 99%. If a Coefficient's t-Statistic exceeds the Critical level, it is considered statistically significant. Alternatively, the p-Value calculates each t-Statistic's probability of occurrence, which means that the smaller the p-Value, the more significant the Coefficient. The usual significant levels for the p-Value are 0.01, 0.05, and 0.10, corresponding to the 99%, 95%, and 90% confidence levels.

The Coefficients with their p-Values highlighted in blue indicate that they are statistically significant at the 90% confidence or 0.10 alpha level, while those highlighted in red indicate that they are not statistically significant at any other alpha levels.

Regression Report II

Analysis of Variance

	Sums of Squares	Mean of Squares	F-Statistic	p-Value
Regression	479388.49	95877.70	4.28	0.0029
Residual	985675.19	22401.71		
Total	1465063.68			

Hypothesis Test

Critical F-statistic (99% confidence with df of 5 and 44)	3.4651
Critical F-statistic (95% confidence with df of 5 and 44)	2.4270
Critical F-statistic (90% confidence with df of 5 and 44)	1.9828

The Analysis of Variance (ANOVA) table provides an F-test of the regression model's overall statistical significance. Instead of looking at individual regressors as in the t-test, the F-test looks at all the estimated Coefficients' statistical properties. The F-Statistic is calculated as the ratio of the Regression's Mean of Squares to the Residual's Mean of Squares. The numerator measures how much of the regression is explained, while the denominator measures how much is unexplained. Hence, the larger the F-Statistic, the more significant the model. The corresponding p-Value is calculated to test the null hypothesis (Ho) where all the Coefficients are simultaneously equal to zero, versus the alternate hypothesis (Ha) that they are all simultaneously different from zero, indicating a significant overall regression model. If the p-Value is smaller than the 0.01, 0.05, or 0.10 alpha significance, then the regression is significant. The same approach can be applied to the F-Statistic by comparing the calculated F-Statistic with the critical F values at various significance levels.

Forecasting

Period	Actual (Y)	Forecast (F)	Error (E)
1	521.0000	299.5124	221.4876
2	367.0000	487.1243	(120.1243)
3	443.0000	353.2789	89.7211
4	365.0000	276.3296	88.6704
5	614.0000	776.1336	(162.1336)
6	385.0000	298.9993	86.0007
7	286.0000	354.8718	(68.8718)
8	397.0000	312.6155	84.3845
9	764.0000	529.7550	234.2450
10	427.0000	347.7034	79.2966
11	153.0000	266.2526	(113.2526)
12	231.0000	264.6375	(33.6375)
13	524.0000	406.8009	117.1991
14	328.0000	272.2226	55.7774
15	240.0000	231.7882	8.2118
16	286.0000	257.8862	28.1138
17	285.0000	314.9521	(29.9521)
18	569.0000	335.3140	233.6860
19	96.0000	282.0356	(186.0356)
20	498.0000	370.2062	127.7938
21	481.0000	340.8742	140.1258
22	468.0000	427.5118	40.4882
23	177.0000	274.5298	(97.5298)

RMSE: 140.4048

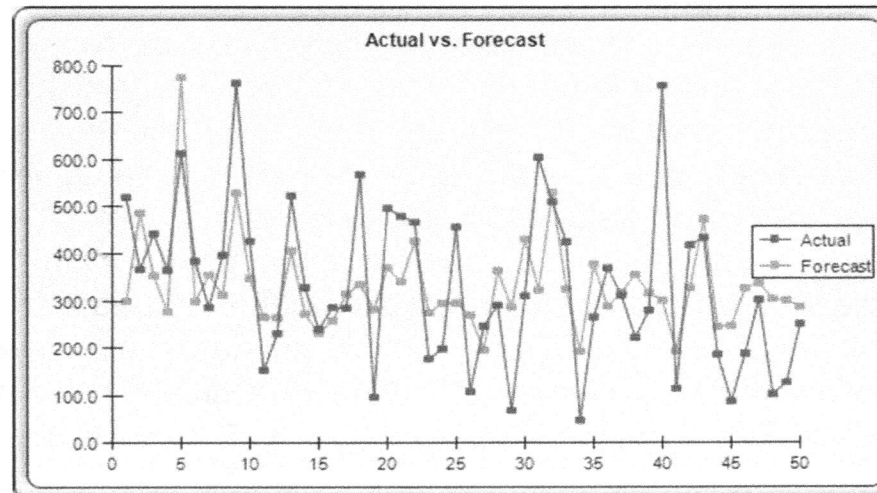

Actual vs. Forecast

Stochastic Process Forecast

- A stochastic process is a mathematically defined equation that can create a series of outcomes over time, outcomes that are not deterministic in nature, that is, an equation or process that does not follow any simple discernible rule, such as price will increase X percent every year or revenues will increase by this factor of X plus Y percent. A stochastic process is nondeterministic, and one can plug numbers into a stochastic process equation and obtain different results every time. For instance, the path of a stock price is stochastic in nature, and one cannot reliably predict the exact stock price path with any certainty. However, the price evolution over time is enveloped in a process that generates these prices. *The process is fixed and predetermined, but the outcomes are not.* Hence, by stochastic simulation, we create multiple pathways of prices, obtain a statistical sampling of these simulations, and make inferences on the potential pathways that the actual price may undertake given the nature and parameters of the stochastic process used to generate the time series. Four stochastic processes are included in Risk Simulator's Forecasting tool, including Geometric Brownian motion or random walk, which is the most common and prevalently used process due to its simplicity and wide-ranging applications. The other three stochastic processes are the mean-reversion process, jump-diffusion process, and a mixed process.

- The interesting thing about stochastic process simulation is that historical data is not necessarily required. That is, the model does not have to fit any sets of historical data. Simply compute the expected returns and the volatility of the historical data or estimate them using comparable external data or make assumptions about these values.

- To run a stochastic process, open Excel and click *Risk Simulator | Forecasting | Stochastic Processes*.

Running a Stochastic Process Forecast

To run a stochastic process forecast:

- Click on *Risk Simulator | Forecasting | Stochastic Processes.*

- Select the required process and enter the requested input parameters and click Update Chart for a sample iteration.

- Click OK to run the analysis.

For more detailed discussions, see Chapter 8 of *Modeling Risk: Applying Monte Carlo Simulation, Strategic Real Options Analysis, Stochastic Forecasting, Portfolio Optimization,* Data Analytics, Business Intelligence, and Decision Modeling, 3rd Edition (2015) by Dr. Johnathan Mun.

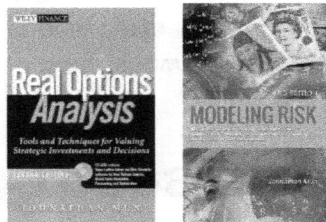

Stochastic Process Forecasting

Stochastic Processes are sequences of events or paths generated by probabilistic laws where random events can occur over time but are governed by specific statistical and probabilistic rules. They are useful for forecasting random events (e.g., stock prices, interest rates, price of electricity).

Methods

- ● Brownian Motion (Random Walk) with Drift
- ○ Exponential Brownian Motion (Random Walk) with Drift
- ○ Mean-Reversion Process with Drift
- ○ Jump-Diffusion Process with Drift
- ○ Jump-Diffusion Process with Drift and Mean-Reversion

Starting Value	100
Growth or Drift Rate (%)	5
Annualized Volatility (%)	25
Forecast Horizon (Years)	10
Reversion Rate (%)	5
Long-Term Value	120
Jump Rate (%)	10
Jump Size	2
Number of Steps	100
Iterations	10
☐ Random Seed	1
☐ Show All Iterations	

Update Chart   OK   Cancel

Stochastic Process Report

The chart shows a sample set of the iterations while the report explains the basics of stochastic processes. In addition, the forecast values (mean and standard deviation) for each time period are provided. Using these values, you can decide which time period is relevant to your analysis, and set assumptions based on these mean and standard deviation values using the normal distribution. These assumptions can then be simulated in your own custom model.

Statistical Summary

A stochastic process is a sequence of events or paths generated by probabilistic laws. That is, random events can occur over time but are governed by specific statistical and probabilistic rules. The main stochastic processes include Random Walk or Brownian Motion, Mean-Reversion, and Jump-Diffusion. These processes can be used to forecast a multitude of variables that seemingly follow random trends but yet are restricted by probabilistic laws.

The Random Walk Brownian Motion process can be used to forecast stock prices, prices of commodities, and other stochastic time-series data given a drift or growth rate and a volatility around the drift path. The Mean-Reversion process can be used to reduce the fluctuations of the Random Walk process by allowing the path to target a long-term value, making it useful for forecasting time-series variables that have a long-term rate such as interest rates and inflation rates (these are long-term target rates by regulatory authorities or the market). The Jump-Diffusion process is useful for forecasting time-series data when the variable can occasionally exhibit random jumps, such as oil prices or price of electricity (discrete exogenous event shocks can make prices jump up or down). Finally, these three stochastic processes can be mixed and matched as required.

The results on the right indicate the mean and standard deviation of all the iterations generated at each time step. If the Show All Iterations option is selected, each iteration pathway will be shown in a separate worksheet. The graph generated below shows a sample set of the iteration pathways.

Stochastic Process: Brownian Motion (Random Walk) with Drift

Start Value	100	Steps	100.00	Jump Rate	N/A
Drift Rate	5.00%	Iterations	10.00	Jump Size	N/A
Volatility	25.00%	Reversion Rate	N/A	Random Seed	890528781
Horizon	10	Long-Term Value	N/A		

Time	Mean	Stdev
0.0000	100.00	0.00
0.1000	100.14	7.51
0.2000	94.23	13.18
0.3000	93.78	18.00
0.4000	94.59	18.69
0.5000	95.04	18.76
0.6000	98.01	19.13
0.7000	100.93	15.18
0.8000	95.13	12.94
0.9000	94.21	14.34
1.0000	92.27	17.43
1.1000	88.07	15.80
1.2000	89.99	20.85
1.3000	89.45	23.97
1.4000	87.54	23.48
1.5000	87.69	26.27
1.6000	91.46	32.68
1.7000	90.56	34.51
1.8000	92.67	32.48
1.9000	94.87	32.59
2.0000	97.74	35.13
2.1000	99.41	39.99
2.2000	100.41	46.41
2.3000	97.83	45.56
2.4000	102.51	47.31
2.5000	99.09	45.15
2.6000	97.74	45.89
2.7000	97.48	48.00
2.8000	96.71	48.70
2.9000	92.94	44.79
3.0000	87.36	35.45
3.1000	82.90	33.71
3.2000	83.65	31.66
3.3000	81.97	27.94
3.4000	83.35	28.85
3.5000	85.10	36.34
3.6000	84.48	38.96
3.7000	84.04	39.05
3.8000	83.48	39.23
3.9000	83.30	38.39
4.0000	86.40	42.17
4.1000	86.00	38.53
4.2000	85.99	41.59
4.3000	84.28	39.44
4.4000	84.58	37.44
4.5000	85.90	43.84
4.6000	85.43	42.69
4.7000	84.45	38.40
4.8000	85.16	39.69
4.9000	90.48	43.07
5.0000	91.25	43.89
5.1000	88.96	42.18
5.2000	89.64	44.90

Stochastic Process

Random Walk Brownian Motion

The Random Walk Brownian Motion process can be used to forecast stock prices, prices of commodities, and other stochastic time-series data given a drift or growth rate and a volatility around the drift path.

Brownian Motion Random Walk Process

The Brownian motion random walk process takes the form of $\frac{\delta S}{S} = \mu(\delta t) + \sigma \varepsilon \sqrt{\delta t}$ for regular options simulation, or a more generic version takes the form of $\frac{\delta S}{S} = (\mu - \sigma^2 / 2)\delta t + \sigma \varepsilon \sqrt{\delta t}$ for a geometric process. For an exponential version, we simply take the exponentials, and as an example, we have $\frac{\delta S}{S} = \exp\left[\mu(\delta t) + \sigma \varepsilon \sqrt{\delta t} \right]$.

The following are the variable definitions:

S as the variable's previous value

δS as the change in the variable's value from one step to the next

μ as the annualized growth or drift rate

σ as the annualized volatility

In order to estimate the parameters from a set of time-series data, the drift rate and volatility can be found by setting μ to be the average of the natural logarithm of the relative returns $ln\frac{S_t}{S_{t-1}}$, while σ is the standard deviation of all $ln\frac{S_t}{S_{t-1}}$ values.

Mean-Reversion Process

The Mean-Reversion process can be used to reduce the fluctuations of the Random Walk process by allowing the path to target a long-term value, making it useful for forecasting time-series variables that have a long-term rate such as interest rates and inflation rates (these are long-term target rates by regulatory authorities or the market).

Mean-Reversion Process

The following describes the mathematical structure of a mean-reverting process with drift: $\frac{\delta S}{S} = \eta(\overline{S}e^{\mu(\delta t)} - S)\delta t + \mu(\delta t) + \sigma\varepsilon\sqrt{\delta t}$. In order to obtain the rate of reversion and long term rate, using the historical data points, run a regression such that $Y_t - Y_{t-1} = \beta_0 + \beta_1 Y_{t-1} + \varepsilon$ and we find $\eta = -\ln[1 + \beta_1]$ and $\overline{S} = -\beta_0 / \beta_1$.

The following are the variable definitions:

η as the rate of reversion to the mean

$\overline{S}$ as the long-term value the process reverts to

Y as the historical data series

β_0 as the intercept coefficient in a regression analysis

β_1 as the slope coefficient in a regression analysis

Jump-Diffusion Process

The Jump-Diffusion process is useful for forecasting time-series data when the variable can occasionally exhibit random jumps, such as oil prices or price of electricity (discrete exogenous event shocks can make prices jump up or down).

Jump Diffusion Process

A jump diffusion process is similar to a random walk process but there is a probability of a jump at any point in time. The occurrences of such jumps are completely random but its probability and magnitude are governed by the process itself. The model is defined as:

$$\frac{\delta S}{S} = \eta(\overline{S}e^{\mu(\delta t)} - S)\delta t + \mu(\delta t) + \sigma\varepsilon\sqrt{\delta t} + \theta F(\lambda)(\delta t)$$ for a jump diffusion process.

The following are the variable definitions:

θ as the jump size of S

$F(\lambda)$ as the inverse of the Poisson cumulative probability distribution

λ as the jump rate of S

The jump size can be found by computing the ratio of the post-jump to the pre-jump levels, and the jump rate can be imputed from past historical data. The other parameters are found the same way as above.

ARIMA

One very powerful advanced times-series forecasting tool is the ARIMA or *Auto Regressive Integrated Moving Average* approach. ARIMA forecasting assembles three separate tools into a comprehensive model. The first tool segment is the autoregressive or "AR" term, which corresponds to the number of lagged value of the residual in the unconditional forecast model. In essence, the model captures the historical variation of actual data to a forecasting model and uses this variation or residual to create a better predicting model. The second tool segment is the integration order or the "I" term. This integration term corresponds to the number of differencing the time series to be forecasted goes through. This element accounts for any nonlinear growth rates existing in the data. The third tool segment is the moving average or "MA" term, which is essentially the moving average of lagged forecast errors. By incorporating the lagged forecast errors, the model in essence learns from its forecast errors or mistakes and corrects for them through a moving average calculation. In addition, ARIMA models can be mixed with exogenous variables, but make sure that the exogenous variables have enough data points to cover the additional number of periods to forecast.

Autoregressive Integrated Moving Average or ARIMA(p,d,q) models are the extension of the AR model that uses three components for modeling the serial correlation in the time series data. The first component is the autoregressive (AR) term. The AR(p) model uses the p lags of the time series in the equation. An AR(p) model has the form: $y_t = a_1 y_{t-1} + \ldots + a_p y_{t-p} + e_t$. The second component is the integration (d) order term. Each integration order corresponds to differencing the time series. I(1) means differencing the data once. I(d) means differencing the data d times. The third component is the moving average (MA) term. The MA(q) model uses the q lags of the forecast errors to improve the forecast. An MA(q) model has the functional form: $y_t = e_t + b_1 e_{t-1} + \ldots + b_q e_{t-q}$. Similarly, an ARMA(p,q) model has the combined functional form: $y_t = a_1 y_{t-1} + \ldots + a_p y_{t-p} + e_t + b_1 e_{t-1} + \ldots + b_q e_{t-q}$.

ARIMA & Auto ARIMA

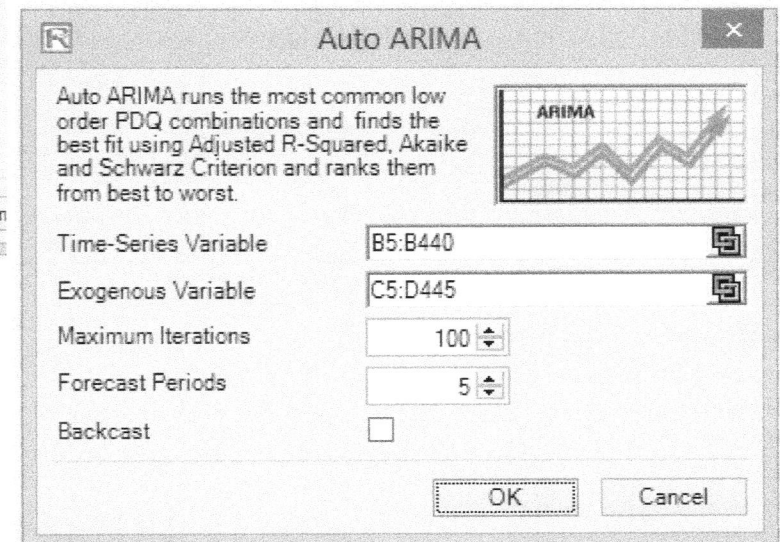

Sample Historical Time-Series Data		
M1	M2	M3
138.90	286.70	289.00
139.40	287.80	290.10
139.70	289.10	291.30
139.70	290.10	292.30
140.70	292.30	294.50
141.20	293.90	296.10
141.70	295.30	297.40
141.90	296.40	298.50
141.00	296.50	298.50
140.50	296.60	298.60
140.40	297.20	299.20
140.00	297.80	299.80
140.00	298.30	300.30
139.90	298.50	300.50
139.80	299.20	301.30
139.60	300.10	302.20
139.60	301.00	303.00
139.60	302.20	304.30
140.20	304.20	306.40
141.30	306.80	309.20
141.20	308.20	310.70
140.90	309.60	312.20
140.90	311.00	313.80
140.70	312.30	315.30
141.10	314.20	317.30
141.60	316.60	320.00

Autoregressive Integrated Moving Average

ARIMA is an advanced modeling technique used to model and forecast time-series data (data that have a time component to them, e.g., interest rates, inflation, sales revenues, gross domestic product).

Time-Series Variable	B5:B440
Exogenous Variable	C5:D445
Autoregressive Order AR(p)	1
Differencing Order I(d)	0
Moving Average Order MA(q)	1
Maximum Iterations	100
Forecast Periods	5
Backcast	☐

OK   Can

Auto ARIMA

Auto ARIMA runs the most common low order PDQ combinations and finds the best fit using Adjusted R-Squared, Akaike and Schwarz Criterion and ranks them from best to worst.

Time-Series Variable	B5:B440
Exogenous Variable	C5:D445
Maximum Iterations	100
Forecast Periods	5
Backcast	☐

OK   Cancel

NOTE: You can run ARIMA using its own historical time-series data only, or add exogenous independent variables. You can forecast as many periods as you desire when using its own time-series data. However, when independent variables are added, the following must hold:

(Forecast Period) ≤ (Number of Independent Variables' Data Rows) – (Number of Time-Series Data Rows)

ARIMA Report (Part I)

ARIMA (Autoregressive Integrated Moving Average)

Regression Statistics

R-Squared (Coefficient of Determination)	0.9999	Akaike Information Criterion (AIC)	4.6213
Adjusted R-Squared	0.9999	Schwarz Criterion (SC)	4.6632
Multiple R (Multiple Correlation Coefficient)	1.0000	Log Likelihood	-1005.13
Standard Error of the Estimates (SEy)	297.52	Durbin-Watson (DW) Statistic	1.8588
Number of Observations	435	Number of Iterations	5

Autoregressive Integrated Moving Average or ARIMA(p,d,q) models are the extension of the AR model that use three components for modeling the serial correlation in the time-series data. The first component is the autoregressive (AR) term. The AR(p) model uses the p lags of the time series in the equation. An AR(p) model has the form: y(t)=a(1)*y(t-1)+...+a(p)*y(t-p)+e(t).The second component is the integration (d) order term. Each integration order corresponds to differencing the time series. I(1) means differencing the data once. I(d) means differencing the data d times. The third component is the moving average (MA) term. The MA(q) model uses the q lags of the forecast errors to improve the forecast. An MA(q) model has the form: y(t)=e(t)+b(1)*e(t-1)+...+b(q)*e(t-q).Finally, an ARMA(p,q) model has the combined form: y(t)=a(1)*y(t-1)+...+a(p)*y(t-p)+e(t)+b(1)*e(t-1)+...+b(q)*e(t-q).

The R-Squared, or Coefficient of Determination, indicates the percent variation in the dependent variable that can be explained and accounted for by the independent variables in this regression analysis. However, in a multiple regression, the Adjusted R-Squared takes into account the existence of additional independent variables or regressors and adjusts this R-Squared value to a more accurate view the regression's explanatory power. However, under some ARIMA modeling circumstances (e.g., with nonconvergence models), the R-Squared tends to be unreliable.

The Multiple Correlation Coefficient (Multiple R) measures the correlation between the actual dependent variable (Y) and the estimated or fitted (Y) based on the regression equation. This correlation is also the square root of the Coefficient of Determination (R-Squared).

The Standard Error of the Estimates (SEy) describes the dispersion of data points above and below the regression line or plane. This value is used as part of the calculation to obtain the confidence interval of the estimates later.

The AIC and SC are often used in model selection. SC imposes a greater penalty for additional coefficients. Generally, the user should select a model with the lowest value of the AIC and SC.

The Durbin-Watson statistic measures the serial correlation in the residuals. Generally, DW less than 2 implies positive serial correlation.

Regression Results

	Intercept	AR(1)	MA(1)
Coefficients	-0.0626	1.0055	0.4936
Standard Error	0.3108	0.0006	0.0420
t-Statistic	-0.2013	1691.1373	11.7633
p-Value	0.8406	0.0000	0.0000
Lower 5%	0.4498	1.0065	0.5628
Upper 95%	-0.5749	1.0046	0.4244

Degrees of Freedom		Hypothesis Test	
Degrees of Freedom for Regression	2	Critical t-Statistic (99% confidence with df of 432)	2.5873
Degrees of Freedom for Residual	432	Critical t-Statistic (95% confidence with df of 432)	1.9655
Total Degrees of Freedom	434	Critical t-Statistic (90% confidence with df of 432)	1.6484

The Coefficients provide the estimated regression intercept and slopes. For instance, the coefficients are estimates of the true; population b values in the following regression equation Y = b0 + b1X1 + b2X2 + ... + bnXn. The Standard Error measures how accurate the predicted Coefficients are, and the t-Statistics are the ratios of each predicted Coefficient to its Standard Error.

The t-Statistic is used in hypothesis testing, where we set the null hypothesis (Ho) such that the real mean of the Coefficient = 0, and the alternate hypothesis (Ha) such that the real mean of the Coefficient is not equal to 0. A t-test is is performed and the calculated t-Statistic is compared to the critical values at the relevant Degrees of Freedom for Residual. The t-test is very important as it calculates if each of the coefficients is statistically significant in the presence of the other regressors. This means that the t-test statistically verifies whether a regressor or independent variable should remain in the regression or it should be dropped.

The Coefficient is statistically significant if its calculated t-Statistic exceeds the Critical t-Statistic at the relevant degrees of freedom (df). The three main confidence levels used to test for significance are 90%, 95% and 99%. If a Coefficient's t-Statistic exceeds the Critical level, it is considered statistically significant. Alternatively, the p-Value calculates each t-Statistic's probability of occurrence, which means that the smaller the p-Value, the more significant the Coefficient. The usual significant levels for the p-Value are 0.01, 0.05, and 0.10, corresponding to the 99%, 95%, and 90% confidence levels.

The Coefficients with their p-Values highlighted in blue indicate that they are statistically significant at the 90% confidence or 0.10 alpha level, while those highlighted in red indicate that they are not statistically significant at any other alpha levels.

ARIMA Report (Part II)

Analysis of Variance

	Sums of Squares	Mean of Squares	F-Statistic	p-Value	Hypothesis Test	
Regression	38415447.53	19207723.76	3171851.1	0.0000	Critical F-statistic (99% confidence with df of 2 and 432)	4.6546
Residual	2616.05	6.06			Critical F-statistic (95% confidence with df of 2 and 432)	3.0166
Total	38418063.58				Critical F-statistic (90% confidence with df of 2 and 432)	2.3149

The Analysis of Variance (ANOVA) table provides an F-test of the regression model's overall statistical significance. Instead of looking at individual regressors as in the t-test, the F-test looks at all the estimated Coefficients' statistical properties. The F-Statistic is calculated as the ratio of the Regression's Mean of Squares to the Residual's Mean of Squares. The numerator measures how much of the regression is explained, while the denominator measures how much is unexplained. Hence, the larger the F-Statistic, the more significant the model. The corresponding p-Value is calculated to test the null hypothesis (Ho) where all the Coefficients are simultaneously equal to zero, versus the alternate hypothesis (Ha) that they are all simultaneously different from zero, indicating a significant overall regression model. If the p-Value is smaller than the 0.01, 0.05, or 0.10 alpha significance, then the regression is significant. The same approach can be applied to the F-Statistic by comparing the calculated F-Statistic with the critical F values at various significance levels.

Autocorrelation

Time Lag	AC	PAC	Lower Bound	pper Bound	Q-Stat	Prob
1	0.9921	0.9921	(0.0958)	0.0958	431.1216	-
2	0.9841	(0.0105)	(0.0958)	0.0958	856.3037	-
3	0.9760	(0.0109)	(0.0958)	0.0958	1,275.4818	-
4	0.9678	(0.0142)	(0.0958)	0.0958	1,688.5499	-
5	0.9594	(0.0098)	(0.0958)	0.0958	2,095.4625	-
6	0.9509	(0.0113)	(0.0958)	0.0958	2,496.1572	-
7	0.9423	(0.0124)	(0.0958)	0.0958	2,890.5594	-
8	0.9336	(0.0147)	(0.0958)	0.0958	3,278.5669	-
9	0.9247	(0.0121)	(0.0958)	0.0958	3,660.1152	-
10	0.9156	(0.0139)	(0.0958)	0.0958	4,035.1192	-

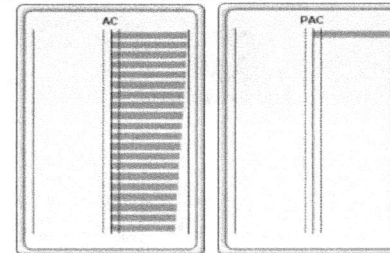

If autocorrelation AC(1) is nonzero, it means that the series is first order serially correlated. If AC(k) dies off more or less geometrically with increasing lag , it implies that the series follows a low-order autoregressive process. If AC(k) drops to zero after a small number of lags, it implies that the series follows a low-order moving-average process. Partial correlation PAC(k) measures the correlation of values that are k periods apart after removing the correlation from the intervening lags. If the pattern of autocorrelation can be captured by an autoregression of order less than k, then the partial autocorrelation at lag k will be close to zero. Ljung-Box Q-statistics and their p-values at lag k has the null hypothesis that there is no autocorrelation up to order k. The dotted lines in the plots of the autocorrelations are the approximate two standard error bounds. If the autocorrelation is within these bounds, it is not significantly different from zero at (approximately) the 5% significance level.

Forecasting

Period	Actual (Y)	Forecast (F)	Error (E)	RMSE:
2	139.4000	139.6056	(0.2056)	2.4523
3	139.7000	140.0069	(0.3069)	
4	139.7000	140.2586	(0.5586)	
5	140.7000	140.1343	0.5657	
6	141.2000	141.6948	(0.4948)	
7	141.7000	141.6741	0.0259	
8	141.9000	142.4339	(0.5339)	
9	141.0000	142.3587	(1.3587)	
10	140.5000	141.0466	(0.5466)	
11	140.4000	140.9447	(0.5447)	
12	140.0000	140.8451	(0.8451)	
13	140.0000	140.2946	(0.2946)	
14	139.9000	140.5663	(0.6663)	
15	139.8000	140.2823	(0.4823)	
16	139.6000	140.2726	(0.6726)	
17	139.6000	139.9775	(0.3775)	
18	139.6000	140.1232	(0.5231)	

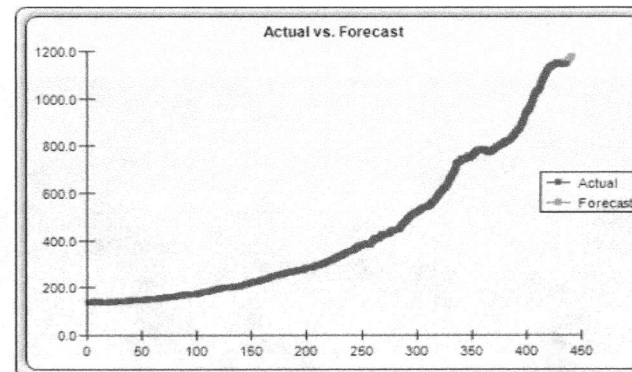

12. Artificial Intelligence and Machine Learning

Dr. Johnathan Mun, Professor of Research
Quantitative Research Methods Course Slides
Seventh Edition, 2026, ROV Press

ARTIFICIAL INTELLIGENCE

Artificial Intelligence (AI) is a broad catch-all term for a group of inorganic computer science technologies that are used to simulate intelligence. The science of AI was established in the 1950s to determine whether inorganic robots could execute human-level intelligence capabilities. Significant interest in AI resurfaced about the same time as Big Data computer capacity became more widely available to researchers and businesses, allowing them to apply the science to a variety of practical applications. Manufacturing robots, smart assistants, proactive healthcare management, illness mapping, automated financial investing, virtual travel-booking agents, social media monitoring, conversational marketing bots, natural language processing tools, and inventory supply chain management are all examples of commercially feasible AI applications.

The timeline of AI and Data Science development reveals a long journey, where mathematical statistics evolved into applied statistics, data science, artificial intelligence, and machine learning (ML). For instance, in 1962, John Tukey's work as a mathematical statistician can be considered one of the early seminal works in data analytics. In 1977, the International Association for Statistical Computing (IASC) was founded to link traditional statistical methodology, modern computer technology, and the knowledge of domain experts to convert data into information and knowledge. Database marketing started a trend in 1994, and by 1996, the term "Data Science" appeared for the first time at the International Federation of Classification Societies in Japan. The inaugural topic was entitled, "Data Science, Classification, and Related Methods." In 1997, Jeff Wu gave an inaugural lecture titled simply "Statistics = Data Science?" In 2001, William Cleveland published "Data Science: An Action Plan for Expanding the Technical Areas of the Field of Statistics." He put forward the notion that data science was an independent discipline and named various areas in which he believed data scientists should be educated: multidisciplinary investigations, models, and methods for data analysis; computing with data; pedagogy; tool evaluation; and theory. By 2008, the term "data scientist" was often attributed to Jeff Hammerbacher and D. J. Patil, then of Facebook and LinkedIn, respectively, and in 2010, the term "data science" had fully infiltrated the vernacular. Between 2011 and 2012, "data scientist" job listings increased by 15,000%. Around 2016, data science started to be entrenched in Machine Learning and Deep Learning. This implies that AI/ML techniques are based solidly on the foundations of traditional mathematical statistics, but with smart algorithmic steps wrapped around these methods.

The term AI typically conjures up the nebulous concept of machine learning, which, in reality, is a subset of AI where a computer system is programmed to identify and categorize external real-world stimuli. AI can be loosely defined as the ability of machines to perform tasks that normally require human intelligence—for example, recognizing patterns, learning from experience, drawing conclusions, making predictions, or taking action—whether digitally or as the smart software behind autonomous physical systems. AI processes that are most appropriate for data science, quantitative research analytics, prediction, and forecast modeling include applications of Machine Learning (ML), Natural Language Processing (NLP), and Robotic Process Automation (RPA).

Whereas AI, in general, involves the use of algorithms exhibiting "smart" behavior, the use of AI algorithms in Machine Learning (ML)— that detect patterns and use them for prediction and decision making—can be broadly divided into supervised and unsupervised methods. *Supervised* learning means that the correct answers are provided by humans to train the algorithm, whereas *unsupervised* learning does not include the correct results. Supervised algorithms are taught patterns using past data and then detect them automatically in new data. For example, a multiple regression model requires historical data of the dependent variable Y and one or more independent variables X_i and because the results (dependent variable) are provided, this is considered a supervised ML algorithm. In contrast, unsupervised algorithms are programmed to detect new and interesting patterns in completely new data. Without supervision, the algorithm is not expected to surface specific correct answers; instead, it looks for logical patterns within raw data. For example, a factor analysis where there are multiple independent variables X_i but the a priori groupings of these variables are not known would be considered an unsupervised method.

AI MACHINE LEARNING

| Natural Language Processing | **ARTIFICIAL INTELLIGENCE** | Deep Learning |

MACHINE LEARNING

Known Groupings or Known Dependent Variables

Unknown Original Groupings

SUPERVISED

UNSUPERVISED

FORECASTING

Linear multivariate regression — **LINEAR FIT**

Customized functional forms — **NONLINEAR FIT**

BAGGING BOOTSTRAP AGGREGATION

One model re-run thousands of times with resampled original data with replacement

Linear multivariate regression — **LINEAR FIT**

Customized functional forms — **NONLINEAR FIT**

FITTING (TRAIN & TEST)

One model fitted using a training dataset for prediction using a testing dataset

Cross-sectional with interactions — **COMMON FIT**

Time-series with interactions — **COMPLEX FIT**

Compares different time-series methods — **TIME-SERIES FIT**

ENSEMBLE LEARNING

Tests thousands of model specifications to find the best fit using the same dataset

COS HYPERBOLIC

HYPERBOLIC

LINEAR

LOGISTIC

NEURAL NETWORK

Forecasting time-series data using multilayered perceptrons

CLASSIFICATION

K-NEAREST NEIGHBOR (KNN)

CLASSIFICATION & FORECASTING

CLASSIFICATION & REGRESSION TREES (CART)

Tree with binary splits

RANDOM FOREST

Bootstraps CART for prediction

SUPPORT VECTOR MACHINES (SVM)

Learns and classifies data into linearly separable segments

GAUSSIAN SVM

LINEAR SVM

POLYNOMIAL SVM

CLASSIFICATION & PROBABILITIES

LOGISTIC (LOGIT)

NORMIT (PROBIT)

Binary dependent variable

DIMENSION REDUCTION

FACTOR ANALYSIS

Eigenvalues, eigenvectors, Varimax rotation, factor scores

PRINCIPAL COMPONENT ANALYSIS (PCA)

Eigenvalues, eigenvectors, reduced data matrix

CLASSIFICATION

GAUSSIAN MIX

Classification probabilities with multivariate normal

K-MEANS

Randomized iterations of classes and groups

PHYLOGENIC TREES

SEGMENTATION CLUSTERING

Clustering with centroids and Euclidean mean distances

CLASSIFICATION & FORECASTING

DISCRIMINANT ANALYSIS

LINEAR LDA

QUADRATIC QDA

AI MACHINE LEARNING: BAGGING LINEAR FIT BOOTSTRAP (SUPERVISED)

This method applies a Bootstrap Aggregation (Bagging) Linear Fit Model of hundreds of models via resampled data to generate the best consensus forecasts. The idea is that in a random selection of data, taking the average forecast of an ensemble of models provides a more accurate prediction than a single sample. In a typical multivariate linear regression, the relationship structure and characteristics of a dependent variable and how it depends on other independent exogenous variables can be modeled. The model can be used to understand the relationship among these variables as well as for the purposes of forecasting and predictive modeling. The accuracy and goodness of fit for this model can also be determined. Similar to a linear multivariate regression model, we first train the algorithm using the training dependent and training independent variables, which will identify the optimized parameters to use on the testing dataset. Then, the dataset is resampled, and the algorithm is again run. This process is repeated or bootstrapped hundreds of times, and the output forecasts will be a consensus of all these bootstrapped models.

In an ensemble forecast, we would apply different models to the same dataset, whereas in a bagging or bootstrap aggregation approach, we use the same model but applied multiple times to a random selection of the existing dataset. The latter's algorithm is trivial. Suppose we have a dependent response variable Y and k number of predictor independent variables $\mathbf{X} = X_1, X_2, \ldots, X_k$, each with N rows of data. Then, we would initialize B, the number of bootstrap models to be fitted, as well as n, the number of data rows to use in the bootstrap, where $n < N$. Starting with $B = 1$, we take a bootstrap resampling of n data rows and fit the model; specifically, we sample with replacement, to fit $\mathbf{X}_B$ to Y_B and obtain a forecast fit $\hat{f}_B(\mathbf{X})$. Repeat the process applying a resampling with replacement and generating the aggregate consensus forecast. Recall that this bootstrap approach assumes that the model is correctly specified, and we are simply re-running the same model specification on resampled data. In contrast, the Ensemble Learning methods such as the AI/ML Ensemble Common Fit and the Ensemble Complex Fit will take the same dataset and apply hundreds or even thousands of models to test for the best-fitting model specification.

```
Model Inputs:
VAR373              Training Y (1 variable)
VAR374:VAR375       Training X (≥ 1 variables)
VAR380:VAR381       Testing X (matches Training X's number of variables)
1000                Number of Bootstraps (1-1000)
45                  Number of Data Points (< number of data rows)
0                   Testing Y (optional, 1 variable)
VAR442              Forecast Save Location (optional, 1 variable)
```

AI Machine Learning: Bagging Linear Fit Bootstrap (Supervised)
Forecasting

Period	Forecast (F)	Min Forecast	Max Forecast
1	380.4235	283.1699	523.8427
2	425.6080	314.7315	615.5356
3	418.1381	309.9623	603.3895
.	. .	. .	. .
30	349.5307	277.0782	440.0635

AI MACHINE LEARNING: BAGGING NONLINEAR FIT BOOTSTRAP (SUPERVISED)

Model Inputs:

VAR373	Training Y (1 variable)
VAR374; (VAR375)^2; LN(VAR376)	Training X (≥ 1 var(s), customized)
VAR380; (VAR381)^2; LN(VAR382)	Testing X (match Training X)
1000	Number of Bootstraps (1-1000)
45	Number of Data Points (< rows)
VARX	Testing Y (optional, 1 variable)
VARX	Forecast Save Location (optional)

AI Machine Learning: Bagging Nonlinear Fit Bootstrap (Supervised)

Period	Forecast (F)	Min Forecast	Max Forecast
1	460.6380	330.5135	624.2640
2	375.6430	196.8459	447.4713
3	432.1997	299.2141	521.3108
4	349.8022	268.4462	436.7163
.	. .	. .	. .
30	378.2814	294.0299	466.1581

AI MACHINE LEARNING: CLASSIFICATION AND REGRESSION TREES CART (SUPERVISED)

The Classification and Regression Trees (CART) model generates branches and subgroups of the categorical dependent Y variable using characteristic X variables. CART is typically used for data mining and constitutes a supervised machine learning approach. This is a classification approach when the dependent variable is categorical, and the tree is used to determine the class or group within which a target testing variable is most likely to fall. The data is split into branches along a tree, and each branch split will be determined using Gini coefficients and information loss coefficients based on the questions asked along the way. Specifically, $Gini = 1 - \sum_{i=1}^{c} p_i^2$. If this Gini index is 0, it means the data are perfectly classified. Therefore, using a recursive algorithm, we can apply the splits that have the lowest Gini index. The final structure looks like a tree with its many branches. Additional splitting and stopping rules are applied along the way, and the terminal branches will provide predictions of the target testing variable.

The next slide provides a visual illustration and the results of a CART model. Simply enter the variables you need to classify and enter the number of clusters desired. The CART model then generates if-then-else rules that are simple to understand and implement as a forecasting tool. The tree can identify patterns that are oftentimes obscured in the complex interactions of the data.

The CART algorithm runs the optimal splits according to the Gini coefficient and then retests the regression tree against the actual Training Y variable to identify its accuracy. If a different set of Testing X variables is entered, it will also project and classify the relevant groupings. The sample data shows the information on 10 individuals, where each individual's preferred transportation mode is the dependent variable (a categorical variable 1, 2, 3 for bus, train, or car). The independent predictors are the individuals' gender (1, 2 for male or female), whether the person owns a car (1, 0 for yes or no), the cost of transportation (1, 2, 3 for cheap, medium, or expensive), and the individual's income level category (1, 2, 3 for low, medium, or high). The tree provides a good visual, with all the relevant splits and Gini coefficients. The tree is then used to back-fit the original data. For the example data, the first individual who ended up taking the Bus (Transportation Mode = 1) has the following dependent variable values: Gender = 1, Car Ownership = 0, Transportation Cost = 1, and Income Level = 1. We start from the top of the tree and see that for cost = 1, we take the first right branch, then going down the next level, we take the right branch where travel cost = 1. Then, we take the left branch where gender = 1. The path is bolded for easier identification. This happens to be the terminal branch, which means the model predicts that the transport mode is 1, corresponding to the original data. All rows of data are fed through this tree according to their own pathways.

```
Model Inputs:
VAR433          Training Y (1 variable)
VAR434:VAR437   Training X (≥ 1 variables)
VAR438:VAR441   Testing X (optional, match Training X's # of variables)
VAR442          Forecast save location (optional, 1 variable)
```

AI MACHINE LEARNING: CLASSIFICATION AND REGRESSION TREES CART (SUPERVISED)

```
                    Node 1      Count    %
                    Class 1      4      40%
                    Class 2      3      30%
                    Class 3      3      30%

Gini = 0.66    Travel Cost = 3        Travel Cost < 3

Terminal 1 Count    %                Node 2      Count    %
Class 1      0      0%               Class 1      4      57%
Class 2      0      0%               Class 2      3      43%
Class 3      3     100%              Class 3      0      0%

Gini = 0.34    Travel Cost = 2        Travel Cost = 1

Terminal 2 Count    %                Node 3      Count    %
Class 1      0      0%               Class 1      4      80%
Class 2      2     100%              Class 2      1      20%
Class 3      0      0%               Class 3      0      0%

Gini = 0.23      Gender = 1                    Gender = 2

Terminal 3 Count    %                Terminal 4 Count    %
Class 1      3     100%              Class 1      1      50%
Class 2      0      0%               Class 2      1      50%
Class 3      0      0%               Class 3      0      0%

Gini = 0.20    Car Owner = 1                  Car Owner = 0

Terminal 3 Count    %                Terminal 4 Count    %
Class 1      0      0%               Class 1      1     100%
Class 2      1     100%              Class 2      0      0%
Class 3      0      0%               Class 3      0      0%
```

The complete results from the algorithm are shown next. The CART method will return the various unique numerical categories in the Training Y set, and, in this example, we have three categories: 1, 2, and 3. It will show the fit of the training dataset, where here we see the actuals versus CART predicted results, with a perfect 100% accuracy match in each category. The actual categories based on the training set are shown, together with the model's predicted categorization. This fitted model and its comparison to actuals allow one to see the accuracy of the model. Then, using this fitted model, if the optional Testing X variables are provided, the algorithm takes this testing dataset and computes the predicted categories.

```
AI Machine Learning: Classification Regression Tree (Supervised)

Category    Actual    Predicted    Accuracy
   1          4           4        100.00%
   2          3           3        100.00%
   3          3           3        100.00%

Training Dataset
Actual      Forecast          Testing Dataset Forecast
1.00         1.00                     1.00
1.00         1.00                     1.00
2.00         2.00                     2.00
1.00         1.00                     1.00
1.00         1.00                     1.00
2.00         2.00                      . .
2.00         2.00
3.00         3.00
3.00         3.00
3.00         3.00
```

	Actual Category is X	Actual Category is Not X
Predicted Category is X	True Positive (TP)	False Positive (FP)
Predicted Category is Not X	False Negative (FN)	True Negative (TN)
	Positive Sensitivity Recall $= TP/(TP+FN)$	Negative Specificity $= TN/(TN+FP)$

AI MACHINE LEARNING: CLASSIFICATION WITH GAUSSIAN MIX & K-MEANS SEGMENTATION (UNSUPERVISED)

The AI Machine Learning Gaussian Mix with K-Means Segmentation model assumes multiple overlaying normal distributions. This is an unsupervised machine learning method that is applicable when we do not know where the clusters come from initially. Typically, the dataset has n rows of data with m columns of multidimensional-space characteristics, and where we typically have $1 \leq m \leq 4$. The results show the probabilities of a certain value belonging to a particular cluster. When there is a single cluster, we would typically perform a distributional fitting routine such as a Kolmogorov–Smirnov model, but when there are multiple such k normal distribution clusters (with μ_k, COV_k mean and covariance), the total probability density is a linear function of the densities across all these clusters, where $p(x) = \sum_{k=1}^{k} \pi_k G(x|\mu_k, COV_k)$ and π_k is the mix-coefficient for the k–th distribution. An expectations maximization algorithm is used to estimate the maximum likelihood function of the fit, while the Bayes Information Criterion is used to automatically select the best covariance parameters.

A Gaussian Mix is related to the K-Means approach and is fairly simple and uses some Naïve Bayes and likelihood estimations. Sometimes the results are not as reliable as, say, a supervised Support Vector Machine (SVM) method. This is because of the Gaussian Mix's unsupervised algorithm, which may not converge. Run the same model several times to see if the model converges (i.e., the results will be the same each time when you click Run). If the results are not identical, try increasing the number of iterations and test again. If the results obtained are not as expected, reduce the number of variables, and increase the number of rows and try again with a higher iteration. The best model is the one with the maximum log-likelihood value (be careful here as log-likelihood is typically a negative value, which means a model with -100 is better than a model with a -300 log-likelihood measure). Alternatively, try the unsupervised AI/ML Segmentation Clustering methodology, which is typically more reliable. Whenever possible and if the data allow for it, the recommendation is to use the supervised SVM methods or the unsupervised AI/ML Segmentation Clustering method.

The results will show both the K-Means Clustering as well as the Gaussian Mix models. As mentioned, if the same model is re-run several times and the results remain the same, the model has converged; otherwise, add more iterations and try again. If the model converges, use the results from that run. If convergence is not achieved, either apply a different method completely or re-run the same model several times and select the one with the maximum log-likelihood value. Also, when the cluster means of K-Means and Gaussian Mix are close to each other, the results are relatively reliable. These means usually do not equal each other as they run different algorithms.

```
Model Inputs:
VAR416:VAR419    The variables to classify
5                The number of clusters to group the data into
1000             Max iterations (Optional=100, Allowed: 1-5000)
VARX             Location to save the forecasted categories
```

AI MACHINE LEARNING: CLASSIFICATION WITH GAUSSIAN MIX & K-MEANS SEGMENTATION (UNSUPERVISED)

```
AI Machine Learning: Classification with Gaussian Mix & K-Means (Unsupervised)
Log-Likelihood:        -532.6046
```

K-Means Average:

	X1	X2	X3	X4
Cluster 1	12.3800	246.6000	67.2000	27.7800
Cluster 2	2.9500	62.7000	53.9000	11.5100
Cluster 3	7.5077	170.3846	71.4615	22.6154
Cluster 4	11.8000	300.8571	68.7143	28.8571
Cluster 5	5.5900	112.4000	65.6000	17.2700

Gaussian Mix Average:

	X1	X2	X3	X4
Cluster 1	12.1347	248.1784	67.3133	27.5988
Cluster 2	2.9546	62.8118	53.9251	11.5229
Cluster 3	7.8164	171.4283	71.0373	22.6710
Cluster 4	11.8121	298.4321	68.9918	29.1794
Cluster 5	5.6117	112.3859	65.5904	17.2776

K-Means Count :

Cluster 1	Cluster 2	Cluster 3	Cluster 4	Cluster 5
10	10	13	7	10

Gaussian Mix Probabilities for Each Row :

Cluster 1	Cluster 2	Cluster 3	Cluster 4	Cluster 5
0.9981	0.0000	0.0019	0.0000	0.0000
1.0000	0.0000	0.0000	0.0000	0.0000
0.0032	0.0000	0.0000	**0.9968**	0.0000
0.0000	0.0000	1.0000	0.0000	0.0000
0.0235	0.0000	0.0000	0.9765	0.0000
0.0013	0.0000	0.9850	0.0136	0.0000
. . .	. . .	. . .	. . .	. . .
0.0000	1.0000	0.0000	0.0000	0.0000
0.0000	1.0000	0.0000	0.0000	0.0000
0.0000	0.0000	1.0000	0.0000	0.0000

K-Means Assignments for Each Row

```
1
1
4
3
4
3
.
2
2
3
```

The K-Means and Gaussian Mix cluster means are provided for the requested 5 clusters (shown as rows in the results) for each of the 4 independent variables (shown as columns). Then, the K-Means counts of the number of states in each category are provided, as are the K-Means assignments of these states into the various categories. The Gaussian Mix results also provide the probabilities that a certain state falls within a specific category. For instance, we see from the results that there are 10 rows grouped into Cluster 1, 10 into Cluster 2, and so forth. The Gaussian Mix probabilities show that there is a 99.81% chance the first row's data fall into Cluster 1, the second row's data has a 100% chance of being in Cluster 1, the third row's data has a 99.68% chance of being in Cluster 4, and so forth You can also run the analysis using AI/ML Cluster Segmentation but be aware that similar rows will be clustered together although the numbering of the clusters may differ due to the different algorithms used. For example, Cluster 1 may be called Cluster 5, and so on.

AI MACHINE LEARNING: CLASSIFICATION WITH K-NEAREST NEIGHBORS (SUPERVISED)

The K-Nearest Neighbor (KNN) algorithm is used to classify and segregate the data into groups. Another name for this method is the k-dimensional tree structure, useful for partitioning data points into a few small dimensions. Simply enter the variables you need to classify and enter the number of clusters desired. KNN results will show the testing points and identify the nearest neighbors. For example, in the first row of the testing data, we have the values 4, 7, 5 and this numerical sequence, as compared to all the other data, is most closely related to 4, 8, 5 (this can be either in the testing set or the training set).

```
Model Inputs:
VAR105:VAR107        Training X (≥ 1 variable)
VAR108:VAR110        Testing X (match Training X's number of variables)
```

AI Machine Learning: Classification with K-Nearest Neighbors (Supervised)

Testing Points			Nearest Neighbor		
[4.00,	7.00,	5.00]	[4.00,	8.00,	5.00]
[3.00,	7.00,	7.00]	[3.00,	8.00,	6.00]
[3.00,	6.00,	7.00]	[3.00,	8.00,	6.00]
[2.00,	8.00,	7.00]	[2.00,	9.00,	7.00]
[4.00,	8.00,	8.00]	[4.00,	8.00,	7.00]
[3.00,	6.00,	6.00]	[3.00,	8.00,	6.00]
. .	. .	. .	. .	. .	. .
[5.00,	8.00,	3.00]	[5.00,	8.00,	3.00]
[4.00,	7.00,	4.00]	[4.00,	8.00,	4.00]
[5.00,	5.00,	6.00]	[5.00,	8.00,	5.00]

AI MACHINE LEARNING: CLASSIFICATION WITH PHYLOGENETIC TREES & HIERARCHICAL CLUSTERING (UNSUPERVISED)

In this method, the algorithm runs phylogenetic trees for data classification by applying a hierarchical clustering algorithm. Phylogenetic trees are typically used in biomedical and genetic research, such as looking at DNA sequences. This method is unsupervised, and the algorithm is applied to figure out how to cluster a set of data that is unordered without being provided with any training data having the correct responses. The result is a hierarchical cluster with multiple fully nested sets where the smallest sets are the individual elements of the set, and the largest set is the entire dataset.

To apply a phylogenetic tree using hierarchical clustering, the dataset is typically a set of sequences or distance matrices. Simply enter the variables you need to classify and enter the number of clusters desired. The input variable is a sample genetic DNA sequence, and the results show a hierarchical 5-level phylogenetic tree. The 5-level tree (vertical lines indicate branching events, and there are 5 vertical lines starting from the first branch to the longest path).

```
Model Inputs:
VAR462        Genetic Chain
0             Chain Name (Optional)
1             Distance Type (Optional, 1-5)
```

DNA Sequence	Names	DNA Sequence	Names
CGGTTGGGAGCT	A	AGGCGGTGCGGG	I
AGGTCGTGAGGT	B	GGGCGGGGCGGG	J
TGGGTGCGAGTT	C	GGGCGCTGCGGG	K
ACGTTTGGGTGA	D	GGACGGAGGCTG	L
AAGGTTGGGGAA	E	GGGTGGGAGCTG	M
GTCTTTCGGGTG	F	AGGAGGCTGATG	N
CACTTGCGGGGG	G	TGGCGGATGATG	O
GCGCGGTGCAGC	H	TGGGTGCGAGTT	P

AI MACHINE LEARNING: CLASSIFICATION WITH SUPPORT VECTOR MACHINES SVM (SUPERVISED)

Support Vector Machines (SVM) is a class of supervised machine learning algorithms used for classification. The term "machine" in SVM might be a misnomer in that it is only a vestige of the term "machine learning." SVM methods are simpler to implement and run than complex neural network algorithms. In supervised learning, we typically start with a set of training data. The algorithm is trained using this dataset (i.e., the parameters are optimized and identified), and then the same model parameters are applied to the testing set, or to a new dataset never before seen by the algorithm. The training dataset comprises m data points, placed as rows in the data grid, where there is an outcome or dependent variable y_i, followed by one or more independent predictors x_i for $i = 1, ..., m$. Each of the dependent (also known as predictor or feature) variables has n dimensions (number of columns). In contrast, there is only a single y_i variable, with a binary outcome (e.g., 1 and 0, or 1 and 2, indicating if an item is in or out of a group). Note that the training set can also be used as the testing set, and the results will typically yield a high level of segregation accuracy. However, in practice, we typically use a smaller subset of the testing dataset as the training dataset and unleash the optimized algorithm on the remaining testing set. One of the few limiting caveats of SVM methods is a requirement that there exists some n-dimensional hyperplane that separates the data.

The hyperplane is defined by an equation $f(\mathbf{x}) = \mathbf{w} \cdot \mathbf{x} + b = 0$, which completely separates the training dataset into two groups. The parameters $\mathbf{w}$ (the normal vector to the hyperplane) and b (an offset parameter such as a virtual intercept) can be scaled as needed, to adjust the forecast back into the original two groups. Applying some analytical geometry, we see that the parameters are best fitted by applying an internal optimization routine to minimize $\frac{1}{2}\mathbf{w} \cdot \mathbf{w}$, which reduces to a Lagrangian problem where we maximize the likelihood of $\mathcal{L}(\alpha, \beta) = \frac{1}{2}f(\mathbf{w}) + \sum_j \alpha_j g_j(\mathbf{w}) + \sum_k \beta_k h_k(\mathbf{w})$, where all parameters are positive.

SVM algorithms are best used in conjunction with a kernel density estimator, and the three most commonly used are the Gaussian, Linear, and Polynomial kernels. Try each of these approaches and see which fits the data the best by reviewing the accuracy of the results.

- **Gaussian SVM.** Applies a normal kernel estimator $exp\left[-\frac{1}{2}|\mathbf{x_i} - \mathbf{x_j}|^2/\sigma^2\right]$.

- **Linear SVM.** Applies a standard linear kernel estimator $\mathbf{x_i} \cdot \mathbf{x_j}$.

- **Polynomial SVM.** Applies a polynomial (e.g., quadratic nonlinear programming) kernel density estimator such as $\left|a\mathbf{x_i} \cdot \mathbf{x_j} + b\right|^c$.

AI MACHINE LEARNING: CLASSIFICATION WITH SUPPORT VECTOR MACHINES SVM (SUPERVISED)

The same procedure applies to all three SVM subclasses. To get started, we use an example dataset where the weights and sizes of 40 fruits were measured. These fruits were either apples or oranges. Recall that SVMs are best used for separations into two groups. The data grid shows VAR408 with the alphanumeric category of the dependent or classified variable (apples or oranges). However, the SVM algorithms require numerical inputs, hence, the dependent groupings have been coded to a numerical value of 1 and 2 in VAR407 (bivariate numerical categories). VAR405 and VAR406 are the predictors or features set (the weights and sizes of the fruits) that we will use as the training set to calibrate and fit the model. These are the first two sets of inputs in the model. Note that we have VAR407 entered in the first row as the training dependent variable and in the second row, VAR405; VAR406 as the training independent variables (predictor feature set). To get started, we use the default Sigma, Lambda, and Omega values of 2, 1000, and 0.5. Depending on the SVM subclass, only some or all three of these will be used. Start with the defaults and change as required. The main variable that impacts the results is the Omega, which is a value between 0 and 1. If you set the Calibrate Option to 1, it will test various Omega values and shows the accuracy levels of each. Select the Omega value with the highest accuracy and rerun the model.

```
Model Inputs:
VAR407              Training dependent variable (1)
VAR405; VAR406      Training independent variables (≥ 1)
2.00                Sigma
1000.00             Lambda
0.50                Omega (this is tested for accuracy)
1.00                Calibrate (1 = calibrate Omega, 0 = do not)
VAR409; VAR410      Testing independent variables
VAR411              Paste the forecast results (optional, can be empty)
VAR412              Paste the grouped results (optional, can be empty)
```

```
AI Machine Learning: Classification with Gaussian SVM (Supervised)
```

Accuracy	85%	85%	85%	100%	100%	100%	100%	100%	100%	100%
Omega	0.10	0.20	0.30	0.40	0.50	0.60	0.70	0.80	0.90	1.00

Forecast	Group	Forecast (Test Vars)	Group (Test Vars)
1.013598	1.00	1.013598	1.00
1.013860	1.00	1.013860	1.00
0.922405	1.00	0.922405	1.00
0.709851	2.00	0.709851	2.00
1.016426	1.00	1.016426	1.00
. . .	. .	. . .	. .
0.670190	2.00	0.670190	2.00

AI MACHINE LEARNING: CLASSIFICATION WITH SUPPORT VECTOR MACHINES SVM (SUPERVISED)

The results provide a series of forecast values and forecast groups for the training set as well as for the testing dataset, showing the numerical segmentation results and the final resulting groups. Note that the example results indicate relatively high goodness of fit to the testing dataset at 95% fit. This fit applies to the training dataset and assuming the same data structure holds, the testing dataset should also have a fit that is close to this result. Typically, only the testing dataset's forecast values and grouping membership are important to the user; hence, you can optionally enter the location in the data grid to save the results, for example, VAR411 and VAR412. If these inputs are left empty, the results will not be saved in the data grid, and they will only be available in the results area.

AI MACHINE LEARNING: CUSTOM FIT MODEL (SUPERVISED)

The AI Machine Learning Custom Fit model is applicable in forecasting time-series and cross-sectional data for modeling relationships among variables. It allows you to create custom-fit multiple regression models. Econometrics refers to a branch of business analytics, modeling, and forecasting techniques for modeling the behavior of or forecasting certain business, financial, economic, physical science, and other variables. Running the Custom Fit model is like regular econometric regression analysis except that the dependent and independent variables can be modified before a regression is run. For more detailed explanations of regression models, see the sections on Linear and Nonlinear Multivariate Regression and Regression Analysis, as well as the associated sections on pitfalls of regression modeling.

As usual, the standard practice is to divide your data into training and testing sets. The training set (one dependent with one or more independent variables) is used to train the algorithm and obtain the best-fitting parameters. In this model, you can create your custom equations. Note that only one variable is allowed as the Training Y Dependent Variable, whereas multiple variables are allowed in the Training X Independent Variables section, separated by a semicolon (;), and that basic mathematical functions can be used (e.g., LN, LOG, LAG, +, -, /, *, TIME, RESIDUAL, DIFF). For instance, you can use your training set's dependent variable as VAR373 and independent variables VAR374; (VAR375)^2; LN(VAR376), and so forth. You need to use the same functional form for the testing set's independent variables as well (but with the same or different variables), otherwise, the model will not run properly. For example, a complementary set of testing independent variables would be VAR380; (VAR381)^2; LN(VAR382). Notice that the same functional form is used but applied to different variables. Applying it to the same variables would be the same as running a customized econometric model instead.

The algorithm also allows you to optionally enter known testing set dependent values. Sometimes these are known and sometimes they are unknown and are to be forecasted. If the values are unknown, simply leave the input empty or enter a 0 in the input if you wish to enter the next input, which is the forecast results save location in the data grid.

```
Model Inputs:
VAR373                          Training set dependent variable
VAR374; (VAR375)^2; LN(VAR376)  Training set custom independent variable(s)
VAR380; (VAR381)^2; LN(VAR382)  Testing set independent (match training set)
{VARx or 0 or empty}            Testing set dependent (optional or 0)
{VARxx or empty}                Forecast results save location (optional)
```

AI MACHINE LEARNING: CUSTOM FIT MODEL (SUPERVISED)

The results interpretation would be similar to that for the basic econometric analysis. The goodness-of-fit results and fitted parameter estimations pertain to the training dataset, whereas the forecast values are based on the testing dataset when applied to these fitted parameters. Sometimes, you may wish to hold some data back from the training dataset and apply it to the testing dataset to test the accuracy of the model and its ability to forecast, as well as to view the forecast errors. In other words, the optional testing set's dependent variable can be used and because these known values are applied, forecast errors can also be generated as a result. For example, the VARx value above can be set to VAR379.

```
AI Machine Learning: Custom Fit Model (Supervised)

Multiple R             0.64492      Maximum Log-Likelihood         -314.63844
R-Square               0.41593      Akaike Info Criterion (AIC)      12.74554
Adjusted R-Square      0.37783      Bayes Schwarz Criterion (BSC)    12.89850
Standard Error       136.39035      Hannan-Quinn Criterion (HQC)     12.80379
Observations              50        Cohen's F-Squared                 0.71211

                 Coeff    Std. Error     T-stat      P-value
Intercept     160.13054    37.08823     4.31756     0.00008
VAR X1         -0.00320     0.00186    -1.72599     0.09106
VAR X2          0.00102     0.00034     2.96002     0.00485
VAR X3        145.42613    38.41272     3.78588     0.00044


ANOVA
                 DF          SS           MS          F        p-Value
Regression        3      609356.63    203118.88   10.91900    0.00002
Residual         46      855707.05     18602.33
Total            49     1465063.68

Forecasting

        Period      Forecast (F)
          1           456.4715
          2           379.5395
          3           436.1389
          .             . .
          30          379.7052
```

AI MACHINE LEARNING: DIMENSION REDUCTION PRINCIPAL COMPONENT ANALYSIS (UNSUPERVISED)

Principal component analysis, or PCA, makes multivariate data easier to model and summarize. To understand PCA, suppose we start with N variables that are unlikely to be independent of one another, such that changing the value of one variable will change another variable. PCA modeling will replace the original N variables with a new set of M variables that are less than N but are uncorrelated to one another, while at the same time, each of these M variables is a linear combination of the original N variables so that most of the variation can be accounted for using fewer explanatory variables.

PCA is a way of identifying patterns in data and recasting the data in such a way as to highlight their similarities and differences. Patterns of data are very difficult to find in high dimensions when multiple variables exist, and higher dimensional graphs are very difficult to represent and interpret. Once the patterns in the data are found, they can be compressed, and the number of dimensions is now reduced. This reduction of data dimensions does not mean much reduction in loss of information. Instead, similar levels of information can now be obtained by a fewer number of variables.

PCA is a statistical method that is used to reduce data dimensionality using covariance analysis among independent variables by applying an orthogonal transformation to convert a set of correlated variables data into a new set of values of linearly uncorrelated variables named principal components. The number of computed principal components will be less than or equal to the number of original variables. This statistical transformation is set up such that the first principal component has the largest possible variance accounting for as much of the variability in the data as possible, and each subsequent component has the highest variance possible under the constraint that it is orthogonal to or uncorrelated with the preceding components. Thus, PCA reveals the internal structure of the data in a way that best explains the variance in the data. Such a dimensional reduction approach is useful to process high-dimensional datasets while still retaining as much of the variance in the dataset as possible. PCA essentially rotates the set of points around their mean to align with the principal components. Therefore, PCA creates variables that are linear combinations of the original variables. The new variables have the property that the variables are all orthogonal. Factor analysis is similar to PCA, in that factor analysis also involves linear combinations of variables using correlations, whereas PCA uses covariance to determine eigenvectors and eigenvalues relevant to the data using a covariance matrix. Eigenvectors can be thought of as preferential directions of a dataset or main patterns in the data. Eigenvalues can be thought of as quantitative assessments of how much a component represents the data. The higher the eigenvalues of a component, the more representative it is of the data.

As an example, PCA is useful when running multiple regression or basic econometrics when the number of independent variables is large or when there is significant multicollinearity in the independent variables. It can be run on the independent variables to reduce the number of variables and to eliminate any linear correlations among the independent variables. The extracted revised data obtained after running PCA can be used to rerun the linear multiple regression or linear basic econometric analysis. The resulting model will usually have slightly lower R-squared values but potentially higher statistical significance (lower p-value). Users can decide to use as many principal components as required based on the cumulative variance.

Suppose there are k variables, X_k, there are exactly k principal components, $Z_i \in i = 1 \ldots k$, and $Z_i = w_{i,1}X_1 + w_{i,2}X_2 + \ldots + w_{i,k}X_k$, where $w_{i,k}$ are the weights or component loadings. The first principal component Z_1 is a linear combination that best explains the total variation, while the second principal component Z_2 is orthogonal or uncorrelated to the first and explains as much as it can of the remaining variation in the data, and so forth, all the way until the final Z_k component.

AI MACHINE LEARNING: DIMENSION REDUCTION PRINCIPAL COMPONENT ANALYSIS (UNSUPERVISED)

Related to another method called Factor Analysis, PCA makes multivariate data easier to model and summarize. An example where we start with 5 independent variables that are unlikely to be independent of one another, such that changing the value of one variable will change another variable. Recall that this multicollinearity effect can cause biases in a multiple regression model. Both principal component and factor analysis can help identify and eventually replace the original independent variables with a new set of smaller variables that are less than the original but are uncorrelated to one another, while, at the same time, each of these new variables is a linear combination of the original variables. This means most of the variation can be accounted for by using fewer explanatory variables. Similarly, factor analysis is used to analyze interrelationships within large numbers of variables and simplifies said factors into a smaller number of common factors. The method condenses information contained in the original set of variables into a smaller set of implicit factor variables with minimal loss of information. The analysis is related to the principal component analysis by using the correlation matrix and applying principal component analysis coupled with a varimax matrix rotation to simplify the factors.

For example, if we have 5 independent variables, which means the factor analysis or principal component analysis results will return a 5×5 matrix of eigenvectors and 5 eigenvalues. Typically, we are only interested in components with eigenvalues >1. Hence, in the results, we are only interested in the first three or four factors or components (some researchers would plot these eigenvalues and call it a scree plot, which can be useful for identifying where the kinks are in the eigenvalues). Notice that the first and second factors (the first two result columns) return a cumulative proportion of 69.88%. This means that using these two factors will explain approximately 70% of the variation in all the independent factors themselves. Next, we look at the absolute values of the eigenvalue matrix. It seems that variables 1 and 3 can be combined into a new variable in factor 1, with variables 4 and 5 as the second factor. This can be done separately and outside of principal component analysis. Notice that the results are not as elegant with only 5 variables. The idea of PCA and Factor Analysis is that the more variables you have, the better the algorithm will perform in terms of reducing the number of data variables or the data dimensionality size.

```
Eigenvalues (Arranged and Ranked):
2.4180       1.0760       0.8665       0.6003       0.0393

Proportions Ranked:
48.36%       21.52%       17.33%       12.01%       0.79%

Cum Proportions Ranked:
48.36%       69.88%       87.21%       99.21%       100.00%

Eigenvectors (Arranged and Ranked):
0.5820      -0.3560      -0.1169       0.1485       0.7063
0.3759       0.1935       0.6864      -0.5911       0.0257
0.5770      -0.3868      -0.1066       0.0858      -0.7062
0.3228       0.6483       0.2073       0.6563      -0.0429
0.2878       0.5157      -0.6789      -0.4364       0.0021

Revised Data:
-0.0652       0.0004      -0.1386      -0.0046       0.0010
0.0740       0.2294       0.2263      -0.4869       0.0050
  . .           . .          . .          . .          . .
-0.0141      -0.0306       0.1469      -0.1321       0.0151
```

NOTE: The results of multiple linear regressions to illustrate how orthogonality works in PCA. For instance, the first multiple regression is run using the original dataset (VAR28 against VAR29:VAR33). The second regression is run based on the revised PCA data (VAR28 against the converted data). Notice that the goodness-of-fit measures such as R-square, Adjusted R-square, Multiple R, and Standard Error of the Estimates are identical. The estimated coefficients will differ because different data were used in each situation. Some of the variables are not significant in the models because this is only meant as an illustration of the PCA method and not about calibrating a good regression model. In fact, using the reduced model, the Adjusted R-square of only using two variables is 23% as opposed to 25% using all 5 independent variables in the original dataset. This showcases the power of PCA, where fewer variables are used while retaining a high level of variability explained.

AI MACHINE LEARNING: DIMENSION REDUCTION FACTOR ANALYSIS (UNSUPERVISED)

This method runs Factor Analysis to analyze interrelationships within large numbers of variables and simplifies said factors into a smaller number of common factors. The method condenses information contained in the original set of variables into a smaller set of implicit factor variables with minimal loss of information. The analysis is related to Principal Component Analysis (PCA) by using the correlation matrix and applying PCA coupled with a Varimax matrix rotation to simplify the factors. The same results interpretation is used for Factor Analysis as for PCA. For instance, an example where we start with 9 independent variables that are unlikely to be independent of one another, such that changing the value of one variable will change another variable. Factor analysis helps identify and eventually replace the original independent variables with a new set of fewer variables that are less than the original but are uncorrelated to one another, while, at the same time, each of these new variables is a linear combination of the original variables. This means most of the variation can be accounted for by using fewer explanatory variables. Factor analysis is therefore used to analyze interrelationships within large numbers of variables and simplifies said factors into a smaller number of common factors. The method condenses information contained in the original set of variables into a smaller set of implicit factor variables with minimal loss of information. The data input requirement is simply the list of variables you want to analyze (separated by semicolons for individual variables or separated by a colon for a contiguous set of variables, such as VAR105:VAR113 for all 9 variables).

```
Model Inputs:
   VAR105:VAR113    The list of variables to analyze
```

AI MACHINE LEARNING: DIMENSION REDUCTION FACTOR ANALYSIS (UNSUPERVISED)

We started with 9 independent variables, which means the factor analysis results will return a 9×9 matrix of eigenvectors and 9 eigenvalues. Typically, we are only interested in components with eigenvalues >1. Hence, in the results, we are only interested in the first four factors or components. Notice that the first four factors (the first four result columns) return a cumulative proportion of 72.31%. This means that using these four factors will explain 72.31% of the variation in all the independent factors themselves. Next, we look at the absolute values of the eigenvalue matrix. It seems that variables 2, 3, 7, 8 can be combined into a new variable in factor 1, with variables 1 and 9 as the second factor, and so forth.

Factor Analysis (Eigenvalues and Eigenvectors)

Eigenvalue	2.8804	1.4387	1.1639	1.0245	0.7052	0.6476	0.5624	0.3452	0.2321
Proportion	0.3200	0.1599	0.1293	0.1138	0.0258	0.0384	0.0784	0.0720	0.0625
Cumulative	0.3200	0.4799	0.6092	**0.7231**	0.7488	0.7872	0.8656	0.9375	1.0000

Eigenvectors	Fact1	Fact2	Fact3	Fact4	Fact5	Fact6	Fact7	Fact8	Fact9
VAR1	0.1087	**-0.6392**	0.2573	0.1138	-0.4171	0.0959	0.4808	0.2842	0.0724
VAR2	**-0.4116**	0.2531	0.1811	-0.2616	-0.3396	-0.0000	0.4365	-0.5925	0.0914
VAR3	**-0.4443**	-0.2907	0.1873	-0.3022	-0.0301	0.1325	-0.3009	0.0640	-0.6918
VAR4	-0.2156	-0.1355	0.1829	0.8396	-0.0282	0.0082	-0.2214	-0.3788	-0.0578
VAR5	-0.3407	-0.0368	-0.4196	0.1560	0.4236	0.5599	0.4245	0.0882	-0.0352
VAR6	-0.1766	-0.0253	-0.7145	0.0630	-0.6325	-0.0296	-0.2161	0.0730	0.0257
VAR7	**-0.4815**	-0.1996	0.1803	-0.1644	0.0891	0.0992	-0.3614	0.1678	0.7016
VAR8	**-0.4053**	-0.0294	-0.1076	0.1162	0.2150	-0.7828	0.2818	0.2591	-0.0651
VAR9	-0.1776	**0.6179**	0.3190	0.2312	-0.2744	0.1903	0.0417	0.5587	-0.0782

AI MACHINE LEARNING: ENSEMBLE COMMON FIT (NONLINEAR) (SUPERVISED)

This algorithm computes thousands of possible nonlinear and interaction models (suitable for cross-sectional data for pattern recognition); it calibrates the best model with the training dataset and forecasts outcomes using the testing dataset. In other words, it performs an ensemble learning approach.

```
Model Inputs:
VAR373              Training Y (1 variable)
VAR374:VAR378       Training X (≥ 1 variables)
VAR380:VAR384       Testing X (optional, match Training X's # of variables)
VAR379              Forecast Save Location (optional, 1 variable)
0.10                P-value Threshold (optional, default at 0.1)
0                   Time Series Lags (optional positive integer, default at 0)
```

The sample results illustrate the ensemble algorithm where over 1,593 combinations of linear, nonlinear, interacting, and mixed models were tested, and the 10 best models are shown. The models are selected based on the independent variables' p-values ≤ 0.10 and ranked by Adjusted R-squares. A stricter p-value can be entered if required.

```
Number of Dependent Variables Tested: 5
Number of Econometric Models Tested: 1593
Number of Best Models Shown: 20
    ADJ R-SQ      MODEL
     0.39034      VAR1;VAR2;LN(VAR3)
     0.38540      LN(VAR3)+LN(VAR5);LN(VAR2)
     0.37892      VAR2*VAR5;LN(VAR3)

      . . .         . . .
     0.34489      LN(VAR2)+LN(VAR5);LN(VAR3)
     0.33791      LN(VAR3)+LN(VAR5)+LN(VAR4);LN(VAR2)
```

```
Top Model Result: VAR1;VAR2;LN(VAR3)
Multiple R           0.65396     Maximum Log-Likelihood          -314.13076
R-Square             0.42767     Akaike Info Criterion (AIC)       12.80523
Adjusted R-Square    0.39034     Bayes Schwarz Criterion (BSC)     13.03467
Standard Error     135.01252     Hannan-Quinn Criterion (HQC)      12.89260
Observations                     Cohen's F-Squared                  0.74723
```

	Coeff	Std. Error	T-stat	P-value
Intercept	59.91680	60.90323	0.98380	0.33036
VAR1	-0.00308	0.00181	-1.70238	0.09543
VAR2	0.70340	0.22372	3.14406	0.00292
LN(VAR3)	138.21002	37.29707	3.70565	0.00056

ANOVA	DF	SS	MS	F	p-Value
Regression	3	626558.21	208852.74	11.45756	0.00001
Residual	46	838505.47	18228.38		
Total	49	1465063.68			

AI MACHINE LEARNING: ENSEMBLE COMPLEX FIT (NONLINEAR) (SUPERVISED)

Using an ensemble learning approach, this model computes thousands of possible nonlinear and interaction models (suitable for time-series data for pattern recognition); it calibrates the best model with the training dataset and forecasts outcomes using the testing dataset.

```
Model Inputs:
VAR373           Training Y (1 variable)
VAR374:VAR378 Training X (≥ 1 variables)
VAR380:VAR384 Testing X (optional, match Training X's # of variables)
VAR379              Forecast Save Location (optional, 1 variable)
0.10               P-value Threshold (optional, default=0.1)
0                  Time Series Lags (optional positive integer, default=0)
0                  Autoregressive AR(p) (optional positive integer, default=0)
```

The results illustrate the complex ensemble model where thousands of combinations of linear, nonlinear, interacting, time-series (lags, rate, and differences), and mixed models were tested, and the best model is shown. The models are selected based on the independent variables' p-values ≤ 0.10 and ranked by Adjusted R-squares. A stricter p-value can be entered if required.

```
Combination List: (14 Variables)

LN(VAR1);DIFF(VAR1);LN(RATE(VAR1));DIFF(VAR2);RATE(VAR2);LN(VAR3);DIFF(VAR4);RATE(VAR5);
LN(RATE(VAR5));VAR1*VAR4;VAR1*VAR5;VAR3*VAR4;VAR3*VAR5;VAR4*VAR5
```

Multiple R	0.90820	Maximum Log-Likelihood	-273.52980	
R-Square	0.82483	Akaike Info Criterion (AIC)	11.40938	
Adjusted R-Square	0.75270	Bayes Schwarz Criterion (BSC)	11.64103	
Standard Error	85.79084	Hannan-Quinn Criterion (HQC)	11.49727	
Observations	49	Cohen's F-Squared	4.70880	

	Coeff	Std. Error	T-stat	P-value
Intercept	3664.81960	805.12137	4.55188	0.00006
LN(VAR1)	-321.07588	83.62231	-3.83960	0.00051
DIFF(VAR1)	-0.00469	0.00144	-3.26953	0.00247
LN(RATE(VAR1))	138.86285	31.87150	4.35696	0.00012
DIFF(VAR2)	0.83499	0.36471	2.28944	0.02839
RATE(VAR2)	-137.48661	77.44510	-1.77528	0.08480
LN(VAR3)	286.43034	66.04043	4.33720	0.00012
DIFF(VAR4)	-0.35191	0.05970	-5.89427	0.00000
RATE(VAR5)	-497.73236	156.06627	-3.18924	0.00306
LN(RATE(VAR5))	431.68094	163.34071	2.64283	0.01234
VAR1*VAR4	0.00004	0.00001	3.46983	0.00143
VAR1*VAR5	-0.00193	0.00077	-2.49557	0.01759
VAR3*VAR4	-0.15513	0.04131	-3.75557	0.00065
VAR3*VAR5	8.92027	2.57281	3.46713	0.00145
VAR4*VAR5	0.03743	0.01553	2.40975	0.02152

AI MACHINE LEARNING: ENSEMBLE TIME-SERIES (SUPERVISED)

This algorithm computes and calibrates an ensemble of different time-series forecast models, selects the best combination, and generates forecasts for the single historical time-series variable. An ensemble of time-series forecast methods such as Holt–Winters, deseasonalized forecasts, ARIMA, and others are applied, the best model combinations are used, and the consensus forecasts are provided. A visual representation of the back-fitting and forecast fit is also provided in the results. An alternative is to run each of these models manually in BizStats.

```
Model Inputs:
VAR64       Historical time series (1 variable)
4           Seasonality (e.g., 1, 4, 12, 250, 365)
8           Forecast periods (positive integer)
VARX        Forecast save location (optional, 1 variable)
```

Another related process is the Combinatorial Fuzzy Logic method available in BizStats. The term fuzzy logic is derived from fuzzy set theory to deal with reasoning that is approximate rather than accurate—as opposed to crisp logic, where binary sets have binary logic, fuzzy logic variables may have a truth value that ranges between 0 and 1 and is not constrained to the two truth values of classic propositional logic. Fuzzy weighting schema is used together with a combinatorial method to yield time-series forecast results.

```
BEST RMSE: 249.495091
Auto ARIMA(Autoregressive Integrated Moving Average)
```

ARIMA(P,D,Q)	Adj R-Sq	AIC	SC	DW Stat	Iter.	Rank
3,2,0	0.975310	10.9575	11.1463	3.00222	0	1
3,3,0	0.974249	12.8944	13.077	3.08095	0	2
3,0,0	0.810734	13.2187	13.4148	3.13092	0	3
. .	. . .	. .	. . .			
0,3,2	0.647397	14.3629	14.5100	1.88313	15	20

```
ARIMA (P, D, Q): 3, 2, 0
R-Squared (Coefficient of Determination)          0.9806010
Adjusted R-Squared                                0.9753100
Multiple R (Multiple Correlation Coefficient)     0.9902530
Standard Error of the Estimates (SEy)             478.74859
Number of Observations                            15
Akaike Information Criterion (AIC)                10.957458
Schwarz Criterion (SC)                           11.146272
Log-Likelihood                                   -78.180937
Durbin-Watson (DW) Statistic                      3.0022200
```

Actual vs. Forecast

	Intercept	AR(1)	AR(2)	AR(3)
Coefficients	27.051029	-1.097853	-1.155977	-1.254295
Standard Error	19.571112	0.052945	0.069607	0.067098
t-Statistic	1.382192	-20.735646	-16.607232	-18.693438
p-Value	0.194334	0.000000	0.000000	0.000000

AI MACHINE LEARNING: LINEAR FIT MODEL (SUPERVISED)

Multivariate linear regression is used to model the relationship structure and characteristics of a certain dependent variable as it depends on other independent exogenous variables. Using the modeled relationship, we can forecast the future values of the dependent variable. The accuracy and goodness of fit for this model can also be determined. Linear and nonlinear models can be fitted in the multiple regression analysis. Similar to the custom fit model, running the Linear Fit model is like regular regression analysis except that we first train the algorithm using the training dependent and training independent variables, which will identify the optimized parameters to use on the testing dataset.

Similar to the custom fit model explained previously, we divide the dataset into a training set and a testing set. The example uses VAR373 as the training dependent variable and VAR374; VAR375 as the training independent variables, making this a form of supervised learning. Using these training data, the model is calibrated, and the parameters estimated. Then, the testing independent variables are entered, such as VAR380; VAR381. Please note that there can only be a single dependent variable versus one or more independent variables. Also, the number of independent variables in the testing set and training set must match.

The algorithm also allows you to optionally enter known testing set dependent values. Sometimes these are known and sometimes they are unknown and are to be forecasted. If the values are unknown, simply leave the input empty or enter a 0 in the input if you wish to enter the next input, which is the forecast results save location in the data grid.

```
Model Inputs:
VAR373                    Training set dependent variable
VAR374; VAR375            Training set independent variable(s)
VAR380; VAR381            Testing set matching dependent variable(s)
{VARx or 0 or empty}      Testing set dependent variable (optional or 0)
{VARxx or empty}          Forecast results save location (optional)
```

The results interpretation would be similar to the multiple linear regression. The goodness-of-fit results and fitted parameter estimations pertain to the training dataset, whereas the forecast values are based on the testing dataset when applied to these fitted parameters. Sometimes, you may wish to hold some data back from the training dataset and apply it to the testing dataset to test the accuracy of the model and its ability to forecast, as well as to view the forecast errors. In other words, the optional testing set's dependent variable can be used and because these known values are applied, forecast errors can also be generated as a result. For example, the VARx value above can be set to VAR379.

Training Fit Results

Multiple R	0.50677	Maximum Log-Likelihood	-320.66137	
R-Square	0.25681	Akaike Info Criterion (AIC)	12.94645	
Adjusted R-Square	0.22519	Bayes Schwarz Criterion (BSC)	13.06118	
Standard Error	152.20473	Hannan-Quinn Criterion (HQC)	12.99014	
Observations	50	Cohen's F-Squared	0.34556	

	Coeff	Std. Error	T-stat	P-value	Std. Beta
Intercept	138.07546	64.40980	2.14370	0.03726	
VAR X1	0.00266	0.00105	2.52933	0.01484	0.33735
VAR X2	0.52024	0.24598	2.11499	0.03976	0.28209

Forecasting

Period	Forecast (F)
1	375.5419
2	420.4133
3	413.4408
4	319.5842
.	. . .
30	347.6475

AI MACHINE LEARNING: MULTIVARIATE DISCRIMINANT ANALYSIS (LINEAR) (SUPERVISED)

A Linear Discriminant Analysis (LDA) approach classifies a categorical dependent Training Y variable using one or more characteristic Training X variables. This supervised method applies maximum linear discriminant ratios (i.e., the ratio of between-class variance to within-class variance), which allows a clear separation or groupings of the Testing X variable. In other words, the separations are obtained through the maximization of $ss_{between}/ss_{within}$ or the sum of squares ratio of a linear combination $w_x x + w_y y + w_z z$. The optimized coefficient results help identify how each of the independent variables contributes towards the categorization. The group assignment will be based on the maximum estimated impact scores. To run the model, enter the variables you need to classify and enter the number of clusters desired. For instance, the required model inputs look like the following:

```
Model Inputs:
VAR444          Training Y (1 variable)
VAR445:VAR447   Training X (≥ 1 variables)
VAR448:VAR450   Testing X (optional, match Training X's # of variables)
VAR451          Forecast save location (optional, 1 variable)
```

The results are self-explanatory in that the group counts are provided, as well as the model's classification ("Put Into Group") compared to the actual group ("True Group") or the training dataset's dependent variable. For instance, we see in the original data of 244 rows (N = 244 or 85 + 93 + 66), that 34.84% were in category 1, 38.11% in category 2, and 27.05% in category 3. Out of the 85 originally in category 1 from the training dataset, the model selected 68 of these into group 1, 13 into group 2, and 4 into group 3, which means there is an 80% accuracy (68/85). In total, there were 185 correctly grouped values out of 244, providing a 75.82% accuracy. The groups' means are also shown, as are the estimated coefficients for the three groups. Recall that LDA uses a linear discriminant model to maximize the sums of squares ratio, and we can use these coefficients in the same manner. For example, suppose the first row for the testing dataset has the following: 15, 18, 16. We can then apply the three groups' coefficients and select the one with the highest discriminant value. Therefore, this first line item belongs to group 3. All other rows of testing data are computed in a similar fashion and categorized appropriately.

$$-23.0975 + 0.6263 \times 15 + 1.2406 \times 18 + 0.6865 \times 16 = 19.6118$$

$$-25.2063 + 0.9966 \times 15 + 1.0380 \times 18 + 0.7956 \times 16 = 21.1563$$

$$-20.7715 + 0.8427 \times 15 + 0.7221 \times 18 + 1.1057 \times 16 = 22.5580$$

AI MACHINE LEARNING: MULTIVARIATE DISCRIMINANT ANALYSIS (LINEAR) (SUPERVISED)

```
AI Machine Learning: Multivariate Discriminant Analysis (Linear) (Supervised)
```

Group	1	2	3
Count	85	93	66
Prior	0.3484	0.3811	0.2705

Classification Results   True Group

Put Into Group	1	2	3
1	68	16	3
2	13	67	13
3	4	10	50
Total N	85	93	66
N Correct	68	67	50
Proportion	0.8000	0.7204	0.7576

N: 244
N Correct: 185
Proportion Correct: 0.758197

VAR	1	2	3
Global Mean Vector	15.6393	20.6762	10.5902

Means of Features in Groups

	1	2	3
1	12.5176	24.2235	9.0235
2	18.5376	21.1398	10.1398
3	15.5758	15.4545	13.2424

Linear Discriminant Function for Groups

Betas1	0.6263	1.2406	0.6865
Intercept1	-23.0975		
Betas2	0.9966	1.0380	0.7956
Intercept2	-25.2063		
Betas3	0.8427	0.7221	1.1057
Intercept3	-20.7715		

Forecast Group
```
    3
    3
    2
    3
    2
    1
    1
```

AI MACHINE LEARNING: MULTIVARIATE DISCRIMINANT ANALYSIS (QUADRATIC) (SUPERVISED)

This approach classifies the categorical dependent Y variable using characteristic X variables via Quadratic Discriminant Analysis (QDA). This method is similar to LDA, but the covariance matrix is used in the group assignment as well as the estimated coefficients because LDA assumes homoskedasticity in the prediction errors whereas QDA allows for some heteroskedasticity. This allows for second-order and second-moment approximations to calibrate the relevant group assignments. To get started, enter the variables you need to classify and enter the number of clusters desired.

```
Model Inputs:
VAR444            Training Y (1 variable)
VAR445:VAR447     Training X (≥ 1 variables)
VAR448:VAR450     Testing X (optional, match Training X's # of variables)
VAR452            Forecast Save Location (optional, 1 variable)
```

Notice that the forecasted classification groups for the QDA model below are identical to the LDA model shown previously. While the LDA model's category is easily predicted using a multiple regression equation and selecting the category with the highest likelihood result, QDA requires the inclusion of the inverse covariance matrix. This means you will have to rely on the results presented and not readily be able to compute the likelihood results directly.

Quadratic Discriminant Analysis (QDA)

Group	1	2	3
Count	85	93	66
Prior	0.3484	0.3811	0.2705

Classification Results

Put Into Group	True Group 1	2	3
1	68	16	3
2	14	68	14
3	3	9	49
Total N	85	93	66
N Correct	68	68	49
Proportion	0.8000	0.7312	0.7424

N : 244
N Correct : 185
Proportion Correct : 0.758197

VAR	1	2	3
Global Mean Vector	15.6393	20.6762	10.5902

Means of Features in Groups

1	12.5176	24.2235	9.0235
2	18.5376	21.1398	10.1398
3	15.5758	15.4545	13.2424

Quadratic Discriminant Function for Groups

Betas1	0.4466	1.0833	0.7536
Intercept1	-24.4522		
Betas2	1.4812	1.1286	0.5873
Intercept2	-33.5319		
Betas3	0.7866	0.9877	0.9219
Intercept3	-25.2082		

Forecast Group
```
3
3
2
3
2
1
1
```

AI MACHINE LEARNING: NEURAL NETWORK (SUPERVISED)

Commonly used to refer to a network or circuit of biological neurons, modern usage of the term *neural network* often refers to artificial neural networks that consist of artificial neurons, or nodes, recreated in a software environment. Such networks attempt to mimic the neurons in the human brain in ways of thinking and identifying patterns and, in our situation, identifying patterns for the purposes of forecasting time-series data.

   Note that the number of hidden layers in the network is an input parameter and will need to be calibrated with your data. Typically, the more complicated the data pattern, the higher the number of hidden layers you would need and the longer it would take to compute. It is recommended that you start at 3 layers. The testing period is simply the number of data points used in the final calibration of the Neural Network model, and we recommend using at least the same number of periods you wish to forecast as the testing period.

- **Linear.** Applies a linear function, where $f(x) = x$.

- **Nonlinear Logistic.** Applies a nonlinear logistic function, where $f(x) = (1 + e^{-x})^{-1}$.

- **Nonlinear Cosine with Hyperbolic Tangent.** Applies a nonlinear cosine with hyperbolic tangent function, where $f(x) = \cos[(e^x - e^{-x})(e^x + e^{-x})^{-1}]$.

- **Nonlinear Hyperbolic Tangent.** Applies a nonlinear hyperbolic tangent function, where

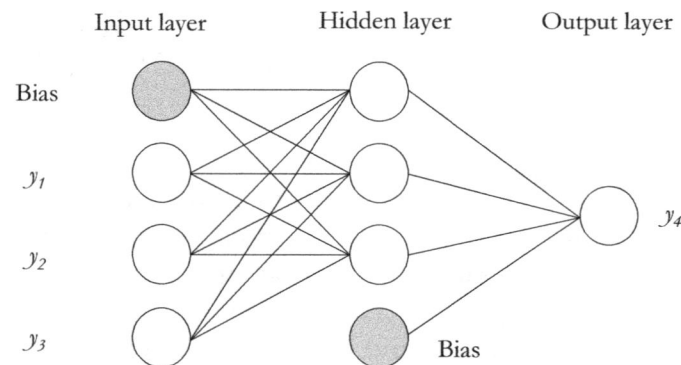

AI MACHINE LEARNING: NEURAL NETWORK (SUPERVISED)

The historical time-series data is entered as the first variable, VAR227. Then, 3 perceptron layers are requested, and 20 data points are used as the testing set. The dataset has 420 data points and entering 2 indicates that we use the first 400 of these data to perform training and calibration on the model, leaving the last 20 data points for testing the model. On completion of the testing, the model is then used to forecast the next future 2 data points. The number of forecast periods has to be ≥ 1. Finally, the model is run through internal multiphasic optimization routines. Setting this to 1 (for "yes") makes it slightly longer to run but provides a more accurate calibration of the results. A chart is also provided in the results to visually examine how good the forecast fit is.

```
Model Inputs:
VAR227      Historical time-series data to fit
3           Number of perceptron layers
20          Testing data points to withhold
2           Number of periods to forecast
1           Apply multiphased optimization (1=Apply, 0=Do not apply)


Neural Network (Cosine with Hyperbolic Tangent)

Sum of Squared Errors (Training): 0.740693
RMSE (Training): 0.043194
Sum of Squared Errors (Modified): 167.402055
RMSE (Modified): 2.893113
```

Actual vs. Forecast

Forecasting Period	Actual (Y)	Forecast (F)	Error (E)
401	650.0200	665.1658	-15.1458
402	662.4900	660.0630	2.4270
403	660.2300	658.6152	1.6148
404	662.3800	659.7383	2.6417
.	. . .	. . .	. . .
420	664.8100	667.3111	-2.5011
421		668.0264	
422		668.9191	

AI MACHINE LEARNING: LOGISTIC BINARY CLASSIFICATION (SUPERVISED)

Limited dependent variables techniques are used to forecast the probability of something occurring given some independent variables (e.g., predicting if a credit line will default given the obligor's characteristics such as age, salary, credit card debt levels; or the probability a patient will have lung cancer based on age and number of cigarettes smoked annually, and so forth). The dependent variable is limited (i.e., binary 1 and 0 for default/cancer, or limited to integer values 1, 2, 3, etc.). Traditional regression analysis will not work as the predicted probability is usually less than 0 or greater than 1, and many of the required regression assumptions are violated (e.g., independence and normality of the errors). We also have a vector of independent variable regressors, X, which are assumed to influence the outcome, Y. A typical ordinary least squares regression approach is invalid because the regression errors are heteroskedastic and non-normal, and the resulting estimated probability estimates will return nonsensical values of above 1 or below 0. This analysis handles these problems using an iterative optimization routine to maximize a log-likelihood function when the dependent variables are limited.

The AI Machine Learning Logistic Binary Classification regression is used for predicting the probability of occurrence of an event by fitting data to a logistic curve. It is a Generalized Linear Model used for binomial regression, and, like many forms of regression analysis, it makes use of several predictor variables that may be either numerical or categorical. Maximum Likelihood Estimation (MLE) is applied in a binary multivariate logistic analysis to determine the expected probability of success of belonging to a certain group.

```
Model Inputs:
VAR421              Training set dependent variable (binary data 0/1)
VAR422:VAR425       Training set independent variables
VAR427:VAR430       Testing set (optional, match independent variables)
VAR432              Forecast probability's save location (optional)
```

The estimated coefficients for the Logistic model are the logarithmic odds ratios and cannot be interpreted directly as probabilities. A quick computation is first required. Specifically, the Logit model is defined as Estimated Y or ($\hat{Y}$) using $\hat{Y} = ln[P_i/(1-P_i)]$ or, conversely, $P_i = e^{\hat{Y}}/(1 + e^{\hat{Y}})$, and the coefficients β_i are the log odds ratios. So, taking the antilog or e^{β_i} we obtain the odds ratio of $P_i/(1-P_i)$. This means that with an increase in a unit of β_i, the log odds ratio increases by this amount. Finally, the rate of change in the probability is $dP/dX = \beta_i P_i(1-P_i)$. The Standard Error measures how accurate the predicted Coefficients are, and the t-Statistics are the ratios of each predicted Coefficient to its Standard Error and are used in the typical regression hypothesis test of the significance of each estimated parameter. To estimate the probability of success of belonging to a certain group (e.g., predicting if a smoker will develop chest complications given the amount smoked per year), simply compute the estimated $\hat{Y}$ value using the MLE coefficients. For example, if the model is $\hat{Y} = 1.1 + 0.005$ (*Cigarettes*), then for someone smoking 100 packs per year, $\hat{Y} = 1.1 + 0.005(100) = 1.6$. Next, compute the inverse antilog of the odds ratio by doing: $e^{\hat{Y}}/[1 + e^{\hat{Y}}] = e^{1.6}/(1 + e^{1.6}) = 0.8320$. So, such a person has an 83.20% chance of developing some chest complications in his or her lifetime.

AI MACHINE LEARNING: LOGISTIC BINARY CLASSIFICATION (SUPERVISED)

The results interpretation is similar to that of a standard multiple regression, with the exception of computing the probability. For example, the first row of the testing variable's data points are 9, 26, 69, 6.7, which means that the $\hat{Y} = -2.047190 - 0.201097(9) - 0.062159(26) + 0.024845(69) + 0.158885(6.7) = -2.6944$. Next, we can compute the inverse antilog of the odds ratio by doing: $e^{\hat{Y}}/[1 + e^{\hat{Y}}] = e^{-2.6944}/(1 + e^{-2.6944}) = 6.33\%$. The remaining rows are similarly computed.

In addition, the results also return a confusion matrix, which lists the true responses based on the training set's dependent variable and the predicted responses. The matrix shows the various positivity and recall rates as well as the specificity, prevalence of false positives, and false negatives. True Positive (TP) is where the actual is 1 and the predicted is 1, and we see that 67.37% of the dataset was predicted correctly as a true positive. The same interpretation applies to False Negatives (FN), False Positives (FP), and True Negatives (TN). In addition, Positive Sensitivity Recall is TP/(TP+FN) and it measures the ability to predict positive outcomes. Negative Specificity is TN/(TN+FP) and it measures the ability to predict negative outcomes. Event Prevalence is the amount of Actual Y=1 and it measures the positive outcomes in the original data. False Positives is FP/(FP+TP) or Type I error. False Negatives is FN/(FN+TN) or Type II error. Positive Precision is TP/(TP+FP) and it measures the accuracy of a predicted positive outcome. Negative Precision is TN/(TN+FN) and it measures the accuracy of a predicted negative outcome. The Accuracy of the overall prediction is the % of TP and TN. Finally, the results show the Receiver Operating Characteristic (ROC) curve. It plots the Positive Sensitivity Rate against the Negative Specificity, where the area under the curve (AUC) is another measure of the accuracy of the classification model. The ROC plots the model's performance at all classification thresholds. AUC ranges from 0%–100%, where 100% indicates a perfect fit. The ROC is available by clicking on the Charts subtab in BizStats while the AUC result is shown as one of the accuracy measures in the Confusion Matrix section.

Generalized Linear Model (Logit with Binary Outcomes)

	Coefficient	Std. Error	Wald Test	P-value	Exp(B)
Intercept	-2.047190	0.301976	45.9592	0.000000	0.129097
VAR1	-0.201097	0.030500	43.4731	0.000000	0.817833
VAR2	-0.062159	0.021873	8.075710	0.004486	0.939734
VAR3	0.024845	0.005846	18.0607	0.000021	1.025156
VAR4	0.158885	0.019759	64.6603	0.000000	1.172203

Log-Likelihood	-214.8162	Positive Sensitivity Recall	49.61%
Restricted Log-Likelihood	-285.4773	Negative Specificity	91.64%
McFadden R-squared	0.247519	Event Prevalence	25.80%
Cox and Snell R-squared	0.246212	False Positives	32.63%
Nagelkerke R-squared	0.361656	False Negatives	16.05%
Raw Akaike Info. Criterion	439.6324	Positive Precision	67.37%
Raw Bayes Criterion	460.7054	Negative Precision	83.95%
Chi-Square	141.3222	Accuracy	80.80%
Degrees of Freedom	4	ROC Curve's AUC Measure	72.61%
P-value	0.000000		

Confusion Matrix

True Response	Predicted Response y = 1	y = 0
y = 1	**True Positive TP**	**False Negative FN**
y = 0	**False Positive FP**	**True Negative TN**

True Response	Predicted Response y = 1	y = 0
y = 1	64	65
y = 0	31	340

True Response	Predicted Response y = 1	y = 0
y = 1	67.37%	16.05%
y = 0	32.63%	83.95%

Forecast Y	Probability
-2.6944	6.33%
-4.1365	1.57%
-0.5931	35.59%
0.6639	66.01%
-2.7523	6.00%
-0.6550	34.19%

AI MACHINE LEARNING: NORMIT PROBIT BINARY CLASSIFICATION (SUPERVISED)

The AI Machine Learning Normit Probit model is a popular alternative specification for the Logistic binary response model. It employs a Normit-Probit function estimated using maximum likelihood estimation and is also sometimes called a Probit regression. The Probit and logistic regression models tend to produce very similar predictions where the parameter estimates in a logistic regression tend to be 1.6 to 1.8 times higher than they are in a corresponding Probit model. The choice of using a Probit or Logit is entirely up to convenience, and the main distinction is that the logistic distribution has a higher kurtosis (fatter tails) to account for extreme values. For example, suppose that house ownership is the decision to be modeled, and this response variable is binary (home purchase or no home purchase) and depends on a series of independent variables X_i such as income, age, and so forth, such that $I_i = \beta_0 + \beta_1 X_1 + \cdots + \beta_n X_n$, where the larger the value of I_i, the higher the probability of homeownership. For each family, a critical threshold I^* exists, where, if exceeded, the house is purchased, otherwise, no home is purchased, and the outcome probability (P) is assumed to be normally distributed, such that $P_i = CDF(I)$ using a standard-normal cumulative distribution function (CDF). Therefore, use the estimated coefficients exactly like that of a regression model and, using the estimated $\hat{Y}$, apply a standard-normal distribution to compute the probability.

```
Model Inputs:
VAR421              Training set dependent variable (binary data 0/1)
VAR422:VAR425       Training set independent variables
VAR427:VAR430       Testing set (optional, match independent variables)
VAR432              Forecast probability's save location (optional)
```

The results interpretation is similar to that of a standard multiple regression and the AI/ML Logistic Binary Classification model, with the exception of computing the probability, which, in the case of a Normit Probit model, requires a standard normal distribution. For example, the first row of the testing variable's data points are 9, 26, 69, 6.7, 3.92, which means that the $\hat{Y} = -1.218323 - 0.113973(9) - 0.033448(26) + 0.013898(69) + 0.092666(6.7) = -1.5339$ (rounded). Next, we can compute the normal cumulative distribution function $\Phi(-1.5339) = 6.25\%$. The resulting forecasted probability for Normit is typically fairly close to the Logit result seen previously. The remaining rows are similarly computed. Finally, the ROC, AUC, and Confusion Matrix results such as positivity, specificity, false positives, false negatives, and so forth, are also computed and their interpretations are identical to the AI/ML Logistic Binary Classification model.

AI MACHINE LEARNING: NORMIT PROBIT BINARY CLASSIFICATION (SUPERVISED)

Generalized Linear Model (Probit with Binary Outcomes)

	Coefficient	Std. Error	Wald Test	P-value	Lower	Upper
Intercept	**-1.218323**	0.170237	51.2172	0.000000	-1.551982	-0.884664
VAR1	**-0.113973**	0.016800	46.0252	0.000000	-0.146900	-0.081046
VAR2	**-0.033448**	0.012279	7.419795	0.006451	-0.057515	-0.009381
VAR3	**0.013898**	0.003350	17.2135	0.000033	0.007333	0.020464
VAR4	**0.092666**	0.010965	71.4226	0.000000	0.071176	0.114157

Log-Likelihood	-214.3784			
Restricted Log-Likelihood	-285.4773			
McFadden R-squared	0.249053			
Cox and Snell R-squared	0.247531	Positive Sensitivity Recall	54.26%	
Nagelkerke R-squared	0.363593	Negative Specificity	89.49%	
Raw Akaike Info. Criterion	438.7567	Event Prevalence	25.80%	
Raw Bayes Criterion	459.8298	False Positives	35.78%	
Chi-Square	142.1979	False Negatives	15.09%	
Degrees of Freedom	4	Positive Precision	64.22%	
P-value	0.000000	Negative Precision	84.91%	
		Accuracy	80.40%	
		ROC Curve's AUC Measure	72.40%	

Forecast Y Probability

-1.5339	**6.25%**
-2.3330	0.98%
-0.3424	36.60%
0.3504	63.70%
-1.5894	5.60%
-0.3880	34.90%
-0.7630	22.27%
-0.5542	28.97%
-1.4084	7.95%
0.8985	81.55%

Confusion Matrix

True Response	Predicted Response y = 1	y = 0
y = 1	True Positive TP	False Negative FN
y = 0	False Positive FP	True Negative TN

True Response	Predicted Response y = 1	y = 0
y = 1	70	59
y = 0	39	332

True Response	Predicted Response y = 1	y = 0
y = 1	64.22%	15.09%
y = 0	35.78%	84.91%

ROC Curve

AI MACHINE LEARNING: RANDOM FOREST (SUPERVISED)

In this approach, bootstraps of regression trees are run multiple times with different combinations of data points and variables to develop a consensus forecast of group assignments. Using a single set of Training Y and Training X variables, the data and variables are bootstrapped and resampled. Each resampling will be run in the CART or classification and regression tree model, and the consensus categorization results will be generated. The benefit of random forests is that it provides a consensus forecast (wisdom of the crowd) through a resampling with replacement of both the variables and the data points. However, the individual CART model and tree process will no longer be available. To get started with this approach, enter the variables you need to classify and enter the number of clusters desired.

```
Model Inputs:
VAR433              Training Y (1 variable)
VAR434:VAR437       Training X (≥ 1 variables)
3                   Min variables (< the total X variables)
9                   Min data points (< the total number of rows)
300                 Max Bootstrap trials (2-1000)
VAR438:VAR441       Testing X (optional)
VARX                Forecast save location (optional)
```

AI MACHINE LEARNING: RANDOM FOREST (SUPERVISED)

Suppose we apply the entire dataset and bootstrapped it (i.e., minimum variables is 4 and the minimum data points to use is 10, which means the entire dataset is utilized), the results will be identical to the AI/ML Classification and Regression Tree CART model. Recall that the CART results had 100% for all three categories. In this random forest model, if we only apply a minimum of 3 variables with 9 data rows, we see the results shown next. Hundreds of CART models are bootstrapped, and the averages of the results are obtained. The testing dataset's categorization shows that the highest probability events are in categories 1, 1, 2, 1, 1, 2, 2, 3, 3, 3, which also corresponds to the single CART model results.

```
AI Machine Learning: Random Forest (Supervised)

    Category       Average Accuracy
     1.00               80.00%
     2.00              103.11%
     3.00               90.22%
```

Training Dataset

Actual	Category 1	Category 2	Category 3
1.00	100.00%	0.00%	0.00%
1.00	75.00%	25.00%	0.00%
2.00	13.33%	86.67%	0.00%
1.00	100.00%	0.00%	0.00%
1.00	71.15%	28.85%	0.00%
2.00	0.00%	100.00%	0.00%
2.00	0.00%	100.00%	0.00%
3.00	0.00%	10.45%	89.55%
3.00	0.00%	0.00%	100.00%
3.00	0.00%	0.00%	100.00%

Testing Dataset

Category 1	Category 2	Category 3
100.00%	0.00%	0.00%
75.00%	25.00%	0.00%
13.33%	86.67%	0.00%
100.00%	0.00%	0.00%
75.00%	25.00%	0.00%
0.00%	100.00%	0.00%
0.00%	100.00%	0.00%
0.00%	10.45%	89.55%
0.00%	0.00%	100.00%
0.00%	9.33%	90.67%

AI MACHINE LEARNING: SEGMENTATION CLUSTERING (UNSUPERVISED)

Taking the original dataset, we run some internal algorithms (a combination of k-means hierarchical clustering and other methods-of-moments to find the best-fitting groups or natural statistical clusters) to statistically divide or segment the original dataset into multiple groups. Segment this dataset into as many groups as you wish. This technique is valuable in a variety of settings including marketing (market segmentation of customers into various customer relationship management groups etc.), physical sciences, engineering, and others.

VAR415 shows the various states, whereas VAR416:VAR419 provides the characteristics in terms of each state's number of murders, number of assaults, the state population in millions, and number of breaking-and-entering events. Using these numerical values (VAR416:VAR419), the states can be segmented into various groups.

```
Model Inputs:
VAR416:VAR419   Variables to cluster
0               Optional (0=Show All Clusters Up To X, 1=Show Cluster X)
5               Cluster X
```

The results from cluster analysis shown next generate clusters of multiple groups partitioned based on data similarity for exploratory data analysis and data mining (e.g., machine learning, pattern recognition, image analysis, bioinformatics, etc.). The objects in the same cluster are more similar to each other than to those in other clusters. In addition, cluster analysis can be used to discover data structures without providing an explanation or interpretation of the relationship among variables. The results will show the cluster membership number as well as the centroid's mean values and counts of members within each cluster subgroup. For example, if we need to segregate the data into 3 segments, we see that one segment has Alaska, Alabama, Arizona, and so forth, while the second segment includes states like Arkansas and so forth (i.e., the 3 Cluster result shows 1, 1, 1, 2, 1, and so forth, indicating that the first three sample rows are categorized into Cluster 1, followed by Cluster 2, and then Cluster 1, etc.). These segments group similar characteristics together as cohorts, where states within these cohorts have the highest amounts of statistical similarities.

AI MACHINE LEARNING: SEGMENTATION CLUSTERING (UNSUPERVISED)

Segmentation Clustering

Sample	X1	X2	X3	X4	Cluster #	2	3	4	5
1	13.20	236.00	58.00	21.20		1	1	1	1
2	10.00	263.00	48.00	44.50		1	1	1	1
3	8.10	294.00	80.00	31.00		1	1	1	2
4	8.80	190.00	50.00	19.50		1	2	3	1
5	9.00	276.00	91.00	40.60		1	1	1	2
..	..	...	...	...		.	.	.	.
46	8.50	156.00	63.00	207.00		1	3	4	5
47	4.00	145.00	73.00	26.20		2	2	3	4
48	5.70	81.00	39.00	9.30		2	2	2	3
49	2.60	53.00	66.00	10.80		2	2	2	3
50	6.80	161.00	60.00	15.60		1	2	3	4

Cluster Centroids [1]

No. of Clusters		2	3	4	5
	1	10.70	11.95	12.14	11.89
	2	7.22	7.32	3.94	11.80
	3		8.50	10.65	2.95
	4			8.50	9.34
	5				8.50

Cluster Centroids [2]

No. of Clusters		2	3	4	5
	1	234.89	261.95	268.94	232.07
	2	95.48	113.50	77.53	300.86
	3		156.00	155.71	62.70
	4			156.00	133.33
	5				156.00

Cluster Centroids [3]

No. of Clusters		2	3	4	5
	1	68.74	69.00	67.82	67.07
	2	61.78	63.43	57.00	68.71
	3		63.00	70.94	53.90
	4			63.00	69.72
	5				63.00

Cluster Centroids [4]

No. of Clusters		2	3	4	5
	1	33.24	28.63	28.22	27.74
	2	15.23	16.56	12.69	28.86
	3		207.00	21.81	11.51
	4			207.00	18.63

Cluster Counts

No. of Clusters		2	3	4	5
	1	27	19	17	14
	2	23	30	15	7
	3		1	17	10
	4			1	18
	5				1

13. Monte Carlo Simulation: On the Shores of Monaco

Dr. Johnathan Mun, Professor of Research
Quantitative Research Methods Course Slides
Seventh Edition, 2026, ROV Press

Monte Carlo Risk Simulation

Simulation (Probability Assumptions)

	Value	Probability
Step 1:	362995	55%
The Assumptions	363522	10%
	252094	10%
	122922	10%
	23572	3%
	305721	3%
	61877	3%
	147322	3%
	179360	3%

Here are the assumed values and their corresponding probabilities of occurrence. The sum of the probabilities have to add up to 100%.

We then translate the assumed values into a set of random numbers bounded by [0,1]. For instance, for a normal distribution, the probability of getting a number between 0.00 and 0.55 is 55% and between 0.56 and 0.65 is 10% and so forth. This is done in Step 2 below.

CELLS $D$15:$F$23

	Minimum	Maximum	Implied
Step 2:	0.00	0.55	362994.83
The Table Setup	0.56	0.65	363522.33
	0.66	0.75	252094
	0.76	0.85	122922.05
	0.86	0.88	23572.39
	0.89	0.91	305721.43
	0.92	0.94	61876.66
	0.95	0.97	147322.19
	0.98	1.00	179359.73

Simulate this for 100 trials and take the average. Then, repeat this for several thousand sets, taking the average on every set. Then, using these thousands of simulated sets, create a probability distribution and calculate its corresponding descriptive statistics (mean, standard deviation, confidence intervals, probabilities, et cetera).

VLOOKUP(RAND(),$D$15:$F$23,3)

Average	297185
90th%	310390

Step 3:	Trials	Set 1	Set 2	Set 3	Set 4	Set 5	Set 100	Set 1000	Set 1500	Set 2000	Set 5000
Simulate	1	147322	122922	252094	362995	362995	362995	252094	362995	61877	363522
	2	362995	362995	362995	362995	147322	61877	61877	362995	122922	179360
	3	252094	362995	362995	122922	362995	252094	61877	362995	362995	362995
	4	362995	362995	252094	362995	362995	362995	61877	179360	179360	122922
	5	252094	362995	363522	362995	363522	122922	363522	252094	147322	362995
	6	362995	362995	363522	122922	252094	363522	362995	179360	122922	179360
	7	122922	362995	363522	362995	362995	122922	122922	252094	61877	122922
	8	363522	362995	362995	122922	362995	122922	122922	122922	362995	61877
	9	362995	362995	362995	252094	252094	362995	362995	362995	179360	363522
	10	122922	122922	363522	362995	305721	362995	252094	61877	362995	362995
	11	305721	362995	362995	362995	252094	362995	252094	363522	362995	362995
	12	362995	362995	362995	362995	252094	362995	362995	252094	362995	122922
Rows 13	95	252094	362995	362995	363522	362995	122922				
to 94 have	96	252094	252094	61877	362995	363522	122922				
been hidden	97	362995	23572	362995	362995	122922	305721				
to conserve	98	362995	362995	362995	147322	362995	252094				
space.	99	122922	362995	362995	362995	362995	362995				
	100	363522	252094	362995	362995	362995	362995				
	Average	275763	282681	318044	292146	300325	299948				

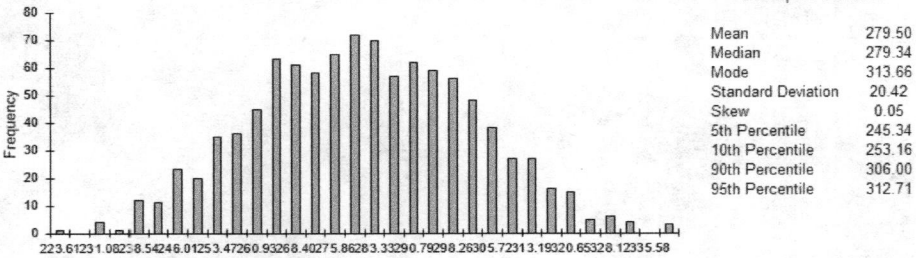

Probability Distribution of Simulated Output

Descriptive Statistics	
Mean	279.50
Median	279.34
Mode	313.66
Standard Deviation	20.42
Skew	0.05
5th Percentile	245.34
10th Percentile	253.16
90th Percentile	306.00
95th Percentile	312.71

Risk Simulator

Discounted Cash Flow / ROI Model

Base Year	2017		Sum PV Net Benefits	$4,762.09		Discount Type	Discrete End-of-Year Discounting ▼	
Start Year	2017		Sum PV Investments	$1,634.22				
Market Risk-Adjusted Discount Rate	15.00%		Net Present Value	$3,127.87		Model	Include Terminal Valuation ▼	
Private-Risk Discount Rate	5.00%		Internal Rate of Return	55.68%				
Terminal Period Growth Rate	2.00%		Return on Investment	191.40%				
Effective Tax Rate	40.00%		Profitability Index	2.91				

	2017	2018	2019	2020	2021	2022	2023	2024	2025	2026
Product A Avg Price/Unit	$10.00	$10.50	$11.00	$11.50	$12.00	$12.50	$13.00	$13.50	$14.00	$14.50
Product B Avg Price/Unit	$12.25	$12.50	$12.75	$13.00	$13.25	$13.50	$13.75	$14.00	$14.25	$14.50
Product C Avg Price/Unit	$15.15	$15.30	$15.45	$15.60	$15.75	$15.90	$16.05	$16.20	$16.35	$16.50
Product A Sale Quantity ('000s)	50	50	50	50	50	50	50	50	50	50
Product B Sale Quantity ('000s)	35	35	35	35	35	35	35	35	35	35
Product C Sale Quantity ('000s)	20	20	20	20	20	20	20	20	20	20
Total Revenues	$1,231.75	$1,268.50	$1,305.25	$1,342.00	$1,378.75	$1,415.50	$1,452.25	$1,489.00	$1,525.75	$1,562.50
Direct Cost of Goods Sold	$184.76	$190.28	$195.79	$201.30	$206.81	$212.33	$217.84	$223.35	$228.86	$234.38
Gross Profit	$1,046.99	$1,078.23	$1,109.46	$1,140.70	$1,171.94	$1,203.18	$1,234.41	$1,265.65	$1,296.89	$1,328.13
Operating Expenses	$157.50	$157.50	$157.50	$157.50	$157.50	$157.50	$157.50	$157.50	$157.50	$157.50
Sales, General and Admin. Costs	$15.75	$15.75	$15.75	$15.75	$15.75	$15.75	$15.75	$15.75	$15.75	$15.75
Operating Income (EBITDA)	$873.74	$904.98	$936.21							
Depreciation	$10.00	$10.00	$10.00							
Amortization	$3.00	$3.00	$3.00							
EBIT	$860.74	$891.98	$923.21							
Interest Payments	$2.00	$2.00	$2.00							
EBT	$858.74	$889.98	$921.21							
Taxes	$343.50	$355.99	$368.49							
Net Income	$515.24	$533.99	$552.73							
Noncash: Depreciation Amortization	$13.00	$13.00	$13.00							
Noncash: Change in Net Working Capital	$0.00	$0.00	$0.00							
Noncash: Capital Expenditures	$0.00	$0.00	$0.00							
Free Cash Flow	$528.24	$546.99	$565.73							
Investment Outlay	$500.00		$1,500.00							
Net Free Cash Flow	($1,105.97)	$546.99	$565.73							
Financial Analysis										
Present Value of Free Cash Flow	$528.24	$475.64	$427.77							
Present Value of Investment Outlay	$500.00	$0.00	$1,134.22							
Discounted Payback Period	3.47 Years									

Assumption Properties — Assumption Name: Revenues

Distributions: Normal, Triangular, Uniform, Custom, Arcsine, Bernoulli, Beta, Beta 3, Beta 4, Binomial, Cauchy, Chi-Square

Mean = 1020.0000
Stdev = 30.8221
Skewness = 0.1913
Kurtosis = -0.6000

Minimum: 950
Most Likely: 1010
Maximum: 1100

● Regular Input
○ Percentile Input

☑ Enable Correlation
☐ Enable Data Boundary
☐ Enable Dynamic Simulations

Minimum: -Infinity
Maximum: Infinity

Triangular Distribution
The triangular distribution describes a situation where you know the minimum, maximum, and most likely values to occur. For example, you could describe the number of cars sold per week when past sales show the minimum, maximum, and usual number of cars sold. The minimum number of items is fixed, the maximum number of items is fixed, and the most likely number of items falls between the...

OK   Cancel

Risk Simulator Results

Probability Distributions

TRIANGULAR
Looks like a triangle, continuous values, tails end at min and max with most likely as its peak. Can be skewed or symmetrical, with negative excess kurtosis (truncated tails). Examples: sales forecasts, subject matter estimates, management assumptions.

NORMAL
Continuous bell curve, a.k.a. Gaussian distribution, infinite tails on both ends, requires mean and standard deviation as inputs. Symmetrical with zero skew and zero excess kurtosis. Examples: stock returns, height, weight, IQ (most are truncated normal with limits).

UNIFORM
Flat continuous area with equal probability of occurrence at any point between the minimum and maximum. Symmetrical with zero skew and negative excess kurtosis (fixed end points). Examples: business forecasts and economic forecasts.

COMMONLY USED DISTRIBUTIONS

BINOMIAL
Discrete events with two mutually exclusive and independent outcomes with fixed probability of success at each successive trial. Symmetrical and approaches normal distribution with high number of trials. Example: tossing a coin multiple times.

POISSON
Discrete events occurring independently with the same average rate of repetition, and measured in time or space (area).
Examples: sales forecasts, subject matter estimates, management assumptions.
Approaches normal with high average rates.

CUSTOM
Empirically fitted discrete distribution when little data is available or when other theoretical distributions fail. Suitable for Delphi methods, can be multimodal or irregular. Examples: subject matter estimates, management assumptions, and qualitative estimates that are converted numerically.

LESS COMMONLY USED BUT IMPORTANT DISTRIBUTIONS

BERNOULLI
Single discrete trial version of Binomial (e.g., simulating success or failure of projects).

BETA 4
Highly flexible continuous distribution capable of taking on multiple shapes and scales.

DISCRETE UNIFORM
Range of discrete events with equal probability of occurrence (e.g., rolling a six-sided die).

EXPONENTIAL 2
High probably of low values, low probability of continuous high values (e.g., wait time).

GUMBEL
Tail-end extreme value simulations of continuous outcomes (e.g., market crashes).

LOGNORMAL
Variables with continuous non-negative and non-zero values (e.g., stock prices).

STUDENT'S T
Continuous-normal with fat tails or higher probability of extremes (e.g., risky returns).

WEIBULL 3
Continuous mean time before failure and reliability estimates (e.g., MTBF of an engine).

OTHER DISTRIBUTIONS: Arcsine, Beta, Beta 3, Cauchy, Chi-square, Cosine, Double Log, Erlang, Exponential, F, Fréchet, Gamma, Geometric, Gumbel Min, Gumbel Max, Hypergeometric, Laplace, Logistic, Lognormal 3, Negative Binomial, Parabolic, Generalized Pareto, Pareto, Pascal, Pearson V, Pearson VI, Pert, Power, Power 3, Rayleigh, Standard-Normal, Standard-T, Weibull

Relationships Among Different Probability Distributions

Simulation, Scenario, Tornado, Bootstrap, and Delphi Custom

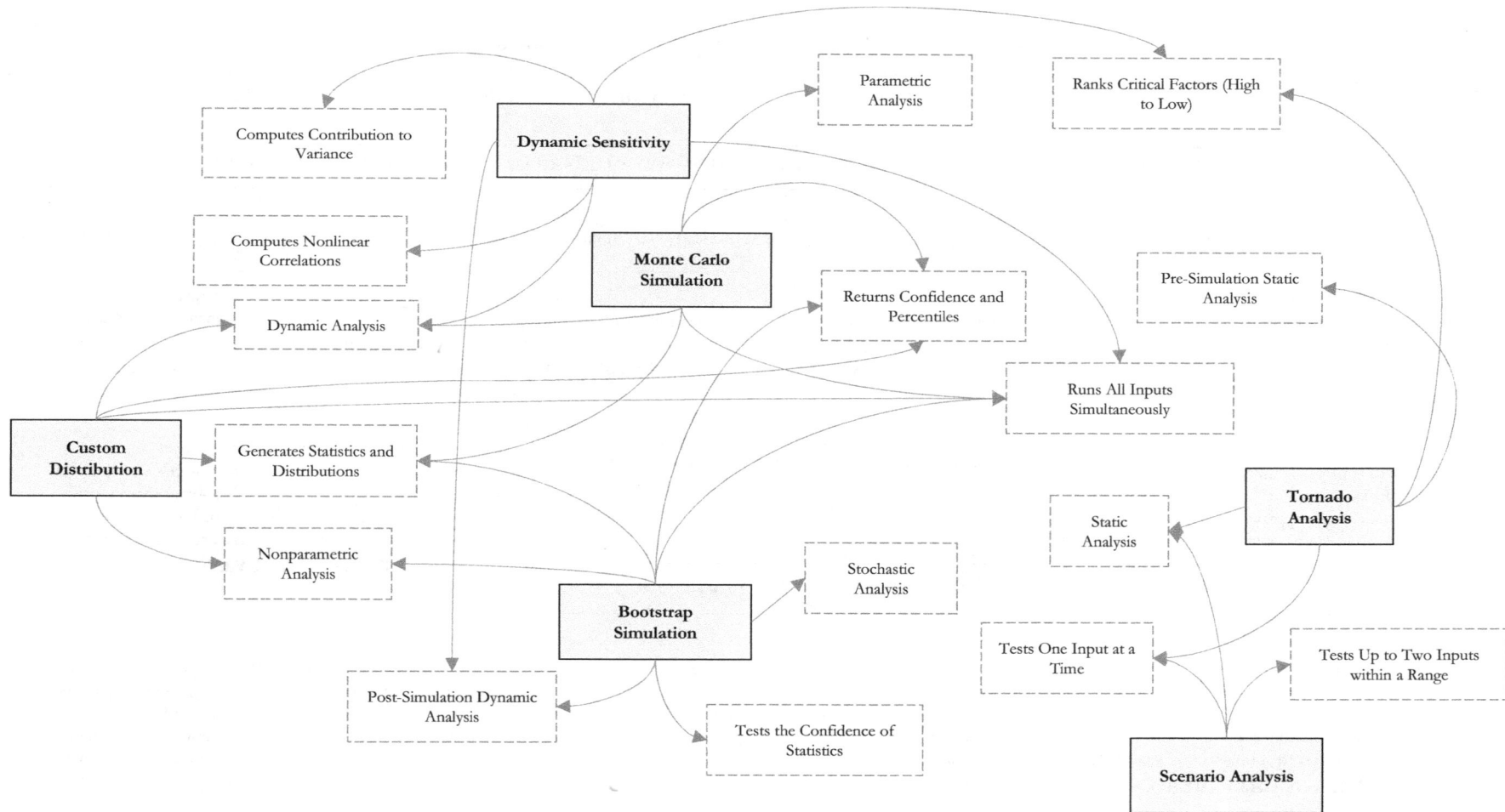

Analytical Methods

DISTRIBUTIONAL FITTING

What distribution and distributional parameters do you use? This technique fits historical empirical data to probability distributions using Akaike Information Criterion (AIC), Anderson–Darling (AD), Chi-Square, Kolmogorov–Smirnov (KS), Kuiper's Statistic, and Schwarz/Bayes Information Criterion (SC/BIC).

DISTRIBUTIONAL ANALYSIS

Distributional Analysis (PDF, CDF, ICDF of 50 distributions). Distributional Charts and Tables (compares PDF & CDF shapes and characteristics). Overlay Charts (overlays empirically simulated output forecasts for a visual comparison of the moments).

CORRELATED SIMULATION

Runs correlated simulations by setting pairwise nonlinear correlations among multiple input assumptions. Normal, T, and Quasi-Normal Copulas are used in the convolution simulation. Correlations affect the second moment or risk of an output forecast distribution.

DATA DIAGNOSTICS

Executes multiple tests on existing dataset to determine its characteristics prior to running forecast models: autocorrelation, heteroskedasticity, lags, micronumerosity, multicollinearity, nonlinearity, and seasonality. Certain tests are relevant only for time-series, cross-sectional, or panel data types.

ANALYTICAL TOOLS

SCENARIO ANALYSIS

Runs multiple scenarios quickly and effortlessly by changing one or two input parameters a prespecified range for a heat map of the output variable.

TORNADO ANALYSIS

Static impacts of each variable on the outcome of the model by perturbing each input variable a preset amount, captures the final result, lists the pre-simulation perturbations ranked from most significant to least. Performed to identify critical factors to set as simulation assumptions to run.

DYNAMIC SENSITIVITY

Applies dynamic perturbations created after simulations and calculates contribution to variance.

HYPOTHESIS TESTS

Determines if two variables are statistically identical or different from one another.

BOOSTRAP SIMULATION

Estimates reliability or accuracy of forecast statistics, answers confidence/precision questions.

OVERLAY CHARTS

Overlays multiple assumptions and simulated forecast charts to compare their characteristics.

OTHER ANALYTICAL TOOLS: Check Model, Data Deseasonalization, Data Diagnostics, Data Open & Import, Distributional Fitting (Single, Multiple, Percentile), Principal Component Analysis, Seasonality Test, Segmentation Clustering, Statistical Tests, and Structural Break

WAYS OF SAVING A MODEL AND RESULTS: Generate live Excel charts after simulation runs, Tornado, and Sensitivity analyses, as well as:

COPY/PASTE CHARTS

Copy and paste the simulation and forecast charts into PowerPoint/Word.

CUSTOM DISTRIBUTION

Create and save nonparametric custom distributions based on actual empirical data.

DATA EXTRACTION

Simulated assumptions and forecasts' raw data can be extracted into Excel or text files.

EXCEL FILE

One file saves all assumptions, forecasts, decisions, constraints, objectives, and profiles.

REPORT GENERATION

Run simulation, forecasting, analytical methods, and optimization reports.

RISK SIMULATOR PROFILE

Create multiple profiles and scenarios of simulation and optimization variable settings.

RISK SIM FILE

Save live Risk Simulator charts for future retrieval without having to re-run simulations.

STATISTICS TABLE

Generate reports of statistical results as tables in Excel for archiving.

Distributional Fitting

Akaike Information Criterion (AIC)
Rewards goodness-of-fit but also includes a penalty that is an increasing function of the number of estimated parameters (although AIC penalizes the number of parameters less strongly than other methods).

Anderson–Darling (AD)
When applied to testing if a normal distribution adequately describes a set of data, it is one of the most powerful statistical tools for detecting departures from normality and is powerful for testing normal tails. However, in non-normal distributions with skew and kurtosis, this test lacks power compared to other methods.

Chi-Square (CS)
Used to exclusively test discrete distributions where data are statistically categorized into various groups. The CS approach cannot be readily used to fit continuous distributions.

DISTRIBUTIONAL FITTING

Kolmogorov–Smirnov (KS)
A nonparametric test for the equality of continuous probability distributions that can be used to compare a sample with a reference probability distribution, making it useful for testing abnormally shaped distributions and non-normal distributions. Use the KS by default if the underlying distribution is unknown.

Kuiper's Statistic (K)
Related to the KS test making it as sensitive in the tails as at the median and also making it invariant under cyclic transformations of the independent variable, rendering it invaluable when testing for cyclic variations over time. In comparison, the AD test provides equal sensitivity at the tails as the median, but it does not provide the cyclic invariance.

Schwarz/Bayes Information Criterion (SC/BIC)
The SC/BIC test introduces a penalty term for the number of parameters in the model with a larger penalty than AIC.

HYPOTHESIS TEST
The null hypothesis being tested is such that the fitted distribution is the same distribution as the population from which the sample data to be fitted comes. Thus, if the computed p-value is lower than a critical alpha level (typically 0.10 or 0.05), then the distribution is the wrong distribution (reject the null hypothesis). Conversely, the higher the p-value, the better the distribution fits the data (do not reject the null hypothesis, which means the fitted distribution is the correct distribution, or null hypothesis of H_0: Error = 0, where error is defined as the difference between the empirical data and the theoretical distribution). Roughly, you can think of p-value as a percentage explained. The higher the p-value, the better the data fits the selected probability distribution.

Continuous PDF and Discrete PMF

Continuous PDF (Area Chart)

Discrete PMF (Bar Chart)

PDF and CDF

Multiple Continuous PDF Overlay Charts

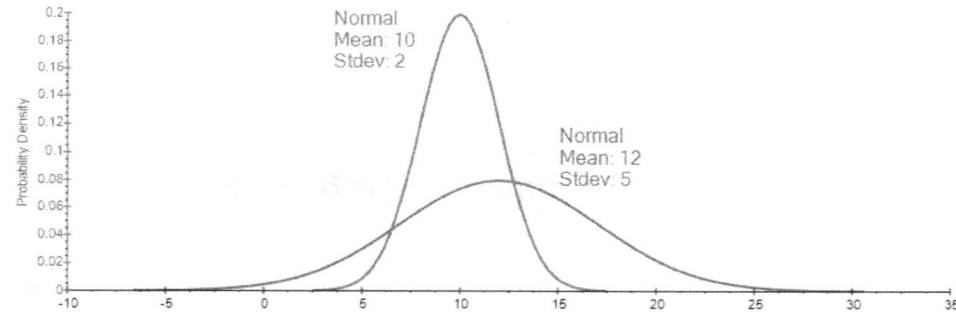

CDF Overlay Charts

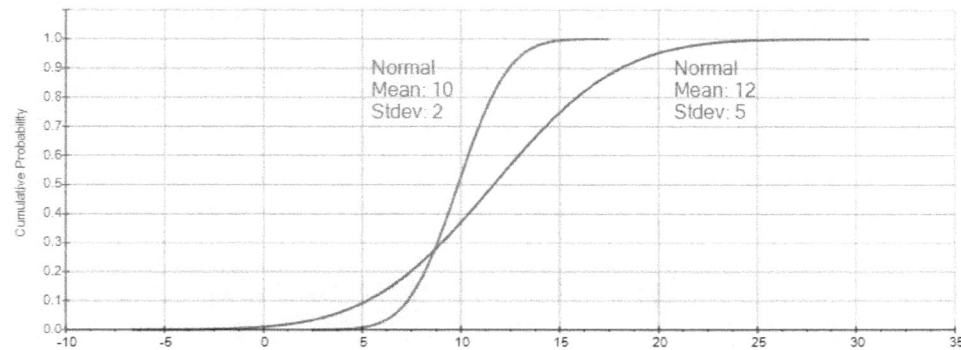

Positively and Negatively Skewed PDFs

PDF Characteristics of the Beta Distribution

PDF of a Negatively Skewed Beta Distribution

Positively and Negatively Skewed CDFs

CDF of a Positively Skewed Distribution

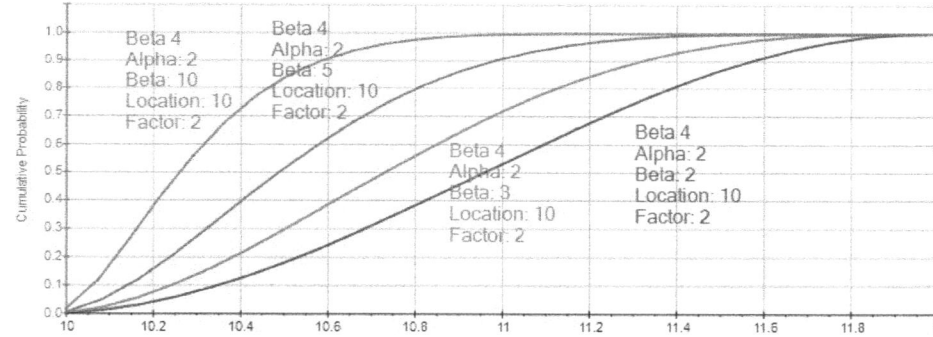

CDF of a Negatively Skewed Distribution

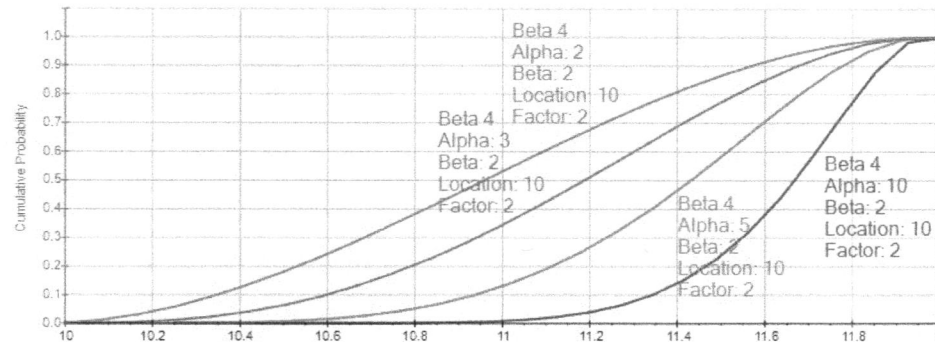

Shifted PDF and CDF

PDF Characteristics of a Shift

CDF Characteristics of a Shift

14. Test Driving Risk Simulator

Dr. Johnathan Mun, Professor of Research
Quantitative Research Methods Course Slides
Seventh Edition, 2026, ROV Press

1. Creating A New Simulation Profile

Enter a relevant title for this simulation

Enter the desired number of simulation trials (default is 1,000)

Simulation Properties

Profile Name First Example Simulation

Simulation Settings

Number of trials 1,000

☐ Pause simulation on error
☑ Turn on correlations
☑ Specify random number sequence (Seed)
999

OK   Cancel

Select if you want correlations to be considered in the simulation (default is checked)

Select if you want the simulation to stop when an error is encountered (default is unchecked)

Select and enter a seed value if you want the simulation to follow a specified random number sequence (default is unchecked)

Notes: A profile stores all your simulation assumptions, forecasts, and optimization settings. The profile is saved inside the Excel model itself as a hidden worksheet. This means your models are self-contained with all the relevant Risk Simulator settings. Finally, you can create multiple profiles and switch among them (this allows you to create various simulation scenarios within the same Excel model).

2. Set Input Assumptions

Different views of distributions exist in this Distribution Gallery

2. Enter the assumption's name

3. Enter the selected distribution's required parameters

1. Select a distribution

Select for alternate parameters

A short description of the distribution is available here

Use this area to add, edit, or remove any correlations among input assumptions

Select for multidimensional simulation

Enter new or leave as is the distributional boundaries

Notes:

Only simple value cells (i.e., cells with numbers and not equations or functions) in Excel can be set as assumptions

3. Set Output Forecasts

Specify the name of the forecast cell

Optional: Specify the forecast precision and error controls

Specify if you want this forecast to be visible

Notes:

You cannot set a forecast on an existing assumption cell.

4. Run Simulation

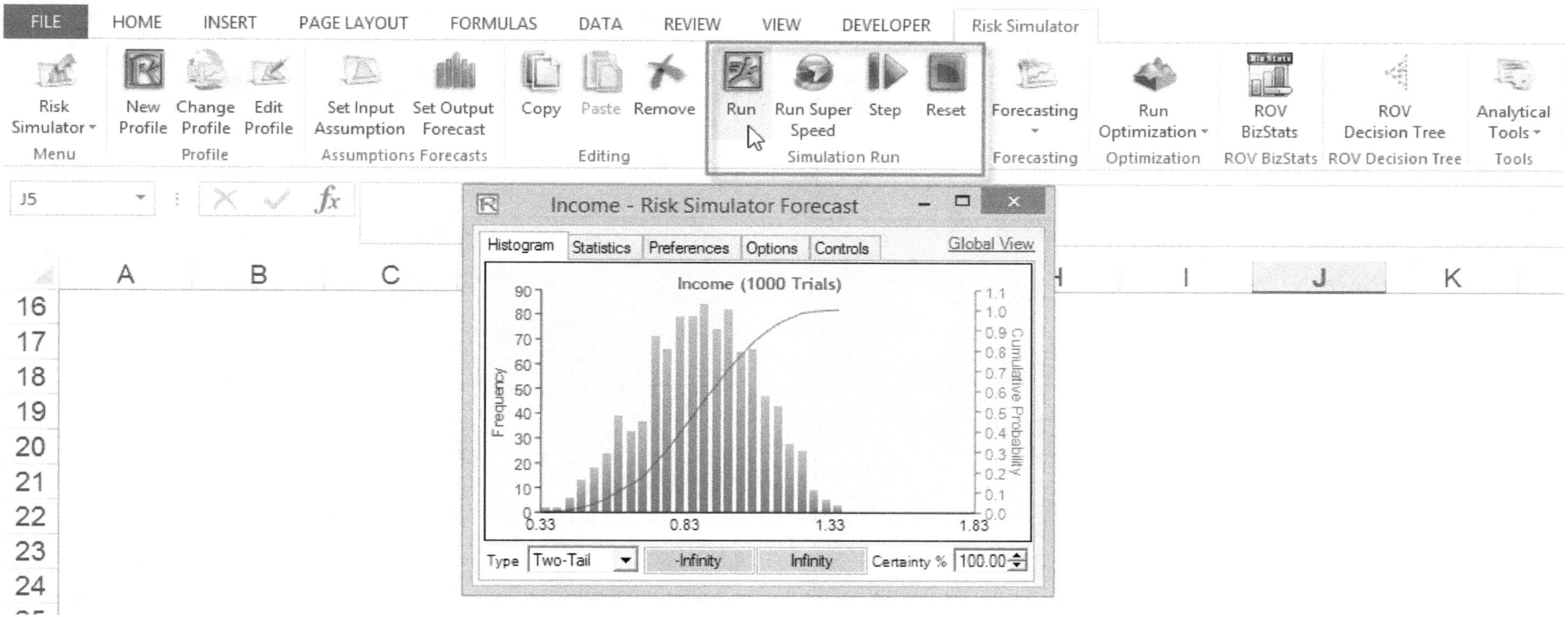

Forecast Charts

Forecast Charts: Other Views

Income - Risk Simulator Forecast

Histogram | **Statistics** | Preferences | Options | Controls — Global View

Statistics	Result
Number of Trials	1000
Mean	0.8626
Median	0.8674
Standard Deviation	0.1933
Variance	0.0374
Coefficient of Variation	0.2241
Maximum	1.3570
Minimum	0.3019
Range	1.0551
Skewness	-0.1157
Kurtosis	-0.4480
25% Percentile	0.7269
75% Percentile	1.0068
Percentage Error Precision at 95% Confidence	1.3888%

Income - Risk Simulator Forecast

Histogram | Statistics | **Preferences** | Options | Controls — Global View

Display
- ☐ Always Show Window On Top
- ☐ Semitransparent When Inactive

Control
- Close All   Excel
- Minimize All
- Copy Chart

Histogram Resolution
Faster Simulation ————————— Higher Resolution

Data Update Interval
Faster Update ————————— Faster Simulation

Income - Risk Simulator Forecast

Histogram | Statistics | Preferences | **Options** | Controls — Global View

Data Filter
- ◉ Show all data
- ○ Show only data between -Infinity and Infinity
- ○ Show only data within 6 standard deviation(s)

Statistic
- Precision level used to calculate the error: 95 %
- Show the following statistic(s) on the histogram:
  - ☐ Mean ☐ Median ☐ 1st Quartile ☐ 3rd Quartile

Show Decimals
- Chart X-Axis 2   Confidence 4   Statistics 4

Income - Risk Simulator Forecast

Histogram | Statistics | Preferences | Options | **Controls** — Global View

Chart Type Bar ▼   Overlay CDF1 ▼   View 1 ▼

	Min	Max	Auto	
X-Axis			☑	Title Income (1000 Trials)
Y-Axis			☑	

Distribution Fitting

	Actual	Theoretical	
Distribution ----			◉ Continuous
	Mean ----	----	○ Discrete
Fit Stats: ----	Stdev ----	----	
	Skew ----	----	2 Decimals
P-Value: ----	Kurt ----	----	Fit

Distributional Fitting

- A powerful simulation tool is distributional fitting. That is, which distribution does an analyst or engineer use for a particular input variable in a model? What are the relevant distributional parameters? If no historical data exist, then the analyst must make assumptions about the variables in question.

- One approach is to use the Delphi method where a group of experts is tasked with estimating the behavior of each variable. For instance, a group of mechanical engineers can be tasked with evaluating the extreme possibilities of a spring coil's diameter through rigorous experimentation or guesstimates. These values can be used as the variable's input parameters (e.g., uniform distribution with extreme values between 0.5 and 1.2). When testing is not possible (e.g., market share and revenue growth rate), management can still make estimates of potential outcomes and provide the best-case, most-likely case, and worst-case scenarios, whereupon a triangular or custom distribution can be created.

- However, if reliable historical, comparable, or contemporaneous data are available, distributional fitting can be accomplished. Assuming that historical patterns hold and that history tends to repeat itself, then historical data can be used to find the best-fitting distribution with their relevant parameters to better define the variables to be simulated.

- The distributional fitting can be run on a single variable or multiple variables.

- The fitting uses advanced statistical tests such as the Kolmogorov–Smirnov, Anderson–Darling, Akaike Criterion, Bayes' Information Criterion, Kuiper's Statistic, and Chi-Square tests coupled with optimization to find the best fitting distribution, which will eliminate any subjective guesses on which distribution is appropriate.

Single Variable Fitting

2. Start Single-Fit, click on *Risk Simulator | Analytical Tools | Distributional Fitting (Single-Variable)*

- Fitting data:
  - Select a column of data to fit to.
  - Start Single Fit.
  - Select fit to continuous or discrete distribution.
  - Either select specific distributions to test or leave the default of testing all distributions.

Notes:

If an existing simulation profile exists, then the distributional fitting will automatically generate the relevant assumption, otherwise, only the distribution type and parameters are provided, and an assumption is not created.

When in doubt, keep the default Kolmogorov–Smirnov approach.

1. Select a column data to fit (can include headers)

3. Select Continuous or Discrete distributions and run the Single Fit

Interpreting Single Fit Results and Report

The null hypothesis (H_0) being tested is such that the fitted distribution is the same distribution as the population from which the sample data to be fitted comes (i.e., H_o: Error = 0, or Fitted – Actual = 0, or that the distribution tested is the correct one). Thus, if the computed p-value is lower than a critical alpha level (typically 0.10 or 0.05), then the distribution is the wrong distribution (reject H_o null hypothesis). Conversely, the *higher the p-value, the better the distribution fits the data* (fail to reject H_o, accept H_o, we say the Fitting Error = 0). Both the results and report show the test statistic, p-value, theoretical statistics (based on the selected distribution), empirical statistics (based on the raw data), the original data (to maintain a record of the data used), and the assumption complete with the relevant distributional parameters (i.e., if you selected the option to automatically generate assumption and if a simulation profile already exists). The results also rank all the selected distributions and how well they fit the data.

Distribution Fitting Result

Distribution	Test Statistics	P-Value	Rank
Normal	0.02	99.96 %	1
Gamma	0.03	98.83 %	2
Lognormal	0.03	98.37 %	3
Lognormal 3	0.03	98.33 %	4
Logistic	0.03	97.19 %	5
Parabolic	0.04	88.55 %	6
Laplace	0.05	76.07 %	7
Gumbel Minimum	0.05	73.91 %	8
Gumbel Maximum	0.05	57.47 %	9
Double Log	0.06	44.25 %	10
Cauchy	0.07	26.58 %	11
Triangular	0.08	15.90 %	12
Chi-Square	0.10	3.11 %	13
Cosine	0.11	1.30 %	14
Exponential 2	0.12	0.67 %	15
Pareto	0.15	0.04 %	16

Statistical Summary

Theoretical vs. Empirical Distribution

Normal
Mean = 100.67
Standard Deviation = 10.40

Kolmogorov-Smirnov Test Statistic
Test Statistic: 0.02
P-Value: 99.96 %

	Actual	Theoretical
Mean	100.61	100.67
Stdev	10.31	10.40
Skewness	0.01	0.00
Kurtosis	-0.13	0.00

☑ Automatically Generate Assumption   OK   Cancel

Single Variable Distributional Fitting

Statistical Summary

Fitted Assumption   100.61

Fitted Distribution **Normal**
Mean   100.67
Standard Deviation   10.40

Kolmogorov-Smirnov Statistic   0.02
P-Value for Test Statistic   0.9996

	Actual	Theoretical
Mean	100.61	100.67
Standard Deviation	10.31	10.40
Skewness	0.01	0.00
Excess Kurtosis	-0.13	0.00

Theoretical vs. Empirical Distribution

Original Fitted Data

73.53	78.21	78.52	79.50	79.72	79.74	81.56	82.08	82.68	82.75	83.34	83.64	84.09
84.66	85.00	85.35	85.51	86.04	86.79	86.82	86.91	87.02	87.03	87.45	87.53	87.66
88.05	88.45	88.51	89.95	90.19	90.54	90.68	90.96	91.25	91.49	91.56	91.94	92.06
92.36	92.41	92.45	92.70	92.80	92.84	93.21	93.26	93.48	93.73	93.75	93.77	93.82
94.00	94.15	94.51	94.57	94.64	94.69	94.95	95.57	95.62	95.71	95.78	95.83	95.97
96.20	96.24	96.40	96.43	96.47	96.81	96.88	97.00	97.07	97.21	97.23	97.48	97.70
97.77	97.85	98.15	98.17	98.24	98.28	98.32	98.33	98.35	98.65	99.03	99.27	99.46
99.47	99.55	99.73	99.96	100.08	100.24	100.36	100.42	100.44	100.48	100.49	100.83	101.17
101.28	101.34	101.45	101.46	101.55	101.73	101.74	101.81	102.29	102.55	102.58	102.60	102.70
103.17	103.21	103.22	103.32	103.34	103.45	103.65	103.66	103.72	103.81	103.90	103.99	104.46
104.57	104.76	105.20	105.44	105.50	105.52	105.58	105.66	105.87	105.90	105.90	106.29	106.35
106.59	107.01	107.68	107.70	107.93	108.17	108.20	108.34	108.42	108.43	108.49	108.70	109.15
109.22	109.35	109.52	109.75	110.04	110.16	110.25	110.54	111.05	111.06	111.44	111.76	111.90
111.95	112.07	112.19	112.29	112.32	112.42	112.48	112.85	112.92	113.50	113.59	113.63	113.70
114.13	114.14	114.21	114.91	114.95	115.40	115.58	115.66	116.58	116.98	117.60	118.67	119.24
119.52	124.14	124.16	124.39	132.30								

Reliability and Validity in Research

- Reliability refers to the repeatability of findings. If the study were repeated, would it yield the same results? If the measurement results are consistent, the data is considered to be reliable. Reliability is the degree to which an assessment tool produces stable and consistent results.

- Two ways in estimating reliability.
  - *Test and Retest*, then compare the similarities of the results of the two tests using correlations or two-sample t-tests and z-tests, or comparable two-variable nonparametric tests.
  - *Internal Consistency* through questioning. Make different sets of questions that measure the same factor. Different people or groups are tasked with answering these questions, and if the results are similar then it is reliable.

- Validity refers to how well a test measures what it is purported to measure (credibility or believability of the research, i.e., are the findings genuine?)

- Validity encompasses the entire experimental concept and establishes whether the results obtained meet all of the requirements of scientific research.

- If reliability is more on consistency, validity is more on how strong the outcomes of the hypothesis are. It answers the question 'are we right?'

- Internal validity dictates how an experimental design is structured and encompasses all of the steps of the scientific research method.

- External validity is the process of examining the results and questioning whether there are any other possible causal relationships.

- Validity can be tested with multivariate models like regression and econometrics.

Reliability vs. Validity
Precision vs. Accuracy

A + P

V + R

NA + P

NV + R

A + NP

**Less V + Less R

NA + NP

NV + NR

Income - Risk Simulator Forecast		— ☐ ✕
Histogram Statistics Preferences Options Controls		Global View
Statistics		Result
Number of Trials		1000
Mean		0.8626
Median		0.8674
Standard Deviation		0.1933
Variance		0.0374
Coefficient of Variation		0.2241
Maximum		1.3570
Minimum		0.3019
Range		1.0551
Skewness		-0.1157
Kurtosis		-0.4480
25% Percentile		0.7269
75% Percentile		1.0068
Percentage Error Precision at 95% Confidence		1.3888%

Define: Population, Sample, Trials, Confidence, Precision, and Accuracy

**If data are valid, they must be reliable.
***If a test is reliable, that does not mean that it is valid.

Precision Control and Reliability Estimation

- Precision control is used to determine how many trials to simulate
- Used in Monte Carlo simulation to determine how many trials are adequate
- Precision and error control consist of two different parts:
  - Precision Confidence Level
  - Precision Error
- The more trials are run, the higher the level of precision…

15. Advanced Data Analytics: Pandora's Toolbox

Dr. Johnathan Mun, Professor of Research
Quantitative Research Methods Course Slides
Seventh Edition, 2026, ROV Press

Distributional Fitting

- A powerful simulation tool is distributional fitting. That is, which distribution does an analyst or engineer use for a particular input variable in a model? What are the relevant distributional parameters? If no historical data exist, then the analyst must make assumptions about the variables in question.

- One approach is to use the Delphi method where a group of experts is tasked with estimating the behavior of each variable. For instance, a group of mechanical engineers can be tasked with evaluating the extreme possibilities of a spring coil's diameter through rigorous experimentation or guesstimates. These values can be used as the variable's input parameters (e.g., uniform distribution with extreme values between 0.5 and 1.2). When testing is not possible (e.g., market share and revenue growth rate), management can still make estimates of potential outcomes and provide the best-case, most-likely case, and worst-case scenarios, whereupon a triangular or custom distribution can be created.

- However, if reliable historical, comparable, or contemporaneous data are available, distributional fitting can be accomplished. Assuming that historical patterns hold and that history tends to repeat itself, then historical data can be used to find the best-fitting distribution with their relevant parameters to better define the variables to be simulated.

- The distributional fitting can be run on a single variable or multiple variables.

- The fitting uses advanced statistical tests such as the Kolmogorov-Smirnov, Anderson-Darling, Akaike Criterion, Bayes' Information Criterion, Kuiper's Statistic, and Chi-Square tests coupled with optimization to find the best fitting distribution, which will eliminate any subjective guesses on which distribution is appropriate.

Single Variable Fitting

2. Start Single-Fit, click on *Risk Simulator | Analytical Tools | Distributional Fitting (Single-Variable)*

1. Select a column data to fit
(can include headers)

3. Select Continuous or Discrete distributions and run the Single Fit

- Fitting data:
  - Select a column of data to fit to.
  - Start Single Fit.
  - Select fit to continuous or discrete distribution.
  - Either select specific distributions to test or leave the default of testing all distributions.

Notes:

If an existing simulation profile exists, then the distributional fitting will automatically generate the relevant assumption, otherwise, only the distribution type and parameters are provided and an assumption is not created.

When in doubt, keep the default Kolmogorov-Smirnov approach.

Interpreting Single Fit Results and Report

The null hypothesis (Ho) being tested is such that the fitted distribution is the same distribution as the population from which the sample data to be fitted comes (i.e., Ho: Error = 0, or Fitted – Actual = 0, or that the distribution tested is the correct one). Thus, if the computed p-value is lower than a critical alpha level (typically 0.10 or 0.05), then the distribution is the wrong distribution (reject Ho null hypothesis). Conversely, the *higher the p-value, the better the distribution fits the data* (fail to reject Ho, accept Ho, we say the Fitting Error = 0). Both the results and report show the test statistic, p-value, theoretical statistics (based on the selected distribution), empirical statistics (based on the raw data), the original data (to maintain a record of the data used), and the assumption complete with the relevant distributional parameters (i.e., if you selected the option to automatically generate assumption and if a simulation profile already exists). The results also rank all the selected distributions and how well they fit the data.

Distribution Fitting Result

Distribution	Test Statistics	P-Value	Rank
Normal	0.02	99.96 %	1
Gamma	0.03	98.83 %	2
Lognormal	0.03	98.37 %	3
Lognormal 3	0.03	98.33 %	4
Logistic	0.03	97.19 %	5
Parabolic	0.04	88.55 %	6
Laplace	0.05	76.07 %	7
Gumbel Minimum	0.05	73.91 %	8
Gumbel Maximum	0.05	57.47 %	9
Double Log	0.06	44.25 %	10
Cauchy	0.07	26.58 %	11
Triangular	0.08	15.90 %	12
Chi-Square	0.10	3.11 %	13
Cosine	0.11	1.30 %	14
Exponential 2	0.12	0.67 %	15
Pareto	0.15	0.04 %	16

Statistical Summary

Theoretical vs. Empirical Distribution

Normal
Mean = 100.67
Standard Deviation = 10.40

Kolmogorov-Smirnov Test Statistic
Test Statistic: 0.02
P-Value: 99.96 %

	Actual	Theoretical
Mean	100.61	100.67
Stdev	10.31	10.40
Skewness	0.01	0.00
Kurtosis	-0.13	0.00

☑ Automatically Generate Assumption   OK   Cancel

Single Variable Distributional Fitting

Statistical Summary

Fitted Assumption   100.61

Fitted Distribution **Normal**
Mean   100.67
Standard Deviation   10.40

Kolmogorov-Smirnov Statistic   0.02
P-Value for Test Statistic   0.9996

	Actual	Theoretical
Mean	100.61	100.67
Standard Deviation	10.31	10.40
Skewness	0.01	0.00
Excess Kurtosis	-0.13	0.00

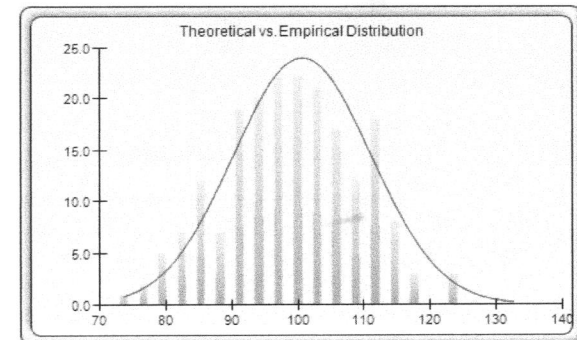

Theoretical vs. Empirical Distribution

Original Fitted Data

73.53	78.21	78.52	79.50	79.72	79.74	81.56	82.08	82.68	82.75	83.34	83.64	84.09
84.66	85.00	85.35	85.51	86.04	86.79	86.82	86.91	87.02	87.03	87.45	87.53	87.66
88.05	88.45	88.51	89.95	90.19	90.54	90.68	90.96	91.25	91.49	91.56	91.94	92.06
92.36	92.41	92.45	92.70	92.80	92.84	93.21	93.26	93.48	93.73	93.75	93.77	93.82
94.00	94.15	94.51	94.57	94.64	94.69	94.95	95.57	95.62	95.71	95.78	95.83	95.97
96.20	96.24	96.40	96.43	96.47	96.81	96.88	97.00	97.07	97.21	97.23	97.48	97.70
97.77	97.85	98.15	98.17	98.24	98.28	98.32	98.33	98.35	98.65	99.03	99.27	99.46
99.47	99.55	99.73	99.96	100.08	100.24	100.36	100.42	100.44	100.48	100.49	100.83	101.17
101.28	101.34	101.45	101.46	101.55	101.73	101.74	101.81	102.29	102.55	102.58	102.60	102.70
103.17	103.21	103.22	103.32	103.34	103.45	103.65	103.66	103.72	103.81	103.90	103.99	104.46
104.57	104.76	105.20	105.44	105.50	105.52	105.58	105.66	105.87	105.90	105.90	106.29	106.35
106.59	107.01	107.68	107.70	107.93	108.17	108.20	108.34	108.42	108.43	108.49	108.70	109.15
109.22	109.35	109.52	109.75	110.04	110.16	110.25	110.54	111.05	111.06	111.44	111.76	111.90
111.95	112.07	112.19	112.29	112.32	112.42	112.48	112.85	112.92	113.50	113.59	113.63	113.70
114.13	114.14	114.21	114.91	114.95	115.40	115.58	115.66	116.58	116.98	117.60	118.67	119.24
119.52	124.14	124.16	124.39	132.30								

Multiple Variable Fitting

For fitting multiple variables, the process is fairly similar to fitting individual variables. However, the data should be arranged in columns (i.e., each variable is arranged as a column) and all the variables are fitted. The same analysis is performed when fitting multiple variables as when single variables are fitted. The difference here is that only the final report will be generated and you do not get to review each variable's distributional rankings. If the rankings are important, run the single variable fitting procedure instead, on one variable at a time. Hypothesis tests of the statistical significance of correlations between variables are also performed. This way, you can decide to use only those correlations that are valid.

Multiple Variable Distributional Fitting

Statistical Summary

	Variable Name	Variable X		Variable Name	Variable Y		Variable Name	Variable Z
	Best-Fit Assumption	99.18		Best-Fit Assumption	49.83		Best-Fit Assumption	6.73

	Fitted Distribution	Normal		Fitted Distribution	Uniform		Fitted Distribution	Binomial
	Mean	99.34		Minimum	44.84		Trials	10.00
	Standard Deviation	10.48		Maximum	54.89		Probability	0.67

	Kolmogorov-Smirnov Statistic	0.03		Kolmogorov-Smirnov Statistic	0.04		Chi-Square Statistic	13.44
	P-Value for Test Statistic	0.9845		P-Value for Test Statistic	0.8110		P-Value for Test Statistic	0.0975

	Actual	Theoretical		Actual	Theoretical		Actual	Theoretical
Mean	99.18	99.34	Mean	49.83	49.87	Mean	6.73	6.72
Standard Deviation	10.33	10.48	Standard Deviation	2.96	2.90	Standard Deviation	1.49	1.48
Skewness	-0.12	0.00	Skewness	0.02	0.00	Skewness	-0.51	-0.23
Excess Kurtosis	0.19	0.00	Excess Kurtosis	-1.32	-1.20	Excess Kurtosis	-0.06	-0.15

Correlation Matrix

	Variable X	Variable Y	Variable Z
Variable X	1.0000		
Variable Y	0.0007	1.0000	
Variable Z	-0.0693	-0.0044	1.0000

Tornado and Spider Analysis

- One of the powerful simulation tools is the tornado analysis—it captures the static impacts of each variable on the outcome of the model. That is, the tool automatically perturbs each variable in the model a preset amount, captures the fluctuation on the model's forecast or final result, and lists the resulting perturbations ranked from the most significant to the least. The question we try to answer here is, what are the critical success drivers that affect the model's output the most?

- The tornado chart tool can be obtained through *Risk Simulator | Analytical Tools | Tornado Analysis*.

- The target cell's precedents in the model are used in creating the tornado chart. Precedents are all the input and intermediate variables that affect the outcome of the model. For instance, if the model consists of $A = B + C$, and where $C = D + E$, then B, D, and E are the precedents for A (C is not a precedent as it is only an intermediate calculated value). If the precedent variables are simple inputs, then the testing range will be a simple perturbation based on the range chosen (e.g., the default is ±10%). Each precedent variable can be perturbed at different percentages if required. A wider range is important as it is better able to test extreme values rather than smaller perturbations around the expected values. In certain circumstances, extreme values may have a larger, smaller, or unbalanced impact (e.g., nonlinearities may occur where increasing or decreasing economies of scale and scope creep in for larger or smaller values of a variable) and only a wider range will capture this nonlinear impact.

- It is important to note that Tornado and Spider Analysis is performed BEFORE running a simulation, in order to identify the critical factors to simulate, as compared to Sensitivity Analysis which is run after a simulation has been completed.

- Tornado and Spider charts are static analyses whereas a Sensitivity Analysis is a dynamic analysis.

Tornado Chart Interpretation

- Tornado chart lists the precedent variable that has the most impact to the least.

- A red bar on the right indicates a negative correlation while a green bar on the right indicates a positive correlation between each input precedent and the result.

- A Tornado analysis report is also generated by the software, complete with an analysis table of the perturbations and results.

Statistical Summary

One of the powerful simulation tools is the tornado chart—it captures the static impacts of each variable on the outcome of the model. That is, the tool automatically perturbs each precedent variable in the model a user-specified preset amount, captures the fluctuation on the model's forecast or final result, and lists the resulting perturbations ranked from the most significant to the least. Precedents are all the input and intermediate variables that affect the outcome of the model. For instance, if the model consists of A = B + C, where C = D + E, then B, D, and E are the precedents for A (C is not a precedent as it is only an intermediate calculated value). The range and number of values perturbed is user-specified and can be set to test extreme values rather than smaller perturbations around the expected values. In certain circumstances, extreme values may have a larger, smaller, or unbalanced impact (e.g., nonlinearities may occur where increasing or decreasing economies of scale and scope creep occurs for larger or smaller values of a variable) and only a wider range will capture this nonlinear impact.

A tornado chart lists all the inputs that drive the model, starting from the input variable that has the most effect on the results. The chart is obtained by perturbing each precedent input at some consistent range (e.g., ±10% from the base case) one at a time, and comparing their results to the base case. A spider chart looks like a spider with a central body and its many legs protruding. The positively sloped lines indicate a positive relationship, while a negatively sloped line indicates a negative relationship. Further, spider charts can be used to visualize linear and nonlinear relationships. The tornado and spider charts help identify the critical success factors of an output cell in order to identify the inputs to simulate. The identified critical variables that are uncertain are the ones that should be simulated. Do not waste time simulating variables that are neither uncertain nor have little impact on the results.

Result

| Precedent Cell | Base Value: 96.6261638553219 | | | Input Changes | | |
	Output Downside	Output Upside	Effective Range	Input Downside	Input Upside	Base Case Value
Investment	$276.63	($83.37)	360.00	$1,620.00	$1,980.00	$1,800.00
Tax Rate	$219.73	($26.47)	246.20	36.00%	44.00%	40.00%
A Price	$3.43	$189.83	186.40	$9.00	$11.00	$10.00
B Price	$16.71	$176.55	159.84	$11.03	$13.48	$12.25
A Quantity	$23.18	$170.07	146.90	45.00	55.00	50.00
B Quantity	$30.53	$162.72	132.19	31.50	38.50	35.00
C Price	$40.15	$153.11	112.96	$13.64	$16.67	$15.15
C Quantity	$48.05	$145.20	97.16	18.00	22.00	20.00
Discount Rate	$138.24	$57.03	81.21	13.50%	16.50%	15.00%
Price Erosion	$116.80	$76.64	40.16	4.50%	5.50%	5.00%
Sales Growth	$90.59	$102.69	12.10	1.80%	2.20%	2.00%
Depreciation	$95.08	$98.17	3.08	$9.00	$11.00	$10.00
Interest	$97.09	$96.16	0.93	$1.80	$2.20	$2.00
Amortization	$96.16	$97.09	0.93	$2.70	$3.30	$3.00
Capex	$96.63	$96.63	0.00	$0.00	$0.00	$0.00
Net Capital	$96.63	$96.63	0.00	$0.00	$0.00	$0.00

Tornado Chart

Spider Chart

Tornado Chart

Spider Chart Interpretation

- Spider charts are like tornado charts, but they also reveal the occurrence of nonlinearities.
- The center of the chart (body of the spider) is the base case condition (the x-axis indicates a 0.00% fluctuation from the base case while the y-axis indicates the starting result base case value).
- Positively sloped lines indicate positive correlations between the precedent variable and the result, while negatively sloped lines indicate negative correlations between the precedent variable and the result.
- The steeper the absolute slope (regardless of direction), the higher the impact that precedent has on the result.

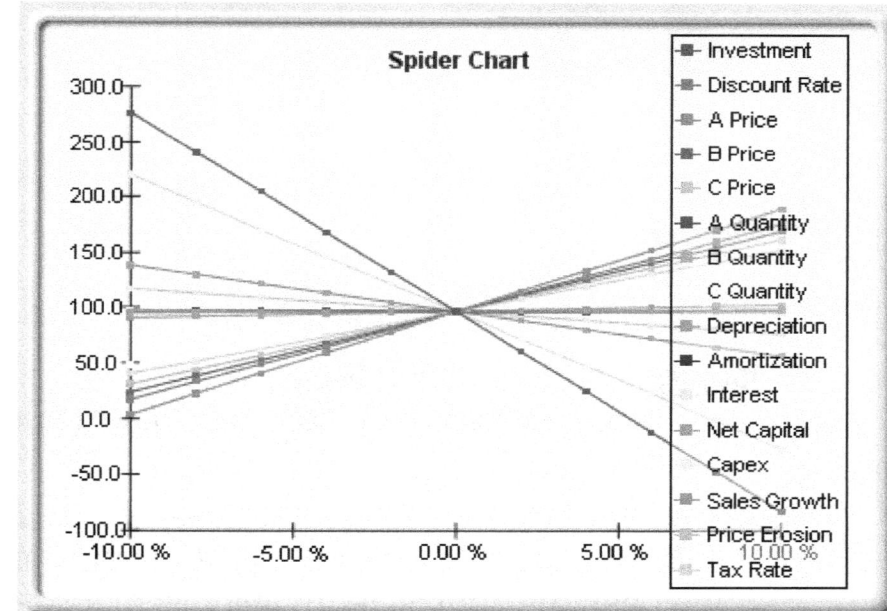

Spider Chart

Legend: Investment, Discount Rate, A Price, B Price, C Price, A Quantity, B Quantity, C Quantity, Depreciation, Amortization, Interest, Net Capital, Capex, Sales Growth, Price Erosion, Tax Rate

Sensitivity Analysis

- Sensitivity charts are dynamic perturbations created after the simulation run. Sensitivity charts are dynamic perturbations in the sense that multiple assumptions are perturbed simultaneously, and their interactions are captured in the fluctuations of the results. In contrast, Tornado and spider charts are static perturbations, meaning that each precedent or assumption variable is perturbed a preset amount and the fluctuations in the results are tabulated. Tornado charts, therefore, identify which variables drive the results the most and hence are suitable for determining which variables to simulate (that is, they are used before a simulation), whereas sensitivity charts identify the impact on the results when multiple interacting variables are simulated together in the model (that is, they are used after a simulation).

- Therefore, in order to run a sensitivity chart, first run a simulation, then click on the Sensitivity Chart icon or *Risk Simulator | Analytical Tools | Sensitivity Analysis*. Select the forecast of choice and run the analysis.

Sensitivity Chart Interpretation

- The Nonlinear Rank Correlation charts indicate the rank correlations between each assumption and the target forecast, and are depicted from the highest absolute value to the lowest absolute value. Positive correlations are shown in green while negative correlations are shown in red. Rank correlation is used instead of a regular correlation coefficient as it captures nonlinear effects between variables.

- In contrast, the Percent Variation Explained computes how much of the variation in the forecast variable can be explained by the variations in each of the assumptions by itself in a dynamic simulated environment. These charts show the sensitivity of the target forecast to the simulated assumptions.

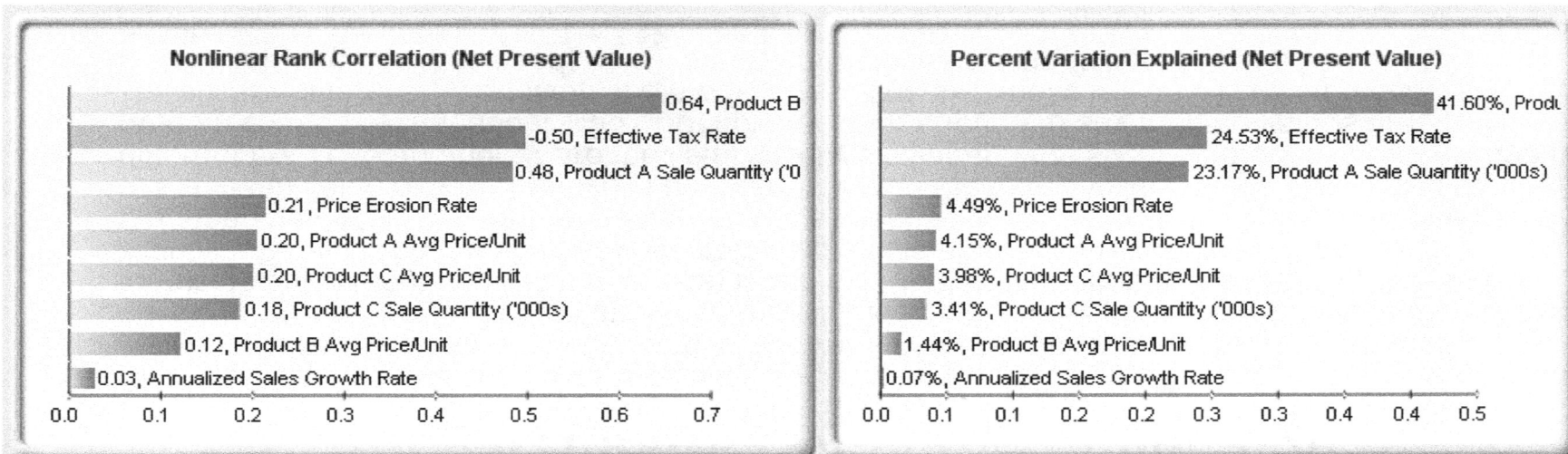

Nonlinear Rank Correlation (Net Present Value)

Value	Assumption
0.64	Product B
-0.50	Effective Tax Rate
0.48	Product A Sale Quantity ('0
0.21	Price Erosion Rate
0.20	Product A Avg Price/Unit
0.20	Product C Avg Price/Unit
0.18	Product C Sale Quantity ('000s)
0.12	Product B Avg Price/Unit
0.03	Annualized Sales Growth Rate

(x-axis: 0.0, 0.1, 0.2, 0.3, 0.4, 0.5, 0.6, 0.7)

Percent Variation Explained (Net Present Value)

Value	Assumption
41.60%	Produ
24.53%	Effective Tax Rate
23.17%	Product A Sale Quantity ('000s)
4.49%	Price Erosion Rate
4.15%	Product A Avg Price/Unit
3.98%	Product C Avg Price/Unit
3.41%	Product C Sale Quantity ('000s)
1.44%	Product B Avg Price/Unit
0.07%	Annualized Sales Growth Rate

(x-axis: 0.0, 0.1, 0.1, 0.2, 0.2, 0.3, 0.3, 0.4, 0.4, 0.5)

Nonparametric Bootstrap Simulation

- Bootstrap simulation estimates the reliability or accuracy of forecast statistics or other sample raw data. Bootstrap simulation can be used to answer a lot of confidence and precision-based questions in simulation. For instance, suppose an identical model (with identical assumptions and forecasts but without any random seeds) is run by 100 different people, the results will clearly be slightly different. The question is, if we collected all the statistics from these 100 people, how will the mean be distributed, or the median, or the skewness or excess kurtosis? Suppose one person has a mean value of say, 1.50 while another 1.52. Are these two values statistically significantly different from one another or are they statistically similar and the slight difference is entirely due to random chance? What about 1.53? So, how far is far enough to say that the values are statistically different? In addition, if a model's resulting skewness is –0.19 is this forecast distribution negatively skewed, or is it statistically close enough to zero to state that this distribution is symmetrical and not skewed?

- If we bootstrapped this forecast 100 times, i.e., run a 1,000-trial simulation for 100 times and collect the 100 skewness coefficient, the skewness distribution would indicate how far zero is away from –0.19. If the 90% confidence on the bootstrapped skewness distribution contains the value zero, then we can state that on a 90% confidence level, this distribution is symmetrical and not skewed, and the value –0.19 is statistically close enough to zero. Otherwise, if zero falls outside of this 90% confidence area, then this distribution is negatively skewed. The same analysis can be applied to excess kurtosis and other statistics.

- Essentially, bootstrap simulation is a hypothesis testing tool. Classical methods used in the past relied on mathematical formulas to describe the accuracy of sample statistics. These methods assume that the distribution of a sample statistic approaches a normal distribution, making the calculation of the statistic's standard error or confidence interval relatively easy. However, when a statistic's sampling distribution is not normally distributed or easily found, these classical methods are difficult to use. In contrast, bootstrapping analyzes sample statistics empirically by repeatedly sampling the data and creating distributions of the different statistics from each sampling. The classical methods of hypothesis testing are available in Risk Simulator and will be explained in the next section. Classical methods provide higher power in their tests but rely on normality assumptions and can only be used to test the mean and variance of a distribution, as compared to bootstrap simulation which provides lower power but is nonparametric and distribution-free, and can be used to test any distributional statistic.

ℝ ☒ Running a Nonparametric Bootstrap Simulation

In order to run a hypothesis test, first, run a simulation, then click on the Bootstrap icon or *Risk Simulator | Analytical Tools | Nonparametric Bootstrap*. Select the forecast of choice, select the statistics you wish to test, enter the number of bootstrap trials, and run the analysis.

MODEL A   MODEL B

Revenue	$200.00	Revenue	$200.00
Cost	$100.00	Cost	$100.00
Income	$100.00	Income	$100.00

To replicate this model, start by creating a Simulation Profile and give it a name (Simulation I New Profile), then, set the random seed to be 123456. Next, select the revenue cells and provide them a Normal distribution with mean of 200 and standard deviation of 20 (select one of the revenue cell and click on Simulation I Set Assumption, select Normal and enter the relevant parameters). Then, define Normal assumptions for each of the cost cells. Finally, define forecast outputs for the two income cells and run the simulation.

Interpreting a Nonparametric Bootstrap Simulation

The bootstrap results are a set of forecast charts of each statistic you selected. Using these forecast charts, you can now determine the confidence intervals of each statistic and perform hypothesis tests.

Precision vs. Accuracy

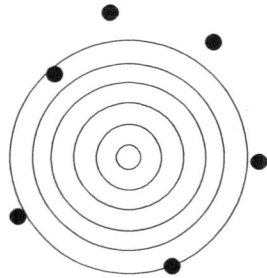

Not Accurate
Not Precise

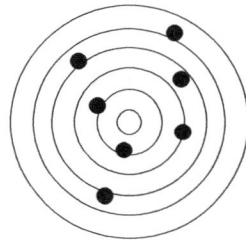

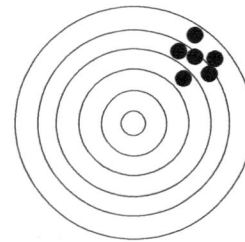

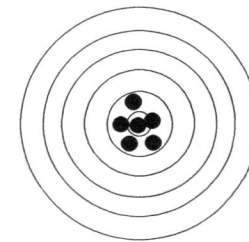

Accurate
Not Precise

Not Accurate
Precise

Accurate
Precise

Income - Risk Simulator Forecast	
Histogram Statistics Preferences Options Controls	Global View

Statistics	Result
Number of Trials	1000
Mean	0.8626
Median	0.8674
Standard Deviation	0.1933
Variance	0.0374
Coefficient of Variation	0.2241
Maximum	1.3570
Minimum	0.3019
Range	1.0551
Skewness	-0.1157
Kurtosis	-0.4480
25% Percentile	0.7269
75% Percentile	1.0068
Percentage Error Precision at 95% Confidence	1.3888%

Define: Population, Sample, Trials, Confidence, Precision, and Accuracy

Precision Control

- Precision control is used to determine how many trials to simulate
- Takes the guesswork out of Monte Carlo simulation and how many trials are adequate
- Precision and error control consist of two different parts:
  - Precision Confidence Level
  - Precision Error
- The more trials are run, the higher the level of precision…

16. Optimization: The Search for the Optimal Decision

Dr. Johnathan Mun, Professor of Research
Quantitative Research Methods Course Slides
Seventh Edition, 2026, ROV Press

What Is Optimization?

An approach used to find the combination of inputs to achieve the best possible output subject to satisfying certain prespecified conditions. For example:

- What stocks to pick in a portfolio, as well as the weights of each stock as a % of the total budget
- Optimal staffing needs for a production line
- Project and strategy selection and prioritization
- Inventory optimization
- Optimal pricing and royalty rates
- Utilization of employees for workforce planning
- Configuration of machines for production scheduling
- Location of facilities for distribution
- Tolerances in manufacturing design
- Treatment policies in waste management

Traveling Financial Planner Problem

- You have to travel and visit clients in New York, Chicago, Seattle.

- You may start from any city and will you stay at your final city, i.e., you will need to purchase two airline tickets for the three cities.

- Your goal is to travel as cheaply as possible.

Airfare Rates

Route	Airfare
Seattle - Chicago	$325
Chicago - Seattle	$225
New York - Seattle	$350
Seattle - New York	$375
Chicago - New York	$325
New York - Chicago	$325

How Do You Solve the Problem?

- Ad Hoc approach – start trying different permutations
- Enumeration – look at all possible alternatives

All The Permutations

Seattle-Chicago-New York	$325 + $325 =	**$650**
Seattle-New York-Chicago	$375 + $325 =	**$700**
Chicago-Seattle-New York	$225 + $375 =	**$600**
Chicago-New York-Seattle	$325 + $350 =	**$675**
New York-Seattle-Chicago	$350 + $325 =	**$675**
New York-Chicago-Seattle	$325 + $225 =	**$550**

Additionally, if you want to visit San Antonio and Denver…

- Five Cities to visit (Seattle, Chicago, New York, San Antonio, and Denver)

  5! = 5 x 4 x 3 x 2 x 1 = 120 possible permutations

How About 100 Different Cities?

100! = 100 x 99 x 98 … x 1 =
93,326,215,443,944,200,000,000,000,000,000,000,00
0,000,000,000,000,000,000,000,000,000,000,000,000
,000,000,000,000,000,000,000,000,000,000,000,000,
000,000,000,000,000,000,000,000,000,000,000,000,000

Or 9.3×10^{157} different combinations

How long would it take to evaluate all these combinations on a Super Computer?

100^{120} Years!!!!!!!!!

Smart Heuristics and Algorithms

Therefore, we need to use optimization software to obtain the solutions. Risk Simulator uses a variety of heuristics and algorithms to find the best and optimal sets of solutions.

Risk Simulator also uses smart algorithms to speed up the search process and intelligently eliminate certain areas that are suboptimal, thereby increasing the search efficiency.

Types of Optimization

Optimizations can be linear or nonlinear, and can be discrete integer or continuous:

A discrete integer optimization can only take on specific integer values such as 0, 1, 2, 3, and so forth.

A continuous optimization can account for continuous decision variables and can take on any value.

Both discrete integer and continuous optimizations can be linear or nonlinear. That is, the objective function and constraints are either all linear or nonlinear.

Steps Required in Optimization

To run an optimization model, several variables have to be first determined and created:

• Objective: The variable to be maximized or minimized (e.g., net present value, catastrophic losses, risk, downtime, etc.)

• Decision Variables and their allowed ranges: Variables you have control over (how much to manufacture, how much to invest, and so forth)

• Constraints: Restrictions or conditions that must be satisfied in the optimization (e.g., budget, time, resources, etc.)

• Simulation Assumptions: Monte Carlo assumptions when running dynamic or stochastic optimizations

Optimization Procedures

- Static Optimization
  - Optimization without simulation: FAST
  - Great starting point before more advanced optimization analysis
- Dynamic Optimization
  - Simulation of N trials, stops, sets up the assumption cells with the simulated statistics, and then optimizes
  - A type of Simulation-Optimization process
  - Accounts for risks and uncertainties
- Stochastic Optimization
  - Simulation of N trials, stops, sets up the assumption cells with the simulated statistics, and then optimizes, then, the entire process is repeated again for T times
  - A series of dynamic optimizations with each decision variable having a forecast distribution
  - A range of optimal values rather than single-point estimates

17. Optimization Under Uncertainty

Dr. Johnathan Mun, Professor of Research
Quantitative Research Methods Course Slides
Seventh Edition, 2026, ROV Press

Diversifying Risk and Efficient Frontier

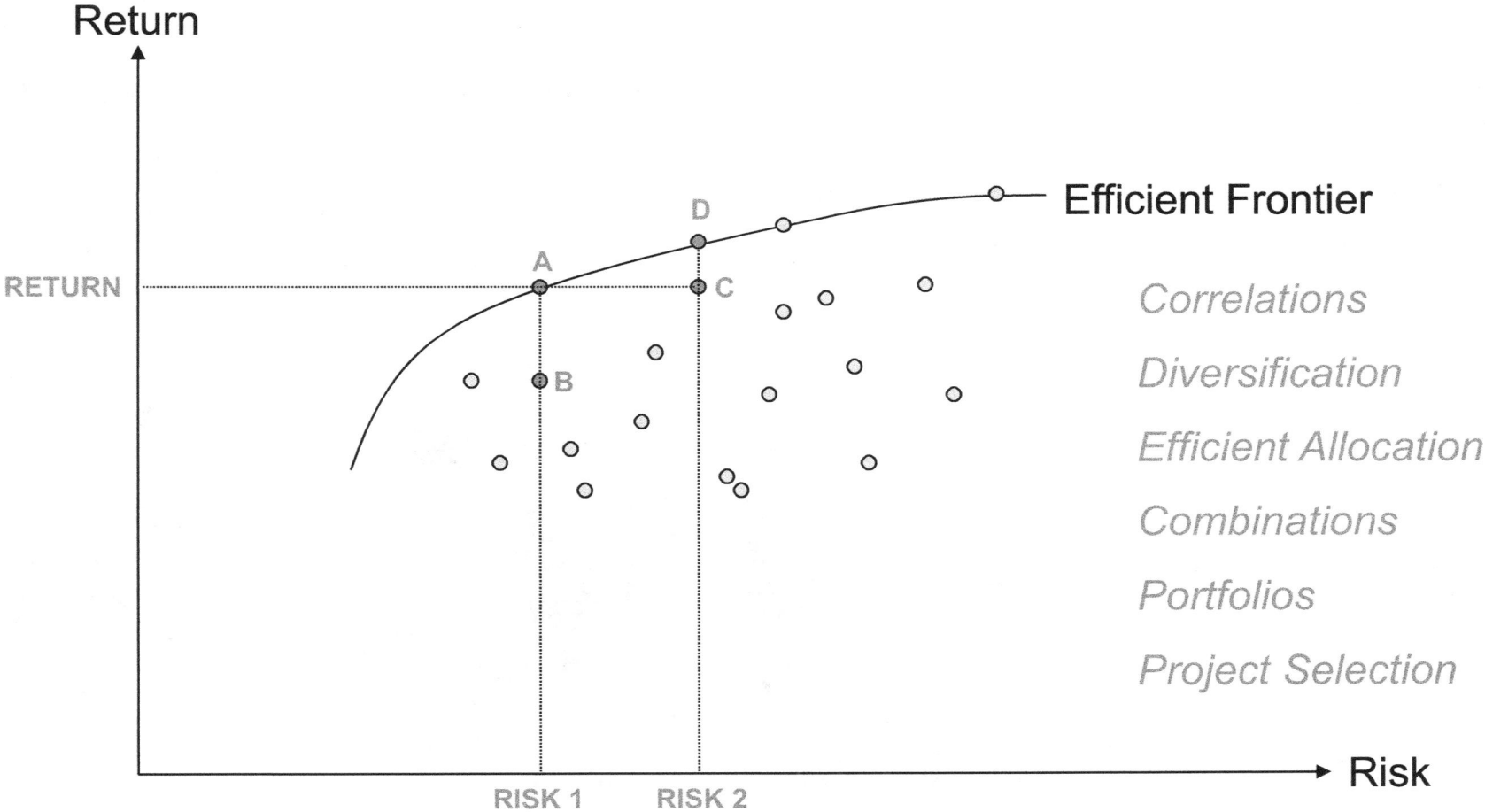

What does this picture tell you?

Optimization Setup

OPTIMAL PROJECT SELECTION FOR A PORTFOLIO WITH EFFICIENT FRONTIER SUBJECT TO CONSTRAINTS

Projects	ENPV	Cost	Risk $	Risk %	Return to Risk Ratio	Profitability Index	Selection
Project 1	$458.00	$1,732.44	$54.96	12.00%	8.33	1.26	1.0000
Project 2	$1,954.00	$859.00	$1,914.92	98.00%	1.02	3.27	1.0000
Project 3	$1,599.00	$1,845.00	$1,551.03	97.00%	1.03	1.87	1.0000
Project 4	$2,251.00	$1,645.00	$1,012.95	45.00%	2.22	2.37	1.0000
Project 5	$849.00	$458.00	$925.41	109.00%	0.92	2.85	1.0000
Project 6	$758.00	$52.00	$560.92	74.00%	1.35	15.58	1.0000
Project 7	$2,845.00	$758.00	$5,633.10	198.00%	0.51	4.75	1.0000
Project 8	$1,235.00	$115.00	$926.25	75.00%	1.33	11.74	1.0000
Project 9	$1,945.00	$125.00	$2,100.60	108.00%	0.93	16.56	1.0000
Project 10	$2,250.00	$458.00	$1,912.50	85.00%	1.18	5.91	1.0000
Project 11	$549.00	$45.00	$263.52	48.00%	2.08	13.20	1.0000
Project 12	$525.00	$105.00	$309.75	59.00%	1.69	6.00	1.0000
Total	$17,218.00	$8,197.44	$7,007	40.70%			12.00
Goal:	MAX	< =$4000					<=6
Sharpe Ratio	2.4573						

ENPV is the expected NPV of each investment or project, while Cost can be the total cost of investment, and Risk is the Coefficient of Variation of the project's ENPV.

Change the Profile to one of the efficient frontier examples in order to run the Efficient Frontier analysis.

Decision Variable Properties

Decision Name: Project 1

Decision Type
- ○ Continuous (e.g., 1.15, 2.35, 10.55)
  - Lower Bound ___ Upper Bound ___
- ○ Integer (e.g., 1, 2, 3)
  - Lower Bound ___ Upper Bound ___
- ◉ Binary (0 or 1)

OK   Cancel

Optimization Objective

Objective Cell: $C$19

Optimization Objective
- ◉ Maximize the value in objective cell
- ○ Minimize the value in objective cell

OK   Cancel

Constraint

Cell: $D$17   <=   Constraint: 4000

OK   Cancel

Constraint

Cell: $J$17   <=   Constraint: 6

OK   Cancel

Optimization Methodologies and Inputs

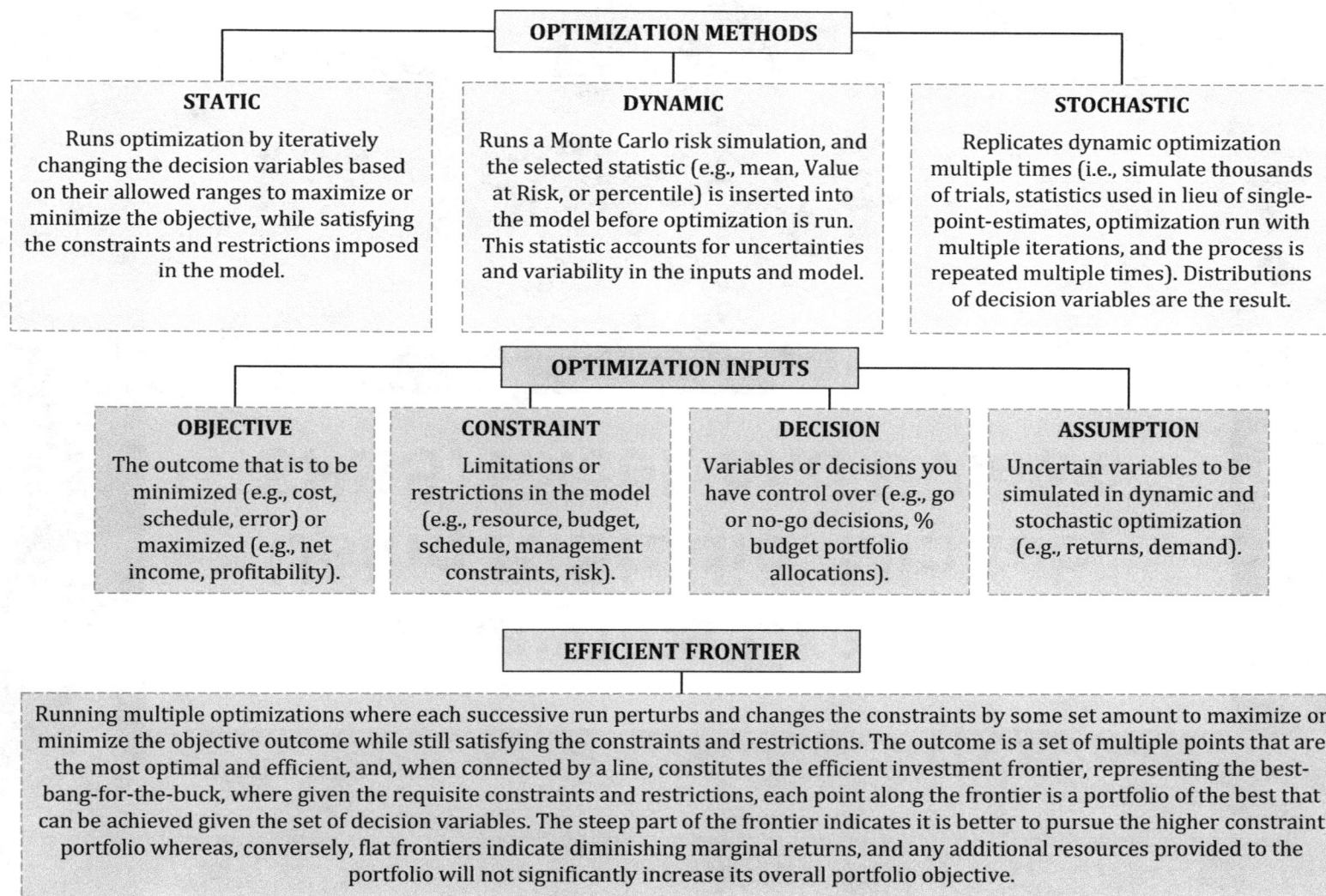

OPTIMIZATION METHODS

STATIC

Runs optimization by iteratively changing the decision variables based on their allowed ranges to maximize or minimize the objective, while satisfying the constraints and restrictions imposed in the model.

DYNAMIC

Runs a Monte Carlo risk simulation, and the selected statistic (e.g., mean, Value at Risk, or percentile) is inserted into the model before optimization is run. This statistic accounts for uncertainties and variability in the inputs and model.

STOCHASTIC

Replicates dynamic optimization multiple times (i.e., simulate thousands of trials, statistics used in lieu of single-point-estimates, optimization run with multiple iterations, and the process is repeated multiple times). Distributions of decision variables are the result.

OPTIMIZATION INPUTS

OBJECTIVE

The outcome that is to be minimized (e.g., cost, schedule, error) or maximized (e.g., net income, profitability).

CONSTRAINT

Limitations or restrictions in the model (e.g., resource, budget, schedule, management constraints, risk).

DECISION

Variables or decisions you have control over (e.g., go or no-go decisions, % budget portfolio allocations).

ASSUMPTION

Uncertain variables to be simulated in dynamic and stochastic optimization (e.g., returns, demand).

EFFICIENT FRONTIER

Running multiple optimizations where each successive run perturbs and changes the constraints by some set amount to maximize or minimize the objective outcome while still satisfying the constraints and restrictions. The outcome is a set of multiple points that are the most optimal and efficient, and, when connected by a line, constitutes the efficient investment frontier, representing the best-bang-for-the-buck, where given the requisite constraints and restrictions, each point along the frontier is a portfolio of the best that can be achieved given the set of decision variables. The steep part of the frontier indicates it is better to pursue the higher constraint portfolio whereas, conversely, flat frontiers indicate diminishing marginal returns, and any additional resources provided to the portfolio will not significantly increase its overall portfolio objective.

Dr. Jonathan Mun, Professor of Research
Quantitative Research Methods Course Slides
Seventh Edition, 2026, ROV Press

18. Analytics Exercises: Using R-Studio, Minitab, SPSS, Excel, and EViews

BIZSTATS (DESCRIPTIVE STATISTICS)

R (DESCRIPTIVE STATISTICS)

```
library(tidyverse)
library(pander)
library(readxl)
mydata <- read_excel ("C:/Users/jcmun/Desktop/mycorrelationdata.xlsx")
summary(mydata)
mean(mydata$Y)
sd(mydata$Y)
max(mydata$Y)
quantile(mydata$Y)
sum(mydata$Y)
```

BIZSTATS (CORRELATIONS, COVARIANCES, CORRELATIONAL SIGNIFICANCE)

MINITAB (CORRELATIONS, COVARIANCES, CORRELATIONAL SIGNIFICANCE)

R (CORRELATIONS, COVARIANCES, CORRELATIONAL SIGNIFICANCE)

```
library(tidyverse)
library(pander)
library(readxl)
mydata <- read_excel("C:/Users/jcmun/Desktop/mycorrelationdata.xlsx")
summary(mydata)
cor(mydata)
cor.test(mydata$Y, mydata$X1)
cov(mydata)
```

Source lines:
```
1  library(tidyverse)
2  library(pander)
3  library(readxl)
4  mydata <- read_excel ("C:/Users/jcmun/Desktop/mycorrelationdata.xlsx")
5  summary(mydata)
6  cor(mydata)
7  cor.test(mydata$Y, mydata$X1)
8  cov(mydata)
9
```

Console:

```
> summary(mydata)
       Y              X1             X2
 Min.   : 47.0   Min.   :1148   Min.   :118.0
 1st Qu.:204.0   1st Qu.: 7229   1st Qu.:191.2
 Median :307.0   Median :15470  Median :240.0
 Mean   :331.9   Mean   :22668  Mean   :261.7
 3rd Qu.:441.0   3rd Qu.:25987  3rd Qu.:302.2
 Max.   :764.0   Max.   :100484 Max.   :600.0

> cor(mydata)
           Y         X1        X2
Y  1.0000000 0.4137718 0.3945292
X1 0.4137718 1.0000000 0.3333145
X2 0.3945292 0.3333145 1.0000000

> cor.test(mydata$Y, mydata$X1)

	Pearson's product-moment correlation

data:  mydata$Y and mydata$X1
t = 3.1327, df = 48, p-value = 0.002762
alternative hypothesis: true correlation is not equal to 0
95 percent confidence interval:
 0.1739051 0.6336378
sample estimates:
      cor
0.4137718

> cov(mydata)
          Y           X1        X2
Y   29939.259  16339381.3  6396.098
X1 16339381.269 4798777330.9 684581.512
X2  6396.098   68458L.5    8790.459
>
```

Environment / History / Connections / Tutorial

Global Environment

Data

myanovadata	24 obs. of 3 variables	
mydata	50 obs. of 3 variables	

User Library

abind	Combine Multidimensional Arrays	1.4-5	
AER	Applied Econometrics with R	1.2-9	
apricom	Tools for the a Priori Comparison of Regression Modelling Strategies	1.0.0	
askpass	Safe Password Entry for R, Git, and SSH	1.1	
assertthat	Easy Pre and Post Assertions	0.2.1	
aTSA	Alternative Time Series Analysis	3.1.2	
backports	Reimplementations of Functions Introduced Since R-3.0.0	1.2.0	
base64enc	Tools for base64 encoding	0.1-3	
BH	Boost C++ Header Files	1.72.0-3	
blob	A Simple S3 Class for Representing Vectors of Binary Data (BLOBS)	1.2.1	
brio	Basic R Input Output	1.1.0	
broom	Convert Statistical Objects into Tidy Tibbles	0.7.2	
callr	Call R from R	3.5.1	
car	Companion to Applied Regression	3.0-10	

BIZSTATS (SINGLE VARIABLE T-TESTS)

MINITAB (SINGLE VARIABLE T-TESTS)

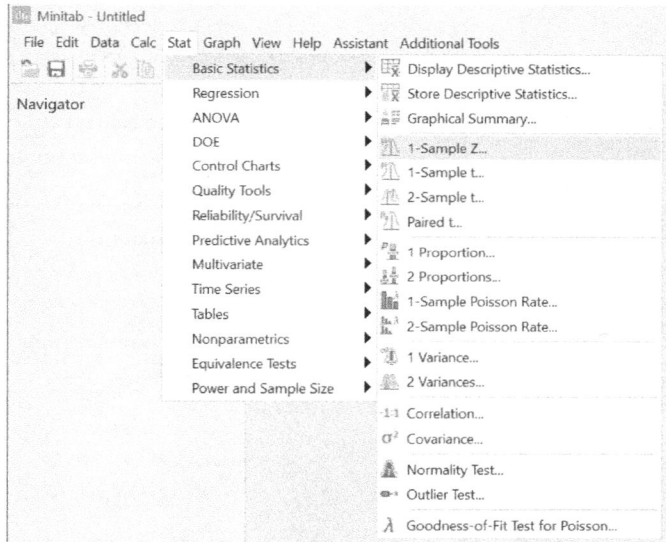

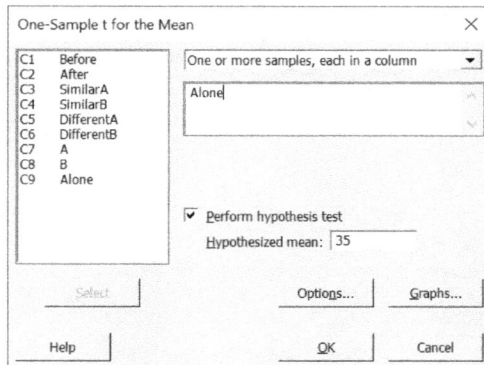

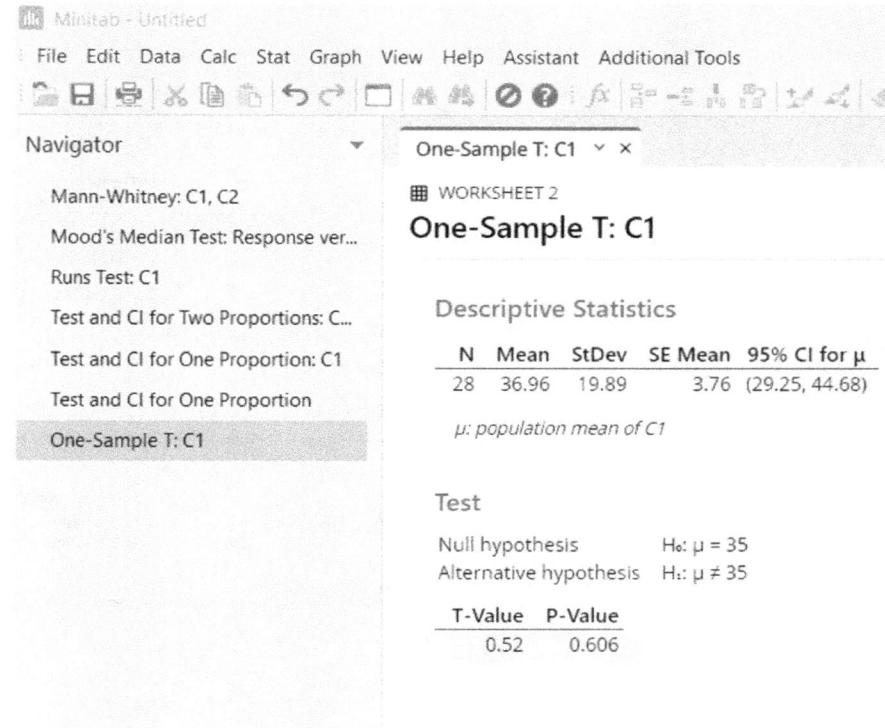

R (SINGLE VARIABLE T-TESTS)

```
library(tidyverse)
library(pander)
library(readxl)
mydata <- read_excel ("C:/Users/jcmun/Desktop/myttestdata.xlsx")
t.test(mydata$Alone,mu=35)
t.test(mydata$Alone,mu=35, alternative="greater")
t.test(mydata$Alone,mu=35, alternative="less")
```

BIZSTATS (INDEPENDENT EQUAL VARIANCE T-TESTS)

SPSS & MINITAB (INDEPENDENT EQUAL VARIANCE T-TESTS)

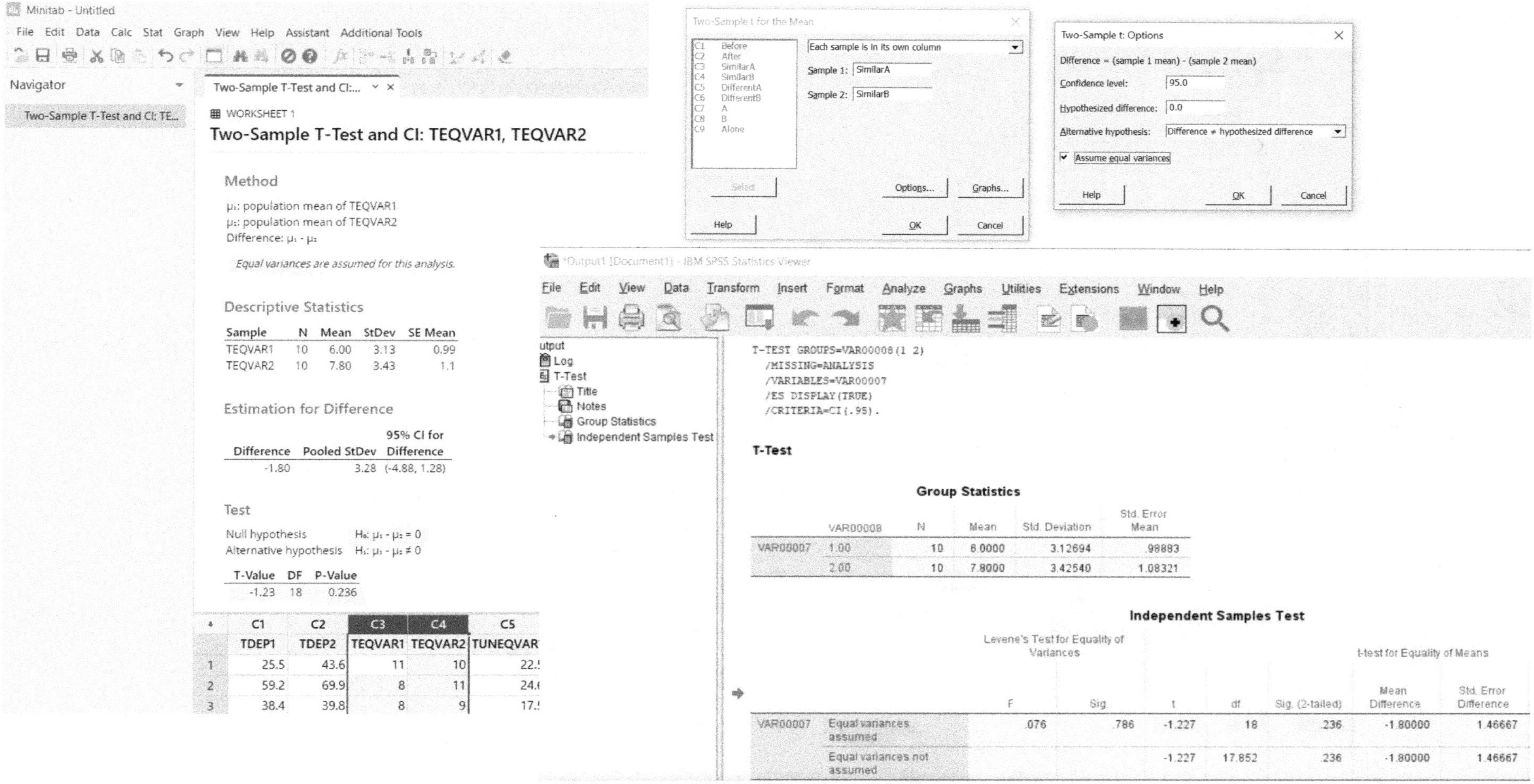

R (INDEPENDENT EQUAL VARIANCE T-TESTS)

```
library(tidyverse)
library(pander)
library(readxl)
mydata <- read_excel ("C:/Users/jcmun/Desktop/myttestdata.xlsx")
t.test(mydata$SimilarA,mydata$SimilarB)
t.test(mydata$SimilarA,mydata$SimilarB,var.equal=TRUE)
```

BIZSTATS (DEPENDENT PAIRED T-TESTS)

SPSS & MINITAB (DEPENDENT PAIRED T-TESTS)

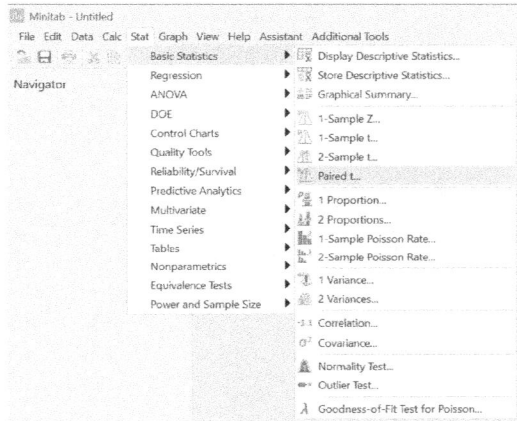

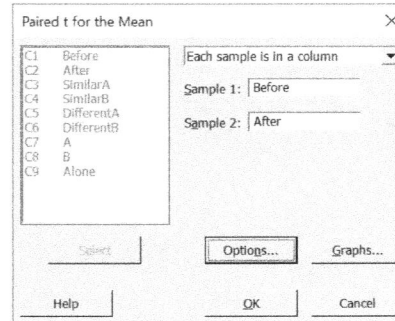

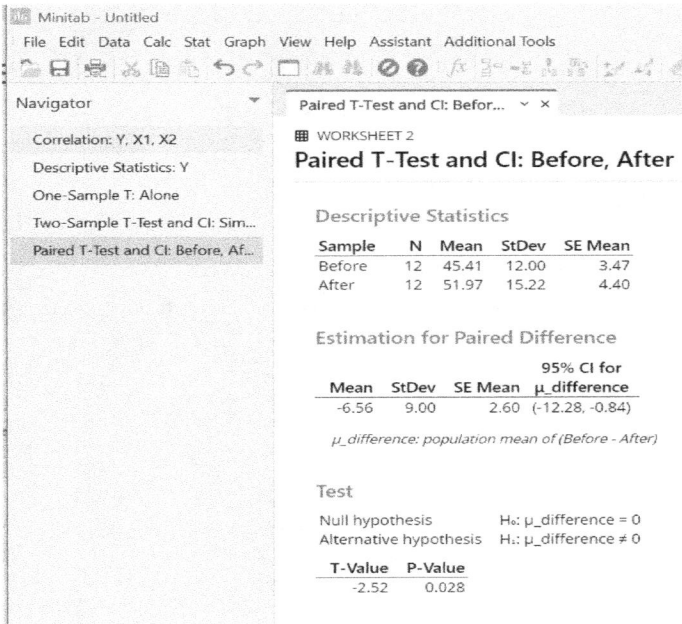

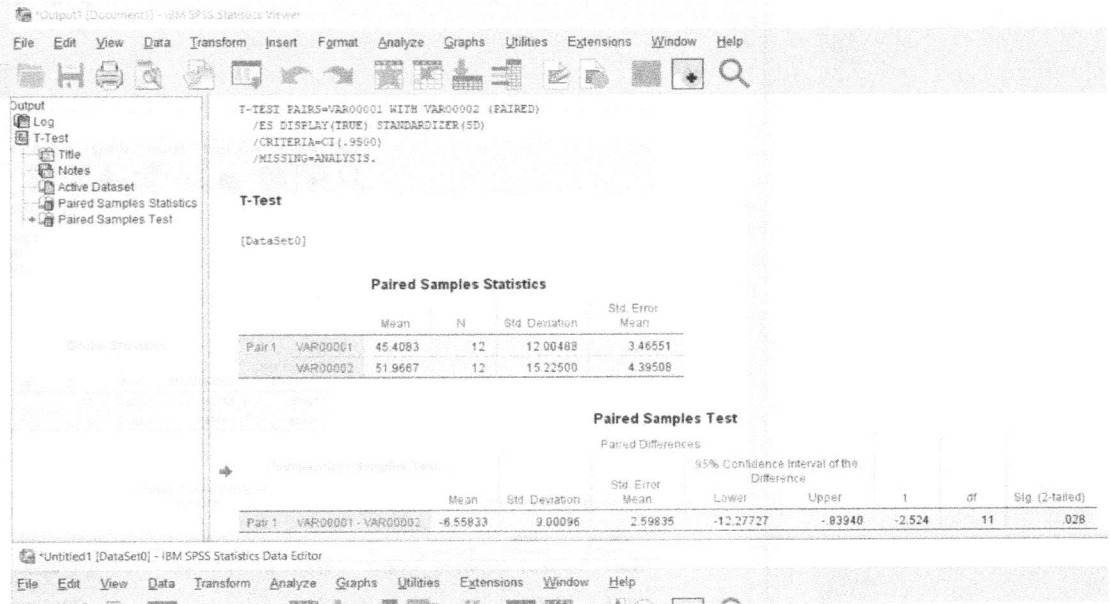

Paired T-Test and CI: Before, After

Descriptive Statistics

Sample	N	Mean	StDev	SE Mean
Before	12	45.41	12.00	3.47
After	12	51.97	15.22	4.40

Estimation for Paired Difference

Mean	StDev	SE Mean	95% CI for μ_difference
-6.56	9.00	2.60	(-12.28, -0.84)

μ_difference: population mean of (Before - After)

Test

Null hypothesis H_0: μ_difference = 0
Alternative hypothesis H_1: μ_difference ≠ 0

T-Value	P-Value
-2.52	0.028

T-TEST PAIRS=VAR00001 WITH VAR00002 (PAIRED)
  /ES DISPLAY(TRUE) STANDARDIZER(SD)
  /CRITERIA=CI(.9500)
  /MISSING=ANALYSIS.

T-Test

[DataSet0]

Paired Samples Statistics

		Mean	N	Std. Deviation	Std. Error Mean
Pair 1	VAR00001	45.4083	12	12.00488	3.46551
	VAR00002	51.9667	12	15.22500	4.39508

Paired Samples Test

		Paired Differences							
				Std. Error	95% Confidence Interval of the Difference				
		Mean	Std. Deviation	Mean	Lower	Upper	t	df	Sig. (2-tailed)
Pair 1	VAR00001 - VAR00002	-6.55833	9.00096	2.59835	-12.27727	-.83940	-2.524	11	.028

R (DEPENDENT PAIRED T-TESTS)

```
library(tidyverse)
library(pander)
library(readxl)
mydata <- read_excel ("C:/Users/jcmun/Desktop/myttestdata.xlsx")
t.test(mydata$Before,mydata$After, paired = TRUE)
t.test(mydata$Before,mydata$After, paired = TRUE, alternative="greater")
```

BIZSTATS (MANN-WHITNEY & WILCOXON SIGNED-RANK TEST)

SPSS (MANN-WHITNEY & WILCOXON SIGNED-RANK TEST)

Mann-Whitney: C2, C3

Method

η_1: median of C2
η_2: median of C3
Difference: $\eta_1 - \eta_2$

Descriptive Statistics

Sample	N	Median
C2	33	39
C3	33	44

Estimation for Difference

Difference	CI for Difference	Achieved Confidence
-0.0000000	(-10, 7)	95.03%

Test

Null hypothesis	H_0: $\eta_1 - \eta_2 = 0$
Alternative hypothesis	H_1: $\eta_1 - \eta_2 \neq 0$

Method	W-Value	P-Value
Not adjusted for ties	1084.00	0.788
Adjusted for ties	1084.00	0.787

R (MANN-WHITNEY & WILCOXON SIGNED-RANK TEST)

```
library(tidyverse)
library(pander)
library(readxl)
mydata <- read_excel ("C:/Users/jcmun/Desktop/myttestdata.xlsx")
wilcox.test(mydata$A,mydata$B)
wilcox.test(mydata$A,mydata$B, exact=FALSE)
wilcox.test(mydata$A,mydata$B, exact=FALSE, alternative="l")
wilcox.test(mydata$A,mydata$B, exact=FALSE, alternative="g")
```

General Linear Models

GENERAL LINEAR MODEL	Dependent Variable(s)	Independent Variable(s)	Notes
ANOVA Single Factor Multiple Treatments	One	One	One factor with multiple treatment types.
ANOVA Single Factor with Repeated Measures	One	One	Repeating similar tests for reliability.
ANOVA with Blocking Variables	One	One	Controls and tests for exogenous impacts.
Two-Way ANOVA	One	Two	Two factors with multiple treatment types each and testing for their interactions.
ANCOVA	One	One	Controls for baselines using covariates.
MANOVA	Multiple	One	Simultaneous ANOVA by testing multiple dependent variables at once.
Two-Way MANOVA	Multiple	Two	Two factors with multiple treatment types each and testing for their interactions on multiple dependent variables at once.

ANOVA for Single Factor Multiple Treatments
1 Dependent Variable vs. 1 Independent Variable (One Factor Multiple Treatments)

Participants	Method 1 Treatment	Method 2 Treatment	Method 3 Treatment
Person 1	58	80	96
Person 2	68	82	92
Person 3	70	88	90
...	...	...	...
...	...	...	...
Person 30	72	86	88

* Method 1: Russian Math; Method 2: Singapore Math; Method 3: U.S. Math
* The Single Factor Tested: Different Teaching Techniques
* Dependent Variable = Math Scores (continuous numerical values in the table)
* Independent Variable = Teaching Techniques (column groups)

ANOVA for Single Factor Repeated Measures
1 Dependent Variable vs. 1 Independent Variable (Repeated Tests)

Participants	Test 1	Test 2	Test 3
Person 1	50	52	50
Person 2	88	90	92
Person 3	60	62	58
...	...	...	...
...	...	...	...
Person 30	78	80	80

* The same treatment is used but the participants are tested multiple times
* Dependent Variable = Math Scores (continuous numerical values in the table)
* The same students are subjected to multiple tests

ANOVA with Blocking Variable
1 Dependent Variable vs. 1 Independent Variable with Blocking Variable

Blocks	Method 1 Treatment	Method 2 Treatment	Method 3 Treatment
Private School	66	82	94
Public School	68	84	90
Home School	70	88	90

* Method 1: Russian Math; Method 2: Singapore Math; Method 3: U.S. Math
* The Single Factor Tested: Different Teaching Techniques
* Dependent Variable = Math Scores (continuous numerical values in the table)
* Independent Variable = Teaching Techniques (column groups)
* Blocking Variable = Type of school (variable to control)

TWO-WAY ANOVA
1 Dependent Variable vs. 2 Independent Variable (One Factor Multiple Treatments)

Factor B	Method 1 Factor A1	Method 2 Factor A2	Method 3 Factor A3
Factor B1: 1 Month	68	82	96
Factor B2: 3 Months	72	84	86
Factor B3: 6 Months	66	90	92

* The Two Factors Tested: Different Teaching Techniques vs. Length of Time Taught
* Factor A:: Method 1: Russian Math; Method 2: Singapore Math; Method 3: U.S. Math
* Factor B:: 1 Month, 3 Month, 6 Months
* Dependent Variable = Math Scores (continuous numerical values in the table)
* This example is a 3 x 3 Factorial Model

MANOVA
Multiple Dependent Variables vs. 1 Independent Variable

Independent Var Schools	Dependent Var 1 Math Scores	Dependent Var 2 Satisfaction	Dependent Var 3 Teacher Ratings
Public	76.7	29.5	7.5
Public	60.5	32.1	6.3
Public	96.1	40.7	4.2
Private	76.9	20.4	3.0
Private	66.9	23.9	1.1
Private	55.4	29.1	5.0
Charter	62.8	25.9	2.9
Charter	45.0	15.9	1.2
Charter	47.8	36.1	4.1
Home School	52.5	39.0	3.1
Home School	80.0	54.2	4.0
Home School	54.7	32.1	5.7

* Multiple Dependent Variables = The numerical values in the table include test scores, student satisfaction survey scores, and teacher ratings
* One Independent Variable = Type of school

TWO WAY MANOVA
Multiple Dependent Variables vs. 2 Independent Variables

Independent Var 1 Schools	Independent Var 2 Economic	Dependent Var 1 Math Scores	Dependent Var 2 Satisfaction	Dependent Var 3 Teacher Ratings
Public	Wealthy	29.50	29.50	7.50
Public	Wealthy	32.10	32.10	6.30
Public	Middle	40.70	40.70	4.20
Public	Middle	29.50	29.50	7.50
Public	Poor	32.10	32.10	6.30
Public	Poor	40.70	40.70	4.20
Private	Wealthy	20.40	20.40	3.00
Private	Wealthy	23.90	23.90	1.10
Private	Middle	29.10	29.10	5.00
Private	Middle	25.90	25.90	2.90
Private	Poor	15.90	15.90	1.20
Private	Poor	36.10	36.10	4.10
Home School	Wealthy	39.00	39.00	3.10
Home School	Wealthy	54.20	54.20	4.00
Home School	Middle	32.10	32.10	5.70
Home School	Middle	39.00	39.00	3.10
Home School	Poor	54.20	54.20	4.00
Home School	Poor	32.10	32.10	5.70

* Multiple Dependent Variables = The numerical values in the table include test scores, student satisfaction survey scores, and teacher ratings
* Two Independent Variable = Type of school vs. Economic status of the school district

SINGLE ANOVA WITH MULTIPLE TREATMENT VARIABLES

The previously described t-tests, z-tests, and F-tests are applied to two variables at a time to determine if their means, proportions, or variances are statistically significantly different or if the small differences are attributable to random chance. When two or more sample means need to be tested at the same time, we resort to Analysis of Variance (ANOVA) tests.

The single ANOVA with multiple treatments tests *one* categorical independent variable (with multiple treatment levels, types, or categories) and *one* numerical dependent variable (randomly allocated into the multiple treatment categories) to determine if their population means are equal. Each data column will have a different treatment (e.g., a new method of manufacturing, a new training regimen, a new technology employed). This test assumes that the treatments are completely and randomly assigned to all the persons in the experiment and the underlying data is normally distributed with equal variance. Note that the nonparametric equivalent is the Kruskal–Wallis test, which is presented later in the chapter.

Example: Nine staff members in an organization were randomly divided into three teams each consisting of three individuals, and each team was provided a different type of training. There are three distinct training courses or treatments in this case. Upon completing the training course, each individual was assigned a task to complete and the time it took to complete the task was recorded and shown in the data grid. Because the selection is random, we use the randomized single ANOVA with multiple treatments the test the following hypotheses:

H_0: $\mu_1 = \mu_2 = \ldots = \mu_t$ for treatments 1 to t (there is no effect in the treatments)
H_a: Population means are not equal (there is an effect in at least one of the treatments)

$$Global\ Average\ \widetilde{x} = \frac{\sum_{j=1}^{t} \sum_{i=1}^{t} x_{ij}}{N} \qquad SS\ Treatment = \sum_{j=1}^{t} n_j (\overline{x}_j - \widetilde{x})^2 \qquad SS\ Error = \sum_{j=1}^{t} \sum_{i=1}^{n_j} (x_{ij} - \overline{x}_j)^2 \qquad SS\ Total = \sum_{j=1}^{t} \sum_{i=1}^{n_j} (x_{ij} - \widetilde{x})^2$$

Mean Squares of Between Treatment (MS Treatment) = (SS Treatment)/(Number of Treatments – 1)

Mean Squares of Errors or Mean Squares Within Treatments (MS Error) = (SS Error)/(Total Observations – Number of Treatments)

F Statistic is computed as MS Treatment / MS Error

EXCEL ADD-IN

	Method 1	Method 2	Method 3
Person 1	15	10	18
Person 2	20	15	19
Person 3	19	11	23

EXCEL ANALYSIS TOOL PAK
Anova: Single Factor

SUMMARY

Groups	Count	Sum	Average	Variance
Column 1	3	54	18	7
Column 2	3	36	12	7
Column 3	3	60	20	7

ANOVA

Source of Variation	SS	df	MS	F	P-value	F crit
Between Groups	104	2	52	7.4286	0.0238	5.1433
Within Groups	42	6	7			
Total	146	8				

BIZSTATS

MANUAL
COMPUTATIONS

ANOVA for Single Factor Multiple Treatments

The specification tested is $x_{ij} = \mu + \tau_j + \varepsilon_{ij}$ and the calculations proceed as follows:

Questions or Participant	Method 1 Treatment	Method 2 Treatment	Method 3 Treatment		Average
Person 1	15	10	18		14.3333
Person 2	20	15	19		18.0000
Person 3	19	11	23		17.6667
Average	18.0000	12.0000	20.0000		16.6667
Rows (N)	3	3	3		

The global average is $\tilde{x} = \dfrac{\sum_{j=1}^{t} \sum_{i=1}^{t} x_{ij}}{N}$

Number of Treatments (Columns)	3	Number of columns
Number of Questions/Participants (Rows)	3	Number of rows
Total Number of Data Points	9	Number of data points

Sum of Squares of Treatment (SS Treatments) is $\sum_{j=1}^{t} n_j (\bar{x}_j - \tilde{x})^2$

Sum of Squares of Error (SS Error) is $\sum_{j=1}^{t} \sum_{i=1}^{n_j} (x_{ij} - \bar{x}_j)^2$

Sum of Squares of the Total (SS Total) is $\sum_{j=1}^{t} \sum_{i=1}^{n_j} (x_{ij} - \tilde{x})^2$

Sums of Squares Between Groups   104.0000   = 3*(18 - 16.6667)^2 + 3*(12 - 16.6667)^2 + 3*(20 - 16.6667)^2

Sums of Squares Within Groups   42.0000   = (15 - 18.0000)^2 + (20 - 18.0000)^2 + (19 - 18.0000)^2 + (10 - 12.0000)^2 + (15 - 12.0000)^2 + (11 - 12.0000)^2 + (18 - 20.0000)^2 + (19 - 20.0000)^2 + (23 - 20.0000)^2

Total Sums of Squares   146.0000   = 104.0000 + 42.0000

Degrees of Freedom Between Groups	2	Number of Columns - 1 (where we have DF = k -1) or 3 - 1
Degrees of Freedom Within Groups	6	Nuber of Data Points - Number of Columns (where DF = N - k) or 9 - 1
Degrees of Freedom Total	8	DF Betwen Groups + DF Within Groups or 2 + 6

Mean Square Between Groups	52.0000	Sums of Squares Between Groups / Mean Square Between Groups or 104.000 / 2
Mean Square Within Groups	7.0000	Sums of Squares Within Groups / Mean Square Within Groups or 42.0000 / 6
Mean Square Total	18.2500	Mean Square Between Groups + Mean Square Within Groups or 146.0000 / 8

F-Statistic	7.4286	Mean Square Between Groups / Mean Square Within Groups or 52.0000 / 7.0000
P-Value	0.0238	F Distribution with DF1 = 2 and DF2 = 6

Eta Squared	0.7123
Omega Squared	0.5882

MINITAB

SPSS

R (MANUAL DATA INPUT)

```
library(tidyverse)
library(pander)

myanovadata <- data.frame(Treatments =
c("Method1","Method1","Method1","Method2","Method2","Method2","Meth
od3","Method3","Method3"), Values = c(15, 20, 19, 10, 15, 11, 18, 19, 23))

print (myanovadata)
print (myanovadata$Values)

pander(summary(aov(data=myanovadata, Values ~ Treatments)))
```

```
Console   Terminal ×   Jobs ×                                        ☐☐
~/ ⬚
> library(tidyverse)
-- Attaching packages ----------------- tidyverse 1.3.0 --
v ggplot2 3.3.2      v purrr   0.3.4
v tibble  3.0.4      v dplyr   1.0.2
v tidyr   1.1.2      v stringr 1.4.0
v readr   1.4.0      v forcats 0.5.0
-- Conflicts ------------------- tidyverse_conflicts() --
x dplyr::filter() masks stats::filter()
x dplyr::lag()    masks stats::lag()
> library(pander)
>
> myanovadata <- data.frame(Treatments = c("Method1","Method1","Method1","Met
hod2","Method2","Method2","Method3","Method3","Method3"), Values = c(15, 20,
 19, 10, 15, 11, 18, 19, 23))
> print(myanovadata)
  Treatments values
1    Method1      15
2    Method1      20
3    Method1      19
4    Method2      10
5    Method2      15
6    Method2      11
7    Method3      18
8    Method3      19
9    Method3      23
> print(myanovadata$values)
[1] 15 20 19 10 15 11 18 19 23
> pander(summary(aov(data=myanovadata, Values ~ Treatments)))
```

	Df	Sum Sq	Mean Sq	F value	Pr(>F)
Treatments	2	104	52	7.429	0.02381
Residuals	6	42	7	NA	NA

Table: Analysis of Variance Model

R (DATA LOAD AND RUNNING ANOVA)

	A	B
1	Treatments	Values
2	Method1	15
3	Method1	20
4	Method1	19
5	Method2	10
6	Method2	15
7	Method2	11
8	Method3	18
9	Method3	19
10	Method3	23
11		

```
library(tidyverse)
library(pander)

library(readxl)
mydata <- read_excel ("C:/Users/jcmun/Desktop/myanovadata.xlsx")
summary(mydata)

pander(summary(aov(Values ~ Treatments, data=mydata)))
```

Table: Analysis of Variance Model

	Df	Sum Sq	Mean Sq	F value	Pr(>F)
Treatments	2	104	52	7.429	0.02381
Residuals	6	42	7	NA	NA

ANOVA WITH RANDOMIZED BLOCK

In the previous single ANOVA test, the assumption was that the treatments were completely and randomly assigned to all the persons in the experiment. This approach may result in overrepresentation and underrepresentation in some treatment groups simply by chance. If the properties or characteristics of the individuals participating in the experiment have a strong influence on the measurements and data obtained, the single ANOVA may end up measuring the differentials inside this experimental group instead of the effects of the treatments. To resolve this issue, ANOVA with Randomized Block can be used. Note that the nonparametric equivalent is the Friedman's test.

The specification tested in this ANOVA is $x_{i,j} = \mu + \tau_j + \beta_i + \varepsilon_{ij}$

H_0: $\tau_j = 0$ for treatments j = 1 to t (there is no effect in the treatments)
H_a: $\tau_j \neq 0$ for at least one treatment j = 1 to t (one or more treatments has an effect)
where τ is the treatments and β is the blocking variable.

Example: Suppose that there are four auto headlamps under development. The manufacturer wishes to test the visibility of each lamp design by measuring how far someone can see using each of these headlamps. Now suppose 12 individuals were randomly selected to participate in this experiment, and suppose we categorize these participants as young (Y), middle aged (M), and old (O). If we completely randomize the selection of these individuals, each of the method may be over- or underrepresented in terms of age groups, as seen in the first data grid below on the left. Now, further suppose that the participants' properties (e.g., age) has an influence on their vision (e.g., older participants cannot see as far as someone much younger). Consequently, completely randomizing the participants into these groups will yield biased results. The better approach is to "block" this intervening age variable. The second data grid below on the right shows how to set up an ANOVA dataset with blocks. In this example, there are three blocks, and the

ANOVA One-Way Randomized Design

	Method 1	Method 2	Method 3	Method 4
Person 1	Y	M	O	Y
Person 2	Y	O	Y	M
Person 3	O	O	M	Y

ANOVA with Blocking Variable

	Method 1	Method 2	Method 3	Method 4
Block 1	Y	Y	Y	Y
Block 2	M	M	M	M
Block 3	O	O	O	O

MANUAL COMPUTATIONS (ANOVA RANDOMIZED BLOCK)

$$Global\ Average = \widetilde{x} = \frac{\sum_{j=1}^{t}\sum_{i=1}^{t} x_{ij}}{N}$$

$$SS\ Treatment = n\sum_{j=1}^{t}(\overline{x}_j - \widetilde{x})^2$$

$$SS\ Block = t\sum_{j=1}^{t}(\overline{x}_i - \widetilde{x})^2$$

$$SS\ Total = \sum_{j=1}^{t}\sum_{i=1}^{n_j}(x_{ij} - \widetilde{x})^2$$

$$SS\ Error = SS\ Total - SS\ Treatment - SS\ Block$$

	A	B	C	D	E	F	G
1		Method 1	Method 2	Method 3	Method 4	Average	
2	Block 1	90	87	93	85	88.7500	
3	Block 2	86	79	87	83	83.7500	
4	Block 3	76	74	77	73	75.0000	
5	Average	84.0000	80.0000	85.6667	80.3333		
6							
7	Global Average	82.5000	=AVERAGE(B2:E4)				
8	Number of Rows (Blocks)	3	=COUNT(B2:B4)				
9	Number of Columns (Treatments)	4	=COUNT(B2:E2)				
10	SS Total	473.0000	=(B2-B7)^2+(B3-B7)^2+(B4-B7)^2+(C2-B7)^2+(C3-B7)^2+(C4-B7)^2+(D2-B7)^2+(D3-B7)^2+(D4-B7)^2+(E2-B7)^2+(E3-B7)^2+(E4-B7)^2				
11	SS Blocking (Rows)	387.5000	=B9*((F2-B7)^2+(F3-B7)^2+(F4-B7)^2)				
12	SS Treatment (Columns)	69.6667	=B8*((B5-B7)^2+(C5-B7)^2+(D5-B7)^2+(E5-B7)^2)				
13	SS Errors	15.8333	=B10-B12-B11				
14	MS Block	193.7500	=B11/B17				
15	MS Treatment	23.2222	=B12/B18				
16	MS Error	2.6389	=B13/B19				
17	DF Block	2	=B8-1				
18	DF Treatment	3	=B9-1				
19	DF Error	6	=B17*B18				
20	F Statistic (Treatment)	8.8000	=B15/B16				
21	P-Value (Treatment)	0.0129	=FDIST(B20,B18,B19)				
22	F Statistic (Blocking)	73.4211	=B14/B16				
23	P-Value (Blocking)	0.0001	=FDIST(B22,B17,B19)				
24	F Critical (Treatment) @ 0.10	3.2888	=FINV(0.1,B18,B19)				
25	F Critical (Treatment) @ 0.05	4.7571	=FINV(0.05,B18,B19)				
26	F Critical (Treatment) @ 0.01	9.7795	=FINV(0.01,B18,B19)				
27	F Critical (Blocking) @ 0.10	3.4633	=FINV(0.1,B17,B19)				
28	F Critical (Blocking) @ 0.05	5.1433	=FINV(0.05,B17,B19)				
29	F Critical (Blocking) @ 0.01	10.9248	=FINV(0.01,B17,B19)				
30	The blocking variable has statistically significant effect at Alpha 5% on at least one of the levels						
31	The treatment variable has statistically significant effect at Alpha 1% on at least one of the levels						

Mean Squares of Between Treatment (MS Treatment) = (SS Treatment)/(Number of Treatments – 1)
Mean Squares of Blocks (MS Block) = (SS Block)/(Total Observations – 1)
Mean Squares of Errors or Mean Squares Within Treatments (MS Error) = (SS Error)/((Total Observations – 1)(Number of Treatments – 1)
F Statistic is computed as MS Treatment / MS Error
F statistic df = (Number of Treatments – 1) in the numerator and (Total Observations – 1)(Number of Treatments – 1) in the denominator

BIZSTATS (ANOVA WITH RANDOMIZED BLOCK)

$$Global\ Average = \widetilde{x} = \frac{\sum_{j=1}^{t} \sum_{i=1}^{t} x_{ij}}{N}$$

$$SS\ Treatment = n\sum_{j=1}^{t} (\overline{x}_j - \widetilde{x})^2$$

$$SS\ Block = t\sum_{j=1}^{t} (\overline{x}_i - \widetilde{x})^2$$

$$SS\ Total = \sum_{j=1}^{t} \sum_{i=1}^{n_j} (x_{ij} - \widetilde{x})^2$$

$$SS\ Error = SS\ Total - SS\ Treatment - SS\ Block$$

Mean Squares of Between Treatment (MS Treatment) = (SS Treatment)/(Number of Treatments – 1)

Mean Squares of Blocks (MS Block) = (SS Block)/(Total Observations – 1)

Mean Squares of Errors or Mean Squares Within Treatments (MS Error) = (SS Error)/((Total Observations – 1)(Number of Treatments – 1)

F Statistic is computed as MS Treatment / MS Error

F statistic df = (Number of Treatments – 1) in the numerator and (Total Observations – 1)(Number of Treatments – 1) in the denominator

MINITAB (ANOVA WITH RANDOMIZED BLOCK)

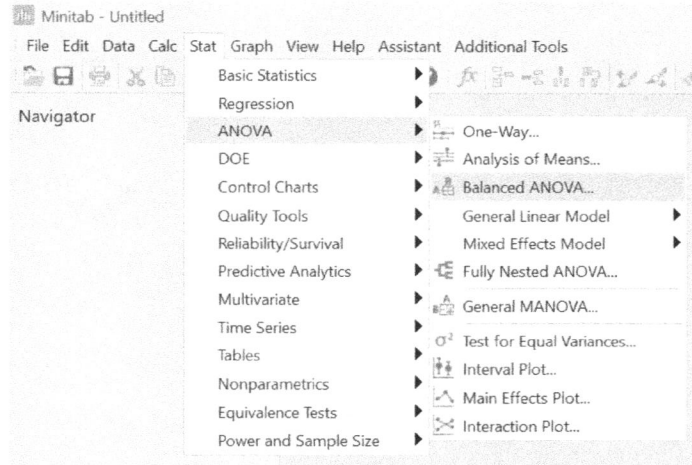

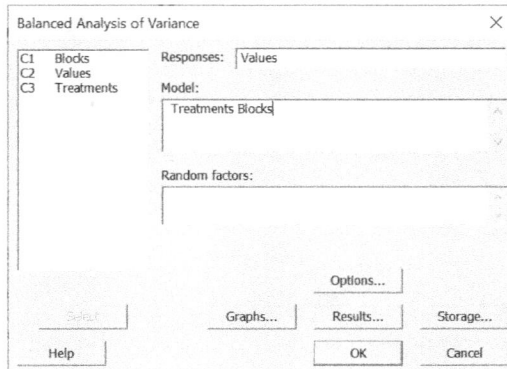

R (MANUAL DATA INPUT FOR ANOVA WITH RANDOMIZED BLOCK)

```
Console   Terminal    Jobs
~/

**Residuals**   6    15.83    2.639    NA    NA
-------------------------------------------------------------

Table: Analysis of Variance Model

> pander(summary(aov(data=myanovadata, Values ~ Block + Method)))

-------------------------------------------------------------
           Df   Sum Sq   Mean Sq   F value   Pr(>F)
-------------  ----  -------  --------  --------  ---------
  **Block**     2    387.5    193.8     73.42     6.05e-05

  **Method**    3    69.67    23.22      8.8      0.01289

 **Residuals**  6    15.83    2.639      NA        NA
-------------------------------------------------------------

Table: Analysis of Variance Model

> myanovadata <- data.frame(
+     Block = c("Block1","Block2","Block3","Block1","Block2","Block3","Block
1","Block2","Block3","Block1","Block2","Block3"),
+     Method = c("Method1","Method1","Method1","Method2","Method2","Method
2","Method3","Method3","Method3","Method4","Method4","Method4"),
+     Values = c(90, 86, 76, 87, 79, 74, 93, 87, 77, 85, 83, 73))
> pander(summary(aov(data=myanovadata, Values ~ Block + Method)))

-------------------------------------------------------------
           Df   Sum Sq   Mean Sq   F value   Pr(>F)
-------------  ----  -------  --------  --------  ---------
  **Block**     2    387.5    193.8     73.42     6.05e-05

  **Method**    3    69.67    23.22      8.8      0.01289

 **Residuals**  6    15.83    2.639      NA        NA
-------------------------------------------------------------

Table: Analysis of Variance Model
```

Dataset for other applications

Block	Values	Method
Block1	90	Method1
Block2	86	Method1
Block3	76	Method1
Block1	87	Method2
Block2	79	Method2
Block3	74	Method2
Block1	93	Method3
Block2	87	Method3
Block3	77	Method3
Block1	85	Method4
Block2	83	Method4
Block3	73	Method4

```
## ANOVA WITH BLOCKING VARIABLES
library(tidyverse)
library(pander)
myanovadata <- data.frame(
  Block =
c("Block1","Block2","Block3","Block1","Block2","Block3","Block1","Blo
ck2","Block3","Block1","Block2","Block3"),
  Method =
c("Method1","Method1","Method1","Method2","Method2","Method2","Me
thod3","Method3","Method3","Method4","Method4","Method4"),
  Values = c(90, 86, 76, 87, 79, 74, 93, 87, 77, 85, 83, 73))
print(myanovadata)
pander(summary(aov(data=myanovadata, Values ~ Block + Method)))
```

R (DATA LOAD FOR ANOVA WITH RANDOMIZED BLOCK)

	A	B	C
1	Blocks	Values	Treatments
2	Block1	90	Method1
3	Block2	86	Method1
4	Block3	76	Method1
5	Block1	87	Method2
6	Block2	79	Method2
7	Block3	74	Method2
8	Block1	93	Method3
9	Block2	87	Method3
10	Block3	77	Method3
11	Block1	85	Method4
12	Block2	83	Method4
13	Block3	73	Method4

```
library(tidyverse)
library(pander)
library(readxl)
mydata <- read_excel ("C:/Users/jcmun/Desktop/myanovablockdata.xlsx")
summary(mydata)
pander(summary(aov(Values ~ Treatments + Blocks, data=mydata)))
```

```
> library(tidyverse)
> library(pander)
> library(readxl)
> mydata <- read_excel ("C:/Users/jcmun/Desktop/myanovablockdata.xlsx")
> summary(mydata)
    Blocks            Values        Treatments
 Length:12        Min.   :73.00   Length:12
 Class :character 1st Qu.:76.75   Class :character
 Mode  :character Median :84.00   Mode  :character
                  Mean   :82.50
                  3rd Qu.:87.00
                  Max.   :93.00
> pander(summary(aov(Values ~ Treatments + Blocks, data=mydata)))
```

	Df	Sum Sq	Mean Sq	F value	Pr(>F)
Treatments	3	69.67	23.22	8.8	0.01289
Blocks	2	387.5	193.8	73.42	6.05e-05
Residuals	6	15.83	2.639	NA	NA

Table: Analysis of Variance Model

Name	Description	Version
User Library		
abind	Combine Multidimensional Arrays	1.4-5
AER	Applied Econometrics with R	1.2-9
apricom	Tools for the a Priori Comparison of Regression Modelling Strategies	1.0.0
askpass	Safe Password Entry for R, Git, and SSH	1.1
assertthat	Easy Pre and Post Assertions	0.2.1
aTSA	Alternative Time Series Analysis	3.1.2
backports	Reimplementations of Functions Introduced Since R-3.0.0	1.2.0
base64enc	Tools for base64 encoding	0.1-3
BH	Boost C++ Header Files	1.72.0-3
blob	A Simple S3 Class for Representing Vectors of Binary Data ('BLOBS')	1.2.1
brio	Basic R Input Output	1.1.0
broom	Convert Statistical Objects into Tidy Tibbles	0.7.2
callr	Call R from R	3.5.1
car	Companion to Applied Regression	3.0-10
carData	Companion to Applied Regression Data Sets	3.0-4

TWO-WAY ANOVA

The one-way ANOVA models presented above look at a single factor on the dependent variable. In this section, we introduce the two-way ANOVA, a method that simultaneously examines the effects of two factors (*two* categorical independent variables) on the *one* numerical dependent variable, as well the interactions of different levels of the two factors. That is, random assignments are made such that two or more participants are subjected to each possible combination of the factor levels. The number of persons or participants within each of these combinations is termed the *number of replications* (r) and r has to be ≥ 2.

The specification tested in this ANOVA is $x_{i,j} = \mu + \alpha_i + \beta_j + (\alpha\beta)_{ij} + \varepsilon_{ijk}$

Testing the main effect, factor A:
H_0: $\alpha_i = 0$ for each level of factor A, for $i = 1$ to a (no level of factor A has an effect)
H_a: $\alpha_i \neq 0$ for at least one value of i, where $i = 1$ to a (at least one level has an effect)

Testing the main effect, factor B:
H_0: $\beta_j = 0$ for each level of factor B, for $j = 1$ to b (no level of factor B has an effect)
H_a: $\beta_j \neq 0$ for at least one value of j, where $j = 1$ to b (at least one level has an effect)

Testing the interaction effects, between levels of factors A and B:
H_0: $\alpha\beta_{ij} = 0$ for each combination of i and j (there are no interaction effects)
H_a: $\alpha\beta_{ij} \neq 0$ for at least one combination of i and j (at least one combination has effect)

Example: Suppose an aircraft manufacturer is testing three different alloys (B1, B2, and B3) for its wing construction of a new plane, and each alloy type can be produced in four different thickness (A1 to A4). The number of twists and flexes are recorded until stress failure is detected.

	Factor B1	Factor B2	Factor B3
Factor A1	804	836	804
Factor A1	816	828	808
Factor A2	819	844	807
Factor A2	813	836	819
Factor A3	820	814	819
Factor A3	821	811	829
Factor A4	806	811	827
Factor A4	805	806	835

$$SSA = rb\sum_{i=1}^{a}(\overline{x}_i - \widetilde{x})^2 \qquad SSB = ra\sum_{j=1}^{b}(\overline{x}_j - \widetilde{x})^2$$

$$SSE = \sum_{i=1}^{a}\sum_{j=1}^{b}\sum_{k=1}^{r}(x_{ijk} - \overline{x}_{ij})^2 \qquad SST = \sum_{i=1}^{a}\sum_{j=1}^{b}\sum_{k=1}^{r}(\overline{x}_{ijk} - \widetilde{x})^2$$

Degrees of freedom (*df*) for factor A is *(a – 1)*, factor B is *(b – 1)*, Interaction AB is *(a – 1)(b – 1)*, Error is *ab(r – 1)*, and Total is *(abr – 1)*.
Mean Squares (MS) for factor A is *SSA/df(A)*, factor B is *SSB/df(B)*, factor AB is *SSAB/df(AB)*, Error is *SSE/df(E)*.
The calculated F Statistic for factor A is MS(A)/MS(E), factor B is MS(B)/MS(E), and AB interaction is MS(AB)/MS(E).

MANUAL COMPUTATIONS (TWO-WAY ANOVA)

	Factor B1	Factor B2	Factor B3	Average		
Factor A1	804	836	804			
Factor A1	816	828	808	816.0000		Two Way ANOVA
Factor A2	819	844	807			
Factor A2	813	836	819	823.0000		Careful with column E. We average the number
Factor A3	820	814	819			of rows based on user input of number of
Factor A3	821	811	829	819.0000		Replication/Rows there are
Factor A4	806	811	827			
Factor A4	805	806	835	815.0000		
Average	813.0000	823.2500	818.5000			

Replication/Rows (User Input)	2	This is a user input	B18=(B2-$B$17)^2+(B3-$B$17)^2+(B4-$B$17)^2+(B5-$B$17)^2+(B6-$B$17)^2+(B7-$B$17)^2+(B8-$B$17)^2+(B9-$B$17)^2+(C2-
Number of Rows	8	=COUNT(B2:B9)	$B$17)^2+(C3-$B$17)^2+(C4-$B$17)^2+(C5-$B$17)^2+(C6-$B$17)^2+(C7-$B$17)^2+(C8-$B$17)^2+(C9-$B$17)^2+(D2-
Factors/Rows	4	=B14/B13	$B$17)^2+(D3-$B$17)^2+(D4-$B$17)^2+(D5-$B$17)^2+(D6-$B$17)^2+(D7-$B$17)^2+(D8-$B$17)^2+(D9-$B$17)^2
Factors/Columns	3	=COUNT(B2:D2)	
Global Average	818.2500	=AVERAGE(B2:D9)	
SS Total	3142.5000	see equation on the right	
SS Factors Rows	232.5000	=B13*B16*((E3-B17)^2+(E5-B17)^2+(E7-B17)^2+(E9-B17)^2)	
SS Factors Columns	421.0000	=B13*B15*((B11-B17)^2+(C11-B17)^2+(D11-B17)^2)	
SS Interaction	2155.0000	=B18-B19-B2C watch out on this one... example has 2 Replication so we average two rows only, if replication 5 then average of all 5 rows and do the difference and square for all five items...	
SS Errors	334.0000	see equation on the right	
MS Factor Rows	77.5000	=B19/(B15-1)	
MS Factor Columns	210.5000	=B20/(B16-1)	'B22=(B2-AVERAGE(B2:B3))^2+(B3-AVERAGE(B2:B3))^2 + (B4-AVERAGE(B4:B5))^2+(B5-AVERAGE(B4:B5))^2 + (B6-
MS Interaction	359.1667	=B21/((B15-1)*(B16-1))	AVERAGE(B6:B7))^2+(B7-AVERAGE(B6:B7))^2 + (B8-AVERAGE(B8:B9))^2+(B9-AVERAGE(B8:B9))^2 + (C2-
MS Errors	27.8333	=B22/(B15*B16*(B13-1))	AVERAGE(C2:C3))^2+(C3-AVERAGE(C2:C3))^2 + (C4-AVERAGE(C4:C5))^2+(C5-AVERAGE(C4:C5))^2 + (C6-
F Statistic for Row Factors	2.7844	=B23/B26	AVERAGE(C6:C7))^2+(C7-AVERAGE(C6:C7))^2 + (C8-AVERAGE(C8:C9))^2+(C9-AVERAGE(C8:C9))^2 + (D2-
F Statistic for Column Factors	7.5629	=B24/B26	AVERAGE(D2:D3))^2+(D3-AVERAGE(D2:D3))^2 + (D4-AVERAGE(D4:D5))^2+(D5-AVERAGE(D4:D5))^2 + (D6-
F Statistic for Interaction	12.9042	=B25/B26	AVERAGE(D6:D7))^2+(D7-AVERAGE(D6:D7))^2 + (D8-AVERAGE(D8:D9))^2+(D9-AVERAGE(D8:D9))^2

			Two Way ANOVA Results					
DF Row Factors	3	=B15-1						
DF Column Factors	2	=B16-1						
DF Interaction	6	=(B15-1)*(B16-1)		DF	SS	MS	F	P
DF Both Factors	12	=B15*B16*(B13-1)	Row Factor	3	232.5000	77.5000	2.7844	0.0864
P-Value for Row Factors	0.0864	=FDIST(B27,B30,B33)	Column Factor	2	421.0000	210.5000	7.5629	0.0075
P-Value for Column Factors	0.0075	=FDIST(B28,B31,B33)	Interaction	6	2155.0000	359.1667	12.9042	0.0001
P-Value for Interaction	0.0001	=FDIST(B29,B32,B33)	Error	12	334.0000	27.8333		

BIZSTATS (TWO-WAY ANOVA)

ROV Biz Stats

File   Data   Language   Help

STEP 1: Data — Manually enter your data, paste from another application, or load an example dataset with analysis   [Example]

STEP 2: Analysis — Choose analysis and enter parameters required (see example inputs below)

Dataset   Visualize   Command

[Visualize]   View: Alphabetical   -

VAR1; VAR2; VAR3
2

- Absolute Values (ABS)
- ANOVA (Randomized Blocks Multiple Treatments)
- ANOVA (Single Factor Multiple Treatments)
- **ANOVA (Two-Way Analysis)**
- ARIMA
- Auto ARIMA
- Auto Econometrics (Detailed)
- Auto Econometrics (Quick)
- Autocorrelation and Partial Autocorrelation
- Average (AVG)
- Charts: 2D Area
- Charts: 2D Bar
- Charts: 2D Line
- Charts: 2D Pareto
- Charts: 2D Point
- Charts: 2D Scatter
- Charts: 3D Area
- Charts: 3D Bar

Data Size (>0):
Var1; Var2; Var3   > 2
> 2

N	VAR1	VAR2	VAR3	VAR4	VAR5	VAR6	VAR7	VAR8	VAR9	VAR10
1	804	836								
2	816	828	808							
3	819	844	807							
4	813	836	819							
5	820	814	819							
6	821	811	829							
7	806	811	827							

STEP 3: Run — Run the current analysis in Step 2 or the selected saved analysis in Step 4; view the results, charts, and statistics; copy the results and charts to clipboard, or generate reports   [Run] [Copy] [Report]

◯ Use All Data   1 ~ 20
◯ Use Rows

Results   Charts

◉ Show New Results Only   ◯ Append Results at the End

DF	Sums of Squares	Mean Square	F Stat	p-Value
3	232.50	77.50	2.7844	0.0664
2	421.00	210.50	7.5629	0.0075
6	2155.00	359.17	12.9042	0.0001
12	334.00	27.83		
23	8142.50			

STEP 4: Save (Optional)   You can save multiple analyses and notes in the profile for future retrieval

Name:
Notes:

[ADD] [EDIT] [DEL] [Save] [Exit]

MINITAB (TWO-WAY ANOVA)

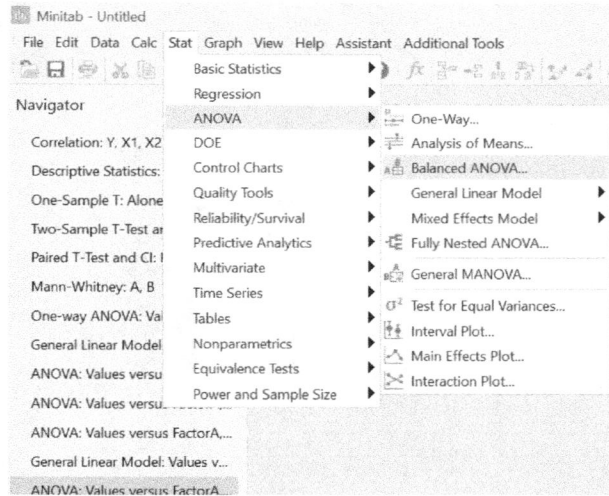

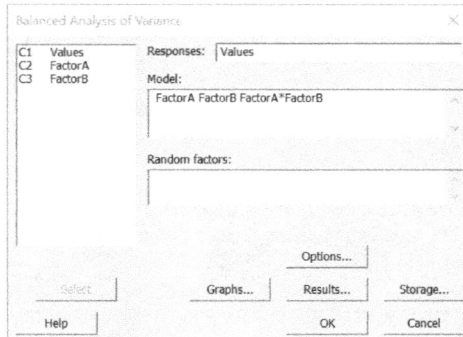

SPSS (TWO-WAY ANOVA)

Univariate Analysis of Variance

Between-Subjects Factors

		N
VAR00004	A1	6
	A2	6
	A3	6
	A4	6
VAR00005	B1	8
	B2	8
	B3	8

Tests of Between-Subjects Effects

Dependent Variable: VAR00001

Source	Type III Sum of Squares	df	Mean Square	F	Sig.
Corrected Model	2808.500[a]	11	255.318	9.173	<.001
Intercept	16068793.50	1	16068793.50	577321.922	<.001
VAR00004	232.500	3	77.500	2.784	.086
VAR00005	421.000	2	210.500	7.563	.007
VAR00004 * VAR00005	2155.000	6	359.167	12.904	<.001
Error	334.000	12	27.833		
Total	16071936.00	24			
Corrected Total	3142.500	23			

a. R Squared = .894 (Adjusted R Squared = .796)

Data Editor values (VAR00001, VAR00004, VAR00005):

	VAR00001	VAR00004	VAR00005
1	804.00	A1	B1
2	816.00	A1	B1
3	819.00	A2	B1
4	813.00	A2	B1
5	820.00	A3	B1
6	821.00	A3	B1
7	806.00	A4	B1
8	805.00	A4	B1
9	836.00	A1	B2
10	828.00	A1	B2
11	844.00	A2	B2
12	836.00	A2	B2
13	814.00	A3	B2
14	811.00	A3	B2
15	811.00	A4	B2
16	806.00	A4	B2
17	804.00	A1	B3
18	808.00	A1	B3
19	807.00	A2	B3
20	819.00	A2	B3
21	819.00	A3	B3
22	829.00	A3	B3
23	827.00	A4	B3
24	835.00	A4	B3

R (MANUAL DATA INPUT FOR TWO-WAY ANOVA)

```
Console  Terminal ×  Jobs ×
~/ <

R version 4.0.3 (2020-10-10) -- "Bunny-Wunnies Freak Out"
Copyright (C) 2020 The R Foundation for Statistical Computing
Platform: x86_64-w64-mingw32/x64 (64-bit)

R is free software and comes with ABSOLUTELY NO WARRANTY.
You are welcome to redistribute it under certain conditions.
Type 'license()' or 'licence()' for distribution details.

  Natural language support but running in an English locale

R is a collaborative project with many contributors.
Type 'contributors()' for more information and
'citation()' on how to cite R or R packages in publications.

Type 'demo()' for some demos, 'help()' for on-line help, or
'help.start()' for an HTML browser interface to help.
Type 'q()' to quit R.

> ## TWO WAY ANOVA
>
> knitr::opts_chunk$set(echo = TRUE)
> library(knitr)
> library(tidyverse)
-- Attaching packages ----------------------------------- tidyverse 1.3.0 --
v ggplot2 3.3.2      v purrr   0.3.4
v tibble  3.0.4      v dplyr   1.0.2
v tidyr   1.1.2      v stringr 1.4.0
v readr   1.4.0      v forcats 0.5.0
-- Conflicts ------------------------------------- tidyverse_conflicts() --
x dplyr::filter() masks stats::filter()
x dplyr::lag()    masks stats::lag()
> library(pander)
> myanovadata <- data.frame(FactorA = c(
+     "FactorA1","FactorA1","FactorA2","FactorA2","FactorA3","FactorA3","FactorA4","FactorA4",
+     "FactorA1","FactorA1","FactorA2","FactorA2","FactorA3","FactorA3","FactorA4","FactorA4",
+     "FactorA1","FactorA1","FactorA2","FactorA2","FactorA3","FactorA3","FactorA4","FactorA4"),
+   FactorB = c(
+     "FactorB1","FactorB1","FactorB1","FactorB1","FactorB1","FactorB1","FactorB1","FactorB1",
+     "FactorB2","FactorB2","FactorB2","FactorB2","FactorB2","FactorB2","FactorB2","FactorB2",
+     "FactorB3","FactorB3","FactorB3","FactorB3","FactorB3","FactorB3","FactorB3","FactorB3"),
+   Values = c(804, 816, 819, 813, 820, 821, 806, 805, 836, 828, 844, 836, 814, 811, 811, 806, 804, 808, 807, 819, 819, 829, 827, 835))
>
> pander(summary(aov(data=myanovadata, Values ~ FactorA*FactorB)))


-----------------------------------------------------------------
               Df   Sum Sq   Mean Sq   F value    Pr(>F)
------------------- ---- -------- --------- --------- -----------
   **FactorA**       3    232.5     77.5      2.784     0.08641

   **FactorB**       2    421      210.5     7.563     0.007495

**FactorA:FactorB**  6    2155     359.2     12.9     0.0001281

  **Residuals**      12   334      27.83      NA         NA
-----------------------------------------------------------------

Table: Analysis of Variance Model
```

library(tidyverse)
library(pander)

myanovadata <- data.frame(FactorA = c(
  "FactorA1","FactorA1","FactorA2","FactorA2","FactorA3","FactorA3","FactorA4","FactorA4",
  "FactorA1","FactorA1","FactorA2","FactorA2","FactorA3","FactorA3","FactorA4","FactorA4",
  "FactorA1","FactorA1","FactorA2","FactorA2","FactorA3","FactorA3","FactorA4","FactorA4"),
  FactorB = c(
  "FactorB1","FactorB1","FactorB1","FactorB1","FactorB1","FactorB1","FactorB1","FactorB1",
  "FactorB2","FactorB2","FactorB2","FactorB2","FactorB2","FactorB2","FactorB2","FactorB2",
  "FactorB3","FactorB3","FactorB3","FactorB3","FactorB3","FactorB3","FactorB3","FactorB3"),
  Values = c(804, 816, 819, 813, 820, 821, 806, 805, 836, 828, 844, 836, 814, 811, 811, 806, 804, 808, 807, 819, 819, 829, 827, 835))
print(myanovadata)
pander(summary(aov(data=myanovadata, Values ~ FactorA*FactorB)))

R (DATA LOAD FOR TWO-WAY ANOVA)

	A	B	C
1	Values	FactorA	FactorB
2	804	A1	B1
3	816	A1	B1
4	819	A2	B1
5	813	A2	B1
6	820	A3	B1
7	821	A3	B1
8	806	A4	B1
9	805	A4	B1
10	836	A1	B2
11	828	A1	B2
12	844	A2	B2
13	836	A2	B2
14	814	A3	B2
15	811	A3	B2
16	811	A4	B2
17	806	A4	B2
18	804	A1	B3
19	808	A1	B3
20	807	A2	B3
21	819	A2	B3
22	819	A3	B3
23	829	A3	B3
24	827	A4	B3
25	835	A4	B3
26			

```
library(tidyverse)
library(pander)
library(readxl)
mydata <- read_excel ("C:/Users/jcmun/Desktop/myanovatwowaydata.xlsx")
summary(mydata)
pander(summary(aov(Values ~ FactorA*FactorB, data=mydata)))
```

Console output:

```
> library(tidyverse)
> library(pander)
> library(readxl)
> mydata <- read_excel ("C:/Users/jcmun/Desktop/myanovatwowaydata.xlsx")
> summary(mydata)
    Values          FactorA            FactorB
 Min.   :804.0   Length:24          Length:24
 1st Qu.:807.8   Class :character   Class :character
 Median :817.5   Mode  :character   Mode  :character
 Mean   :818.2
 3rd Qu.:827.2
 Max.   :844.0
> pander(summary(aov(Values ~ FactorA*FactorB, data=mydata)))
```

	Df	Sum Sq	Mean Sq	F value	Pr(>F)
FactorA	3	232.5	77.5	2.784	0.08641
FactorB	2	421	210.5	7.563	0.007495
FactorA:FactorB	6	2155	359.2	12.9	0.0001281
Residuals	12	334	27.83	NA	NA

Table: Analysis of Variance Model

BIZSTATS (MANOVA)

```
Model Inputs:
VAR9
VAR10; VAR11; VAR12
Category
Treatment 1, Treatment 2, Treatment 3


General Linear Model: MANOVA


                  Stat          F        DF1        DF2     P-
value
Pillai Trace    0.53450     2.02340     9.00      84.00
0.04641
Wilk's Lambda   0.48941     2.40496     9.00      63.43
0.02047
Hotelling Trace 0.99464     2.72605     9.00      74.00
0.00840
Roy's Root      0.94364


Null hypothesis: There is zero mean difference among all the variables.


SSCP Matrix Adjusted for Type (H)
           911.41594           62.97406          162.45969
            62.97406          121.90594           23.64531
           162.45969           23.64531           32.34844


SSCP Matrix Adjusted for Error (E)
          4057.45125          713.71625         -272.65125
           713.71625         2833.98625          122.69375
          -272.65125          122.69375          112.43625


Covariance Matrix
          4968.86719          776.69031         -110.19156
           776.69031         2955.89219          146.33906
          -110.19156          146.33906          144.78469
```

MINITAB (MANOVA)

General Linear Model: Values1, Values2, Values3 versus Treatments

MANOVA Tests for Treatments

Criterion	Test Statistic	Approx F	DF Num	DF Denom	P
Wilks'	0.48941	2.405	9	63	0.021
Lawley-Hotelling	0.99464	2.726	9	74	0.008
Pillai's	0.53450	2.023	9	84	0.046
Roy's	0.94364				

$s = 3$ $m = -0.5$ $n = 12$

SPSS (MANOVA)

General Linear Model: yield, water, herbicide versus Type

MANOVA Tests for Type

Criterion	Test Statistic	Approx F	DF Num	DF Denom	P
Wilks'	0.48941	2.405	9	63	0.021
Lawley-Hotelling	0.99464	2.726	9	74	0.008
Pillai's	0.53450	2.023	9	84	0.046
Roy's	0.94364				

$s = 3$ $m = -0.5$ $n = 12.0$

SSCP Matrix (adjusted) for Type

	yield	water	herbicide
yield	911.42	62.97	162.46
water	62.97	121.91	23.65
herbicide	162.46	23.65	32.35

SSCP Matrix (adjusted) for Error

	yield	water	herbicide
yield	4057.5	713.7	-272.7
water	713.7	2834.0	122.7
herbicide	-272.7	122.7	112.4

Partial Correlations for the Error SSCP Matrix

	yield	water	herbicide
yield	1.00000	0.21047	-0.40367
water	0.21047	1.00000	0.21736
herbicide	-0.40367	0.21736	1.00000

EIGEN Analysis for Type

Eigenvalue	0.9436	0.04531	0.00568
Proportion	0.9487	0.04556	0.00571
Cumulative	0.9487	0.99429	1.00000

Eigenvector	1	2	3
yield	0.015260	-0.003933	0.00911
water	-0.007106	0.018140	0.00611
herbicide	0.095727	0.013190	-0.05156

R (DATA LOAD FOR MANOVA)

```
library(tidyverse)
library(pander)
library(readxl)
mydata <- read_excel ("C:/Users/jcmun/Desktop/mymanovadata.xlsx")
summary(mydata)
pander(summary(manova(cbind(Values1, Values2, Values3) ~ Treatments,
data=mydata)))
```

BIZSTATS (TWO-WAY MANOVA)

MINITAB (TWO-WAY MANOVA)

General Linear Model: kindness, optimism versus gender, economic

MANOVA Tests for gender

Criterion	Test Statistic	F	DF Num	DF Denom	P
Wilks'	0.58825	5.950	2	17	0.011
Lawley-Hotelling	0.69995	5.950	2	17	0.011
Pillai's	0.41175	5.950	2	17	0.011
Roy's	0.69995				

$s = 1$ $m = 0$ $n = 7.5$

MANOVA Tests for economic

Criterion	Test Statistic	F	DF Num	DF Denom	P
Wilks'	0.50412	3.472	4	34	0.018
Lawley-Hotelling	0.94119	3.765	4	32	0.013
Pillai's	0.51728	3.140	4	36	0.026
Roy's	0.89368				

$s = 2$ $m = -0.5$ $n = 7.5$

MANOVA Tests for gender*economic

Criterion	Test Statistic	F	DF Num	DF Denom	P
Wilks'	0.38703	5.163	4	34	0.002
Lawley-Hotelling	1.34909	5.396	4	32	0.002
Pillai's	0.70379	4.887	4	36	0.003
Roy's	1.14396				

$s = 2$ $m = -0.5$ $n = 7.5$

SPSS (TWO-WAY MANOVA)

Multivariate Tests[a]

Effect		Value	F	Hypothesis df	Error df	Sig.
VAR00006	Pillai's Trace	.412	5.950[b]	2.000	17.000	.011
	Wilks' Lambda	.588	5.950[b]	2.000	17.000	.011
	Hotelling's Trace	.700	5.950[b]	2.000	17.000	.011
	Roy's Largest Root	.700	5.950[b]	2.000	17.000	.011
VAR00007	Pillai's Trace	.517	3.140	4.000	36.000	.026
	Wilks' Lambda	.504	3.472[b]	4.000	34.000	.018
	Hotelling's Trace	.941	3.765	4.000	32.000	.013
	Roy's Largest Root	.894	8.043[c]	2.000	18.000	.003
VAR00006 * VAR00007	Pillai's Trace	.704	4.887	4.000	36.000	.003
	Wilks' Lambda	.387	5.163[b]	4.000	34.000	.002
	Hotelling's Trace	1.349	5.396	4.000	32.000	.002
	Roy's Largest Root	1.144	10.296[c]	2.000	18.000	.001

a. Design: VAR00006 + VAR00007 + VAR00006 * VAR00007

b. Exact statistic

c. The statistic is an upper bound on F that yields a lower bound on the significance level.

Tests of Between-Subjects Effects

Source	Dependent Variable	Type III Sum of Squares	df	Mean Square	F	Sig.
Model	VAR00008	661.750[a]	6	110.292	37.282	<.001
	VAR00009	691.250[b]	6	115.208	61.444	<.001
VAR00006	VAR00008	12.042	1	12.042	4.070	.059
	VAR00009	22.042	1	22.042	11.756	.003
VAR00007	VAR00008	28.583	2	14.292	4.831	.021
	VAR00009	23.083	2	11.542	6.156	.009
VAR00006 * VAR00007	VAR00008	11.083	2	5.542	1.873	.182
	VAR00009	36.083	2	18.042	9.622	.001
Error	VAR00008	53.250	18	2.958		
	VAR00009	33.750	18	1.875		
Total	VAR00008	715.000	24			
	VAR00009	725.000	24			

a. R Squared = .926 (Adjusted R Squared = .901)

b. R Squared = .953 (Adjusted R Squared = .938)

BIZSTATS (MULTIPLE LINEAR REGRESSION)

VAR28	VAR29	VAR30	VAR31	VAR32	VAR33
Y	X1	X2	X3	X4	X5
521	18308	185	4.041	79.6	7.2
367	1148	600	0.55	1	8.5
443	18068	372	3.665	32.3	5.7
365	7729	142	2.351	45.1	7.3
614	100484	432	29.76	190.8	7.5
385	16728	290	3.294	31.8	5
286	14630	346	3.287	678.4	6.7
397	4008	328	0.666	340.8	6.2
764	38927	354	12.938	239.6	7.3
427	22322	266	6.478	111.9	5
153	3711	320	1.108	172.5	2.8
231	3136	197	1.007	12.2	6.1
524	50508	266	11.431	205.6	7.1
328	28886	173	5.544	154.6	5.9
240	16996	190	2.777	49.7	4.6
286	13035	239	2.478	30.3	4.4
285	12973	190	3.685	92.8	7.4
569	16309	241	4.22	96.9	7.1
96	5227	189	1.228	39.8	7.5
498	19235	358	4.781	489.2	5.9
481	44487	315	6.016	767.6	9
468	44213	303	9.295	163.6	9.2
177	23619	228	4.375	55	5.1
198	9106	134	2.573	54.9	8.6
458	24917	189	5.117	74.3	6.6
108	3872	196	0.799	5.5	6.9
246	8945	183	1.578	20.5	2.7
291	2373	417	1.202	10.9	5.5
68	7128	233	1.109	123.7	7.2
311	23624	349	7.73	1042	6.6
606	5242	284	1.515	12.5	6.9
512	92629	499	17.99	381	7.2
426	28795	231	6.629	136.1	5.8
47	4487	143	0.639	9.3	4.1
265	48799	249	10.847	264.9	6.4
370	14067	195	3.146	45.8	6.7
312	12693	288	2.842	29.6	6
222	62184	229	11.882	265.1	6.9
280	9153	287	1.003	960.3	8.5
759	14250	224	3.487	115.8	6.2
114	3680	161	0.696	9.2	3.4
419	18063	221	4.877	118.3	6.6
435	65112	237	16.987	64.9	6.6
186	11340	220	1.723	21	4.9
87	4553	185	0.563	60.8	6.4
188	28960	260	6.187	156.3	5.8
303	19201	261	4.867	73.1	6.3
102	7533	118	1.793	74.5	10.5
127	26343	268	4.892	90.1	5.4
251	1641	300	0.454	4.7	5.1

[EXAMPLE] - ROV Biz Stats

File   Data   Language   Help

STEP 1: Data   Manually enter your data, paste from another application, or load an example dataset with analysis

STEP 2: Analysis   Choose analysis and enter parameters required (see example inputs below)

Dataset   Visualize   Command   View: All Methods

N	VAR28	VAR29	VAR30	VAR31	VAR32	VAR33	VAR34	VAR35	VAR36	VAR
NOTES	Y	X1	X2	X3	X4	X5	Type 1	Type 2	Type 3	Type
1	521	18308	185	4.041	79.6	7.2	6	8	3	5
2	367	1148	600	0.55	1	8.5	6	7	3	4
3	443	18068	372	3.665	32.3	5.7	5	7	1	4
4	365	7729	142	2.351	45.1	7.3	10	9	8	4
5	614	100484	432	29.76	190.8	7.5	7	9	7	6
6	385	16728	290	3.294	31.8	5	6	6	3	9
7	286	14630	346	3.287	678.4	6.7	5	8	6	7

Hotelling T-Square: 2 VAR Indep. Equal Variance with Related Measures
Hotelling T-Square: 2 VAR Indep. Unequal Variance with Related Measures
Inter-rater Reliability: Cohen's Kappa
Inter-rater Reliability: Inter Class Correlation (ICC)
Inter-rater Reliability: Kendall's W (No Ties)
Inter-rater Reliability: Kendall's W (With Ties)
Inter-rater Reliability: Kuder-Richardson
Internal Consistency Reliability: Cronbach's Alpha (Dichotomous Data)
Internal Consistency Reliability: Guttman's Lambda and Spilt Half Model
Kendall's Tau Correlation (No Ties)
Kendall's Tau Correlation (With Ties)
Linear Interpolation
Logistic S Curve
Mahalanobis Distance
Markov Chain
Markov Chain Transition Risk Matrix
Multiple Poisson Regression (Population and Frequency)
Multiple Regression (Deming Regression with Known Variance)
Multiple Regression (Linear)
Multiple Regression (Nonlinear)

VAR28
VAR29:VAR33

Dependent Variable, Independent Variables:
> Var1
> Var2; Var3; Var4

Runs a multiple linear regression.

STEP 3: Run   [Run]   Run the current analysis in Step 2 or the selected saved analysis in Step 4; view the results, charts and statistics; copy the results and charts to clipboard; or generate reports

● Use All Data
○ Use Rows   1 ~ 20

[Copy]   [Report]

☑ Show Input Variables

STEP 4: Save (Optional)
You can save multiple analyses and notes in the profile for future retrieval

Results   Charts

● Show New Results Only   ○ Append Results at the End

```
OVERALL FIT
Multiple R             0.57203   Maximum Log Likelihood          -318.17341
R-Square               0.32721   Akaike Info Criterion (AIC)       12.96694
Adjusted R-Square      0.25076   Bayes Schwarz Criterion (BSC)     13.19638
Standard Error       149.67200   Hannan-Quinn Criterion (HQC)      13.05431
Observations                50   Cohen's F-Squared                  0.48636

              Coeff   Std. Error   T-stat    P-value   Lower 5%    Upper 95%   Std. Beta
Intercept   57.95550  108.79014   0.53273   0.59690  -161.29661   277.20762
VAR X1      -0.00354    0.00352   -1.00656   0.31965    -0.01064     0.00355   -0.44890
VAR X2       0.46437    0.25353    1.83159   0.07379    -0.04659     0.97533    0.25179
VAR X3      25.23770   14.11723    1.78772   0.08071    -3.21371    53.68911    0.79688
VAR X4      -0.00856    0.10156   -0.08433   0.93317    -0.21325     0.19612   -0.01165
VAR X5      16.55792   14.79957    1.11881   0.26929   -13.26866    46.38449    0.14710
```

Name: Multiple Regression (Linear)
Notes:

[ADD]   [EDIT]   [DEL]   [Save]   [Exit]

Mahalanobis Distance
Markov Chain
Markov Chain Transition Matrix
Multiple Poisson Regression (Population and Freq)
Multiple Regression (Deming Regression Known V...
Multiple Regression (Linear)
Multiple Regression (Nonlinear)
Multiple Regression (Ordinal Logistic)
Multiple Regression (Through Origin)
Multiple Regression (2VAR Functional Forms)
Multiple Ridge Regression (High VIF Bias)

MINITAB (MULTIPLE LINEAR REGRESSION)

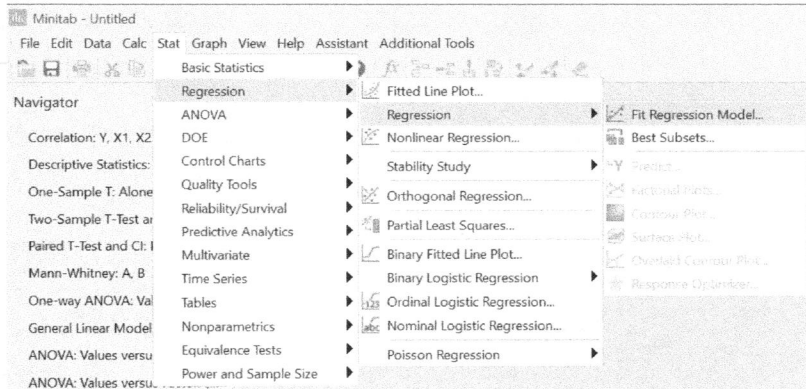

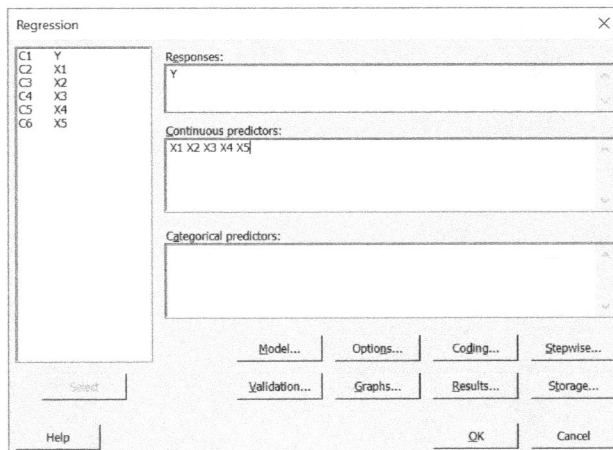

Regression Analysis: Y versus X1, X2, X3, X4, X5

Regression Equation

Y = 58 - 0.00354 X1 + 0.464 X2 + 25.2 X3 - 0.009 X4 + 16.6 X5

Coefficients

Term	Coef	SE Coef	T-Value	P-Value	VIF
Constant	58	109	0.53	0.597	
X1	-0.00354	0.00352	-1.01	0.320	13.01
X2	0.464	0.254	1.83	0.074	1.24
X3	25.2	14.1	1.79	0.081	12.99
X4	-0.009	0.102	-0.08	0.933	1.25
X5	16.6	14.8	1.12	0.269	1.13

Model Summary

S	R-sq	R-sq(adj)	R-sq(pred)
149.672	32.72%	25.08%	6.38%

Analysis of Variance

Source	DF	Adj SS	Adj MS	F-Value	P-Value
Regression	5	479388	95877.7	4.28	0.003
X1	1	22696	22696.4	1.01	0.320
X2	1	75152	75151.7	3.35	0.074
X3	1	71595	71594.8	3.20	0.081
X4	1	159	159.3	0.01	0.933
X5	1	28041	28041.1	1.25	0.269
Error	44	985675	22401.7		
Total	49	1465064			

R (MULTIPLE LINEAR REGRESSION)

```
library(tidyverse)
library(pander)
library(readxl)
mydata <- read_excel ("C:/Users/jcmun/Desktop/myregressiondata.xlsx")
summary(mydata)
pander(summary(lm(formula=Y~X1+X2+X3+X4+X5, data=mydata)))
```

BIZSTATS (MULTIPLE NONLINEAR REGRESSION)

[EXAMPLE] - ROV Biz Stats

File Data Language Help

STEP 1: Data   Manually enter your data, paste from another application, or load an example dataset with analysis

Example

STEP 2: Analysis   Choose analysis and enter parameters required (see example inputs below)

Dataset Visualize Command

Visualize

View   All Methods

N	VAR28	VAR29	VAR30	VAR31	VAR32	VAR33	VAR34	VAR35	VAR36	VAR
NOTES	Y	X1	X2	X3	X4	X5	Type 1	Type 2	Type 3	Type
1	521	18308	185	4.041	79.6	7.2	6	8	3	5
2	367	1148	600	0.55	1	8.5	6	7	3	4
3	443	18068	372	3.665	32.3	5.7	5	7	1	4
4	365	7729	142	2.351	45.1	7.3	10	9	8	4
5	614	100484	432	29.76	190.8	7.5	7	9	7	6
6	385	16728	290	3.294	31.8	5	6	6	3	9
7	286	14630	346	3.287	678.4	6.7	5	8	6	7

Inter-rater Reliability: Cohen's Kappa
Inter-rater Reliability: Inter Class Correlation (ICC)
Inter-rater Reliability: Kendall's W (No Ties)
Inter-rater Reliability: Kendall's W (With Ties)
Inter-rater Reliability: Kuder-Richardson
Internal Consistency Reliability: Cronbach's Alpha (Dichotomous Data)
Internal Consistency Reliability: Guttman's Lambda and Split Half Model
Kendall's Tau Correlation (No Ties)
Kendall's Tau Correlation (With Ties)
Linear Interpolation
Logistic S Curve
Mahalanobis Distance
Markov Chain
Markov Chain Transition Risk Matrix
Multiple Poisson Regression (Population and Frequency)
Multiple Regression (Deming Regression with Known Variance)
Multiple Regression (Linear)
Multiple Regression (Nonlinear)
Multiple Regression (Ordered Multinomial Logistic Regression)
Multiple Regression (Through Origin)

VAR28
VAR29:VAR33

Dependent Variable, Independent Variables:
> Var1
> Var2; Var3; Var4

STEP 3: Run

Run

Run the current analysis in Step 2 or the selected saved analysis in Step 4; view the results, charts, and statistics; copy the results and charts to clipboard; or generate reports

Copy

Report

Runs a multiple nonlinear regression.

○ Use All Data
○ Use Rows   1 ~ 20

Results Charts

☑ Show Input Variables

STEP 4: Save (Optional)
You can save multiple analyses and notes in the profile for future retrieval

○ Show New Results Only   ○ Append Results at the End

Regression Results

OVERALL FIT
Multiple R   0.66490   Maximum Log Likelihood   -313.49239
R-Square   0.44210   Akaike Info Criterion (AIC)   12.77970
Adjusted R-Square   0.37870   Bayes Schwarz Criterion (BSC)   13.00914
Standard Error   136.29559   Hannan-Quinn Criterion (HQC)   12.86707
Observations   50   Cohen's F-Squared   0.79242

	Coeff	Std. Error	T-stat	P-value	Lower 5%	Upper 95%	Std. Beta
Intercept	98.92897	844.72688	0.11711	0.90730	-1603.50617	1801.36412	
VAR X1	-91.46394	77.75790	-1.17627	0.24581	-248.17469	65.24681	-0.54387
VAR X2	139.51590	63.57364	2.19456	0.03352	11.39165	267.64015	0.27105
VAR X3	165.97844	74.25607	2.23522	0.03053	16.32517	315.63170	0.97706
VAR X4	-1.71352	19.32712	-0.08866	0.92976	-40.66477	37.23774	-0.01430
VAR X5	86.05091	77.47353	1.11071	0.27272	-70.08673	242.18856	0.13382

Name: Multiple Regression (Nonlinear)
Notes:

ADD
EDIT
DEL
Save

Mahalanobis Distance
Markov Chain
Markov Chain Transition Matrix
Multiple Poisson Regression (Population and Freq)
Multiple Regression (Deming Regression Known V...
Multiple Regression (Linear)
Multiple Regression (Nonlinear)
Multiple Regression (Ordinal Logistic)
Multiple Regression (Through Origin)
Multiple Regression (2VAR Functional Forms)
Multiple Ridge Regression (High VIF Bias)

Exit

MINITAB (MULTIPLE NONLINEAR REGRESSION)

Minitab - Untitled

File Edit Data Calc Stat Graph View Help Assistant Additional Tools

Navigator

One-way ANOVA: Response versus...
Regression Analysis: C1 versus C2, ...
Discriminant Analysis: job versus o...
Discriminant Analysis: job versus o...
Discriminant Analysis: job versus o...
Regression Analysis: Y versus X1, X...
Regression Analysis: Y versus X1, X...

Regression Analysis: Y vers... ✓ ×

WORKSHEET 1

Regression Analysis: Y versus X1, X2, X3, X4, X5

Regression Equation

$Y = 99 - 91.5 X1 + 139.5 X2 + 166.0 X3 - 1.7 X4 + 86.1 X5$

Coefficients

Term	Coef	SE Coef	T-Value	P-Value	VIF
Constant	99	845	0.12	0.907	
X1	-91.5	77.8	-1.18	0.246	16.86
X2	139.5	63.6	2.19	0.034	1.20
X3	166.0	74.3	2.24	0.031	15.07
X4	-1.7	19.3	-0.09	0.930	2.05
X5	86.1	77.5	1.11	0.273	1.14

Model Summary

S	R-sq	R-sq(adj)	R-sq(pred)
136.296	44.21%	37.87%	31.39%

Analysis of Variance

Source	DF	Adj SS	Adj MS	F-Value	P-Value
Regression	5	647698	129540	6.97	0.000
X1	1	25702	25702	1.38	0.246
X2	1	89466	89466	4.82	0.034
X3	1	92812	92812	5.00	0.031
X4	1	146	146	0.01	0.930
X5	1	22918	22918	1.23	0.273

Data will have to be first pre-processed:

↓	C1	C2	C3	C4	C5	C6
	Y	X1	X2	X3	X4	X5
1	521	9.8151	5.22036	1.39649	4.37701	1.97408
2	367	7.0458	6.39693	-0.59784	0.00000	2.14007
3	443	9.8019	5.91889	1.29883	3.47507	1.74047
4	365	8.9527	4.95583	0.85484	3.80888	1.98787
5	614	11.5178	6.06843	3.39317	5.25123	2.01490
6	385	9.7248	5.66988	1.19210	3.45947	1.60944
7	286	9.5908	5.84644	1.18998	6.51974	1.90211
8	397	8.2960	5.79301	-0.40647	5.83130	1.82455
9	764	10.5694	5.86930	2.56017	5.47897	1.98787
10	427	10.0133	5.58350	1.86841	4.71761	1.60944
11	153	8.2191	5.76832	0.10256	5.15040	1.02962
12	231	8.0507	5.28320	0.00698	2.50144	1.80829
13	524	10.8299	5.58350	2.43633	5.32593	1.96009
14	328	10.2711	5.15329	1.71272	5.04084	1.77495
15	240	9.7407	5.24702	1.02137	3.90600	1.52606
16	286	9.4754	5.47646	0.90745	3.41115	1.48160
17	285	9.4706	5.24702	1.30427	4.53045	2.00148
18	569	9.6995	5.48480	1.43984	4.57368	1.96009
19	96	8.5616	5.24175	0.20539	3.68387	2.01490

R (MULTIPLE NONLINEAR REGRESSION)

```
library(tidyverse)
library(pander)
library(readxl)
mydata <- read_excel ("C:/Users/jcmun/Desktop/myregressiondata.xlsx")
summary(mydata)
summary(lm(formula=Y~log(X1)+log(X2)+log(X3)+log(X4)+log(X5), data=mydata))
```

Console output:

```
> summary(mydata)
      Y             X1            X2            X3            X4            X5
Min.   : 47.0  Min.   : 1148  Min.   :118.0  Min.   : 0.454  Min.   :   1.00  Min.   : 2.700
1st Qu.:204.0  1st Qu.: 7229  1st Qu.:191.2  1st Qu.: 1.300  1st Qu.:  31.93  1st Qu.: 5.550
Median :307.0  Median :15470  Median :240.0  Median : 3.390  Median :  77.05  Median : 6.500
Mean   :331.9  Mean   :21668  Mean   :261.7  Mean   : 4.962  Mean   : 166.12  Mean   : 6.366
3rd Qu.:441.0  3rd Qu.:25987  3rd Qu.:302.2  3rd Qu.: 5.898  3rd Qu.: 170.28  3rd Qu.: 7.200
Max.   :764.0  Max.   :100484 Max.   :600.0  Max.   :29.760  Max.   :1042.00  Max.   :10.500
> pander(summary(lm(formula=Y~log(X1)+log(X2)+log(X3)+log(X4)+log(X5), data=mydata)))
```

	Estimate	Std. Error	t value	Pr(>|t|)
(Intercept)	98.93	844.7	0.1171	0.9073
log(X1)	-91.46	77.76	-1.176	0.2458
log(X2)	139.5	63.57	2.195	0.03352
log(X3)	166	74.26	2.235	0.03053
log(X4)	-1.714	19.33	-0.08866	0.9298
log(X5)	86.05	77.47	1.111	0.2727

Observations	Residual Std. Error	R^2	Adjusted R^2
50	136.3	0.4421	0.3787

Table: Fitting linear model: Y ~ log(X1) + log(X2) + log(X3) + log(X4) + log(X5)

BIZSTATS (REGRESSION THROUGH THE ORIGIN)

R (REGRESSION THROUGH THE ORIGIN)

```
library(tidyverse)
library(pander)
library(readxl)
mydata <- read_excel
("C:/Users/jcmun/Desktop/myregressiondata.xlsx")
summary(model <- lm(mydata$Y ~ 0 + mydata$X1))
anova(model)
```

BIZSTATS (LOGISTIC REGRESSION)

MINITAB (LOGISTIC REGRESSION)

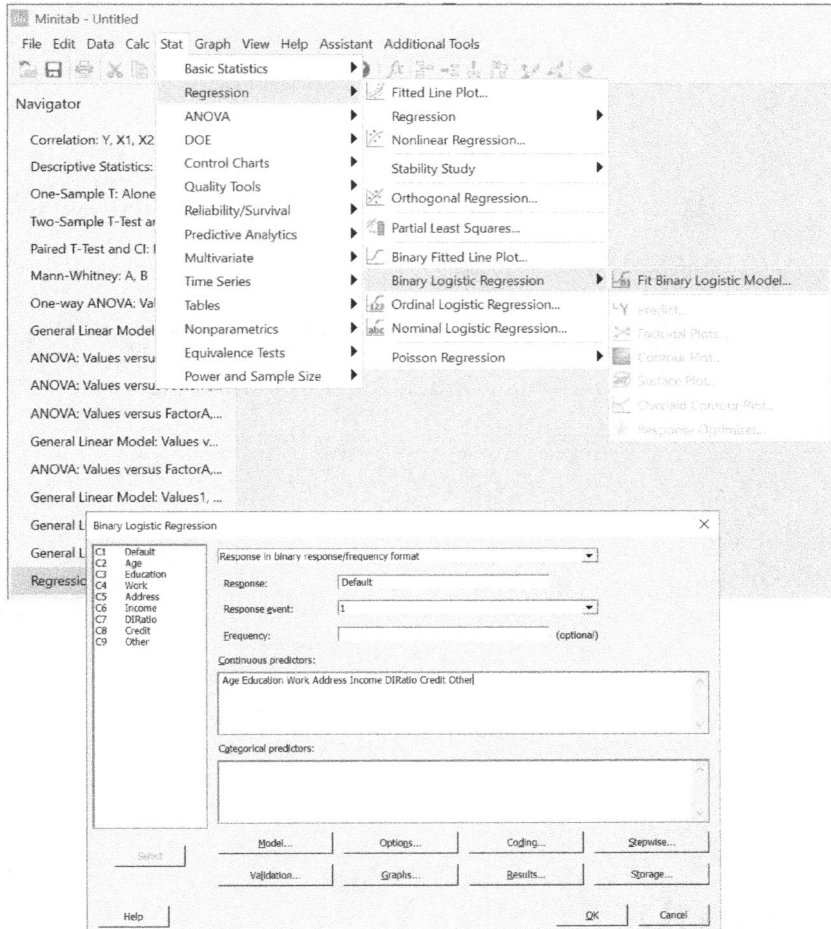

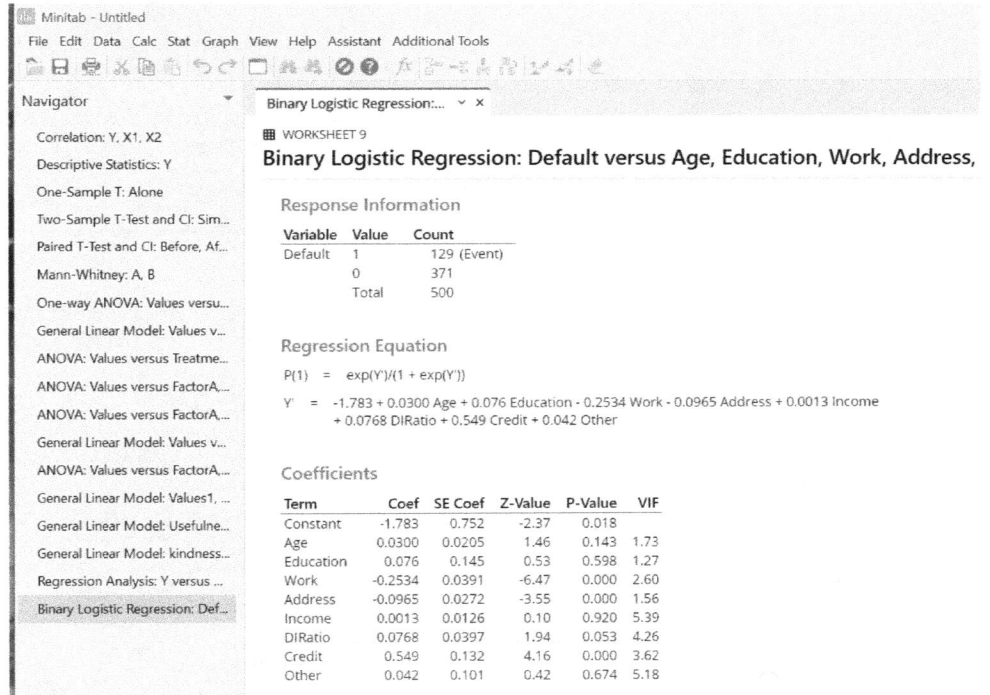

R (LOGISTIC REGRESSION)

```
library(tidyverse)
library(pander)
library(readxl)
mydata <- read_excel ("C:/Users/jcmun/Desktop/mylogitdata.xlsx")
summary(glm(data=mydata, Default~., family = "binomial"))
```

R (USING I() IN CUSTOM NONLINEAR REGRESSION)

R (USING : IN INTERACTION ECONOMETRIC MODELS)

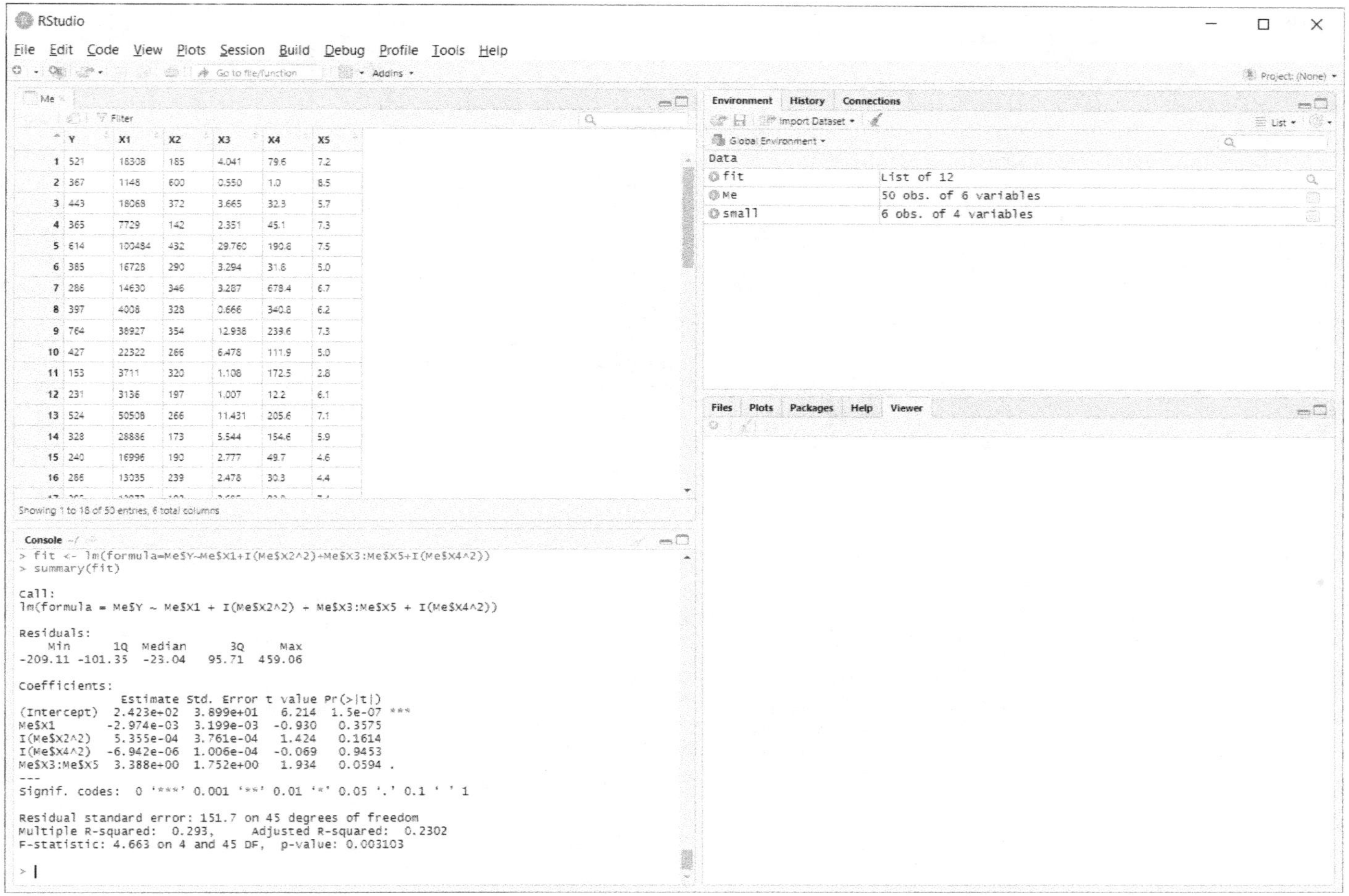

R (BASIC DATA MANIPULATION)

# Setting main working directory:
setwd("M:/Software/R")

# Quick data and analysis:
age <- c(1,3,5,2,11,9,3,9,12,3)
weight <- c(4.4,5.3,7.2,5.2,8.5,7.3,6.0,10.4,10.2,6.1)
mean(weight)
cor(age,weight)
plot(age,weight)

#Creating your own data matrix:
x <- matrix(1:10, nrow=2)
x

```
        [,1] [,2] [,3] [,4] [,5]
[1,]   1    3    5    7    9
[2,]   2    4    6    8    10
```

x[2,]

```
2 4 6 8 10
```

x[,2]

```
3 4
```

x[1,4]

```
7
```

x[1,c(4,5)]

```
7 9
```

dim1 <- c("A1", "A2")
dim2 <- c("B1", "B2", "B3")
dim3 <- c("C1", "C2", "C3", "C4")
z <- array(1:24, c(2,3,4), dimnames=list(dim1, dim2, dim3))
z

```
, , C1                          , , C3

   B1 B2 B3                        B1 B2 B3
A1  1  3  5                     A1 13 15 17
A2  2  4  6                     A2 14 16 18

, , C2                          , , C4

   B1 B2 B3                        B1 B2 B3
A1  7  9 11                     A1 19 21 23
A2  8 10 12                     A2 20 22 24
```

R (BASIC DATA MANIPULATION)

# Manually generate data variables and then edit them:
mydata <- data.frame(age=numeric(0), gender=character(0), weight=numeric(0))
mydata <- edit(mydata) # This opens an editable table (see screenshot)

# Read existing CSV file and see the data:
read.csv("C:/Users/jcmun/Desktop/mysampledata.csv")
mydata <- read.table("C:/Users/jcmun/Desktop/mysampledata.csv", header=TRUE, sep=",")
summary(mydata)
str(mydata)
print(mydata)

R (BASIC DATA MANIPULATION)

library(readxl)
Me <- read_excel("C:/Users/jcmun/Desktop/mysampledata.xlsx")
view(Me)
mean(Me$age)
mean(Me$weight)
sd(Me$weight)
summary(Me)

It is simpler to use RStudio to import dataset and databases

	A	B	C
1	age	gender	weight
2	10	male	85
3	11	male	90
4	15	female	90
5	16	female	110
6	18	male	145
7	20	female	110

19. Capital Budgeting and Portfolio Optimization

Dr. Johnathan Mun, Professor of Research
Quantitative Research Methods Course Slides
Seventh Edition, 2026, ROV Press

Why Is Risk Important?

Name of Project	Cost	Returns	Risk
Project X	$50	$50	$25
Project Y	$250	$200	$200
Project Z	$100	$100	$10

Project X for the Cost- and Budget-Constrained Manager

Project Y for the Returns-Driven and Non-Resource-Constrained Manager

Project Z for the Risk-Averse Manager

Project Z for the Smart Manager

WHY?

Name of Project	Cost	Returns	Risk
Project X	$50	$50	$25
Project Y	$250	$200	$200
Project Z	$100	$100	$10

Adding an Element of Risk...

Looking at Bang for the Buck, X (2), Y (1), Z (10), Project Z should be chosen... with a $1,000 budget, the following can be obtained:

Project X: 20 Project Xs returning $1,000, with $500 risk
Project Y: 4 Project Ys returning $800, with $800 risk
Project Z: 10 Project Zs returning $1,000, with $100 risk

Project X: For each $1 return, $0.5 risk is taken
Project Y: For each $1 return, $1.0 risk is taken
Project Z: For each $1 return, $0.1 risk is taken

Project X: For each $1 of risk taken, $2 return is obtained
Project Y: For each $1 of risk taken, $1 return is obtained
Project Z: For each $1 of risk taken, $10 return is obtained

Conclusion:
Risk is important. Forgoing risks results in making the wrong decision.

Diversifying Risk

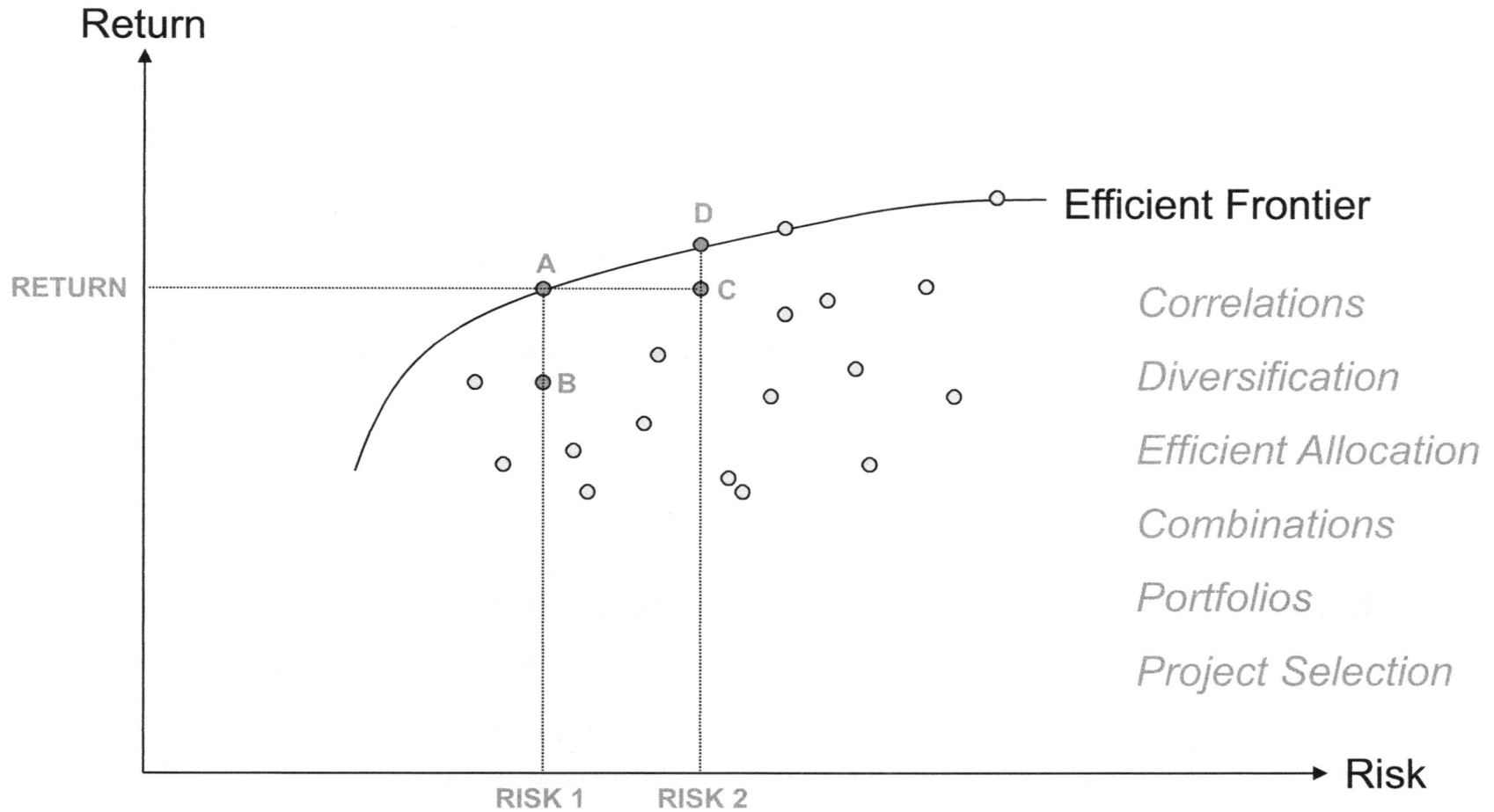

What does this picture tell you?

Potential Value Metrics: Operational/Logistics

- **Inherent Availability** (IA). Measures operational percentage in an ideal support environment per design specifications.

$$IA = \frac{MTBF}{MTBF+MTTR}$$

- **Effective Availability** (EA). Probability a ship's system is available at any instant during the maximum operational period, accounting for all critical failures, reparable and nonrepairable at sea, and preventive maintenance.

$$EA = 1 - \frac{MTTR}{MTBF+MTTR} - \frac{MDT}{MT} - 0.5\frac{MT}{MTTF}$$

- **Mission Reliability** (MR). Operational Ready Rate (ORR) at the start of a mission compared to its Inherent Reliability (IR).

$$MR = ORR * IR$$

- **Operational Dependability** (OD). Probability a system can be used to perform a specified mission when desired.

$$OD = \frac{MTTF}{MTBF}$$

- **Mean Down Time** (MDT), **Mean Maintenance Time** (MMT), **Logistics Delay Time** (LDT). and their combinations.

- **Achieved Availability** (AA), **Operational Availability** (OA), **Mission Availability** (MA)

- Others… TBD based on research to be performed.

Potential Value Metrics: Financial/Economics

- **Cost Deterrence and Avoidance**. Soft or shadow-revenue (cost savings) over the economic and operational life of the program or system. Milestone A, B, C.

- Traditional Financial Metrics. **Net Present Value** (NPV), **Internal Rate of Return** (IRR), **Return on Investment** (ROI), and other metrics, as long as there are financial and monetary values.

- **Budget Constraint**. FY Budget limitations and probabilities of budgetary overruns.

- **Total Ownership Cost** (TOC) and **Total Lifecycle Cost** (TLC). Accounting for the cost of developing, producing, deploying, maintaining, operating, and disposing of a system over its entire lifespan. Uses **Work Breakout Structures** (WBS), **Cost Estimating Categories** (CEC), and **Cost Element Structures** (CES).

- **Knowledge Value Added** (KVA). Monetizing **Learning Time**, **Number of Times Executed**, **Automation**, **Training Time**, and **Knowledge Content**.

- Others… TBD based on research to be performed.

Potential Value Metrics: Strategic & Capability

- Multiple value metrics can be determined from **Subject Matter Experts** (SME):
  - **Expected Military Value**
  - **Strategic Value**
  - **Future Weapon Strategy**
  - Others… TBD based on research to be performed.
- **Capability Measures** (CM). Difficult to quantify and needs SME judgment:
  - Innovation Index, Conversion Capability, Ability to Meet Future Threats
  - Force Structure (size/units), Modernization (technical sophistication), Combat Readiness, Sustainability
  - Future Readiness (ability to meet evolving threats, ability to integrate future weapons systems)
- **Domain Capabilities** (DC)
  - Portfolios are divided into different domains, and each domain is optimized separately, and then combined into the enterprise level and re-optimized; for example, Coastal Defense, Anti-Air Surface Warfare, Anti-Surface Warfare, Anti-Submarine Warfare, Naval Strike, Multi-Mission Air Control, Sea Control, Deep Strike, Missile Defense, etc.
  - We can add constraints whereby each domain needs to have a minimum amount of capability or systems, and within each domain, we can utilize different "value" parameters.

Recommended Approach

- Review approaches (e.g., Preference Ranking Organization Methods for Enrichment Evaluations [PROMETHEE], Elimination and Choice Expressing the Reality [ELECTRE] Methods, Multi-Criteria Analysis [MCA], Portfolio Optimization, Hierarchical Scoring-Ranking, etc.).

- Provide recommendations for methodology and military value (something that has consensus from decision makers with practical applications and reusability across domains).

- Obtain SME estimates to run case examples. We create the engine (methods and models) but require the fuel (data) to make it run.

- Come up with several methodologies to triangulate a consensus portfolio that reduces game-playing or gaming the system/model. We compare results from multiple approaches to develop a consensus portfolio.

- Compare the results with heuristics such as a commander's estimates of nominal capability requirements to support specific missions.

- Need to also consider World Scenarios (peace, war); Military Outcomes Strategy (nation building, deterrence, innovation, evolving threats); and Domains (balancing force structure: surface, undersea, air, training, future weapons, missile defense) to determine Value Measures (effectiveness and lethality measures depend on war gaming outcomes) that roll up into the Enterprise Level.

Integrated Risk Management Process

1 QUALITATIVE MANAGEMENT SCREENING

RISK IDENTIFICATION

A
B
C
D

Start with a list of projects or strategies to be evaluated that have already been through qualitative screening…

2 FORECAST PREDICTION MODELING

RISK PREDICTION

Back-fitting, Forecasting, and Scenario Analysis

ARIMA, GARCH, Fuzzy Logic, Markov Chains, Time Series Models…

…with the assistance of forecasting algorithms, future outcomes can be predicted…

3 BASE CASE STATIC MODELS

RISK MODELING

Traditional analysis stops here!

…create traditional static base case financial or economic models for each project…

4 DYNAMIC MONTE CARLO RISK SIMULATION

RISK ANALYSIS

Simulate thousands of scenario outcomes

Tornado   Simulation

…Tornado analysis identifies critical success factors, then dynamic sensitivities and Monte Carlo risk simulations are run…

5 REAL OPTIONS PROBLEM FRAMING

RISK MITIGATION

Strategy Trees

Dynamic Decision Trees

…strategic real options are framed to hedge and mitigate downside risks and take advantage of upside potential…

6 REAL OPTIONS VALUATION AND MODELING

RISK HEDGING

Simulation

$$\frac{\delta S}{S} = \mu \delta t + \sigma \varepsilon \sqrt{\delta t}$$

Differential Equations

Binomial Lattices

…the real options are valued using binomial lattices and closed-form partial-differential models with simulation…

7 PORTFOLIO AND RESOURCE OPTIMIZATION

RISK DIVERSIFICATION

Efficient Frontier

Delay cost
Other opportunities
Loss revenues
Loss cost reduction

Revenue enhancement
Cost reduction
Strategic options value
Strategic competitiveness

Constrained Allocations → Decision ← Competing Objectives

…stochastic optimization on multiple projects for efficient asset allocation subject to resource constraints…

8 REPORTS, PRESENTATION, AND UPDATES

RISK MANAGEMENT

Revenue enhancement
Cost reduction
Strategic options value
Strategic competitiveness

…create reports, make decisions, and update analysis iteratively when uncertainty is resolved over time…

Time Value of Money

- Most financial decisions involve situations in which someone pays money at one point in time and receives money at some later time. The values of dollars paid or received at two different points in time are different; that is, the value of money changes over time. This difference in value is recognized and accounted for by *Time Value of Money* (TVM) analysis.

- *Compounding* is the process of determining the Future Value (FV) of a cash flow or a series of cash flows. The compounded amount, or future value, is equal to the beginning amount plus the interest earned.

- *Discounting* is the process of finding the Present Value (PV) of a future cash flow or a series of cash flows; it is the reciprocal, or reverse, of compounding.

- Future Value and Present Value are the basic building blocks.

- Given any three of the four (PV, FV, i, n) variables, you can solve for the missing variable. (Note that there will be a fifth variable, PMT, coming up shortly in the annuities section).

Future Value

As an example, if you saved $100 today in a savings account yielding 5% a year, how much will you have at the end of 3 years?

DEFINITIONS:

o   *FV*: Future Value amount (the amount you will have in the future, sometimes denoted with a subscript n to indicate n-periods into the future).

o   *n*: Some time period n in the future. (This can be hours, days, months, quarters, years, etc., but to get started, we will simplify and use *years*. Later, we will run different compounding periods.)

o   *i*: Interest rate or discount rate, the rate used to compound the value to the future, or to discount a future value to the present.

o   *PV*: Present Value amount (the amount you currently have, sometimes denoted with a subscript 0 to indicate time zero, or now).

o   *FVIF*: Future Value Interest Factor (usually for a combination of specific time n and interest rate i denoted as subscripts). This is the FV of one unit ($1) of some present value for some time and interest rate.

o   *PVIF*: Present Value Interest Factor (usually for a combination of specific time n and interest rate i denoted as subscripts). This is the PV of one unit ($1) of some future value for some time and interest rate.

Year 0	Year 1	Year2	Year 3

PV = 100

$FV_1 = 100(1+0.05)$
$= 105$

$FV_1 = PV(1+i)^1$

$FV_2 = 100(1+0.05)(1+0.05)$
$= PV(1+0.05)^2$
$= 110.25$

$FV_2 = PV(1+i)^2$

$FV_3 = 100(1+0.05)(1+0.05)(1+0.05)$
$= PV(1+0.05)^3$
$= 115.76$

$FV_3 = PV(1+i)^3$

$$FV_3 = FV_2(1+i)^1 = FV_1(1+i)^1(1+i)^1 = PV_0(1+i)^1(1+i)^1(1+i)^1 = PV_0(1+i)^3$$

This conforms to the equation: $FV_n = PV_0(1+i)^n = PV_0[FVIF_{i,n}]$

As another example, we can compute FV manually (using Excel, of course, but entering the equations manually) or using Excel's *FV* function:

	A	B	C	D	E	F
1	1. How much would you have if you invested $1000 now for 5 years at 10% per year.					
2						
3		Hard way:	$ 1,610.51	<<< Equation: =1000*(1+0.1)^5		
4						
5		PV	-1000			
6	Solve:	FV	$1,610.51	<<< Excel: =FV(C8,C7,C9,C5)		
7		N	5			
8		INT	10%			
9		PMT	0			

Present Value

Similarly, we can compute the PV manually as well as by using Excel's *PV* function:

	A	B	C	D	E	F	G
12	2. You need to save enough right now to buy a car in 10 years that costs $50,000 at a savings rate of 7%.						
13	How much do you need to save today?						
14							
15		Hard way:	$ 25,417.46	<<< Equation: =50000/(1+0.07)^10			
16							
17	Solve:	PV	($25,417.46)	<<< Excel: =PV(C20,C19,C21,C18)			
18		FV	$50,000.00				
19		N	10				
20		INT	7%				
21		PMT	0				

$$PV_0 = \frac{FV_n}{(1+i)^n} = \frac{50,000}{(1+0.07)^{10}} = 25,417.46$$

Questions:

1. Why are cells C5 and C17 in the previous two figures negative values?
2. If we wanted the result to be positive (such that it matches the manual result and to have it make more sense), what do we need to do?
3. What is PMT?
4. Why is PMT set to 0 for the two examples above?

Rate of Return and Interest Rates

As mentioned, given any four out of the five variables, we can compute the missing variable. The next example below shows how Interest Rate i can be computed.

	A	B	C	D	E	F	G
23	3. What investment interest rate would I need if I have $100,000 now and want to have $2 Million in 15 years?						
24							
25		Hard way:	22.1055%	<<< Equation: =10^(LOG(-C28/C27)/C29)-1			
26							
27		PV	($100,000.00)				
28		FV	$2,000,000.00				
29		N	15				
30	Solve:	INT	22.1055%	<<< Excel: =RATE(C27,C29,C25,C26)			
31		PMT	0				

Now, how about doing this manually?
$FV = PV(1 + i)^n$
$2,000,000 = 100,000(1 + i)^{15}$
$20 = (1+i)^{15}$
$\log(20) = 15 \log(1 + i)$
$\log(20) / 15 = \log(1 + i) = 0.086735$
$10^{0.086735} = (1 + i) = 1.221055$
$i = 1.221055 - 1 = 0.221055 = \mathbf{22.1055\%}$
This can be summarized as $=10^\wedge(LOG(-C28/C27)/C29)-1$ as seen above.

$$i = 10^{\log\left[\frac{-FV_n}{PV_0}\right]/n} - 1$$

Investment Periods

Similarly, we can compute the *n* manually as well as by using Excel's *NPER* function:

	A	B	C	D	E	F	G
33	4. Suppose you want to have a $2,000,000 retirement amount in the future and currently have $500,000 invested in						
34	a guaranteed fund paying 7% per year before taxes. How long do you have to wait before you can retire?						
35							
36		Hard way:	20.4895	<<< Equation: = LOG(-C39/C38)/LOG(1+C41)			
37							
38		PV	($500,000.00)				
39		FV	$2,000,000.00				
40		N	20.4895	<<< Excel: =NPER(C41,C42,C38,C39)			
41	Solve:	INT	7%				
42		PMT	0				

$$FV = PV(1 + i)^n$$
$$2{,}000{,}000 = 500{,}000(1 + 0.07)^n$$
$$4 = 1.07^n$$
$$\log(4) = n \log(1.07)$$
$$n = \log(4) / \log(1.07) = \textbf{20.4895 Years}$$

This can be summarized as = *LOG(−C39/C38)/LOG(1+C41)* as seen above.

$$n = \frac{\log\left[\frac{FV_n}{PV_0}\right]}{\log(1 + i)}$$

Multiple Cash Flows and Annuities

- An annuity is defined as a series of equal periodic payments (PMT) for a specified number of periods. We can compute both the FV and PV of an annuity.
- An annuity whose payments occur at the end of each period is called an **ordinary** annuity.

$$FVA_n = PMT_1(1+i)^4 + PMT_2(1+i)^3 + PMT_3(1+i)^2 + PMT_4(1+i)^1 + PMT_5(1+i)^0$$

Since this is an annuity,

$$PMT_1 = PMT_2 = PMT_3 = PMT_4 = PMT_5$$

$$FVA_n = PMT\left[\sum_{t=1}^{n}(1+i)^{n-t}\right] = PMT\left[\frac{(1+i)^n}{i} - \frac{1}{i}\right] = PMT[FVIFA_{i,n}]$$

$$PVA_0 = \sum_{t=1}^{n}\frac{PMT}{(1+i)^t} = PMT\left(\frac{1}{i} - \frac{1}{i(1+i)^n}\right) = PMT[PVIFA_{i,n}]$$

Multiple Cash Flows and Annuities

	A	B	C	D	E	F	G	H
44	5. I have a house mortgage loan of $300,000 at 7% per year. How much is my *monthly* payment for the next 30 years?							
45								
46		Hard way:	$1,995.91	<<<Equation: =C48/(1/C51-1/(C51*(1+C51)^C50))				
47								
48		PV	$300,000.00					
49		FV	$0.00					
50		N	360					
51		INT	0.58%					
52	Solve:	PMT	($1,995.91)	<<< Excel: =PMT(C49,C48,C46,C47)				

Questions:

1. How do we use the PMT function in Excel? What did we need to modify in terms of periodic inputs (for this "monthly" mortgage payment) compared to previous examples with annual periodicities?
2. Explain the manual computations performed in the example above. That is, which equation was used and modified?
3. Why do we usually use PVA instead of FVA to compute a periodic loan payment such as a mortgage in the example above?

Amortization

You decide to open your own fast-food restaurant. You decide to borrow $48,040 from a local bank charging you annual interest at 11.9959%. How much do you have to pay a year assuming you want to pay off the loan in 3 years? Show the amortization table.

Step 1: Calculate the recurring payment necessary:

Year 0	1	2	3
$48,040	− PMT	− PMT	− PMT

...
...
...

SUM = $0

$$PVA_0 = \sum_{i=1}^{n} \frac{PMT}{(1+i)^t} = PMT\left(\frac{1}{i} - \frac{1}{i(1+i)^n}\right) = PMT[PVIFA_{i,n}]$$

$$PVA_0 = PMT\left(\frac{1}{i} - \frac{1}{i(1+i)^n}\right)$$

$$PMT = \frac{PVA_0}{\frac{1}{i} - \frac{1}{i(1+i)^n}} = \frac{48,040}{\frac{1}{0.119959} - \frac{1}{0.119959(1+0.119959)^3}} = 20,000$$

Excel's PMT function: PMT (*Rate, N, PV, FV*): PMT (0.119959, 3, 48040, 0)

Step 2: Set up the amortization schedule (replicate this, use rounded 12% interest):

Year	Payment	=	Interest	+	Principal	Balance
1	20,000		5,764.80		14,235.20	33,804.80
2	20,000		4,056.58		15,943.42	17,861.38
3	20,000		2,143.37		17,861.38	0

Interest is computed by 12% (48,040), 12% (33,804), 12% (17,861.38)
Last payment of 20,000 is distributed: 2,143.37 Interest and 17,861.38 Principal

Amortization Table				
SUM::	$ 718,526.69	$ 418,526.69	$ 300,000.00	
Period	Starting	Payment	Interest	Principal	Remaining
1	$ 300,000.00	$1,995.91	$ 1,750.00	$245.91	$ 299,754.09
2	$ 299,754.09	$1,995.91	$ 1,748.57	$247.34	$ 299,506.75
3	$ 299,506.75	$1,995.91	$ 1,747.12	$248.78	$ 299,257.97
4	$ 299,257.97	$1,995.91	$ 1,745.67	$250.24	$ 299,007.73
5	$ 299,007.73	$1,995.91	$ 1,744.21	$251.70	$ 298,756.03
6	$ 298,756.03	$1,995.91	$ 1,742.74	$253.16	$ 298,502.87
7	$ 298,502.87	$1,995.91	$ 1,741.27	$254.64	$ 298,248.23
355	$ 11,734.70	$1,995.91	$ 68.46	$1,927.46	$ 9,807.25
356	$ 9,807.25	$1,995.91	$ 67.21	$1,938.70	$ 7,868.55
357	$ 7,868.55	$1,995.91	$ 45.90	$1,950.01	$ 5,918.54
358	$ 5,918.54	$1,995.91	$ 34.52	$1,961.38	$ 3,957.16
359	$ 3,957.16	$1,995.91	$ 23.08	$1,972.82	$ 1,984.33
360	$ 1,984.33	$1,995.91	$ 11.58	$1,984.33	$ 0.00

Amount going to..

(Chart with y-axis: $0, $250, $500, $750, $1,000, $1,250, $1,500, $1,750, $2,000, $2,250; x-axis periods 1 to 353)
Legend: —— Interest ····· Principal

What Is Optimization?

An approach used to find the combination of inputs to achieve the best possible output subject to satisfying certain prespecified conditions; for example:

- Which military capabilities do I select subject to budgetary constraints, risks and uncertainties on outcomes, and different strategic and operational points of view?
- What stocks to pick in a portfolio, as well as the weights of each stock as a % of the total budget
- Optimal staffing needs for a production line
- Project and strategy selection and prioritization
- Inventory optimization
- Optimal pricing and royalty rates
- Utilization of employees for workforce planning
- Configuration of machines for production scheduling
- Location of facilities for distribution
- Tolerances in manufacturing design
- Treatment policies in waste management

Traveling Financial Planner Problem

- You have to travel and visit clients in New York, Chicago, and Seattle.

- You may start from any city and you will stay at your final city, i.e., you will need to purchase two airline tickets for the three cities.

- Your goal is to travel as cheaply as possible.

Airfare Rates

Route	Airfare
Seattle - Chicago	$325
Chicago - Seattle	$225
New York - Seattle	$350
Seattle - New York	$375
Chicago - New York	$325
New York - Chicago	$325

How Do You Solve the Problem?

- Ad Hoc approach – start trying different permutations
- Enumeration – look at all possible alternatives
- Algorithms

All The Permutations

Seattle-Chicago-New York	$325 + $325 =	**$650**
Seattle-New York-Chicago	$375 + $325 =	**$700**
Chicago-Seattle-New York	$225 + $375 =	**$600**
Chicago-New York-Seattle	$325 + $350 =	**$675**
New York-Seattle-Chicago	$350 + $325 =	**$675**
New York-Chicago-Seattle	$325 + $225 =	**$550**

Additionally, if you want to visit San Antonio and Denver...

- Five Cities to visit: Seattle, Chicago, New York, San Antonio & Denver

  5! = 5 x 4 x 3 x 2 x 1 = 120 possible permutations

How About 100 Different Cities?

100! = 100 x 99 x 98 ... x 1 =
93,326,215,443,944,200,000,000,000,000,000,000,000,00
0,000,000,000,000,000,000,000,000,000,000,000,000,000
,000,000,000,000,000,000,000,000,000,000,000,000,000,
000,000,000,000,000,000,000,000,000,000,000,000,000

or 9.3×10^{157} different combinations

How long would it take to evaluate all these combinations on a Super Computer?

100^{120} Years!!!!!!!!!!

This is why computer-based analytical algorithms are critical to solving large portfolios!

Financial and Economic Portfolios

In instances where cost savings and other financial/economic metrics are applicable, we can model the Total Ownership Cost and Lifecycle Cost for each program or capability. The standard financial metrics in capital budgeting approaches can be easily calculated.

1. Discounted Cash Flow Model (DCF) 2. Cash Flow Ratios 3. Economic Results 4. Information and Details

DCF Starting Year: 2016 DCF Ending Year: 2043 Discount Rate (%): 10.00%

Revenues: 1 Rows   Direct Costs: 3 Rows   Indirect Expenses: 2 Rows   View Full Grid

Year	2016	2017	2018	2019	2020	2021	2022
Revenues	1,742.50	11,737.14	225,850.12	225,850.12	225,850.12	225,850.12	225,850.12
Cost Deferred (Shadow Revenues)	1,742.50	11,737.14	225,850.12	225,850.12	225,850.12	225,850.12	225,850.12
Direct Costs	1,141.09	1,141.09	25,337.25	25,337.25	25,337.25	25,401.31	25,777.82
Mission Support	1,110.26	1,110.26	24,896.68	24,896.68	24,896.68	24,896.68	24,896.68
Combat Systems Integration	18.50	18.50	414.95	414.95	414.95	453.38	829.89
Operations and Maintenance	12.33	12.33	25.62	25.62	25.62	51.25	51.25
Gross Profit (Operating Income)	601.41	10,596.05	200,512.87	200,512.87	200,512.87	200,448.81	200,072.30
Indirect Expenses (General & Administrative)	0	31.00	703.00	703.00	703.00	703.00	703.00
Procurement and Inventory Spares for MTBF EOQ	0.00	31.00	703.00	703.00	703.00	703.00	703.00
Sensor Integration and Technology Insertion	0.00	0.00	0.00	0.00	0.00	0.00	0.00
EBITDA: Earnings Before Interest, Taxes, Depreciation, and Amortization	601.41	10,565.05	199,809.87	199,809.87	199,809.87	199,745.81	199,369.30
Depreciation	0.00	9,874.00	39,827.00	39,074.00	38,161.00	37,206.00	36,172.00
Amortization	0.00	0.00	0.00	0.00	0.00	0.00	0.00
EBIT: Earnings Before Interest and Taxes	601.41	691.05	159,982.87	160,735.87	161,648.87	162,539.81	163,197.30
Interest	0.00	6,779.32	25,892.66	22,767.15	19,224.35	15,842.53	13,062.00
EBT: Earnings Before Taxes	601.41	-6,088.27	134,090.21	137,968.72	142,424.52	146,697.28	150,135.30
Corporate Taxes	171.40	-1,735.16	38,215.71	39,321.09	40,590.99	41,808.72	42,788.56
NET INCOME	430.01	-4,353.11	95,874.50	98,647.63	101,833.53	104,888.56	107,346.74
Total Noncash Expense Items	0	9,874.00	39,827.00	39,074.00	38,161.00	37,206.00	36,172.00
Change in Net Working Capital	0.00	0.00	0.00	0.00	0.00	0.00	0.00
Capital Expenditures	0.00	0.00	0.00	0.00	0.00	0.00	0.00

Custom (xls1) Project 1 Project 2 Project 3 Project 4 Project 5 Project 6 Project 7 Project 8 Project 9 Project 10 Portfol

- Analysis of Alternatives (No Base Case)
- Incremental Analysis (Choose Base Case):

Project 1

Update

Economic Results	Project 1	Project 2	Project 3	Project 4
Net Present Value (NPV)	608,388.29	205,972.62	31,361.10	30,667.51
Net Present Value (NPV) with Terminal Value	726,488.72	310,848.95	59,306.45	52,893.78
Internal Rate of Return (IRR)	29.31%	10.58%	14.75%	16.80%
Modified Internal Rate of Return (MIRR)	15.07%	10.21%	11.91%	12.50%
Profitability Index (PI)	3.43	1.07	1.29	1.39
Return on Investment (ROI)	243.36%	6.68%	28.72%	39.46%
Payback Period (PP)	3.7982	11.2820	6.8823	6.1294
Discounted Payback Period (DPP)	4.7988	26.5103	11.1445	9.3080

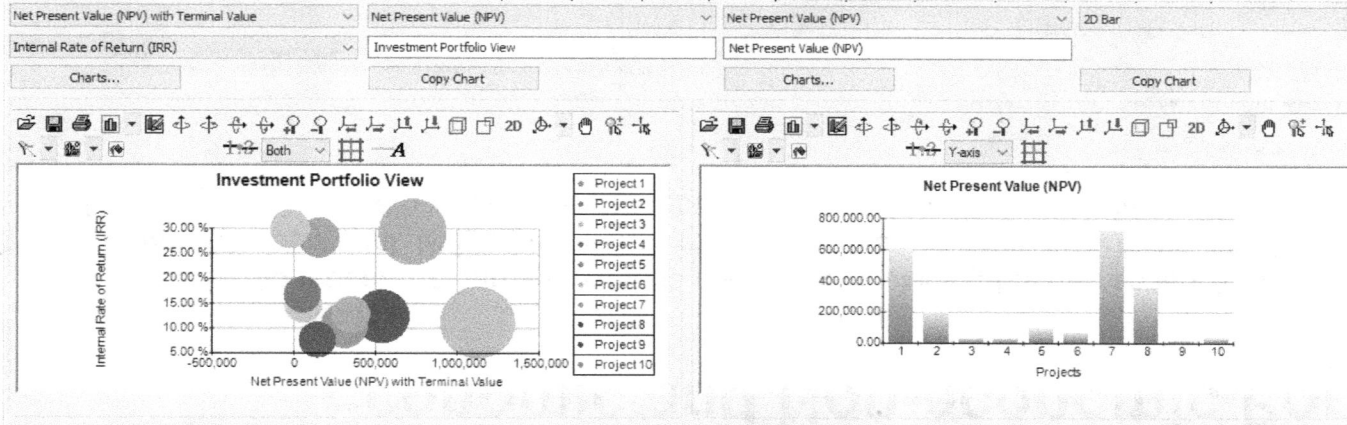

Show on Charts

Net Present Value (NPV) with Terminal Value   Net Present Value (NPV)   Net Present Value (NPV)   2D Bar
Internal Rate of Return (IRR)   Investment Portfolio View   Net Present Value (NPV)
Charts...   Copy Chart   Charts...   Copy Chart

Investment Portfolio View

Project 1, Project 2, Project 3, Project 4, Project 5, Project 6, Project 7, Project 8, Project 9, Project 10

Net Present Value (NPV)

Economic and Non-economic Portfolios

In the portfolio model, we can add various constraints including budget, schedule, risk, cost, and human resources, as well as additional SME judgmental military values. Various algorithms will be used and tested, including Newtonian search methods, gradient reduction, genetic algorithm, and others.

Slice and Dice – Multicriteria Portfolios

- We have multiple Military Values (e.g., economic, non-economic, strategic, operational, logistic).

- Portfolio selection and optimization can be run to maximize each of these value metrics to create a cross-tabulation matrix (below). Each "model" below is an optimal portfolio under each military value metric.

- We then prioritize the program/capability by the Count (a high count indicates that regardless of what value metric we use, that specific capability is still dominant). The portfolios are also constrained portfolios (subject to cost, schedule, risk, budget, and other constraints).

✂ Compare Model Results

Index	1	2	3	4	5	Count
Model	Model 1	Model 2	Model 3	Model 4	Model 5	
Objective Function	55.6000	59.3000	55.6000	33.0600	38.9000	
Optimized Constraint 1	7.0000	7.0000	7.0000	7.0000	7.0000	
Optimized Constraint 2	2,588,872.3394	2,413,054.1576	2,588,872.3394	2,585,326.8849	2,413,054.1576	
Option 1	1	0	1	1	0	3
Option 2	0	0	0	0	0	0
Option 3	1	1	1	1	1	5
Option 4	1	1	1	0	1	4
Option 5	1	1	1	1	1	5
Option 6	0	1	0	1	1	3
Option 7	0	0	0	0	0	0
Option 8	1	1	1	1	1	5
Option 9	1	1	1	1	1	5
Option 10	1	1	1	1	1	5

1 = Selected Program/Capability

0 = Rejected Program/Capability

Models 1 to 5 are run based on five different military values, where each portfolio is still subject to multiple constraints and limitations (budget and risk).

Count shows the number of times a specific Program/Capability Option is selected under various military value objectives.

Budgetary Constraints

- Portfolios are optimized based on constraints and limitations; for example, budgetary levels can be applied (below).

- The Investment Efficient Frontier analysis based on the budget will show different programs/options that should be added or replaced based on various budgetary levels.

- The analysis can be done on any military values.

Objective Function	6.1286	6.7465	6.9478	6.9478	6.9478
Frontier Variable	2,000,000	2,500,000	3,000,000	3,500,000	4,000,000
Optimized Constraint	1,978,818	2,487,042	2,718,646	2,718,646	2,718,646
Option1	1	1	1	1	1
Option2	0	1	1	1	1
Option3	1	1	1	1	1
Option4	1	1	1	1	1
Option5	1	0	1	1	1
Option6	0	0	1	1	1
Option7	0	0	0	0	0
Option8	1	1	1	1	1
Option9	0	0	1	1	1
Option10	0	1	1	1	1

Investment Efficient Frontier

The x-axis shows budgetary levels and constraints.

Each point along the frontier is an optimal portfolio for that budgetary level (combinations of programs and capabilities are chosen at that budget level).

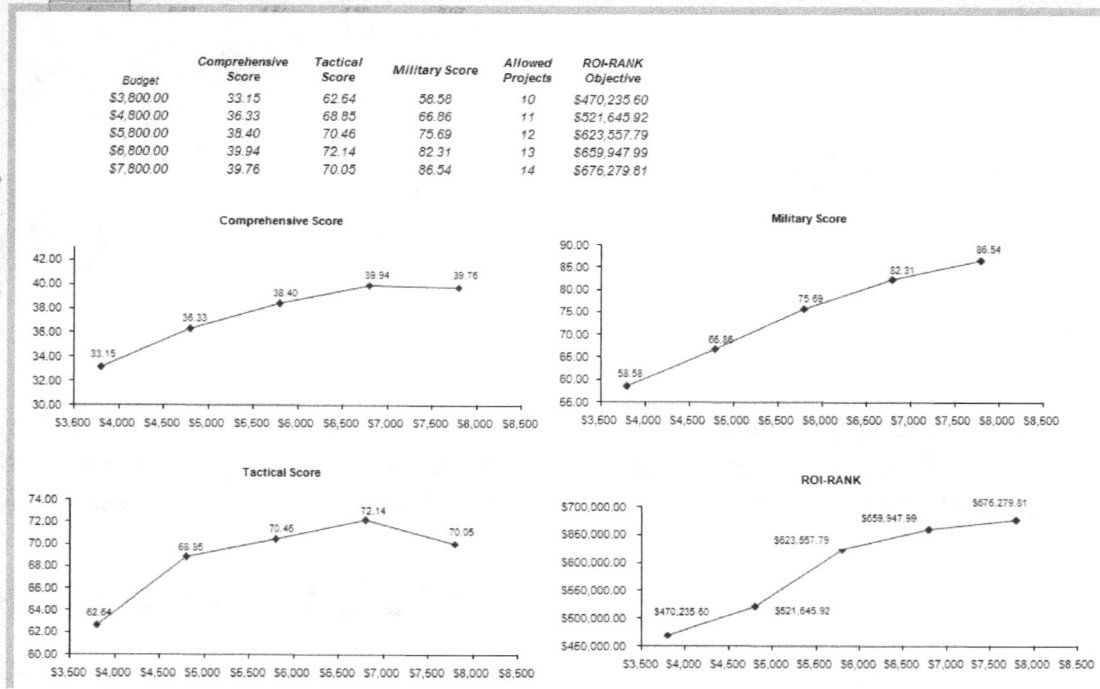

Military Portfolio Optimization

Project Name	ENPV	NPV	Cost	Strategy Ranking	Return to Rank Ratio	Profitability Index	Selection	Military Score	Tactical Score	FTE Resources	Comprehensive Score
Project 1	$458.00	$150.76	$1,732.44	1.20	381.67	1.09	1	8.10	2.31	1.20	1.98
Project 2	$1,954.00	$245.00	$859.00	9.80	199.39	1.29	1	1.27	4.83	2.50	1.76
Project 3	$1,599.00	$458.00	$1,845.00	9.70	164.85	1.25	1	9.88	4.75	3.60	2.77
Project 4	$2,251.00	$529.00	$1,645.00	4.50	500.22	1.32					
Project 5	$849.00	$564.00	$458.00	10.90	77.89	2.23					
Project 6	$758.00	$135.00	$52.00	7.40	102.43	3.60					
Project 7	$2,845.00	$311.00	$758.00	19.80	143.69	1.41					
Project 8	$1,235.00	$754.00	$115.00	7.50	164.67	7.56					
Project 9	$1,945.00	$198.00	$125.00	10.80	180.09	2.58					
Project 10	$2,250.00	$785.00	$458.00	8.50	264.71	2.71					
Project 11	$549.00	$35.00	$45.00	4.80	114.38	1.78					
Project 12	$525.00	$75.00	$105.00	5.90	88.98	1.71					
Project 13	$516.00	$451.00	$48.00	2.80	184.29	10.40					
Project 14	$499.00	$458.00	$351.00	9.40	53.09	2.30					
Project 15	$859.00	$125.00	$421.00	6.50	132.15	1.30					
Project 16	$884.00	$458.00	$124.00	3.90	226.67	4.69					
Project 17	$956.00	$124.00	$521.00	15.40	62.08	1.24					
Project 18	$854.00	$164.00	$512.00	21.00	40.67	1.32					
Project 19	$195.00	$45.00	$5.00	1.20	162.50	10.00					
Project 20	$210.00	$85.00	$21.00	1.00	210.00	5.05					
Total	$22,191.00		$10,200.44	162.00							
Profit/Rank	$136.98										
Profit*Score	$1,244,365.33		Maximize	<=$3800	<=100						

Budget	Comprehensive Score	Tactical Score	Military Score	Allowed Projects	ROI-RANK Objective
$3,800.00	33.15	62.64	58.58	10	$470,235.60
$4,800.00	36.33	68.85	66.86	11	$521,645.92
$5,800.00	38.40	70.46	75.69	12	$623,557.79
$6,800.00	39.94	72.14	82.31	13	$659,947.99
$7,800.00	39.76	70.05	86.54	14	$676,279.81

Time-Sequenced Optimized Portfolios

In some instances, a list of capabilities or programs/options can be considered for execution in the future. In fact, some programs and systems may require sequencing (platform or base systems need to be up and running before add-on systems can be implemented) or initial proofs of concept (Milestone A before additional funding is authorized for Milestones B and C).

Capability		Optimal on Budget	Optimal Cost-Risk	BMD Must-Have	BMD Cost-Risk
Capability 1		ACB16	ACB16	ACB16	ACB18
Capability 2		ACB18	Later	ACB14	ACB14
Capability 3		Later	Later	Later	Later
Capability 4		ACB14	ACB14	ACB16	ACB16
Capability 5		ACB16	ACB14	ACB16	ACB16
Capability 6		ACB14	ACB16	ACB18	ACB18
Capability 7		ACB14	ACB14	ACB16	ACB16
Capability 8		Later	ACB18	ACB18	Later
Capability 9		ACB16	ACB14	ACB18	ACB16
Capability 10		ACB14	ACB14	ACB16	ACB16
Capability 11		ACB14	ACB14	ACB14	ACB14
Capability 12		ACB16	ACB16	ACB18	ACB18
Capability 13		ACB14	ACB14	ACB16	ACB16
Capability 14		ACB14	ACB14	ACB16	ACB16
Capability 15		ACB14	ACB16	ACB16	ACB18
Capability 16		ACB14	ACB14	ACB14	ACB16
Capability 17		ACB14	ACB14	ACB14	ACB16
Capability 18		ACB14	ACB14	ACB14	ACB16
Capability 19		ACB16	ACB18	Later	Later
Capability 20		ACB16	ACB16	Later	ACB18
Capability 21		ACB16	ACB16	Later	ACB18
Capability 22		Later	Later	Later	Later
Capability 23		ACB16	ACB16	ACB16	ACB18

(Actual Capabilities Redacted)

ACB 14 + ACB 16 + ACB 18
*rounded to the nearest 0.1

	Optimal on Budget	Optimal Cost-Risk	BMD Must-Have	BMD Cost-Risk
Total Capabilities ACB14	11	11	5	2
Total Capabilities ACB16	8	7	9	10
Total Capabilities ACB18	1	2	4	7
EMV ACB14	310.98	299.74	115.56	61.02
EMV ACB16	149.87	151.58	268.03	280.96
EMV ACB18	42.24	57.94	127.93	151.58
Total Cost ACB14	$146.00	$139.00	$149.00	$129.00
Total Cost ACB16	$141.00	$129.00	$150.00	$137.00
Total Cost ACB18	$126.00	$95.00	$141.00	$129.00
Total Spent on ACB14-18	$413.00	$363.00	$440.00	$395.00
Probability of Under Budget ACB14	29.70%	97.90%	41.50%	90.80%
Probability of Under Budget ACB16	72.23%	90.90%	16.25%	99.90%
Probability of Under Budget ACB18	94.80%	99.90%	72.90%	90.90%
ACB14 Median 50th Percentile on Budget	$153.20	$142.90	$152.60	$132.30
ACB14 Median 85th Percentile on Budget	$160.22	$146.60	$166.60	$146.30
ACB14 Median 95th Percentile on Budget	$164.30	$148.70	$173.90	$153.50
ACB16 Median 50th Percentile on Budget	$145.40	$137.90	$156.50	$139.50
ACB16 Median 85th Percentile on Budget	$153.50	$147.30	$164.80	$143.30
ACB16 Median 95th Percentile on Budget	$157.80	$152.70	$169.20	$145.30
ACB18 Median 50th Percentile on Budget	$128.90	$95.30	$145.10	$137.90
ACB18 Median 85th Percentile on Budget	$142.90	$101.30	$153.50	$147.30
ACB18 Median 95th Percentile on Budget	$150.20	$104.30	$158.40	$152.70

Risk and Uncertainty in Input Assumptions and Projected Outcomes

In many instances, SME judgment and input assumptions are fraught with uncertainties and risks. Before running optimization and capital budgeting analytics, we will be applying sensitivity analysis (see Tornado chart below) to identify which input assumptions and data points have the highest impact on the results. More detailed analysis and additional data refinement will be performed on these inputs.

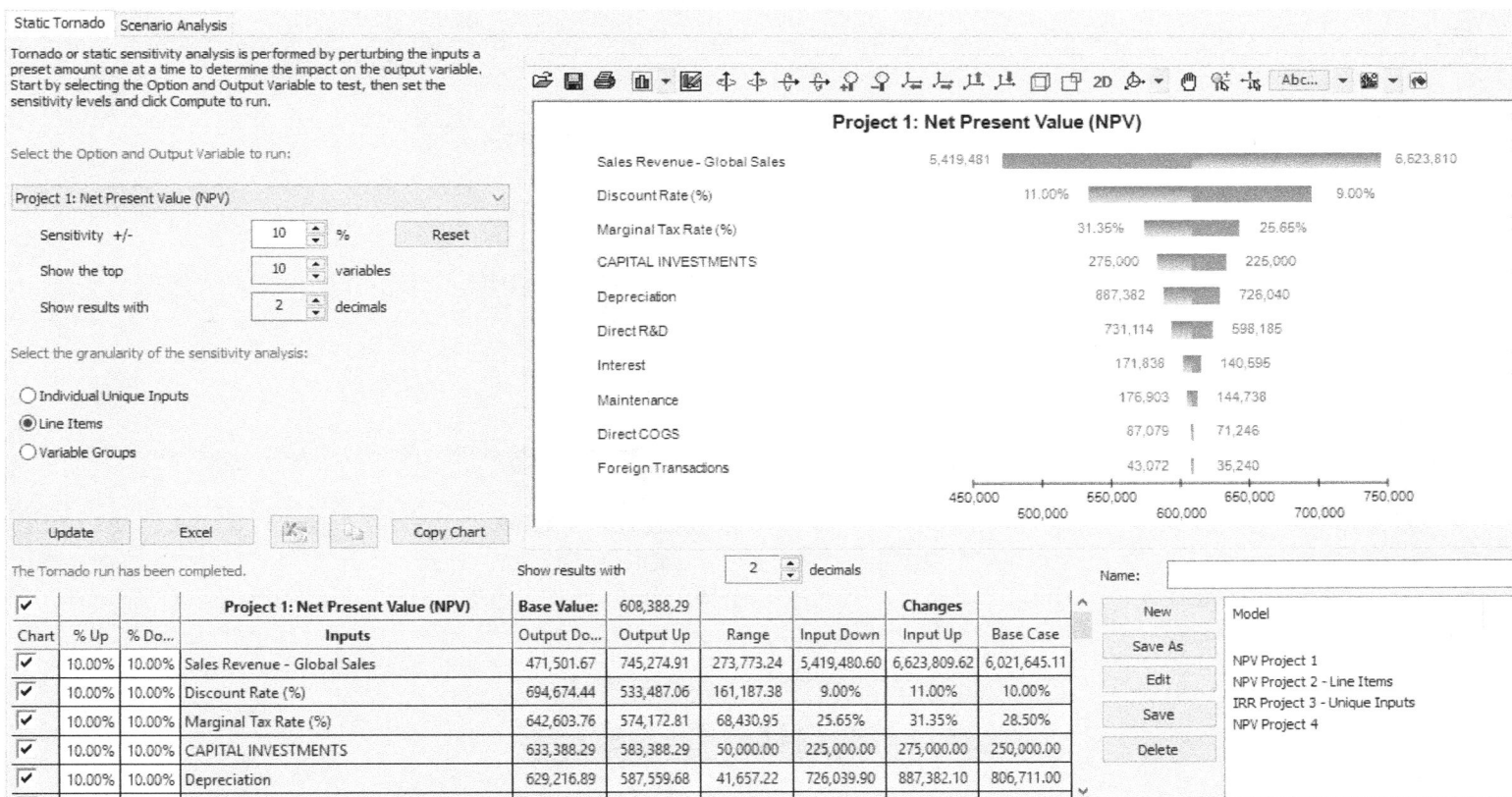

Risk Simulation

Monte Carlo risk simulation of millions of trials will be performed on uncertain inputs to obtain probability distributions instead of single point estimates. These distributions are then used in the portfolio optimization process. We can then determine the probability that a portfolio will be under or over budget, the chances of a schedule overrun and by how much, and the levels of uncertainty and risk of each portfolio.

Optimization

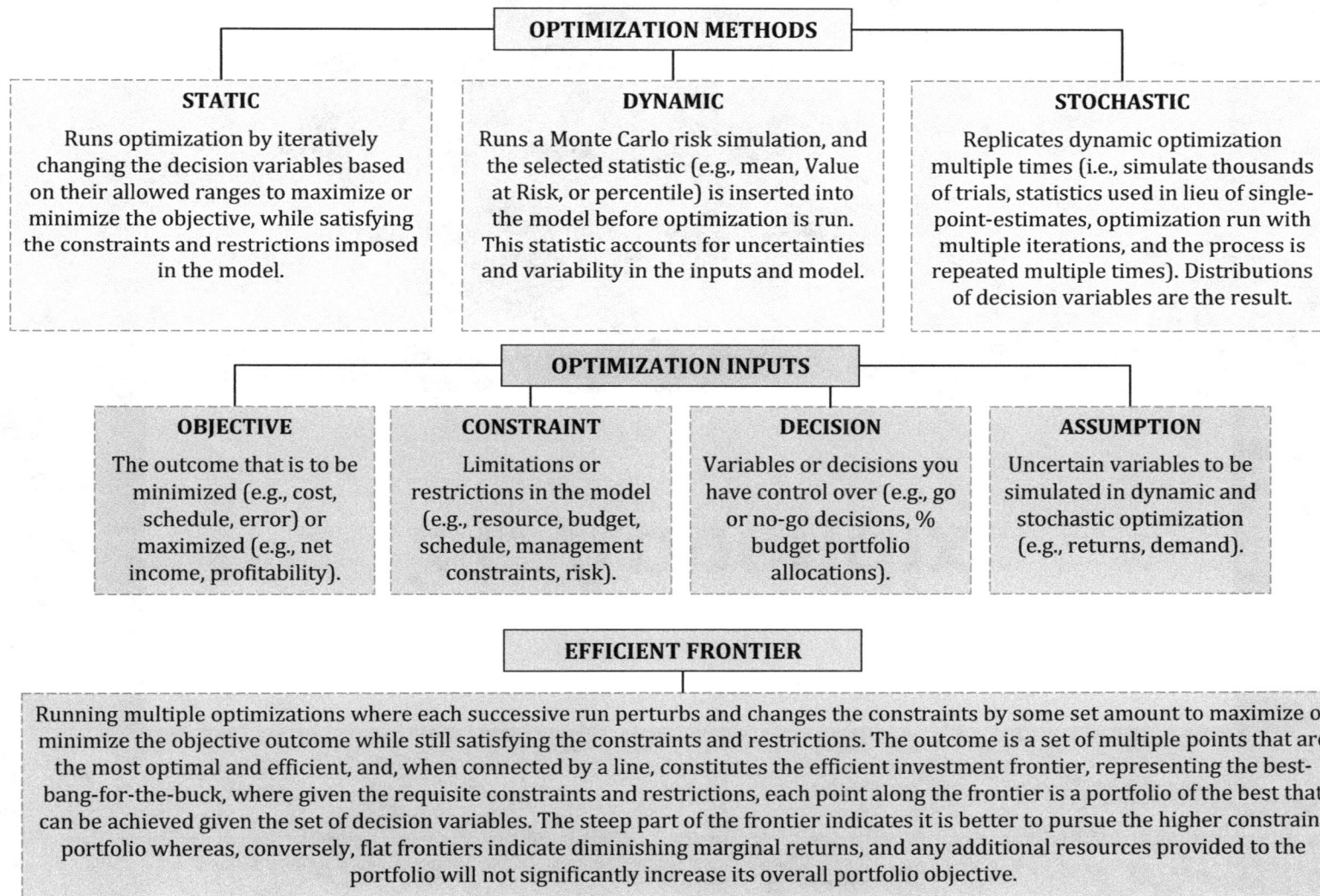

OPTIMIZATION METHODS

STATIC

Runs optimization by iteratively changing the decision variables based on their allowed ranges to maximize or minimize the objective, while satisfying the constraints and restrictions imposed in the model.

DYNAMIC

Runs a Monte Carlo risk simulation, and the selected statistic (e.g., mean, Value at Risk, or percentile) is inserted into the model before optimization is run. This statistic accounts for uncertainties and variability in the inputs and model.

STOCHASTIC

Replicates dynamic optimization multiple times (i.e., simulate thousands of trials, statistics used in lieu of single-point-estimates, optimization run with multiple iterations, and the process is repeated multiple times). Distributions of decision variables are the result.

OPTIMIZATION INPUTS

OBJECTIVE

The outcome that is to be minimized (e.g., cost, schedule, error) or maximized (e.g., net income, profitability).

CONSTRAINT

Limitations or restrictions in the model (e.g., resource, budget, schedule, management constraints, risk).

DECISION

Variables or decisions you have control over (e.g., go or no-go decisions, % budget portfolio allocations).

ASSUMPTION

Uncertain variables to be simulated in dynamic and stochastic optimization (e.g., returns, demand).

EFFICIENT FRONTIER

Running multiple optimizations where each successive run perturbs and changes the constraints by some set amount to maximize or minimize the objective outcome while still satisfying the constraints and restrictions. The outcome is a set of multiple points that are the most optimal and efficient, and, when connected by a line, constitutes the efficient investment frontier, representing the best-bang-for-the-buck, where given the requisite constraints and restrictions, each point along the frontier is a portfolio of the best that can be achieved given the set of decision variables. The steep part of the frontier indicates it is better to pursue the higher constraint portfolio whereas, conversely, flat frontiers indicate diminishing marginal returns, and any additional resources provided to the portfolio will not significantly increase its overall portfolio objective.

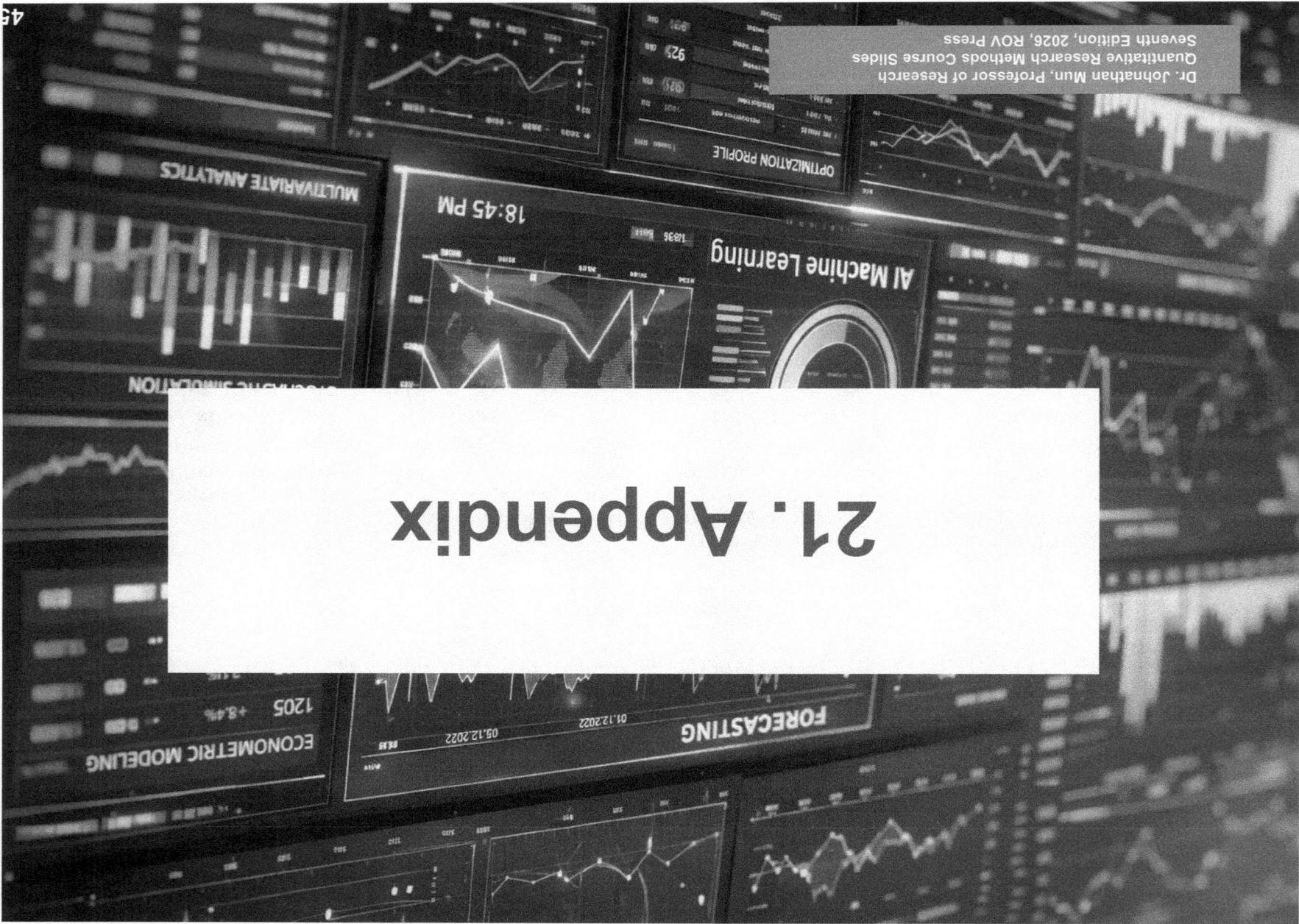

21. Appendix

Dr. Jonathan Mun, Professor of Research
Quantitative Research Methods Course Slides
Seventh Edition, 2026, ROV Press

Z STANDARD NORMAL(0,1) DISTRIBUTION

Standard Normal Distribution

Z	0.00	0.01	0.02	0.03	0.04	0.05	0.06	0.07	0.08	0.09
0.0	0.5000	0.5040	0.5080	0.5120	0.5160	0.5199	0.5239	0.5279	0.5319	0.5359
0.1	0.5398	0.5438	0.5478	0.5517	0.5557	0.5596	0.5636	0.5675	0.5714	0.5753
0.2	0.5793	0.5832	0.5871	0.5910	0.5948	0.5987	0.6026	0.6064	0.6103	0.6141
0.3	0.6179	0.6217	0.6255	0.6293	0.6331	0.6368	0.6406	0.6443	0.6480	0.6517
0.4	0.6554	0.6591	0.6628	0.6664	0.6700	0.6736	0.6772	0.6808	0.6844	0.6879
0.5	0.6915	0.6950	0.6985	0.7019	0.7054	0.7088	0.7123	0.7157	0.7190	0.7224
0.6	0.7257	0.7291	0.7324	0.7357	0.7389	0.7422	0.7454	0.7486	0.7517	0.7549
0.7	0.7580	0.7611	0.7642	0.7673	0.7704	0.7734	0.7764	0.7794	0.7823	0.7852
0.8	0.7881	0.7910	0.7939	0.7967	0.7995	0.8023	0.8051	0.8078	0.8106	0.8133
0.9	0.8159	0.8186	0.8212	0.8238	0.8264	0.8289	0.8315	0.8340	0.8365	0.8389
1.0	0.8413	0.8438	0.8461	0.8485	0.8508	0.8531	0.8554	0.8577	0.8599	0.8621
1.1	0.8643	0.8665	0.8686	0.8708	0.8729	0.8749	0.8770	0.8790	0.8810	0.8830
1.2	0.8849	0.8869	0.8888	0.8907	0.8925	0.8944	0.8962	0.8980	0.8997	0.9015
1.3	0.9032	0.9049	0.9066	0.9082	0.9099	0.9115	0.9131	0.9147	0.9162	0.9177
1.4	0.9192	0.9207	0.9222	0.9236	0.9251	0.9265	0.9279	0.9292	0.9306	0.9319
1.5	0.9332	0.9345	0.9357	0.9370	0.9382	0.9394	0.9406	0.9418	0.9429	0.9441
1.6	0.9452	0.9463	0.9474	0.9484	0.9495	0.9505	0.9515	0.9525	0.9535	0.9545
1.7	0.9554	0.9564	0.9573	0.9582	0.9591	0.9599	0.9608	0.9616	0.9625	0.9633
1.8	0.9641	0.9649	0.9656	0.9664	0.9671	0.9678	0.9686	0.9693	0.9699	0.9706
1.9	0.9713	0.9719	0.9726	0.9732	0.9738	0.9744	0.9750	0.9756	0.9761	0.9767
2.0	0.9772	0.9778	0.9783	0.9788	0.9793	0.9798	0.9803	0.9808	0.9812	0.9817
2.1	0.9821	0.9826	0.9830	0.9834	0.9838	0.9842	0.9846	0.9850	0.9854	0.9857
2.2	0.9861	0.9864	0.9868	0.9871	0.9875	0.9878	0.9881	0.9884	0.9887	0.9890
2.3	0.9893	0.9896	0.9898	0.9901	0.9904	0.9906	0.9909	0.9911	0.9913	0.9916
2.4	0.9918	0.9920	0.9922	0.9925	0.9927	0.9929	0.9931	0.9932	0.9934	0.9936
2.5	0.9938	0.9940	0.9941	0.9943	0.9945	0.9946	0.9948	0.9949	0.9951	0.9952
2.6	0.9953	0.9955	0.9956	0.9957	0.9959	0.9960	0.9961	0.9962	0.9963	0.9964
2.7	0.9965	0.9966	0.9967	0.9968	0.9969	0.9970	0.9971	0.9972	0.9973	0.9974
2.8	0.9974	0.9975	0.9976	0.9977	0.9977	0.9978	0.9979	0.9979	0.9980	0.9981
2.9	0.9981	0.9982	0.9982	0.9983	0.9984	0.9984	0.9985	0.9985	0.9986	0.9986
3.0	0.9987	0.9987	0.9987	0.9988	0.9988	0.9989	0.9989	0.9989	0.9990	0.9990

Example: For a Z-value of 2.33, refer to the 2.3 row and 0.03 column for the area of 0.99. This means there is 99% in the shaded region and 1% in the one-sided left or right tail.

DISTRIBUTIONAL ANALYSIS TOOL FOR CDF AND 1-CDF

Left Panel — Distribution Analysis

This tool generates the probability density function (PDF), cumulative distribution function (CDF) and the Inverse CDF (ICDF) of all the distributions in Risk Simulator, including theoretical moments and probability chart.

Field	Value
Distribution	Normal
Mean	0
Standard Deviation	1
Chart type	PDF
Type	CDF & 1-CDF
Formatting	0.000000
Single Value / Value X	
Range of Values	(selected)
Lower Bound	0
Upper Bound	3
Step Size	0.1

Chart: Mean = 0.0000, Stdev = 1.0000, Skewness = 0.0000, Kurtosis = 0.0000

X	CDF	1-CDF
0.000000	0.500000	0.500000
0.100000	0.539828	0.460172
0.200000	0.579260	0.420740
0.300000	0.617911	0.382089
0.400000	0.655422	0.344578
0.500000	0.691462	0.308538
0.600000	0.725747	0.274253
0.700000	0.758036	0.241964
0.800000	0.788145	0.211855
0.900000	0.815940	0.184060
1.000000	0.841345	0.158655
1.100000	0.864334	0.135666
1.200000	0.884930	0.115070
1.300000	0.903200	0.096800
1.400000	0.919243	0.080757
1.500000	0.933193	0.066807
1.600000	0.945201	0.054799
1.700000	0.955435	0.044565
1.800000	0.964070	0.035930
1.900000	0.971283	0.028717
2.000000	0.977250	0.022750
2.100000	0.982136	0.017864
2.200000	0.986097	0.013903
2.300000	0.989276	0.010724
2.400000	0.991802	0.008198
2.500000	0.993790	0.006210
2.600000	0.995339	0.004661
2.700000	0.996533	0.003467
2.800000	0.997445	0.002555
2.900000	0.998134	0.001866

Right Panel — Distribution Analysis

This tool generates the probability density function (PDF), cumulative distribution function (CDF) and the Inverse CDF (ICDF) of all the distributions in Risk Simulator, including theoretical moments and probability chart.

Field	Value
Distribution	Normal
Mean	0
Standard Deviation	1
Chart type	PDF
Type	CDF & 1-CDF
Formatting	0.000000
Single Value / Value X	
Range of Values	(selected)
Lower Bound	0
Upper Bound	1
Step Size	0.01

Chart: Mean = 0.0000, Stdev = 1.0000, Skewness = 0.0000, Kurtosis = 0.0000

X	CDF	1-CDF
0.000000	0.500000	0.500000
0.010000	0.503989	0.496011
0.020000	0.507978	0.492022
0.030000	0.511966	0.488034
0.040000	0.515953	0.484047
0.050000	0.519939	0.480061
0.060000	0.523922	0.476078
0.070000	0.527903	0.472097
0.080000	0.531881	0.468119
0.090000	0.535856	0.464144
0.100000	0.539828	0.460172
0.110000	0.543795	0.456205
0.120000	0.547758	0.452242
0.130000	0.551717	0.448283
0.140000	0.555670	0.444330
0.150000	0.559618	0.440382
0.160000	0.563559	0.436441
0.170000	0.567495	0.432505
0.180000	0.571424	0.428576
0.190000	0.575345	0.424655
0.200000	0.579260	0.420740
0.210000	0.583166	0.416834
0.220000	0.587064	0.412936
0.230000	0.590954	0.409046
0.240000	0.594835	0.405165
0.250000	0.598706	0.401294
0.260000	0.602568	0.397432
0.270000	0.606420	0.393580
0.280000	0.610261	0.389739
0.290000	0.614092	0.385908
0.300000	0.617911	0.382089

STUDENT'S T DISTRIBUTION

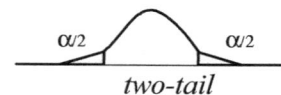

t-Distribution

alpha	0.1	0.05	0.025	0.01	0.005		alpha	0.1	0.05	0.025	0.01	0.005
			one-tail							two-tail		
df = 1	3.0777	6.3137	12.7062	31.8210	63.6559		df = 1	6.3137	12.7062	25.4519	63.6559	127.3211
2	1.8856	2.9200	4.3027	6.9645	9.9250		2	2.9200	4.3027	6.2054	9.9250	14.0892
3	1.6377	2.3534	3.1824	4.5407	5.8408		3	2.3534	3.1824	4.1765	5.8408	7.4532
4	1.5332	2.1318	2.7765	3.7469	4.6041		4	2.1318	2.7765	3.4954	4.6041	5.5975
5	1.4759	2.0150	2.5706	3.3649	4.0321		5	2.0150	2.5706	3.1634	4.0321	4.7733
6	1.4398	1.9432	2.4469	3.1427	3.7074		6	1.9432	2.4469	2.9687	3.7074	4.3168
7	1.4149	1.8946	2.3646	2.9979	3.4995		7	1.8946	2.3646	2.8412	3.4995	4.0294
8	1.3968	1.8595	2.3060	2.8965	3.3554		8	1.8595	2.3060	2.7515	3.3554	3.8325
9	1.3830	1.8331	2.2622	2.8214	3.2498		9	1.8331	2.2622	2.6850	3.2498	3.6896
10	1.3722	1.8125	2.2281	2.7638	3.1693		10	1.8125	2.2281	2.6338	3.1693	3.5814
15	1.3406	1.7531	2.1315	2.6025	2.9467		15	1.7531	2.1315	2.4899	2.9467	3.2860
20	1.3253	1.7247	2.0860	2.5280	2.8453		20	1.7247	2.0860	2.4231	2.8453	3.1534
25	1.3163	1.7081	2.0595	2.4851	2.7874		25	1.7081	2.0595	2.3846	2.7874	3.0782
30	1.3104	1.6973	2.0423	2.4573	2.7500		30	1.6973	2.0423	2.3596	2.7500	3.0298
35	1.3062	1.6896	2.0301	2.4377	2.7238		35	1.6896	2.0301	2.3420	2.7238	2.9961
40	1.3031	1.6839	2.0211	2.4233	2.7045		40	1.6839	2.0211	2.3289	2.7045	2.9712
45	1.3007	1.6794	2.0141	2.4121	2.6896		45	1.6794	2.0141	2.3189	2.6896	2.9521
50	1.2987	1.6759	2.0086	2.4033	2.6778		50	1.6759	2.0086	2.3109	2.6778	2.9370
100	1.2901	1.6602	1.9840	2.3642	2.6259		100	1.6602	1.9840	2.2757	2.6259	2.8707
200	1.2858	1.6525	1.9719	2.3451	2.6006		200	1.6525	1.9719	2.2584	2.6006	2.8385
300	1.2844	1.6499	1.9679	2.3388	2.5923		300	1.6499	1.9679	2.2527	2.5923	2.8279
500	1.2832	1.6479	1.9647	2.3338	2.5857		500	1.6479	1.9647	2.2482	2.5857	2.8195
100000	1.2816	1.6449	1.9600	2.3264	2.5759		100000	1.6449	1.9600	2.2414	2.5759	2.8071

Example: For an alpha in the single right tail area of 2.5% with 15 degrees of freedom, the critical-t value is 2.1315.

PROBABILITY CHARTS AND TABLES TOOL IN RISK SIMULATOR

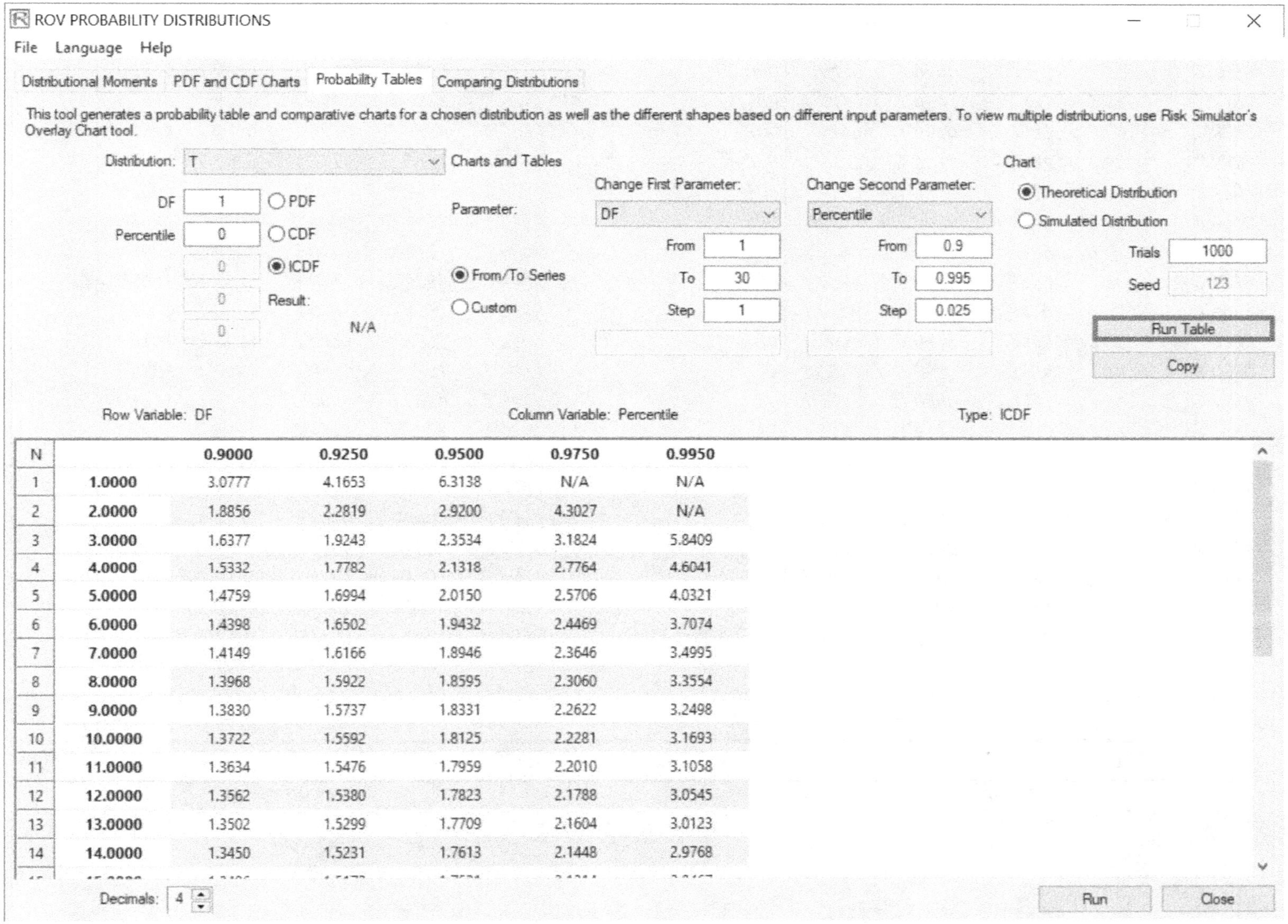

N		0.9000	0.9250	0.9500	0.9750	0.9950
1	1.0000	3.0777	4.1653	6.3138	N/A	N/A
2	2.0000	1.8856	2.2819	2.9200	4.3027	N/A
3	3.0000	1.6377	1.9243	2.3534	3.1824	5.8409
4	4.0000	1.5332	1.7782	2.1318	2.7764	4.6041
5	5.0000	1.4759	1.6994	2.0150	2.5706	4.0321
6	6.0000	1.4398	1.6502	1.9432	2.4469	3.7074
7	7.0000	1.4149	1.6166	1.8946	2.3646	3.4995
8	8.0000	1.3968	1.5922	1.8595	2.3060	3.3554
9	9.0000	1.3830	1.5737	1.8331	2.2622	3.2498
10	10.0000	1.3722	1.5592	1.8125	2.2281	3.1693
11	11.0000	1.3634	1.5476	1.7959	2.2010	3.1058
12	12.0000	1.3562	1.5380	1.7823	2.1788	3.0545
13	13.0000	1.3502	1.5299	1.7709	2.1604	3.0123
14	14.0000	1.3450	1.5231	1.7613	2.1448	2.9768

Sample Comprehensive and Oral Exam Questions

1. Provide an example of a problem statement. What are some of the required elements and characteristics of a well-written problem statement?

2. Provide an example of a research thesis or dissertation layout. Describe each of the sections or chapters involved.

3. Explain what Bayesian analysis is and how it works. You can use Bayes' Theorem as an illustration of the approach. What are some of the main requirements to run a Bayesian analysis?

4. What is conditional probability and how does it work? Are conditional probabilities important in situations where there is dependence or independence between events?

5. What is the difference between descriptive statistics used in deduction versus inferential statistics used for induction purposes? How do inferential statistics work in terms of using statistical samples?

6. Explain some basic sampling methods (e.g., stratified sampling, random sampling) and how one might control or block for intervening variables. What about proper population representation, spread, and diversity?

7. What is the definition of a hypothesis? What does it mean and how is it usually constructed?

8. Provide examples of directional vs. nondirectional hypotheses. What happens to the alpha significance levels and the computed p-values when we change from a one-tail to a two-tailed test and vice versa?

9. What are the four levels of data measurement? Provide some examples. Under which levels of measurement would degrees Fahrenheit, binary conditional outcomes, placement in a race, kilograms, time, and stock prices fall?

10. What is the difference between a parameter and a statistic of distributional moments? How can you tell the difference? Which ones would have a larger uncertainty?

11. What is a standard deviation? What is a coefficient of variation? When is each used? Which is a relative measure, and which would be an absolute measure? Provide examples to support your response.

12. What are the differences among arithmetic average, geometric average, moving average, weighted average, and harmonic average? When do you use each?

13. What are the assumptions surrounding the use of a binomial distribution versus a Poisson distribution? Provide examples for each distribution.

14. Provide an example of how a hypergeometric distribution may be applied. Is this a discrete or continuous distribution? Does this distribution have event memory or is it considered memoryless? Why or why not?

15. What are the four distributional moments and what do they each measure? What are IQR, Beta, and VaR, and what moments are these?

16. What does a high kurtosis in your data imply? Does a triangular distribution have positive, negative, or zero kurtosis? What about a uniform distribution and normal distribution? Is high kurtosis a good thing or a concern for someone working in Six Sigma quality control?

Sample Comprehensive and Oral Exam Questions

17. What do you use to measure the spread and dispersion of a dataset? What information does dispersion provide? How is dispersion used in hypothesis tests?

18. What is the main difference between combinations and permutations? In determining the number of required pairwise correlations of a variable set, which would we use?

19. What do PDF, CDF, ICDF stand for and how are they used? Explain how you can identify the four moments from the shape of a CDF S-curve.

20. When is a Z-score used and when might it be appropriate? What are the required main assumptions for a Z-score model? Provide an example of how a Z-score model works.

21. What are the main characteristics of a normal distribution and why is normality so important in quantitative research methods?

22. What are Type I, Type II, Type III, and Type IV errors? Which can we control directly and which ones of these errors might be a false positive or false negative?

23. What is the statistical power of a test and how is it computed? Which error types might statistical power be related to?

24. What is the difference between accuracy and precision, and which can you possibly exert control over and how? Explain the differences: accurate and precise, accurate but not precise, not accurate but precise, and not accurate and not precise.

25. Does risk lead to uncertainty or does uncertainty lead to risk? What are some measures of risk and uncertainty?

26. What is the central limit theorem, how does it work, and why is it important? Provide an example of statistical sampling as it pertains to the central limit theorem.

27. What is a sampling distribution and how does it work? Provide an example of a full-scale sample versus statistical sampling.

28. Explain what the following terms mean and how they might be tested: data reliability, consistency, and credibility. What is inter-rater versus intra-rater reliability?

29. How would you measure a model's internal validity and external validity? What are some of the statistical measures you can use?

30. What is predictive validity? How is that measured or quantified?

31. When and why are nonparametrics employed? How are the hypotheses different? What are the strengths and weaknesses of nonparametrics versus parametric methods?

32. Why do nonparametric methods use medians instead of means? Which has higher statistical power?

33. Does correlation imply causality? Does causality imply correlation? How do you test for causality?

34. What test do you apply to see if there is a statistically significant difference of an effect? Specifically, if you wanted to test a before-and-after effect of a new vaccine or viral therapeutic treatment, what approach would you use and why?

35. How do you test if two variables are statistically independent of one another? Is correlation a good way to measure statistical dependence and statistical independence? If not, what other tests or approaches might you use and why?

36. What is the difference between a Spearman and Pearson correlation? How do you compute a Spearman correlation using the Pearson's approach?

Sample Comprehensive and Oral Exam Questions

37. Compare and contrast the various ANOVA models. Specifically, explain what each model is used for and under what conditions.

38. What do the Hotelling and Bonferroni methods do? Why could we not simply use multiple standard tests instead of these larger and bulkier tests?

39. Provide an example of how ANOVA with blocking variables might be used, and why we might run into data and modeling biases if this method is not used. What are these variable blocks?

40. What does a two-way ANOVA factorial model with replication look like? Can we test for interactions between factors using this method?

41. Multivariate regression has two main uses. What are they? What are the pros and cons of a multivariate linear regression?

42. What is a unit root and why might it be important? Is this applicable for time-series or cross-section data or both?

43. Do independent variables need to be independent of the dependent variable or from other independent variables? Why or why not? What happens if the requirement is violated?

44. Compare and contrast the following terms: binary, binomial, bivariate, bimodal.

45. What are some examples of bivariate regression model specifications?

46. Can you run a regular multivariate regression when the independent variable is binary or truncated? What about when the dependent variable is binary or truncated?

47. What are some of the assumptions required in running an ordinary least squares multivariate regression? What are some of the potential errors in a regression model?

48. What are autocorrelation, multicollinearity, and heteroskedasticity?

49. What are Logit and Probit models and when are they applicable? What are the differences and similarities between these two methods?

50. What are random walks, Brownian motion, mean reversion, and jump-diffusion processes? Are these dynamic or stochastic processes and what are they used for?

51. How do you measure the accuracy of a forecast model? What about the model precision of in a forecast? Compare and contrast these two terms.

52. What is a Runs test used for and how does it work? Is it a powerful test? What are some alternatives to the Runs test?

53. What are the Cronbach's Alpha and Kendall's W tests used for? Provide an example of how these methods may be applicable.

54. Why is normality in the data such an important thing? How do you know if the data are normal? If not normal, what happens then? Are statistical results still valid? What do we do if the data are not normal?

55. What are the Lilliefors test, Shapiro–Wilk–Royston test, and D'Agostino–Pearson test used for? What about the Kuiper's model or Akaike models?

56. In a Kolmogorov–Smirnov distributional fitting routine, what is the null hypothesis tested, would you look for a low or high p-value, and why?

57. What are some examples of errors and biases in your data and in your model?

Sample Comprehensive and Oral Exam Questions

58. If your data are nonlinear and non-normal, how would you linearize or normalize them and why would you bother?

59. Explain what the following means: heteroskedasticity, multicollinearity, nonlinearity, outliers, micronumerosity, structural breaks.

60. What is data stationarity and why is it important to know? What issues might you encounter and how would you handle the issues if your data are stationary versus nonstationary?

61. What are inter-rater reliability and intra-rater reliability? How would you test these?

62. What is the Kruskal–Wallis test and what is the Friedman's test?

63. What is the Wilcoxon test used for?

64. How would you identify and model cause and effect? How do you identify and know if you run into a causality loop? How would Granger causality models help?

65. A hypothesis is usually an induction or inference to the population from a sample, as opposed to a deduction with constructs and propositions. Can one truly with absolute confidence reject a hypothesis or accept a hypothesis? Which action is easier? Can you provide an example?

66. What are some examples of data and modeling biases? Provide details.

67. What do calculations such as the Akaike Information Criterion (AIC), Bayes and Schwarz Criterion (BSC), and Hannan–Quinn Criterion (HQC) measure?

68. Explain self-selection bias and survivorship bias. Provide examples.

69. Computational Monte Carlo simulations and stochastic models were performed to generate data from experiments or theoretical constructs. Provide some examples of where you might run into the need to do this in future research?

70. What is Granger causality? Explain leading, lagging, and coincident indicators. How would one use the results from the Granger model?

71. How does a statistical process control chart work? What are SPC charts used for? Can I use SPC to identify normality, outliers, and extreme events?

72. Describe some examples of potential data and modeling errors that may exist in a multivariate regression.

73. How do you test for the randomness of data? Is the approach valid for time-series, cross-sectional, mixed panel data, or some combination thereof?

74. What is the difference between an ARIMA and a GARCH model? What are each used for, what types of data are most appropriate, and why use these models as compared to other methods? What might be the limitations and advantages of these methods?

75. How would you model interactions among various independent variables? Are the same approaches applicable for time-series data as cross-sectional data?

76. If you find a high variance inflation factor in your model, is it a good thing or a bad thing? How would you solve any potential issues that might occur with a high VIF?

77. If asked to model a presidential election or some other national election results, describe the steps and methodology you would take.

78. What is a neural network model and how does it work?

Sample Comprehensive and Oral Exam Questions

79. Is heteroskedasticity critical in both time-series and cross-sectional models? Why or why not? How would you fix heteroskedasticity?

80. The Akaike Information Criterion and the Bayes Schwartz Criterion are used in a variety of models. What do these two methods actually do?

81. Name some of the various types of multivariate regression and when each one might be used and under what conditions?

82. When is a mean-reversion model most appropriately used?

83. What is the Kolmogorov–Smirnov test used for? Explain the idea behind this method.

84. What is the difference between precision and accuracy? Which can you control for in a computational Monte Carlo simulation model?

85. What is a seed value used for? How does it work and how will the results change?

86. All time-series data can be decomposed into three fundamental elements. What are these elements and how do they work in combination to help generate a forecast?

87. Compare and contrast among the following methods: tornado analysis, scenario analysis, dynamic sensitivity analysis, bootstrap simulation, computational Monte Carlo simulation, and spider analysis.

88. Explain the differences among static analysis, dynamic analysis, and stochastic analysis in terms of computational Monte Carlo simulation and nonlinear optimization.

89. What types of data and what data properties might be best suited for a Holt–Winters model? What is this model used for?

90. What is a dynamic model and what is a stochastic process model? How are they similar or different? When would you use each?

91. Under what circumstances would an exponential curve or a logistic curve be more appropriate to use?

92. Discuss the various types of stepwise regression and how they work (e.g., forward, backward, forward–backward, correlation, and others).

93. What are the four typical input parameters required to run a stochastic optimization? Provide examples of a stochastic optimization and how you would obtain these inputs.

94. What is a two-stage least squares 2SLS model and how do you use instrumental variables to model it? What is endogeneity in this case?

95. Is seasonality or cyclicality in a dataset easier to model? Why? Are cross-sectional data susceptible to these changes? What about mixed panel data?

96. Explain factor analysis and principal component analysis. What does each do? Explain how you would use the computed eigenvalues and eigenvectors.

97. How does a Markov chain work? What would a multi-state Markov chain be used for?

98. What is a cubic spline? Provide an example of how this method would apply.

99. What is combinatorial fuzzy logic? What is fuzzy logic in general and why would someone use this method?

100. What are simultaneous equations model and structural equation model? Provide an example of when each method might be applicable.

To access BizStats and Risk Simulator, please visit:

www.realoptionsvaluation.com

SOFTWARE INSTALLATION